ABORTION

ABORTION

[a reader]

edited by Lloyd Steffen

The Pilgrim Library of Ethics

THE PILGRIM PRESS, *Cleveland, Ohio*

The Pilgrim Press, Cleveland, Ohio 44115
© 1996 by Lloyd Steffen

All rights reserved. Published 1996

Printed in the United States of America on acid-free paper

01   00   99   98   97   96   5   4   3   2   1

Library of Congress Cataloging-in-Publication Data

Abortion : a reader / edited by Lloyd Steffen.
      p.   cm. — (The Pilgrim library of ethics.)
    Includes bibliographical references.
    ISBN 0-8298-1117-6 (alk. paper)
    1. Abortion—Moral and ethical aspects.   I. Steffen, Lloyd H.,
1951–   . II. Series.
HQ767.15.A24   1996
363.4'6—dc20   95-51169
                                                                    CIP

Contents

PART THREE
Abortion and Faith: Moral Analysis in Christian Perspective

PART FOUR
Abortion and Society: Justice, Law, and Public Policy

Preface

THIS BOOK IS A COLLECTION of readings on the issue of abortion. That such a book should be assembled is not surprising given the prominent place abortion holds in the American political and social consciousness—not to mention in the headlines. What is surprising, given the numerous books available on the abortion issue, is that one more book should present itself for addition to an already sagging shelf. For over the last three decades many anthologies and collections of readings have appeared, addressing abortion from a variety of perspectives, including practical philosophy, social and medical ethics, rhetoric and law. That such books keep appearing testifies to the continuing importance of the abortion debate in our cultural life, and every editor hopes to contribute to elevating the tone of that debate by providing materials that will be of use to students, academics and professional persons, as well as to citizens who might turn to such pages to keep themselves abreast of the current state of the abortion question.

And what a troubling issue this is. Offering a book that hopes to contribute to meaningful conversation about abortion seems to fly in the face of cultural reality. Abortion, after all, has incited violence—a sad, even tragic state of affairs. And dialogue over abortion, while a worthy goal, seems out of the question. After all, sides have been chosen and battle lines drawn: debates over abortion do not feature arguments but the hurling of incommensurate conclusions that pass one another in rhetorical flight.

There is no doubt that we are a society divided over abortion, and this division is apparent throughout the abortion literature. But the division itself is not mysterious. The cultural conflict we have experienced over abortion can be traced to a lack of consensus over moral meaning. Our deepest problems with abortion stem from the moral questions that we, in American society, have failed to answer definitively or categorically as a moral community.

Abortion poses problems of moral meaning: this volume addresses those moral problems. And for the purposes of this volume, that moral focus is itself qualified. This particular collection will not reprint one more time Judith Jarvis Thomson's well-known "A Defense of Abortion" with its celebrated violin player (though there will be references to it in various selections). The focus on moral issues here is religious and theological rather than strictly philosophical. That is, those who address the abortion issue in the following pages do so either from within their religious or theological tradition, or they do so against a backdrop of religious or theological concerns that we as readers need to take seriously, for religious thought and value illuminate what these authors have to say about abortion.[1]

This volume has been assembled with an eye toward presenting selections—some old, some new—on abortion as a moral and religious issue. These selections, all of which have previously appeared in print, do not share a common point of view on the particularities of the position they describe, argue for, advance or present. They do, however, share one thing in common: they raise issues of moral complexity. This complexity can appear in particular selections by all that an author is trying to do in generating an argument. But some selections are focused, even single-minded. Now the complexity surfaces when the essays are read in relation to one another, when the full extent of the diversity of religious and moral issues emerges, when emphasis in value and meaning shifts from one selection to the next, when moral concerns are highlighted in one place and diminished in others.

Abortion provokes moral issues in the context of religiously diverse perspectives and value commitments, and when read as a whole, the essays in this volume help that diversity to emerge.

In most cases, as in the Official Vatican "1974 Declaration on Procured Abortion," the religious backdrop for the ethical position advanced is explicit and unmistakable. But in other cases, the religious or theological backdrop must be inferred or actually brought to bear in indirect ways. The first two articles in the volume, for example, tell stories of persons involved in the experience of abortion, one being a woman's reflection on having gone through the abortion procedure, the other being a story about a black woman who was denied abortion services. If the reader keeps in mind that feminist theology has argued forcefully and convincingly that human experience—the experience of women—must inform theological thinking, then the relevance of these two apparently non-religious, non-theological selections should become clear. It is hoped that the inclusion of such pieces will supply experiential data for reflection and complement the more explicit theological and moral analyses that other scholars—many of them women—will offer throughout the volume.

So the religious is not everywhere in every selection the explicit focus of attention. But whether the piece is from a *Harper's Magazine* feature, a legal article by the attorney who argued *Roe v. Wade* before the Supreme Court (Sarah Ragle Weddington), an analysis of the debate over federal funding for abortion (Mary C. Segers), or a moral analysis made against the backdrop of a "just war" model of thinking grounded in the Roman Catholic moral tradition, the religious is everywhere at issue. It is even at issue in the letter (reprinted here) from the anonymous Pensacola bomber who claims religion had nothing to do with what she did. (Why, one wonders, does that need to be said?)

The question can naturally arise, "What is distinctive about this collection?" and to that question I can respond by specifying three objectives that have guided the work of assembling this particular collection.

First, the attention paid to the moral meaning of abortion in this volume accepts the viewpoint that the moral meaning of abortion, as a practical matter, rarely arises without an assist from religious thought, so that included in this volume are writings that keep religious thought in play with ethical analysis. This interconnectedness continues to press itself on those who would seek to address adequately and clearly "the state of the question." At issue are certain presumptions about how the abortion issue is to be understood. The editor of this volume holds that the moral meaning of abortion cannot be easily extracted from the religious matrix that has given rise to so many of the issues that perplex us about abortion: the meaning of personhood, the developmental moment of personhood, the meaning of innocence, the conflict of rights between fetus and mother, the meaning of the value of life, the permissibility of killing and the possibility of justified killing. The rhetoric over abortion has tended in recent years to simplify some of these issues. The present volume is dedicated toward restoring abortion to its rightful place as a morally complex, even befuddling issue that demands consideration not only as a public policy issue, but as a serious moral issue involving a conflict between desired goods, and as a religious issue involving deep faith commitments among people of passion living in a religiously diverse, pluralist society.

Second, in the interests of balance, this volume has sought to include some more traditional authors and classic arguments on abortion, recognizing that males have often held authoritative positions from which to pronounce on questions of moral meaning. But in the interests of balance, the volume has also sought to include the voices of women on this issue, recognizing that women have not always been afforded a hearing, because of various kinds of exclusions, including the lack of position from which to present professional analyses. That situation has changed, and an effort has been made to make sure that women's voices are heard throughout this book, which is also to say that the collection has not isolated or inadvertently marginalized women by offering a separate section on women's contributions to the abortion debate.

A third explicit objective of this volume has been to include a diversity of religious positions, including the non-Christian. This deserves a brief comment.

The American abortion debate has often proceeded as if the Christian community were the only tradition that had a viewpoint on abortion. The assumption that America is a Christian nation and that the abortion conflict is a purely internal conflict within the Christian community—which is coterminous with America itself—as if the viewpoints of other religious traditions need receive no hearing, is a bizarre assumption at this moment in our cultural history, and a sadly shortsighted view. And it is a mistaken view. Christianity has been affected by the reality of religious pluralism just as it has been affected by feminist theology. For Christians not to engage other religious traditions on an issue as central to Christian ethics as abortion is not to take our many inter-faith initiatives with requisite seriousness. So in addition to providing in these pages official statements and pronouncements from religious organizations indicating internal diversity within the Christian community, an effort has been made to invite other religious traditions into the conversation over moral meaning. Some readers may find themselves reflecting on the fact that abortion has been a topic of serious moral and religious reflection in an array of non-Christian religious traditions—Judaism, Islam, Buddhism, for example—and that may lead to reflection on this issue: that all of the faith traditions represented here happen to be included in the American religious patchwork. That should mean that they enjoy, one would have to assume, First Amendment religious freedom guarantees and protections. It is an interesting issue to consider: what does the diversity of viewpoints emerging from this patchwork of religious perspectives mean for constitutional interpretation? For if the state should determine by fiat (and not by empirical evidence; the moral meaning of personhood is not a biological or scientific issue) that a conceptus/zygote/embryo is a person from the moment of conception, would that imposition of belief by governmental action infringe and restrict the right of, say, Jews and Muslims, and many Protestant Christians—who on religious grounds do not hold such a view and find no compelling reason to do so—to freely practice their religion? The important selection by Peter Wenz sheds light on this issue.

Having laid out the objectives that guided the work of assembling this volume and that indicate where any distinctiveness must lie, it must now be said by way of disclaimer that this volume makes no claim to being exhaustive. This book seeks to overview the abortion issue from the viewpoint of religious ethics and to gather viewpoints that survey significant, responsible and diverse perspectives on an issue of great moral tension—even violence—in contemporary American society.

Why this book? What's the point? What more is there to add?

If this volume can contribute to restoring through a balance of thoughtful articles a sense of the moral complexity provoked by this troubling, even dangerous issue—and highlight the role of religion in shaping that complexity—then that complexity will, as an answer to the questions asked, suffice.

Notes

1. If many books treat abortion in the context of treating other issues in philosophy, ethics, medicine, or law, it is important to note that numerous books focused exclusively on abortion are available, with a few centered directly on theological issues and religious ethics. Outstanding examples of the latter would include the 1982 Pilgrim Press reader *Abortion: The Moral Issues*, edited by Edward Batchelor Jr., which presented various Christian theological and ethical responses to abortion, and the more recent collection focused on Roman Catholic theological response, edited by Patricia Beattie Jung and Thomas Shannon, *Abortion and Catholicism: The American Debate* (New York: Crossroad, 1988).

Acknowledgments

I WOULD LIKE TO acknowledge the assistance of several persons in assembling this volume. For their gracious advice and suggestions, I wish to thank Lisa Sowle Cahill, Stanley Hauerwas, Paul Lauritzen, and John P. Reeder. None of these individuals is in any way responsible for the final collection, though each offered helpful comments and critical suggestions that made this, I hope, a better, more useful collection than it might otherwise have been. For their attention I am most grateful.

A thank-you also to Richard Brown of The Pilgrim Press, who encouraged me to undertake this project and who helped in many ways to bring it to completion. I am grateful for the help I received from Kelley Baker at Pilgrim.

I also wish to thank my colleagues in the Religion Studies Department at Lehigh University, particularly Michael Raposa, chair of religion studies, for his continued support of this project. Thanks also to my other colleagues at Lehigh, particularly Rev. Al Schlert, who answered questions and helped me acquire crucial materials for inclusion in the volume; Sally Schray, for assistance with some of the secretarial work involved in putting the volume together; and to some of our students, especially Rob Johnson, who also helped me in the project. I must also thank the librarians, especially the interlibrary loan department at Lehigh University, for invaluable assistance; and to the students in Lehigh's computer center who provided me with needed help at crucial moments.

For all of her support, a special word of thanks must go to Emmajane Finney, who is part of all I am and all I do.

PART ONE

THE LANGUAGE OF ABORTION

The Personal/The Public

[1]

Abortion: A Personal Moral Dilemma

Linda Bird Francke

"JANE DOE," THIRTY-EIGHT, had an abortion in New York City in 1973. The mother of three children, then three, five, and eleven, Jane had just started a full-time job in publishing. She and her husband, an investment banker, decided together that another baby would add an almost unbearable strain to their lives, which were already overfull. What Jane had not anticipated was the guilt and sadness that followed the abortion. She wrote about the experience shortly thereafter and filed the story away. Three years later she reread it and decided it might be helpful to other women who experience the ambivalence of abortion. The *New York Times* ran it on their Op-Ed page in May 1976. This is what she wrote:

We were sitting in a bar on Lexington Avenue when I told my husband I was pregnant. It is not a memory I like to dwell on. Instead of the champagne and hope which had heralded the impending births of the first, second and third child, the news of this one was greeted with shocked silence and Scotch. "Jesus," my husband kept saying to himself, stirring the ice cubes around and around. "Oh, Jesus."

Oh, how we tried to rationalize it that night as the starting time for the movie came and went. My husband talked about his plans for a career change in

SOURCE: From *The Ambivalence of Abortion* by Linda Bird Francke. Copyright © 1978 by Linda Bird Francke. Reprinted by permission of Random House, Inc. "There Just Wasn't Room . . ." by L. B. Francke, Op-Ed, May 14, 1976. Copyright © 1976 by the New York Times Company. Reprinted by permission.

the next year, to stem the staleness that fourteen years with the same investment-banking firm had brought him. A new baby would preclude that option.

The timing wasn't right for me either. Having juggled pregnancies and child care with what freelance jobs I could fit in between feedings, I had just taken on a full-time job. A new baby would put me right back in the nursery just when our youngest child was finally school age. It was time for *us*, we tried to rationalize. There just wasn't room in our lives now for another baby. We both agreed. And agreed. And agreed.

How very considerate they are at the Women's Services, known formally as the Center for Reproductive and Sexual Health. Yes, indeed, I could have an abortion that very Saturday morning and be out in time to drive to the country that afternoon. Bring a first morning urine specimen, a sanitary belt and napkins, a money order or $125 cash—and a friend.

My friend turned out to be my husband, standing awkwardly and ill at ease as men always do in places that are exclusively for women, as I checked in at nine A.M. Other men hovered around just as anxiously, knowing they had to be there, wishing they weren't. No one spoke to each other. When I would be cycled out of there four hours later, the same men would be slumped in their same seats, locked downcast in their cells of embarrassment.

The Saturday morning women's group was more dispirited than the men in the waiting room. There were around fifteen of us, a mixture of races, ages and backgrounds. Three didn't speak English at all and a fourth, a pregnant Puerto Rican girl around eighteen, translated for them.

There were six black women and a hodge-podge of whites, among them a T-shirted teenager who kept leaving the room to throw up and a puzzled middle-aged woman from Queens with three grown children.

"What form of birth control were you using?" the volunteer asked each one of us. The answer was inevitably "none." She then went on to describe the various forms of birth control available at the clinic, and offered them to each of us.

The youngest Puerto Rican girl was asked through the interpreter which she'd like to use: the loop, diaphragm, or pill. She shook her head "no" three times. "You don't want to come back here again, do you?" the volunteer pressed. The girl's head was so low her chin rested on her breastbone. "*Sí*," she whispered.

We had been there two hours by that time, filling out endless forms, giving blood and urine, receiving lectures. But unlike any other group of women I've been in, we didn't talk. Our common denominator, the one which usually floods across language and economic barriers into familiarity, today was one of shame. We were losing life that day, not giving it.

The group kept getting cut back to smaller, more workable units, and finally I was put in a small waiting room with just two other women. We changed into paper bathrobes and paper slippers, and we rustled whenever we moved. One of the women in my room was shivering and an aide brought her a blanket.

"What's the matter?" the aide asked her. "I'm scared," the woman said. "How much will it hurt?" The aide smiled. "Oh, nothing worse than a couple of bad cramps," she said. "This afternoon you'll be dancing a jig."

I began to panic. Suddenly the rhetoric, the abortion marches I'd walked in, the telegrams sent to Albany to counteract the Friends of the Fetus, the Zero Population Growth buttons I'd worn, peeled away, and I was all alone with my microscopic baby. There were just the two of us there, and soon, because it was more convenient for me and my husband, there would be one again.

How could it be that I, who am so neurotic about life that I step over bugs rather than on them, who spend hours planting flowers and vegetables in the spring even though we rent out the house and never see them, who make sure the children are vaccinated and inoculated and filled with vitamin C, could so arbitrarily decide that this life shouldn't be?

"It's not a life," my husband had argued, more to convince himself than me. "It's a bunch of cells smaller than my fingernail."

But any woman who has had children knows that certain feeling in her taut, swollen breasts, and the slight but constant ache in her uterus that signals the arrival of a life. Though I would march myself into blisters for a woman's right to exercise the option of motherhood, I discovered there in the waiting room that I was not the modern woman I thought I was.

When my name was called, my body felt so heavy the nurse had to help me into the examining room. I waited for my husband to burst through the door and yell "stop," but of course he didn't. I concentrated on three black spots in the acoustic ceiling until they grew in size to the shape of saucers, while the doctor swabbed my insides with antiseptic.

"You're going to feel a burning sensation now," he said, injecting the Novocaine into the neck of the womb. The pain was swift and severe, and I twisted to get away from him. He was hurting my baby, I reasoned, and the black saucers quivered in the air. "Stop," I cried. "Please stop." He shook his head, busy with his equipment. "It's too late to stop now," he said. "It'll just take a few more seconds."

What good sports we women are. And how obedient. Physically the pain passed even before the hum of the machine signaled that the vacuuming of my uterus was completed, my baby sucked up like ashes after a cocktail party. Ten minutes start to finish. And I was back on the arm of the nurse.

There were twelve beds in the recovery room. Each one had a gaily flowered draw sheet and a soft green or blue thermal blanket. It was all very feminine. Lying on these beds for an hour or more were the shocked victims of their sex, their full wombs now stripped clean, their futures less encumbered.

It was very quiet in that room. The only voice was that of the nurse, locating the new women who had just come in so she could monitor their blood pressure, and checking out the recovered women who were free to leave.

Juice was being passed about, and I found myself sipping a Dixie cup of Hawaiian Punch. An older woman with tightly curled bleached hair was just getting up from the next bed. "That was no goddamn snap," she said, resting before putting on her miniskirt and high white boots. Other women came and went, some walking out as dazed as they had entered, others with a bounce that signaled they were going right back to Bloomingdale's.

Finally then, it was time for me to leave. I checked out, making an appointment to return in two weeks for an IUD insertion. My husband was slumped in the waiting room, clutching a single yellow rose wrapped in a wet paper towel and stuffed into a baggie.

We didn't talk the whole way home, but just held hands very tightly. At home there were more yellow roses and a tray in bed for me and the children's curiosity to divert.

It had certainly been a successful operation. I didn't bleed at all for two days just as they had predicted, and then I bled only moderately for another four days. Within a week my breasts had subsided and the tenderness vanished, and my body felt mine again instead of the eggshell it becomes when it's protecting someone else.

My husband and I are back to planning our summer vacation and his career switch.

And it certainly does make more sense not to be having a baby right now— we say that to each other all the time. But I have this ghost now. A very little ghost that only appears when I'm seeing something beautiful, like the full moon on the ocean last weekend. And the baby waves at me. And I wave at the baby. "Of course, we have room," I cry to the ghost. "Of course, we do."

I am "Jane Doe." Using a pseudonym was not the act of cowardice some have said it was, but rather an act of sympathy for the feelings of my family. My daughters were too young then to understand what an abortion was, and my twelve-year-old son (my husband's stepson) reacted angrily when I even broached the subject of abortion to him. Andrew was deeply moralistic, as many children are at that age, and still young enough to feel threatened by the actions of adults; his replies to my "suppose I had an abortion" queries were devastating. "I think abortion is okay if the boy and girl aren't married, and they just made a mistake," he said. "But if you had an abortion, that would be different. You're married, and there is no reason for you not to have another baby. How could you just kill something—no matter how little it is—that's going to grow and have legs and wiggle its fingers?

"I would be furious with you if you had an abortion. I'd lose all respect for you for being so selfish. I'd make you suffer and remind you of it all the time. I would think of ways to be mean. Maybe I'd give you the silent treatment or something.

"If God had meant women to have abortions, He would have put buttons on their stomachs."

I decided to wait until he was older before we discussed it again.

There were other considerations as well. My husband and I had chosen not to tell our parents about the abortion. My mother was very ill at the time and not up to a barrage of phone calls from her friends about "what Linda had written in the newspaper." And there were my parents-in-law, who had always hoped for a male grandchild to carry on the family name. So I avoided the confessional and simply wrote what I thought would be a helpful piece for other women who might have shared my experience.

The result was almost great enough to be recorded on a seismograph. Interpreting the piece as anti-abortion grist, the Right-to-Lifers reproduced it by the thousands and sent it to everyone on their mailing lists. In one Catholic mailing, two sentences were deleted from the article: one that said I was planning to return to the clinic for an IUD insertion, and the other the quote from a middle-aged woman, "That was no goddamn snap." Papers around the country and in Canada ran it, culminating in its appearance in the Canadian edition of the *Reader's Digest,* whose staff took it upon their editorial selves to delete the last paragraph about the "little ghost" because they considered it "mawkish." They also changed the title from "There Just Wasn't Room in Our Lives for Another Baby" to "A Successful Operation" in the hopes that it would change their magazine's pro-abortion image.

Hundreds of letters poured into the *New York Times,* some from Right-to-Lifers, who predictably called me a "murderer," and others from pro-choice zealots who had decided the article was a "plant" and might even have been written by a man. Women wrote about their own abortions, some of which had been positive experiences and some disastrous. One woman even wrote that she wished her own mother had had an abortion instead of subjecting her to a childhood that was "brutal and crushing." Many of the respondents criticized me, quite rightly, for not using birth control in the first place. I was stunned, and so was the *New York Times.* A few weeks later they ran a sampling of the letters and my reply, which follows:

> The varied reactions to my abortion article do not surprise me at all. They are all right. And they are all wrong. There is no issue so fundamental as the giving of life, or the cessation of it. These decisions are the most personal one can ever make and each person facing them reacts in her own way. It is not black-and-white as the laws governing abortion are forced to be. Rather it is the gray area whose core touches our definition of ourselves that produces "little ghosts" in some, and a sense of relief in others.
>
> I admire the woman who chose not to bear her fourth child because she and her husband could not afford to give that child the future they felt necessary. I admire the women who were outraged that I had failed to use any form of contraception. And I ache for the woman whose mother had given birth to her even though she was not wanted, and thus spent an empty, lonely childhood. It takes

courage to take the life of someone else in your own hands, and even more courage to assume responsibility for your own.

I had my abortion over two years ago. And I wrote about it shortly thereafter. It was only recently, however, that I decided to publish it. I felt it was important to share how one person's abortion had affected her, rather than just sit by while the pro and con groups haggled over legislation.

The effect has indeed been profound. Though my husband was very supportive of me, and I, I think, of him, our relationship slowly faltered. As our children are girls, my husband anguished at the possibility that I had been carrying a son. Just a case of male macho, many would argue. But still, that's the way he feels, and it is important. I hope we can get back on a loving track again.

Needless to say, I have an IUD now, instead of the diaphragm that is too easily forgotten. I do not begrudge my husband his lack of contraception. Condoms are awkward. Neither do I feel he should have a vasectomy. It is profoundly difficult for him to face the possibility that he might never have that son. Nor do I regret having the abortion. I am just as much an avid supporter of children by choice as I ever was.

My only regret is the sheer irresponsibility on my part to become pregnant in the first place. I pray to God that it will never happen again. But if it does, I will be equally thankful that the law provides women the dignity to choose whether to bring a new life into the world or not.

I had obviously and unintentionally touched a national nerve. With abortion becoming an everyday occurrence since the Supreme Court ruling in 1973, which overturned the right of individual states to intervene in a woman's decision to abort in the first trimester (twelve weeks) of pregnancy and to intervene in the second trimester (twenty-four weeks) only to ensure medical practices "reasonably related to maternal health," American women of all ages, races, and backgrounds were facing the same sort of dilemma I had. . . .

So much has happened in the short time since abortion was legalized that only now is there an opportunity to draw breath and begin to evaluate what the 1973 Supreme Court decision has wrought, and what repercussions the 1977 Supreme Court decision upholding states' rights to withhold abortion funding for the poor will have. Abortion is not new by any means. But confronting the fact of it without furtiveness and danger is. The quantum leap from women's age-old need and desire to control their reproductive lives to their sanctioned ability finally to do so has raised questions of ethics and morality that have yet to be answered. Perhaps they never will be.

[2]

The Right Not to Be Born

Marion K. Sanders

THE SMITHS ARE A strikingly handsome couple; an astute TV pro-
ducer might well choose them as stars of a poignant documentary about up-
ward-mobile young blacks in the urban jungle. Beatrice is small-boned, with
the delicately rounded features of an elegant African carving. Her husband,
Richard, is a craggy six-footer who works nights and weekends, goes to college
by day, and hopes eventually to study medicine. Though they have lived in New
York for eight years—first in Harlem, now in the seedy Crown Heights section
of Brooklyn—they still speak in the accents of their native North Carolina.
Their strapping six-year-old daughter, Rosemary, has inherited her parents'
good looks plus an added component of outgoing vivacity. The Smiths also
have a younger child, Ruth. And Ruth is the reason why in the autumn of 1968
the Smiths find themselves spending ten anxious days in a Brooklyn courtroom.
This is a civil action, a suit for damages. The plaintiffs are Ruth and her parents;
the defendant is Long Island College Hospital where Ruth was born on January
4, 1965. The searing personal tragedy which resulted in this litigation is set
forth in stark detail in the trial transcript on which this report is based.

The Smiths' attorney, Norman Roy Grutman, an earnest, highly articulate
man, is skilled in the dramatic flourishes which are the hallmark of the trial
lawyer. He specializes in negligence law, notably medical malpractice—a

profitable field. The Smith case is not, however, likely to prove lucrative. It is, indeed, a very long shot. For the issue to be adjudicated is whether Ruth should have been born at all.

No doctor or hospital in the United States has ever been penalized for failing to terminate a pregnancy. On the contrary, it takes nerve and a flexible interpretation of the law to perform an abortion openly in a New York hospital where—as in most states—the operation is unlawful unless performed by a doctor under a reasonable belief that it is required to preserve the life of the mother. Consequently the Smith case, at the outset, seems to Long Island College Hospital more of a nuisance suit than a serious threat.

The plaintiffs counsel, Grutman, views the matter differently. He has already tried and lost a somewhat similar suit, and his sympathies as well as his professional pride are engaged. He also sees this as a potential "landmark case" with portentous social consequences. But the outlook is not promising. As the veniremen are chosen, he exhausts his challenges to dismiss those who either admit, or convey the impression, that they regard the termination of pregnancy for any reason as murder. Among the twelve men finally in the jury box—who look like a random collection of subway riders—there are still five Catholics. (One juror is black, as is one alternate.) The presiding judge, Charles J. Beckinella, who rules his courtroom with a firm hand, is also a Catholic.

With considerable passion, Grutman defines the issue in his opening statement. Beatrice Smith was admitted to Long Island College Hospital on June 8, 1964, for the purpose of having a therapeutic abortion. It was never performed. Why not? The preceding sequence of events is not disputed. In the spring of 1964, New York City experienced the worst epidemic of German measles—known medically as rubella—in thirty-five years. One of those who came down with it was Rosemary Smith. As is the custom of New Yorkers who want "the best" medical care for their children but cannot afford private pediatricians' fees, her mother took her to the nearest pediatric clinic, at Brookdale Hospital. There the diagnosis was made. Shortly afterward, Beatrice Smith found herself with the same symptoms—a rash, swollen glands, sore throat, and fever. She also suspected that she might be pregnant—the Smiths had been planning a second child around this time. When she was feeling well enough to go out, she called on a local general practitioner who had treated her once before for a minor ailment, Dr. Wolf J. Domsky. The standard test confirmed her pregnancy.

On the witness stand, Mrs. Smith haltingly recalls her visit to Dr. Domsky: "I told him I had read an article concerning German measles and the pregnant mother. And I explained to him that—well he knew that I had the German measles. . . . "

Dr. Domsky recommended therapeutic abortion: a course of action now approved in standard medical-school obstetrical textbooks when the infection occurs in the first eight weeks of pregnancy. (The connection between rubella and birth defects first became known in 1942 when an Australian ophthalmologist, Dr. Norman Gregg, reported an astounding number of congenital cataracts in babies whose mothers had a history of German measles early in pregnancy. The mechanism is well understood today: the pregnant woman, like anyone else, gets rid of the virus in a few weeks but the fetus remains infected, with a strong likelihood of damage to the developing cells.)

The Smiths are devout people with stern moral standards. They still attend the Pentecostal church in Harlem which they joined when they first came to New York although it is more than an hour's subway ride from their present home in Brooklyn.

"I discussed it with my husband and with the minister of our church, Reverend M. V. Solomon," Mrs. Smith continues on the stand. The decision finally was that therapeutic abortion would be "the right thing." Dr. Domsky, who like many general practitioners in New York had no hospital connection himself, recommended that she apply to the obstetrical clinic of the nearest city hospital, Kings County. City hospitals in New York, chronically overcrowded and understaffed and chronically deferential to the politically potent Roman Catholic hierarchy, are less than cordial to pregnant black ladies who walk in off the street demanding abortions for any reason. (In 1964, more than 500 in-hospital abortions were performed on ward and private patients in New York's voluntary institutions, but only 32 in municipal hospitals—statistics which explain why botched abortions are the major cause of maternal deaths among the city's black women.)

Armed with a letter from Dr. Domsky, Mrs. Smith applies for a therapeutic abortion at Kings County. After a second visit, she is told that a certification from the City Board of Health would be desirable. In due course, the Smiths manage to obtain this document. Nearly a month has now gone by. Considerably worried, they seek out Dr. Domsky again. Hoping to fare better, Mrs. Smith now applies to Long Island College Hospital where she is known because Rosemary was born there. To her immense relief she is admitted. The hospital record is Exhibit 3 in the court proceedings.

> *. . . 22 yr. old Negro girl . . . pregnancy & German measles . . . 23rd of April patient developed Rubella. She [is in] for therapeutic abortion. . . . —[signed] Mayerson [an intern]*

On the witness stand, Richard Smith recalls the encounter. "The doctor said they would admit her and that they would do the therapeutic abortion," he testifies. "I think he said there had to be some signing. The doctors had to approve. . . . "

At Long Island College Hospital, where there was no standing committee on therapeutic abortion, the senior attending obstetricians would make the decision. Their opinions are entered on Beatrice Smith's chart.

6/9/64 Attending's Note
Pt. seen by Dr. H. Freedman who feels that the history of rubella from the patient combined with the letter from the B of H plus the note confirming the diagnosis of rubella from the pt.'s MD are all confirmatory evidence of rubella infection having occurred at the 5th amenorrheic week. Dr. Freedman feels therefore that a therapeutic AB is indicated. Pt. reveals the uterus to be enlarged to about 16 wks. size & the method employed to be "salting out." To be seen by Dr. MacGregor today. —J.P. Jones [chief resident]

6/9/64 Agree to recommendation for interruption in view of history of rubella in 5th wk. of gestation. —C.H. Taffeen [attending obstetrician]

6/10 . . . Awaiting Dr. MacGregor

6/11. Pt. appears depressed . . . discussion as to . . . th. AB. —Czallorn [an intern]

5[sic]/12/64 Consultation sheet
The history would indicate the probability of German measles in this patient occurring at about the fifth week of pregnancy. My only hesitancy in recommending therapeutic abortion is that this patient was not seen by a physician during the acute stage of rubella.—Consultant A.J. MacGregor

(On the witness stand, Dr. Freedman reaffirms his opinion. Drs. Taffeen and MacGregor are not called. Dr. Domsky cannot be called because he died several months before the trial began.)

It is June 13, Beatrice Smith's fifth day in the hospital. Her husband has visited her daily.

"I was working at night and some mornings I would work a few hours overtime," Richard Smith testifies. "And this [June 13] was one of the mornings when I worked overtime, and when I got home the hospital called and they told me that I had to sign the papers before they could go through with the operation so I rushed to the hospital. . . . "

The paper, Exhibit 3C, is written in longhand on the hospital's letterhead.

This is to certify that we are fully aware of the procedure (amniocentesis) being done. The abortion is being done because of having contracted Rubella during the first trimester of pregnancy. —[Richard Smith] —[Beatrice Smith]

"Was the procedure, amniocentesis, explained to you?" Grutman asks Smith.

"He didn't give the name of it, but he told me they were going to do it by a process where they would inject a needle into my wife and that she would drop—"

(The jury by this time has been educated in the various methods of terminating pregnancies—explicitly spelled out at the Judge's insistence by several expert witnesses: dilation and curettage—the scraping out of the products of conception from the womb—safe up to about the third month of pregnancy; amniocentesis, the method of choice at sixteen weeks, injecting saline or another solution into the uterus, which subsequently ejects the fetus; hysterotomy, a kind of miniature cesarean for later pregnancies. Dr. Irvin Cushner, an attending obstetrician at Johns Hopkins, has testified that eight hundred amniocentesis procedures have been done there without untoward incidents.)

On the morning of June 13 Mrs. Smith is given an injection of 100 milligrams of Demerol and taken to the operating room, "a large room with a lot of light. A big light shining down with a mirror," she testifies. She lies there alone for some time. Then a nurse arrives.

"She told me that I could go home now," Mrs. Smith continues. "I was wheeled back into the bedroom. . . . [The doctor] told me I didn't need a therapeutic abortion, don't worry, that the baby would be all right. And not to go to any place to try to have one; to continue in their clinic."

At this point the courtroom begins to acquire some of the atmosphere of a mystery play. For at the start of the trial, the Judge and jury have been shown the child who would be "all right."

Dr. Louis Z. Cooper, a young pediatrician who directs an experimental program for rubella babies, is on the stand. In his arms is Ruth Smith, a pretty three-year-old with the limp body and limbs of a rag doll. The only sound she makes is an animal-like wail.

"Doctor," Grutman asks, "what is the condition of this child?"

"This child has congenital rubella," Cooper says. "She has retardation of both the intellectual and motor skills. . . . I think you can see that Ruth's left eye is much smaller than her right eye . . . it has a dense, pearly-looking cataract which films her pupil and prevents her from using that eye. Her right eye appears to be normal. If you examine this eye with an ophthalmoscope you would see what looks like someone peppered this retina with a pepper shaker. . . . And this is caused by the virus actually infecting various parts of the eye. . . . Instead of talking, which you would expect for a child of this age, her sounds consist just of some noises. . . . She tests as deaf to the routine tests that are available. . . . She has long leg braces with a pelvic band . . . whereby with proper training, first parallel bars and support, and then with canes of her own . . . she might be able to walk. . . .

"In our clinic as of last year, we had roughly sixty children we called the bottom of the barrel. . . . Ruth was among this group whose handicaps were so severe and multiple that we couldn't get any existing school or facility to accept her for education and rehabilitation. And so she became eligible for this experimental program that included a teacher of the deaf, a teacher of the blind, a teacher of the brain-damaged, working right in Bellevue Hospital. . . . "

Dr. Cooper explains that, although Ruth also has a congenital heart defect, it is not serious enough to impair her life expectancy, which is normal.

All this was almost immediately apparent to the doctors who delivered Ruth.

"Did you learn anything about your child on the night or early in the morning of the day that she came into the world?" Grutman asks Richard Smith.

"Well, he first just congratulated me and told me about the defects . . . he said that my daughter, there is a cataract on one of her eyes and that there seemed to be some problem with her heart, that she may have a heart condition. That was all I was told that night."

"Were you disturbed?"

"I was hurt."

An account of Ruth's disabilities is set forth on her own record at Long Island College Hospital—"classic rubella syndrome" is the overall description.

As the trial nears its end, the mystery of how Ruth came to be is finally dissipated. The witness is Dr. Robert Gordon, director of the Department of Obstetrics and Gynecology. In this capacity, as one of his colleagues testifies, he "has the ultimate decision . . . to do or not to do." Dr. Gordon's opinion—curiously dated 6/14, the day after Beatrice Smith left the hospital—is part of Exhibit 3 in the Court record.

6/14/64 Pt. has a history of German measles occurring at about the 5th week. The history is definite but pt. was not seen by a physician until after the German measles had subsided. Pt. now has a uterus about 16 weeks size. In view of the fact that: 1.) The diagnosis was not substantiated by a physician 2.) The uterus is too large for termination to be carried out by a simple curettage, then I would recommend that no abortion be done. —Robert E. Gordon, M.D.

Throughout his direct examination, Dr. Gordon stoutly insists that the overriding reason for his decision was the fact that Beatrice Smith was not seen by a doctor while she had the German measles rash. It was also his view in 1964 that amniocentesis was a highly hazardous procedure.

Grutman starts his cross-examination on a different tack, which quickly puts his tightlipped, crew-cut witness on the defensive.

"Dr. Gordon," he asks, "in the first twelve years that you had been practicing medicine up to 1964, had you ever performed an abortion?"

"No."

"Is there any reason for that?"

"I am a Catholic, and as such I don't do abortions."

"The note that you wrote on the chart is dated June 14th; that is a mistake, isn't it?"

"I guess so."

"When Mrs. Smith was there in June of 1964, you didn't think that she had German measles did you?"

"I didn't think it was documented."

" . . . That was a mistake too, wasn't it?"

"I don't know that."

Grutman confronts Gordon with records of his own hospital which characterize Ruth's case as "classic rubella syndrome." Dr. Gordon places the risk of abnormality in rubella at around 30 percent. Grutman cites studies placing the risk much higher, summed up in a comprehensive article in *Scientific American.*

"Do you recognize the *Scientific American* as an authoritative journal?"

"I have never read that."

Grutman hammers away at the admitted fact that neither Gordon nor any of his assistants telephoned Dr. Domsky for information beyond his brief letter. Nor did her hospital history include the fact that Beatrice's daughter Rosemary had had German measles, a clue of vital pertinence in an epidemic year. Dr. Gordon dismisses the paper the Smiths signed as a "routine consent."

Grutman refers to a poll of the nation's leading obstetricians who agree overwhelmingly that when rubella occurs in the first trimester of pregnancy therapeutic abortion is the "proper medical procedure if the husband and wife do not wish to take the obvious risks involved."

"I don't think that applies in this case," Gordon says. (Medical opinion is so nearly unanimous on this question that the defense never fell back on the fact that in New York, under a literal interpretation of the law, an abortion performed because of rubella is illegal.)

Grutman elicits Dr. Gordon's views on the hazards of amniocentesis. At Long Island College Hospital, the witness testified earlier, "we had never done one, to my knowledge, and there was very little experience with this procedure around Brooklyn."

Gordon insists that Beatrice Smith was admitted to the hospital only for "work-up or evaluation." Why then was she given an injection of Demerol and taken to the operating room?

"What do you give Demerol for?" Grutman asks.

"I would give it for a lot of things," Gordon replies. "We use Demerol in labor. We use Demerol preoperatively. We use Demerol for any kind of pain."

The jury is well aware that Mrs. Smith was neither in labor nor in pain.

Finally, Grutman zeroes in on the keystone in Gordon's position—his firm conviction that only a rash witnessed by a physician is conclusive evidence of rubella.

"Foremost in your mind was the fact that nobody had specifically reported that Mrs. Smith had a rash, is that correct?"

"That's correct." . . .

"Doctor, what color is the rash? On Caucasians?"

"What?"

"On Caucasians it is red?"

"That's true."

"Have you ever seen it on non-Caucasians?"

"Do you mean on—"

Judge Beckinella intervenes. "A colored person, an Oriental or Negro," he explains.

"I have seen regular measles. I don't think that I have ever seen rubella in a Negro."

Grutman reads from Holt's *Diseases of Infancy and Childhood*, a standard text: "The diagnosis of rubella can seldom be made with assurance unless the disease is prevailing epidemically. . . . The first cases in an epidemic are usually overlooked. . . . Its identification in Negroes is almost impossible."

"I have no opinion on that," Gordon says.

At this point, Grutman has won his case. The testimony of subsequent witnesses, the summing up by opposing counsel, and the Judge's charge are somewhat anticlimactic recapitulations of a now-familiar tale.

The jury's verdict is unanimous. An award of $10,000 to Beatrice Smith, $1 to Richard Smith, and $100,000 to Ruth Smith.

Judge Beckinella ponders the matter for two months. Then, he sets aside the verdict favoring Ruth. "The proof adduced demonstrated beyond any doubt that the infant's birth defects were the consequence of the child's mother having contracted rubella (German measles) during the early stages of her pregnancy," he says. "The proof showed that the only way the infant could have been spared being born without birth defects was not to have been born at all. . . . This court cannot weigh the value of life with impairments against the nonexistence of life itself. . . . "

When one has seen Ruth and others like her doomed to be crushing burdens to their families, until they move up on the waiting lists of nightmarishly overcrowded institutions for the severely retarded, Judge Beckinella's reasoning seems tortuous. But even to those who share his doubts on this point, Beatrice

Smith's ordeal is a clear example of a law which distorts the relationship between doctor and patient and, in fact, prevents physicians from practicing medicine in accordance with the highest prevailing standards of medical knowledge.

The Smith case is now being appealed in New York's higher Courts and may eventually reach the U.S. Supreme Court. Currently several other cases are challenging statutory prohibitions against abortion on constitutional grounds. (By the time the Smith case is finally adjudicated the specific problem of "rubella babies" could be on the way to becoming academic. An effective antirubella vaccine has been developed in the past year and a program has been started for the mass immunization of young children who might pass the disease on to their pregnant mothers. But unfortunately the public funds so far allocated are far from sufficient to wipe out a disease which produced 200,000 defective babies after the 1964 epidemic.)

Opponents of the present abortion laws in New York and the other 39 states with similar laws are now generally convinced that the remedy should be sought in judicial as well as legislative action. Heartened by some recent court decisions they are also painfully aware of the extreme difficulty of persuading state legislatures to act in this area. The going has proved particularly rough in states like New York where the Catholic Church wields formidable power and influential upstate rural legislators have shown little interest in the problem.

Last year, a moderate abortion reform bill sponsored by Assemblyman Albert Blumenthal, which was backed by the Governor and supported by most of the state's civic and welfare organizations (with the exception of course, of Catholic groups), would have permitted abortion for rubella and other causes of grave abnormalities. It went down to defeat after an emotionally charged debate in which wavering legislators succumbed to the tearful appeal of one of their number—a polio victim on crutches—defending his right to exist (a right not in jeopardy since he contracted the disease well after birth).

This year a bill calling for total repeal of the abortion law was introduced. Its supporters are disillusioned by the experience in several states where so-called "reform" statutes have been enacted within the past few years. Fearful of acquiring the stigma of becoming known as "abortion mills," some of these states have set up elaborate precautions including expensive psychiatric consultations. None of the new laws openly recognizes that the chief motivation for abortion is the unwillingness of a couple to have a child at a particular time. Where pregnancy due to rape has been made a legitimate reason for abortions, certification by a district attorney is generally required—and is often not forthcoming.

Most of the new statutes are patterned after the model adopted by the American Law Institute in 1959 which permits a licensed physician to terminate a pregnancy, not only to save the life of the mother, but also (1) if there is substantial risk to the physical or mental health of the mother, (2) if there is substantial risk that the child be born with grave physical or mental defects, (3) if the pregnancy resulted from rape or incest.

Only Oregon (which passed its reform bill last summer) has gone as far as the British Abortion Act of 1967, which provides that "in determining whether or not there is substantial risk [to the woman's physical or mental health] account may be taken of the mother's total environment actual or reasonably foreseeable."

On the other hand, in California, the clause dealing with potentially defective offspring was stricken out of the bill at the insistence of Governor Reagan, who threatened a veto unless it was omitted. Thus ironically, at the very time the Smiths were suing Long Island College Hospital for permitting the birth of a rubella baby, nine distinguished California doctors were called up for disciplinary action for performing abortions for precisely this reason.

The problem of potentially defective offspring is, however, statistically minor. Demographers estimate that no more than 10 per cent of the "unwanted babies" born in the United States annually are physically or mentally abnormal and defects can seldom be accurately predicted before birth.

In very few cases of unwanted pregnancy is the physical health of the mother threatened, for modern medicine has learned to cope effectively with most of the ills which formerly made pregnancy hazardous. The escape clause—for those who can afford psychiatric consultations—is a threat to mental health. Thus in California, during the first year in which the new law became operative, approximately 87 per cent of all therapeutic abortions were performed for psychiatric mental-health reasons.

"Some of our psychiatrists are balking at the suddenly increased load of consultations—in a matter which for most is a distasteful business," Dr. Edmund W. Overstreet, Professor of Obstetrics and Gynecology at the University of California School of Medicine, told a recent conference of Planned Parenthood physicians. "Individual [hospital] committee practices are extremely variable; some meet frequently and discuss each case meticulously; others simply rubber-stamp the patient's application and consultation papers. . . . [There is] a kind of geographic discrimination in the practice of therapeutic abortion in California. Thus, the nine counties surrounding San Francisco account for only 23 per cent of California's births; yet 63 per cent of California's therapeutic abortions are done there. By contrast, the two counties of the Los Angeles metropolitan area, with almost twice this share of babies (44 per cent), account for only 19 percent of its therapeutic abortions. . . .

"One of the continuing problems in many hospital committees," Dr. Overstreet added, "is the member physician who manifests a punitive attitude toward the results of illicit sex activity." (You've had your fun, now pay for it, continues to be the expressed or implicit sentiment of many medical professionals.)

"The economics of therapeutic abortion in California is something of a shambles," Dr. Overstreet said. "Because of the consultation system the total cost to a private patient ranges anywhere from $600 up into the thousands. . . . Hospitals discourage the indigent patients by not assisting them in clearance for Medi-Cal while eagerly doing so for other gynecological surgical patients." Nor has the new law solved the problem of criminal abortion. "Our projected 4,100 therapeutic abortions annually scarcely make a dent" in the estimated figure of 100,000 criminal abortions a year in California with an average of thirty related deaths, Dr. Overstreet said. "And the problem of the sociologically unwanted pregnancy has scarcely been touched by the new California law. . . . California's experience with it is not a happy one, and the law really satisfies no one."

Similarly in Colorado there is widespread dissatisfaction with the liberalized law passed in 1967. "This is a rich lady's law," Dr. Harvey Cohen, a Denver obstetrician, told a *New York Times* reporter. He estimated the Colorado price tag as at least $500. Colorado Blue Cross and Blue Shield have paid for only 2 per cent of the legal abortions performed since the new law was passed although 40 per cent of the state's residents have health insurance.

As disenchantment with "liberalized" laws has mounted, there have been surprising developments on the judicial level. This turn of events was anticipated by very few of the proponents of abortion-law reform who have been keenly sensitive to the emotions and prejudices of legislators. But now judicial "repeal" seems to be on the horizon.

The first startling decision was handed down in September of last year by the California Supreme Court which reversed the conviction of Dr. Leon P. Belous for conspiring to perform an illegal abortion. A Beverly Hills obstetrician and gynecologist who has campaigned vigorously for abortion-law reform, Dr. Belous was consulted by a pregnant college girl and her fiancé, also a student. Both were determined not to have a baby until the young man had completed his education. If all else failed, the girl said she would go to a notoriously dangerous Tijuana abortion mill. Dr. Belous referred her to a physician in whose competence he had confidence and who was licensed to practice in Mexico but not in California. Dr. Belous was convicted on a conspiracy charge.

Reversing his conviction on appeal, the state Supreme Court held by a 4 to 3 vote that the California statute infringed on a number of constitutional rights including a woman's right of privacy and her right to decide whether to have a child. The Court found the old California law unconstitutionally vague in that there was no way of determining when an abortion is "necessary to pre-serve life."

"The problem caused by the vagueness of the statue," the Court held, "is accentuated because under the statute the doctor is, in effect, delegated the duty to determine whether a pregnant woman has a right to an abortion and the physician acts at his peril if he determines the woman is entitled to an abortion. He is subject to prosecution for a felony and to deprivation of his right to practice medicine if his decision is wrong. Rather than being impar-tial, the physician has a 'direct, personal, substantial pecuniary interest' in reaching a conclusion that the woman should not have an abortion. The dele-gation of decision-making power to a directly involved individual violates the Fourteenth Amendment. . . . The state . . . has skewed the penalties in one di-rection: *no* criminal penalties are imposed where the doctor refuses to perform a necessary operation, even if the woman should in fact die because the opera-tion was not performed. . . . "

Dr. Belous was tried before California's abortion law was liberalized and convicted under a statute enacted in 1850. At that time, the Court pointed out, before surgical asepsis, abortion, like all surgery, was a highly hazardous procedure. Today, in contrast, "it is safer for a woman to have a hospital thera-peutic abortion than to bear a child. . . . [Yet] criminal abortions are the most common single cause of maternal death in California . . . the incidence of se-vere infection is very much greater. . . . The Los Angeles County Hospital alone, for example, in 1961 admitted over 3,500 patients treated for such abortions. . . . "

On the heels of the California decision, in November, in United States Dis-trict Court in Washington, D.C., Judge Gerhard A. Gesell held that a local law prohibiting doctors from performing abortions except when the expectant mother's life or health was in danger was unconstitutional on essentially the same grounds as those set forth by the California Court. By this ruling, he barred the trial in Washington of Dr. Milan Vuitch on charges of performing an abortion.

Paradoxically, ten days later, in neighboring Silver Spring, Maryland, Dr. Vuitch was sentenced to a year in jail and fined $5,000 on the same charge. Maryland is one of the states which liberalized its abortion laws in 1968; the new statute requires, however, that the operation be performed in a hospital. Dr. Vuitch, who had done abortions in his office, is something of a local hero. He has courted arrest more than a dozen times for defiantly performing abor-tions. To emphasize the absurdity of his predicament he announced that he would soon purchase a hospital where he could operate legally. He has also vol-unteered for service at an abortion clinic in Washington "open to women all over the country" which a national committee proposes to establish. The Justice Department is appealing Judge Gesell's opinion and, pending the outcome, most doctors in the area are discreetly silent.

Meanwhile, in New York, a suit has been filed in the federal District Court in behalf of four distinguished physicians challenging the constitutionality of the state's abortion statutes. The first round was won on November 5, when Judge Edward Weinfeld ordered a three-judge court to decide the case.

Thus there is, as of this writing, a very real possibility that the U.S. Supreme Court will decide that the question of whether or not to terminate a pregnancy is a private matter to be decided by a woman and her physician. This would be a giant forward step; however, as happened after the school integration decision of 1964, it is unlikely to produce an instant solution of the problem.

Catholic doctors and hospitals certainly show no signs of deviating from the historic position of their church, which holds that life begins either at the moment of conception or of implantation in the womb and that destruction of the fetus at any stage is infanticide, although no code of lay law upholds this thesis. Possibly some of the distinguished Catholics who have endorsed the birth-control pill might modify their position if, as some scientists hope, current reproductive research produces a technique for preventing the fertilized ovum from moving from the fallopian tubes to the uterus. Another promising and not too remote scientific possibility is a safe morning-after or once-a-month pill which would, in all probability, be a biochemical abortifacient. But until such a product is perfected, surgical abortion will continue to be a widely used alternative method of birth control—because of contraceptive failures and the unwillingness of a considerable number of women to use contraceptives at all for a variety of psychological reasons. So far as Catholic women are concerned—many take the pill in defiance of their church and a number flout the even more stringent ban against abortion. In Colorado, for example, where 22 per cent of the population is Catholic, 17 per cent of the applicants for therapeutic abortion, since the law was liberalized in 1967, were Catholics.

No one can compel Catholics—or anyone else who regards abortions as sinful—to have them. But is there any reason to give weight to the views of one religious group in framing secular law? Catholics, however, are not entirely alone in their aversion to abortion.

"I think we have to face the fact that if you got pregnant by rubbing a cloth across your cheek, there would be no abortion act or bill in the law and there would be no concern about terminating a pregnancy," Dr. Allan Barnes of Johns Hopkins, who was one of the prime movers in Maryland's abortion-reform movement, said on a recent TV program. "It's the fact that you get pregnant through sexual intercourse, and sex is different, sex is worrisome to some people, sex bothers them. . . ."

And certainly no one is more mightily bothered on the subject than the average physician. Some observers of medical attitudes theorize that men are attracted to the study of medicine, in part, because of a special fear of dying. Conceiving of their role as a continuous contest against death, they find the destruction of life, at any stage, peculiarly repugnant. Dr. Robert B. White, a Texas psychiatrist, offered another explanation in a paper presented to the Houston Psychiatric Society.

"Why," he asked, "are we as physicians so adamant in our anxious determination to put great obstacles in the way of women who want to terminate a pregnancy . . . ? Perhaps we have some primordial dread that lowering the taboo will lead to racial extinction. There is, however, at least one other deep motive . . . a fear on the part of the male physician of granting a woman a greater say in whether she will or will not keep the pregnancy. . . . Is it possible that the pregnant woman symbolizes the proof of male potency and that if we loosen our rule over women and grant them the right to dispose of that proof when *they* want to, we men then feel terribly threatened lest women can at will rob us of the proof of our potency and masculinity?"

If indeed such irrational factors are at work, then the current insistence of some militant feminists on making the right to abortion strictly a "women's issue" may be a questionable strategy. The presumption seems to be that the act which made the woman pregnant was something to which she "submitted"— surely an anachronism in this age of "sexual equality." It implies also that the man who impregnated her is, in all probability, an irresponsible cad who has no concern about whether or not he fathers a child. This is a libel on the American male.

A doctor can scarcely be forced to operate against his wishes, no matter what the courts may decide. He may object to "abortion on demand" on the grounds that he does not perform any other type of surgery at the patient's demand; the decision, theoretically a joint one, is largely his. Questions of malpractice can arise, however, if he fails to treat a patient competently or fails to refer the patient to another physician. The outcome of the Smith case may move some to reconsider their policies on abortion.

Granting that the physical burden of "compulsory pregnancy" falls upon women, the issue, in fact, affects all human beings, not just one sex. The gravity of the population crisis is now almost universally acknowledged. The battle lines are currently being drawn between champions of voluntary family planning and hard-line demographers who advocate compulsory population control as a matter of social policy, enforced through a variety of tax incentives (or disincentives) and techniques for sterilizing entire populations, making childbirth possible only by special permit. The goal of this movement is Zero Population Growth—that is, an exact equalization of the birth and death rate.

Civil libertarians argue persuasively that the time is hardly ripe for such draconian measures when an estimated five million American women do not have access to contraceptive information and when the difficulty of procuring abortions results in the birth of an estimated quarter of a million unwanted babies in this country every year.

The fiction that there is no "unwanted" child, that every human life—actual or potential—is equally precious and cherished, dies hard. We look back with horror upon the ancient and primitive societies which openly practiced infanticide. But in the not far distant past this was precisely the function of Britain's "baby farms," which received illegitimate babies and the unwanted off-spring of impoverished millhands without question on payment of a lump sum. The more babies that died, the more profitable the business, and the rampant infectious diseases of the day did the job handily in overcrowded nurseries. (When Little Buttercup sang in *HMS Pinafore*, "A many years ago/ When I was young and charming/ As some of you may know/ I practiced baby farming," Victorian audiences well understood why the chorus responded by finding, "This is most alarming!" In Germany, baby farmers were known as "angel makers.") The situation in Britain was so scandalous by 1871 that the House of Commons appointed a select committee "to enquire as to the best means of preventing the destruction of the lives of infants put out to nurse for hire by their parents." By the turn of the century considerable protective legislation had been enacted. However, as recently as the decade ending in 1927 the British Society for the Prevention of Cruelty to Children reported an annual average of 13 baby-farming cases involving 28 children.

"Parents have now taken over the executioner's role—not many parents but too many," says Garrett Hardin, a University of California biologist. "Child-ridden, impoverished, and desperate parents are responsible for thousands of 'battered babies' every year and perhaps some hundreds of dead ones. . . . But we should not focus our attention exclusively on the physical mayhem and murder. How many more unwanted children, never physically harmed by their parents, have their hearts broken every year?"

In the case of illegitimate babies, adoption has long been the favored solution in this country, and for many years there were far more would-be adoptive parents than available infants, a fact which may account for the long silence of social workers on the question of abortion. There has, however, always been an oversupply of "unadoptable babies," the ugly, the stupid, the crippled or emotionally disturbed, those whose skin is the wrong color or those who become "unwanted" by their parents when they are no longer adorable cuddly infants or toddlers, but unruly and unmanageable adolescents.

These are the unwanted children who keep venerable buildings known as "shelters" in cities like New York filled most of the time to 150 per cent of capacity. The official intention is to make these temporary way-stations until foster homes can be found. But foster homes are in short supply, even for babies, and there are few foster parents who can cope with troublesome adolescents. So many of the children remain for years in the "temporary" shelters. Among them are many long-rejected young girls whose conscious or unconscious yearning for something of their own to love propels them into pregnancy at the age of fourteen or earlier. Few of these child mothers have any prospect of supporting or rearing their offspring. Thus another generation fated to become "unwanted" is spawned.

In view of our society's callous unconcern for existing children who are, in fact, unwanted, it is hard to listen tolerantly to the hypocritical cant which defends the "rights" of minute cells of human tissue which have had the mischance to be fertilized.

Despite the dramatic gains of genetics in recent years, there will probably always be human beings misshapen in mind or body because of heredity, accident, disease, war, famine, or the lack of loving nurture. To them, a humane people owes the kind of support and rehabilitative effort which is now no more than a utopian dream. Surely it is a form of madness to insist on adding to this still-unaccepted burden responsibility for thousands of children, rejected even before they are born.

In his appeals brief, Attorney Grutman has included an eloquent quotation from Dr. N. J. Berill's recent book, *The Person in the Womb:* "If a human right exists at all it is the right to be born with a normal body and mind, with the prospect of developing further to fulfillment. If this is to be denied, then life and conscience are mockery and a chance should be made for another throw of the ovarian dice."

[3]

The Woman's Right of Privacy

Sarah Ragle Weddington

My topic, "The Woman's Right of Privacy," has two facets: the constitutional protection of the privacy of our citizens, and the particular concern of women regarding pregnancy.

On January 22, 1973, the U.S. Supreme Court decided the case of *Roe v. Wade.* That decision specifically holds that a woman's right of privacy extends to the decision of whether to continue or terminate an unwanted pregnancy. The case is truly a landmark decision. Before discussing the basis for and the impact of the decision, I would like to make a few general remarks.

First, regarding the topic of abortion, it is important to divide what is said from the manner in which it is said. Those of us who favor availability of choice are at a disadvantage concerning semantics. Those who oppose availability of choice emphasize being pro-life. All of us would affirm the sanctity of life, the joy of life, the value of life. The points on which we divide include the definition of human life, the weighing of concerns for the pregnant woman and for the fertilized ovum, and the implications of constitutional law.

Second, those of us who favor the availability of alternatives are not "for" abortion. We are *for* such things as preventing unwanted pregnancies; I personally have sponsored legislation to make contraceptive measures more widely available. We *do not* advocate, for example, that every woman should

Source: Originally published in *The Perkins Journal,* fall 1973. Copyright © by Sarah Ragle Weddington. Reprinted by permission of the author.

seek an abortion; we *do* advocate that the alternative of abortion be an alternative available to pregnant women.

Discussion regarding abortion so often centers on the fertilized ovum and omits any focus on the woman involved. My remarks will focus on the woman.

Pregnancy unquestionably has an impact on the woman involved. *Roe v. Wade* established that the impact of pregnancy is of such a nature and extent that the woman is entitled to constitutional protection in being able to choose among alternatives that include abortion.

The main plaintiff in the case, Jane Roe, at the time she filed suit was an unmarried adult. She filed on behalf of herself and "all other women who have sought, are seeking, or in the future will seek" a legal, medically safe abortion. She had not finished high school, had difficulty holding a job, and had no money for medical care associated with the pregnancy. Jane Roe had sought an abortion but had been refused since she was in good health and Texas law allowed abortion only for the purpose of saving the life of the woman.

Mary and John Doe, a childless married couple, were also plaintiffs. Mary Doe's health, but not life, would be seriously affected by pregnancy. Because of a neural-chemical disorder, she had been advised not to use oral contraceptives and not to get pregnant. The Does also filed a class action, pointing out that according to the 1965 National Fertility Study, among *married* couples in the United States, nearly 20 percent of all recent births were unwanted.[1]

The Constitution does not specifically enumerate a "right to seek abortion" or a "right of privacy." That such rights are not enumerated in the Constitution is no impediment to the existence of the rights. Other rights not specifically enumerated have been recognized as fundamental rights entitled to constitutional protection[2] including the right to marry,[3] the right to have offspring,[4] the right to use contraceptives to avoid having offspring,[5] the right to direct the upbringing and education of one's children,[6] as well as the right to travel.[7]

The plaintiff in *Roe v. Wade* sought to establish the right of individuals to seek and receive health care unhindered by arbitrary state restraint, the right of married couples and of women to privacy and autonomy in the control of reproduction, and the right of physicians to practice medicine according to the highest professional standards.

The federal district court agreed that a right of privacy was involved.

On the merits, plaintiffs argue as their principal contention that the Texas Abortion Laws must be declared unconstitutional because they deprive single women and married couples of their right, secured by the Ninth Amendment, to choose whether to have children. We agree.

The essence of the interest sought to be protected here is the right of choice over events that, by their character and consequences, bear in a fundamental manner on the privacy of individuals.

That view has been shared by a number of other courts which have considered the question and have affirmed the fundamental right involved. The progression of decisions by courts which have indicated their recognition of abortion as an aspect of protected privacy rights includes the following:

> The fundamental right of the woman to choose whether to bear children follows from the Supreme Court's and this court's repeated acknowledgment of a "right of privacy" or "liberty" in matters related to marriage, family, and sex.[8]
>
> For whatever reason, the concept of personal liberty embodies a right to privacy which apparently is also broad enough to include the decision to abort a pregnancy. Like the decision to use contraceptive devices, the decision to terminate an unwanted pregnancy is sheltered from state regulation which seeks broadly to limit the reasons for which an abortion may be legally obtained.[9]
>
> It is as true after conception as before that "there is no topic more closely interwoven with the intimacy of the home and marriage than that which relates to the conception and bearing of progeny." We believe that Griswold and related cases establish that matters pertaining to procreation, as well as to marriage, the family, and sex are surrounded by a zone of privacy which protects activities concerning such matters from unjustified governmental intrusion.[10]

Without the ability to control their reproductive capacity, women and couples are largely unable to control determinative aspects of their lives and marriages. If the concept of "fundamental rights" means anything, it must surely include the right to determine when and under what circumstances to have children.

All too frequently it is presumed that people have access to and are able to use highly effective contraceptives, and are themselves at fault in cases of unwanted or unplanned pregnancy. This assumption could not be further from medical reality. First, there still is no such thing as a contraceptive device that is 100 percent safe and 100 percent effective. Second, there are still those in the United States who financially do not have access to medical care and contraceptives.

The California Supreme Court has recognized that "childbirth involves the risk of death."[11]

Nearly ten years ago a medical expert reported that "the risk to life from an abortion, performed by an experienced physician in a hospital on a healthy woman in the first trimester of pregnancy is far smaller than the risk ordinarily associated with pregnancy and childbirth."[12] A recent study of the death rate from childbirth in the United States revealed that twenty deaths per 100,000 pregnancies occur among American women.[13] The same study reported that the death rate due to legalized abortions performed in hospitals in Eastern Europe is three per 100,000 pregnancies. Thus, in the United States today, giving birth is nearly seven times more dangerous than a therapeutic abortion.

Further, women who have been unable to end an unwanted pregnancy by other means have sometimes resorted to illegal abortions performed by persons with little or no medical training. There is no need to detail the emotional and medical consequences.

From the moment a woman becomes pregnant her status in society changes as a result of both direct and indirect actions of the government and because of social mores.

Pregnancy, from the moment of conception, severely limits a woman's liberty. In many cases of both public and private employment, women are forced to temporarily or permanently leave their employment when they become pregnant. The employer has no duty to transfer a pregnant woman to a less arduous job during any stage of pregnancy (should the woman or her doctor consider this advisable); nor is there any statutory duty to rehire the woman after she gives birth.

Until 1972, a woman who became pregnant and was employed in Texas state government was forced to quit. She was not allowed to use accumulated sick leave or vacation time; she had no right to get her job back; and if she were rehired, she came back in the status of a new employee. This was true even if she wished to continue working and her doctor certified the advisability of such. Regardless of whether the woman wishes and/or needs to continue working, regardless of whether she is physically capable of working, she may nonetheless be required to stop working solely because of her pregnancy. In many if not most states, women who are public employees continue to be compelled to terminate their employment at some arbitrary date during pregnancy regardless of whether they are capable of continuing work.

In Connecticut a directive from the Attorney General in 1938 stated that a pregnant woman could not be employed "during the four weeks previous to and following her confinement." This rule still exists. In fact, such employment is a criminal offense directed against the employer.[14]

This denial of liberty in one's work is accompanied by an unconstitutional taking of property, for Connecticut provides no maternity benefits. A woman is also denied unemployment compensation during her last two months of pregnancy, even when her unemployment is due to some reason other than pregnancy. If "total or partial unemployment is due to pregnancy," the woman is completely ineligible for benefits.

In Louisiana an amendment in 1968 of L.S.A.—R.S. 23: 1601(6)(b) enables a woman who is forced to leave her employment either by contract or otherwise because of pregnancy to qualify for unemployment compensation. But as illustrated in the case of *Grape v. Brown,* 231 So. 2d 663 (Ct. App. La., 1970), the unemployment compensation in no way adequately compensates either for the actual wages lost or for the denial of liberty that forces a woman to receive unemployment compensation. Mary Grape was employed as a key-punch operator by Southwestern Electric Power Company. When she became pregnant she was advised that the company policy required expectant mothers to terminate employment no later than the end of the 150th day of pregnancy and that no leaves of absence would be granted. She was forced onto unemployment compensation and had lost her job.

Thus, the pregnant woman loses her job, her source of income, and is *forced* to become economically *dependent* on others. The law is harshest on pregnant women who are heads of households, and depended upon as breadwinners. Statistics show that a high percentage of working women are in this position, i.e., they *must* work to support themselves and/or their children.

But restrictions on a woman's liberty and property only *begin* with pregnancy. A woman worker with children is considered "unavailable for work" (which means she cannot qualify for unemployment compensation) if she restricts her hours of availability to late afternoon and night shifts so she may care for her children during the day. Connecticut courts have often held that "domestic responsibilities" are "personal reasons unrelated to employment"[15] or "entirely disconnected from any attribute of employment."[16] In one decision the court said that a woman had just *five weeks* to rearrange her life and domestic responsibilities to try to make herself "available for work" according to Connecticut standards (i.e., ready for work at all hours of the day).

Once a woman has given birth, according to the Court of Appeals for the Fifth Circuit, she may still be barred from employment as long as she has preschool children.[17] If she needs or merely wishes to work while she has preschool children she cannot, unless she is fortunate enough to have a family who will care for the children or is wealthy enough to hire help. And although a housekeeper, nurse, or baby-sitter is a necessary expense, enabling her to work, she has not been able to deduct the salary of this person from her income tax [26 U.S.C. 214] and thus is normally left with little, if any, of her pay after these expenses are covered.

A further denial of liberty results from the fact that women are generally forced to arbitrarily end their education because of pregnancy. Until recently, girls who became pregnant were often forced to drop out of public school. Many women are also deprived of higher education because of college rules requiring that pregnant women leave school.

The importance of education in modern society has been stressed and re-stressed in recent years. It has been recognized that there are special problems for women in obtaining education, for although "men and women are equally in need of continuing education . . . at present women's opportunities are more limited than men's."[18] Nonetheless, women may be robbed of their education and opportunity for any development and self-fulfillment because of an unwanted pregnancy.

The incursions on the liberty of an unmarried woman who becomes pregnant are even more severe. She too may be fired from her job and is even more likely to be compelled to discontinue her education. Unable to terminate her pregnancy, she is often forced into marriage against her will and better judgment in an attempt to cope with the new economic and social realities of her life.

Of course, frequently, the man who is responsible for the pregnancy refuses to marry her. In Texas the illegitimate father has no common-law or statutory responsibility to provide support. The woman may be forced to become a welfare recipient, become part of this cycle of poverty, and expose herself to the personal humiliation, loss of personal liberty, and inadequate income this entails.

A woman who has a child is subject to a whole range of *de jure* and *de facto* punishments, disabilities, and limitations to her freedom from the earliest stages of pregnancy. In the most obvious sense she alone must bear the pains and hazards of pregnancy and childbirth. She may be suspended or expelled from school and thus robbed of her opportunity for education and self-development. She may be fired or suspended from her employment and thereby denied the right to earn a living and, if single and without independent income, forced into the degrading position of living on welfare.

Having been forced to give birth to a child she did not want, a woman may be subject to criminal sanctions for child neglect, e.g., D.C. Code §22-902, if she does not care for the child to the satisfaction of the state. In some states even here the disabilities for the woman are greater than for the man. The New York courts seem to have found as a matter of law that the mother has a greater responsibility for the child than the father. In the case of *People v. Edwards*, 42 Misc. 2d 930, 249 N.Y.S. 2d 325 (1964), although the father and mother were jointly indicted for failure to provide shelter and medical attention for their baby, the court held that only the mother could be punished for failing to bring the baby to a doctor when a condition that began with a diaper rash resulted in the child's death.

The impact of pregnancy is not restricted to economic and educational areas. Certainly there is a physical impact, as well as the emotional reaction to an unwanted pregnancy. These aspects are obvious, and I will not belabor the point.

The Supreme Court in its opinion in *Roe v. Wade* said:

This right of privacy, whether it be founded in the Fourteenth Amendment's concept of personal liberty and restrictions upon state action, as we feel it is, or, as the District Court determined, in the Ninth Amendment's reservation of rights to the people, is broad enough to encompass a woman's decision whether or not to terminate her pregnancy. The detriment that the State would impose upon the pregnant woman by denying this choice altogether is apparent. Specific and direct harm medically diagnosable even in early pregnancy may be involved. Maternity, or additional offspring, may force upon the woman a distressful life and future. Psychological harm may be imminent. Mental and physical health may be taxed by child care. There is also the distress, for all concerned, associated with the unwanted child, and there is the problem of bringing a child into a family already unable, psychologically and otherwise, to care for it. In other cases, as in this one, the additional difficulties and continuing stigma of unwed motherhood may be involved. All these are factors the woman and her responsible physician necessarily will consider in consultation.

Thus, a woman's right of privacy extends to abortion. Can the state prove a compelling reason to regulate? No.

Briefly, Texas law has never treated prior-to-birth and after-birth the same. Murder, in Texas, is defined as the killing of one who has been born. Murder carries a penalty of up to life. Abortion was a completely separate offense punishable by a maximum of five years, unless the *woman's* consent to the procedure was not obtained, in which event the penalty was doubled. Texas courts had specifically held self-abortion was not a crime, and one case regarding abortion stated that the woman was the victim of the crime. Tort and property rights in Texas are contingent on being born alive.

The Court responded to the State's argument as follows:

Texas urges that, apart from the Fourteenth Amendment, life begins at conception and is present throughout pregnancy, and that, therefore, the State has a compelling interest in protecting that life from and after conception. We need not resolve the difficult question of when life begins. When those trained in the respective disciplines of medicine, philosophy, and theology are unable to arrive at any consensus, the judiciary, at this point in the development of man's knowledge, is not in a position to speculate as to the answer.

It should be sufficient to note briefly the wide divergence of thinking on this most sensitive and difficult question. There has always been strong support for the view that life does not begin until live birth. This was the belief of the Stoics. It appears to be the predominant, though not the unanimous, attitude of the Jewish faith. It may be taken to represent also the position of a large segment of the Protestant community, insofar as that can be ascertained; organized groups that have taken a formal position on the abortion issue have generally regarded abortion as a matter for the conscience of the individual and her family. As we have noted, the common law found greater significance in quickening. Physicians and their scientific colleagues have regarded that event with less interest and have tended to focus either upon conception or upon live birth or upon the interim point at which the fetus becomes "viable," that is, potentially able to live outside the mother's womb, albeit with artificial aid. Viability is usually placed at above seven months (28 weeks) but may occur earlier, even at 24 weeks. The Aristotelian theory of "mediate animation," that held sway throughout the Middle Ages and the Renaissance in Europe, continued to be official Roman Catholic dogma until the 19th century, despite opposition to this "ensoulment" theory from those in the Church who would recognize the existence of life from the moment of conception. The latter is now, of course, the official belief of the Catholic Church. As one of the briefs *amicus* discloses, this is a view strongly held by many non-Catholics as well, and by many physicians. Substantial problems for precise definition of this view are posed, however, by new embryological data that purport to indicate that conception is a "process" over time, rather than an event, and by new medical techniques such as menstrual extraction, the "morning-after" pill, implantation of embryos, artificial insemination, and even artificial wombs.

In areas other than criminal abortion the law has been reluctant to endorse any theory that life, as we recognize it, begins before live birth or to accord legal rights to the unborn except in narrowly defined situations and except when the rights are contingent upon live birth. For example, the traditional rule of tort law had denied recovery for prenatal injuries even though the child was born alive. That rule has been changed in almost every jurisdiction. In most States recovery is said to be permitted only if the fetus was viable, or at least quick, when the injuries were sustained, though few courts have squarely so held. In a recent development, generally opposed by the commentators, some States permit the parents of a stillborn child to maintain an action for wrongful death because of prenatal injuries. Such an action, however, would appear to be one to vindicate the parents' interest and is thus consistent with the view that the fetus, at most, represents only the potentiality of life. Similarly, unborn children have been recognized as acquiring rights or interests by way of inheritance or other devolution of property, and have been represented by guardians *ad litem*. Perfection of the interests involved, again, has generally been contingent upon live birth. In short, the unborn have never been recognized in the law as persons in the whole sense.

In view of all this, we do not agree that, by adopting one theory of life, Texas may override the rights of the pregnant woman that are at stake.

The Court, however, did not recognize an absolute right of privacy. Rather, it stated, for example, that the state could constitutionally regulate to require that abortions be performed by licensed practitioners, that second trimester abortions be performed in hospitals, and that third trimester abortions be done only for the purpose of saving the life or health of the woman.

Pregnancy does affect a woman directly and profoundly. The Supreme Court therefore held that the constitutional right of privacy would extend to the choice of whether to continue or terminate a pregnancy. The state then failed to meet its burden of proving a compelling state interest; the great diversity of opinion that exists demonstrates the obvious difficulty of proof.

The year 1973 began with the establishment of a woman's right of privacy extending to the choice of whether to continue or terminate a pregnancy. However, as a practical matter, many women who seek medical services have great difficulty finding them. There are various moves in Congress to amend the Constitution to end the woman's right of privacy. Whether the right will become a reality soon remains to be seen.

Notes

1. Larry Bumpass and Charles F. Westoff, "The Perfect Contraceptive Population," *Science* 169, no. 3951 (18 September 1970): 1177, 1180.

2. "The association of people is not mentioned in the Constitution nor in the Bill of Rights. The right to educate a child in a school of the parents' choice—whether public or private or parochial—is also not mentioned. Nor is the right to study any particular subject or any foreign language. Yet the First Amendment has been construed to include certain of those rights." *Griswold v. Connecticut,* 381 U.S. 479, 482 (1965).

3. *Loving v. Commonwealth,* 388 U.S. 1, 12 (1967) (alternate ground of decision).

4. *Skinner v. Oklahoma,* 316 U.S. 535, 536 (1942).

5. *Griswold v. Connecticut,* 381 U.S. 479 (1965).

6. *Pierce v. Society of Sisters,* 268 U.S. 510 (1925).

7. *United States v. Guest,* 383 U.S. 745 (1966).

8. *California v. Belous,* 71 Cal. 2d 954, 458 P.2d 194, 199, 80 Cal. Rptr. 354 (1969), cert. denied, 397 U.S. 915 (1970).

9. *Doe v. Bolton,* 319 F. Supp. 1048, 1055 (N. D. Ga. 1970) (per curiam).

10. *Doe v. Scott,* 321 F. Supp. 1385, 1389–90 (N.D. Ill.) appeal docketed sub nom. *Hanrahan v. Doe,* 39 U.S.L.W. 3438 (U.S. Mar. 29, 1971) (No. 70–105, 1971 Term).

11. *California v. Belous,* 80 Cal. Rptr. 354, 359 (1969) cert. denied, 397 U.S. 915 (1970).

12. Christopher Tietze, "Legal Abortion in Eastern Europe," *Journal of the American Medical Association* (April 1961).

13. *Studies in Family Planning* (New York: Population Council), vol. 34 (September 1969): 6–8.

14. CGST 31-236(5), *Janello v. Administrator, Unemployment Compensation Act,* 178 A.2d 282, 23 Conn. Supp. 155 (1961).

15. *Lukienchuk v. Administrator, Unemp. Comp. Act,* 176 A.2d 892, 23 Conn. Supp. 85 (Super. Ct., 1961).

16. *Lenz v. Administrator, Unemp. Comp. Act,* 17 Conn. Supp. 315 (Super. Ct., 1951).

17. *Phillips v. Martin Marietta Corp.,* 411 F.2d 1 (5th Cir., 1969).

18. *American Women:* Report of the President's Commission on the Status of Women (1963), 11.

[4]

Rules for Abortion Debate

Richard A. McCormick, S.J.

THERE ARE A MILLION legal abortions performed annually in the United States. If this is what many people think it is (unjustified killing of human beings, in most cases), then it certainly constitutes the major moral tragedy of our country. In contrast, over many years fifty thousand Americans were lost in Vietnam. About the problem of abortion and its regulation, Americans are profoundly polarized, and there seems little hope of unlocking deeply protected positions to reach any kind of national consensus. Yet surely this is desirable on an issue so grave.

I have been professionally involved in this problem for well over twenty years, on podium, in print, and above all, in many hundreds of hours of conversation. Such experiences do not necessarily increase wisdom. But they do generate some rather clear impressions about the quality of discourse on the problem of abortion. I have to conclude, regrettably, that the level of conversation is deplorably low. On both sides, slogans are used as if they were arguments; the sound level rises as verbal bludgeoning and interruptions multiply; the dialogue of the deaf continues. Some of the most prestigious organizations of the news media (for example, *The New York Times, The Washington Post*) support policies that stem from moral positions whose premises and assumptions they have not sufficiently examined, let alone argued. The same can be

SOURCE: Copyright © 1978 by Richard A. McCormick, S.J. Reprinted from the July 22, 1978 issue of *America* by permission of the author.

said of some antiabortionists in the policies they propose. An executive assistant in the Senate told me recently that the two most obnoxious lobbies on the Hill are the antiabortionists and the proabortionists. Briefly, civil conversation on this subject has all but disappeared. Perhaps this is as it should be. Perhaps now is the time for camping in abortion clinics or beneath office windows of the secretary of Health and Human Services. But I think not, at least in the sense that such tactics should not replace disciplined argument.

Many of us have become bone weary of this discussion. But to yield to such fatigue would be to run from a problem, not wrestle with it. If stay we ought and must, then it may be of help to propose a set of rules for conversation, the observance of which could nudge us toward more communicative conversation. This is surely a modest achievement, but where the level of discourse is as chaotic and sclerotic as it is, modesty recommends itself, especially when so many begged questions and non sequiturs are traceable to violations of some of the fundamental points raised below. I do not believe these guidelines call for compromise or abandonment of anyone's moral conviction. At least they are not deliberately calculated to do this. Basic moral convictions have roots, after all, in some rather nonrational (which is not to say irrational) layers of our being. Rather, these suggestions are but attempts to vent and circumvent the frustrations that cling to bad arguments. In qualifying certain arguments as "bad," one unavoidably gives his or her position away at some point. But that is neither here nor there if the points made have independent validity. Perhaps the following can be helpful.

Attempt to identify areas of agreement. Where issues are urgent and disputants have enormous personal stakes and investments, there is a tendency to draw sharp lines very quickly and begin the shootout. Anything else strikes the frank, let-it-hang-out American mind as hypocrisy. We have, it is argued, seen too many instances where a spade is called a shovel. Serious moral issues only get postponed by such politesse. Well and good. But this misses an important point: There are broad areas of agreement in this matter, and explicitly speaking of them at times will at least soften the din of conversation and soundproof the atmosphere. Some of these areas are the following.

Both those who find abortion morally repugnant and those who do not would agree that abortion is, in most cases, tragic and undesirable. It is not a tooth extraction, although some heavy doses of wishful thinking and sanitized language ("the procedure") sometimes present it this way. Therefore, all discussants should be clearheadedly and wholeheartedly behind policies that attempt to frustrate the personal and social causes of abortion. One thinks immediately of better sex education (which is not equivalent to so-called plumbing instructions), better prenatal and perinatal care, reduced poverty, various forms of family support, more adequate institutional care of developmentally disabled children, etc. Furthermore, anyone who sees abortion as a sometimes tragic necessity should in consistency be practically supportive of alternatives to this procedure. While these two areas of agreement will not eliminate differences, they will—especially in combination with an overall concern for the quality of life at all stages—inspire the stirrings of mutual respect that improve the climate of discussion. This is no little achievement in this area.

Avoid the use of slogans. Slogans are the weapons of the crusader, one who sees his or her role as warfare, generally against those sharply defined as "the enemy." Fighting for good causes clearly has its place, as do slogans. The political rally or the protest demonstration are good examples. But slogans are not very enlightening conversational tools, simply because they bypass and effectively subvert the process of communication.

I have in mind two current examples. One is the use of the word murder to describe abortion. "Murder" is a composite value term that means (morally) unjustified killing of another person. There are also legal qualifiers to what is to count as murder. To use this word does not clarify an argument if the very issue at stake is justifiability. Rather, it brands a position and, incidentally, those who hold it. It is a conversation-stopper. Moreover, the word murder is absolutely unnecessary in the defense of the traditional Christian position on abortion.

The other example is "a woman has a right to her own body." This is not an argument; it is the conclusion of an often unexamined argument and therefore a slogan with some highly questionable assumptions. For instance: that the fetus is, for these purposes, a part of the woman's body; that rights over one's body are absolute; that abortion has nothing to do with a husband, etc. To rattle some of these assumptions, it is sufficient to point out that few would grant that a woman's rights over her own body include the right to take thalidomide during pregnancy. The U.S. Supreme Court has gone pretty far in endorsing some of these assumptions. But even justices not above the use of a little "raw judicial power" would choke, I think, on the above slogan as an apt way to summarize the issue.

Represent the opposing position accurately and fairly. Even to mention this seems something of an insult. It contains an implied accusation. Unfortunately, the accusation is too often on target. For instance, those opposed to abortion sometimes argue that the woman who has an abortion is antilife or has no concern for her fetus. This may be the case sometimes, but I believe it does not take sufficient account of the sense of desperate conflict experienced by many women who seek abortions. A sense of tragedy would not exist if women had no concern for their intrauterine offspring.

However, those who disagree with a highly restrictive moral position on abortion sometimes describe this position as "absolutist" and say that it involves "total preoccupation with the status of the unborn." This is the wording of the unfortunate "Call to Concern," which was aimed explicitly at the American Catholic hierarchy.[1] The track record of the hierarchy on social concerns over a broad range of issues is enough to reveal the calumnious character of such protests. As Notre Dame's James Burtchaell wrote apropos of this manifesto: "Ethicians are expected to restrain themselves from misrepresenting positions with which they disagree."[2]

Distinguish the pairs right-wrong, good-bad. Repeatedly I have heard discussants say of a woman who has had an abortion, "She thought at the time and afterward that it was not morally wrong." Or, "She is convinced she made the right decision." It is then immediately added that the moral character of an action depends above all on the perceptions of the person performing it.

Indeed it does. But the term "moral character" needs a further distinction. One who desires to do and intends to do what is supportive and promotive of others (beneficence) performs a *good* act. This person may actually and mistakenly do what is unfortunately harmful, and then the action is morally *wrong*, but it is morally *good*. On the contrary, one who acts from motives of selfishness, hatred, envy, performs an evil, or *bad* act. Thus a surgeon may act out of the most selfish and despicable motives as he performs brilliant lifesaving surgery. His action is morally *bad* but morally *right*. One's action can, therefore, be morally good but still be morally wrong. It can be morally right but morally bad.

The discussion about abortion concerns moral rightness and wrongness. This argument is not settled or even much enlightened by appealing to what a person thought of it at the time, or thinks of it afterward. Nor is it settled by the good and upright intentions of the woman or the physician. Those who destroyed villages in Vietnam to liberate them often undoubtedly acted from the best of intentions but were morally wrong.

Not only is this distinction important in itself; beyond its own importance, it allows one to disagree agreeably, that is, without implying, suggesting, or predicating moral evil of the person one believes to be morally wrong. This would be a precious gain in a discussion that often witnesses this particular and serious collapse of courtesy.

Try to identify the core issue at stake. Many issues cluster around the subject of abortion, issues such as health (fetal, maternal), family stability, justice (for example, rape), and illegitimacy. These are all genuine concerns and can represent sources of real hardship and suffering. Those who believe abortion is sometimes justifiable have made a judgment that the hardships of the woman or family take precedence over nascent life in moral calculation. Those who take an opposing view weight the scales differently.

The core issue is, therefore, the evaluation of nascent life. By this I do not refer to the question about the beginning of personhood; this is a legitimate and important discussion. But the definition of person is often elaborated with a purpose in mind—that is, one defines and then grants or does not grant personhood in terms of what one wants to do and thinks it appropriate to do with nonpersons. That this can be a dog-chasing-tail definition is quite clear. As Princeton's Paul Ramsey is fond of saying, "Does one really need a Ph.D. from Harvard to be a person, or is a functioning cerebral cortex quite sufficient?"

The core issue, then, concerns the moral claims the nascent human being (what Pope Paul VI, in a brilliant finesse, referred to as *personne en devenir* [a person in the process of becoming])[3] makes on us. Do these frequently or only very rarely yield to what appear to be extremely difficult alternatives? And above all, why or why not? This is, in my judgment, the heart of the abortion debate. It must be met head on. It is illumined neither by flat statements about the inviolable rights of fetuses nor by assertions about a woman's freedom of choice. These promulgate a conclusion. They do not share with us how one arrived at it.

Admit doubts, difficulties, and weaknesses in one's own position. When people are passionately concerned with a subject, as they should be in this case, they tend to overlook or even closet their own doubts and problems. Understandable as this is—who will cast the first stone?—it is not a service to the truth or to good moral argument.

For instance, those with permissive views on abortion (who often favor Medicaid funding for it) sometimes argue that denial of Medicaid funding means a return to the back-alley butchers for many thousands of poor. This is deceptively appealing to a sensitive social conscience. But it fails to deal with the fact that in some, perhaps many places, there is precious little price differential between the butchers and the clinics that now offer abortion services. So why go to the butchers? Furthermore, it conveniently overlooks the fact, noted by Daniel Callahan,[4] that the woman most commonly seeking an abortion is not the poor, overburdened mother of many children, but "an unmarried, very young woman of modest, or relatively affluent means whose main 'indication' for abortion will be her expressed wish not to have a [this] child [now]."

Or, again, it is occasionally argued that in a pluralistic society we should refrain from imposing our moral views on others. This was the solution of *The New York Times*[5] when it welcomed the *Wade* and *Bolton* decisions of the Supreme Court. The *Times* stated: "Nothing in the Court's approach ought to give affront to persons who oppose all abortion for reasons of religion or individual conviction. They can stand as firmly as ever for those principles, provided they do not seek to impede the freedom of those with an opposite view."

I agree with Union Theological's Roger Shinn when he says that this view is simplistic and disguises its own weaknesses. He wrote: "If a person or group honestly believes that abortion is the killing of persons, there is no moral comfort in being told, 'Nobody requires you to kill. We are only giving permission to others to do what you consider killing.'" The protester ought surely to reply that one key function of law is to protect minorities of all types: political, racial, religious, and, as here, unborn.[6]

The traditional Christian view on abortion (until recently, universally proposed by the Christian churches) was that the fetus was inviolable from the moment of conception. I believe that certain phenomena in the preimplantation period raise doubts and questions about evaluation, and that is all—namely, they do not yield certainties. I have in mind the twinning process, the estimated number of spontaneous abortions (thought to be huge), and above all, the rare process of recombination of two fertilized ova into one. To admit that such phenomena raise serious evaluative problems is quite in place, if as a matter of fact they do. Indeed, I would argue that it is a disservice to the overall health and viability of the traditional Christian evaluation to extend its clarity and certainty into areas where there are grounds for residual and nagging doubts.

Distinguish the formulation and the substance of a moral conviction. This may seem a refined, even supertechnical and sophisticated guideline better left in the footnotes of the ethical elite. Actually, I believe it is enormously important for bringing conversationalists out of their trenches. And it applies to both sides of the national debate.

For instance, not a few antiabortionists appeal to the formulations of recent official Catholic leaders in stating their moral convictions. Specifically, Pius XI and Pius XII both stated (and, with them, traditional Catholic ethical treatises on abortion) that direct abortion was never permissible, even to save the life of the mother. As this was understood, it meant simply and drastically, better two deaths than one murder. Concretely, if the only alternatives facing a woman and a physician were either abort or lose both mother and child, the conclusion was drawn that even then the direct disposing of the fetus was morally wrong.

This is a formulation—and almost no one, whether liberal or conservative, endorses the conclusion as an adequate and accurate way of communicating the basic value judgment (substance) of the matter. Some moral theologians would say, in contrast to the popes, that in this instance the abortion is indirect and permissible. Others would say, again in contrast to the popes, that it is direct but still permissible. For instance, the Catholic bishop of Augsburg, Josef Stimpfle, stated: "He who performs an abortion, except to save the life of the mother, sins gravely and burdens his conscience with the killing of human life."[7] A similar statement was made by the entire Belgian hierarchy in its 1973 declaration on abortion. Of those rare and desperate conflict instances, the Belgian bishops stated: "The moral principle which ought to govern the intervention can be formulated as follows: Since two lives are at stake, one will, while doing everything possible to save both, attempt to save one rather than to allow two to perish."[8] What is clear is that all would arrive at a conclusion different from the official one, even though the language might differ in each case.

The point here is, of course, that ethical formulations—being the product of human language, philosophy, and imperfection—are only more or less adequate to the substance of our moral convictions at a given time. Ethical formulations will always show the imprint of human handling. This was explicitly acknowledged by Pope John XXIII in his speech (October 11, 1962) opening the Vatican Council II. It was echoed by Vatican II in *Gaudium et spes:* "Furthermore, while adhering to the methods and requirements proper to theology, theologians are invited to seek continually for more suitable ways of communicating doctrine to the men of their times. For the deposit of faith or revealed truths are one thing; the manner in which they are formulated without violence to their meaning and significance is another."[9]

This statement must be properly understood. Otherwise theology could easily be reduced to word shuffling. If there is a distinction between substance and formulation, there is also an extremely close—indeed, inseparable—connection. One might say they are related as are body and soul. The connection is so intimate it is difficult to know just what the substance is amid variation of formulation. The formulation can easily betray the substance. Furthermore, because of this close connection, it is frequently difficult to know just what is changeable, what permanent. Where abortion is concerned, one could argue that the Roman Catholic Church's *substantial* conviction is that abortion is tolerable only when it is lifesaving, therefore also life-serving, intervention. Be that as it may, to conduct discussion as if substance and formulation were identical is to get enslaved to formulations. Such captivity forecloses conversations.

Something similar must be said of the 1973 abortion decisions of the U.S. Supreme Court. The court was evolutionary in interpreting the notion of liberty enacted in 1868 as the Fourteenth Amendment to the Constitution. No evidence exists that the Congress and the states understood this amendment to include the liberty to abort. Yet the court asserts that "liberty" there must be read in a way consistent with the demands of the present day. Therefore, it concluded that the right to terminate pregnancy is "implicit in the concept of ordered liberty."

This is but a formulation of the notion of constitutionally assured liberty, and to treat it as more than that, as an ironclad edict, is to preempt legal development. Indeed, the court itself gives this away when it treats the word person in the Constitution in a static and nondevelopmental way, as John Noonan has repeatedly pointed out. It looks at the meaning of the word at the time of the adoption of the Constitution and freezes it there—just the opposite of what it does with the word liberty. Such vagaries reveal that the court's decisions and dicta are hardly identical with the substance of the Constitution. To argue as if they were is to confuse legal substance and legal formulations, and to choke off conversation. In brief, we must know and treasure our traditions without being enslaved by them.

Distinguish morality and public policy. It is the temptation of the Anglo-American tradition to identify these two. We are a pragmatic and litigious people for whom law is the answer to all problems, the only answer and a fully adequate answer. Thus many people confuse morality and public policy. If something is removed from the penal code, it is viewed as morally right and permissible. And if an act is seen as morally wrong, many want it made illegal. Behold the there-ought-to-be-a-law syndrome.

This is not only conceptually wrong, it is also conversationally mischievous. It gets people with strong moral convictions locked into debates about public policy, as if only one public policy were possible given a certain moral position. This is simplistic. While morality and law are intimately related, they are obviously not identical. The closer we get to basic human rights, the closer the relationship ought to be in a well-ordered society. It is quite possible for those with permissive moral convictions on abortion to believe that more regulation is required than is presently provided in the *Wade* and *Bolton* decisions. Contrarily, it is possible for those with more stringent moral persuasions to argue that there are several ways in which these might be mirrored in public policy.

I am not arguing here for this or that public policy (although personally I am deeply dissatisfied with the present one on nearly all grounds). The point, rather, is that public discourse would be immeasurably purified if care were taken by disputants to relate morality and public policy in a more nuanced way than now prevails.

Distinguish morality and pastoral care or practice. A moral statement is one that attempts to summarize the moral right or wrong, and then invites to its realization in our conduct. As the well-known Redemptorist theologian Bernard Häring words it: Moral theology operates on a level "where questions are raised about general rules or considerations that would justify a particular moral judgment."[10] A moral statement is thus an abstract statement, not in the sense that it has nothing to do with real life or with particular decisions, but in the sense that it abstracts or prescinds from the ability of this or that person to understand it and live it.

Pastoral care (and pastoral statements), by contrast, looks to the art of the possible. It deals with an individual where this person is in terms of his or her strengths, perceptions, biography, circumstances (financial, medical, educational, familial, psychological). Although pastoral care attempts to expand perspectives and maximize strengths, it recognizes at times the limits of these attempts.

Concretely, one with strong convictions about the moral wrongfulness of abortion could and should be one who realizes that there are many who by education, familial and religious background, and economic circumstances are, or appear to be, simply incapable in those circumstances of assimilating such convictions and living them out, at least here and now. This means that compassion and understanding extended to the woman who is contemplating an abortion or has had one need by no means require abandonment of one's moral convictions. Similarly, it means that a strong and unswerving adherence to a moral position need not connote the absence of pastoral compassion, and deafness to the resonances of tragic circumstances. I believe that if more people understood this, the abortion discussion would occur in an atmosphere of greater tranquillity, sensitivity, and humaneness—and therefore contain more genuine communication.

Incorporate the woman's perspective, or women's perspectives. I include this because, well, frankly, I have been told to. And I am sure that there are many who will complain: "Yes, and you put it last." To which a single response is appropriate: "Yes, for emphasis." In the many discussions I have had on abortion where women have been involved in the discussion, one thing is clear: Women feel they have been left out of the discussion. This seems true of both so-called prochoice women and so-called prolife adherents.

But being told to is hardly a decisive reason for urging this point. And it is not my chief reason. Women rightly, if at times one-sidedly and abrasively, insist they are the ones who carry pregnancies and sometimes feel all but compelled to have abortions. Thus they argue two things: (1) They ought to have an influential voice in this discussion. (2) Up to and including the present, they feel they have not had such a voice.

All kinds of shouts will be heard when this suggestion is raised. We are familiar with most of them. For instance, some will argue paternal rights against the U.S. Supreme Court's 1976 *Planned Parenthood v. Danforth* decision. Others will ask: Which women are you talking about, prolife or prochoice? And then, of course, they will begin issuing passes to the discussion on the basis of predetermined positions. Still others will wonder why the fetus does not have a proxy with at least equal say. And so on. One can see and admit the point in all these ripostes. Nothing in femaleness as such makes women more or less vulnerable to error or bias in moral discourse than men, yet when all is shrieked and done, the basic point remains valid: The abortion discussion proceeds at its own peril if it ignores women's perspectives. As Martin I. Silvermann remarked in an issue of *Sh'ma,* "The arguments change when you must face the women."[11]

One need not make premature peace with radical feminists or knee-jerk proabortionists to say this. Quite the contrary. One need only be familiar with the growing body of literature on abortion by women (for example, Linda Bird

Francke's *The Ambivalence of Abortion*[12] or Sidney Callahan's essays on abortion) to believe that the woman's perspective is an important ingredient in this discussion. To those who feel this is tantamount to conferring infallibility on Gloria Steinem, it must be pointed out that in nearly every national poll, women test out more conservatively than men on the morality of abortion.

These are but a few guidelines for discussion. I am sure there are many more, perhaps some of even greater importance than the ones mentioned. Be that as it may, I am convinced that attention to these points cannot hurt the national debate. It may even help. Specifically, it may prevent good people from making bad arguments—chief of which, of course, is that it is only bad people who make bad ones.

Notes

1. "Call to Concern," *Christianity and Crisis* 37 (1977): 222.
2. James Burtchaell, "A Call and a Reply," *Christianity and Crisis* 37 (1977): 221–22.
3. Pope Paul VI, "Pourquoi l'église ne peut accepter l'avortement," *Documentation Catholique* 70 (1973): 4–5.
4. Daniel Callahan, "Abortion: Thinking and Experiencing," *Christianity and Crisis* 32 (1973): 295–98.
5. *The New York Times,* 23 January 1973, editorial.
6. Roger L. Shinn, "Personal Decisions and Social Policies in a Pluralist Society," *Perkins Journal* 27 (1973): 58–63.
7. This statement is cited in Franz Scholz, "Durch ethische Grentzsituationem aufworfene Normenprobleme," *Theologisch-praktische Quartalschrift* 123 (1975): 342.
8. "Déclaration des évêques belges sur l'avortement," *Documentation Catholique* 70 (1973): 432–38.
9. Vatican Council II, "Pastoral Constitution on the Church in the Modern World" (*Gaudium et spes*), translated from the Latin and reprinted in Walter M. Abbott, ed., *The Documents of Vatican II*, no. 62 (New York: Herder & Herder/Association Press, 1966), 199–308.
10. Bernard Häring, *Medical Ethics* (Notre Dame, Ind.: Fides, 1973), 89.
11. Martin I. Silverman, *Sh'ma,* January 20, 1978.
12. Linda Bird Francke, *The Ambivalence of Abortion* (New York: Random House, 1978).

[5]

A "Right to Life"?

Celeste Michelle Condit

THE ISSUE OF WHETHER or not a fetus has a Right to Life and the implications of such a right for the abortion debate are important but have been dealt with only indirectly to this point (i.e., with regard to the image of the fetus). This issue must be more fully addressed because the Right-to-Life movement has made it a central question on the public agenda. They have been able to do so, in part, because the persuasive value of their pictures and films derives from a real material entity with more or less substantial being— the fetus. Deciding the status of the fetus is, therefore, a real question that has colored the story I have told here (for I have tried to be non-judgmental in describing the path of the public argument, whereas one who accepted the Right to Life of the fetus probably would have condemned the path of the controversy between 1960 and 1985).[1] I believe it is an issue yet unresolved, and since its full impact on the abortion controversy is yet to be unraveled, I can analyze only the current stasis of the issue.

Life vs. Choice

The first substantive question might seem to be, Does the fetus have the Right to Life? Before addressing that issue, however, I wish to make clear that this

SOURCE: From *Decoding Abortion Rhetoric: Communicating Social Change* by Celeste Michelle Condit (Urbana: University of Illinois Press, 1990). © 1990 by the Board of Trustees of the University of Illinois. Used with the permission of the author and of the University of Illinois Press.

question is not itself simple or decisive. As several feminists have pointed out, the Right to Life does not entail the right to use the body of another human being.[2] Few would want to endorse the principle that the state can coerce some people to allow others to use their bodies (e.g., kidneys, bone marrow, blood), even to maintain the life of the others. Such a principle would leave us the nightmarish possibility of a state that decides which of us shall be sliced up for the benefit of others.[3] Thus, even if the fetus has a Right to Life, the pregnant woman does not necessarily lose the right to abort the fetus. Numerous concerns affect the final outcome of this issue, including the special responsibility a woman may or may not have to a fetus—an issue which entails one's view of sexuality—and the active nature of abortion as opposed to the more passive character of most other types of refusal to support others. Further, the fact that many pro-Life advocates support exceptions to a ban on abortion (usually for cases of rape, incest, and threat to the pregnant woman's life) indicates clearly that they also believe that the existence of the Right to Life of the fetus is not determinative.

Therefore, even if we were to find that a fetus has a Right to Life, this would not necessarily mean that a fetus had the right to use the body of a woman. A fetus's right does not necessarily outweigh a woman's Right to Choice, even though the Life of the fetus may seem to some to be a more serious value than the Choice of the woman. In a legal system built on principle and individual rights, we cannot reach judgment by choosing which of two entities the society weighs as more serious (the woman's Choice or the fetal Life). Instead, judgments are based on the spheres covered by individual rights. In this case, the fetal right may not reach far enough to abrogate the woman's right. Nonetheless, we ought to examine the claim that a fetus has a Right to Life.

A Right to Life?

After examining the arguments presented by pro-Life activists on the status of the fetus, I believe that there is an important core to this argument. Pro-Life arguments contend that the human fetus is a being of value, deserving consideration in the abortion issue. Because of this value, an abortion always contains morally undesirable elements. There are, however, incontrovertible differences between fetuses and human persons, and therefore the pro-Life movement's claim that a fetus is identical to a human being/person from the period of conception is not true. Moreover, the advocates have yet to establish the lesser claim that, in spite of the differences between a human fetus and a human person, we should *weigh* a fetus as a full human being (although this is a proposition that they might someday be able to establish with added grounds and warrants). To explain these conclusions, I will review here the argument about the status of the fetus in some detail.

Because the fetus has characteristics both like and unlike those of a human being, the classification of the fetus is a contingent matter, rationally undecidable and rhetorically constructed, rather than a basic fact of nature. As a consequence, rather than relying on some natural, logical classification, we must *choose* how to count the fetus.

Such classifications can be a matter of social *choice* rather than grammatical or logical necessity. This is not the case in all classifications (I am not maintaining an utter relativism here); for example, the classification of "red" as a "color" is a necessary one.[4] Natural and necessary classifications are usually either tautologies or built on analogies that are fundamentally profound, meaning that no overriding differences generate inconsistencies and that to deny the essentiality of the similarities of the compared objects would result in evident contradictions. Some definitional sets operate like that. If we define color with reference to blue and yellow, the analogy between red and blue and yellow makes it impossible to deny that red is a color. More formal definitions, focusing on wavelengths of light, similarly entail that red is a color because of the way both *red* and *color* are defined in terms of wavelengths of light. Such neat classifications are usually found in science, but some are also found in social language use.

In social life, however, many classifications are not so neat. The choices made in these cases (e.g., whether people are "adults" and so to be permitted adult rights such as drinking at age eighteen or at twenty-one) are precisely that—social choices. They are not "mere rhetoric" in the sense that journalists fling that term around, for the choices are based on the careful weighing of a host of relevant facts and values through public discussion ("rhetoric" in the classical sense). Because such social definitions are subject to a "weighing" process, they will be decided differently by different groups who must, quite rationally, weigh things through their own ideologies and conditions. Wherever there are both significant similarities and significant differences, therefore, we are thrown back on social choices rather than upon natural, logical, or necessary classifications. Clearly, if the fetus has major characteristics both like "human beings/persons" and unlike "human beings/persons," the classification of a fetus is such a matter of rational, deliberative choice (either for individuals or for the society).

Before analyzing the characteristics of the fetus, the contest over labels must be clarified. Pro-Choice advocates prefer the term *person* and pro-Life rhetors prefer the label *human being*. Even after arguing for hours over the status of the "personhood" of the fetus, pro-Life rhetors will charge that their opponents "never disagree with us that the fetus is a human being"; therefore, we will have to explore the implications of both labels. However, neither label establishes that fetuses before viability have, by grammatical, logical, biological, or historical *necessity*, a Right to Life.

The fetus clearly does not have, and cannot have, status as a full person on legal grounds. The Supreme Court's ruling that the constitutional usages of "person" have not included the unborn is convincing. Most simply, the constitutional protections spoken about usually refer to things that can only apply to those "persons *born* or naturalized in the United States of America." More important, the legal problems that would be generated by declaring a fetus a person are legion. Fetuses would have to be counted as dependents for tax purposes, covered by the census and apportionment, and treated as "persons" in dozens of other ways where it is simply not possible to treat them "the same as" persons (e.g., in assault laws). Although exceptions and modifications or special bills could be written on issues such as inheritance, taxes, and assault laws, the very fact that exceptional laws would *have* to be written indicates quite clearly that the fetus cannot share *the same legal status* as "persons." The law *must* treat the fetus differently from other persons because of the objective material differences between persons and the fetus. Legally, then, a fetus cannot be "a full human person" to be treated exactly as all human persons. Even a legal declaration that a fetus was a human person by the Supreme Court, a constitutional amendment, or Congress could not make it fully true, for exceptional laws that denied the claim would also have to be written.

This legal limitation arises from a biological fact. Legally, to have a "right" requires that one be an individual, and until birth, or until a viable separation from the mother, the fetus has not been individuated; biologically, it remains, absolutely, physiologically, a part of the mother. One cannot have a right *to life* unless one is capable of life, and the fetus before viability is not individually capable of life. Pro-Life advocates object to this standard of viability on two grounds—that the period of viability is changing to an ever-earlier stage and that no human being lives "independently," so the presumed independence of the fetus at viability is a chimera.

The first objection—that medical science can alter the point of viability—is valid only if we believe that some unalterable, permanent time-line determines the status of the fetus. The general pro-Life worldview maintains such a view—that things "are" permanently.[5] Essence cannot change. But this Platonic view offers only one possible set of criteria. A broad range of scholars in the twentieth century have pointed out the contingency of language as well as the radical changes in meanings of terms over time.[6] For those able to see that words unceasingly change *some* elements of their denotations through time, the fact that the numerical referent of viability may change does not invalidate it as a logically necessary standard for a Right to Life.

The second objection to viability arises from the concept of "independence." Viability provides an appealing standard for demarcating the transition from mere fetus to "person" because at that point the fetus is capable of independent life. In response, pro-Life advocates point out that no human being can really live independently; we all depend on others at some point in our lives. But, of course, this is not the kind of dependence at issue. To survive, a nonviable fetus must depend on precisely one other person's body; no other human being can offer the fetus what it needs. Moreover, what the fetus requires is *the substance* of the mother's body. That clearly is a unique kind of dependence, to which human beings are not otherwise subject. That difference is recognized in the law: even when a given person is dependent on precisely one other human being for a donated organ (e.g., a kidney) because only one other person can provide a good and timely match, the law and society refuse to compel that potential donor to give up the kidney for another, even if the donor is dead. The fetus thus has at least one substantial biological difference from the rest of us (others will be explored in the discussion of "human beings").

Therefore it is viability—the point at which the fetus can survive *without* absolute dependence on precisely one other person—not conception, that marks the biological point at which it is reasonable to conclude that, like all human beings, the fetus has a Right to Life because it is capable of sustaining life in the same way all human persons are capable of sustaining independent life. This statement might be taken to imply that, once medical science can keep a fetus alive from conception to viability outside the womb, the fetus may have a biologically based Right to Life from conception. The fact that personal physical independence is a necessary condition for a Right to Life does not mean that it is also a sufficient condition and that issue has not yet been much explored.

If the standard of viability is taken to be a sufficient condition, there are serious implications. A woman does not have the Right to Choose the death of a technologically viable human just because she does not want to have it in her body any longer.[7] Therefore, if technology allows removal of a fetus, even at very early stages of pregnancy, without killing the fetus, then, assuming that the physical risk to the woman is the same, she should forego abortion for removal. Some women will not like this requirement because they may continue to feel more responsibility and want legal control. In addition to creating moral dilemmas, this technological capability will generate a whole host of new policy problems—including issues of overpopulation and of financial responsibility for such children (and I believe that the state cannot coerce such artificial births AND require the woman to assume financial responsibility for it NOR place the fetus in an "orphanage" situation). If viability is accepted as a logically necessary *and* sufficient standard, however, we will have eventually to face such issues.

Currently, however, on both legal and biological grounds, there are clear differences between fetuses and human persons which deny the statement "The fetus IS a person" status as a simple, non-problematic fact. The final grounds on this issue are historical. For indeed, language is an historical entity, and if our culture had always said "the fetus is a person," then the claim, although not a necessary natural fact, would have presumption as a true statement because it would reflect a prior classification, made through history by the society. But this also is not the case.

American society has systematically treated a fetus as different from a person. Aside from the legal factors mentioned above, custom has treated the fetus differently. Persons in our society have names, and we have never given fetuses names. The naming as a unique individual person occurs at birth. Additionally, persons in our society are given ritualized burials, but outside of the Catholic church (and even here, by necessity, the fetus is treated somewhat differently), miscarriages have not generally been given the same funeral and burial customary in the society. This, of course, is especially true for the thousands of early miscarriages that occur each year. Moreover, in terms of the response of individuals, an early miscarriage is generally not as crushing a blow as the death of a newborn infant. Thus, our culture has not, historically, treated the fetus as a person.

On historical, legal, and biological grounds, therefore, the statement that a fetus is a person from the moment of conception is not apparently a simple statement of fact. Rather, it is a rhetorical suggestion, an urging that we make such a classification. The tactic used is "classification by denial of classification." Pro-Life rhetors seek to get their classification accepted as a fact by "naturalizing" the issue; denying that they are proposing a classification, they pretend instead that the "fact" is self-evident and inescapable. Instead of claiming that the fetus should be classified or treated as a human person, they claim that the fetus IS a human person. By mere assertion of factual status, they gain the persuasiveness of factual status.

The pro-Life movement, however, prefers to rest its case not on the claim that the fetus is a person but rather on the grounds that the fetus is a human being. Arguing to the effect that the fetus is both human and a being, they indicate that the conclusion is inescapable that the fetus is a human being. Here, we should begin with Abe Lincoln's caution that just because you have a chestnut and you have a horse does not mean that you have a chestnut horse. In a fallacy of composition and division, pro-Life rhetors elide the non-technical meaning of "human" and "being" with the richly embedded cultural meanings of "human being." This move once again relies on careful rhetorical construction.

The core of the pro-Life argument in this area has been vivid pictures of fetuses and the claim that science has discovered that the fetus is a human being *from the moment of conception*. The "discoveries" are the early-nineteenth-century finding that the fetus begins to grow after the joining of sperm and egg, nine months before its birth, and the twentieth-century investigations into the genetic makeup of the fetus from conception.

Although science has indeed discovered that the fetus has a unique, human set of chromosomes from the moment of conception, a problem arises when we try to link this fact with the larger claim that, therefore, because of its chromosomes, a blastocyst, embryo, or fetus is a human being. For example, after conception the "human being" may turn into twins, which might even recombine or dissolve later. According to the pro-Life definition, we have *a* unique person suddenly constituting two unique individuals and then, perhaps, back to one again. In addition, studies suggest that, for perfectly natural causes, as many as a third of all conceptions do not come to term. It seems extremely awkward to our conceptual system to suggest that a third of all "human beings" never get even to the developmental stage of viability. Finally, in addition to genetics other factors determine the characteristics of a fetus carried to term. What the pregnant woman ingests—food, drugs, germs, cigarette smoke, industrial chemicals—and what she does—physical activity, listening to music, natural vs. caesarean birth—will have a huge impact on the specific human being the fetus becomes. A conceptus with chromosomes that would allow musical brilliance or mathematical facility might be born grossly incompetent in these areas if its mother is deprived of a few small vitamins. Consequently, nourishment and history are as crucial as chromosomes in shaping the human personality.

One of the major reasons that genetics appears determinative for pro-Life advocates, even though it provides only a partial account, derives from their underlying belief structure. For different belief groups, the essence or "being" of a thing has been identified with its "substance" (physical or material), with its "spirit" (or "idea"), or with the unique fusion of substance, idea, and, perhaps, history. Because of their religious ideology, pro-Life advocates work from a rhetorical system in which "spirit" or "idea" is the sole important element. Genetic structure, taken as a "code" with information possibilities at its core, fits the concept of "idea" or "spirit" reasonably well. Consequently, the point at which this "idea" is fixed appears to pro-Life advocates to be the point at which the fetus has its "essential" element. All other characteristics are merely accidental. Hence their statement that "anything with a human set of chromosomes is a human being."

Again, however, such a rhetorical structure is not a necessary one. Others view material being as more important or consider idea and material as of equal importance. From either of these alternate perspectives, unless the fetus has a certain material being, it cannot be a human being. The pro-Life claim that once conception has occurred "all that is added is nutrition" thus glosses a major issue. For "mere nutrition" (i.e., physical substance), along with the substance of a personal history, might well be considered necessary components of human nature. This, of course, is a common element of the layperson's objection to anti-abortion laws. The lay statement that the fetus is just a "small blob of cells" captures the sense in which the materiality and history of the fetus are too insubstantial to allow it to count as a human being. . . . In sum, the conclusion that the fetus is a human being *because* it has a full set of human chromosomes is logical only for those who constitute being solely through "idea" or spirit, supplied in this case by genes.

The pro-Life rhetors have other arguments, however, which attempt to address the issue of "substance" to some extent. In pictures and verbal descriptions they emphasize the substantial elements of the fetus, citing the developmental stages at which its "heart" begins to function, when it has "brain waves," and so on. Here too, however, the pro-Life rhetoric uses metaphorical language that pretends to be literal. When they say that "the heartbeat begins between the eighteenth to twenty-fifth day,"[8] they refer to the early fetal "pulse" which, while definitely an analogy and forerunner of the human heart, does not have the four developed major compartments of the human heart or the developed arteries and veins and pumps at a tenth of the relative force. Therefore, when they say an early fetus has a "heartbeat," they conjure up the image of a beating human heart, but the *substance* of a "human heart" is not really there. Even when referencing material acts, the pro-Life rhetors refer to idea alone.

The same is true of "brain waves." Although electrical impulses can be measured in the embryo as early as forty days, these do not have the full complex patterns of adult brain waves, nor does the embryo have the substantial parts of a human brain. Not until somewhere between the twentieth and fortieth weeks do fetuses even begin to have the kind of brain development that would allow perceptions such as awareness of pain. Once again, the pro-Life rhetoric effectively asserts an analogy as a literal identity. This elision occurs because they take "idea" or "potential" as subsuming substance.

The genetic argument for claiming a fetus to be a human being is therefore internally sound but inadequate because it is incomplete: human beings are not mere chromosome content or "spirit."

The other major pro-Life argument derives from the pictures of fetuses. . . . On their own visual grounds the pictures demonstrate that until at least eight to twelve weeks, and perhaps even later, the fetus does not look much like a human being or have much substance. It is difficult to draw lines here—

another woman might not be deterred by the appearance of the fetus until as late as sixteen to twenty weeks—but clearly, if visual evidence is the grounds for decision, the early fetus does not meet the criterion required of a full human being. The fact that the pictures circulated in the early eighties by pro-Life rhetors in national magazines were of nineteen-week-old fetuses, not two-week-old fetuses, is a clear sign of their partisanship here.

The pro-Life position that the fetus is a human being from the moment of conception is not a simple statement of natural fact but a highly constructed claim. However, this does not mean that we have no rational grounds for *choosing* to count the fetus as a human being/person, for the partial grounds of the pro-Life rhetors are nonetheless strong grounds. Ultimately, then, we may *choose* to classify the fetus as a human. Our choice to do so, however, will be based on the weighing of the similarities between "fetus" and "human being/person" against the differences. To this point, there has been no public consensus (nor much discussion) about this weighing process.

One last argument is of interest on the pro-Life side. In public, especially on a national scale, pro-Life rhetors are usually careful to avoid citing religious tradition as a reason for their claims; in fact, pro-Life advocates generally deny the religious foundations of their beliefs in public. However, since these religious foundations are an absolutely essential component motivating the movement, it is important to address the Christian Bible.[9]

I do not wish to suggest that the Bible is an adequate authority in the *public* controversy. Although this nation was founded as a set of Christian theocracies, we have evolved past such city-state tyrannies into a secular state in which Moslems, Jews, deists, Hindus, Buddhists, and atheists all have their rights, and arguments based on the Bible can hold no public authority over these groups. The pro-Life rhetors recognize this fact in their vehement denials of a religious base to their arguments.

Nonetheless, in spite of vehement in-group assertions by pro-Life activists to the contrary, the Bible itself does not explicitly ban abortion. To support their claim, pro-Life advocates cite only the general commandment against killing, vague and metaphorical passages about the beginning of life in the womb, and one ambiguous passage about accidentally induced miscarriage. These proofs are surprising for the conspicuousness of their weakness and indirection. None mentions abortion explicitly. The religious proscription of abortion is not, therefore, the result of clear Biblical commandment but a by-product of Catholic tradition and the recent fundamentalist politics that have combined to construct a set of interpretations that cast moral and religious opprobrium on abortion.

On a multiplicity of grounds, the pro-Life advocates' assertion that the "fetus is a human being and therefore abortion is murder" is not a "true" claim but a rhetorical tactic—an effort to establish the claim as a social choice *disguised* as a statement of fact. There is slippage between the solid grounds employed by the pro-Life movement and the overclaiming they do on the basis of those grounds, and this slippage may be part of the reason that their position has not been fully successful in legal and other realms.

Until recently the pro-Choice movement has been reticent in addressing this issue. Because they argue that the issue is a matter of individual Choice, they have refused to "take a position" on the status of the fetus. While ideologically consistent, that refusal allows the pro-Life claims to go uncontested. In the long run, this may result in the adoption of the pro-Life "choice" about the status of the fetus by a majority of individuals. This could lead to legislative coercion to compel all individuals to act on the pro-Life definition. The pro-Choice movement's discursive choice may, therefore, also form part of the long-term outcome of the controversy.

Even if we dismiss, at least for now, the pro-Life claim that a fetus is a person with a Right to Life, we should not dismiss the grounds they offer us (that kind of either/or response is as partisan as the pro-Life over-claiming). If, indeed, we block out their partisan overstatement and concentrate on the substance of what is left, the pro-Life rhetoric indicates with gleaming clarity that the fetus has value in its material being, its potential, and its "spirit." It seems inhumane to look at the pro-Life pictures, watch their movies, listen to their descriptions of fetal development, and conclude that a fetus is, throughout its development, nothing but a blob of tissue. The human fetus is a living, growing thing, increasingly precious as it develops, gains substance, and builds relationships to the pregnant woman and, through her, to the social world. The pro-Life argument forces us to face the real violence in abortion, and their truths are necessary to keep us morally responsible. They prevent us from seeing abortion as a casual act of birth control; they remind us, powerfully, that we ought to take serious measures as individuals and as a society to reduce or eliminate abortions, even if we must do so through means that do not violate the rights of women.[10]

Notes

1. My analysis of this still-current political issue of the status of the fetus is influenced by my own predispositions, and so I will indicate what my assumptions and premises are. I define myself as a "substantive liberal"; . . . I tend further to oppose the use of state power for enforcing morality.

   My background influences the way I interpret the issues in the abortion debate, but my position is a centrist position in the United States today. Hence, the "bias" in this analysis is one that is probably the most generally taken one. There is, however, one crucial caveat. One fundamental stumbling stone in the abortion debate is the issue of religious worldviews. . . . [R]eligion has been the underlying motivation and worldview of most pro-Life activists, but religious discourse has not formed the overt center-post of their public argumentation. The following analyses do not accept any overt or covert assumptions deriving from religious views. Consequently, those who look at the issues from a religious foundation will not find these suggestions comforting. The same, however, is true on the other side of the issue for feminists. Although some of the feminist worldview has been part of the public argument, and I share it, that view has not been willing to incorporate the contributions of the pro-Life argument, and I have attempted to do so. In sum, my position ends up pleasing neither pro-Choice nor pro-Life activists, but it probably will end up offering alternatives least acceptable to religious activists.

2. For example, see Beverly Wildung Harrison, *Our Right to Choose: Toward a New Abortion Ethic* (Boston: Beacon Press, 1983).

3. Our government does, in fact, take it upon itself to act coercively, in disregard for individual rights in some instances, most notably for the draft and for taxation. I am partially convinced that it should not do so in these cases. However, I believe that a simple distinction between such cases and those of the fetus vs. the woman is that in these other cases the "social good" done is a tangible one for the person whose rights are deprived as well as for others. Taxes provide services directly to the individual taxed. Even the draft, in theory at least, is undertaken to protect the Freedom of the individual drafted as well as others. This is clearly not the case in the abortion controversy. The reason for the abrogation of the woman's right is not a social good but the competing individual interest of the fetus (except where criminalization of abortion is justified on explicitly pro-natalist grounds, but that would raise an entirely different frame for the issue).

4. For the theoretical underpinnings of this view, see Celeste Condit Railsback, "Beyond Rhetorical Relativism: A Structural-Material Model of Truth and Objective Reality," *Quarterly Journal of Speech* 69 (1983): 351–63.

5. There is not yet published an adequate description of the philosophical pinnings of the pro-Life view, but for partial development see Celeste Condit Railsback, "Pro-Life, Pro-Choice: Different Conceptions of Value," *Women's Studies in Communication* 5 (spring 1982): 16–28; Randall Lake, "Order and Disorder in Anti-Abortion Rhetoric: A Logological View," *Quarterly Journal of Speech* 70 (1984): 425–43; Kristin Luker, *Abortion and the Politics of Motherhood* (Berkeley: University of California Press, 1984).

6. For example, Ludwig Wittgenstein, *Philosophical Investigations,* trans. C. E. M. Anscombe (Oxford: Basil Blackwell, 1963), 83, 31e–32e; Alfred Korzybski, *Science and Sanity,* 4th ed. (Lakeville, Conn.: The Institute of General Semantics, 1958); Jacques Derrida, *Of Grammatology* (Baltimore: Johns Hopkins University Press, 1976); Jean-François Lyotard, *The Postmodern*

Condition: A Report on Knowledge, trans. Geoff Bennington and Brian Massumi (Minneapolis: University of Minnesota Press, 1984). For a concrete example see Michael Calvin McGee, "The Origins of 'Liberty': A Feminization of Power," *Communication Monographs* 47 (1980): 23–45; or McGee, "An Essay on the Flip Side of Privacy," in *Argument in Transition: Proceedings of the Third Summer Conference on Argumentation,* ed. David Zarefsky, Malcolm O. Sillars, and Jack Rhodes (Annandale, Va.: Speech Communication Association, 1983), 105–15.

7. The reason for this has been eloquently implied by women who argue against the destruction of disabled fetuses or female fetuses (femicide). Clearly implied in their arguments is the assumption of the unique value even of pre-humans. See, for example, Anne Finger, "Claiming All Our Bodies: Reproductive Rights and Disabilities," and Viola Rogencamp, "Abortion of a Special Kind: Male Sex Selection in India," both in *Test Tube Women,* ed. Rita Arditti, Renate Duelli-Klein, and Shelley Minden (London, Boston: Pandora Press, 1984), 81–97, 266–78.

8. For an example of such claims, see Dr. and Mrs. J. C. Willke, *Handbook on Abortion* (Cincinnati, Ohio: Hayes, 1979), 18.

9. I have already cited several examples of this, but consider, for example, the case of Joseph M. Scheidler. In public media he argues pointedly that his position is based not on religion but on science. "Discussion," *Christian Century,* 18 July 1979, 738. In in-group rhetoric, however, Scheidler's discourse is some of the most thoroughgoingly Christian I have seen. He argues the necessity of saving the *souls* of women and abortionists *for God,* even against their own will; for example, "We want the abortionists to be converted, returned to God, and be saved," or "We do not want anyone to lose his soul. We do not want the abortionists to be punished in hell for eternity." Scheidler, *Abortion: Opposing Viewpoints* (St. Paul, Minn.: Greenhaven Press, 1986), 171–75.

10. Policies which would protect Life through Choice would include intensified education, especially for young males, about the consequences of intercourse, the reasons for abstinence, the available contraceptive options, along with the provision of more attractive alternatives than young, unwed motherhood to economically deprived teenagers and the provision of maternal care, day care, and other child-raising support mechanisms to women who desire to have children.

[6]

Concerning Abortion: An Attempt at a Rational View

Charles Hartshorne

My ONETIME COLLEAGUE T. V. Smith once wrote a book called *Beyond Conscience,* in which he waxed eloquent in showing "the harm that good men do." To live according to one's conscience may be a fine thing, but what if A's conscience leads A to try to compel B and C to live, not according to B's or C's conscience, but according to A's? That is what many opponents of abortion are trying to do. To propose a constitutional amendment to this effect is one of the most outrageous attempts to tyrannize over others that I can recall in my long lifetime as an American citizen. Proponents of the antiabortion amendment make their case, if possible, even worse when they defend themselves with the contention "It isn't my conscience only—it is a commandment of religion." For now one particular form of religion (certainly not the only form) is being used in an attempt to tyrannize over other forms of religious or philosophical belief. The separation of church and state evidently means little to such people.

In What Sense "Human"?

Ours is a country that has many diverse religious groups, and many people who cannot find truth in any organized religious body. It is a country that has

SOURCE: Copyright 1981 by Christian Century Foundation. Reprinted by permission from the January 21, 1981 issue of *The Christian Century.*

great difficulty in effectively opposing forms of killing that *everyone* admits to be wrong. Those who would saddle the legal system with matters about which consciences sincerely and strongly differ show a disregard of the country's primary needs. (The same is to be said about crusades to make things difficult for homosexuals.) There can be little freedom if we lose sight of the vital distinction between moral questions and legal ones. The law compels and coerces, with the implicit threat of violence; morals seek to persuade. It is a poor society that forgets this difference.

What is the *moral* question regarding abortion? We are told that the fetus is alive and that therefore killing it is wrong. Since mosquitoes, bacteria, apes and whales are also alive, the argument is less than clear. Even plants are alive. I am not impressed by the rebuttal, "But plants, mosquitoes, bacteria and whales are not human, and the fetus is." For the issue now becomes, in *what sense* is the fetus human? No one denies that its origin is human, as is its *possible* destiny. But the same is true of every unfertilized egg in the body of a nun. Is it wrong that some such eggs are not made or allowed to become human individuals?

Granted that a fetus is human in origin and possible destiny, in what further sense is it human? The entire problem lies here. If there are pro-life activists who have thrown much light on this question, I do not know their names.

One theologian who writes on the subject—Paul Ramsey—thinks that a human egg cell becomes a human individual with a moral claim to survive if it has been fertilized. Yet this egg cell has none of the qualities that we have in mind when we proclaim our superior worth to the chimpanzees or dolphins. It cannot speak, reason or judge between right and wrong. It cannot have personal relations, without which a person is not functionally a person at all, until months—and not, except minimally, until years—have passed. And even then, it will not be a person in the normal sense unless some who are already fully persons have taken pains to help it become a human being in the full value sense, functioning as such. The antiabortionist is commanding some person or persons to undertake this effort. For without it, the fetus will *never* be human in the relevant sense. It will be human only in origin, but otherwise a subhuman animal.

The fertilized egg is an individual egg, but not an individual human being. For such a being is, in its body, a multicellular organism, a *metazoan*—to use the scientific Greek—and the egg is a single cell. The first thing the egg cell does is to begin dividing into many cells. For some weeks the fetus is not a single individual at all, but a colony of cells. During its first weeks there seems to be no ground for regarding the fetus as comparable to an individual animal. Only in possible or probable destiny is it an individual. Otherwise it is an organized society of single-celled individuals.

A possible individual person is one thing; an actual person is another. If this difference is not important, what is? There is in the long run no room in the solar system, or even in the known universe, for all human eggs—even all fertilized eggs, as things now stand—to become human persons. Indeed, it is mathematically demonstrable that the present rate of population growth must be lowered somehow. It is not a moral imperative that all possibilities of human persons become actual persons.

Of course, some may say that the fertilized egg already has a human soul, but on what evidence? The evidence of soul in the relevant sense is the capacity to reason, judge right and wrong, and the like.

Genetic and Other Influences

One may also say that since the fertilized egg has a combination of genes (the units of physical inheritance) from both parents, in this sense it is already a human individual. There are two objections, either one in my opinion conclusive but only one of which is taken into account by Ramsey. The one he does mention is that identical twins have the same gene combination. The theologian does not see this as decisive, but I do.

The other objection is that it amounts to a very crude form of materialism to identify individuality with the gene-combination. Genes are the chemical bearers of inherited traits. This chemical basis of inheritance presumably influences everything about the development of the individual—*influences,* but does not fully determine. To say that the entire life of the person is determined by heredity is a theory of unfreedom that my religious conviction can only regard as monstrous. And there are biophysicists and neurophysiologists who agree with me.

From the gene-determined chemistry to a human person is a long, long step. As soon as the nervous system forming in the embryo begins to function as a whole—and not before—the cell colony begins to turn into a genuinely individual animal. One may reasonably suppose that this change is accompanied by some extremely primitive individual animal feelings. They cannot be recognizably human feelings, much less human thoughts, and cannot compare with the feelings of a porpoise or chimpanzee in level of consciousness. That much seems as certain as anything about the fetus except its origin and possible destiny. The nervous system of a very premature baby has been compared by an expert to that of a pig. And we know, if we know anything about this matter, that it is the nervous system that counts where individuality is concerned.

Identical twins are different individuals, each unique in consciousness. Though having the same genetic makeup, they will have been differently situated in the womb and hence will have received different stimuli. For that reason, if for no other, they will have developed differently, especially in their brains and nervous systems.

But there are additional reasons for the difference in development. One is the role of chance, which takes many forms. We are passing through a great cultural change in which the idea, long dominant in science, that chance is "only a word for our ignorance of causes" is being replaced by the view that the real laws of nature are probabilistic and allow for aspects of genuine chance.

Another reason is that it is reasonable to admit a reverse influence of the developing life of feelings in the fetus on the nervous system, as well as of the system on the feelings. And since I, along with some famous philosophers and scientists, believe in freedom (not solely of mature human beings but—in some slight degree—of all individuals in nature, down to the atoms and farther), I hold that even in the fetus the incipient individual is unconsciously making what on higher levels we call "decisions." These decisions influence the developing nervous system. Thus to a certain extent we *make our own bodies* by our feelings and thoughts. An English poet with Platonic ideas expressed this concept as follows:

> *The body from the soul its form doth take,*
> *For soul is form and doth the body make.*

The word soul is, for me, incidental. The point is that feelings, thoughts, experiences react on the body and partly mold its development.

The Rights of Persons

Paul Ramsey argues (as does William Buckley in a letter to me) that if a fetus is not fully human, then neither is an infant. Of course an infant is not fully human. No one thinks it can, while an infant, be taught to speak, reason or judge right and wrong. But it is much closer to that stage than is a three-month fetus. It is beginning to have primitive social relations not open to a fetus; and since there is no sharp line anywhere between an infant and a child able to speak a few words, or between the latter and a child able to speak very many words, we have to regard the infant as significantly different from a three-month or four-month fetus. Nevertheless, I have little sympathy with the idea that infanticide is just another form of murder. Persons who are already functionally persons in the full sense have more important rights even than infants. Infanticide can be wrong without being fully comparable to the killing of persons in the full sense.

Does this distinction apply to the killing of a hopelessly senile person (or one in a permanent coma)? For me it does. I hope that no one will think that if, God forbid, I ever reach that stage, it must be for my sake that I should be treated with the respect due to normal human beings. Rather, it is for the sake of others that such respect may be imperative. Symbolically, one who has been a person may have to be treated as a person. There are difficulties and hazards in not so treating such individuals.

Religious people (I would so describe myself) may argue that once a fetus starts to develop, it is for God, not human beings, to decide whether the fetus survives and how long it lives. This argument assumes, against all evidence, that human life-spans are independent of human decisions. Our medical hygiene has radically altered the original "balance of nature." Hence the population explosion. Our technology makes pregnancy more and more a matter of human decision; more and more our choices are influencing the weal and woe of the animals on this earth. It is an awesome responsibility, but one that we cannot avoid. And, after all, the book of Genesis essentially predicted our dominion over terrestrial life. In addition, no one is proposing to make abortion compulsory for those morally opposed to it. I add that everyone who smokes is taking a hand in deciding how long he or she will live. Also everyone who, by failing to exercise reasonably, allows his or her heart to lose its vigor. Our destinies are not simply "acts of God."

I may be told that if I value my life I must be glad that I was not aborted. Yes, I am glad, but this expression does not constitute a claim to having already had a "right," against which no other right could prevail, to the life I have enjoyed. I feel no indignation or horror at contemplating the idea that the world might have had to do without me. The world could have managed, and as for what I would have missed, there would have been no such "I" to miss it.

Potential, Not Actual

With almost everything they say, the fanatics against abortion show that they will not, or cannot, face the known facts of this matter. The inability of a fetus to say "I" is not merely a lack of skill; there is nothing there to which the pronoun could properly refer. A fetus is not a person but a *potential* person. The "life" to which "pro-life" refers is nonpersonal, by any criterion that makes sense to some of us. It is subpersonal animal life only. The mother, however, *is* a person.

I resent strongly the way many males tend to dictate to females their behavior, even though many females encourage them in this. Of course, the male parent of a fetus also has certain rights, but it remains true that the female parent is the one most directly and vitally concerned.

I shall not forget talking about this whole matter to a wonderful woman, the widow of a philosopher known for his idealism. She was doing social work with young women and had come to the conclusion that abortion is, in some cases, the lesser evil. She told me that her late husband had said, when she broached the subject to him, "But you can't do that." "My darling," she replied, "we *are* doing it." I see no reason to rate the consciences of the pro-lifers higher than this woman's conscience. She knew what the problem was for certain mothers. In a society that flaunts sex (its pleasures more than its serious hazards, problems and spiritual values) in all the media, makes it difficult for the young to avoid unwanted pregnancy, and does little to help them with the most difficult of all problems of self-discipline, we tell young persons that they are murderers if they resort to abortion. And so we should not be surprised that Margaret Mead, that clear-sighted observer of our society (and of other societies), should say, "Abortion is a nasty thing, but our society deserves it." Alas, it is too true.

I share something of the disgust of hard-core opponents of abortion that contraceptives, combined with the availability of abortion, may deprive sexual intercourse of spiritual meaning. For me the sacramental view of marriage has always had appeal, and my life has been lived accordingly. Abortion is indeed a nasty thing, but unfortunately there are in our society many even nastier things, like the fact that some children are growing up unwanted. This for my conscience is a great deal nastier, and truly horrible. An overcrowded world is also nasty, and could in a few decades become truly catastrophic.

The argument against abortion (used, I am sorry to say, by Pearl Buck) that the fetus may be a potential genius has to be balanced against the much more probable chance of its being a mediocrity, or a destructive enemy of society. Every egg cell is a possible genius and also a possible monster in human form. Where do we stop in calculating such possibilities?

If some who object to abortion work to diminish the number of unwanted, inappropriate pregnancies, or to make bearing a child for adoption by persons able to be its loving foster parents more attractive than it now is, and do this with a minimum of coercion, all honor to them. In my view of the population problem, the first of these remedies should have high priority.

Above all, the coercive power of our legal system, already stretched thin, must be used with caution and chiefly against evils about which there is some-thing like universal consensus. That persons have rights is a universal belief in our society, but that a fetus is already an actual person—about that there is and there can be no consensus. Coercion in such matters is tyranny. Alas for our dangerously fragmented and alienated society if we persist in such tyranny.

[7]
What Is Sacred?

Ronald Dworkin

THE LIFE OF A single human organism commands respect and protection, then, no matter in what form or shape, because of the complex creative investment it represents and because of our wonder at the divine or evolutionary processes that produce new lives from old ones, at the processes of nation and community and language through which a human being will come to absorb and continue hundreds of generations of cultures and forms of life and value, and, finally, when mental life has begun and flourishes, at the process of internal personal creation and judgment by which a person will make and remake himself, a mysterious, inescapable process in which we each participate, and which is therefore the most powerful and inevitable source of empathy and communion we have with every other creature who faces the same frightening challenge. The horror we feel in the willful destruction of a human life reflects our shared inarticulate sense of the intrinsic importance of each of these dimensions of investment.

The Metric of Disrespect

I must now try to show how this understanding of the sacredness of human life allows us better to explain the two opposing attitudes toward abortion than

SOURCE: From *Life's Dominion* (New York: Random House, Vintage Books, 1993, 1994). Copyright © 1993 by Ronald Dworkin. Reprinted by permission of Alfred A. Knopf Inc. and the author.

does the traditional account, which supposes that these attitudes are based on different views about whether and when a fetus is a person with a right to life. I shall assume that conservatives and liberals all accept that in principle human life is inviolable in the sense I have defined, that any abortion involves a waste of human life and is therefore, in itself, a bad thing to happen, a shame. And I shall try to show how that assumption explains why the two sides both agree and disagree in the ways that they do.

I begin with their agreement. Conservatives and liberals both suppose, as I said, that though abortion is always morally problematic and often morally wrong, it is worse on some occasions than on others. They suppose, in other words, that there are degrees of badness in the waste of human life. What measure are they assuming in those judgments? Let us put that question in a more general form. We all assume that some cases of premature death are greater tragedies than others, not only when we are puzzling about abortion, but in the context of many other events as well. Most of us would think it worse when a young woman dies in a plane crash than when an elderly man does, for example, or a boy than a middle-aged man. What measure of tragedy are we assuming when we think this? What measure should we assume?

This is not the question moral philosophers and medical ethicists often write about—the question of what *rights* different sorts of people have to live, or of how relatively wicked it is to deny them lifesaving resources or to kill them. We might believe that it is worse—that there has been a greater waste of life—when a young person dies than when an old one does, or when an emotionally healthy person dies than a suicidal one, or when a man with young children dies than a bachelor, without suggesting that it would be any less wicked to kill an old than a young person, or a depressive than a happy one, or a bachelor than a father. Nor even—though this is obviously a different and harder question—that it would be any fairer to deny an old man scarce lifesaving resources, like kidney machines, when there is not enough for everyone who needs them, or to deny those resources to depressives and bachelors so that they could be used for spirited fathers of six.

These judgments about murder and fairness belong to the system of rights and interests, the system of ideas I said could not explain our most common convictions about abortion. Most people think (and our laws certainly insist) that people have an equal right to life, and that the murder of a depressive handicapped octogenarian misanthrope is as heinous, and must be punished as seriously, as the murder of anyone younger or healthier or more valuable to others. Any other view would strike us as monstrous. It is more complicated, as I just conceded, how these differences between people should affect the distribution of scarce medical resources. Doctors in most countries assume that such resources should be devoted to younger rather than older people, and for many doctors, quality of life and value to others come into the equation as well. But even these questions of fairness are different from the question of the intrinsic goodness or badness of events that we are considering. We might insist, for example, that the interests of a seriously depressed and gravely handicapped person should be respected just as much as those of an emotionally healthy person in allocating scarce medical resources, and yet think (as some people might, though many do not) that it is a greater tragedy when the latter dies young than the former. I am now asking, then, not about justice or rights or fairness, but about tragedy and the waste of life. How should we measure and compare the waste of life, and therefore the insult to the sanctity of life, on different occasions?

We should consider, first, a simple and perhaps natural answer to that question. Life is wasted, on this simple view, when life is lost, so that the question of how much has been wasted by a premature death is answered by estimating how long the life cut short would probably otherwise have lasted. This simple answer seems to fit many of our intuitive convictions. It seems to explain the opinion I just mentioned, for example: that the death of a young woman in an airplane crash is worse than the death of an old man would be. The young woman would probably otherwise have had many more years left to live.

The simple answer is incomplete, because we can measure life—and therefore loss of life—in different ways. Should we take into account only the duration of life lost with no regard to its quality? Or should we take quality into account as well? Should we say that the loss of the young woman who died in the crash would be greater if she had been looking forward to a life full of promise and pleasure than if she was physically or psychologically handicapped in some permanent and grave way? Should we also take into account the loss her death would cause to the lives of others? Is the death of a parent of young children, or of a brilliant employer of large numbers of people, or of a musical genius, a worse waste of life than the death at the same age of someone whose life was equally satisfying to himself but less valuable to others?

We should not puzzle over these alternatives, however, because this simple answer, which measures waste of life only in terms of life lost, is unacceptable whether we define that loss only as duration of life or include quality of life or benefit to others. It is unacceptable, in any of these forms, for two compelling reasons.

First, though the simple answer seems to fit some of our convictions, it contradicts other important and deeply held ones. If the waste of life were to be measured only in chronological terms, for example, then an early-stage abortion would be a worse insult to the sanctity of life, a worse instance of life being wasted, than a late-stage abortion. But almost everyone holds the contrary assumption: that the later the abortion—the more like a child the aborted fetus has already become—the worse it is. We take a similar view about the death of young children. It is terrible when an infant dies but worse, most people think, when a three-year-old child dies and worse still when an adolescent does. Almost no one thinks that the tragedy of premature death decreases in a linear way as age increases. Most people's sense of that tragedy, if it were rendered as a graph relating the degree of tragedy to the age at which death occurs, would slope upward from birth to some point in late childhood or early adolescence, then follow a flat line until at least very early middle age, and then slope down again toward extreme old age. Richard's murder of the princes in the Tower could have no parallel, for horror, in any act of infanticide.

Nor does the simple interpretation of how death wastes life fit our feelings better in the more elaborate forms I mentioned. Our common view that it is worse when a late-stage fetus is aborted or miscarries than an early-stage one, and worse when a ten-year-old child dies than an infant, makes no assumptions about the quality of the lives lost or their value for others.

The simple view of wasted life fails for a second, equally important reason. It wholly fails to explain the important truth I have several times emphasized: that though we treat human life as sacred, we do not treat it as incrementally good; we do not believe abstractly that the more human lives that are lived the better. The simple claim that a premature death is tragic only because life is lost—only because some period of life that might have been lived by someone will not be—gives us no more reason to grieve over an abortion or any premature death than we have to grieve over contraception or any other form of birth control. In both cases, less human life is lived than might otherwise be.

The "simple loss" view we have been considering is inadequate because it focuses only on future possibilities, on what will or will not happen in the future. It ignores the crucial truth that waste of life is often greater and more tragic because of what has already happened in the past. The death of an adolescent girl is worse than the death of an infant girl because the adolescent's death frustrates the investments she and others have already made in her life— the ambitions and expectations she constructed, the plans and projects she made, the love and interest and emotional involvement she formed for and with others, and they for and with her.

I shall use "frustration" (though the word has other associations) to describe this more complex measure of the waste of life because I can think of no better word to suggest the combination of past and future considerations that figure in our assessment of a tragic death. Most of us hold to something like the following set of instinctive assumptions about death and tragedy. We believe, as I said, that a successful human life has a certain natural course. It starts in mere biological development—conception, fetal development, and infancy—but it then extends into childhood, adolescence, and adult life in ways that are determined not just by biological formation but by social and individual training and choice, and that culminate in satisfying relationships and achievements of different kinds. It ends, after a normal life span, in a natural death. It is a waste of the natural and human creative investments that make up the story of a normal life when this normal progression is frustrated by premature death or in other ways. But how bad this is—how great the frustration—depends on the stage of life in which it occurs, because the frustration is greater if it takes place after rather than before the person has made a significant personal investment in his own life, and less if it occurs after any investment has been substantially fulfilled, or as substantially fulfilled as is anyway likely.

This more complex structure fits our convictions about tragedy better than the simple loss-of-life measure does. It explains why the death of an adolescent seems to us worse in most circumstances than the death of an infant. It also explains how we can consistently maintain that it is sometimes undesirable to create new human lives while still insisting that it is bad when any human life, once begun, ends prematurely. No frustration of life is involved when fewer rather than more human beings are born, because there is no creative investment in lives that never exist. But once a human life starts, a process has begun, and interrupting that process frustrates an adventure already under way.

So the idea that we deplore the frustration of life, not its mere absence, seems adequately to fit our general convictions about life, death, and tragedy. It also explains much of what we think about the particular tragedy of abortion. Both conservatives and liberals assume that in some circumstances abortion is more serious and more likely to be unjustifiable than in others. Notably, both agree that a late-term abortion is graver than an early-term one. We cannot explain this shared conviction simply on the ground that fetuses more closely resemble infants as pregnancy continues. People believe that abortion is not just emotionally more difficult but morally worse the later in pregnancy it occurs, and increasing resemblance alone has no moral significance. Nor can we explain the shared conviction by noticing that at some point in pregnancy a fetus becomes sentient. Most people think that abortion is morally worse early in the second trimester—well before sentience is possible—than early in the first one (several European nations, which permit abortion in the first but not the second trimester, have made that distinction part of their criminal law). And though that widely shared belief cannot be explained by the simple lost-life theory, the frustration thesis gives us a natural and compelling justification of it. Fetal development is a continuing creative process, a process that has barely begun at the instant of conception. Indeed, since genetic individuation is not yet complete at that point, we might say that the development of a unique human being has not started until approximately fourteen days later, at implantation. But after implantation, as fetal growth continues, the natural investment that would be wasted in an abortion grows steadily larger and more significant.

Human and Divine

So our sense that frustration rather than just loss compromises the inviolability of human life does seem helpful in explaining what unites most people about abortion. The more difficult question is whether it also helps in explaining what divides them. Let us begin our answer by posing another question. I just described a natural course of human life—beginning in conception, extending through birth and childhood, culminating in successful and engaged adulthood in which the natural biological investment and the personal human investment in that life are realized, and finally ending in natural death after a normal span of years. Life so understood can be frustrated in two main ways. It can be frustrated by premature death, which leaves any previous natural and personal investment unrealized. Or it can be frustrated by other forms of failure: by handicaps or poverty or misconceived projects or irredeemable mistakes or lack of training or even brute bad luck; any one of these may in different ways frustrate a person's opportunity to redeem his ambitions or otherwise to lead a full and flourishing life. Is premature death always, inevitably, a more serious frustration of life than any of these other forms of failure?

Decisions about abortion often raise this question. Suppose parents discover, early in the mother's pregnancy, that the fetus is genetically so deformed that the life it would lead after birth will inevitably be both short and sharply limited. They must decide whether it is a worse frustration of life if the gravely deformed fetus were to die at once—wasting the miracle of its creation and its development so far—or if it were to continue to grow in utero, to be born, and to live only a short and crippled life. We know that people divide about that question, and we now have a way to describe the division. On one view, immediate death of the fetus, even in a case like this one, is a more terrible frustration of the miracle of life than even a sharply diminished and brief infant life would be, for the latter would at least redeem some small part, however limited, of the natural investment. On the rival view, it would be a worse frustration of life to allow this fetal life to continue because that would add, to the sad waste of a deformed human's biological creation, the further, heartbreaking waste of personal emotional investments made in that life by others but principally by the child himself before his inevitable early death.

We should therefore consider this hypothesis: though almost everyone accepts the abstract principle that it is intrinsically bad when human life, once begun, is frustrated, people disagree about the best answer to the question of whether avoidable premature death is always or invariably the most serious possible frustration of life. Very conservative opinion, on this hypothesis, is grounded in the conviction that immediate death is inevitably a more serious frustration than any option that postpones death, even at the cost of greater frustration in other respects. Liberal opinion, on the same hypothesis, is grounded in the opposite conviction: that in some cases, at least, a choice for premature death minimizes the frustration of life and is therefore not a compromise of the principle that human life is sacred but, on the contrary, best respects that principle.

What reasons do people have for embracing one rather than the other of these positions? It seems plain that whatever they are, they are deep reasons, drawn consciously or unconsciously from a great network of other convictions about the point of life and the moral significance of death. If the hypothesis I just described holds—if conservatives and liberals disagree on whether premature death is always the worst frustration of life—then the disagreement must be in virtue of a more general contrast between religious and philosophical orientations.

So I offer another hypothesis. Almost everyone recognizes, as I have suggested, that a normal, successful human life is the product of two morally significant modes of creative investment in that life, the natural and the human. But people disagree about the relative importance of these modes, not just when abortion is in question but on many other mortal occasions as well. If you believe that the natural investment in a human life is transcendently important, that the gift of life itself is infinitely more significant than anything the person whose life it is may do for himself, important though that may be, you will also believe that a deliberate, premature death is the greatest frustration of life possible, no matter how limited or cramped or unsuccessful the continued life would be.[1] On the other hand, if you assign much greater relative importance to the human contribution to life's creative value, then you will consider the frustration of that contribution to be a more serious evil, and will accordingly see more point in deciding that life should end before further significant human investment is doomed to frustration.

We can best understand some of our serious disagreements about abortion, in other words, as reflecting deep differences about the relative moral importance of the natural and human contributions to the inviolability of individual human lives. In fact, we can make a bolder version of that claim: we can best understand the full range of opinion about abortion, from the most conservative to the most liberal, by ranking each opinion about the relative gravity of the two forms of frustration along a range extending from one extreme position to the other—from treating any frustration of the biological investment as worse than any possible frustration of human investment, through more moderate and complex balances, to the opinion that frustrating mere biological investment in human life barely matters and that frustrating a human investment is always worse.

If we look at the controversy this way, it is hardly surprising that many people who hold views on the natural or biological end of that spectrum are fundamentalist or Roman Catholic or strongly religious in some other orthodox religious faith—people who believe that God is the author of everything natural and that each human fetus is a distinct instance of His most sublime achievement. Our hypothesis explains how orthodox religion can play a crucial role in forming people's opinions about abortion even if they do not believe that a fetus is a person with its own right to life.

That is a significant point. It is widely thought that religious opposition to abortion is premised on the conviction that every human fetus is a person with rights and interests of its own. It is therefore important to see that religious opposition to abortion need not be based on that assumption. I said that many religious traditions, including Roman Catholicism for most of its history, based their opposition to abortion on the different assumption that human life has intrinsic value. The present hypothesis shows how that assumption can ground very fierce, even absolute, opposition to abortion. A strongly orthodox or fundamentalist person can insist that abortion is always morally wrong because the deliberate destruction of something created as sacred by God can never be redeemed by any human benefit.

This is not to suggest, however, that only conventionally religious people who believe in a creator God are conservatives about abortion. Many other people stand in awe of human reproduction as a natural miracle. Some of them, as I said, embrace the mysterious but apparently powerful idea that the natural order is in itself purposive and commands respect as sacred. Some prominent conservationists, for example, though hardly religious in the conventional sense, seem to be deeply religious in that one and may be drawn a considerable distance toward the conservative end of the spectrum of opinion I described. They may well think that any frustration of the natural investment in human life is so grave a matter that it is rarely if ever justified—that the pulse in the mud is more profound than any other source of life's value. They might therefore be just as firmly opposed to aborting a seriously deformed fetus as any religiously orthodox conservative would be.

Nor does it follow, on the other hand, that everyone who is religious in an orthodox way or everyone who reveres nature is therefore conservative about abortion. As we have seen, many such people, who agree that unnecessary death is a great evil, are also sensitive to and emphatic about the intrinsic badness of the waste of human investment in life. They believe that the frustration of that contribution—for example, in the birth of a grievously deformed fetus whose investment in its own life is doomed to be frustrated—may in some circumstances be the worse of two evils, and they believe that their religious conviction or reverence for nature is not only consistent with but actually requires that position. Some of them take the same view about what many believe to be an even more problematic case: they say that their religious convictions entail that a woman should choose abortion rather than bear a child when that would jeopardize her investment in her *own* life.

I described extreme positions at two ends of the spectrum: that only natural investment counts in deciding whether abortion wastes human life, and that only human investment counts. In fact, very few people take either of these extreme positions. For most people, the balance is more complex and involves compromise and accommodation rather than giving absolute priority to avoiding frustration of either the natural or the human investment. People's opinions become progressively less conservative and more liberal as the balance they strike gives more weight to the importance of not frustrating the human investment in life; more liberal views emphasize, in various degrees, that a human life is created not just by divine or natural forces but also, in a different but still central way, by personal choice, training, commitment, and decision. The shift in emphasis leads liberals to see the crucial creative investment in life, the investment that must not be frustrated if at all possible, as extending far beyond conception and biological growth and well into a human being's adult life. On that liberal opinion, as I have already suggested, it may be more frustrating of life's miracle when an adult's ambitions, talents, training, and expectations are wasted because of an unforeseen and unwanted pregnancy than when a fetus dies before any significant investment of that kind has been made.

That is an exceptionally abstract description of my understanding of the controversy between conservative and liberal opinion. But it will become less abstract, for I shall try to show how the familiar differences between conservative and liberal views on abortion can be explained by the hypothesis that conservatives and liberals rank the two forms of frustration differently. We must not exaggerate that difference, however. It is a difference in emphasis, though an important one. Most people who take what I call a liberal view of abortion do not deny that the conception of a human life and its steady fetal development toward recognizable human form are matters of great moral importance that count as creative investments. That is why they agree with conservatives that as this natural investment continues, and the fetus develops toward the shape and capacity of an infant, abortion, which wastes that investment, is progressively an event more to be avoided or regretted. Many people who hold conservative opinions about abortion, for their part, recognize the importance of personal creative contributions to a human life; they, too, recognize that a premature death is worse when it occurs not in early infancy but after distinctly human investments of ambition and expectation and love have been made. Conservatives and liberals disagree not because one side wholly rejects a value the other thinks cardinal, but because they take different—sometimes dramatically different—positions about the relative importance of these values, which both recognize as fundamental and profound.

Conservative Exceptions: Reconsidering the Natural

I am defending the view that the debate over abortion should be understood as essentially about the following philosophical issue: is the frustration of a biological life, which wastes human life, nevertheless sometimes justified in order to avoid frustrating a human contribution to that life or to other people's lives, which would be a different kind of waste? If so, when and why? People who are very conservative about abortion answer the first of these questions No.

There is an even more extreme position, which holds that abortion is never justified, even when necessary to save the life of the mother. Though that is the official view of the Catholic church and of some other religious groups, only a small minority even of devout Catholics accept it, and even Justice Rehnquist, who dissented in *Roe v. Wade,* said that he had little doubt that it would be unconstitutional for states to prohibit abortion when a mother's life was at stake. So I have defined "very conservative" opinion to permit abortion in this circumstance. This exceedingly popular exception would be unacceptable to all conservatives, as I have said, if they really thought that a fetus is a person with protected rights and interests. It is morally and legally impermissible for any third party, such as a doctor, to murder one innocent person even to save the life of another one. But the exception is easily explicable if we understand conservative opinion as based on a view of the sanctity of life that gives strict priority to the divine or natural investment in life. If either the mother or the fetus must die, then the tragedy of avoidable death and the loss of nature's investment in life is inevitable. But a choice in favor of the mother may well seem justified to very conservative people on the ground that a choice against her would in addition frustrate the personal and social investments in her life; even they want only to minimize the overall frustration of human life, and that requires saving the mother's life in this terrible situation.

The important debate is therefore between people who believe that abortion is permissible *only* when it is necessary to save the mother's life and people who believe that abortion may be morally permissible in other circumstances as well. I shall consider the further exceptions the latter group of people claim, beginning with those that are accepted even by people who regard themselves as moderately conservative about abortion and continuing to those associated with a distinctly liberal position.

Moderate conservatives believe that abortion is morally permissible to end a pregnancy that began in rape. Governor Buddy Roemer of Louisiana, for example, who has declared himself in favor of a ban on abortion, nevertheless vetoed an anti-abortion statue in 1991 because it excepted rape victims only in a manner that he said "dishonors women . . . and unduly traumatizes victims of rape."[2] On the a-fetus-is-a-person view, an exception for rape is even harder to justify than an exception to protect the life of the mother. Why should a fetus be made to forfeit its right to live, and pay with its life, for the wrongdoing of someone else? But once again, the exception is much easier to understand when we shift from the claim of fetal personhood to a concern for protecting the divine or natural investment in human life. Very conservative people, who believe that the divine contribution to a human life is everything and the human contribution almost nothing beside it, believe that abortion is automatically and in every case the worst possible compromise of life's inviolability, and they do not recognize an exception for rape. But moderately conservative people, who believe that the natural contribution normally *outweighs* the human contribution, will find two features of rape that argue for an exception.

First, according to every prominent religion, rape is itself a brutal violation of God's law and will, and abortion may well seem less insulting to God's creative power when the life it ends itself began in such an insult. Though rape would not justify violating the rights of an innocent person, it could well diminish the horror conservatives feel at an abortion's deliberate frustration of God's investment in life. In his opinion in *McRae v. Califano,* . . . Judge John Dooling summarized testimony by Rabbi David Feldman: "In the stricter Jewish view abortion is a very serious matter permitted only where there is a threat to life, or to sanity, or a grave threat to mental health and physical well-being. Abortion for rape victims would be allowed, using a field and seed analogy: involuntary implantation of the seed imposes no duty to nourish the alien seed."[3]

Second, rape is a terrible desecration of its victim's investment in her own life, and even those who count a human investment in life as less important than God's or nature's may nevertheless recoil from so violent a frustration of that human investment. Rape is sickeningly, comprehensively contemptuous because it reduces a woman to a physical convenience, a creature whose importance is exhausted by her genital use, someone whose love and sense of self—aspects of personality particularly at stake in sex—have no significance whatsoever except as vehicles for sadistic degradation.

Requiring a woman to bear a child conceived in such an assault is especially destructive to her self-realization because it frustrates her creative choice not only in sex but in reproduction as well. In the ideal case, reproduction is a joint decision rooted in love and in a desire to continue one's life mixed with the life of another person. In Catholic tradition, and in the imagination of many people who are not Catholics, it is itself an offense against the sanctity of life to make love without that desire: that is the basis of many people's moral opposition to contraception. But we can dispute that sex is valuable only for reproduction, or creative only in that way—as most people do—while yet believing that sex is maximally creative when reproduction is contemplated and desired, and that reproduction frustrates creative power when it is neither. Of course, people in love often conceive by accident, and people not in love sometimes conceive deliberately, perhaps out of a misguided hope of finding love through children. Rape is not just the absence of contemplation and desire, however. For the victim, rape is the direct opposite of these, and if a child is conceived, it will be not only without the victim's desire to reproduce but in circumstances made especially horrible because of that possibility.

Moderate conservatives therefore find it difficult to insist that abortion is impermissible in cases of rape. It is sometimes said that conservatives who allow the rape exception but not, for example, an exception for unmarried teenagers whose lives would be ruined by childbirth must be motivated by a desire to punish unmarried women who have sex voluntarily. Though some conservatives may indeed believe that pregnancy is a fit punishment for sexual immorality, our hypothesis shows why conservatives who make only the rape exception do not necessarily hold that appalling view. The grounds on which I said conservatives might make an exception for rape do not extend so forcefully to pregnancies that follow voluntary intercourse. Though many religious people do think that unmarried sex also violates God's will, few consider it as grave as rape, and the argument that an unwanted pregnancy grotesquely frustrates a woman's creative role in framing her own life is weaker when the pregnancy follows voluntary sex. Of course, the difference would not be pertinent at all, as I said, if a fetus were a person with rights and interests of its own, because that person would be completely innocent whatever the nature or level of its mother's guilt.

Liberal Exceptions: Protecting Life in Earnest

Other, more permissive exceptions to the principle that abortion is wrong are associated with a generally liberal attitude toward abortion, and we should therefore expect, on the basis of the hypothesis we are testing, that they will reflect a greater respect for the human contribution to life and a correspondingly diminished concern with the natural. But we must not forget that people's attitudes about abortion range over a gradually changing spectrum from one extreme to the other, and that any sharp distinction between conservative and liberal camps is just an expository convenience.

Liberals think that abortion is permissible when the birth of a fetus would have a very bad effect on the quality of lives. The exceptions liberals recognize on that ground fall into two main groups: those that seek to avoid frustration of the life of the child, and those that seek to prevent frustration of the life of the mother and other family members.

Liberals believe that abortion is justified when it seems inevitable that the fetus, if born, will have a seriously frustrated life. That kind of justification is strongest, according to most liberals, when the frustration is caused by a very grave physical deformity that would make any life deprived, painful, frustrating for both child and parent, and, in any case, short. But many liberals also believe that abortion is justified when the family circumstances are so economically barren, or otherwise so unpromising, that any new life would be seriously stunted for that reason. It is important to understand that these exceptions are not based, as they might seem to be, on concern for the rights or interests of the fetus. It is a mistake to suppose that an early fetus has interests of its own; it especially makes no sense to argue that it might have an interest in being aborted. Perhaps we could understand that latter argument to mean that if the fetus does develop into a child, that child would be better off dead. But many liberals find abortion justified even when this is not so. I do not mean to deny that sometimes people would be better off dead—when they are in great and terminal pain, for example, or because their lives are otherwise irremediably frustrated. . . . But this is rarely true of children born into even very great poverty. Nor is it necessarily true even of children born with terrible, crippling handicaps who are doomed shortly to die; sometimes such children establish relationships and manage achievements that give content and meaning to their lives, and it becomes plain that it is in their interests, and in the interests of those who love and care for them, that they continue living as long as possible. The liberal judgment that abortion is justified when the prospects for life are especially bleak is based on a more impersonal judgment: that the child's existence would be intrinsically a bad thing, that it is regrettable that such a deprived and difficult life must be lived.

Sometimes this liberal judgment is wrongly taken to imply contempt for the lives of handicapped children or adults, or even as a suggestion, associated with loathsome Nazi eugenics, that society would be improved by the death of such people. That is a mistake twice over. First, as I insisted earlier, . . . the general question of the relative intrinsic tragedy of different events is very different from any question about the *rights* of people now living or about how they should be treated. The former is a question about the intrinsic goodness or evil of events, the latter about rights and fairness. Second, in any case, the liberal opinion about abortion of deformed fetuses in no way implies that it would be better if even grievously handicapped people were now to die. On the contrary, the very concern the liberal judgment embodies—respect for the human contribution to life and anxiety that it not be frustrated—normally sponsors exactly the opposite conclusion. The investment a seriously handicapped person makes in his own life, in his struggle to overcome his handicap as best he can, is intense, and the investment his family and others make is likely to be intense as well. The liberal position insists that these investments in life should be realized as fully as possible, for as long and as successfully as the handicapped person and his community together can manage; and liberals are even more likely than conservatives to support social legislation that promotes that end. One may think that in the worst of such cases it would have been better had the life in question never begun, that the investment we are so eager to redeem should never have been necessary. But that judgment does not detract from concern for handicapped people; on the contrary, it is rooted in the same fundamental respect for human investment in human life, the same horror at the investment being wasted.

The second distinctly liberal group of exceptions, which take into account the effects of pregnancy and childbirth on the lives of mothers and other family members, are even harder to justify on any presumption that includes the idea that a fetus is a person with rights and interests. But the popularity of these exceptions is immediately explicable once we recognize that they are based on respect for the intrinsic value of human life. Liberals are especially concerned about the waste of the human contribution to that value, and they believe that the waste of life, measured in frustration rather than mere loss, is very much greater when a teenage single mother's life is wrecked than when an early-stage fetus, in whose life human investment has thus far been negligible, ceases to live. That judgment does not, of course, depend on comparing the quality of the mother's life, if her fetus is aborted, with that of the child, had it been allowed to live. Recognizing the sanctity of life does not mean attempting to engineer fate so that the best possible lives are lived overall; it means, rather, not frustrating investments in life that have already been made. For that reason, liberal opinion cares more about the lives that people are now leading, lives in earnest, than about the possibility of other lives to come.

The prospects of a child and of its mother for a fulfilling life obviously each depend very much on the prospects of the other. A child whose birth frustrates the chances of its mother to redeem her own life or jeopardizes her ability to care for the rest of her family is likely, just for that reason, to have a more frustrating life itself. And though many people have become superb parents to disabled or disadvantaged children, and some extraordinary ones have found a special vocation in that responsibility, it will sometimes be a devastating blow to a parent's prospects to have a crippled child rather than a normal one, or a child whose bearing and care will seriously strain family resources.

This is only another instance of the difficulty any theoretical analysis of an intricate personal and social problem, like abortion, must face. Analysis can proceed only by abstraction, but abstraction, which ignores the complexity and interdependencies of real life, obscures much of the content on which each actual, concrete decision is made. So we have no formulas for actual decision but only, at best, a schema for understanding the arguments and decisions that we and other people make in real life. I have argued that we do badly, in understanding and evaluating these decisions and arguments, if we try to match them to procrustean assumptions about fetal personhood or rights. We do better to see them as reflecting more nuanced and individual judgments about how and why human life is sacred, and about which decision of life and death, in all the concrete circumstances, most respects what is really important about life.

There will be disagreement in these judgments, not only between large parties of opinion, like those I have been calling conservative and liberal, but within these parties as well. Indeed, very few people, even those who share the same religion and social and intellectual background, will agree in every case. Nor is it possible for anyone to compose a general theory of abortion, some careful weighing of different kinds or modes of life's frustration from which particular decisions could be generated to fit every concrete case. On the contrary, we discover what we think about these grave matters not in advance of having to decide on particular occasions, but in the course of and by making them.

Notes

1. Many people who hold that view will make exceptions: for capital punishment, for example, and for killing the enemy in war. I cannot consider, in this essay, the large and important question of how far these exceptions contradict the principle. But people who believe that the natural contribution to life is paramount for a particular reason—that God has created all life—will obviously not count these as contradictions if they also believe that executing murderers or killing enemy soldiers in a just war is also God's will.

2. See "Nation's Strictest Abortion Law Enacted in Louisiana Over Veto," *The New York Times,* 19 June 1991. The Louisiana legislature overrode Governor Roemer's veto, and the strict anti-abortion law it enacted has been held unconstitutional by two federal courts. See "Court Backs Overturning of Strict Abortion Law," *The New York Times,* 23 September 1992. In 1992, the Supreme Court refused to review a lower-court decision striking down a similar Guam statute. See Linda Greenhouse, "Guam Abortion Law; High Court Reaffirms Right to Regulate, but Not to Ban," *The New York Times,* 6 December 1992, D2.

3. 491 F. Supp. 630 (1980), 696.

PART TWO

DEFINING STATEMENTS

Religious Positions

ROMAN CATHOLICISM

[8]

The Roman Catholic Position

Daniel Callahan

Two points need to be distinguished in talking about the Church's present position. The first concerns the matter of the *method* of the argument, and the second the *substance* of the argument. In general, as the position is argued in papal statements and manuals of moral theology, the method is deductive. Fundamental general principles are laid down; specific conclusions, applicable to abortion cases, are then drawn. The principles function as axioms, the conclusions, as consequences derived from the axioms. While this style of argumentation is most obvious in the manuals, where it is explicitly used, it is also present in the papal and conciliar statements. It is possible to look on this method in two ways. Viewed benignly, it represents simply a common method of moral argumentation: General principles are established and specific applications are made. Viewed more critically, it can fall under the kind of charge leveled by Protestant theologian James M. Gustafson and echoed by many contemporary Catholic moralists about the method of Catholic moral theology. Gustafson has pointed out, perceptively, that Catholic arguments about abortion are (1)"arguments made by an *external judge*"; (2)"are made on a basically *juridical model*"; (3)"largely confine the relevant data to *the physical*"; (4)"are limited by concerning themselves almost *exclusively with the physician and the patient* at the time of a particular pregnancy, isolating these two

Source: Reprinted with permission of Simon & Schuster, Inc., from *Abortion: Law, Choice, and Morality* by Daniel Callahan. Copyright © 1970 by Daniel Callahan.

from the multiple relationships and responsibilities each has to and for others over long periods of time"; (5) "are *rationalistic*"; and further that (6) "the traditional perspective seeks to develop arguments based on *natural law*, and thus ought to be persuasive and binding on all men."[1] Yet, while a general characterization of this kind is accurate, not all who argue the Catholic position necessarily argue in this fashion; instead, one can now find commonly employed a variety of styles (which will be indicated in the ensuing discussion).

The substance of the Catholic position can be summed up in the following principles, which are sometimes developed in a theological way, sometimes philosophically, and sometimes mixed together: (1) God alone is the Lord of life. (2) Human beings do not have the right to take the lives of other (innocent) human beings. (3) Human life begins at the moment of conception. (4) Abortion, at whatever the stage of development of the conceptus, is the taking of innocent human life. The conclusion follows: Abortion is wrong. The only exception to this conclusion is in the case of an abortion that is the indirect result of an otherwise moral and legitimate medical procedure (e.g., the treatment of an ectopic pregnancy and cancerous uterus).

God alone is the Lord of life. When the Catholic position is argued theologically, this is a key proposition. "Only God is Lord of the Life of a man who is not guilty of a crime punishable with death," Pius XII said on one occasion, and, on another, "Every human being, even the child in its mother's womb, receives its right to life directly from God" (as quoted above). Norman St. John-Stevas argues in a similar way, as do other Catholic authors.[2] Variantly, this argument is often couched in terms of the right to life, especially when the inviolability of human life is approached from a philosophical–natural-law–perspective. Thus Fr. Thomas J. O'Donnell contends that the purposeful termination of a pregnancy "contains the moral malice of the violation of man's most fundamental human right—the right to life itself."[3] Other authors, although more rarely, have also seen in abortion the thwarting of the ends of nature, in this instance that of frustrating the good of the species in favor of the good of an individual (the mother).[4]

I am critical of the use of the principle of God's lordship as a premise in a consideration of the morality of abortion. To recapitulate, it presupposes that God intervenes directly in natural and human affairs as the primary causative agent of life and death. Not only is this theologically dubious, it also has the effect of obscuring the necessity that human beings define terms, make decisions, and take responsibility for the direct care of human life. Moreover, to say that God is the ultimate source of the right to life, which is less objectionable theologically, still does not solve the problem of *how* human beings ought to respect that right or how they are to balance a conflict of rights. Normally speaking, the right to life takes primacy over other rights, since without life no other rights can be exercised. But abortion problems normally arise because other important rights appear to be in conflict with this right; unless a prior and fixed decision has been made to give always and in every circumstance the right to life a primacy over all other human rights, it is not clear how, without begging some important questions, the right to life can be invoked as the sole right in question in abortion decisions. But this is the procedure of many Catholic moralists when it comes to abortion.

Human beings do not have the right to take the lives of other (innocent) human beings. This proposition is consistent both with Christian ethics, in the theological sense, and with Catholic natural-law morality. The word innocent, however, is crucial here. Traditional Catholic morality has defended the just war, i.e., defensive, limited war waged for the preservation of life or the protection of vital human rights. These wars have been justified even though they result, often enough, in the foreseen taking of innocent life, particularly the lives of noncombatants. The justification for thus taking innocent life is governed by the principle of double effect. Thus, innocent (noncombatant) lives cannot be taken unless, for the strict demands of self-defense, these lives are taken only indirectly, that is, by an action "designed and intended solely to achieve some other purpose(s) even though death is foreseen as a concomitant effect. Death therefore is not positively willed, but is reluctantly permitted as an unavoidable by-product."[5] Thus, while the proposition concerning the absence of the right of one human being to take the life of another is basic to Catholic morality, when argued both theologically and in terms of natural law, it admits of an important exception in two circumstances: when the life to be taken is *not* innocent human life (as in punishment for capital crimes and in the case of a just defensive war) and when it is innocent life but the taking of life is indirect.

Human life begins at the moment of conception. Whereas the first two propositions were general moral principles, this one is a specific proposition about the nature of the life in question in abortion decisions. While some Catholic moralists are attempting to revive the earlier distinction between the formed and the unformed fetus, the general trend in recent decades has been to eliminate the distinction and count as human the immediate product of conception.[6] Thus, Pius XII: "Even the child, even the unborn child, is a human being in the same degree and by the same title as its mother." These words were consistent with the words of Pope Pius XI, who had spoken of the conceptus as "an innocent child" and "an innocent human being." In line with phrases of this kind, the Catholic Hospital Association of the United States and Canada has specified as one of its principles: "Every unborn child must be regarded as a human person, with all the rights of a human person, from the moment of conception."[7] When speaking cautiously, many theologians would say that, in the absence of a philosophical or scientific demonstration that a conceptus is human, respect for life requires us to treat it as if it were.

It goes without saying that a decision to call a conceptus, whatever the stage of development, a human being or a human person presumes certain convictions about the proper way to read biological evidence. While the papal statements do not give the reasoning behind this decision, it is safe to assume that the ultimate motive behind so reading the evidence in this fashion is to extend protection to the earliest reaches of individual human life. It represents a moral policy, one which has chosen one possible way of reading the data and chosen this way, the safest way, as the most compatible with the moral aim: the protection of all innocent life. In addition, in a way consistent with the Catholic tradition, Catholic authors overwhelmingly tend to make the problem of the beginning of human life the major, indeed overriding, particular factual question to be answered in any approach to abortion. Once it is determined (as the tradition has determined) that the right to life is the fundamental human right, and that innocent life may not be taken, then the only remaining question of consequence is whether the conceptus ought to be considered human life. As Fr. Robert Drinan has put it, "Every discussion of abortion must, in the final analysis, begin and end with a definition of what one thinks of a human embryo or fetus."[8] For John T. Noonan Jr., "the most fundamental question involved in the long history of thought on abortion is: How do you determine the humanity of a being?"[9] David Granfield felt that the centrality of the question warranted beginning his book on abortion with it. For that matter, whether dealt with in terms of the question of the moment of animation or ensoulment or in some other more contemporary form, it is a question that has traditionally been given primacy.[10] This characteristic of Catholic argumentation is important because, by so ordering the priority of the questions to be asked, all other questions are thrown into a subsidiary position. Actually this makes it exceedingly difficult, within the Catholic problematic, to try and weigh other values—the mother's duty toward her children, her psychological state and freedom, her economic situation—or to raise or answer the other kinds of questions; the first question asked tends to preempt the others. An important aspect of the one-dimensionality of the Catholic position is thus its tendency to narrow the issues considered legitimate and important to very few; issues that, it turns out, bear almost exclusively (with the noted exceptions) on the status of the conceptus. No room is left for the integration of a full range of rights, personal and communal.

Abortion, at whatever the stage of development of the conceptus, is the taking of innocent human life. Once the question of whether the conceptus from the moment of conception is human life has been answered in the affirmative, then it is only a short, indeed tautological step to state that abortion is the taking of innocent human life. While, as Noonan has shown, there have been theologians who have tried to develop the argument that, in some cases, the fetus can be counted as an aggressor, this line has had scant papal or theological support. The net result is that the act of abortion is, in the end, defined as an act that takes innocent human life, and thus by definition an act to be condemned and proscribed. If one stays within the framework of the Catholic argument, proceeding from premises 1 to 3, then this is a logical deduction and thus unexceptionable. With premise 2 taken as a principle of the natural law and the conceptus judged factually (biologically) to be human, no other conclusion is possible than a condemnation of abortion. As Josef Fuchs, S.J., has argued (exhibiting both the style and the substance of the argument):

> *Any principle of the natural law remains efficacious in every situation that realizes the facts involved by this principle.* For example, it can never happen that the prohibition of a direct destruction of unborn life—a principle of the natural law—could cease to be an absolute demand even in difficult concrete situations, or out of charitable consideration for a mother and her family.[11]

Put in terms of the four propositions above, the structure of the Catholic argument is comparatively simple and straightforward. It rests on no *obscure* arguments (even if they may strike many as fallacious), requires no elaborate steps to carry it off (as, for instance, Catholic natural-law arguments against contraception do) and draws on few idiosyncratic Catholic ways of arguing moral issues (conservative Protestant and Jewish arguments are not that dissimilar). But it seems to me that one cannot fully appreciate the Catholic position (or the vehemence with which it is supported) without observing a number of collateral arguments commonly brought to bear in support of it. Most commonly, it is contended that a justification of abortion has the force of a justification for treating all human beings as expendable and introducing a principle of expediency into human relations. As David Granfield has put it:

> Abortion is forbidden morally because it is an abuse of human power. It is a destruction of a human being by another human being, and as such it strikes at the heart of human dignity. The usurpation of authority which is abortion is not wrong simply because it kills unborn children, but because it results in the vilification of all men. To give moral justification to abortion is to condemn all men to the level of expendable things. Morally, the fight against abortion is not primarily to protect the human dignity of the unborn, but is above all to safeguard that dignity in all men.[12]

For Father Drinan, an acceptance of the American Law Institute's Model Penal Code on abortion would have the consequence of overthrowing a fundamental value of Anglo-Saxon law, the inviolability of human life: "At no time and under no circumstances has Anglo-American law ever sanctioned the destruction of one human being—however useless and unwanted such a person may be—for the purpose of securing or increasing the health or happiness of other individuals."[13] For Father O'Donnell, doctors who perform therapeutic abortions have adopted a philosophy of "medical expediency" that they are willing to place above any other moral standard.[14] Bernard Häring sees the possibility of a fundamental threat to motherhood: "If it were to become an accepted principle of moral teaching on motherhood to permit a mother whose life was endangered simply to 'sacrifice' the life of her child in order to save her own, motherhood would no longer mean absolute dedication to each and every child."[15] For Noonan, "abortion violates the rational humanist tenet of the equality of human lives."[16] Finally, it is not unfitting to mention that some older manuals of moral theology—still in use in some places—condemned abortion on the added (but theologically dubious) ground that "it deprives the soul of eternal life."[17]

Extrapolations of this kind, which often strike the non-Catholic as red herrings if not bizarre, make considerable logical sense once one realizes that the premises of the Catholic argument have *defined* abortion as the taking of innocent human life. At stake, in the Catholic view, is the principle of the right to life: if the principle is breached in one place, it could well be breached in another—a precedent has been established for violating the principle. One may object (as I will) to the premises, but it is important to see that, once adopted, the conclusions Catholics draw from them are consistent. The practice of envisioning further erosions of respect for life if abortion is accepted is, in the Catholic view, a perfectly legitimate philosophical procedure, a way of trying to chart the consequences of a change in what are taken to be fundamental moral principles. It is a procedure, moreover, used commonly in all forms of moral argumentation and by no means restricted to Catholics; it is only to say, as others say when their own ox is gored, that the social consequences of a change in basic moral principles can be enormously harmful. Given the Catholic premises, it should at least be understandable (even if not acceptable) why many Catholics cannot but view with alarm the prospect of a moral acceptance of abortion. State the case as bluntly as John Marshall has done and it is easy to see social disaster as a consequence of an acceptance of abortion: "Direct abortion . . . is gravely wrong, because it constitutes the direct killing of an innocent human being."[18] It ought to be understandable why Catholics, given their premises, can envision the antiabortion cause as an attempt to hold on to very basic Western values, values by no means exclusively their own but rather the patrimony of the entire culture. A quotation from Fr. Richard A. McCormick will help to drive the point home: "The question 'What am I doing?' is the first question to be asked about induced abortion. It is all the more urgent because it is precisely the question our society nearly always neglects."[19] The Catholic answer is that the act being performed in abortion is the killing of an innocent human being; once reached, a conclusion of this kind dictates, at the cost of inconsistency and moral irresponsibility, vigorous opposition to abortion.

The principle of double effect. Within the framework of traditional Catholic morality, it is exceedingly difficult for a Catholic—even if he or she would like to do so—to find a way of taking exception to the received teaching. This is, no doubt, one reason why few efforts have been mounted to change the teaching. With the exception of the premise that human life begins at conception (which can at any rate be challenged on biological grounds, where the evidence is open to varying interpretations), the other premises seem either securely fixed by the Christian tradition or represent straightforward deductions from natural-law premises already accepted. If, then, the traditional teaching is to be challenged within a Catholic framework (and, of course, it is simple to challenge it from an entirely different theological or philosophical framework), it must be done by a critical examination of (1) the premises themselves, (2) the validity of the conclusions drawn from the premises, and (3) the details and methods of argumentation. As for the premises, a number of objections have already been leveled at the theological belief that the lordship of God takes the matter of abortion decisions out of human hands, and at the philosophical belief that the right to life necessarily takes precedence over all other rights. Once this much has been seen and the premises thrown into question (but only that), then the way is open to dispute the conclusion drawn from these premises: that the direct taking of innocent fetal (or embryonic) life is always and necessarily immoral.

One detail in particular of the traditional Catholic argument opens the way for such a disputation: the principle of double effect. As noted, the only exceptions to the absolute prohibition of abortion are in the case of an ectopic pregnancy or a cancerous uterus. In both of these instances, the justification for the exception is that the indicated medical procedure to save the life of the mother (the removal of the tube or of the uterus) has as its direct intention the saving of the life of the mother; the death of the fetus is the foreseen but unintended and indirect result of the lifesaving surgery performed on the mother. By a use of this distinction, then, an abortion can be performed in the specified cases without directly violating the moral law that innocent life cannot be killed. The basis for the principle is the commonsense observation that an action can have a good and a bad effect or result. As a theological distinction, it was first employed by Thomas Aquinas, who built on it a justification for the taking of life in self-defense.[20] In essence, the point of the principle is this: An action that has both a good and a bad effect may be performed if the good effect accomplished is greater than the evil effect and if, in addition, at least four other conditions are met: (1) the act must itself be either good or indifferent, or at least not forbidden with a view to preventing just that effect; (2) the evil effect cannot be a means to the good, but must be equally immediate or at least must result from the good effect; (3) the foreseen evil effect must not be intended or approved, merely permitted—for even a good act is vitiated if accompanied by an evil intent; (4) there must be a proportionately serious reason for exercising the cause and allowing the evil effect.[21] The problem of an ectopic pregnancy illustrates what is considered a legitimate use of the principle:

> The removal of a pregnant fallopian tube containing a non-viable living fetus, even before the external rupture of the tube, can be done in such a way that the consequent death of the fetus will be produced only indirectly. Such an operation will be licitly performed if all the circumstances are such that the necessity for the operation is, in moral estimation, proportionate to the evil effect permitted.[22]

In this instance, the intent of the operation itself is good (as standard operation to save life); although the fetus is killed, this effect, although foreseen, is not the intention of the operation (thus the death of the fetus is indirectly caused); the evil effect (the death of the fetus) is not the means to the good end (the saving of the life of the woman), but only the indirect result of the means (the tubal removal) necessary to save the life of the woman. Thus, the conditions for an application of the principle are met. By contrast, a fetal craniotomy to save the life of the woman would not be licit because, in this case, the life of the fetus is taken directly by the act of crushing its skull. The intention is good (saving the life of the woman), but the means employed are evil (directly taking the life of an innocent fetus); hence, fetal craniotomy is forbidden.[23]

Now, it has been contended that, far from being impersonal and legalistic, the principle of double effect represents "an attempt on the part of theologians to free us to do as much as possible, even though indirectly intended evil—in this case, the death of the unborn—results."[24] For Noonan, the making of exceptions on the basis of the principle represents an attempt to achieve a balance: "In Catholic moral theology, as it developed, life even of the innocent was not taken as an absolute. Judgments on acts affecting life issued from a process of weighing. In the weighing, the fetus was always given a greater value than zero, always a value separate and independent from its parents."[25] One feels compelled to comment, however, that the weighing in question is decisively one-sided, takes physical life alone as the only value at stake, leaving no real room for even investigating any other considerations that might come into play. It is evident, moreover, that a theology that would countenance the death of the fetus and the woman (rare in fact but pertinent in principle) rather than directly take the life of the fetus is one geared heavily to a preoccupation with preserving individuals from sin or crime. Its real interest in the extreme case of letting both woman and fetus die turns out, in effect, not to be the good of the mother (for, hypothetically, a fetal craniotomy would save her life), but the good conscience of those who might but do not act to save her. The basic moral principle of "Do good and avoid evil" is efficaciously rendered into the avoiding of evil alone.

The way in which a conflict of rights between a woman and a fetus is treated is illuminating of the consequences of this style of moral reckoning; for it is at this point that the style most clearly shows itself. Pope Pius XII in a statement has said that "neither the life of the mother nor that of the child can be subjected to an act of direct suppression. In the one case as in the other, there can be but one obligation: to make every effort to save the lives of both, of the mother and the child." But it is, of course, precisely the supposition of the hypothesis in these situations (however rare medically) that, unless the fetus is killed, the mother will die also: both lives cannot be saved. The assumption behind this form of reasoning is that there exists a fixed order of rights, before which humans must passively stand, whatever the physical consequences of their passivity. A passage from Josef Fuchs's book brings this out:

> The difficulty of a conflict of rights can *easily* [my italics] be solved if one understands that there are no heterogeneous orders and demands of the natural law placed side by side without any relation to one another. There exists indeed *an order* of goods and values, of commands and demands through the very nature of things, so that there can be no true conflict of rights but at most an apparent conflict. The two obligations concerning a pathological birth, to preserve the life of the mother and not to kill the child, only seem to contradict one another. There is in fact no commandment to save the mother at all costs. There is only an obligation to save her in a morally permissible way and such a way is not envisaged in stating this given situation. Consequently only one obligation remains: to save the mother without attempting to kill the child.[26]

What seems apparent here is that, despite acknowledgment of an obligation to the mother, the *primary* obligation is fulfillment of the moral law, which exists independently of the obligations owed to particular human beings. Once the primary obligation has been discharged, fidelity to the moral law, no human obligations remain; the woman may be allowed to die. One consequence of a morality that centers obligation and responsibility in preservation of the law is to posit a sharp distinction between physical and moral evils. "Two natural deaths," David Granfield has written, "are a lesser evil than one murder. In the conflict of interests between mother and child, the rights of both to live must be preserved. The conflict cannot be resolved morally by the killing of the weaker party without thereby destroying all morality."[27] Even if one assumes the killing of the child in the instance of a moral conflict would be "murder," one has to ask why this "murder" would be a greater evil than the death of both. Would it not be a moral evil to let the woman die (when she could be saved), and an even greater moral evil if there were others (husband, other children) dependent on her? To imply that such an evil is physical is to posit a moral helplessness and lack of human responsibility in the face of natural disasters. On the contrary, it seems to me perfectly reasonable to say that what is initially a physical situation (an event in nature) becomes a moral situation when it enters the realm of potential human action. A choice not to act in the face of a physical evil for the sake of saving another becomes—assuming human responsibility—a moral choice.

In a rigid natural-law formulation the terms of the choice seem dictated by laws supposedly transcendent to the human beings affected by them. In Granfield's instance the preservation of the rights of both to life becomes nothing more than sheer formalism. For, when one or more human beings refuse to save the mother by the "murder" of the fetus, she is being refused by other human beings the de facto right to life; her rights are nullified. To say that "all morality" would be destroyed "by the killing of the weaker party" is only possible if one presumes that morality consists in observing a moral law regardless of the consequences for individual human beings. The range of human responsibility is thus narrowed to a point where the good conscience of those who could act and the abstract demands of the law take precedence over every other consideration. It becomes, at this point, virtually meaningless to speak, as Noonan has done, of the work of the moralists as one of "the weighing of fetal rights against other human rights."[28] For the terms allowable in the weighing are such as to ensure that, once the fetus has been defined as innocent human life, the weighing entirely favors the fetus. That two exceptions are admitted (and those medically uncommon) can hardly be said to constitute "balance." And it goes without saving, of course, that when the only aspects of the balance even worthy of consideration are those of physical life, then the whole network of other responsibilities the mother may have becomes morally irrelevant.

Notes

1. James M. Gustafson, "A Christian Approach to the Ethics of Abortion," *The Dublin Review* 514 (winter 1967–68): 347–50.

2. See, for instance, Bernard Häring, *The Law of Christ,* vol. III (Westminster, Md.: Newman Press, 1966), 209: "God alone is the author of life and death.

No physician may pass and execute the sentence of death on one who is innocent. . . . If despite all his sincere efforts . . . he is not successful, then God Himself has rendered the decision and passed the verdict on a human life." Fr. Charles McFadden, in line with many other Catholic moralists, argues that only those who are theists can understand this kind of point (*Medical Ethics,* 3d ed. [Philadelphia, F. A. Davis Co., 1955], 165).

3. Thomas J. O'Donnell, "Abortion, II (Moral Aspect)," in *New Catholic Encyclopedia,* vol. 1 (New York: McGraw-Hill, 1967), 29.

4. I. Aertnys et al., *Theologiae Moralis,* 17th ed. (Turin, Italy: Marietti, 1956), 547–49.

5. Richard A. McCormick, "Morality of War," in *New Catholic Encyclopedia,* vol. 14 (New York: McGraw-Hill, 1967), 805; see Jonathan Bennett, "Whatever the Consequences," *Analysis* (January 1966): 83–102.

6. Cf. John P. Kenny, *Principles of Medical Ethics* (Westminster, Md.: Newman Press, 1952), 131; Giuseppe Bosio, "Animazione," *Enciclopedia Cattolica* (Rome: Città del Vaticano, 1948), cols. 1352–54; H. Noldin et al., *Summa Theologica Moralis,* 34th ed., vol. 2 (Innsbruck: F. Rauch, 1963), 313; Rudolph Joseph Gerber, "When Is the Human Soul Infused?," *Laval Théologique et Philosophique* 22 (1966): 234–47.

7. *Ethical and Religious Directives for Catholic Hospitals* (St. Louis: The Catholic Hospital Association of the United States and Canada, 1965), 4; see also Karl Rahner, *Schriften zur Theologie* (Einsiedeln: Benziger Verlag, 1966), 317, where the unborn child is called a human being.

8. Robert F. Drinan, "The Inviolability of the Right to Be Born," *Abortion and the Law,* ed. David T. Smith (Cleveland: Western Reserve University Press, 1967), 107.

9. John T. Noonan Jr., "Abortion and the Catholic Church: A Summary History," *Natural Law Forum* 12 (1967): 125

10. David Granfield, "The Scientific Background," in *The Abortion Decision* (New York: Doubleday, 1969), 15–41.

11. Josef Fuchs, *Natural Law,* trans. H. Reckter and J. A. Dowling (New York: Sheed and Ward, 1965), 123. A standard manual of moral theology that argues in the same fashion is E. Genicot, J. Salsmans, A. Gortebecke, and J. Beyer, *Institutiones Theologiae Moralis,* 17th ed., vol. 1 ([Beyer] Louvain: Desclee de Brouwer, 1964), 304–5.

12. Granfield, *The Abortion Decision,* 144.

13. Robert F. Drinan, "The Right of the Foetus to Be Born," *The Dublin Review* 514 (winter 1967–68), 377.

14. O'Donnell, "Abortion, II," 219.

15. Häring, *The Law of Christ,* 209.

16. Noonan, "Abortion and the Catholic Church," 131.

17. I. Aertnys et al., *Theologiae Moralis,* 547.

18. John Marshall, *The Ethics of Medical Practice* (London: Darton, Longman & Todd, 1960), 103.

19. Richard A. McCormick, *America* 117 (9 December 1967): 717.

20. *S. T.,* IIa–IIae. q. 64, art. 7.

21. This set of specifications has been taken from Noldin et al., *Summa Theologica Moralis,* 84ff.; for an application to abortion decisions, see A. Vermeersch, *Theologiae Moralis,* 4th ed., vol. 1 (Rome: Gregorian University Press, 1967), 105–7; F. Hurth, *De Statibus* (Rome: Gregorian University Press, 1946), 325; E. Genicot et al., *Institutiones Theologiae Moralis,* 305–6; "Aborto," *Enciclopedia Cattolica* (Rome: Città del Vaticano, 1948), col. 107.

22. A. Bouscaren, *Ethics of Ectopic Operations,* 2d ed. (Milwaukee: Bruce, 1943), 1–2. Bouscaren's book remains the most thorough treatment of the subject of ectopic operations. See also Gerard Kelly, *Medico-Moral Problems* (St. Louis: The Catholic Hospital Association, 1958), 26; Joseph J. Farraher, "Notes on Moral Theology," *TS* 22 (December 1961): 622; John J. Lynch, "Ectopic Pregnancy: A Theological Review," *TS* 28 (February 1961): 12.

23. See Noldin et al., *Summa Theologica Moralis,* 340ff.

24. Granfield, *The Abortion Decision,* 139.

25. Noonan, "Abortion and the Catholic Church," 130.

26. Fuchs, *Natural Law,* 131.

27. Granfield, *The Abortion Decision,* 143.

28. Noonan, "Abortion and the Catholic Church," 130.

[9]

Condemnation of Abortion and Infanticide in the Early Church

James Tunstead Burtchaell, C.S.C.

THE JEWISH SCRIPTURES SEEM to have regarded the unborn as paternal property. A monetary indemnity was due to the father from anyone who caused his wife to abort. The rabbinical tradition, which sired the long legal continuity of later Judaism, is also relatively silent on the subject of abortion.

But at the time of Jesus there was an alternative Jewish tradition, associated with the Greek idiom, that was articulating a strenuous prohibition against both abortion and infanticide. It was this Hellenistic Jewish moral tradition that was in many respects to be both parent and sibling of the nascent Christian belief.[1] Jews and their sympathizers were commonly enjoined not to abort or to expose their children, but to bear and rear them: the defense and nurture of the unborn and newborn was put forth as a notable moral duty.

Hecataeus of Abdera writes:

[Moses] required those who dwelt in the land to rear their children [in contrast with the Greeks who exposed unwanted newborns].[2]

Pseudo-Phocylides concurs:

SOURCE: From *The Giving and Taking of Life: Essays Ethical* by James T. Burtchaell. © 1989 by the University of Notre Dame Press. Reprinted by permission.

A woman should not destroy the unborn babe in her belly; nor after its birth throw it before the dogs and the vultures as a prey.[3]

Philo of Alexandria gives this injunction:

He must not make abortive the generative power of men by gelding nor that of women by sterilizing drugs and other devices. . . . no destroying of their seed nor defrauding their offspring.[4]

Flavius Josephus deals with the same theme:

The Law orders all offspring to be brought up, and forbids women either to cause abortion or to make away with the foetus; a woman convicted of this is regarded as an infanticide, because she destroys a soul and diminishes the race.[5]

A Jewish portion of the *Third Sybil* joins the doctrine:

Foster your offspring instead of killing them: for the fury of the Eternal threatens one who commits such crimes.[6]

Roman law in the same era offered no protection against either abortion or infanticide, both of which were within the prerogatives of the male head-of-household. Neither tradition offered a protection for infants reliable enough to suit the first Christians, and they soon stated their own conviction which was to the point.

The most ancient Christian document we possess, besides the New Testament, is *The Didache, The Instruction of the Twelve Apostles*. Already in this first century catechism, the obligation to protect the unborn and the infant was included within the roster of essential moral duties:

You shall not commit murder; you shall not commit adultery; you shall not prey upon boys; you shall not fornicate; you shall not deal in magic; you shall not practice sorcery; you shall not murder a child by abortion, or kill a newborn; you shall not covet your neighbor's goods. You shall not break your oath; you shall not give perjured evidence; you shall not speak damagingly of others; you shall not bear a grudge.[7]

In a later passage the instruction describes what it calls "the way of death":

It is the path of those who persecute the innocent, despise the truth, find their ease in lying . . . those who have no generosity for the poor, nor concern for the oppressed, nor any knowledge of who it was who made them; they are killers of children, destroyers of God's handiwork; they turn their backs on the needy and take advantage of the afflicted; they are cozy with the affluent but ruthless judges of the poor: sinners to the core. Children, may you be kept safe from it all![8]

The Greek is as straightforward as my translation, bluntly choosing words like "kill" (*apokteinein*) and "murder" (*phoneuein*). Its word for abortion, *phthora*, means, literally, "destruction," and the one destroyed is called "child," *teknon*, the same gentle word used in the final sentence to address the readers themselves.[9]

Shortly before or after the turn of the second century, the *Letter of Barnabas* repeats the *Didache*'s injunction against abortion and infanticide in virtually the same words, and laments that they destroy small images of God.[10]

The second century had not advanced far before the Christian movement had achieved momentum enough to arouse antagonism from Roman society. Some of the most articulate writers of that age were apologists defending their fellow Christians against libel. And one of the slanders that outraged them most was the rumor that Christians slew infants to obtain blood for their eucharistic rites. What made the lie particularly galling was the fact that protection of the young had become such a Christian priority. They did not conceal their contempt for the surrounding pagan society that was willing to destroy its young by choice.

One early apologist, writing in the *Letter to Diognetus,* notes that his fellow Christians stand out from their neighbors, not by citizenship or language or social style, but by their moral convictions.

Every foreign land is their home, and every home a foreign land. They marry like all others and beget children; but they do not expose their offspring. Their board they spread for all, but not their bed. . . . They obey the established laws, but in their private lives they go well beyond the laws.[11]

Minucius Felix, a Roman attorney of African origin, states the contrast even more irascibly:

There is a man I should now like to address, and that is the one who claims, or believes, that our initiations take place by means of the slaughter and blood of a baby. Do you think it possible to inflict fatal wounds on a baby so tender and tiny? That there could be anyone who would butcher a newborn babe, hardly yet a human being, who would shed and drain its blood? The only person capable of believing this is one capable of actually perpetrating it. And, in fact, it is a practice of yours, I observe, to expose your own children to birds and wild beasts, or at times to smother and strangle them—a pitiful way to die; and there are women who swallow drugs to stifle in their womb the beginnings of a human on the way—committing infanticide even before they give birth to their infant.[12]

The same rumor was challenged by Athenagoras of Athens. How could Christians be accused of murder when they refused even to attend the circus events where humans perished as gladiators or as victims of wild beasts? Christians consider, he wrote, that even standing by and tolerating murder is much the same as murder itself. He then continues:

> We call it murder and say it will be accountable to God if women use instruments to procure abortion: how shall we be called murderers ourselves? The same person cannot regard that which a woman carries in her womb as a living creature, and therefore as an object of value to God, and then slay the creature that has come forth to the light of day. The same person cannot forbid the exposure of children, equating such exposure with child-murder, and then slay a child that has found one to bring it up. No, we are always consistent, everywhere the same, governed by the truth and not coercing it to serve us.[13]

Tertullian, a teacher in Rome, was perhaps the most eloquent of the second century apologists. He repeatedly opposed the teaching of the Stoics that children are not yet alive in the womb, and that their soul is given them at birth. Arguing from philosophical more than biological grounds, he insisted that the body and soul grow together from the beginning.

> We have established the principle that all the natural potentialities of the soul with regard to sensation and intelligence are inherent in its very substance, as a result of the intrinsic nature of the soul. As the various stages of life pass, these powers develop, each in its own way, under the influence of circumstances, whether of education, environment, or the supreme powers.[14]

Abortion, he said, was not only homicide, it was parricide: the slaying of one's own flesh and blood.

> With us, murder is forbidden once for all. We are not free to destroy anyone conceived in the womb, while the blood is still being absorbed to build up the human being. To prevent the birth of a child is simply a swifter way to murder. It makes no difference whether one destroys a soul already born or interferes with it on its way to birth. It is a human being and one who will be a human being, for every fruit is there present in the seed.[15]

Even in the case of a child whose uterine presentation makes birth impossible, when Tertullian would accept dismemberment to save at least the mother's life, he bluntly says the child is being "butchered by unavoidable savagery" (*trucidatur necessaria crudelitate*).[16]

Those were statements which Christian apologists were making to outsiders. Among themselves, abortion continued to be reviled as a procedure unthinkable for believers. Clement of Alexandria, perhaps the leading theologian of the second century, wrote:

> If we would only control our lusts at the start, and if we would refrain from killing off the human race born or developing according to the divine plan, then our entire lives would be lived in harmony with nature as well. But women who resort to some sort of deadly abortion drug slay not only the embryo but, along with it, all human love (*philanthropia*).[17]

Early in the next century Hippolytus of Rome condemned bishop Callistus for his readiness to encourage marriage, legal or otherwise, between affluent women and lower-class or slave-class men. Such unions, he observed, had only tended to encourage abortion.

> Women who pass for believers began to resort to drugs to induce sterility, and to bind their abdomens tightly so as to abort the conceptus, because they did not want to have a child by a slave or lower-class type, for the sake of their family pride and their excessive wealth. Look what abuse of duty this lawless man has encouraged, by inciting them both to adultery and to murder. And after such outrageous activity they have the nerve to call themselves a Catholic church![18]

Those were forthright voices from the first and formative Christian years, all arguing that the destruction of the child, unborn or newborn, is infamy for those who follow Christ.

The Character of This Conviction

One is confronted by five facts: five aspects of that early Christian conviction which must in some way be foundational for Christian ethics.

First, the repudiation of abortion was not an isolated or esoteric doctrine. It formed part of an obligation by all believers to protect the four categories of people whom they now saw as peculiarly exposed to the whim and will of their fellow humans: the slave, the enemy, the wife and the infant, unborn or newborn. These were at great risk, as were the four traditional protégés: the pauper, the alien, the widow, and the orphan. And this fourfold obligation was preached across the full expanse of the church: from Carthage to Egypt and up into Syria, then across Greece and in Rome.

Second, this was not a program for the more strenuous. It was presented as the imperative agenda for the church, the test for all discipleship. Believers were warned away from abortion just as they were from adultery, murder, greed and theft: they were all ways to spiritual death. The four Christian innovations were offered as the classic new signs of authenticity. If theirs was not a community where Jew and gentile (divided by such ancient hostility), where man and woman, where slave and free could show forth as one, then it had failed as Christian. That was their test. Paul sends Onesimus the slave back to his master Philemon and tells him to receive him as a brother, and then charges him: "So if you grant me any fellowship with yourself, welcome him as you would me." That was their test. If this be heroism, it is a heroism exacted of every person who would walk the new Way.

A third thing one must observe is that though these exhortations show a sensitive and compassionate sympathy for the victims, their principal moral concern is for the oppressors. It is the husband that bullies his wife whose person dwindles even more sadly than hers. The master or mistress who abuses the slave sustains an injury even greater than what the slave experiences. It is the mother who eliminates her son that Clement cares about, because she must destroy her *philanthropia* as well, her love for humankind, in order to do it. The disease of character that follows from exploitation of others was seen, in Christian perspective, to be more hideously incapacitating than the worst that befell the victims. It could be a death far worse than death. Even when they enter the contemporary dispute over the animation of the unborn, these writers dismiss it as a quibble when it comes to abortion: it is the same ruthless willingness to eliminate unwelcome others that shows itself in the slaying of the unborn, the newborn, or the parent. In truest Christian perspective, it is the oppressor that is destroyed.

Fourthly: these writers know well that any true protection of the helpless and exploited calls for a stable empowerment, so that those same people would not continue to be victimized. This means that the Christian moral agenda demands a price. Oppressors must give up their advantage. It little matters whether the advantage was seized purposefully or inherited unwittingly. There is a forfeiture to be accepted by those in power if the disadvantaged and helpless are to be afforded true protection.

But there is a further sacrifice to be made. The victims must accept suffering as well. The price they must pay—if they are to be Christians—is that they must forgo resentment and hatred. Empowerment cannot be grasped as the means to take revenge or, still worse, as the way to begin to be an exploiter oneself. The victims must gaze directly upon those who had taken advantage of them, and recognize them as brothers and sisters who themselves may have been pressed by distress of one kind or another. So there is no moral accomplishment possible unless reconciliation extends the hand of fellowship across the battleline of suffering. There will be heavy and sometimes bitter things to accept if hatred is to be extinguished, and not merely aimed in a new direction.

Fifth, we must note that this was a rigorous duty presented to the church's Christian ancestors. The light was dazzling, and they often preferred to draw back into the cover of darkness. Christians have sinned against that light and continued to relish and even to justify hatred against their enemies. They did not set the slaves free. Women were not welcomed into full and equal status. And parents continued to destroy their young.

A Fourfold Moral Movement Today

Yet every person interested enough to follow this debate must be aware that we live in an extraordinary age in the life of the world and the church. Four great movements have stirred the church round the world:

1. A movement for world peace that is more than a weariness of war; it is making bold and positive ventures towards the reduction of enmity and distrust.
2. Another movement for the relief of bondage of every kind: freedom from slavery and from racial subjection, dignity for the worker, status for the migrant.
3. Another movement for equality of women and a more integrated companionship with men, so that family and work can be humanized for each and for both together.
4. And a fourth movement to rescue the children from abortion, prenatal neglect, infanticide, infant mortality, and every sort of abuse and predatory danger.

In the trough of some of the most genocidal carnage and oppressive bondage and degradation of women and slaughter of children, our era may be unusual in the readiness of some to listen to that bold and visionary Christian age whose teaching I have been holding up for recollection.

Each of these movements is bent on empowerment. If the exploited do arise and claim their rightful places, will they take power like Spartacus or Robespierre or Pol Pot? Or will they take power like Mahatma Gandhi or Nelson Mandela . . . or like Jesus? Christians may make the difference. This fourfold phalanx of conscience on the march is only partly Christian in origin. But Christians will mean much to these movements of grace, and these movements must mean much to the Christian community.

Christians, possibly more than others, should immediately recognize that these various struggles are in alliance with each other. None can be pitted against another. The United States, for instance, must never imagine that enmity between nations will be subdued if our neighbors are in bondage to us. Enslavement and enmity must both vanish; one must never be forfeited for the sake of the other. Likewise, the movement of enhancement for women must never be furthered by making their children expendable. In America today abortion is said to resolve a conflict of rights, a conflict of interests between women and their children. But a Christian must hold suspect any human right which must be guaranteed by another human's elimination.

Another Christian contribution will be to tell all those who stand to lose bully power that it is in their highest interest to do so. For they have truly withered under the weight of their exploitative advantages. To say this to them with any credibility, one must first be utterly persuaded that oppressors suffer an even more tragic injury than their victims. Are we really ready to believe that the staff of Auschwitz perished in a worse tragedy than those they exterminated? Do you mourn more for the 2,000 or so abortionists in America than for the 20,000,000 or so infants they have efficiently destroyed? Were you more dismayed about Bull Connor than about Martin Luther King Jr.? Only if you do believe that can you say believably that it is the mothers who destroy their unborn children you care much for, for they stand to lose even more than do their tragically destroyed offspring.

A Characteristically Christian Insight

There is another characteristic Christian insight needed in the abortion dispute. Christians must see and say how often it is that women who victimize their children are themselves handicapped by never having enjoyed control over their own lives. They are victims—even though they are victims who destroy others.

How often it is that some helpless group is savaged by aggressors who have themselves been victims. They are survivors of outrage, and they now seek to relieve their stress and suffering by turning on others who are weaker still. Victims exploiting victims.

Who are those who want to close the nation's gates against impoverished and threatened refugees? Those groups who have long been trampled underfoot by the economy, and who fear new rivals just as they see for themselves a hope for betterment and security at last. Victims pushing aside victims.

What is the background of parents who abuse and batter their children? A childhood of violence, incest, contempt. Victims lashing out at victims.

And who are aborting their daughters and sons today? Women and men who are alienated, abused, spoiled, poor, who are at a loss to manage their own lives or intimacies. Victims destroyed, destroying victims.

Hate them—hate any victimizers—and you are simply cheering on the cycle of abuse and violence. Suppress your rage well enough to look closely and humanely at drug dealers, at rapists, at pathological prison guards, and you may see it there too: the same pathetic look of the battered spirit, preying on others wantonly.

Women who are desperate or autistic enough to destroy their children are among society's most abused victims. We owe them every help. But a truly compassionate support could never invite them to assuage their own anger by exterminating those more helpless still. It is by breaking the savage cycle of violence that victimization is laid to rest.

When you grasp the uplifted hand to prevent one injured person from striking out at another, you must do so in love, not in anger, for you are asking that person to absorb suffering rather than pass it on to another. And, to be a peacemaker, you must be as ready to sustain as you are to restrain. One must be more than just to accept undeserved injury, yet deal out undeserved favor.

The church's belief is in a Lord who was the innocent victim of injustice. Yet Christ caught the impact of that injustice in his own body, his own self. He deadened it and refused to pass it on; he refused to let the hatred go on ricocheting through humankind. If we truly follow him we are committed to doing the same. And the truest test of that faith is whether we have the gumption to share it with others, with those who are treating others unjustly, but especially with people who are victims. Christians must prevail upon them to let us help them catch the impact of their distress in their own bodies, and in our own selves alongside theirs, without permitting the cycle of violence to carry on.

The fire of Pentecost rapidly enflamed the Christian community to a sense of what they were about. They were in so many ways an observant Jewish movement: in their worship, their hopes, their moral way of life. But in two great matters they burst forth as men and women possessed by a new Spirit. They witnessed to the resurrection: Jesus, during whose unjust execution they had been inert and disengaged, was risen to power as Messiah and Lord. That was the first great matter. The second was like it. They too had been raised to unexpected power, and they stated with vehemence that they would no longer be passive before affliction. That determination was embodied in the distinctive and innovative moral commitment to befriend the enemy, to embrother the slave, to raise up the wife, and to welcome the child. Their own lives were at stake, for these Christians believed that they would perish in their persons if they proved nonchalant about the suffering of any of these most vulnerable brothers and sisters. But they rushed to their task, for many lives depended on them: the lives of those so powerful they could crush others without noticing; and the lives of their victims—unnoticed, undefended, even unnamed.

I have been asking whether recent developments and reflection give us authentic reasons to reconsider what the *Didache* and Athenagoras and Tertullian and other ancestors in faith held to be essential. We have never had more reasons to reconsider their teaching. And I say that their teaching has never rung more defiantly as the prophetic call of Christ.

The revolt against abortion was no primitive and narrow dogma that a more sophisticated church has now outgrown. It was in the very nucleus of the moral insight by which the church first defined itself before the Lord and before the world. The community has not yet approached it, while some speak of having surpassed it. Those first disciples who reverenced every unwanted child, born or unborn, would have been stupefied by the sight of their own children in the faith gainsaying this or any of that fourfold commitment. Were that community to forswear the hated enemy, the enslaved laborer, the subjected woman, or the defenseless infant, and do that in his name, Christ would have died in vain.

Notes

1. John J. Collins has described this pre-Christian development in Hellenistic Judaism that framed ethical duty in less particularist ways; see *Between Athens and Jerusalem: Jewish Identity in the Hellenistic Diaspora* (New York: Crossroad, 1983), 142–48.

2. Hecataeus of Abdera (reported by Diodorus Siculus, *Library of History* 40: 3, 8); see *Diodorus of Sicily*, trans. Francis R. Walton, 12 (Cambridge: Harvard University Press, 1967), 284.

3. Pseudo-Phocyclides, *Sentences* 184–85; see *The Sentences of Pseudo-Phocyclides*, P. W. van der Horst (Leiden: Brill, 1978), 232.

4. Philo of Alexandria, *Hypothetica*, 7:7; see *The Works of Philo of Alexandria*, ed. Francis Henry Colson et al. (New York: Putnam, 1929–62), 9:428.

5. Flavius Josephus, *Contra Apionem* 2:202; see *The Works of Flavius Josephus*, ed. Henry St. John Thackeray et al. (Cambridge: Harvard University Press, 1962-65), 1:372–74.

6. *Sibylline Oracles* 3:765–66.

7. *Didache* 2:2–3.

8. Ibid., 5:2.

9. This vocabulary carries over from the hellenistic Jewish documents quoted above.

10. *Letter of Barnabas* 19:5; 20:2.

11. *Letter to Diognetus* 5:6–7, 10.

12. Marcus Minucius Felix, *Octavius* 30:1–2.

13. Athenagoras of Athens, *Embassy for the Christians*, 35.

14. Tertullian, *De Anima* 38:1; see also 37.

15. Tertullian, *Apologeticum* 9:8; see also 9:4–7.
16. Tertullian, *De Anima* 25:4.
17. Clement of Alexandria, *The Pegagogue,* 96.
18. Hippolytus of Rome, *Refutation of All Heresies* 9:12:25.

[10]

Respect for Life in the Womb: Address to the Medical Association of Western Flanders (April 23, 1977)

Pope Paul VI

MODERN MEDICINE IS BECOMING more and more remote from the uninitiated because both its techniques and its language have become so complicated. At the same time, however, the high scientific level every physician should attain must not be allowed to overshadow or lessen that sense of the human reality and that attention to persons which have always characterized the medical profession and been the source of its greatness.

In the matter of medical ethics, We wish to insist once again on the foundation of everything else, namely, an unconditional respect for life from its very beginnings. It is important to understand why this principle, so essential to every civilization worthy of the name, is today being challenged and why we must firmly oppose what is being improperly termed a "liberalization."

The Catholic Church has always regarded abortion as an abominable crime because unqualified respect for even the very beginnings of life is a logical consequence of the mysteries of creation and redemption. In our Lord Jesus Christ every human being, even one whose physical life is utterly wretched, is called to the dignity of a child of God. That is what our faith teaches us.

SOURCE: From *The Pope Speaks* 22 (fall 1977). Reprinted by permission of Our Sunday Visitor, Inc.

Every Christian must draw the necessary conclusions from this premise and not let himself be blinded by what are claimed to be social or political necessities.

Still less may he excuse himself on the ground that he must respect the opinions of those who do not share his convictions for, in this area, the Christian faith simply casts a further, supernatural light on a moral attitude which is a universal and basic demand imposed by every rightly formed conscience and which is, therefore, legitimately regarded as a requirement of humanness itself, that is, of human nature in the philosophical sense of the term.

Every Christian must attribute the proper importance to this higher morality, this unwritten law which exists in the very heart of man and alone can provide a basis for an authentic social consensus and a legislation worthy of the name.

As doctors, moreover, as men and women who know the scientific and ethical norms of your profession, you have a special and very important role to play in informing and forming others, each of you according to your special competence, and in pointing out the serious errors on which propaganda for abortion is based. Who more than you are frequently in a position to denounce the manipulation of statistics, the overhasty claims in the area of biology and the disastrous physiological and psychological repercussions of abortion?

In encouraging you to fight on behalf of life, We do not forget—as We are sure you realize—the serious problems you face in the exercise of your profession. You need an enlightened conscience if you are to find practical solutions, often painful to implement, which will not sacrifice any of the values at stake. Is it not in this way that the role of physician, which is based on but involves more than technical competence, takes on its full dimensions: the role, We mean, of being a person to whom nothing human is alien?

In your researches may you advance equally in knowledge and in awareness of your responsibilities! You can be sure that We lift up your intentions to the Lord, asking him to bless you, your families and all who come to seek your help.

[11]

1974 Declaration on Procured Abortion

The Vatican

I. Introduction

1. The problem of procured abortion and of its possible legal liberalization has become almost everywhere the subject of impassioned discussions. These debates would be less grave were it not a question of human life, a primordial value, which must be protected and promoted. Everyone understands this, although many look for reasons, even against all evidence, to promote the use of abortion. One cannot but be astonished to see on the one hand an increase of unqualified protests against the death penalty and every form of war and on the other hand the vindication of the liberalization of abortion, either in its entirety or in ever broader indications. The Church is too conscious of the fact that it belongs to her vocation to defend man against everything that could disintegrate or lessen his dignity to remain silent on such a topic. Because the Son of God became man, there is no man who is not his brother in humanity and who is not called to become a Christian in order to receive salvation from him.

2. In many countries the public authorities which resist the liberalization of abortion laws are the object of powerful pressures aimed at leading them to

SOURCE: From Sacred Congregation for the Doctrine of Faith, *Declaration on Abortion* (November 18, 1974), published 1975.

this goal. This, it is said, would violate no one's conscience, for each individual would be left free to follow his own opinion, while being prevented from imposing it on others. Ethical pluralism is claimed to be a normal consequence of ideological pluralism. There is, however, a great difference between the one and the other, for action affects the interests of others more quickly than does mere opinion. Moreover, one can never claim freedom of opinion as a pretext for attacking the rights of others, most especially the right to life.

3. Numerous Christian lay people, especially doctors, but also parents' associations, statesmen, or leading figures in posts of responsibility have vigorously reacted against this propaganda campaign. Above all, many episcopal conferences and many bishops acting in their own name have judged it opportune to recall very strongly the traditional doctrine of the Church.[1] With a striking convergence these documents admirably emphasize an attitude of respect for life which is at the same time human and Christian. Nevertheless it has happened that several of these documents here or there have encountered reservation or even opposition.

4. Charged with the promotion and the defence of faith and morals in the universal Church,[2] the Sacred Congregation for the Doctrine of the Faith proposes to recall this teaching in its essential aspects to all the faithful. Thus, in showing the unity of the Church, it will confirm by the authority proper to the Holy See what the bishops have opportunely undertaken. It hopes that all the faithful, including those who might have been unsettled by the controversies and new opinions, will understand that it is not a question of opposing one opinion to another, but of transmitting to the faithful a constant teaching of the supreme Magisterium, which teaches moral norms in the light of faith.[3] It is therefore clear that this Declaration necessarily entails a grave obligation for Christian consciences.[4] May God deign to enlighten also all men who strive with their whole heart to "act in truth" (Jn. 3:21).

II. In the Light of Faith

5. "Death was not God's doing, he takes no pleasure in the extinction of the living" (Wis. 1:13). Certainly God has created beings who have only one lifetime and physical death cannot be absent from the world of those with a bodily existence. But what is immediately willed is life, and in the visible universe everything has been made for man, who is the image of God and the world's crowning glory (cf. Gen. 1:26–28). On the human level, "it was the devil's envy that brought death into the world" (Wis. 2:24). Introduced by sin, death remains bound up with it: death is the sign and fruit of sin. But there is no final triumph for death. Confirming faith in the Resurrection, the Lord pro-

claims in the Gospel: "God is God, not of the dead, but of the living" (Matt. 22:32). And death like sin will be definitively defeated by resurrection in Christ (cf. 1 Cor. 15:20–27). Thus we understand that human life, even on this earth, is precious. Infused by the Creator,[5] life is again taken back by him (cf. Gen. 2:7; Wis. 15:11). It remains under his protection: man's blood cries out to him (cf. Gen. 4:10) and he will demand an account of it, "for in the image of God man was made" (Gen. 9:5–6). The commandment of God is formal: "You shall not kill" (Exod. 20:13). Life is at the same time a gift and a responsibility. It is received as a "talent" (cf. Matt. 25:14–30); it must be put to proper use. In order that life may bring forth fruit, many tasks are offered to man in this world and he must not shirk them. More important still, the Christian knows that eternal life depends on what, with the grace of God, he does with his life on earth.

6. The tradition of the Church has always held that human life must be protected and favored from the beginning, just as at the various stages of its development. Opposing the morals of the Greco-Roman world, the Church of the first centuries insisted on the difference that exists on this point between those morals and Christian morals. In the Didache it is clearly said: "You shall not kill the fetus by abortion and you shall not murder the infant already born."[6] Athenagoras emphasizes that Christians consider as murderers those women who take medicines to procure an abortion; he condemns the killers of children, including those still living in their mother's womb, "where they are already the object of the care of divine Providence."[7] Tertullian did not always perhaps use the same language; he nevertheless clearly affirms the essential principle: "To prevent birth is anticipated murder; it makes little difference whether one destroys a life already born or does away with it in its nascent stage. The one who will be a man is already one."[8]

7. In the course of history, the Fathers of the Church, her Pastors and her Doctors have taught the same doctrine—the various opinions on the infusion of the spiritual soul did not introduce any doubt about the illicitness of abortion. It is true that in the Middle Ages, when the opinion was generally held that the spiritual soul was not present until after the first few weeks, a distinction was made in the evaluation of the sin and the gravity of penal sanctions. Excellent authors allowed for this first period more lenient case solutions which they rejected for following periods. But it was never denied at that time that procured abortion, even during the first days, was objectively a grave fault. This condemnation was in fact unanimous. Among the many documents it is sufficient to recall certain ones. The first Council of Mainz in 847 reconsiders the penalties against abortion which had been established by preceding Councils. It decided that the most rigorous penance would be imposed "on women who procure the elimination of the fruit conceived in their womb."[9] The De-

cree of Gratian reports the following words of Pope Stephen V: "That person is a murderer who causes to perish by abortion what has been conceived."[10] Saint Thomas, the Common Doctor of the Church, teaches that abortion is a grave sin against the natural law.[11] At the time of the Renaissance Pope Sixtus V condemned abortion with the greatest severity.[12] A century later, Innocent XI rejected the propositions of certain lax canonists who sought to excuse an abortion procured before the moment accepted by some as the moment of the spiritual animation of the new being.[13] In our days the recent Roman Pontiffs have proclaimed the same doctrine with the greatest clarity. Pius XI explicitly answered the most serious objections.[14] Pius XII clearly excluded all direct abortion, that is, abortion which is either an end or a means.[15] John XXIII recalled the teaching of the Fathers on the sacred character of life "which from its beginning demands the action of God the Creator."[16] Most recently, the Second Vatican Council, presided over by Paul VI, has most severely condemned abortion: "Life must be safeguarded with extreme care from conception; abortion and infanticide are abominable crimes."[17] The same Paul VI, speaking on this subject on many occasions, has not been afraid to declare that this teaching of the Church "has not changed and is unchangeable."[18]

III. In the Additional Light of Reason

8. Respect for human life is not just a Christian obligation. Human reason is sufficient to impose it on the basis of the analysis of what a human person is and should be. Constituted by a rational nature, man is a personal subject, capable of reflecting on himself and of determining his acts and hence his own destiny: he is free. He is consequently master of himself, or rather, because this takes place in the course of time, he has the means of becoming so: this is his task. Created immediately by God, man's soul is spiritual and therefore immortal. Hence man is open to God; he finds his fulfillment only in him. But man lives in the community of his equals; he is nourished by interpersonal communication with men in the indispensable social setting. In the fact of society and other men, each human person possesses himself, he possesses life and different goods; he has these as a right. It is this that strict justice demands from all in his regard.

9. Nevertheless, temporal life lived in this world is not identified with the person. The person possesses as his own a level of life that is more profound and that cannot end. Bodily life is a fundamental good; here below it is the condition for all other goods. But there are higher values for which it could be legitimate or even necessary to be willing to expose oneself to the risk of losing bodily life. In a society of persons the common good is for each individual an

end which he must serve and to which he must subordinate his particular interest. But it is not his last end and, from this point of view, it is society which is at the service of the person, because the person will not fulfill his destiny except in God. The person can be definitively subordinated only to God. Man can never be treated simply as a means to be disposed of in order to obtain a higher end.

10. In regard to the mutual rights and duties of the person and of society, it belongs to moral teaching to enlighten consciences, it belongs to the law to specify and organize external behavior. In fact, there are a certain number of rights which society is not in a position to grant since these rights precede society; but society has the function to preserve and to enforce them. These are the greater part of those which are today called "human rights" and which our age boasts of having formulated.

11. The first right of the human person is the right to life. He has other goods of which some are more precious, but this one is fundamental—the condition of all the others. Hence it must be protected above all others. It does not belong to society, nor does it belong to public authority in any form to recognize this right for some and not for others: all discrimination is evil, whether it be founded on race, sex, color or religion. It is not recognition by another that constitutes this right. This right is antecedent to its recognition; it demands recognition and it is strictly unjust to refuse it.

12. Any discrimination based on the various stages of life is no more justified than any other discrimination. The right to life remains complete in an old person, even one greatly weakened, it is not lost by one who is incurably sick. The right to life is no less to be respected in the small infant just born than in the mature person. In reality, respect for human life is called for from the time that the process of generation begins. From the time that the ovum is fertilized, a life is begun which is neither that of the father nor of the mother; it is rather the life of a new human being with his or her own growth. It would never be made human if it were not human already.

13. To this perpetual evidence—perfectly independent of the discussions on the moment of animation[19]—modern genetic science brings valuable confirmation. It has demonstrated that, from the first instant there is established the programme of what this living being will be: a man, this individual man with his characteristic aspects already well determined. Right from fertilization is begun the adventure of a human life, and each of its capacities requires time—a rather lengthy time—to find its place and to be in a position to act. The least that can be said is that present science, in its most evolved state, does not give any substantial support to those who defend abortion. Moreover, it is not up to biological sciences to make a definitive judgment on questions which are properly philosophical and moral, such as the moment when a hu-

man person is constituted or the legitimacy of abortion. From a moral point of view this is certain: even if a doubt existed concerning whether the fruit of conception is already a human person, it is objectively a grave sin to dare to risk murder. "The one who will be a man is already one."[20]

IV. Reply to Some Objections

14. Divine law and natural reason, therefore, exclude all right to the direct killing of an innocent man. However, if the reasons given to justify an abortion were always manifestly evil and valueless the problem would not be so dramatic. The gravity of the problem comes from the fact that in certain cases, perhaps in quite a considerable number of cases by denying abortion one endangers important values to which it is normal to attach great value, and which may sometimes even seem to have priority. We do not deny these very great difficulties. It may be a serious question of health, sometimes of life or death, for the mother; it may be the burden represented by an additional child, especially if there are good reasons to fear that the child will be abnormal or retarded; it may be the importance attributed in different classes of society to considerations of honor or dishonor, of loss of social standing, and so forth. We proclaim only that none of these reasons can ever objectively confer the right to dispose of another's life, even when that life is only beginning. With regard to the future unhappiness of the child, no one, not even the father or mother, can act as its substitute, even if it is still in the embryonic stage, to choose in the child's name, life or death. The child itself, when grown up, will never have the right to choose suicide; no more may his parents choose death for the child while it is not of an age to decide for itself. Life is too fundamental a value to be weighed against even very serious disadvantages.[21]

15. The movement for the emancipation of women, in so far as it seeks essentially to free them from all unjust discrimination, is on perfectly sound ground.[22] In the different forms of cultural background there is a great deal to be done in this regard. But one cannot change nature. Nor can one exempt women, any more than men, from what nature demands of them. Furthermore, all publicly recognized freedom is always limited by the certain rights of others.

16. The same must be said of the claim to sexual freedom. If by this expression one is to understand the mastery progressively acquired by reason and by authentic love over instinctive impulse, without diminishing pleasure but keeping it in its proper place—and in this sphere this is the only authentic freedom—then there is nothing to object to. But this kind of freedom will always be careful not to violate justice. If, on the contrary, one is to understand that

men and women are "free" to seek sexual pleasures to the point of satiety, without taking into account any law or the essential orientation of sexual life to its fruits of fertility,[23] then this idea has nothing Christian in it. It is even unworthy of man. In any case it does not confer any right to dispose of human life—even if embryonic—or to suppress it on the pretext that it is burdensome.

17. Scientific progress is opening to technology—and will open still more —the possibility of delicate interventions, the consequences of which can be very serious, for good as well as for evil. These are achievements of the human spirit which in themselves are admirable. But technology can never be independent of the criterion of morality, since technology exists for man and must respect his finality. Just as there is no right to use nuclear energy for every possible purpose, so there is no right to manipulate human life in every possible direction. Technology must be at the service of man, so as better to ensure the functioning of his normal abilities, to prevent or to cure his illnesses, to contribute to his better human development. It is true that the evolution of technology makes early abortion more and more easy, but the moral evaluation is in no way modified because of this.

18. We know what seriousness the problem of birth control can assume for some families and for some countries. That is why the last Council and subsequently the Encyclical *Humanae Vitae* of July 25, 1968, spoke of "responsible parenthood."[24] What we wish to say again with emphasis, as was pointed out in the conciliar Constitution *Gaudium et Spes,* in the Encyclical *Populorum Progressio* and in other papal documents, is that never, under any pretext, may abortion be resorted to, either by a family or by the political authority, as a legitimate means of regulating births.[25] The damage to moral values is always a greater evil for the common good than any disadvantage in the economic or demographic order.

V. Morality and Law

19. The moral discussion is being accompanied more or less everywhere by serious juridical debates. There is no country where legislation does not forbid and punish homicide. Furthermore, many countries had specifically applied this condemnation and these penalties to the particular case of procured abortion. In these days a vast body of opinion petitions the liberalization of this latter prohibition. There already exists a fairly general tendency which seeks to limit as far as possible all restrictive legislation, especially when it seems to touch upon private life. The argument of pluralism is also used. Although many citizens, in particular the Catholic faithful, condemn abortion, many others hold that it is licit, at least as a lesser evil. Why force them to follow an

opinion which is not theirs, especially in a country where they are in the majority? In addition it is apparent that, where they still exist, the laws condemning abortion appear difficult to apply. The crime has become too common for it to be punished every time, and the public authorities often find that it is wiser to close their eyes to it. But the preservation of a law which is not applied is always to the detriment of authority and of all other laws. It must be added that clandestine abortion puts women who resign themselves to it and have recourse to it in the most serious dangers for future pregnancies and also in many cases for their lives. Even if the legislator continues to regard abortion as an evil, may he not propose to restrict its damage?

20. These arguments and others in addition that are heard from varying quarters are not conclusive. It is true that civil law cannot expect to cover the whole field of morality or to punish all faults. No one expects it to do so. It must often tolerate what is in fact a lesser evil, in order to avoid a greater one. One must, however, be attentive to what a change in legislation can represent. Many will take as authorization what is perhaps only the abstention from punishment. Even more, in the present case, this very renunciation seems at the very least to admit that the legislator no longer considers abortion a crime against human life, since murder is still always severely punished. It is true that it is not the task of the law to choose between points of view or to impose one rather than another. But the life of the child takes precedence over all opinions. One cannot invoke freedom of thought to destroy this life.

21. The role of law is not to record what is done, but to help in promoting improvement. It is at all times the task of the State to preserve each person's rights and to protect the weakest. In order to do so the State will have to right many wrongs. The law is not obliged to sanction everything, but it cannot act contrary to a law which is deeper and more majestic than any human law: the natural law engraved in men's hearts by the Creator as a norm which reason clarifies and strives to formulate properly, and which one must always struggle to understand better, but which it is always wrong to contradict. Human law can abstain from punishment, but it cannot declare to be right what would be opposed to the natural law, for this opposition suffices to give the assurance that a law is not a law at all.

22. It must in any case be clearly understood that whatever may be laid down by civil law in this matter, man can never obey a law which is in itself immoral, and such is the case of a law which would admit in principle the liceity of abortion. Nor can he take part in a propaganda campaign in favour of such a law, or vote for it. Moreover, he may not collaborate in its application. It is, for instance, inadmissible that doctors or nurses should find themselves obliged to cooperate closely in abortions and have to choose between the law of God and their professional situation.

23. On the contrary it is the task of law to pursue a reform of society and of conditions of life in all milieux, starting with the most deprived, so that always and everywhere it may be possible to give every child coming into this world a welcome worthy of a person. Help for families and for unmarried mothers, assured grants for children, a statute for illegitimate children and reasonable arrangements for adoption—a whole positive policy must be put into force so that there will always be a concrete, honorable and possible alternative to abortion.

VI. Conclusion

24. Following one's conscience in obedience to the law of God is not always the easy way. One must not fail to recognize the weight of the sacrifices and the burdens which it can impose. Heroism is sometimes called for in order to remain faithful to the requirements of the divine law. Therefore we must emphasize that the path of true progress of the human person passes through this constant fidelity to a conscience maintained in uprightness and truth; and we must exhort all those who are able to do so to lighten the burdens still crushing so many men and women, families and children, who are placed in situations to which in human terms there is no solution.

25. A Christian's outlook cannot be limited to the horizon of life in this world. He knows that during the present life another one is being prepared, one of such importance that it is in its light that judgments must be made.[26] From this viewpoint there is no absolute misfortune here below, not even the terrible sorrow of bringing up a handicapped child. This is the contradiction proclaimed by the Lord: "Happy those who mourn: they shall be comforted" (Matt. 5:5). To measure happiness by the absence of sorrow and misery in this world is to turn one's back on the Gospel.

26. But this does not mean that one can remain indifferent to these sorrows and miseries. Every man and woman with feeling, and certainly every Christian, must be ready to do what he can to remedy them. This is the law of charity, of which the first preoccupation must always be the establishment of justice. One can never approve of abortion; but it is above all necessary to combat its causes. This includes political action, which will be in particular the task of the law. But it is necessary at the same time to influence morality and to do everything possible to help families, mothers and children. Considerable progress in the service of life has been accomplished by medicine. One can hope that such progress will continue, in accordance with the vocation of doctors, which is not to suppress life but to care for it and favor it as much as possible. It is equally desirable that, in suitable institutions, or, in their absence, in

the outpouring of Christian generosity and charity every form of assistance should be developed.

27. There will be no effective action on the level of morality unless at the same time an effort is made on the level of ideas. A point of view—or even more perhaps a way of thinking—which considers fertility as an evil cannot be allowed to spread without contradiction. It is true that not all forms of culture are equally in favor of large families. Such families come up against much greater difficulties in an industrial and urban civilization. Thus the Church has in recent times insisted on the idea of responsible parenthood, the exercise of true human and Christian prudence. Such prudence would not be authentic if it did not include generosity. It must preserve awareness of the grandeur of the task of cooperating with the Creator in the transmission of life, which gives new members to society and new children to the Church. Christ's Church has the fundamental solicitude of protecting and favoring life. She certainly thinks before all else of the life which Christ came to bring: "I have come so that they may have life and have it to the full" (Jn. 10:10). But life at all its levels comes from God, and bodily life is for man the indispensable beginning. In this life on earth sin has introduced, multiplied and made harder to bear suffering and death. But in taking their burden upon himself Jesus Christ has transformed them: for whoever believes in him, suffering and death itself become instruments of resurrection. Hence Saint Paul can say: "I think that what we suffer in this life can never be compared to the glory, as yet unrevealed, which is waiting for us" (Rom. 8:18). And, if we make this comparison we shall add with him: "Yes, the troubles which are soon over, though they weigh little, train us for the carrying of a weight of eternal glory which is out of all proportion to them" (2 Cor. 4:17).

The Supreme Pontiff Pope Paul VI, in an audience granted to the undersigned Secretary of the Sacred Congregation for the Doctrine of the Faith on June 28, 1974 has ratified this Declaration on Procured Abortion and has confirmed it and ordered it to be promulgated.

Given in Rome, at the Sacred Congregation for the Doctrine of the Faith, on November 18, the Commemoration of the Dedication of the Basilicas of Saints Peter and Paul, in the year 1974.

Franciscus. Card. Seper
Prefect

Hieronymus Hamer
Titular Archbishop of Lorium
Secretary

Notes

1. A certain number of bishops' documents are to be found in Gr. Caprile, *Non Uccidere: Il magistero della Chiesa sull'aborto*, Part II (Rome, 1973), 47–300.

2. *Regimini Ecclesiae Universae*, III, 1, 29. Cf. Ibid., 31 (AAS 59, 1967): 897. On the Sacred Congregation for the Doctrine of the Faith depend all the questions which are related to faith and morals or which are bound up with the faith.

3. *Lumen Gentium* 12 (AAS 57, 1965): 16–17. The present Declaration does not envisage all the questions which can arise in connection with abortion: it is for theologians to examine and discuss them. Only certain basic principles are here recalled which must be for the theologians themselves a guide and a rule, and confirm certain fundamental truths of Catholic doctrine for all Christians.

4. *Lumen Gentium* 25 (*AAS* 57, 1965): 29–31.

5. The authors of Scripture do not make any philosophical observations on when life begins but they speak of the period of life which precedes birth as being the object of God's attention: he creates and forms the human being, like that which is moulded by his hand (cf. Ps. 118:73). It would seem that this theme finds expression for the first time in Jr. 1:5. It appears later in many other texts. Cf. Isa. 49:1, 5; 46:3; Job 10:8–12; Ps. 22:10, 71:6, 139:13. In the Gospels we read in Luke 1:44: "For the moment your greeting reached my ears, the child in my womb leapt for joy."

6. *Didache Apostolorum*, edition Funk, *Patres Apostolici*, V, 2. The *Epistle of Barnabas*, XIX, 5 uses the same expressions (cf. Funk, l.c., 91–93).

7. Athenagoras, *A Plea on Behalf of Christians*, 35 (cf. PG 6,970: S.C. 3, pp. 166–67). One may also consult the *Epistle to Diognetus*, V, 6 Funk, o.c., I, 399: S.C. 33), where it says of Christians: "They procreate children, but they do not reject the foetus."

8. Tertullian, *Apologeticum*, IX, 8 PL 1, 371–72: *Corp. Christ.* I, 103, 1.31–36.

9. Canon 21 (Mansi, 14, p. 909). cf. Council of Elvira, canon 63 (Mansi, 2, p. 16) and the Council of Ancyra, canon 21 (ibid., 519). See also the decree of Gregory III regarding the penance to be imposed upon those who are culpable of this crime (Mansi 13, 292, c. 17).

10. Gratian, *Concordantia Discordantium Canonum*, c. 20, C. 2, q. 2. During the Middle Ages appeal was often made to the authority of Saint Augustine who wrote as follows in regard to this matter in *De Nuptiis et Concupiscentiis*, c. 15: "Sometimes this sexually indulgent cruelty or this cruel sexual indulgence goes so far as to procure potions which produce sterility. If the desired result is not achieved, the mother terminates the life and expels the foetus which was in her womb in such a way that the child dies before having lived or, if the baby was living already in its mother's womb, it is killed before being born" (PL 44, 423-424: CSEL 33, 619). Cf. the *Decree of Gratian* q. 2, C 32, c. 7.

11. *Commentary on the Sentences,* book IV, dist. 31, exposition of the text.

12. Constitutio *Effraenatum* in 1588 (*Bullarium Romanum,* V, 1, 25–27; *Fontes Iuris Canonici,* 1, no. 165, 308–11.

13. Dz-Sch 1184. Cf. also the Constitution *Apostolicae Sedis* of Pius IX (Acta Pii · IX, V, 55-72; *ASS* 5 (1869), 305–31; *Fontes Iuris Canonici* III, no. 552, 24–31.

14. Encyclical *Casti Connubii,* (*AAS* 22, 1930), 562–65; Dz-Sch. 3719–21.

15. The statements of Pius XII are express, precise and numerous; they would require a whole study on their own. We quote only this one from the Discourse to the Saint Luke Union of Italian Doctors of November 12, 1944, because it formulates the principle in all its universality: "As long as a man is not guilty, his life is untouchable, and therefore any act directly tending to destroy it is illicit, whether such destruction is intended as an end in itself or only as a means to an end, whether it is a question of life in the embryonic stage or in a stage of full development or already in its final stages" (Discourses and Radio-messages, VI, 183 ff.).

16. Encyclical *Mater et Magistra* (*AAS* 53, 1961), 447.

17. *Gaudium et Spes* 51. Cf. 27 (*AAS* 58, 1966): 1072; cf. 1047.

18. The Speech: *Salutiamo con paterna effusione,* 9 December 1972, *AAS* 64, 777. Among the witnesses of this unchangeable doctrine one will recall the declaration of the Holy Office, condemning direct abortion (Denzinger 1890, *AAS* 17 (1884): 556; 22 (1888–1890), 748; Dz–Sch 3258).

19. This declaration expressly leaves aside the question of the moment when the spiritual soul is infused. There is not a unanimous tradition on this point and authors are as yet in disagreement. For some it dates from the first instant, for others it could not at least precede nidation. It is not within the competence of science to decide between these views, because the existence of an immortal soul is not a question in its field. It is a philosophical problem from which our moral affirmation remains independent for two reasons: (1) supposing a belated animation, there is still nothing less than a *human* life, preparing for and calling for a soul in which the nature received from parents is completed; (2) on the other hand it suffices that this presence of the soul be probable (and one can never prove the contrary) in order that the taking of life involve accepting the risk of killing a man, not only waiting for, but already in possession of his soul.

20. Tertullian, cited in note 8.

21. Cardinal Villot, Secretary of State, wrote on 10 October 1973 to Cardinal Döpfner, regarding the protection of human life: "(Die Kirche) kann jedoch sur Behebung solcher Notsituationen weder empfängnisverhütende Mittel noch erst recht nicht die Abtreibung als sittlich erlaubt erkennen" (*L'Osservatore Romano,* German edition, 26 October 1973), 3.

22. Encyclical *Pacem in Terris* (*AAS* 55, 1963), 267. Constitution *Gaudium et Spes* 29. Speech of Paul VI, *Salutiamo* (*AAS* 64, 1972), 779.

23. *Gaudium et Spes* 48: "Indole autem sua naturali, ipsum institutum matrimonii amorque coniugalis ad procreationem et educationem prolis ordinantur, iisque veluti suo fastigio coronantur." Also paragraph 50: "Matrimonium et amor coniugalis indole sua ad prolem procreandam et educandam ordinantur."

24. *Gaudium et Spes* 50–51. Paul VI, Encyclical *Humanae Vitae* 10 (*AAS* 60, 1968): 487.

25. *Gaudium et Spes* 87. Paul VI, Encyclical *Populorum Progressio* 31: Address to the United Nations (*AAS* 57, 1965): 883. John XXIII, *Mater et Magistra* (*AAS* 53, 1961): 445–48. Responsible parenthood supposes the use of only morally licit methods of birth regulation. cf. *Humanae Vitae* 14 (ibid., 490).

26. Cardinal Villot, Secretary of State, wrote to the World Congress of Catholic Doctors held in Barcelona, 26 May 1974:

    Por lo que a la vida humana se refiere, esta non es ciertamente univoca; más bien se podria decir que es un haz de vidas. No se puede reducir, sin mutilarlas gravemente, las zonas de su ser, que, en su estrecha dependencia e interacción están ordenadas las unas a las otras: zona corporal, zona afectiva, zona mental, y ese transfondo del alma donde la vida divina, recibida por la gracia, puede desplegarse mediante los dones del Espiritu Santo." (*L'Osservatore Romano,* 29 May 1974)

[12]

Catholics for a Free Choice

Although the Roman Catholic Church has pronounced on the abortion issue officially through the Church hierarchy, not all Roman Catholics accept the Church's position. Catholics for a Free Choice represents a prominent organized response by Roman Catholics to the Church's official stance on abortion. Among members of its board of directors are the American Roman Catholic theologians Daniel Maguire, Giles Milhaven, and Rosemary Radford Ruether. Its official mission statement follows.

Catholics for a Free Choice shapes and advances sexual and reproductive ethics that are based on justice, reflect a commitment to women's well-being, and respect and affirm the moral capacity of women and men to make sound and responsible decisions about their lives.

Engaging in discourse, education and advocacy, CFFC works in the United States and internationally to infuse these values into public policy, community life, feminist analysis, and Catholic social thinking and teaching.

We believe in:

The Moral Agency of Women

Women are to be respected as moral agents. They can be trusted to make decisions that support the well being of their families, children and society and enhance their own integrity and health.

SOURCE: Catholics for a Free Choice, 1436 U Street, N.W., Washington, D.C. 20009-3997. Used by permission.

The Primacy of Informed Conscience

A Catholic who is convinced that her conscience is correct, in spite of a conflict with magisterial Church teaching, not only may, but must follow the dictates of conscience rather than the teaching of the magisterium.

The Right to Dissent

The teaching of the hierarchical magisterium on moral issues related to human reproduction, while serious, is not infallible. Catholics have the right to dissent from such non-infallible teachings without fear of reprisal from the institutional Church.

Religious Freedom

Faith groups in the United States hold a number of different beliefs on both the morality and legality of abortion. Catholics need to respect this diversity of legitimate views. We must not seek legislation that would limit the freedom of members of these faith groups to practice their religion.

Social Justice

Catholic principles of social justice speak to a preferential option for the poor. Poor women are entitled to public funding for abortion and family planning as well as for childbearing and child-rearing. Denial of such funding is discriminatory and unjust.

[13]

Abortion: A Question of Catholic Honesty

Daniel C. Maguire

"In the 'already but not yet' of Christian existence, members of the church choose different paths to move toward the realization of the kingdom in history. Distinct moral options coexist as legitimate expressions of Christian choice." This "prochoice" statement recently made by the Catholic bishops of the United States has nothing to do with abortion. Rather, it addresses the possibility of ending life on earth through nuclear war. On that cataclysmic issue, the bishops' pastoral letter on peace warns against giving "a simple answer to complex questions." It calls for "dialogue." Hand-wringingly sensitive to divergent views, the bishops give all sides a hearing, even the winnable nuclear war hypothesis—a position they themselves find abhorrent. At times they merely raise questions when, given their own views, they might well have roundly condemned.

Change the topic to abortion, and nothing is the same. On this issue, the bishops move from the theological mainstream to the radical religious right. Here they have only a single word to offer us: No! No abortion ever—yesterday, today or tomorrow. No conceivable tragic complexity could ever make abortion moral. Here the eschaton is reached: there is no "already but not yet"; there is only "already." "Distinct moral options" do not exist; only unqualified oppo-

Source: Copyright 1983 by the Christian Century Foundation. Reprinted by permission from the September 14–21, 1983 issue of *The Christian Century.*

sition to all abortions moves toward "the realization of the kingdom in history." There is no need for dialogue with those who hold other views or with women who have faced abortion decisions. Indeed, as Marquette University theologian Dennis Doherty wrote some years ago, there seems to be no need even for prayer, since no further illumination, divine or otherwise, is anticipated.

Here we have no first, second, third and fourth drafts, no quibbles over "curbing" or "halting." Here we have only "a simple answer to complex questions." The fact that most Catholics, Protestants and Jews disagree with this un-nuanced absolutism is irrelevant. The moral position of those who hold that not every abortion is murder is treated as worthless. Moreover, the bishops would outlaw all disagreement with their view if they could, whether by way of the Buckley-Hatfield amendment, the Helms-Hyde bill, or the Hatch amendment.

As a Catholic theologian, I find this situation abhorrent and unworthy of the richness of the Roman Catholic traditions that have nourished me. I indict not only the bishops, but also the "petulant silence" (Beverly Harrison's phrase) or indifference of many Catholic theologians who recognize the morality of certain abortions, but will not address the subject publicly. I indict also the male-dominated liberal Catholic press which does too little to dissipate the myth of a Catholic monolith on abortion. It is a theological fact of life that there is no *one* normative Catholic position on abortion. The truth is insufficiently known in the American polity because it is insufficiently acknowledged by American Catholic voices.

This misconception leads not only to injustice but to civil threat, since non-Catholic as well as Catholic citizens are affected by it. The erroneous belief that the Catholic quarter of the American citizenry unanimously opposes all abortions influences legislative and judicial decisions, including specific choices such as denying abortion funding for poor women. The general public is also affected in those communities where Catholic hospitals are the only health care facilities. The reproductive rights of people living in such communities are curtailed if (as is common) their hospital is administratively locked into the ul-traconservative view on abortion, and even on such reproductive issues as tubal ligation and contraception. Physicians practicing at such hospitals are compromised. Academic freedom is frequently inhibited at Catholic universities and colleges—public agencies that often are federal contractors—with consequent injustice to the students and to the taxpayers. (In the face of all of this, non-Catholic citizens have been surprisingly and—I dare aver—uncourageously polite.)

Ten years ago, Catholic theologian Charles E. Curran stated in the *Jurist* (32:183 [1973]) that "there is a sizable and growing number of Catholic theologians who do disagree with some aspects of the officially proposed Catholic teaching that direct abortion from the time of conception is always wrong."

That "sizable number" has been growing since then despite the inhibiting atmosphere. It is safe to say that only a minority of Catholic theologians would argue that all abortions are immoral, though many will not touch the subject for fear of losing their academic positions. (As one woman professor at a large eastern Catholic university said, "I could announce that I had become a communist without causing a stir, but if I defended *Roe v. Wade* [the 1973 Supreme Court decision legalizing abortion in the United States], I would not get tenure.")

To many, the expression "Catholic pluralism" sounds like a contradiction in terms. The Catholic system, however, does have a method for ensuring a liberal pluralism in moral matters: a system called "probabilism." While it is virtually unknown to most Catholics, probabilism became standard equipment in Catholic moral theology during the 17th century. It applies to situations where a rigorous consensus breaks down and people begin to ask when they may in good conscience act on the liberal dissenting view—precisely the situation with regard to abortion today.

Probabilism was based on the insight that a doubtful moral obligation may not be imposed as though it were certain. "Where there is doubt, there is freedom" (*Ubi dubium, ibi libertas*) was its cardinal principle. It gave Catholics the right to dissent from hierarchical church teaching on a moral matter, if they could achieve "solid probability," a technical term. Solid probability could come about in two ways: *intrinsically*, in a do-it-yourself fashion, when a person prayerfully discovered in his or her conscience "cogent," nonfrivolous reasons for dissenting from the hierarchically supported view; or *extrinsically*, when "five or six" theologians of stature held the liberal dissenting view, even though all other Catholic theologians, including the pope, disagreed. Church discipline required priest confessors who knew that a probable opinion existed to so advise persons in confession even if they themselves disagreed with it.

In a very traditional book, *Moral and Pastoral Theology*, written 50 years ago for the training of seminarians, Henry Davis, S.J., touched on the wisdom of probabilism by admitting that since "we cannot always get metaphysical certainty" in moral matters, we must settle for consenting "freely and reasonably, to sufficiently cogent reasons."

Three things are noteworthy about probabilism: (1) a probable opinion which allows dissent from the hierarchically maintained rigorous view is entirely based on *insight*—one's own or that of at least five or six experts. It is not based on permissions, and it cannot be forbidden. (2) No moral debate—and that includes the abortion debate—is beyond the scope of a probabilistic solution. To quote Father Davis again: "It is the merit of Probabilism that there are no exceptions whatever to its application: once given a really probable reason for the lawfulness of an action in a particular case, though contrary reasons may be stronger, there are no occasions on which I may not act in accordance with the good probable reason that I have found." (3) Probabilism is theologically deep, going back to John and Paul's scriptural teaching that Spirit-filled persons are "taught of God," and to Thomas Aquinas's doctrine that the primary law for the believer is the grace of the Holy Spirit poured into the heart, while all written law—including even Scripture, as well as the teachings of the popes and councils—is secondary. Probabilism allows one to dissent from the secondary through appeal to the primary teaching of the Spirit of God. It is dangerous, of course, but it is also biblical and thoroughly Catholic.

There are far more than five or six Catholic theologians today who approve abortions under a range of circumstances, and there are many spiritual and good people who find "cogent," nonfrivolous reasons to disagree with the hierarchy's absolutism on this issue. This makes their disagreement a "solidly probable" and thoroughly respectable Catholic viewpoint. Abortion is always tragic, but the tragedy of abortion is not always immoral.

Teilhard de Chardin, S.J., pointed out that nothing is intelligible outside of its history. I would add that no conclusion is intelligible unless one knows the history and method of thought that produced it, since moral opinions do not pop out of a void. Whence the moral taboo on all abortions?

The Bible does not forbid abortion. Rather, the prohibition came from theological and biological views that were seriously deficient in a number of ways and that have been largely abandoned. There are at least nine reasons why the old taboo has lost its footing in today's Catholic moral theology. In a 1970 article "A Protestant Ethical Approach," in *The Morality of Abortion* (with which few Catholic theologians would quarrel), Protestant theologian James Gustafson pointed out five of the foundational defects in the traditional Catholic arguments against all abortions: (1) These arguments relied on "an external judge" who would paternalistically "claim the right to judge the past actions of others as morally right or wrong," with insufficient concern for the experience of and impact on mothers, physicians, families and society. (2) The old arguments were heavily "juridical," and, as such, marked by "a low tolerance for moral ambiguity." (3) The traditional arguments were excessively "physical" in focus, with insufficient attention to "other aspects of human life." (I would add that the tradition did not have the advantage of modern efforts to define personhood more relationally. The definition of person is obviously central to the abortion question.) (4) The arguments were "rationalistic," with necessary nuances "squeezed out" by "timeless abstractions" which took the traditional Catholic reasoning "far from life." (5) The arguments were naturalistic and did not put "the great themes of the Christian faith at a more central place in the discussion." It would be possible to parallel Gustafson's fair and careful criticisms with exhortations from the Second Vatican Council, which urged correctives in precisely these areas.

Other criticisms can be added to Gustafson's list: (6) The theology that produced the traditional ban on all abortions was not ecumenically sensitive. The witness of Protestant Christians was, to say the least, underesteemed. Vatican II condemned such an approach and insisted that Protestants are "joined with us in the Holy Spirit, for to them also He gives His gifts and graces, and is thereby operative among them with His sanctifying power." The bishops and others who condemn all abortion *tout court* should show some honest readiness to listen in the halls of conscience to Protestant views on abortion before they try to outlaw them in the halls of Congress.

(7) Furthermore, the old theology of abortion proceeded from a primitive knowledge of biology. The ovum was not discovered until the 19th century. Because modern embryology was unknown to the tradition, the traditional arguments were spawned in ignorance of such things as twinning and recombination in primitive fetal tissue and of the development of the cortex.

On the other hand, the teachings about abortion contained some remarkable scientific premonitions, including the insight that the early fetus could not have personal status. Said St. Augustine: "The law does not provide that the act [abortion] pertains to homicide. For there cannot yet be said to be a live soul in a body that lacks sensation when it is not formed in flesh and so is not endowed with sense." As Joseph Donceel, S.J., notes, up until the end of the 18th century "the law of the Roman Catholic Church forbade one to baptize an aborted fetus that showed no human shape or outline." If it were a personal human being, it would deserve baptism. On the question of a rational soul entering the fetus, Donceel notes that Thomas Aquinas "spoke of six weeks for the male embryo and three months for the female embryo." In Aquinas's hylomorphic theory, the *matter* had to be ready to receive the appropriate *form*. According to such principles, as Rosemary Ruether points out, "Thomas Aquinas might well have had to place the point of human ensoulment in the last trimester if he had been acquainted with modern embryology."

If the bishops and other negative absolutists would speak of tradition, let them speak of it in its full ambiguity and subtlety, instead of acting as though the tradition were a simplistic, Platonic negative floating through time untouched by contradiction, nuance or complexity.

(8) Vatican II urged priests and church officers to have "continuous dialogue with the laity." The arguments prohibiting all abortion did not grow out of such dialogue, nor are the bishops in dialogue today. If they were, they would find that few are dancing to the episcopal piping. A November 1982 Yankelovich poll of Catholic women shows that fewer than one-fifth would call abortion morally wrong if a woman has been raped, if her health is at risk, or if she is carrying a genetically damaged fetus. Only 27 per cent judge abortion as wrong when a physically handicapped woman becomes pregnant. A majority

of Catholic women would allow a teen-ager, a welfare mother who can't work, or a married woman who already has a large family to have an abortion.

Since the tradition has been shaped by the inseminators of the species (all Catholic theologians, priests and bishops have been men), is the implication that there is no value in the witness of the bearers? Why has all authority on this issue been assumed by men, who have not been assigned by biology to bear children or by history to rear them? Are the Catholic women who disagree with the bishops all weak-minded or evil? Is it possible that not a single Catholic bishop can see any ambiguity in any abortion decision? The bishops are not unsubtle or unintelligent, and their pastoral letter on peace shows a surefooted approach to complexity. Their apparent 100 per cent unanimity against all abortion is neither admirable nor even plausible. It seems, rather, imposed.

(9) This leads to the question of sin and sexism. Beverly Harrison (professor of Christian ethics at Union Theological Seminary in New York) charges that "much discussion of abortion betrays the heavy hand of the hatred of women." Are the negative absolutists sinlessly immune to that criticism? Since the so-called "prolife" movement is not dominated by vegetarian pacifists who find even nonpersonal life sacred, is the "prolife" fetal fixation innocent? Does it not make the fertilized egg the legal and moral peer of a woman? Indeed, in the moral calculus of those who oppose all abortion, does not the *potential* person outweigh the *actual* person of the woman? Why is the intense concern over the 1.5 million abortions not matched by an equal concern over the male-related causes of those 1.5 million unwanted pregnancies? Has the abortion ban been miraculously immune to the sexism rife in Christian history?

Feminist scholars have documented the long record of men's efforts to control the sexuality and reproductivity of women. Laws showcase our biases. Is there no sexist bias in the new Catholic Code of Canon Law? Is the code *for* life or *against* women's control of their reproductivity? After all, canon law excommunicates a person for aborting a fertilized egg, but not for killing a baby after birth. One senses here an agenda other than the simple concern for life. What obsessions are operating? A person could push the nuclear button and blow the ozone lid off the earth or assassinate the president (but not the pope) without being excommunicated. But aborting a five-week-old precerebrate, prepersonal fetus would excommunicate him or her. May we uncritically allow such an embarrassing position to posture as "prolife"? Does it not assume that women cannot be trusted to make honorable decisions, and that only male-made laws and male-controlled funding can make women responsible and moral about their reproductivity?

The moral dilemma of choosing whether to have an abortion faces only some women between their teens and their 40s. The self-styled "prolife" movement is made up mainly of men and postfertile women. Is there nothing suspicious about passionately locating one's orthodoxy in an area where one will never be personally challenged or inconvenienced?

Prohibition was wrong because it attempted to impose a private moral position on a pluralistic society. The prohibition of abortion is wrong for the same reason. Society must allow for the debate of valid issues, and then for freedom of choice, not coercion. Some moral positions are not within the pale of respectability, and we properly use coercion to prohibit them. Refusing to educate children, denying sick children blood transfusions, keeping snakes in a church for faith-testing are not respectable options, and we forbid them. But most abortions are not in that category. Abortion is an issue deserving respectable debate.

A moral opinion merits respectable debate if it is supported by serious reasons which commend themselves to many people and if it has been endorsed by a number of reputable religious or other humanitarian bodies. Note the two requirements: *good reasons* and *reliable authorities*. The principle of respectable debate is based on some confidence in the capacity of free minds to come to the truth, and on a distrust of authoritarian short-cuts to consensus and uniformity. This principle is integral to American political thought and to the Catholic doctrine of probabilism. On the other hand, prohibition represents a despairing effort to compel those whom one cannot convince; it can only raise new and unnecessary doubts about Catholic compatibility with democratic political life.

But what of legislators who personally believe that all abortion is wrong? Those legislators must recognize that it is not their function to impose their own private moral beliefs on a pluralistic society. St. Augustine and St. Thomas Aquinas both found prostitution morally repugnant, but felt that it should be legalized for the greater good of the society. St. Thomas wryly but wisely suggested that a good legislator should imitate God, who could eliminate certain evils but does not do so for the sake of the greater good. The greater good supported by the principle of respectable debate is the good of a free society where conscience is not unduly constrained on complex matters where good persons disagree. Thus a Catholic legislator who judges all abortions to be immoral may in good conscience support the decisions of *Roe v. Wade,* since that ruling is permissive rather than coercive. It forces no one to have an abortion, while it respects the moral freedom of those who judge some abortions to be moral.

Good government insists that essential freedoms be denied to no one. Essential freedoms concern basic goods such as the right to marry, the right to a trial by jury, the right to vote, the right to some education and the right to bear *or not to bear* children. The right not to bear children includes abortion as a means of last resort. Concerning such goods, government should not act to limit freedom along income lines, and should ensure that poverty takes no essential freedoms from any citizen. Furthermore, the denial of abortion funding to poor women is not a neutral stance, but a natalist one. The government takes sides on the abortion debate by continuing to pay for births while denying poor women funds for the abortion alternative that is available to the rich. Funding cutbacks are also forcing many to have later abortions, since they have to spend some months scraping up the funds denied them by the government. The denial of funding is an elitist denial of moral freedom to the poor and a stimulus for later or unsafe abortions.

Abortion has become the Catholic orthodoxy's stakeout. In January 1983, California Bishop Joseph Madera threatened excommunication for "lawmakers who support the effective ejection from the womb of an unviable fetus." (His warning also extended to "owners and managers of drugstores" where abortion-related materials are sold.) In a bypass of due process, Sister Agnes Mary Mansour was pressured out of her identity as a Sister of Mercy because her work for the poor of Michigan involved some funding for abortions. Despite his distinguished record in working for justice and peace, Robert Drinan, S.J., was ordered out of politics by the most politically involved pope of recent memory. I am not alone in seeing a link between this and the antecedent right-wing furor over Father Drinan's position on abortion funding. The 4,000 Sisters of Mercy (who operate the second-largest hospital system in the U.S., after the Veterans Administration) were ordered, under threat of ecclesiastical penalties, to abandon their plan to permit tubal ligations in their hospitals. A Washington, D.C., group called Catholics for Free Choice had its paid advertisements turned down by *Commonweal,* the *National Catholic Reporter* and *America.* This group is not promoting abortions, but simply honestly acknowledging Catholic pluralism on the issue. (Interestingly, the only "secular" magazine to refuse their advertisement was the *National Review.*) In June 1983, Lynn Hilliard, a part-time nurse in a Winnipeg, Manitoba, clinic where abortions are performed, had her planned marriage in a Catholic parish peremptorily canceled by Archbishop Adam Exner two weeks before the event, even though the archbishop admitted he did not know whether Ms. Hilliard was formally responsible for any abortions. In the face of all this injustice, Catholic theologians remain remarkably silent; they exhibit no signs of anger. Seven hundred years ago, Thomas Aquinas lamented that we had no name for the virtue of anger in our religious lexicon. He quoted the words of St. John Chrysostom, words that are still pertinent today: "Whoever is without anger, when there is cause for anger, sins."

[14]

Abortion Issue Far from Black-and-White

Archbishop Rembert Weakland

THE ABORTION ISSUE IS one of the most divisive in our society and also in our church. It is an issue that touches our faith because it forces us to articulate how we view God's relationship to human life. It is, moreover, so sensitive that people are hesitant to speak frankly about how they feel on the issue, especially if they sense that the other person may not be on the same side of the argument.

Rational discourse seems to have vanished in favor of slogans. It is not easy in the public forum to have a calm discussion about the moral principles involved.

The church's official position has been clear for decades now: Abortion is seen as the taking of human life and, thus, morally wrong. It could also be said that the church would like to see its moral position become the legal position in the nation as well. Listening is also an important part of any teaching process: The church's need to listen is no exception.

But this unequivocal position does not have the full support of many Catholics, especially of many women, because it seems to be too simplistic an answer to a complicated and emotional question and does not resolve all the concomitant problems surrounding the issue raised in a pluralistic society, es-

SOURCE: Excerpted from Milwaukee Archbishop Rembert Weakland's response to six listening sessions on abortion he held with the women of his archdiocese. From the *National Catholic Reporter* 26 (June 1, 1990). Reprinted with permission of the *Milwaukee Catholic Herald.*

pecially where there is no political and societal consensus on the issue, neither in its moral dimension nor in its legal embodiment.

Moreover, this issue is often indicative of how women view their own identity and see their role in society, so that it has become the symbol for many other issues that touch feminism today.

For these reasons I felt that I had to do more listening to the voices of faithful women in the archdiocese. I have faith and trust in their wisdom and honesty. I knew I had much to learn from them that I had not heard yet. Listening seemed absolutely necessary to me. From the sessions, I gained a clearer idea of why some women do not accept in its totality the church's official teaching. . . .

I did not hear one Catholic woman defend abortion as a good in itself; they all considered it a tragedy in our society, a procedure that no one should have to resort to. Perhaps there were no representatives in favor of abortion-on-demand without grave cause present, or perhaps they decided not to speak; but I feel my observation is correct when I say that there were so many women troubled by this issue and seeking some kind of shared common ground through a more profound and more sensitive dialogue than we have had up to now. Through such dialogue it was hoped that one could slowly begin to arrive at some here-and-now practical wisdom. . . .

Some felt that these sessions, because I listened to those who did not accept fully the church's official position, may have given the impression that the church was weak in its teaching. They expected me to take the opportunity of these listening sessions to come down hard and forcefully on those who disagree with the explicitness of the church's teaching on this issue. That would have negated the whole purpose of listening. I would have learned nothing. I always feel that those who are afraid to hear points of view that differ from their own are not really very secure in their positions.

One point was clear and emphasized by all: The church must maintain more consistency between its teaching and its actions. It must do more to help and encourage women facing most difficult life decisions, especially those carrying to term unplanned pregnancies.

It has to take seriously the consistent life ethic if it is to be credible in its teaching on abortion. I heard . . . how many women applauded the U.S. bishops' emphasis on this consistent ethic of life as a means of showing that all life is sacred and that, thus, the taking of even one life is a serious moral decision, whether it be through abortion, war, or capital punishment. They supported the teaching that each Christian has a responsibility, personally and socially, of protecting and preserving the sanctity of all life from womb to natural death, and of fighting to eliminate in society all those structures and situations that deprive others of their rightful dignity and development.

At times I heard the pro-life movement criticized in this regard: It was felt that life was not consistently held in the same esteem after birth by some in that group. Others pointed out that the church excommunicates those involved in abortion but not in other attacks on human life. Women asked if the church was being consistent in admitting some circumstances that justify the taking of human life in other contexts (the just war theory, unjust aggressors, etc.) but not in this instance. They called for further study of traditional teaching on such items as the principle of double effect and other moral teachings that could be helpful in forming the consciences of all the faithful—without retreating from the position of respect for human life as such. . . .

Some members of the pro-life movement asked me why so many priests hesitate to preach publicly on the church's official teaching and do not support their political activity in favor of changing the present laws on abortion. It is true: I, too, know so many wonderful pastoral priests who do not want to be identified with the pro-life movement, even though they are solidly against abortion on demand. I have talked many times to our priests in private about this question.

Although what I say may seem harsh, it is important that we all listen to such criticism. Many dislike the narrowness of so many in the pro-life movement, their tactics, their nonacceptance of the consistent life ethic approach, their lack of compassion, their alliances with groups that often are very anti-Catholic in other areas, their lack of civility, and so on.

In other words, such a perception of the pro-life movement does not lend itself to attracting not just priests but so many others who are searching for what is best for our society. Many priests, moreover, feel uncomfortable with some of the political and other aggressive activities of the pro-life movement. Some of the rhetoric and literature seem ugly and demeaning. Further discussion on these observations is truly needed so the root reasons for lack of support can be verified.

My ears are still ringing after hearing so many women say bluntly that they are angry about the church's stance on birth control. The listening sessions were not about that question, but it kept coming up over and over again. I did not sense that there was much support, even among those who were strong in their opposition to abortion, for the church's position about contraception. Even those advocating natural family planning as a solution seemed at times to approach the question with a contraceptive mentality, with little discussion of motives and intentions. . . .

I could not help but notice some strong cultural differences that seemed to accompany the position taken on abortion. Women who saw their identity as women in childbearing, in raising a family, in being a homemaker tended to be stronger in their convictions and stances on the pro-life spectrum. Those who saw childbearing as important but only one aspect of their full identity as women and who were concerned about developing other aspects of their gifts through involvement in world and society tended to be more open on the issue. I could not help but reflect on the fact that this latter group seemed to dominate on our college faculties and could represent the thinking of many of the younger women they come into contact with daily.

Likewise, I noticed cultural influences I had not thought about previously on the part of those who were more favorably disposed to a more open stance on the issue of abortion. From the literature, but less so among the participants at the listening sessions, I noticed that some seemed to fall into the Cartesian dualism between body and soul that looks upon the body as a machine or instrument to be controlled as one wills. The church has never accepted this point of view, namely, that one has control over one's body to do with it what one wants. The body is not a mannequin nor a machine. Cutting off any part of the body just to show that one has control over this "machine" is contrary to the whole approach our faith takes to the body as integral to the identity of the whole person. Control over the forces that affect one's life made more sense to me.

One heard also an occasional reference to "rights" over one's body, or "rights to an abortion." We all use expressions such as this. It is true that in common speech we have come to use that word "rights" for almost anything we wish, so that it has begun to lose its full meaning. In a discussion as serious as this one about abortion I see the need for us Catholics to be very precise in its use. I was never quite sure how the term was being used. . . .

I came away from the listening sessions making a few resolutions. I would never be so glib in talking about the "moment of conception" since from a medical point of view that is far from accurate: Conception is a long process, not a moment. I have learned much from letters and from the discussion among the health-care women that the first days and weeks of the growth of a fetus are, from a medical point of view, anything but simple. I know I must be more precise and correct in talking about those stages of development.

I also learned from listening to women to be more careful about the need to treat in a pastoral fashion infertility and miscarriages. Especially in the latter case, I sensed that for many women such grieving is needed and a sense of loss can be very real. Nor will I talk so glibly about bringing the baby to term and then "just give it up for adoption," since I learned that there can be so much grieving here, too, and a deep sense of loss that often needs to be faced. . . .

From the discussion I became aware of the implications of the terms pro-choice and pro-life. . . .

Some said they felt many in the pro-life movement were really just anti-abortion because of their lack of support for a total range of life issues. In each case this would have to be verified.

The term pro-choice was much more ambiguous and the term itself did not seem to cover the range of differences. Abortion on demand was one extreme. Some used it in a legal way, implying the right to the process of choice, even though they did not feel they personally could have an abortion; the choice, however, would be theirs and not the government's. . . .

In any case, I will continue to use the term pro-life for the church's position and try to distinguish the ranges of meaning within the pro-choice groups to do justice to the variety of points of view found there.

I was disappointed that the pro-life women who were politically involved in trying to reverse present laws and legally to eliminate all abortions in the land were not more articulate for me about what the consequences of such a total prohibition would be in our society. Would the wealthy, because they could afford to do so, then go to other countries where abortions would be permitted? Would there be again the back alley, illegal practitioners? These are urgent questions, especially if there is no clear consensus of the population on this issue.

I was surprised and disturbed by the strong influence of fundamentalist positions on some of the pro-life women who have been politically involved in this issue. I say disturbed because they did not seem to know the Catholic approach to scripture and fell into proof-texting in ways that are not our tradition. I will have to talk much with the priests and other pastoral ministers in the diocese about this unwholesome influence and what it means. It might also account for some of the narrowness of vision on the part of some of the pro-life people one meets. . . .

I recognize that there is some legitimate frustration on the part of the pro-life advocates within the church because they feel a need for a broader support and find it lacking. They, too, will have to do some self-examination in a humble way of the causes of this nonsupport. In so many ways, I have come to see that the success of the pro-life movement will depend on its ability to change the perceptions so many have of it as one of a narrowness that takes a single-issue approach. . . .

I would like to call all Catholics to civil and respectful discourse on this potentially divisive issue. Such a type of reasoned debate is both in the true spirit of our democratic processes as well as of our tradition of faith built on reason. . . .

At the end of the listening sessions, I came to the conclusion that no ideal situation will evolve quickly in our culture so that this thorny societal and moral issue can be resolved. . . .

Indeed, the church must do more to teach about the dignity of all people and fight against all human degradation—racism, stereotyping, permissiveness, promiscuity, and violence and abuse toward women and children. . . .

Economic deprivation also has its negative effects on the dignity and worth of people and can be the hidden cause of so many evils, including abortion. The burdens that single women who are the heads of households must carry are enormous and often almost impossible. Support systems are indeed needed but also advocacy for alleviating their hardships. At the same time we support family structures and do everything to help married couples stay together and raise a family.

PROTESTANTISM

[15]

Protestant Attitudes toward Abortion

James B. Nelson

EARLY PROTESTANT ATTITUDES TOWARD abortion show considerable continuity with those of the pre–sixteenth-century church. The major
Reformers—Martin Luther (1483–1546), Philip Melanchthon (1497–1560),
and John Calvin (1509–1564)—were at least as conservative as their Roman
Catholic counterparts on the issues of ensoulment and the gravity of abortion.
Indeed, some historians believe that these Reformers indirectly but significantly contributed to the present papal position on the subject.[1]

The Reformers insisted upon the full humanity of the fetus from the time
of conception. Their insistence arose, however, less from attention to the abortion issue itself than from their concern about the doctrines of original sin and
predestination. Full humanity of the conceptus was believed necessary if the
mind and spirit as well as the body of nascent life were to be involved in the
consequences of the human fall.

Luther reclaimed the traducian position of the early Church Fathers in regard to ensoulment. This position held that the soul of the fetus along with
its body was inherited from its parents. Influenced by the embryology of Aristotle and Galen, however, Luther assumed that the semen alone contained life
and that the woman provided only nourishment for that life. Hence the father
(through the power of God) was the source of the fetal soul. Melanchthon's

SOURCE: From *Between Two Gardens: Reflections on Sexuality and Religious Experience* by James B. Nelson.
Copyright © 1983 by The Pilgrim Press. Reprinted by permission.

theory of ensoulment was creationist, the belief that God directly creates the soul of each nascent life. Both of these Reformers, however, insisted upon the full humanity of the conceptus regardless of its gestational stage.

With Melanchthon, Calvin was creationist concerning ensoulment. With Luther, Calvin was concerned about the depth of human need and the radical nature of God's grace in the face of original sin. His particularly strong doctrine of predestination gave additional force to the contention that the fetus from its earliest stage was already *homo,* fully a person, for this life was believed to be primordially destined to be saved or damned.

The major Reformers, then, were rigorously opposed to abortion at any stage of pregnancy. Moreover, they had significantly enhanced the fetal status for reasons more basically doctrinal than for ethical reasons against abortion. Regarding fetal status, they were more conservative than the sixteenth-century Roman Catholic Church, which still maintained the Septuagint's distinction between the "unformed" and the "formed" fetus, and with it a consequent distinction in the gravity of abortion, depending on its timing. The Reformation's strong affirmations of justification by grace and forgiveness of sin, however, were to provide many later Protestants with theological perspectives and religious resources for dealing with abortion as a situation of ambiguity, compromise, and value conflict.

In seventeenth-century England, both Anglicans and Puritans continued to oppose abortion, but made the distinction between the unformed and the formed fetus. At the same time, the English Puritans initiated changes in the traditional understanding of marriage. Companionship was now seen as marriage's primary end, to which the ends of procreation and the restraint of lust were believed subordinate. This companionate view gradually became the dominant Protestant interpretation, and with it came the groundwork for justifiable abortions in cases of mortal conflict between woman and fetus. Indeed, by the late eighteenth century, English physicians were commonly urging and performing abortions to save threatened women.

Eighteenth and Nineteenth Centuries

American Protestantism manifested at least three major developments relevant to the abortion issue during the eighteenth and nineteenth centuries. One was a loss of interest in the human status of the fetus. Puritan predestinationists pressed Calvin's position on salvation, but with different results. Convinced that the individual's eternal destiny was fixed well before conception and gestation, the Puritans saw little to be gained from speculation about fetal ontology. Protestants generally lost touch with the earlier traditions on abortion and were inclined to appeal directly to scripture, where the early Jewish view and most subsequent texts supported full humanity only at birth. The pietist and revivalist groups of this period were disinclined to reflect about fetal humanity, for they were principally concerned with adult conversion. While they continued the typical Protestant opposition to abortion, their emphasis was often more restricted and practical: abortion was wrong because it was used, frequently at least, as a cover-up for sexual sins.

A strongly pro-fertility norm emerged in large segments of nineteenth-century American Protestantism, further buttressing antiabortion sentiments. Women must bear children if they were to be fulfilled as women. Furthermore, as God's New Israel, America had a crucial destiny in the world's salvation, and population growth was desirable to that end. Abortion thus was not simply an individual sin but also a social evil that denied society its needed citizens, economic producers, and defenders.

A significant countervailing influence on the abortion issue also emerged in nineteenth-century American Protestantism, however: the rise of social idealism and the Social Gospel movement. Those trends were less concerned about abortion than about the more visibly disadvantaged. But their particular concern for women's dignity, expressed in the suffrage movement, laid important foundations for later theories of both justifiable abortion and abortion on request.

Twentieth-century Influences

During the first half of the twentieth century, while official American Protestant opposition to abortion largely continued, the attitudes of numerous Protestant individuals were gradually being altered by several factors.[2] Under the impact of secularization, certainties that once had undergirded theological opposition to abortion became less certain. If to earlier Protestants the presence of each fetus in the womb was an expression of God's mysterious providence, to later Protestants the fetal presence was explained by natural processes, including human mistakes as well as human planning.

Furthermore, the mid-century abortion reform movement drew upon themes of great importance to the Protestant tradition itself, particularly human self-determination and the obligation to exercise rational control over nature. While the latter-day view of self-determination may have been a highly individualistic and secularized version of the Reformation's image of Christian liberty, it is nevertheless inexplicable apart from that historical connection.

A third factor was the waning vision of a Protestant America. The failure of the Protestant-inspired prohibition law was a reminder that religious pluralism had replaced Protestant hegemony. America was no longer a society in which moral convictions that arose from particular Protestant theologies could be sanctioned by legislation. Thus, the distinction between a sin and a crime gained currency: what a particular religious group deemed sinful on its own doctrinal grounds ought not to be socially legislated as criminal without a much broader moral consensus on the issue. This distinction was further to erode Protestant support for antiabortion legislation.

Patterns in Contemporary Protestant Thought

In their theological reasoning, Protestants tend to take the church's tradition less seriously than they take the Bible. Those Protestants who look to scripture for specific moral instruction rather than for more general ethical principles, however, discover an absence of biblical texts specifically forbidding or permitting induced abortions. Indeed, the Old Testament does not typically view the fetus as fully human life. Exodus 21:22–25, for example, simply demands monetary compensation from the guilty party who causes a woman's miscarriage. Only if the woman herself dies does the charge become homicide, the offender being sentenced to death. Nevertheless, there are significant themes in both Old and New Testaments upon which Protestants typically draw for guidance in the abortion question. Life is a gift from God, and human reproduction is a process of sharing in God's creative powers (Psalm 139:13). Human beings are created not simply for comfort and pleasure but more basically for fulfillment, which often involves sacrifice for others (John 15:13). Life and death belong to God's providence, and there is no human right to extinguish life apart from persuasive evidence that such action expresses God's will in a tragic situation (Philippians 1:21–24). However general these biblical principles are, many Protestants insist that even they must be understood within the framework provided by the central ethical norm of scripture: the love commandment, which includes the dimensions of justice and mercy.

The major historical positions and influences mentioned earlier are present in the contemporary configurations of Protestant opinion on abortion. The perspectives range along a continuum from antiabortion to abortion on request, with perhaps the larger number of ethicists and Protestant groups affirming the justifiable-but-tragic abortion in certain situations of value conflict.

The antiabortion position is voiced by Dietrich Bonhoeffer, Paul Ramsey, Helmut Thielicke, and, with qualification, Karl Barth. Regarding the ensoulment issue, these ethicists maintain that it is not necessary to describe the fetus as a person. Rather, it is crucial that the fetus be recognized as a human individual; it is en route to becoming personal, but at all times it possesses the full sanctity of human life. Thus, two arguments are interwoven. First, biological data, especially at the stage of segmentation, establish human individuality. Second, Christian faith insists that the dignity of human life is not founded upon the individual's utility but rather is an alien dignity conferred by God and not admitting relative degrees of worth. While additional antiabortion arguments are typically added to the two above, the central issue is held to be the inviolable right to life of the fetus as a human individual, and not the weighing of competing values. Antiabortion Protestants, however, usually incorporate some version of the traditional Roman Catholic "principle of double effect" to argue that in certain extreme situations abortion is permitted because it is not the direct and willful taking of innocent life but rather the indirect result of saving life.

Abortion on request is more recent in the literature of Protestant ethics, although it has its articulate defenders. Proponents of this position argue that only wanted babies should be born. They typically maintain that permissive legal systems better protect women's lives and health, minimize social discrimination, and protect the autonomy of the medical profession. Here the principal concern is the woman's right to control over her own body and its reproductive processes, against those double standards that would permit others (usually males) to make choices on her behalf. As Joseph Fletcher observed some years ago, "Maybe an unexpressed and powerful objection is that responsible abortion, especially upon request, may give women the final control over reproduction."[3] The earlier Protestant emphases on self-determination, rational control of nature, equality, social justice, and the dignity of women enter strongly into this position. The real question, proponents argue, is not so much how we can justify abortion, but rather how we can justify compulsory childbearing.

The third general approach, sometimes called the justifiable abortion, lies somewhere between the first two, affirming arguments of each but differing from both. Rights of both fetus and woman are to be highly valued, but in theory and in practice neither ought to be absolutized. The elevation of one single right, it is argued, removes the inherent moral ambiguity of abortion decisions and oversimplifies other relevant moral factors. Instead of absolute rights, it is better to speak of competing rights and values. Together with the woman's right to self-determination and the value of human fetal life, a complex range of relational, social, medical, economic, and psychological values must be weighed, inasmuch as God cares for all these dimensions. Thus, each problem pregnancy has its own uniqueness, its own moral tragedy, and its possible alternatives. Christians must rely on God's grace and forgiveness as they make these ambiguous decisions.[4]

A Direction for the Future:
A Pro-choice Theology in Feminist Perspective

Protestant feminists have charted new directions for the ethics of abortion in recent times by uncovering the misogyny embedded in the mainstream religious discussion of the issue.[5] They have argued that the "pro-life" position is more accurately described as "pro-fetus," and that the "pro-choice" position is actually "pro-woman." The former position has its origin in the ecclesiastical and sexual struggle over the control of procreative power: will men control it, or will women? For centuries the men have won in that struggle. But the pro-woman position finds its grounding in significantly different values. It is not a pro-abortion posture. It recognizes the moral ambiguity of every abortion decision. It clearly acknowledges that those who affirm procreative choice as an important moral good do not maintain that resorting to abortion is ever a desirable way of expressing such choice. They insist that the desirability of abortion's availability not be confused with the desirability of the act as such.

Certain critical assumptions in pro-choice theology differ from those common to the Christian tradition on the issue.[6] According to pro-woman arguments, life does not begin at the moment of fertilization or viability, but, morally speaking, with the woman's life prior to the conception. Moreover, the fetus's life cannot be considered simply as a separate entity detached from the woman, but must be viewed as a new dimension of life in addition to an already fully alive person. Furthermore, the decision to terminate a pregnancy must be seen as one that can express deep reverence for life, not only for the woman herself but also for the quality of potential life.

Feminist Protestant ethics are now uncovering distortions in the male-shaped historical record of the abortion discussion. Males have romanticized biological procreation as the central metaphor for divine blessing. Even so, there is overall in Christian history a relative disinterest in the question of abortion; it has not been a major ethical preoccupation. Protestant clergy did not rally in support of the proposed nineteenth-century antiabortion laws in the United States. Until the latter part of the last century, both natural-law tradition and Protestant biblical interpretations strongly tended to define abortion as the interruption of pregnancy *after* ensoulment, that is after quickening or feeling of fetal movement; thus early termination of pregnancy was not perceived as abortion. Finally, prior to the development of safe medical abortion procedures, one of the principal objections to abortion was the concern for the woman's health—an argument that now is voiced by the pro-choice side.

The core of the feminist argument is this: The moral status of the fetus simply does not deserve greater standing than does that of the pregnant woman.

As Beverly Wildung Harrison says:

> The distinctly human power is not our biologic capacity to bear children, but our power actively to love, to nurture, to care for one another and to shape one another's existence in cultural and social interaction. To equate a biologic process with full normative humanity is crass biologic reductionism, and such reductionism is never practiced in religious ethics except when women's lives and well-being are involved.[7]

What, then, is a responsible Christian position, indeed an authentic pro-life position? Feminist Protestants maintain that such a position would genuinely enhance women's well-being and minimize the necessity for abortions. The necessity for abortions will be reduced only when the causes of problem pregnancy are directly addressed: contraceptive failure within marriage, the results of sexual violence, and the results of "coercive sexuality" (young males are typically taught that sexual prowess is the measure of their masculinity without responsibility for the consequences, and young females are taught that sexual appeal is the measure of their femininity, with total responsibility for the sexual consequences).[8]

Official Church Positions

A variety of public policy issues on abortion have concerned Protestant ethicists. Does a pro-choice public policy tend to cheapen or to enhance human dignity and the value of human life generally, and how can the evidence be assessed? Does a pro-choice public policy enhance racial equality or is it a disguised attack on racial minorities? What should be the relation of abortion policies to the population problem? What abortion policies best protect the freedoms of religion and conscience both of women with problem pregnancies and of medical personnel?

During the 1950s and 1960s several American Protestant denominations and ecumenical groups publicly affirmed positions on abortion. Since the 1973 U.S. Supreme Court rulings (*Roe v. Wade, Doe v. Bolton*), there have been additional Protestant policy statements. Most of these have acknowledged the moral ambiguity in abortion decisions. Most have recognized that the rights of both the fetus and the woman are important, and that neither should be absolutized. Most have acknowledged that the attempt to legislate a particular theological doctrine is a violation of religious liberty.

The statements have yet to go beyond the dilemma of the particular abortion decision itself. The churches need to adopt a *genuinely* pro-life position, in the broadest, most inclusive sense of that term. Such a position will enhance women's well-being and minimize the necessity of abortions. It will support more medical research into reliable contraception for males as well as for females. It will insist on more adequate control of the production and distribution of contraception materials (some of which have been dangerously misleading and hence tragically destructive). It will support education for male responsibility in contraception, in procreation, and in long-term child care and nurture. It will support more widespread and effective sexuality education. It will challenge the destructive masculinist myths that women exist primarily to meet the sexual needs of men and that they are really fulfilled only through their procreative capacities.

Some Protestant denominations have remained officially silent on the abortion issue, encouraging their members to exercise prayerful freedom of conscience in such decisions. On the one hand, this seems to be a very appropriate respect for religious liberty. On the other hand, it is a retreat—a regrettable retreat—from engagement with the roots of the problem. When the churches fully face up to the thinly disguised oppression of women in the current abortion debate, a more genuine respect-for-life ethos may emerge.

Notes

1. See, for example, George Huntston Williams, "Religious Residues and Presuppositions in the American Debate on Abortion," *Theological Studies* 31 (1970): 13, 41.

2. See Ralph B. Potter Jr., "The Abortion Debate," in *Updating Life and Death: Essays in Ethics and Medicine,* ed. Donald R. Cutler (Boston: Beacon Press, 1968), 88f; and Wilson Yates, *Family Planning on a Crowded Planet* (Minneapolis: Augsburg, 1971), 63–78.

3. Joseph F. Fletcher, "A Protestant Minister's View," *Abortion in a Changing World,* vol. 1, ed. Robert E. Hall (New York: Columbia University Press, 1970), 27.

4. James M. Gustafson, "A Protestant Ethical Approach," in *The Morality of Abortion: Legal and Historical Perspectives,* ed. John Thomas Noonan (Cambridge: Harvard University Press, 1970).

5. Beverly Wildung Harrison, "Theology of Pro-Choice: A Feminist Perspective," in *Abortion: The Moral Issues,* ed. Edward Batchelor Jr. (New York: Pilgrim Press, 1982); and Joy K. Bussert, "Woman or Fetus: A Call for Compassion," monograph published by the Minnesota Council of Churches, 1982. While there are a number of feminist theologians writing on the abortion issue at this time, I particularly want to acknowledge my debt to Professor Harrison for both personal conversation and printed word, and I want to

celebrate the significance of her new book on this issue, *Our Right to Choose* (Boston: Beacon Press, 1983).

6. Bussert, "Woman or Fetus," 3.

7. Harrison, "Theology of Pro-Choice," 220.

8. Bussert, "Woman or Fetus," 4.

[16]

The Protection of Life

Karl Barth

THE PROBLEM OF THE deliberate interruption of pregnancy, usually called abortion (*abortus,* the suppression of the fruit of the body), arises when conception has taken place but for varying reasons the birth and existence of the child are not desired and are perhaps even feared. The persons concerned are the mother, who either carries out the act, or desires or permits it; the more or less informed amateurs who assist her; perhaps the scientifically and technically trained physician; the father, relatives, or other third parties who allow, promote, assist, or favor the execution of the act and therefore share responsibility; and in a wider but no less strict sense the society whose conditions and mentality directly or indirectly call for such acts and whose laws may even permit them. The means employed vary from the most primitive to relatively sophisticated, but these need not concern us in the first instance. Our first contention must be that no pretext can alter the fact that the whole circle of those concerned is in the strict sense engaged in the killing of human life. For the unborn child is from the very first a child. It is still developing and has no independent life. But it is a person and not a thing, nor a mere part of the mother's body.

The embryo has its own autonomy, its own brain, its own nervous system, its own blood circulation. If its life is affected by that of the mother, it also affects hers. It can have its own illnesses in which the mother has no part. Con-

SOURCE: Reprinted from *Church Dogmatics,* part III, vol. 4, 415–22, by permission of the publisher, T. & T. Clark, Ltd., Edinburgh.

versely, it may be quite healthy even though the mother is seriously ill. It may die while the mother continues to live. It may also continue to live after its mother's death, and be eventually saved by a timely operation on her dead body. In short, it is a human being in its own right. I take this and other information from the book by Charlot Strasser, *Der Arzt und das keimende Leben*, 1948 (cf. also Alfred Labhardt, *Die Abtreibungsfrage*, 1926).

Before proceeding, we must underline the fact that one who destroys germinating life kills a person and thus ventures the monstrous thing of decreeing concerning the life and death of a fellow human being, whose life is given by God and therefore, like his or her own, belongs to God. This person desires to discharge a divine office or, even if not, accepts responsibility for such discharge by daring to have the last word on at least the temporal form of the life of a fellow human. Those directly or indirectly involved cannot escape this responsibility.

At this point we have first and supremely to hear the great summons to halt issued by the command. Can we accept this responsibility? May this thing be? Must it be? Whatever arguments may be brought against the birth and existence of the child, is it the child's fault that he or she is here? What has the child done to its mother or to any of the others that they wish to deprive it of its germinating life and punish it with death? Does not the child's utter defenselessness and helplessness, or the question whom they are destroying, to whom they are denying a future even before he or she has breathed and seen the light of the world, wrest the weapon from the hand of the mother first, and then from all the others, thwarting their will to use it? Moreover, this child is a person for whose life the Son of God has died, for whose unavoidable part in the guilt of all humanity and future individual guilt he has already paid the price. The true light of the world shines already in the darkness of the mother's womb. And yet they want to kill the child deliberately because certain reasons that have nothing to do with the child itself favor the view that it had better not be born! Is there any emergency that can justify this? It must surely be clear to us that until the question is put in all its gravity a serious discussion of the position cannot even begin, let alone lead to serious results.

The mediaeval period, which in this case extended right up to the end of the eighteenth century, was therefore quite right in its presuppositions when it regarded and punished abortion as murder. It is indeed an action that in innumerable cases obviously has the character of murder, of an irresponsible killing which is both callous and wicked, and in which one or more or perhaps all the participants play more or less consciously an objectively horrible game. If only the rigor with which the past judged and acted in this matter, as in child murder strictly speaking, had been itself more just and not directed against the relatively least guilty instead of the relatively most guilty! If only its draconian attitude had at least made an impression on the consciousness of the people and formed even in later recollection an effective dyke against this crime! But it obviously failed to do this. For no sooner had this attitude decayed externally than its inner strength also collapsed, and transgression swept in full flood over the land.

In the circumstances there is something almost horribly respectable in the attitude of the Roman Church. Never sparing in its extreme demands on women, it has to this day remained inveterate and never changed its course an inch in this matter. In the encyclical *Casti connubii* of 1930,[1] deliberate abortion is absolutely forbidden on any grounds, so that even Roman Catholic nuns raped when the Russians invaded Germany in 1945 were not allowed to free themselves from the consequences in this way.

This attitude of the Roman Church is undoubtedly impressive in contrast to the terrible deterioration, to what one might almost call the secret and open mass murder, which is the modern vogue and custom in this respect among so-called civilized peoples. This can be partly explained by the social and psychological conditions in which modern man finds himself, and by the estrangement from the Church and palpable paganism of the modern masses, the age of the *corpus Christianum* being now, as it seems, quite definitely a thing of the past. But there is more to it than this. It concerns both the rich and the poor, both those who suffer and are physically in danger and innumerable others who are in full or at least adequate possession of their spiritual balance. Nor is it restricted to the so-called world; it continues to penetrate deeply into the Christian community. It is a simple fact that the automatic restraint of the recognition that every deliberate interruption of pregnancy, whatever the circumstances, is a taking of human life, seems to have been strangely set aside in the widest circles in spite of our increasing biological appreciation of the facts. Even worse, the possibility of deliberate killing is sometimes treated as if it were just a ready expedient and remedy in a moment of embarrassment, nothing more being at issue than an unfortunate operation like so many others. In short, it can be and is done. Even official statistics tell us in a striking way how it can be and is done; and we may well suspect that these figures fall far short of the reality. It remains to be seen how legal regulation will finally work out where it is introduced, but the first result always seems to be a violent campaign for the widest possible interpretation.

Who is to say where the error and wickedness operative in this matter have their ultimate origin? Are they to be traced to the morality or immorality of the women and girls who are obviously for some reason troubled or distressed at their condition? Do they lie in the brutality or thoughtlessness of the men concerned? Are they to be sought in the offer of the sinister gentleman who makes use of both? Are we to look to the involved lack of conscientiousness in some medical circles? Do they originate in a general increase of self-pity in face of the injustices of life, which were surely just as great in the past as they are today? Or do they arise from a general decline in the individual and collective sense of responsibility?

We certainly cannot close our eyes to these happenings. Nor can we possibly concur in this development. Nevertheless, there can be no doubt that the abstract prohibition which was pronounced in the past, and which is still the only contribution of Roman Catholicism in this matter, is far too forbidding and sterile to promise any effective help.

The fact that a definite No must be the presupposition of all further discussion cannot be contested, least of all today. The question arises how this No is to be established and stated if it is to be a truly effective No. In face of the wicked violation of the sanctity of human life that is always seriously at issue in abortion, and that is always present when it is carried out thoughtlessly and callously, the only thing that can help is the power of the wholly new and radical feeling of awe at the mystery of all human life as this is commanded by God as its creator and giver. Legal prohibitions and restrictions of a civil, moral, and supposedly spiritual kind are obviously inadequate to instill this awe. Nor does mere churchmanship, whether Romanist or Protestant, provide the atmosphere in which this awe can thrive. The command of God is based on grace. God summons people to the freedom in which they may live instead of having to live. At root, persons who think they must live cannot and will not respect life, whether their own or that of others, far less the life of an unborn child. If it is for them a case of "must" rather than "may," they lack perspective and understanding in relation to what life is. They are already burdened and afflicted with their own lives. They will only too readily explore and exploit all the supposed possibilities by which to shield themselves from life that is basically hostile. They will also fall into the mistake of thinking that the life of the unborn child is not really human life at all, and thus draw the inference that they have been given a free hand to maintain or destroy it. Mothers, fathers, advisers, doctors, lawgivers, judges, and others whom it may concern to desire, permit, execute, or approve this action, will act and think in true understanding of the meaning of human life, and therefore with serious reluctance to take such a step, only if they themselves realize that human life is not something enforced but permitted, i.e., that it is freedom and grace. In these circumstances they will not be at odds with life, whether their own or that of others. They will not always desire to be as comfortable as possible in relation to it. They will not simply take the line of least resistance in what they think and do concerning it. Those who live by mercy will always be disposed to practice mercy, especially to a human being who is so dependent on the mercy of others as the unborn child.

This brings us back to the point at which we cannot evade the question where was and is the witness of the Protestant Church in face of this rising flood of disaster. This Church knows and has the Word of the free mercy of

God which also ascribes and grants freedom to man. It could and can tell and show a humanity which is tormented by life because it thinks it must live it, that it may do so. It could and can give it this testimony of freedom, and thus appeal effectively for the protection of life, inscribing upon its heart and conscience a salutary and resolute No to all and therefore to this particular destruction of human life. Hence it neither could nor can range itself with the Roman Catholic Church and its hard preaching of the Law. It must proclaim its own message in this matter, namely, the gospel. In so doing, however, it must not underbid the severity of the Roman Catholic No. It must overbid its abstract and negative: "Thou shalt not," by the force of its positive: "Thou mayest," in which, of course, the corresponding: "Thou mayest not," is included, the No having the force not merely of the word of man but of the Word of God. The Protestant Church had and has this Word of God for man but against his depravity in so far as its task was and is to bear witness to it. For this reason it cannot have clean hands in face of the disastrous development. It need not enquire whether or not it has restrained this development, or may still do so. The truth is plain that it has not been faithful to its own commission in the past, but that its attitude has resembled far too closely that of the Roman Church, i.e., that it has been primarily a teacher of the Law. The truth is also plain that only now is it beginning to understand its commission, and that it has not yet grasped it with a firm hand. It is still almost with joy that we hear perspicacious doctors, perhaps of very different beliefs (cf. Lk. 16:8), express a view which the Protestant Church, if it had listened and borne witness to the Word of God, ought to have stated and championed long since, namely, the kindly and understanding No which will prevail as such.

At this point it may be interjected that when this No is established as a divine No, namely, when it is in virtue of the liberating grace of God that deliberate abortion is irrefutably seen to be sin, murder, and transgression, it cannot possibly be maintained that there is no forgiveness for this sin. However dangerous it might sound in relation to all that has been said thus far, it must also be said that in faith, and in a vicariously intercessory faith for others too, there is a forgiveness that can be appropriated even for this sin, even for the great modern sin of abortion. God the Creator, who by grace acquits and liberates humans that they may live and let live in the most serious sense, who in and by this liberation claims humans incontestably as the great protectors of life, who inexorably reveals the true character of human transgression as sin—this God is our Parent in Jesus Christ, in whom God has not rejected sinful persons but chosen them and reconciled them, in whom God has intervened for sinful persons who have violated God's command, in order that the latter may not be lost to them even in and by reason of this terrible transgression. God sees and understands and loves even modern humans in and in spite of all the dreadful confusions and entanglements of their collective and individual existence, including this one. Those who see themselves placed by the gospel in the light of the relevant command, and are thus forced to admit that they, too, are in some degree entangled in this particular transgression, and are willing, therefore, to accept solidarity with more blatant transgressors, cannot and will not let go the fact, nor withhold it from others, that the same gospel that reveals this with such dreadful clarity is the gospel that, proclaiming the kingdom of God to all, summons all to repentance and promises and offers forgiveness to all. Nor does it weaken the command and its unconditional requirement that the one free grace, which in its one dimension unmasks sin as such, implies in the other that God has loved this sinful world in such a way that God has given the Son, and in him God, on its behalf, that it should not perish. Without this second dimension we cannot really understand the first. Indeed, only those who really grasp the promise of divine forgiveness will necessarily realize that sin as such is inexorably opposed by the divine No, and will never be able to keep this either from themselves or others.

If the No is securely grounded as seen from this angle, it inevitably raises here, too, the problem of the exception. Human life, and therefore the life of the unborn child, is not an absolute, so that, while it can be protected by the commandment, it can be so only within the limits of God, who issues it. It cannot claim to be preserved in all circumstances, whether in relation to God or to other persons, i.e., in this case to the mother, father, doctor, and others involved. In grace God can will to preserve the life that has been given, and in grace God can will to take it again. Either way, it is not lost. Humans cannot exercise the same sovereignty in relation to it. It does not really lie in their power even to preserve it. And only by an abuse of their power, by a sinister act of overweening arrogance, can they willfully take it. But they do have the power, and are thus commissioned, to do in the service of God and for the preservation of life that which is humanly possible if not finally decisive. Trained in the freedom that derives from the grace of God, they can choose and will only the one thing. In the case of the unborn, the mother, father, doctor (whose very vocation is to serve the preservation and development of life), and all concerned can desire only its life and healthy birth. How can they possibly will the opposite? They can do so only on the presupposition of their own blindness toward life, in bondage to the opinion that they must live rather than that they may live, and therefore out of anxiety, i.e., out of gracelessness and therefore godlessness.

However, they cannot set their wills absolutely on the preservation of this life, or rather on the service of its preservation. They all stand in the service of God, who orders them to serve its preservation and therefore the future birth of the child. There is an almost infinite number of objections to the possibility of willing anything else in obedience to God. But it is not quite infinite. If an individual knows that she or he is in God's service and wills to be obedient to God, can this person really swear that she or he will never on any occasion will anything else as God may require? What grounds have we for the absolute thesis that in no circumstances can God will anything but the preservation of a germinating life, or make any other demand from the mother, father, doctor, or others involved? If God can will that this germinating life should die in some other way, might God not occasionally do so in such a way as to involve the active participation of others? How can we deny absolutely that God might have commissioned them to serve in this way, and that their actions have thus been performed, and had to be performed, in this service? How, then, can we indict them in these circumstances?

This is the exceptional case that calls for discussion. In squarely facing it, we are not opening a side door to the crime that is so rampant in this sphere. We refer to God's possibility and specific command. We cannot try to exclude this. Otherwise the No that has to be pronounced in every other case is robbed of its force. For, as we have seen, it is truly effective only as the divine No. Hence no human No can or should be given the last word. The human No must let itself be limited. God can limit this human No, and, if this happens, it is simply human obstinacy and obduracy and transgression to be absolutely logical and to try to execute the No unconditionally. Let us be quite frank and say that there are situations in which the killing of germinating life does not constitute murder but is in fact commanded.

I hasten to lay down some decisive qualifications. For these will be situations in which all the arguments for preservation have been carefully considered and properly weighed, and yet abortion remains as *ultima ratio*. If all the possibilities of avoiding this have not been taken into account in this decision, then murder is done. Genuine exceptions will thus be rare. If they occur too often, and thus become a kind of second rule, we have good reason to suspect that collective and individual transgression and guilt are entailed. Again, they will be situations in which all those concerned must answer before God in great loneliness and secrecy, and make their decisions accordingly. If the decisions have any other source, if they are only the results of their subjective reflection and agreement, this fact alone is enough to show that we are not dealing with the genuine exception in which this action is permitted and commanded. With these qualifications, there are undoubtedly situations of this kind.

And we can and must add that, even if only in general terms and in the sense of a guiding line, these situations may always be known by the concrete fact that in them a choice must be made for the protection of life, one life being balanced against another, i.e., the life of the unborn child against the life or health of the mother, the sacrifice of either the one or the other being unavoidable. It is hard to see why in such cases the life of the child should always be given absolute preference, as maintained in Roman Catholic ethics. To be sure, we cannot and must not maintain, on the basis of the commandment, that the life and health of the mother must always be saved at the expense of the life of the child. There may well be mothers who for their part are ready to take any risk for their unborn children, and how can we forbid them to do so? On the basis of the command, however, we can learn that when a choice has to be made between the life or health of the mother and that of the child, the destruction of the child in the mother's womb might be permitted and commanded, and with the qualifications already mentioned a human decision might thus be taken to this effect. It goes without saying that the greatest possible care must be exercised in its practical execution. That is to say, it cannot be left to the mother herself or to quacks but is a matter for the experienced and trained physician. More detailed consideration would take us rather beyond the sphere of ethics. The question obviously arises in what particular circumstances and from what standpoint the life of the mother might be regarded as in peril and therefore this alternative indicated. To try to answer this question, however, is to expose oneself to the risk of making assertions that inevitably prove to be either too broad or too narrow from the standpoint of ethics, especially theological ethics. We must be content, therefore, simply to make our general point.

Physicians and lawyers speak in terms of the "indication" of abortion, a distinction being made between medical (whether somatic or psychiatric) on the one side and social on the other. The Swiss Penal Code regards it as nonindictable in an emergency, generally defined as a danger to life, body, freedom, honor or capacity, which cannot be averted in any other way.[2] In practice, however, it allows it only where there exists an immediate danger which cannot otherwise be warded off, or the risk of severe and permanent injury to the health of the pregnant woman. It also insists that it be undertaken by a certified doctor who is under obligation to report it to the responsible cantonal authorities.[3] It will be seen that this is in line with what we have just said. It must be remembered, however, that by no means every action allowed and exempted from punishment even on a strict, less alone a laxer, interpretation of these rules is for this reason permitted and enjoined ethically, i.e., by the command of God, as if those involved did not have to keep to a much narrower restriction of "indication" than that of the law. On the other hand, while Swiss legislation finds valid reason for abortion in an emergency affecting the life or body of the pregnant woman, the same does not hold good of an emergency affecting her freedom, honor or capacity. This means that, whereas medical "indication" is fully accepted, sound reasons are seen for not including social, and therefore for its implicit rejection. It does not follow, however, that a doctor is generally and radically guilty of transgressing the command of God, though he may expose himself to legal penalty, if he thinks he should urge a socio-medical "indication," i.e., in terms of a threat presented to the physical or mental life of the mother, or of economic or environmental conditions. For occasionally the command of God may impose a judgment and action which go beyond what is sanctioned by the law, and this may sometimes serve as a summons to all of us to consider that a sound social policy might well be a most powerful weapon in the struggle against criminal abortion. The legal rules are obviously useful, and even have an indirect ethical value as general directions to those involved, particularly doctors and judges. On the other hand, they are not adapted to serve as ethical criteria, since obedience to the command of God must have the freedom to move within limits which may sometimes be narrower and sometimes broader than even the best civil law. The exceptional case in the ethical sense is in general something very different from an extension of the permissible and valid possibilities established by human law.

The required calculation and venture in the decision between life and death obviously cannot be subject to any human law, because no such law can grasp the fullness of healthy or sick, happy or unhappy, preserved or neglected human life, let alone the freedom of the divine command the obedience which we owe to it. Hence we shall have to be content with the following observations: (1) For all concerned what must be at stake must be life against life, nothing other nor less, if the decision is not to be a wrong decision and the resultant action murder either of the child or the mother. (2) There is always required the most scrupulous calculation and yet also a resolute venture with a conscience that is bound and therefore free. Where such thought as is given is only careless or clouded, and the decision weak and hesitant, sin crouches at the door. (3) The calculation and venture must take place before God and in responsibility to God. Otherwise, how can there possibly be obedience, and how can the content be good and right, even though apparently good human reasons and justification might be found in one direction or another? (4) Since the calculation and venture, the conviction that we are dealing with the exception, are always so dangerous, they surely cannot be executed with the necessary assurance and joy except in faith that God will forgive the elements of human sin involved.

Notes

1. *E.S.* No. 2242f.
2. *Swiss Penal Code,* §34.
3. Ibid., §120.

[17]

The Book of Discipline of The United Methodist Church, 1992

ABORTION.—THE BEGINNING OF life and the ending of life are the God-given boundaries of human existence. While individuals have always had some degree of control over when they would die, they now have the awesome power to determine when and even whether new individuals will be born. Our belief in the sanctity of unborn human life makes us reluctant to approve abortion. But we are equally bound to respect the sacredness of the life and well-being of the mother, for whom devastating damage may result from an unacceptable pregnancy. In continuity with past Christian teaching, we recognize tragic conflicts of life with life that may justify abortion, and in such cases support the legal option of abortion under proper medical procedures. We cannot affirm abortion as an acceptable means of birth control, and we unconditionally reject it as a means of gender selection. We call all Christians to a searching and prayerful inquiry into the sorts of conditions that may warrant abortion. We call for the Church to provide nurturing ministries to those persons who terminate a pregnancy. We encourage the Church to provide nurturing ministries to those who give birth. Governmental laws and regulations do not provide all the guidance required by the informed Christian conscience. Therefore, a decision concerning abortion should be made only after thoughtful and prayerful consideration by the parties involved, with medical, pastoral, and other appropriate counsel.

SOURCE: From Section H of #71–72 of page 92, *The Book of Discipline of The United Methodist Church— 1992.* Copyright © 1992 by The United Methodist Publishing House. Reprinted by permission.

[18]

Human Beginnings: Deciding about Life in the Presence of God

Craigville VI Theological Colloquy

Witness to Our Sisters and Brothers in the United Church of Christ

Responding to the invitation extended to all members of the United Church of Christ and the Church at large to engage in theological dialogue on the topic "Human Beginnings: Deciding About Life in the Presence of God," we, the participants of Craigville Colloquy VI, August 13–18, 1989, now write this statement, intending it to be used by the churches for information, dialogue, and a call to action. The central focus of our discussion was the issue of abortion, studying and responding to the document *Ethics and the Search for Christian Unity: Two Statements by the Roman Catholic/Presbyterian-Reformed Consultation* (1980).

We recognize that the ultimate authority for our moral decisions must be God's will as it is revealed in Scripture, understood in the light of Jesus Christ, and interpreted through experience, reason, and tradition. Our beginnings are sanctified by the Holy Spirit whose presence was known at the conception of Jesus Christ. Although we vary widely in their interpretation and application, we affirm specific biblical motifs as central to our discussion. These include creation, covenant, stewardship, community, the fall, and grace.

SOURCE: From *Human Beginnings: Deciding about Life in the Presence of God* (1989). Reprinted by permission of the Craigville Conference Center.

With anguish and uncertainty we have struggled with the subject of human beginnings and abortion. We sought to engage each other in the spirit of love, although we did not always succeed. We acknowledge that we have radically different perspectives, but we affirm that as human beings our efforts alone are not enough for the crucial decisions of life. We constantly stand in need of grace, revealed in the suffering love of God in Jesus Christ. Despite our struggle, anguish, and uncertainty, we feel compelled to speak about abortion from the perspective of our Christian faith and our life together in the United Church of Christ.

Traditionally, abortion has been defined as the termination of pregnancy, but with modern reproductive technology, it has become increasingly difficult to define either pregnancy or abortion. For example, *in vitro* fertilization and frozen embryos have complicated the definition of pregnancy; and abortifacient birth control pills and devices confuse the definition of abortion. For the purpose of this witness statement the term abortion will be used in its traditional meaning.

Some areas of agreement include the following:

1. We affirm the sanctity of God's whole creation and of human life as uniquely made in the image and likeness of God.
2. The ultimate responsibility for moral decision making rests with the individual conscience guided by Scripture, reason, experience, tradition and grace.
3. We do not make moral decisions in isolation but rather within the web of our human relationships and our relationship with God.
4. As members of the Body of Christ, we are called to responsible sexual behavior.
5. Judicial and legislative standards are not always coterminous with moral demands, and therefore neither legislation nor prohibition of abortion itself absolve the Christian conscience of moral responsibility.
6. Religious groups have the moral right to use just means to influence public policy.

Some areas in which agreement was not reached include the following:

1. Abortion poses a moral dilemma. For some, this choice would never be considered a viable option; for others, it is a viable option. Abortion involves death, but for some this choice becomes a decision for life.
2. Similarly, while some say that there should be no civil laws in matters pertaining to abortion, others would encourage the government to keep abortion legal, and still others would urge the government to prohibit most or all abortions.

3. As we were unable to reach consensus about the moment and meaning of personhood, we could not agree upon the rights of the unborn or the rights of the unborn in situations where the rights of mother, father, grandparents, or others are in conflict.

After several days of deliberations we realize our conversations are just the beginning as it is not enough for one colloquy of concerned Christians to wrestle with this issue. It is imperative that the whole Church become involved in the struggle for justice and peace. We therefore call upon the Church at all levels

1. to become a community based on love and forgiveness,
2. to develop comprehensive Christian education programs enabling persons to make responsible decisions in the areas of sexuality, reproduction, and parenting,
3. to provide pastoral counseling to persons before, during, and after pregnancy,
4. to be present with women and families engaged in difficult choices and situations,
5. to continue and expand services to people in crisis,
6. to train lay persons to be effective care-givers in the community,
7. to work toward economic and social justice for all persons.

Our Christian hope is for a new heaven and a new earth, in which God's ultimate will reigns. Because we now live in a fallen world in which we are faced with difficult choices, our ability to discern what is good, right, and fitting is limited by our sinfulness and lack of right relationship with God. However, we acknowledge that shame and guilt are God-given and desirable emotions which can lead us to repentance and healing within the Body of Christ. We are grateful for the gift of God's grace and the knowledge that nothing can separate us from the love of God in Christ Jesus.

God's mercy and forgiveness allow us to hope for the future, and we live toward the day when the trauma of abortion will no longer exist. We strive for a society in which all people are able to reach their full potential without fear or discrimination. We dream of a day when each pregnancy will be a cause for celebration and each child will be loved, cherished, and cared for in the embrace of God's promised Shalom.

In Christ,
The Participants in the Craigville VI Theological Colloquy
August 18, 1989
(This Witness Statement was voted by Colloquy participants at the final plenary August 18th. The statement took form from reports of five individual

discussion groups meeting throughout the Colloquy. The papers of these groups were presented to plenary then to a witness drafting committee of seven, five chosen by lot, and two appointed by the Convening Committee. The draft statement was presented initially Thursday evening and then reviewed, amended, and editorially refined in a three hour plenary session before adoption with two negative votes and three abstentions.)

ORTHODOXY

[19]

A Statement on Abortion

Greek Orthodox Archdiocese of
North and South America

THE MOST DIVINE GIFT bestowed by God upon mankind is the gift of life itself, and throughout the centuries the sacredness of human life has been undisputed by responsible men and women of all persuasions.

We are currently confronted with a controversy surrounding the liberalization of abortion statutes stemming from the initiative of various groups and individuals whose actions, although predicated upon sincere and humanitarian motives, are nevertheless in conflict with divine law. Their position evolves from the general contention that the termination of unborn human life is justifiable when medical opinion believes there is substantial risk that continuance of the pregnancy would impair the physical or mental health of the mother, or that the child would be born with grave physical or mental defects, or if the pregnancy resulted from rape or incest.

It has been the position of the Orthodox Church over the centuries that the taking of unborn life is morally wrong. This is based upon divine law which is the most difficult law for man to comprehend for it transcends the boundaries of human frailty due to its source of divine authority. No law is perfect, and man in his diverse interpretations of the law is continually reminded of his human limitations. Even in such basic law as "Thou Shalt Not Kill": we can take

SOURCE: This statement reprinted by permission of the Greek Orthodox Archdiocese of North and South America, 10 East 79th Street, New York, NY 10021.

no pride in its exceptions which justify war and self-defense, for they serve only to becloud our unceasing efforts toward shaping man in the image of God. This same principle of exception also extends to the unborn child. When the unborn child places the life of its mother in jeopardy, then and only then can this life be sacrificed for the welfare of its mother. To move beyond this exception would be transgressing man's duty in the protection of human life as understood and interpreted by the Orthodox Church.

We are profoundly aware that the discipline of divine law sometimes creates inequities that are difficult for human comprehension to accept, but the eternal values of divine law were not created for *a* man, but for mankind.

The solution to our vexing problem of an increasing need for abortion does not lie in reinterpreting the law to meet the needs of our present-day morality, but rather challenges us to find a more effective eternal protector of human life.

[20]

On the Sanctity of Life

Ninth All-American Council
of the Orthodox Church in America

WHEREAS THE ORTHODOX CHURCH in America has consistently spoken out in defence of the sanctity of life, and has done so in connection with contemporary threats to the life of the unborn, the handicapped, the infirm, and the elderly; and

WHEREAS abortion in all cases has been condemned by the Orthodox Church in America unequivocally on the basis of Orthodox theology, which faithfully reflects for today nearly two thousand years of Christian doctrine and ethical teaching; and

WHEREAS, before the end of this century, "do-it-yourself" abortion will more than likely be commonplace (the RU 486 pill), and legislation will have little effect on whether or not a woman brings her child to term;

BE IT THEREFORE RESOLVED THAT the Ninth All-American Council of the Orthodox Church in America strongly *reaffirms* the Orthodox Church's opposition to abortion in all cases, and that it does so on theological and moral grounds; *commends* the efforts of Orthodox bishops, clergy, and laity to bear witness to the sanctity of life in the public arena, especially noting in this connection the work and witness of Orthodox Christians for Life; and

SOURCE: From *On the Sanctity of Life*, resolution by the Ninth All-American Council of the Orthodox Church in America. Reprinted by permission of the Orthodox Church in America.

commits the Orthodox Church in America to continued witness on behalf of the God-given sanctity of life;

BE IT FURTHER RESOLVED THAT the Orthodox Church in America recognizes that opposition to and condemnation of abortion in all cases is not enough, and that the Orthodox Church and Orthodox Christians have a moral obligation to work for the creation and maintenance of Orthodox adoption agencies and for the facilitation of adoption procedures for families to consider adopting a homeless or unwanted or disabled infant, regardless of the child's racial or ethnic background in the realization that the Church as a whole and the parish community in particular is called to give active material and spiritual support to those who accept the responsibility of adoption;

BE IT FURTHER RESOLVED THAT this Council affirms and supports the work of the Orthodox Christian Adoption Referral Service and encourages parishes and members of the Orthodox Church in America to give their material and moral support to this organization;

FINALLY, BE IT FURTHER RESOLVED THAT this Council recognizes and affirms spiritual, pastoral and educational efforts towards moral persuasion, directed to the father as much as to the mother, to help stem the present hemorrhaging of unborn and unwanted human persons and lives.

Resolution on Sanctity of Life Sunday

WHEREAS the Orthodox Church in America has always respected the right to life of all men and women from conception to the time of natural death, and

WHEREAS the Supreme Court of the United States of America has allowed legalized abortions since January 22, 1973, leading to the deaths of 1,500,000 unborn children each year,

WE HEREBY PROCLAIM the Sunday in January falling on or before January 22 each year to be called Sanctity of Life Sunday in all churches of the Orthodox Church in America, and that on this Sunday a letter from our primate be read in all churches, and special petitions be taken at Liturgy, proclaiming our respect as a Church, for all human life.

ECUMENICAL ISSUES

[21]

Abortion: An Ecumenical Dilemma

Gregory Baum

BECAUSE OF THE DELICATE nature of the topic, I wish to begin with a personal remark. Emotionally I am strongly opposed to abortions. When I argue about the issue in my mind, I tend to conjure up selfish and insensitive opponents who are exclusively interested in their comfort and career. I tend to connect the trend toward abortions with the hostility to little children that characterizes our highly rational culture. In my mind, the demand for abortions becomes a symptom of an ultimate capitalism where people claim total control not only over their property, but over their bodies, a kind of *reductio ad absurdum* of the individualism our economic system has generated. What has been lost, I then feel, is a sense of wonder before life itself and the hidden forces operative within it.

I

It is only when I engage in more serious reflection that I remember that among the people who regard abortion under certain circumstances as a licit, moral, even if regrettable and extreme, form of birth control, are Christian thinkers and in fact several Christian churches. Many Protestant theologians whose

SOURCE: Reprinted with permission of *Commonweal* (November 30, 1973). Copyright © 1973.

work I admire and whose moral judgment I respect look on abortion under certain circumstances as a moral choice. In some cases, according to them, it could even be a duty. I have read these theological essays and studied the ecclesiastical documents; while I always win the argument when I discuss the issue in my mind with the imaginary opponents, selfish and insensitive as they are, I must admit that I respect the reflections of Protestant thinkers and take the teaching of their churches seriously.

As an ecumenical theologian I must ask myself whether one should regard the moral teaching of these Christian churches, even though they differ from the traditional position, as a Christian witness. Of course, the possibility exists that churches betray the substance of the gospel. We recall the blindness of the so-called German Christians under the Hitler regime. Yet at that time, the new ecclesiastical trend was repudiated by other Christian churches outside the country and by courageous Christians in Germany. No one received the position of the German Christians as an authentic witness to gospel morality. Their nationalistic stand was a brief episode in the life of the church, which should never be forgotten, but there is no analogy here whatever to the position on abortion adopted by many Christian churches in the industrialized world. Here Christian thinkers, on grounds they regard as responsible, tested, and in keeping with the gospel, come to conclusions on abortion that differ from traditional teaching but are shared by great numbers of Christians in the highly developed countries, whose moral judgments on other issues, even if untraditional, deserve the greatest respect. This break with the moral tradition of the past, then, does not resemble the kind of betrayal mentioned above: it recalls, rather, the break with the tradition that has taken place on many moral issues in recent decades. Even when we disagree with the view on abortion, defended by many Protestant thinkers, we must respect it as part of the Christian conversation about the meaning of the gospel for modern life.

Vatican Council II has acknowledged this ecumenical dilemma. In the Decree on Ecumenism, in the section dealing with the attitude of Catholics to Protestant Christians, we read, "If in moral matters there are many (Protestant) Christians who do not always understand the gospel in the same way as Catholics, and do not admit the same solutions for the more difficult problems of modern society, nevertheless they share our desire to cling to Christ's words as the source of Christian virtue [No. 23]." When Catholics disagree with the teaching on abortion adopted by some Protestant churches and many Christian thinkers, they should respect this Protestant position as an attempt to deal in a Christian way with a difficult moral problem.

This respect, I propose, is all the more necessary because the Anglican and Protestant churches have exercised moral leadership in contemporary society on many issues, on which the Catholic Church still defended the moral stance of a previous age. We all remember the repeated papal condemnations of religious liberty that, as late as the fifties of this century, caused a good deal of trouble to the late John Courtney Murray. Similarly in regard to birth control, I hold that the Anglican and Protestant churches gave moral leadership in the conditions of modern life with all its ambiguities, at a time when the Catholic Church continued to teach moral norms from the cultural experience of the premodern age. From my own personal contact with Protestant moral thinkers, I have acquired great admiration for them and thus I do not find the words of Vatican Council II exaggerated when they recall that Protestant thinkers look to Christ as the source of moral wisdom.

I realize, of course, that Protestant thinkers are divided on the abortion issue. My point is that we must respect their various positions as part of the significant Christian conversation. It is my personal experience that the Protestant authors who repudiate abortion altogether and agree with the common Catholic position often entertain moral views on other issues, such as authority, obedience, war, private property, socialism, etc., that greatly differ from my own. I suppose it is inevitable that we test the strength of a moral argument offered by a thinker by turning to the moral conclusions to which her or his reflections have led on other issues. This may not be philosophically sound, but in the concrete conditions of life we do rely on the moral counsel of persons whose moral judgment we approve in many areas.

The first conclusion I draw from the above reflections is that one cannot approve of the language and the arguments adopted by Catholics in their defense of the traditional position, which imply that the defenders of abortion are immoral, selfish, insensitive, cruel, lacking in respect for life, or worse. Yet such language is found even in statements made by bishops and popes. While I am quite sure there are unprincipled people arguing in favor of abortion, people who have lost a sense of morality and look on life in a materialist, comfort-oriented way, it would be quite unjust, and therefore immoral, for Catholics to suppose that all people who favor abortion under certain circumstances, including Christian groups and thinkers, share this materialistic outlook on life. The dilemma is that there are Christians who think a liberal position on abortion is more moral, more in keeping with God's will, than the traditional one.

Since no one claims that the traditional position is revealed by God, Catholics should not adopt a tone of voice as if their position is beyond challenge. Catholics may hold that, from their point of view, a liberal position on abortion is immoral, possibly due to false consciousness induced by the social conditions of industrial society, but they have no right whatever to suggest that the thinkers who differ from them are immoral, that their position reflects a lack of virtue, and that the theologians and the theologically oriented among them have refused to search the gospel to find God's will in regard to this contemporary problem.

The ecumenical ecclesiology, found in the Decree on Ecumenism, which has been commonly adopted by Catholic theologians in North America, demands that we regard the abortion issue as a complex one. While Catholics may repudiate certain extreme positions on abortion with vehemence and passion, I do not see how they can do this to the more nuanced and careful positions of Christian thinkers and their churches. The idea that Catholics can solve the moral and pastoral problems of the present age by themselves, without relying on ecumenical dialogue and cooperation and without hoping that wisdom and insight will be exchanged among various Christian communities, living as they do in such varied circumstances, seems, to me, contrary to the ecclesial foundation of the Christian faith. The first conclusion of this essay, then, is that Catholics should not employ language and arguments against abortion that do not recognize the ecumenical dimension of the problem.

II

How is it possible that Christians who take the gospel seriously come to such different conclusions? This, I think, demands an explanation. For it would not do to say that Catholics on the whole are wiser, and more moral, than Anglicans and Protestants. Nor has anyone suggested that we are dealing with a revealed truth that Catholics and some Protestants have preserved but which the major Protestant churches have abandoned. The reason why the position of the Catholic Church differs from that of many other churches is related to a difference in social and cultural background. While a theologian does not wish to reduce significant moral stands to diverse social conditions, he or she must recognize that the conditions of modern life have produced a changed outlook on such traditional issues as birth control, extramarital sex, divorce, etc. in the Anglican and Protestant churches, and that these same conditions are leading Catholic theologians in the highly industrialized parts of the world, encouraged by the present pluralism in the Catholic Church, to raise the same issues and come to similar conclusions. Abortion, however, is such a serious matter that every reflection on it is pushed to its very foundation.

To understand the difference between the traditional position, defended by the Catholic Church, and the position adopted by some Protestant churches, we must place the respective moral judgments into the wider vision of human life, to which they belong and from which they try to derive their validity. Individual moral norms never stand alone; they belong to a more total understanding of human life, to a more complete ideal of what human existence is about.

Thanks to my conversations with Protestant theologian Herbert Richardson, my colleague at St. Michael's College in the University of Toronto, I have begun to understand more clearly the two diverse world views, traditional and new, in which the abortion question has been raised.

The traditional Catholic position, with roots in the ancient past, was dominated by the concept of nature. Here sexuality and procreation were understood as being part of nature, watched over by divine providence. I wish to call this position Model A. According to Model A, sexuality is a biological function directed toward the procreation of the human race. While there is pleasure attached to sexuality, it is oriented by its very nature to the begetting of children. Sexual intercourse outside of marriage is therefore sinful. The conception of children is part of the natural process, watched over by God's providence. It is not for parents to choose the number of children. To practice birth control or to provoke an abortion is an interference with the order of nature and hence gravely sinful. From this perspective, abortion is seen among the sins against nature, touching on the procreative process of human life.

Since in recent years the Catholic arguments against nonprocreative sexual expressions have become less convincing, especially since the traditional position on birth control is no longer accepted, it has been necessary to find new and stronger arguments against abortion. The arguments now given see it as a destruction of fetal life destined to become fully human or, according to some thinkers, even the destruction of human life simply speaking. What was condemned and abhorred in the past as a sin against the order of nature is today often described as the taking of innocent life or murder. Yet the Catholic tradition shows it is possible to oppose abortion and regard it as a grave moral evil, without solving the question of when fetal life in the mother's womb should properly be called a human person. No official teaching on this matter has been established; it is unlikely that this is a matter on which the Christian church is able to offer definitive teaching.

The more liberal position on abortion, adopted by some Protestant churches, fits into a world picture that is dominated by the concept of history. I shall call this position Model B. People do not enter into their destiny by conforming to a given order of nature, but by assuming responsibility for themselves and their environment and by creating their own future. God's providence is here not a guidance from above, but a gracious action within human life, freeing and enabling people ever to expand the area of their responsibility. Sexuality, conception, and procreation, while grounded in biology, belong properly to the sphere of history. Humans are called on by God to assume responsibility for them. Sexuality is here seen not just under its biological aspect: it is a wider human reality, with deep meaning and power, and men and women are summoned to integrate the sexual dimension into their lives in a healing, joyful, and reconciling manner. The biological orientation of sexuality toward procreation cannot be used as an argument against extramarital sexuality. Moralists here do not speak of the pleasure that accompanies sexuality, but of the multileveled meaning and power it has in bringing about responsible human growth and community. Here the number of children is the responsibility of the parents. God's providence is believed to be operative through the grace-sustained free choice of mother and father.

According to Model B, abortion is an extreme interference in the life process, prompted by people's responsibility for the future, which to many thinkers seems justified, at least under certain circumstances. They think the parents' responsibility includes the authority, in cases of emergency, to interrupt a pregnancy with a clinical intervention. We note, however, that the moral approval of abortion is by no means a necessary consequence of Model B. It is possible to adopt Model B for the understanding of sexual life and procreation, without acknowledging abortion as a moral option. Nonetheless, it is the world view of humankind's ever increasing responsibility for the future, for the number of children born and for the kinds of lives these children will have, that explains how theologians and Christian churches can come to acknowledge abortion as a moral choice in extreme cases.

The distinction between the two models enables me to make a significant point. I hold that the Catholic Church at Vatican Council II has shifted from Model A to Model B. This was done, not in a fully consistent manner in regard to all its consequences, but in regard to two significant issues. First, ecclesiastical teaching at Vatican Council II abandoned the view that children are the primary end of marriage: quite apart from its procreative role, sexuality is credited with an important function in the building up of the family in love. Second, Vatican Council II unambiguously adopted the ideal of responsible parenthood: divine providence can no longer be invoked as dispensing people from assuming responsibility for their procreative role. Since then, and despite the papal teaching reproving contraception, Catholic theologians have, on the whole, opted for Model B and developed its full implications for a new theological approach to sexuality.

This leads me to the second conclusion of this essay. The opposition of Catholics against abortion should place itself frankly on the side of humans' historical responsibility for their sexual lives. Catholics should argue against abortion out of the presuppositions of Model B. I am uneasy with a movement against abortion that does not advocate sexual education and birth control. The attempt of Catholics to use their opposition to abortion as a subtle way of returning to Model A, that is, of going back to a purely biological-procreative view of sexuality and to the traditional sexual morality corresponding to this, I regard as theologically indefensible. It is my view that since Catholics are against abortion and want to help to reduce the number of abortions, they should favor the spread of sexual information, the availability of birth control, and an enlightened attitude that increases people's sense of responsibility for their own sexual lives.

Catholic groups and ecclesiastical leaders fighting against abortion often adopt a language and a style of argument that promote the view that sexuality is primarily and essentially procreative. In addition to opposing abortions, they advocate the traditional view of sexuality. Their struggle against abortion thus pursues two ends. While they do not always admit it, they wish to achieve two distinct goals with their campaign. But by linking their opposition to abortion to a highly biological view of sexuality, they weaken their arguments. We occasionally meet people involved in a movement against abortion with a certain passion, adopting a certain style and tone of voice, that give the impression that their main concern is not really human life (they were not greatly upset about the deaths during the war), but sexual morality. They are greatly upset by a sexual morality that acknowledges the quest for sexual freedom within the bounds of reason and love. By linking a special view of sexuality to their struggle against abortions, their arguments actually lose credibility.

The argument of some groups that wherever more sexual information and ready access to contraception are available the result has always been more abortions rather than less, is not the point. What is involved, I think, is a matter of principle. Since I hold that the Catholic Church has moved over to Model B and since I am convinced that the older view of sexuality, however adequate it may have been for the culture that generated it, is harmful for the present day, it is for me a matter of principle to defend the right and duty of men and women to choose with responsibility the form and pattern of their sexual lives. In this sense we must hope that more adequate, more human, and more reliable methods of contraception will be invented. Society must overcome the violence of abortions by increasing the sense of power and responsibility people have over their sexual lives.

III

Moral theology usually puts the burden of freedom and guilt on the individual. From the study of sociology, however, it would appear that the social and cultural conditions in which people live create a certain mind-set that must also be taken in consideration when evaluating people's actions. These two aspects are dialectically related: there is an interaction between the consciousness induced by social institutions and the freedom to transcend their limitations. The Roman Catholic Church's preaching on the whole has paid attention mainly to the aspect of personal freedom, thus sparing the institutions from a critical analysis and exempting them from moral guilt. While moral theologians usually acknowledge that institutional pressures reduce personal freedom and limit culpability, they do not sufficiently appreciate the formative influence of institutions on human consciousness.

Moralists in church and society tend to lament people's selfishness, their lack of generosity, and their bad will without analyzing to what extent the crimes committed by them are related to the mind-set induced by the contradictions within society. Can we confine an analysis of why people steal to a consideration of their private lives? Or must we not also analyze the society that produces an impoverished proletariat, bombards these same people with advertisements for the easy life, and creates conditions of loneliness and personal alienation in which drug addiction thrives? If we only take a firm stand against robbery without submitting society to a critical analysis, we disguise the true causes of evil in society, defend the injustices implicit in the present social system, and perpetuate the individualistic illusion that is related to the problem. The moralistic preaching of church and society is here seen as a defense of the established order.

After the October 1970 crisis in French Canada—the kidnapping of two government officials and the accidental murder of one of them—the French Canadian bishops published a statement expressing their dismay at the outbreak of violence in their midst. Let us remember, they wrote, that violence is nourished by injustice.

If the root of evil is twofold, in personal consciousness and in the social institutions made by people, then we must learn to repudiate abortions in this dialectical manner. We cannot place all the blame on the trapped people who desperately seek a way out of their predicaments. If it is true that violence is nourished by injustice, then we must ask what are the social injustices that make people interfere with the life-giving process in a violent manner. The repudiation of abortion should then be accompanied by a critique of society that tries to define the contradictions operative within it that foster the violence of abortion. Few moralists have done this.

Even a cursory analysis reveals two kinds of oppression in society favoring abortion. First and foremost, it seems to me, is the alienation imposed on people, especially, although not exclusively, on the underprivileged, by the money- and profit-oriented, maximizing economic system. The present system, through its various institutions, tries to make people into customers. From childhood on, people are taught to dream of buying goods and symbolizing affluence through ostentatious consumption. As they become part of the world of consumers, be it only in their dreams, they become estranged from the deep things of life, from love, truth, and fidelity. Institutionally summoned to a false life, they fall into emotional and sexual chaos. The confusion, isolation, and terror created among the urban dispossessed, coupled with an authentic desire for ecstasy, traps vast numbers of women in unwanted pregnancies. And while they are quite incapable of looking after themselves, society expects them to look after their children.

A second contradiction, operative in another section of the population, is the oppression of women. In our generation, women have discovered that much of the emphasis that they are mothers and achieve their highest fulfillment as mothers looking after a family, is an ideology that prevents them from experiencing the self-realization that is open to men. They sense that what is involved in much of the opposition to abortion is the hidden trend of the male-dominated society, endorsed by many women, to keep the power relations between men and women as they are. Women struggling for their liberation regard any form of unwanted motherhood as an unjust imposition of society.

It is the task of the moral theologian—this is the third conclusion of this essay—to institute a detailed critique of society to see more precisely how violence is nourished by injustice. The secular liberal approach to abortion, represented by the recent decision of the U.S. Supreme Court, which regards the interruption of pregnancies as a purely private matter, refuses to recognize in the abortive practices a symptom of social ills and alienation. The secular liberal approach intends to persuade us that nothing is basically wrong with society. The moralist who puts the blame for abortion on the people who seek it or commit it, and who refuses to deal critically with the social system, also disguises the full cause of evil in society. What the moral theologian will have to find, through a more detailed analysis of society, is a set of arguments repudiating abortions, that do not strengthen the oppressions working in the social order but promote social change and the liberation of men and women. Only too often is the call for a return to virtue an attempt to make people look away from the discrepancies in the institutions and is thus a disguise for a reactionary political outlook. The opposition to abortion could thus go hand in hand with the continued oppression of women and with the approval of an individualistic, profit-oriented, money-centered, customer-producing society. Catholic theologians will want to make their rejection of violence as a licit means of birth control a statement that is politically and culturally responsible and that raises the consciousness of the community in regard to the contradictions operative in it.

[22]

Ethics and the Search for Christian Unity: Statement by the Roman Catholic/Presbyterian-Reformed Consultation

The Statement on Abortion

Touched by the tragic personal and social dimensions of decisions regarding abortion, the members of the Roman Catholic/Presbyterian-Reformed Consultation wish to express our common concern. We are conscious of the need for our churches to call attention to the profound moral dimensions of the situation and to identify the individual and societal factors which give rise to the issue and make resolutions so difficult. We believe that our differing traditions have much to contribute through dialogue towards the clarification of principles and the exercise of charity in this matter.

We live in a moral universe. Our human capacity and even willingness to know or apply moral principles in situations of conflict are limited and make us conscious of our human finitude and brokenness and of our need for graced guidance and open inquiry.

These limitations have sometimes prevented us from recognizing the wealth of Christian resources for pastoral guidance concerning responsible sexuality, family planning, and public witness on moral issues. At the same time, we affirm the importance of drawing upon our traditions in dealing with these issues. The proper structuring of family life, the honoring of the gift of the covenant of mar-

SOURCE: Copyright © 1981 by the Publications Office, United States Catholic Conference, 1221 Massachusetts Avenue, N.W., Washington, D.C. 20017. Reprinted by permission.

riage, the demands of caring for future generations, and the protecting of the weak and the vulnerable must be part of any discerning moral position.

Abortion decisions exist in a milieu of closely related social evils which limit peoples' choices. Social, educational, and economical inequities suffered by women are part of the problem. Any discussion of abortion in our times should proceed with a recognition of the pervasive bias of cultural and ecclesial traditions which devalue women. Until these factors are acknowledged there will not be a climate in which a morally and humanly satisfactory resolution to abortion can be effected. Women are too narrowly regarded in terms of their reproductive functions. Women encounter problems of poverty, inequality of opportunity, and sexual exploitation. If our churches are to be credible in addressing abortion, they must take the lead in accepting women as full and contributing members of the human and ecclesial communities. They must work to develop supportive networks to which pregnant women have a rightful claim. We recommend extensive, open discussion in the churches on the reproductive functions, on responsible sexuality, on the social aspects of pregnancy and child rearing, and on the new problems raised by prenatal diagnostic information as well as the pervasive sexual bias influencing many of our ecclesial and societal structures and institutions.

Moral and spiritual formation of conscience, in which the churches have an important role, pertains to many questions concerning the value of life, of which abortion is only one. Those who face abortion decisions are moral agents and therefore free to make responsible decisions with due regard for the unborn, the pregnant woman, the family, the society, and the faith community. Considering an abortion places on everyone involved a serious moral responsibility.

Some of the basic principles on which the Consultation was able to reach agreement include the following:

1. the transcendent basis for respect for human life is the image and likeness of God in which human beings are created;
2. the ultimate responsibility for moral decision making rests with the individual conscience guided by reason and grace;
3. authentic moral decisions can never be exclusively subjective or individualistic but must take account of the insights and concerns of the broader religious, social and familial community;
4. judicial and legislative standards are not always coterminous with moral demands, and therefore the legalization of abortion does not of itself absolve the Christian conscience from moral responsibility; and
5. religious groups have the right to use licit means to influence civil policy regarding abortion.

Some of the areas in which substantial differences were discovered and which call for further dialogue between our two traditions include the following:

1. the moment and meaning of personhood;
2. the rights of the unborn in situations where rights are in conflict;
3. the role of civil law in matters pertaining to abortion; and
4. the interrelation of individual versus communal factors in decision making.

In the light of our common Christian heritage and in recognition of our real differences, our ministry, with regard to abortion, will be characterized by the following: we will attempt to clarify the basic principles pertinent to decision making in this area. We will always respect the personal dignity of those involved in making decisions about abortion. Regardless of the ultimate decisions reached, we will offer pastoral support insofar as our personal conscience and moral convictions allow. We will not resort to stereotypes and abusive language. We will work to transform societal arrangements which press people into untenable moral dilemmas. We will attempt to create compassionate community which overcomes alienation, loneliness, and rejection and which makes real a genuine community of moral discourse and decision. We will take responsibility as part of the mission of the church to create an ethos which values all life and which works toward a society where abortion need not occur.

JUDAISM

[23]

Abortion—A Jewish View

Rabbi Isaac Klein

WHILE THE PROBLEM OF abortion is an old one, it has become particularly pressing today because of many new social, scientific and religious developments. Attention is focused on the problem particularly now because of the proposed legislation to liberalize the laws of abortion and because of the pressures from many quarters to change the existing laws.

Because the question is not new, various traditions and religious principles have had an opportunity to cluster around it and to crystallize definite attitudes to the subjects and views on the problems that it poses.

In this paper, I shall endeavour to present the Jewish attitude as it has developed in the religious tradition of the Jewish people.

I shall preface my presentation of the subject with two general statements:

(a) The Bible states: "See, I have set before thee this day life and good, and death and evil" (Deut. x, 15). Another relevant statement is: "Ye shall therefore keep my statutes and my judgements which if a man shall do, he shall live by them" (Lev. xviii, 15).

In these two verses, life is equated with the good, and the observance of the commandments with the enhancement of life. This identification has been a cardinal principle in Judaism. The Rabbis repeatedly emphasized that the words, "he shall live by them" meant that God's commandments are to be a

SOURCE: From *The Dublin Review* 514 (winter 1967–68). Copyright © by *The Month*, London. Reprinted by permission.

means for the furtherance of life and not for its destruction. Therefore, with the exception of three prohibitions, all commandments of the Torah are in abeyance whenever their performance would endanger life. The exceptions are idolatry, murder and adultery.

(b) The written sources upon which Jewish life is based are divided into two categories, the Halakhic and the Aggadic. The Halakhic is normative and contains that which was accepted as the prescribed standard of conduct. The Aggadah is not normative but expresses the ideals, values and aspirations of the people and its teachers which often went beyond the law. While not normative, the Aggadic affirmations do touch on ethical problems and may furnish guidance or suggest lines of development. Both, the Halachah and the Aggadah, find their major expression in the Talmud, which after the Bible is the main source and authority for Jewish practice.

The classical source for the Jewish attitude to abortion is found in the Mishnah, a code of laws that dates back to the second century and which forms the basis of the Talmud. It states: "A woman that is having difficulty in giving birth, it is permitted to cut up the child inside her womb and take it out limb by limb because her life takes precedence. If the greater part of the child has come out, it must not be touched because one life must not be taken to save another" (M. Ahiloth vii, 6).

The Bible does not speak about abortion but does have reference to that status of a foetus in the following passage: "If men strive, and hurt a woman with child, so that her fruit depart from her, and yet no mischief follow: he shall surely be punished according as the woman's husband will lay upon him; and he shall pay as the judge determine. And if any mischief follow, then thou shalt give life for life" (Exod. xxi, 22–23).

The mischief refers to the death of the woman. It is only in the case if death to the mother results from the hurt that capital punishment is inflicted. The death of the unborn is punishable by fine only, because the unborn child is not accounted as a living thing.

Philo and Josephus also deal with abortion, but their statements are confused and inconsistent. Furthermore, these have not been in the mainstream of Jewish Tradition and have not influenced its development. (See Jacobovitz, *Jewish Medical Ethics*, p. 179 f.)

We must, therefore, go to the Talmud and its commentators for guidance.

The statement of the Mishnah is repeated in the Tosefta, a contemporary Rabbinic work, with slight variations (Tosefta Yebamoth ix, 9).

The Talmud explains the reason for the statement of Mishnah in this fashion: "Once its head has come forth [while the Mishnah requires extrusion of the greater part of the child the Tosefta speaks about the extrusion of the head] it may not be harmed because one life may not be taken to save another. But why so? Is he not a pursuer? There it is different, for she is pursued by heaven" (B. Sanhedrin 72b).

This passage explains the distinction between the case where the mother's life takes precedence and where it does not. Rashi, the preeminent commentator of the Bible and the Talmud (eleventh century) explains the Talmudic passage thusly: "For as long as the child did not come out into the world it is not called a living thing and it is therefore permissible to take its life in order to save the life of its mother. Once the head of the child has come out, the child may not be harmed because it is considered as fully born, and one life may not be taken to save another."

According to Rashi's interpretation the reason for the permission to take the life of the unborn child is that the embryo is not considered a living thing, and hence taking its life cannot be called murder.

This view is supported by the Biblical law concerning harm done to a pregnant woman, that we quoted above. The unborn child is not considered there as a living being.

Maimonides, in his Code, explains that the reason for the position of the Mishnah is that the child in this case endangers the life of the mother and is therefore subject to the law of the "pursuer." He says therefore: "This is moreover a negative commandment, that we have no pity on the life of a pursuer. Consequently, the Sages have ruled that if a woman with child is having difficulty in giving birth, the child inside her may be taken out either by drugs or by surgery, because it is regarded as one pursuing her and trying to kill her. But once its head has appeared, it must not be touched, for we may not set aside one human life to save another" (Maimonides, Laws of the Murderer i, 9).

From this difference in interpretation of the Mishnah may also result a difference in legal decisions. According to Maimonides, we would permit abortion only where there is clear danger to the life of the mother. According to the interpretation of Rashi, there may be other reasons besides a threat to the life of the mother that would be considered adequate.

The contemporary discussion of the problem seems to centre around the question whether the foetus is considered a living being. This would view the question as Rashi did. However, the opinion of Maimonides is also relevant because much of the discussion today also hinges on the welfare of the mother and the family.

These are the main Halakhic sources for the problem of abortion. We shall bring one relevant statement from Aggadic sources. The Talmud reports the following conversation between Rabbi Judah the Prince and Antoninus the Roman Emperor. "Antoninus said to Rabbi Judah, 'When is the soul given unto man, at the time that the embryo is formed, or at the time of conception?' He replied, 'At the time of conception.' The Emperor objected: 'Is it possible for a piece of meat to stay for three days without salt and not putrefy? It must therefore be at conception.' Said Rabbi Judah: 'This thing Antoninus taught me and Scripture supports him, as it is said; and thy visitation has preserved my spirit'" (Job x, 12) (Sanhedrin 91b).

If this discussion sounds naive and irrelevant let me remind you that this controversy still goes on today; only the terminology has changed. It was also a point of argument among the Greek philosophers. According to Aristotle the rational soul is infused the fortieth day after conception in the case of a male and the eightieth day in the case of a female. According to the Platonic tradition the soul entered at conception. The Stoics believed that the soul entered at birth.

Roman jurists followed the Stoics and maintained therefore that abortion was not murder. According to common law also taking a life is punishable only after there has been complete extrusion of the child from the body of the mother.

The difference of attitude between the various religious traditions regarding abortion reflects this difference between Plato, Aristotle and the Stoics.

Surprisingly, medical science considers the foetus a living thing from the moment the ovum is fertilized (Joseph B. Lee, *Obstetrics,* 4th ed., p. 274).

Actually being a living thing and being a separate entity are not the same thing. Even if we say that the foetus is a living thing, we can maintain that it is *pars viscera matrum,* or as the Talmud expresses it, the foetus is accounted as the loin of its mother. When abortion is therapeutic, therefore, there can be no objection to it because it is like any surgery where we sacrifice a part for the whole.

This is the attitude the Rabbis have taken. Abortion is not murder under any circumstances. Since, however, it is the destruction of potential life it is not permitted except if it is therapeutic.

The problem now is to define therapeutic. We shall cite a number of practical cases that came before the Rabbis the past few centuries. Their answers will give us guidance to a definition of therapeutic.

The example cited in the Mishnah would indicate that permission is limited to where there is a direct threat to the mother's life. Later literature has examples indicating that the area has been widened.

Rabbi Yair Hayyim Bachrach (1639–1702), the author of a collection of Responsa entitled *Havoth Yair,* reports this strange case in one of his responsa. A married woman committed adultery and became pregnant. She had pangs of remorse and now wants to do penance. She asked whether she could swallow a drug in order to get rid of the "evil fruit" in her womb. In his answer Rabbi Bachrach makes it clear immediately, that the question of the permissibility of abortion has nothing to do with the legitimacy of the child to be born. The only question involved is whether abortion is accounted as taking a life or not. He draws distinctions between the various stages of the development of the foetus, i.e. forty days after conception, three months after conception. Rabbi Bachrach then concludes that theoretically abortion might be permitted at the early stages of the pregnancy, but we do not do so because of the custom adopted by both the Jewish and the general community.

Rabbi Meir Eisenstadt (1670–1744) in his collection of responsa entitled *Panim Me-iroth* has the following question. A woman had difficulty in giving birth, and the child came out feet first, is it permitted to cut up the child limb by limb in order to save the mother?

This seems to be the very case stated in the Mishnah. The difficulty arises when we read how this case is restated in Maimonides. Whereas the Mishnah mentions that if the greater part of the child has come out we do not take the life of the child to save the mother, Maimonides, following the text of the Tosefta, says that if the head of the child or the majority thereof came out first it is considered as born and we do not take its life in order to save the mother.

The commentators tried to resolve this contradiction by saying that the extrusion of the head or the majority thereof, or in the case where the head came out last, the extrusion of the majority of the body, constitutes birth.

The author then poses the question whether if at this stage, should we let nature take its course, death would result to both, the mother and the child, is it still forbidden to take the life of the child in order to save the mother? He leaves the question unanswered. A later authority is very explicit and answers that in this case, too, we save the mother.

Rabbi Eliezer Deutsch (1850–1916), the author of a collection of responsa entitled *Revi Ha-sadah* treats the following problem. A woman who has been pregnant a few weeks begins to spit blood. Expert physicians say she must drink a drug in order to bring about a miscarriage. Should she wait, it will become necessary to bring out the child by cutting it up and also endanger the life of the mother, whereas now it is possible to bring forth the child with a drug. Is it permissible to do so?

Rabbi Deutsch answers that in such a case, it is certainly permissible to do so. He also draws a distinction between the various stages in the development of the foetus, between the use of drugs and the use of surgery, and between another person doing it or the woman herself. He concludes that abortion is permitted in this case for three reasons: (a) Before three months after conception there is not even a foetus; (b) There is no overt act involved in this abortion; The woman herself is doing it and it is thus an act of self-preservation.

Obviously, current Halakhic literature also faced the question. This is reflected again in current responsa literature. Most eminent among the authorities that dealt with the question are Rabbi B. H. Uziel, the late Chief Rabbi of the Sephardic community of Israel, and Rabbi I. J. Unterman, the present Chief Rabbi of the Ashkenazic community of Israel.

Rabbi Uziel treats the case of a pregnant woman who was threatened with deafness if she were to go through with the pregnancy. He decided that since the foetus is not an independent life (nefesh) but only a part of the mother, there is no sin in destroying it for the sake of the mother (B. H. Uziel, Mishpetei Uziel 11; see, 46, 47).

Rabbi Unterman dealt with the question of abortion in the case where the expectant mother contracted German measles, and it is feared that the child may be born with serious physical and mental abnormalities (Noam v, 6, 5723). Rabbi Unterman is unalterably opposed to any abortion except if it is, like the case mentioned in the Mishnah, a direct threat to the mother's life.

I will bring two more contemporary responsa because of the light they will shed on the problem. Rabbi Isaac Oelbaum, formerly of Czechoslovakia and now in Toronto, Canada, treats this case. A woman has a weak child. According to the doctors it will not live unless it is breast-fed by the mother. The mother has now been pregnant four weeks and has felt that there was a change in her milk. Could she destroy the child, they asked, by means of an injection in order to save the child that she nursed?

The author discusses first the reliability of doctors in these things (they sometimes exaggerate and are overcautious), and whether a way out could be found with substituting a proper formula for bottle feeding.

He concludes that if there is expert evidence that danger may result if there be no abortion, it is permitted (Sh'eilot Yitzhok Sec. 64).

The other responsum is by Rabbi Gedaliah Felder, also of Toronto. The case concerns a pregnant woman who is afflicted with cancer of the lungs. The doctors say that if a premature birth will not be effected, the cancer will spread faster and hasten her death. Is it permissible to have an abortion where the mother is saved only temporarily? (Kol Torah, Hershvan 5719).

From the case we brought it is evident that the main factor in determining the permissibility of abortion is whether allowing the pregnancy to take its natural course will constitute a threat to the mother.

The classic case of the Mishnah would indicate that only when it is a direct threat to the life of the mother. The later responsa widen the meaning of the word threat to include a threat to the health of the mother.

Another consideration is the question of the psychological factors involved. All the cases that we have mentioned speak of health in terms of the physical. A very large number of the cases that involve abortion today have to do with mental anguish, and threats to the mental health of the mother or the child. While mental anguish is not now with us, we know more about its deleterious consequences today. Attacks of hysteria and suicidal tendencies are as much of a threat to the life of the mother as the cases mentioned before that involve only physical ailment.

I came across one responsum going back to the seventeenth century that deals with the problem. Rabbi Israel Meir Mizrahi permitted abortion when it was feared that the mother would otherwise suffer an attack of hysteria (Peri Ha-aretz Yoreh Deah Sec. 21). (See also I. J. Unterman, Hatorah V'Ha-Medinah, pp. 25, 29.)

Contemporary authorities have dealt with cases that involved the thalidomide babies, victims of rape, and mothers of large families that just cannot afford physically to enlarge the family.

The authorities, with a few notable exceptions, agree that a child once conceived has a right to live even if there is a chance for it to be born malformed or in poor health. We introduce, however, the question of what this does to the mother in terms of mental anguish, psychological disturbances, attacks of hysteria and suicidal tendencies. Examples of such results are abundant (I. Jacobovitz, The Jewish Review, London, 14 November 1962).

From the foregoing we would make the following conclusions, suggested by the weight of opinions quoted as well as by present sociologic and medical factors.

There is a distinction between the early stages and the later stages of pregnancy.

In the later stages, we would permit abortion only when the birth of the foetus would be a direct threat to the life of the mother. This threat should be interpreted to also include cases where if the pregnancy should be allowed to continue it would have such debilitating effect, whether psychological or otherwise, on the mother as to present a hazard to her life, however remote such danger may be.

In the earlier stages, we would allow therapeutic abortions whenever there is any threat to the health of the mother, directly or indirectly, physically and psychologically.

Since this is very flexible and therefore subject to abuse, the facts have to be established by reliable medical evidence.

We would therefore permit abortion in the case of the thalidomide babies, cases of rape, and the like, not because such a foetus has no right to life, but because it constitutes a threat to the health of the mother.

This is the area of controversy where many authorities would disagree and limit abortion to cases where the threat to the life of the mother is direct.

We would exclude abortions that are prompted merely by the desire of the mother not to have another child.

Those who advocate the permission of all abortion and to leave the decision completely to the mother have taken this stand because it is an answer to the problem of the widespread practice of criminal abortions resulting often in sickness and death of the mother, and also the problem of the population explosion.

While we recognize the gravity of these problems, we are of the opinion that there are other and equally effective methods of dealing with them which do not have this moral stigma. At the present time, when life has lost so much of its sanctity, we dare not add measures that will increase disregard for it. A prominent obstetrician of Buffalo called my attention to this passage in a medical textbook of over thirty years ago.

> There is abundant evidence that the frequency of criminal induction of abortion is increasing at an alarming rate, although accurate statistics cannot be obtained. Numerous reasons may be advanced for this deplorable situation, the most probable being: (1) Twentieth-century standards of living have made children an economic liability for a large percentage of the population. This may be contrasted with more primitive rural conditions where a large family was considered an economic asset. (2) As a by-product of the woman's freedom movement, a very large number of women have come to believe that pregnancy should be regulated by their personal desires. (3) The present-day lack of religious feeling and the wide teaching that pregnancy may be controlled, have contributed to a lowering of moral standards among women, with a resulting increase in the number of undesired pregnancies (Carl Henry Davis, *Gynaecology and Obstetrics,* Ch. X, p. 1).

Thirty years is a comparatively short time when we are speaking about the history of man. The last thirty years' period, however, has been the most momentous in the annals of man. It has witnessed World War II, the rise of many new nations, the awakening of Africa, the re-awakening of Asia, the birth of the nuclear age, the advent of the space age, and the imminence of the population explosion. And yet in the case of abortion the analysis of the good doctor is still relevant, and the situation that he described has become aggravated rather than changed. Giving a carte-blanche to all abortions would spell a moral defeatism, that buys time at the sacrifice of moral values. When proposing legislation, we must balance one against the other. We, therefore, favour only therapeutic abortion, liberally interpreted, and believe also that is the view of the religious tradition of Judaism.

[24]

Abortion in Jewish Law

Rachel Biale

JEWISH LAW (HALAKHA) HAS no single coherent position on abortion. Instead it presents a number of central opinions that, when carried to their logical conclusions, lead to a range of possible rulings on abortion and to internal contradiction.

Abortion appears in biblical legislation only in the case of accidental miscarriage: "When men fight and one of them pushes a pregnant woman and a miscarriage results, but no other harm ensues, the perpetrator shall be fined whatever the woman's husband may exact from him" (Exodus 21:22). Accidentally induced abortion is treated as a civil matter, and the husband is compensated for his loss of progeny (since, according to biblical law, all his wife's "products" are his property). If, however, "other harm" occurs, namely, the woman is killed or injured, "the penalty shall be life for life" (ibid.). The destruction of a fetus is not considered a capital crime, and therefore, later sources conclude, a fetus is not considered a living person. In fact, the fetus is defined as a part of its mother's body: "*ubar yerekh immo*" ("a fetus is [like] its mother's thigh," Hulin 58a, Gittin 23b).

The fetus has no independent rights, and it may be destroyed to save the mother's life, even as late as the birth process itself: "If a woman is having difficulty giving birth, one cuts up the fetus within her and takes it out limb by

---

SOURCE: From *Tikkun* 4 (July–August 1989). Reprinted with permission of *Tikkun* magazine, a Bimonthly Jewish Critique of Politics, Culture, and Society.

limb because her life takes precedence over its life. Once its greater part has emerged, you do not touch it because you may not set aside one life for another" (Mishna Oholot 7:6). Thus the fetus becomes an independent person only when its head or most of its body has emerged (Sanhedrin 72b). In fact, a newborn is not considered fully viable until thirty days after birth, and a neonate's death before thirty days is not mourned like other deaths.

Nevertheless, the fetus is valued as a *potential* life, and thus one may violate the law in order to save its life—for example, carrying a knife on the Sabbath in order to operate and assist in the delivery (Yoma 85b). Consequently, even those halakhic authorities who base their ruling on the principle that a fetus is not a person allow abortion only in the gravest circumstances.

In fact, most halakhic authorities permit abortion only to save the life of the mother. They follow, in one way or another, Maimonides's argument that the fetus is a pursuer (*rodef*) who, like a murderer chasing a victim, may be killed to save the life of the pursued: "Therefore the Sages have ruled that when a woman has difficulty in giving birth one may dismember the child within her womb, either by drugs or by surgery, because he is a pursuer seeking to kill her" (Mishneh Torah, Hilkhot Rotze'akh U-Shmirat Nefesh 1:9).

Maimonides's ruling that the fetus is a "pursuer" implicitly undermines the argument that a fetus is not a person. In other words, if the only reason that the fetus can be destroyed is that it is a pursuer, the implication is that it might be considered a person. Although Maimonides did not explicitly draw this conclusion, subsequent authorities did. Rabbi Hayyim Soloveitchik makes this argument more radically than other halakhists when he states: "The reason for the opinion of Maimonides here . . . is that he believed that the fetus falls into the general category in the Torah of *pikuakh nefesh* [saving life], since the fetus, too, is considered a *nefesh* and is not put aside for the life of others" (Hiddushei Rabbi Hayyim Soloveitchik to Mishneh Torah, Hilkhot Rotze'akh, 1:9). In any case, whether one accepts the talmudic or the Maimonidean position on the status of the fetus, abortion is permitted—required—to save the life of the mother.

In addition to allowing abortion to save the mother's life, the Talmud cites another situation when abortion is permitted: "If a woman is about to be executed, one does not wait for her until she gives birth. . . . One strikes her against her womb so that the child may die first, to avoid her being disgraced" (Arakhin 7a–b). Thus, the dignity of a condemned woman takes precedence over the life of the fetus, as does the mental anguish she would experience if she were to wait for the execution in order to complete the pregnancy. The implication of this ruling, in the opinion of the more permissive legal authorities, is that abortion may be actively sought and induced in order to save a woman from great suffering, even if that suffering is only psychological. Thus, the eighteenth-century halakhist Jacob Emden allowed a woman who conceived a child through adultery to have an abortion because of her "great need," namely, her anguish at "the thought of giving birth to a *mamzer* [bastard]" (She'elat Ya'avetz No. 43).

However, unlike Emden, most halakhists—even "lenient" ones—allow abortion only when there is a *physical* (not psychological) hazard to the mother. Ben Zion Uziel, for example, Ashkenazic chief rabbi of Israel in the 1950s, permitted abortion in a case where a pregnant woman would become deaf if she did not have an abortion (Mishpetei Uziel, Hoshen Mishpat 3:46).

A minority of halakhists, however, follow Emden's example of allowing abortion to prevent psychological harm to the mother. Among more contemporary halakhists, Rabbi Yehiel Jacob Weinberg in Switzerland permitted abortion of a fetus conceived by a woman infected with rubella, and Rabbi Eliezer Waldenberg in Israel ruled that a Tay-Sachs fetus may be aborted. Neither of these halakhists justified their rulings on the basis of the expected suffering of the baby, a halakhically unacceptable argument since there is no halakhic permission for euthanasia based on arguments of "quality of life." Rather, these rabbis based their decision on the *mother's* anguish at the prospect of bearing a fatally ill or deformed child, for, as Waldenberg argues, "psychological suffering is in many ways much greater than the suffering of the flesh" (Responsa Tzitz Eliezer, Part 13, No. 102).

In short, the halakha does clearly state that the fetus is not a person, not just until the end of the second trimester of pregnancy but until the actual moment of birth. Yet the principle of protecting potential life and the justification of abortion on the grounds that the fetus is a "pursuer" limit even the most lenient halakhic authorities to sanctioning abortion only in circumstances of grave physical or psychological threat to the mother.

The question remains how the halakhic discussion of abortion relates to the constitutional issues raised by *Roe v. Wade*. Much of the discussion of *Roe v. Wade* focuses on the question of whether abortion should be immune from legislative interference based on the rights of privacy and individual freedom. The halakha does not adhere precisely to the constitutional categories of privacy and individual freedom, but some analogies seem evident. One of the halakha's fundamental "metarulings" is: "We do not make a ruling [*gezeyra*] unless the majority of the community can abide by it" (Baba Kama 79b). Indeed, one of the major "pragmatic" arguments in favor of legal abortion has been that the majority of women who seek abortion would not abide by a prohibition; they would resort to illegal abortion. Such abortions force women to put their lives in significant danger, and endangering one's life is forbidden by the halakha. One is required to violate any commandment in order to save one's life, with the exception of the prohibitions against murder, idolatry, and illicit sexual relations. Thus, even if an unambiguous ethical argument could be made against abortion, the lack of public consensus and the prohibition against endangering one's life would raise significant halakhic problems.

The halakha may also be implying that a woman has the right to determine her own fate and the future of her pregnancy when it insists on exempting women from the legal duty of procreation. While men are bound by the mitzvah (commandment) of procreation based on Genesis 1:28 ("be fruitful and multiply") and Genesis 9:7 (the blessing/commandment of procreation to Noah and his sons after the flood), the Rabbis engaged in hermeneutical acrobatics in order to exempt women from that duty (Yevamot 65b). Although the exact rationale for this exemption is only alluded to, it is clear that the Rabbis felt it necessary not to require women to do something that "puts their lives on the line." The Rabbis were concerned primarily with the physical dangers of childbirth, but they were also aware of the emotional and social dimensions: the ways in which women's lives were devoted to and determined by childbearing.

The Rabbis' determination to exempt women from the duty to procreate left a significant halakhic opening for the practice of contraception (Yevamot 12b). Perhaps the fact that the talmudic statement regarding contraception is descriptive, not prescriptive (which has led to much controversy in post-talmudic rulings on contraception), was on purpose. Just as the Rabbis intentionally refrained from prescriptive rulings on matters of pregnancy and birth, so too did they refrain from offering such rulings about conception and childbearing. Thus we may point to halakhic justifications for the argument that the state or any other legal authority should not legislate in those areas that require a woman to endanger her life.

[25]

Conservative Judaism Statements from the Rabbinical Assembly and the Women's League for Conservative Judaism

The Rabbinical Assembly

Resolution on Abortion Rights

Whereas Jewish law, though promoting the highest respect for human life, does *not* categorically or universally oppose an option to terminate certain pregnancies, and

Whereas Jewish law does in fact, in a number of circumstances, *sanction* abortion, basing its view of permissibility upon the belief that a foetus is not an autonomous person, and

Whereas the Committee on Jewish Law and Standards of The Rabbinical Assembly has affirmed the right of a woman to choose an abortion in cases where "continuation of a pregnancy might cause the mother severe physical or psychological harm, or when the foetus is judged by competent medical opinion as severely defective," and

Whereas our Movement has consistently advocated a separation "between church and state" meant to inhibit the government from imposing a restrictive legal stance in matters of personal moral choice where citizens of differing faiths may in good conscience honorably disagree, and

Whereas members of The Rabbinical Assembly have lent their support to issues of social justice,

Therefore Be It Resolved that The Rabbinical Assembly call upon Federal and State courts, the United States Congress and the legislatures of the several states to maintain a woman's right to abortion as established in the 1973 Supreme Court decision *Roe v. Wade,* and

Be It Further Resolved that members of The Rabbinical Assembly, acting as leaders in their respective communities, be authorized through the power of this resolution to represent the Conservative rabbinate's position on this matter in those fora where their voices need to be heard, and

Be It Further Resolved that The Rabbinical Assembly, in pursuit of the advancement of the goals defined above, officially affiliate with the Religious Coalition on Abortion Rights as a sponsoring organization, and

Be It Further Resolved that The Rabbinical Assembly, in pursuit of the goals defined above, call upon the Canadian Government not to recriminalize abortion in the Dominion of Canada.

SOURCE: Passed by the Rabbinical Assembly Plenary on May 14, 1990 and reprinted with permission of the Rabbinical Assembly, 3080 Broadway, New York, NY 10027.

Resolution on the Politics and Halakhah of Abortion

Whereas the Rabbinical Assembly has repeatedly affirmed, and continues to affirm, a woman's right to legal abortion as established in the 1973 Supreme Court decision *Roe v. Wade,* and

Whereas the free exercise of a legal right, like abortion, may, under certain circumstances, violate halakhic standards,

Therefore Be It Resolved that the Rabbinical Assembly take pains to distinguish, in the media and from the pulpit, between the politics and the Halakhah of abortion, and

Be It Further Resolved that the Rabbinical Assembly membership encourage thoughtful reflection among the laity on the tension between the legality of abortion in American jurisprudence and the considerations which guide a halakhically-sensitive Conservative community.

SOURCE: Passed by the Rabbinical Assembly Plenary on May 1, 1991 and reprinted with permission of the Rabbinical Assembly, 3080 Broadway, New York, NY 10027.

Resolution on Reproductive Freedom

Whereas Jewish law does not permit abortion on demand, yet does not categorically or universally oppose the termination of certain pregnancies; and

Whereas the Committee on Jewish Law and Standards of the Rabbinical Assembly has affirmed the right of a woman to choose an abortion in cases where "continuation of a pregnancy might cause the mother severe physical or psychological harm, or when the fetus is judged by competent medical opinion as severely defective"; and

Whereas the Rabbinical Assembly has in past years, urged courts, parliaments, and legislatures in State, Provincial, and Federal governments in the United States and Canada to preserve women's legal access to abortion services; therefore be it

Resolved that the Rabbinical Assembly commends President Clinton for his removal of the "Gag Order" on Federally funded family planning agencies; and be it further

Resolved that the Rabbinical Assembly urges the Congress of the United States to pass the "Freedom of Choice Act"; and be it further

Resolved that the Rabbinical Assembly urges courts and legislatures on all levels of government in the United States and Canada to remove legal impediments to women's free exercise of reproductive freedom; and be it further

Resolved that the RA urges local, state, and federal law enforcement agencies to take measures to insure the safety and physical well-being of doctors and other health care professionals who work with family planning agencies and clinics.

SOURCE: Resolution adopted April 1993 and is reprinted here with the permission of the Rabbinical Assembly, 3080 Broadway, New York, NY 10027.

Women's League for Conservative Judaism: Social Action— Background Paper on Abortion

"There is no single Jewish attitude toward abortion. A few generalizations can be made, however. First, in Jewish law, a fetus does not have the status of a human being. Second, if a choice has to be made. . . . the mother's life always takes precedence." —Francine Klagsbrun, from *Voices of Wisdom* (Pantheon Books, 1980)

"If a woman is having difficulty giving birth, the fetus within her womb may be cut up and brought out limb by limb, because her life takes precedence over its life.

"But if the greater part has already been born, it may not be touched, for we do not set aside one person's life for that of another." —Mishnah, tractate Oholot

"Abortion in Jewish law and morality is primarily for the mother's physical or mental welfare.

"In speaking of the mother's welfare one could make a rough generalization about Jewish law. . . . If a woman were to come before the rabbi and say, 'I took thalidomide or I had rubella during pregnancy. There is a fifty-fifty chance my child is going to be deformed. What kind of life is that for a person? Therefore I want an abortion,' the rabbi would say no. However, if the same woman in the same circumstances came to the same rabbi . . . and formulated the question differently, saying, 'I took thalidomide or I had German measles. There is a fifty-fifty chance that the child is going to be deformed, and that *possibility* is driving me to distraction and grave mental anguish,' then the rabbi would say, "Well, go have an abortion, you poor woman.'

"The difference is clear. In the first formulation the woman is speaking about the fetus and what *might* be. . . . In the second formulation, however, she is not talking about the potential, about the fetus, and what *might* be. She is talking about the *actual*, namely, the mother, and when you talk about the actual and you talk about a person, especially a woman, then the entire burden of Jewish law in all these areas—birth control, abortion, sterilization, marital sex, and so on—is weighed in favor of the woman." —David M. Feldman, from "Abortion and Ethics," in *Conservative Judaism* (summer 1975)

"The law on abortion is and should be liberal, to meet genuine cases of hardship and misery that are not soluble in any other way. But society has an obligation to educate its members to ethical standards that rise above the level of abortion on demand. In other words, abortion should be *legally available but ethically restricted*, to be practiced only for very good reasons. Men and women must be persuaded that though the abortion of a fetus is not equivalent to taking an actual life, it does represent the destruction of potential life and must not be undertaken lightly or flippantly." —Robert Gordis, from *Love and Sex: A Modern Jewish Perspective*

Resolution on Abortion

Women's League for Conservative Judaism believes that freedom of choice is inherent in the civil rights of women. We also believe that the welfare of the mother must always be our primary concern.

We therefore urge our Sisterhoods to oppose any legislative attempts through Constitutional amendments, the deprivation of Medicaid, family services and other current welfare services, to weaken the force of the Supreme Court's decision permitting abortions.

Women's League for Conservative Judaism: Amended Resolution on Abortion (1982)

Reverence for life is the cornerstone of our Jewish heritage. Since abortion in Jewish law is primarily for the mother's physical or mental welfare, we deplore the burgeoning casual use of abortion. Abortion should be "legally available, but ethically restricted. Though the abortion of a fetus is not equivalent to taking an *actual* life, it does represent the destruction of *potential* life and must not be undertaken lightly. . . . "

However, Women's League also believes that the practice of the principle of the separation of Church and State guaranteed by our Constitution has kept our nation strong and preserved full freedom for the individual. Women's League believes that transmitting religious values is the responsibility of the religious sector.

Women's League for Conservative Judaism urges its Sisterhoods to oppose any legislative attempts through Constitutional amendments, the deprivation of Medicaid, family services and/or other current welfare services, to weaken the force of the Supreme Court's decision permitting abortions.

United Synagogue of Conservative Judaism

WHEREAS, Jewish tradition cherishes the sanctity of life, even the potential of life which a pregnant woman carries within her; and

WHEREAS, under certain unfortunate circumstances, such as when the life or health of the mother are in jeopardy, Judaism sanctions, even mandates, abortion, although Judaism does not condone or permit abortion for contraceptive purposes; and

WHEREAS, Judaism does not believe that personhood and human rights begin with conception (the premise that personhood begins with conception is founded on a religious position which is not identical with Jewish tradition); and

WHEREAS, under special circumstances, Judaism chooses and requires abortion as an act which reaffirms and protects the life, well being and health of the mother; and

WHEREAS, to deny a Jewish woman and her family the ability to obtain a safe, legal abortion when so mandated by Jewish tradition, is to deprive Jews of their fundamental right of religious freedom;

NOW, THEREFORE, BE IT RESOLVED that the UNITED SYNA-GOGUE OF CONSERVATIVE JUDAISM continues to affirm its strong opposition to any further weakening, limitation, or withdrawal of the 1973 Supreme Court decision of *Roe v. Wade;* and

BE IT FURTHER RESOLVED that the UNITED SYNAGOGUE OF CONSERVATIVE JUDAISM in light of the recent Supreme Court decision and the efforts of the U.S. government to limit the choices available to most Americans, must be diligent in efforts to safeguard and preserve the full personal and religious freedom given to the American people; and

BE IT FURTHER RESOLVED that the UNITED SYNAGOGUE OF CONSERVATIVE JUDAISM opposes any legislative attempt through constitutional amendments, the deprivation of Medicaid, family services and/or other current welfare services, to weaken the force of the United States Supreme Court's decision permitting choice; and

BE IT FURTHER RESOLVED that the UNITED SYNAGOGUE OF CONSERVATIVE JUDAISM encourages the various provinces of Canada and the Canadian government to preserve the rights of all women to legal abortions.

SOURCE: Resolution approved by the 1991 Biennial Convention of the United Synagogue of Conservative Judaism and is reprinted with permission of the United Synagogue of Conservative Judaism, Commission on Social Action and Public Policy.

ISLAM

[26]

Birth and Abortion in Islam

Fazlur Rahman

Birth

The process of pregnancy and birth is stated in the Qur'an: "We have created man out of an extraction of clay [the origin of semen]; then we turn it into semen and settle it in a firm receptacle. We then turn semen into a clot [literally, something hanging, that is, from the womb] which we then transmute into a lump. We then create bones which we clothe with flesh. Then we transmute it into a new mode [of ensoulment]—blessed be then Allah the best of creators" (23, 12–14; see also 22, 5). The Qur'an thus looks upon the process of the creation of a fetus as a series of genuine transformations or "creations," the last being the "ensoulment." In both passages referred to here, the Qur'an also reminds one of resurrection, which will be another fundamental transformation (re-creation) *on the basis of one's conduct in this world* which is, therefore, organically related to the coming form or level of transformation in the eyes of the Qur'an.

To the formation of the child, both spouses contribute. Although the Qur'an does not say anything on this issue, the Hadīth explicitly states that the child is formed from the semen of both the male and female: "The semen

SOURCE: Fazlur Rahman, *Health and Medicine in the Islamic Tradition.* Copyright © 1987 by Lutheran General Health Care System. Reprinted by permission of the Crossroad Publishing Company.

of the male being white and that of the female being yellowish."[1] The Ḥadīth is therefore more in line with the Galenic view on the contribution of both the male and the female, although the Ḥadīth does not speak of the female ovaries as Galen does. This is radically different from the Aristotelian doctrine that the male gives the active principle while the female is passive and only provides the place for the activity of the male semen. This doctrine, of course, flows directly from the Aristotelian doctrine (which he applies universally to explain all phenomena) of form and matter, the active and the passive principle, where the passive factor, "the matter," is not something negative, however, but has a positive "tendency" to "become" something, while the active factor, "the form," fashions matter into that something. Although Aristotle believed that the woman contributed only the menstrual blood that fashioned the body of the child and that its soul came from the male, according to the Islamic doctrine the contributions of both spouses produce the entire organism of the child; in a deeper sense, of course, the entire process is the *creation* of God.

In Islamic medical history, Ibn Sīnā, who was basically Aristotelian but had to account for the discovery of the female ovaries, transformed the Galenic theory to fit it into an Aristotelian framework. He believed that it was not just the female menses, but primarily the female semen (which was much more "concocted" that the rest of the menstrual blood) that constituted the effective female contribution to the formation of the fetus. Yet Ibn Sīnā regarded the male semen alone as formative while the female's semen was passive. Ibn Sīnā had to do this, for otherwise the fundamental Aristotelian doctrine of form and matter, as a universal explanatory principle, would be violated. On this issue, however, the Ḥadīth followed its own course based on the principle of the contributions of both male and female. The Prophetic Medicine works, based as they were primarily on Ḥadīth, also followed the same direction. To the question "From what is the child created?" the Prophet is said to have replied, "It is created from both the semen of the man and the semen of the woman. The man's semen is thick and forms the bones and tendons, while the woman's is fine and forms the flesh and blood."[2] The Qur'an, as shown above, states that the body is formed of the male semen. Again, "Let a human see from what he or she has been created. He or she has been created from water that gushes out from between the back and the chest bones" (86, 5–7). The Qur'an, therefore, prima facie would agree more with Aristotle than with Galen, except that it also states, without elaboration, that humankind is created from both male and female (49, 13; cf. 3, 1). Nevertheless, for subsequent theological doctrine, the Ḥadīth was decisive because the Qur'an was held to be less explicit on the matter. Mixed with the Ḥadīth is, of course, the Greek medical tradition, as has been shown by Bāsim Musallam in his *Sex and Society in Islam*.

Before presenting and discussing in some detail the Galen-Aristotle debate on the issue, Ibn Qayyim al Jauzīya, in his *Kitāb al-Tibyān* narrates this Ḥadīth: ʿĀyisha and Umm Salmā, two wives of the Prophet, asked him the same question, and in his answer, the Prophet "established the female semen": "Should a woman wash [her clothes] after nocturnal emission *[idhā īhtala-mat]*?" The Prophet said that she should if there is a trace of the fluid. They asked again: "Do women have nocturnal emissions?" The Prophet retorted, "How else do their children resemble them?" Ibn Qayyim also quotes another version of the Ḥadīth with the following addition: "Do you think that there is any other reason for the resemblance?" Said the Prophet: "When her semen dominates the man's semen the child [boy] will look like her brothers and when the man's se-men dominates her semen the child [boy] will look like his brothers."[3]

The principle that the fetus owes itself to both parents' contribution has not had much effect on doctrines of conception control, as we shall see below. But here some important laws may be noted on the status of the fetus and the baby. After the fetus becomes "ensouled," which happens after 120 days of preg-nancy, it becomes a "person" in a legal sense, and it has "rights." It may not be aborted, and its abortion counts as homicide. Also, it inherits just as any other living human does, except that until its sex is known, its precise share of inher-itance cannot be determined. The actual determination and disposal of inheri-tance must await birth, in fact, because a pregnancy may result in twins or triplets. Although the Qur'an stresses filial piety for both parents, it is especially tender toward the mother, for "in affliction did she carry him and in affliction did she deliver him" (46, 15). A Ḥadīth from the Prophet says, "The Paradise is under the feet of your mother." For this reason, the Prophet assigned the baby to its mother: "A woman said to the Prophet, 'this son of mine I carried in my womb, I suckled him with my breast and my lap has been his playground, but his father has divorced me and wants to take him away from me!' The Prophet said, 'You have a greater right over him so long as you do not marry.'"[4]

Contraception and Abortion

Conception control was practiced in pre-Islamic Arabia mostly by *coitus inter-ruptus* (*ʿazl*). But Ḥadīth is contradictory about whether Islam allows it.[5] There is a Ḥadīth according to which the Prophet said that contraception (*coitus interruptus*) is a "lesser infanticide." But according to another Ḥadīth, a man came to the Prophet and said, "We practice *coitus interruptus,* but we have some Jewish neighbors who say that this is a lesser infanticide." "They are ly-ing," retorted the Prophet. "It is not lesser infanticide; you may practice it, but if God has predetermined for a child to be born, it will be born." After some time, the man reported that his wife had become pregnant, upon which the Prophet said, "Did I not tell you that if a child is predetermined by God to be born it will be born?" It is most probable that neither of these contradictory Ḥadīths emanates from the Prophet but that both arise from a controversy ensuing in Islam after his death, when Arabs conquered neighboring lands and settled in garrison towns. For example, we have the report of a Friday sermon (khuṭba), given in Fustāt, the capital and garrison town of Egypt; in his sermon ʿAmr ibn al-ʿĀs (d. 663), the governor of Egypt after its conquest, stressed that the Arabs exercise restraint in reproduction.[6] The words of the Qurʾan in 4, 3, commonly understood by Muslims to mean "[Marry only one wife], *so that you will likely not go wrong*," have been interpreted by al-Shāfiʿī to mean "so that you will likely not have many children." The words in Arabic (*dhālik adnā an-lā-taʿūlū*) are capable of both interpretations.

There is, however, a third Ḥadīth which seems to have a ring of historical authenticity about it and according to which a companion of the Prophet reported, "We used to practice *coitus interruptus* [during the Prophet's lifetime] and he knew about it while the Qurʾan was also being revealed, but the Qurʾan did not prohibit it." It therefore seems plausible to hold that the common pre-Islamic practice of contraception was allowed to stand by the Prophet as it was, without his saying anything about it, although it would have been possible for him to ban it, if he had thought fit. The question was, however, consciously raised after him, when some people objected to it on certain grounds. It must be noted first of all that the Qurʾan, if it does not command reproduction, nevertheless was understood as encouraging it: "Your women are your tilth," it declares (2, 223). Although it denounces excessive attachment to property and sons as "mere tinsel of this worldly life" (18, 46)—particularly because pagan Arabs set such high priority on them—it nevertheless regards them as blessings of God. But an additional argument was brought by religious leaders to support large-scale reproduction: A Ḥadīth reports the Prophet as saying that, on the Day of Resurrection, he would be proud of the numbers of his community compared with other communities and portrays him as admonishing his followers, "So reproduce and increase in number."[7]

Notwithstanding this general policy statement, many prominent theologians and lawyers permitted contraception and some even abortion within the first four months of pregnancy before the fetus is "infused with life." Such "family planning" was, however, left to individuals and was never adopted as a general social policy.[8] Among the schools of law, the Ẓāhirī or the "literalist" school—which had few followers although it had some very prominent jurists, and which is currently rising to prominence in the Arab Middle East—absolutely forbids contraception and abortion. The Shāfiʿī school allows contraception unconditionally *to the husband,* who need not do it with the consent of the wife, for they contend that a wife even if she be free and not a slave has no automatic right to children but only to orgasm. This shows that the biological theory outlined above, according to which both spouses contribute to the generation of the fetus, had little effect on doctrines and laws about contraception, which were essentially based on considerations of social issues. Many lawyers of the other legal schools of Islam allow contraception only with the consent of both spouses, except in the case of a slave-wife. Most considered a slave-wife to be entitled to orgasm but not to ejaculation. According to some, however, the consent of a slave-wife is also necessary, while still others think that the consent of the owner of the slave-wife is necessary and not of the slave-wife because the child would belong to her owner (where the owner is not also the husband): the main reason behind reluctance to reproduce from slave women—and even to marry them—was that their children would also be slaves, which was not desirable.[9]

Among the authorities who allow contraception the most eminent is the Shāfiʿī jurist, theologian, and Sufi al-Ghazālī. Al-Ghazālī held that a truly pious person who has attained to "trust in God" (among the highest spiritual "stations" of Sufism) cannot resort to contraception because he or she *knows* that God, who has created a soul, will not leave it without sustenance. Therefore, for such a person to exercise conception control is *unlawful*. But people who have this kind of trust in God are very rare, while the average person is always haunted by worldly considerations. For such people, it is permitted to exercise conception control to free them of economic worries. Further, if a person fears that having children might force him or her to obtain livelihood by foul means like stealing or robbery, it is *mandatory* that he or she avoid having children in order to avoid the distinct possibility of committing sins. Al-Ghazālī goes so far as to hold that a man who fears that if his wife has children, her health or good looks might be affected *and he might come to dislike her* should refrain from having children.[10]

The impulse to procreate, a pervasive biological need, seems to be especially strong in the East. Particularly sons were considered to be a socioeconomic and moral, if not a biological, necessity. Although it is not so strong in Islam as, for example, in Hinduism, nevertheless, judging from the Qur'an, the Arabs' desire for sons was exceptionally great. This and other social factors coupled with the Prophet's Ḥadīth that Muslims must have large families and that he would be proud of their numbers on the Day of Resurrection, made for a high rate of fertility. Among the important social factors was the fact that generally neither the husband nor the wife had much amusement except each other as well as the fact that sons are regarded as old-age insurance. The number of Muslims in the world is estimated to be around nine hundred million and according to some claims exceeds one billion. The first responsibility of Muslim nations, given these numbers, is to control the flood of population growth, to improve the quality of life, and to distribute the resources of nature more equitably and conscientiously.

Since the 1960s, most Muslim governments have instituted family planning educational programs and have provided facilities to make the programs a success. However, these programs have not been successful. In fact, since March 1984, the government of Pakistan has put a virtual ban on family planning on "moral grounds." This is part of the sociomoral scene in Pakistan since the seizure of power by General Zia Ul-Haq, whose systematically retrogressive policies have almost annihilated the gains made during earlier, more liberal regimes. Khomeini's Iran is, of course, far worse in this respect than Pakistan. Khomeini has sacrificed (and is determined to continue to do so) such large numbers of young boys in the Iran-Iraq war that he can hardly afford to encourage family planning, even if he were inclined to do so (which, of course, he is not). Indeed, the Shi'a practice of *mut'a* or temporary marriage (banned by Umar I and made unlawful in Sunni Islam, but continued under the Shi'a law as even meritorious), although ignored by the late Shah's government, is getting high priority treatment from Khomeini's government, which has embarked upon a program of systemic "education of the public" in the doctrine and practice of *mut'a*.

As for the moral argument against the use of contraceptives, it is infructuous: it is not the contraceptives themselves that are immoral but their misuse. Family planning, however, is their correct use just as *coitus interruptus* was a correct method to achieve this very end. But if modern contraceptives can be misused for extramarital intercourse so could the *coitus interruptus*. It is, therefore, sheer confusion to regard the presence of modern contraceptive devices as immoral. It is analogous to the argument given by many Muslims which says that the abolition or restriction of polygamy would lead to sexual permissiveness just as in the West monogamy had led to or contributed to it. It is true that during the recent decades there has been increasing sexual permissiveness in the West, but it is not at all certain that monogamy had led to it or contributed to it materially. Nor is there any factual evidence nor any claim on the part of the Qur'an that polygamy confers any immunity from sexual deviancy. The ban on contraceptives imposed in Pakistan is apparently based on the legal-moral concept of "blocking the way to sin" (*sadd al-dharā'i'*) propounded by classical Muslim lawyers. This doctrine means that not only must sin be prevented but also the path or means to it must be blocked. It is on this basis that many religious leaders in the latter part of the 1900s and early decades of this century sought to prevent the public education of women; once women went beyond the protective four walls of the house, it was believed, their chastity would be threatened. This principle, although it does have a sound point, is obviously often taken to absurd lengths: when pushed far enough, its logic would require that one live on the mountains rather than in the cities where opportunities for sin abound. There are really no legal provisions sufficient to create a bulwark against errancy if the moral fiber is not strong enough, and, given strong moral training, legal defenses do not count for much.

In the Muslim countries, the only program acknowledged to be effective by the United Nations is that of Indonesia, although reports of the United Nations depend on the data supplied by the governments of the countries being studied. When I worked in Pakistan and was connected with the religious aspects of the implementation of the program for family planning (1964–68), my study showed that theological aspects were of limited importance. Of course, officials sought to bolster their policies with the opinions of religious authorities like al-Ghazālī, while the opposition exploited the opposite opinions. But I found those arguments were relevant only to the urban middle class and especially the lower middle classes, whose education was not high but who could read well enough to be largely influenced by the religious opposition to the family planning campaign. The higher middle and upper classes were generally convinced of the utility and even necessity of population control. But the bulk of the population lives in the countryside; there, as a matter of fact, peasants understood the force of the *economic* argument if it was cogently put forward, and the available evidence suggested that the program was fairly effective in places where it had been well communicated.

In the Muslim world as a whole, two types of religious opinions exist and work at two levels. The higher 'Ulama, who have a solid base in religious learning, generally allow family planning as an individual family's decision but strongly oppose it as an official policy. This is connected with a widespread belief, political in nature, that the idea of population control has originated in the West, which is frightened by the rising tide of the Third World population and therefore wants to control its growth. This argument has had powerful appeal on the urban masses in Third World countries and effectively counteracts official policies where they exist. "A child born in the United States," people are told, "consumes twenty times the resources a child in the Third World does." For every American child, then, the Third World can afford twenty. The moral overtones of the argument are obvious.

It has often been held that no policy of population control can be effective unless abortion is legalized, as in Japan. According to the 1969 United Nations estimate, the Japanese population was declining at a rate which if continued, would render the Japanese race extinct in three hundred years. But in the past decade, Japanese population has registered an increase, probably due to the extraordinary pace of industrialization. In Islam, as said above, several medieval jurists had permitted abortion within four months of pregnancy before the fetus was "ensouled," although the majority opposed it because the fetus was "going to be ensouled" and the coming into being of new life was not, therefore, a remote possibility but a ripe potentiality which could not be destroyed. A policy like the one adopted by the current Chinese Communists, under which mature fetuses are aborted under official aegis, will never succeed in Islam. But all this means that *individuals* have to be made conscious of what is at stake *for them* primarily, and only secondarily for the collective existence of Muslims, and that there is no conflict between the two but, rather, a coalescing of both interests. There does exist, it seems, the possibility of general acceptance of abortion within four months of pregnancy, which will go a long way in making population control effective.[11]

Notes

1. For this discussion, see Bāsim F. Musallam, *Sex and Society in Islam* (Cambridge: Cambridge University Press, 1983), 39ff., 46, 50.

2. Ibid., 39, 46.

3. Ibid., 50.

4. *Mishkāt,* 293 (Robson), 719–20.

5. Rahman, "Islam and Medicine," 591–92.

6. The *Khutba* of 'Amr ibn al-'Ās, in *Tārīkh 'Amr ibn al-'Ās* (Biography of 'Amr ibn al- 'Ās), by Hasan Ibrāhīm Hasan, 2d ed. (Cairo, 1926), 140–41; Abul Hasan Zaid Fārūqī, *Islam and Family Planning,* 3d ed. (New Delhi, 1976), 68.

7. Rahman, "Islam and Medicine," 592.

8. Musallam, *Sex and Society in Islam;* for Islamic law, 57–59; for medical practice, 69–71.

9. Rahman, "Status of Women," 290.

10. Rahman, "Islam and Medicine," 592.

11. Musallam, *Sex and Society in Islam,* 57–59.

BUDDHISM/HINDUISM

[27]

A Buddhist View of Abortion

Phillip A. Lecso

This essay examines the abortion issue from a Buddhist perspective. As the consciousness is held to enter the embryo at conception, it is felt to be fully human at that moment. Thus, Buddhism strongly discourages abortion except in the situation of an immediate threat to the mother's life. Though Buddhism has clearly a "pro-life" position on abortion, the final decision should be left to the pregnant woman.

The abortion debate rages on. Many different secular and religious viewpoints have been expressed. To this date, little has been written from the standpoint of the Buddhist teachings. I will attempt in this paper to present Buddhist aspects of the abortion issue. First will be a more traditional discussion based on standard teachings within Mahayana Buddhist scripture and commentary. To my knowledge there are no specific teachings per se within the voluminous Buddhist scriptures and commentaries on abortion, so that one must extrapolate from ethical and cosmological positions implicit within them. Following this discussion, I will undertake a short examination of the political implications of the abortion issue from the Buddhist perspective.

Within this paper I have drawn mainly from Tibetan Buddhist sources for two main reasons. First, there now exists a substantial body of works translated into English, available for a general audience. Second, Tibetan works, especially

SOURCE: From *Journal of Religion and Health* 26 (fall 1987). Copyright © 1987 by Human Sciences Press. Reprinted by permission.

those of the Gelugpa sect, are known for their scholarly and philosophical clarity. It is a commonly held misconception that Tibetan Buddhism is an unusual form of Buddhism off of the mainstream. Most Buddhist scholars now accept that Tibetan Buddhism is solidly based on traditional Mahayana Buddhist teachings and its main difference is in the cultural expression, not in substance.

As with all religious traditions, there are varying opinions amongst Buddhists, especially Western Buddhists, concerning abortion. Abortion is widely performed in some countries in which Buddhism is influential, such as Japan and South Korea. In other Buddhist countries, such as Sri Lanka, Thailand, and Burma, abortion is more restricted. There seems to be a trend toward increased abortion practices directly related to increased industrialization and movement away from traditional values.

The writings of Western proponents of Buddhism vary on the topic of abortion. Robert Aitken, a teacher of the Japanese Zen tradition, focuses on the woman's dilemma but is unclear on the ethical issues.[1] Roshi Philip Kapleau, also a teacher of the Japanese Zen tradition, states that "abortion is a grave matter."[2] However, he goes on to say, "There is no absolute right or wrong, no clear-cut solution."[3] A more clear stance has been taken by the Buddhist Churches of America, a Japanese Shin Buddhist sect. In a recent position paper on abortion, they state that "abortion, the taking of a human life, is fundamentally wrong and must be rejected by Buddhists."[4]

Key to the arguments in the abortion debate is the central question of when human life begins. The answer to this question has many times been obscured by the introduction of such concepts as viability or functionality of a central nervous system. Buddhist teachings are explicit as to when human life begins. This is in clear contradistinction to the following comment published from a symposium on the abortion issue, " . . . although Buddhism, the predominant religion, condemns 'killing of life,' it defines the commencement of life rather loosely."[5] Buddhist teaching holds that human life starts at conception.

From the moment of conception on, the embryo is already a human being.[6]

The cornerstone of Buddhist cosmology is a belief in rebirth. All sentient beings constantly undergo the cycle of birth-death-rebirth and have done so from beginningless time. They will do so through the foreseeable future until ended by the realization of enlightenment, the goal of Buddhism. Between consecutive lives, one's mental continuum passes through an intermediate state, known in the Tibetan tradition as the Bardo.[7] The following passage describes the emergence from the intermediate state to a new rebirth.

> After that, these drops of semen and blood, which definitely do emerge from both male and female, are mixed in the mother's womb. The consciousness of the dying intermediate being enters into the middle of this. . . . [8]

Thus, the mental continuum enters at the moment of conception and consequently the embryo is felt to be fully human. As opposed to the current materialistic viewpoint of consciousness as dependent upon the central nervous system for its existence, Buddhism teaches that this is not the case. Consciousness exists prior to the physical form. Therefore, arguments based on either development or functionality of a central nervous system as a basis for defining human life are not acceptable. This does not deny that there is a qualitative difference in the functionality of a fetus as it grows, but this carries no moral weight in argumentation concerning abortion. Consciousness is a whole, and its expression, not its development, follows along with the increasing complexity of the fetus.

It is quite difficult to defend logically any position that argues that one becomes human at any other time than at conception. A single human life starts at conception and ends at death. This is true of any sexually reproduced organism. It is interesting to note that one would be hard pressed to find a scientist who would argue that a dog fetus is not really a dog until some arbitrarily designated time period has elapsed. As pointed out by Mary Meehan, many of the arguments put forth in defense of abortion "appear to be guided by sociopolitical goals rather than scientific interest."[9] Life is a continuum that one can arbitrarily divide into phases such as embryo-fetus-infant-adult. However, these are mere conventions, and to base actions on these relative and arbitrary designations is quite logically unjustified.

Thus, to destroy an embryo or fetus would entail the taking of a human life. This is in direct opposition to the first Buddhist precept, which enjoins us to refrain from destroying life.[10] Does this apply to the "special circumstances" common in the abortion debate: rape, fetal deformity or disease, a threat to the mother's physical or mental health? These are difficult and complex issues.

We are all the same in that we wish to avoid suffering and desire to increase our happiness. In the "special circumstances," situations are such that in order to relieve her own suffering, a mother may seek an abortion. Where does this leave the life within her? In the case of rape, the conception occurs during a violent assault, placing the woman in the difficult situation of carrying the child of her assailant. Does her suffering justify the taking of the human life within her as the means of resolving the problem? The Buddhist would argue against this, basing the position on the high value placed upon the human rebirth. The human rebirth is "a life form hard to find and once found, very meaningful; a treasure more precious than a wishfulfilling gem."[11] Also:

> This body, the complete, opportune, fortunate basis, is of immense value, in no way to be conveyed even by such an example as finding a system of realms thrice-thousandfold, all full of precious jewels.[12]

Thus, the human rebirth is considered rare, difficult to obtain, and to be highly protected. This in no way relieves the woman of her suffering but is meant to encourage her to protect the life within her. Buddhism encourages altruistic attitudes emphasizing the benefit of others as opposed to our own narrow self-interest. Concern for the other life and its inherent value and potential may prevent the woman from adding another injustice to the situation.

The issue of fetal malformation and/or disease is basically one of euthanasia for the Buddhist. I have dealt with this issue in more detail elsewhere.[13] In cases such as Down's syndrome or spina bifida where a meaningful life is possible, Buddhism is strongly against aborting these individuals. There is insufficient reason to abort their existence merely because they cannot function as fully endowed human beings. More difficult are cases concerning problems such as anencephaly or Tay-Sachs disease. In these situations where viable extrauterine life is neither possible nor of prolonged duration, for some it would seem justifiable to terminate the life early. However, Buddhism teaches that life and life's events are complex, karmic interactions and undue interference in natural processes is to be avoided.

Last is the issue of a threat to maternal health. If the mother's life is truly endangered by continuation of the pregnancy so that both lives are at stake, it is permissible to abort the fetus.[14] Much less clear is the situation of implied threat to the mother's mental health. Here it is extremely difficult to predict the outcome upon her health and, therefore, aborting the fetus would not be permissible. It does not seem reasonable that one could predict inexorable and permanent mental injury from a completed pregnancy to the extent that the taking of another's life would be justifiable.

Thus it is clear that Buddhism has a "pro-life" position on abortion. However, unlike many fundamentalist Christian positions, Buddhism does not agree with attempts to legislate individual morality. It is recognized that we live in a pluralistic world and society in which toleration of divergent views is encouraged. As stated by his Holiness the XIV Dalai Lama:

> With the basic understanding of all humans as brothers and sisters, we can appreciate the usefulness of different systems and ideologies that can accommodate different dispositions, different tastes. For certain people under certain conditions, a certain ideology or cultural heritage is more useful. Each person has the right to choose whatever is most suitable. This is the individual's business on the basis of deep understanding of all other persons as brothers and sisters.[15]

Also:

> At the same time, we must openly accept all ideologies and systems as means of solving humanity's problems. One country, one nation, one ideology, one sys-

tem is not sufficient. It is helpful to have a variety of different approaches on the basis of a deep feeling of the basic sameness of humanity.[16]

Specifically on the issue of abortion, I will again quote from the Buddhist Churches of America position paper:

Although others may be involved in the decision-making, it is the woman carrying the fetus, and no one else, who must in the end make this most difficult decision and live with it the rest of her life. As Buddhists, we can only encourage her to make a decision that is both thoughtful and compassionate.[17]

To summarize, Buddhism is firmly against abortion, only clearly allowing it in the unusual circumstance of a physical threat to the mother's existence. Human rebirth is rare, of great value, and filled with potential. As has been shown, Buddhism rejects the arguments favoring abortion and argues strongly for protecting all human life. However, the decision concerning abortion should be left with the pregnant woman.

Notes

1. R. Aitken, *The Mind of Clover* (San Francisco: North Point Press, 1984), 21–22.

2. P. Kapleau, *Zen: Dawn in the West* (Garden City, N.Y.: Anchor Press/Doubleday, 1980), 248.

3. Ibid., 249–50.

4. Buddhist Churches of America Social Issues Committee, "A Shin Buddhist Stance on Abortion," *Buddhist Peace Fellowship Newsletter* 6, July 1984, 3, 6.

5. L. P. Chow, "Abortion in Taiwan," in *Abortion in a Changing World,* ed. R. E. Hall, vol. 1 (New York and London: Columbia University Press, 1970), 251.

6. G. Rabten, *The Essential Nectar,* ed. and verse trans. M. Willson (London: Wisdom Publications, 1984), 122.

7. *The Tibetan Book of the Dead,* trans. F. Fremantle and C. Trungpa (Berkeley and London: Shambhala Publications, 1975).

8. L. Rinbochay and J. Hopkins, *Death, Intermediate State, and Rebirth in Tibetan Buddhism* (Valois and New York: Gabriel/Snow Lion, 1980), 60.

9. M. Meehan, "More Trouble Than They're Worth? Children and Abortion," in *Abortion: Understanding Differences,* ed. D. and S. Callahan (New York and London: Plenum Press, 1984), 149.

10. T. Gyatso, *The Opening of the Wisdom-Eye* (Wheaton, Ill.: The Theosophical Publishing House, 1974), 53–64.

11. *Essence of Refined Gold*, trans. and ed. G. H. Mullin (Ithaca, N.Y.: Gabriel/Snow Lion, 1982), 58.

12. G. Rabten, *The Essential Nectar*, 197.

13. P. Lecso, "Euthanasia: A Buddhist Perspective," *Journal of Religion and Health* 25: 1, 51–55.

14. Based on an audience with His Holiness Ganden Tri Rinpoche (Jamphal Shenphen) during his recent North American tour at Washington, New Jersey, September 1985.

15. T. Gyatso, *Kindness, Clarity and Insight*, trans. and ed. J. Hopkins (Ithaca, N.Y.: Snow Lion Publications, 1984), 60.

16. Ibid., 60.

17. Buddhist Churches of America, 7.

[28]

Mizuko Kuyō: Abortion Ritual in Japan

William R. LaFleur

TODAY THE MIZUKO KUYŌ can be performed in many different ways. It comes in a wide variety of sizes, types, and costs. And monetary cost, of course, is usually directly correlated to the elaborateness of the ceremony and whether religious experts—priests and the like—are to officiate.

The simplest rite of all is probably the one with the oldest pedigree—that is, the one carried out by local women who have organized themselves into a confraternity to take care of the local Jizō shrine or shrines. This involves a kind of perpetual care for a simple sculpture or sculptures at a junction of streets—or at a roadside. The care involves putting out flowers in front of the icon, washing it down from time to time, and lighting a few sticks of incense once in a while. These Jizō shrines, whose otherworldly protection extends both to deceased children and aborted fetuses, are as close as possible to whole communities. It takes very little effort for anyone with concerns about such departed children to stop and bow at such sites. In the Japanese countryside and even in the residential sections of a metropolis such as Tokyo, such shrines can be found in abundance; from time to time people of the neighborhood, most likely women, will be seen stopping for a momentary act of kuyō.

Also very simple will be the rite at the household shrine. Fairly often today the mizuko will be remembered as if it were merely another "ancestor"—

SOURCE: William R. LaFleur, *Liquid Life: Abortion and Buddhism in Japan.* Copyright © 1992 by Princeton University Press. Reprinted by permission of Princeton University Press.

although technically it is not. When fine distinctions are not made, the fetus, which did not precede the living, is treated as an ancestor and will be remembered along with them at the Buddhist altar in those households that have them. In homes a small icon of Jizō can be placed on the altar and reverential bows can be made to it. If a bit more pious and concerned for such things, members of the family may also recite the words of the "Heart Sutra"[1] or a prayer addressed simultaneously to Jizō and the invisible dead fetus.

The next level of complexity involves paying for a stone image of Jizō and having it properly enshrined at one of the many cemeteries specializing in this. Such cemeteries can, as noted above, increasingly be found connected to temples of the established Buddhist denominations. During the past couple of decades, however, there has—in connection with the "mizuko boom"—been a large growth in the number of independent temples that deal exclusively in mizuko memorializing; often such institutions have little or no antiquity and may even be regarded as semiprivate *business* ventures. Their commercial aspects are patent. Persons who initially visit such places are often presented with stories of others who experienced tragedy when they "neglected" their mizuko, and such stories are soon followed by an outline of the temple's services and the fees charged. For a price, a concerned parent can have what in these cemeteries is tantamount to the "perpetual care" in American mortuary contexts. Periodic rites for the mizuko can be purchased—and it is not strictly necessary for the parent to be personally present on such occasions. The requiem then is vicariously performed.

Within the context of many established Buddhist temples, there is often a large Jizō icon or a set of six or more smaller ones bedecked with red bibs. There a parent can perform simple rites—largely bowing, observing reverential silence, lighting a candle, and maybe saying prayers or chanting. Some temples have an alcove filled with dolls and other items that in their own way relate to the departed child or fetus. Others have Jizō cemeteries or, in special instances, a collection of look-alike and rough-hewn stones that are designated as the Riverbank of Sai. Candles can be lit and coins deposited in such places. More and more, however, the mizuko kuyō is moving inside the temple as well. Many temples now have special days set aside for mizuko remembrance rites. Robed priests will then officiate, and the concerned parents will join a larger congregation of persons—the "parents" of mizuko—like themselves.

In fact, the mizuko rite now has an important role even outside of Buddhism; some of the "new religions" have made them a part of the panoply of services offered. Helen Hardacre vividly describes such a rite in the Oi church of Kurozumikyō, on the outskirts of Okayama City. In this case it is one offered to nonmembers:

The woman making the request, invariably the one who would have been the mother of the child, comes to the church, and a minister prepares an ancestral tablet [*mitama bashira*] for each aborted or miscarried child, writing a name and approximate date on each slip of white wood. Initially this is placed on a small movable altar adjacent to the ancestral altar of the church. The church's ancestral altar is decorated with particularly colorful flowers and food offerings and with a large red and white paper streamer, representing a symbolic offering of clothes for the child. Before the ancestral altar, the ministers recite the Great Purification Prayer and read a *norito* to console the child's spirit, directing it to enter the ancestral tablet previously prepared. The officiating minister, who has donned a paper mask covering the mouth, and an assistant then move to a temporary altar on which the tablet rests. The officiating minister directs the spirit of the child to enter the tablet as the assistant intones a long "Ooooo" indicating the spirit's passage into the tablet. Then the tablet is removed to the ancestral altar, and all assembled offer *tamagushi* before it while music is played.[2]

Here, as in many of the new religions of Japan, there is mix of Buddhist, Shinto, and even Christian elements. Much of the terminology of the rite just described is Shinto; moreover in that context, according to Hardacre, the soul of the unborn has to be purified, because in abortion or miscarriage it has been polluted by contact with blood—a distinctively Shinto theme. The institution performing this kind of mizuko kuyō is, significantly, a "church" and its officiant a "minister."

This confirms the fact that the impulse to deal with abortion through a ritual such as this comes from deep roots in Japanese culture. Although the practice has historically centered around the figure of Jizō and the largely Buddhist kuyō rituals, it can with apparently little difficulty now enter into the religious context of the new religions. There is, it seems, a deeply sensed need for such rituals and, when abortion is practiced across denominational and religious lines, so too, it seems, will rituals emerge.

Perhaps one of the most fascinating questions is whether mizuko ritual will enter into Japanese Christianity—or whether it has already begun to do so. Japanese researchers have already noted what seems an undue interest in the mizuko ritual by Western Catholics residing in Japan.[3] Some of the very few studies of mizuko in English have been published in a journal that is based at Nanzan University, a Catholic institution in Nagoya. Although this does not necessarily reflect institutional or even editorial policy, it is at least interesting to note that these studies have moved from initial criticism to an enlarged "understanding" and contextualization of these rites.[4]

It is not unreasonable to expect that in Japan what begins as the Christians' effort to understand phenomena within Japanese culture eventually may, with great caution, be accepted into the Christian context itself. Many Protestants have done just that with respect to rites for ancestors: although since the Meiji period, many Protestants in Japan scorned the kuyō for ancestors as compromises with false religion, in recent years even foreign missionaries in Japan have, according to reports in Japanese newspapers, been exploring the importance of ancestor rituals for family coherence. That is, once the Japanese family is understood to be—in its basic structure—even stronger than that of the Christian cultures of the West, it seems to some wasteful not to make an accommodation to the practices that make it so.

Mizuko kuyō may, in time, prove to be a context wherein the Catholic Church's adamant opposition to abortion comes—at least in Japan—face to face with what some perceive to be the emotional and ritual needs of persons who, rightly or wrongly, have had abortions. If this happens in Japan, even non-Catholics will have reason to watch with great interest.

And perhaps the underlying question will then become: Is such a rite merely something that arose to fit the peculiar and idiosyncratic needs of one culture, that of Japan, or does it accord with more generally human needs?

. . . In keeping with Gabrielle Taylor's analysis of guilt, I suggest that many Japanese who make ritual apology to an aborted fetus do so to retain their sense of their own humanity. . . . There clearly are instances of people being badgered into exacerbated guilt over mizuko. Still, the majority of those who do mizuko kuyō may do so, at least in part, because they want very much to keep on believing that they are sensitive, conscience-controlled persons—even though in undergoing an abortion they have felt virtually compelled to do something that would seem to fly in the face of that self-assessment.

This is to say, the terrible fact of abortion makes it all the more important for the "parent" of the fetus to find concrete evidence that she—and sometimes he as well—still remains a person who cares and who has human feelings. The hardness of the fetus-destroying act makes the excavation of a fundamental softness in the actor a matter of crucial importance. The guilt, then, can be a welcome sign, a gratifying testimony to the perdurance of a humanizing sensitivity still at the center of the self. The Japanese have a very basic word for this softness; they call it *kokoro*. Very often tears will be the outward signal of its presence.

Rituals, especially rituals of guilt and apology, are often the forms that confirm the sense that, in spite of everything, the person that one wants oneself to be is *still intact*. They are the arena of self-assessment. In Japan it is simply assumed that such rituals are given by the culture; they are simply available there as forms (*kata*) into which the individual can enter in order to be reaffirmed. But this does not mean they are mere externalities—as if without also a deep personal introspection such rituals would have no value. As a matter of fact, the participation in ritual is itself a mirror that the person holds up to herself or himself to prove thereby that she or he "cares" enough to be participating. The rite is self-reflexive. To be in ritual is, as Confucius suggested, to already *be* in Goodness. As noted by David L. Hall and Roger T. Ames, in their superb exposition of Confucian thought, "Ritual actions are not only performed *by* people, but, because they actively evoke a certain kind of response, in an important sense they 'perform' people."[5]

Sweaters, Not Lawyers

Persons in the West have trouble with this. Over recent centuries we have built into our own intellectual and social climate a many-layered set of objections and impatiences vis-à-vis both guilt and ritual. This puts us in a double bind in trying to understand this kind of practice in Japan. We expect that what is ritualized is likely to be concealing something nefarious. It *must,* we feel, be false. Ritual is suspect. Ritual is waste.

This is what is most likely to make things difficult for Westerners to see why Japanese who have had abortions are often quite willing to expend some of their valuable time and even make an outlay of cash to apologize to their mizuko. Perhaps the modern Western fantasy of finding a guilt-free culture or of turning oneself into a person no longer "burdened" by guilt is connected to the wish to have a culture without rituals. Our notions of what it means be rational and to be freed from the religious components in our own culture's past often include beliefs about an *economical* use of our time, our emotions, and our wealth. Guilt and rites do not fit well in such beliefs. Guilt has become an emotion many in our society are simply embarrassed to find in themselves.

What may be peculiar about the West is not that it had an unduly stressed concept of guilt but, rather, that in its modern phase it gave wide credence to the belief that guilt itself was and ought to be completely dispensable and there should be no need whatsoever for rituals in a truly rational society.

We will not find that in Japan—at least not to any comparable extent. And perhaps, then, we cannot really fault the Japanese for trying, sometimes a bit forcedly, to retain certain practices of the past, especially if such practices throw into relief the contrast with the West's rather rigid notions of what modernization means and what of the past is necessarily pared away to make for it. The Japanese, to the dismay of some critics in the West, are sometimes quite willing to be less consistently "modern" or even eagerly postmodern. And if the model of a normative modernity is fixed, this will make much of Japan—including certainly practices such as the mizuko kuyō—look like kitsch or like pastiche.

The practices of the past that the Japanese have intentionally retained cannot all be accounted for in terms of ideological manipulation. Many of the

Japanese social customs that have been selected for retention are things that we need to view as more than merely interesting, quaint survivals but also as other than the camouflage used by a political ideology. Even when we have noticed that it is usually political conservatives who beat the drums most loudly for the preservation of past culture, we have not fully *explained* that preservation.

The retention of ritual is a case in point. The Japanese have simply never subscribed to the modern Western notion that ritual is in conflict with a truly economic modernization and with rapid economic development. The paring away of such "uneconomical" social etiquette has not proven to be a necessity in Japan. Large amounts of time and energy still go into such things.

The deliberate refusal to allow litigation to become a deep and pervasive cultural pattern is another. With a still relatively small ratio of lawyers to the total population, Japan in the eyes of many of its people functions fairly well—and with just about as much social justice as anywhere in the world, perhaps quite a bit more than in most of it. This is a boat that does not, many feel, need rocking. To train and pour in a higher percentage of lawyers would be to fix something not perceived as really broken. On the other hand, the *disadvantages* of a society given over to pervasive and deep litigation are all too obvious to the Japanese. The notion that where there is more law there is more modern efficiency is, in the eyes of many, one of the odder myths of the modern West.

The notion that religion is somehow inimical to modernization is another idea cherished by many Westerners but openly and emphatically rejected by a lot of Japanese. That is so even if the practice of religion costs money—sometimes a good deal of it. Individuals will often complain about the outrageous cost of religious funerals and the like; still they go on paying and praying. Emiko Ohnuki-Tierney correctly observes, "To the Japanese, who may literally throw ten-thousand yen or hundred-yen coins to deities and Buddhas when they go to shrines and temples, the commercial side of contemporary religious establishments is quite within tradition—they have always paid for religious services."[6]

Much of what is given seems, even to many in Japan, not quite necessary. Yet people go on doing it. The society, at least as judged by the sheer quantity of its religious activities, still thinks of religion as important in public and private life. The contrast with its Marxist-Maoist continental neighbor could not be sharper. But that contrast, many Japanese people will privately suggest, only shows that the wise culture is the one that does not get rid of the gods too quickly. The gods and Buddhas, they often nowadays say with a laugh, seem—when it comes right down to it—to have done their own part in making the Japanese rich.

In the kuyō for mizuko a number of these things come into focus. Guilt and rite are still present and used. My point is that this is precisely why the practice of the rites for the mizuko arose in Japan—and came in as *the* Japanese way of handling the moral dilemma posed by the practice of abortion. Such rites both express and tap into a deeply enculturated pattern of thinking and behaving. Such cultural "inventions" are not accidental.

The pragmatic retention of religion is involved here too. In essence the Japanese, seeing abortion as a moral problem, have brought that problem directly into the arena of religious practice and tried to work out their own solution there. It is a problem that has its legal dimension, but in Japan there is not the sense that the problem might be somehow *solved* in the domain of law and litigation. The courts are not usually where consciences are treated.

The existence of the old kuyō concept and its adaptability for memorializing the large number of fetuses aborted in modern times constitute the Japanese "solution" in another sense too. They make it possible for many Japanese to tolerate the practice of abortion and still think of themselves as moral and even as "sensitive"—both individually and collectively. Kuyō demonstrates that the practitioner and, collectively, the culture still have *kokoro*—the capacity to be moved. That is, through this ritual their moral options are not limited to either categorically forbidding abortion or, at the exact opposite pole, treating the fetus as so much inert matter to be dispensed with guiltlessly.

The mizuko ritual gave another alternative. Although it involved the discomfort of feeling guilty for a while, it also permitted the involved parent both to have the abortion and to retain a self-image as humane and caring. The presence of guilt was an index to the presence of such admirable emotions, and the performance of the rite was an enacted bodily expression of the same.

Abortion was in this way neither forbidden nor treated lightly. It is an act that by definition objectifies, instrumentalizes, and even on one level rends a relationship—the one of the parent and child—that is ordinarily the epitome of what ought *not* be objectified, instrumentalized, or rent. Everywhere the mother-child relationship is ordinarily the paradigmatic expression of intimacy, of emotional and bodily closeness, of noninstrumentalized life together.

This is probably why the mizuko kuyō bends over backwards on every level of its multiple meanings to reassert the reality of the *bond of emotional intimacy* between the parent and the deceased child. In many small ways, the rite says that the fetus was not considered a mere "thing" and ought not, wherever it is, to harbor the feeling that its now-distant parents regard it as a thing. The whole language of the ritual is to negate any suggestion of thingness, any hint that the child in question was objectified and instrumentalized.

Thus there is so much attention paid to kuyō rituals, why prayers are chanted to remind the fetus that "out of sight" on the Riverbank of Sai does not mean "out of mind," why pinwheels are placed next to the statue that serves both as Jizō and surrogate child, why sweaters are lovingly knitted to keep the masonry icon from catching cold, why money is paid to the temple for the sake of the deceased child's "educational" needs, why the fetus's siblings in "this world" are brought to the cemetery for introductions, and why there can even be the equivalent of "graveside" conversations about going together to see the film "E.T." Even when absurd, and when "kitschy" from the usual Western perspective, the *importance* of these things to those directly involved cannot be denied. Kitsch can easily come under criticism when we apply aesthetic standards, but these may not be appropriate here. To the degree that it becomes the tangible focus of sentiment that, at least to the person most directly involved, seems to prove anew that there is a "softness" deep down, the usual criteria of aesthetics are inadequate.

Notes

1. Known as the *Hannya shingyō* in Japanese. An English translation can be found in William R. LaFleur, *Buddhism: A Cultural Perspective*, 82–83.

2. Helen Hardacre, *Kurozumikyō and the New Religions of Japan* (Princeton: Princeton University Press, 1986), 151.

3. Hashimoto Mitsuru, "Fuan no shakai ni motomeru shūkyō: mizuko kuyō," *Gendai shakai–gaku* 13:1 (1987): 42.

4. *Japanese Journal of Religious Studies,* in sequence these studies are: Anne Page Brooks, "'Mizuko Kuyō' and Japanese Buddhism," 8:3–4 (Sept.–Dec. 1981): 119–47; Hoshino Eiki and Takeda Dosho, "Indebtedness and Comfort: The Undercurrents of *Mizuko Kuyō* in Contemporary Japan," 14:4 (December 1987): 305–20; and Bardwell Smith, "Buddhism and Abortion in Contemporary Japan: *Mizuko Kuyō* and the Confrontation with Death," 15:1 (March 1988): 3–24.

5. David L. Hall and Roger T. Ames, *Thinking through Confucius* (Albany: State University of New York Press, 1987), 274. The impact of this aspect of Confucian thinking on Japan was probably deep. Nevertheless, Ogyū Sorai, although a Confucian, was so preoccupied with uneconomical "waste" that he could not see how Buddhist ritual could also be an act that "performs" people.

6. Emiko Ohnuki-Tierney, *Illness and Culture,* 144.

[29]

The Hindu Perspective

S. Cromwell Crawford

THE PRESENT STUDY WILL attempt to shed new light on aspects of the abortion issue from the perspective of the Hindu tradition. It is basically a religio-philosophical exploration based on classical texts, with no pretensions to any sociological claims.

The most important texts for our purpose are the medical manuals of Caraka and Suśruta which date from the beginning of the Christian era. The medical science they represent was known as *Āyurveda*, which has had a new lease on life in our own day. Semantically the word is significant for our study because the first term *(āyur)* defines the purpose of classical Indian medicine as the *prolongation* and *preservation* of life, and second term *(veda)* anchors the science within the religious tradition of the Hindus. Āyurveda was designated as a secondary science *(upānga)* linked to the Atharvaveda. This means that it looks upon science as collaborative with religion so that the cultivation of a sound body and mind is seen as ensuring the welfare of the soul.

From ancient times, the tradition out of which the medical manuals speak placed the highest premium on life in the womb. Feticide was killing. Correspondingly, there developed a system of supportive values, buttressed by rewards and punishments in this life and the next. Pregnant women were subjects of solicitude and were treated with kindness and care.

SOURCE: Reprinted from *Dilemmas of Life and Death: Hindu Ethics in a North American Context* by S. Cromwell Crawford, by permission of the State University of New York Press. © 1995 State University of New York.

Before we examine the tradition, we shall be spared some confusion by noting, as Julius Lipner points out in his seminal article on abortion, "the distinction implied in the Sanskrit between the terms for abortion *(garbha-, bhrūna-: hatyā, vadha)* and those for (involuntary) miscarriage. The former terms assume that a morally reprehensible killing (hatyā) has taken place, rather than an ethically neutral evacuation, dislodging, or excision, for example, while . . . the standard Sanskrit words for miscarriage refer simply to a falling or emission (of the embryo)."[1]

The *Śruti* Literature

The earliest Vedic literature provides us with an attitudinal framework, plus certain specific injunctions, that give us definite clues to Vedic views on abortion.

The Āyurvedic ideal of longevity is a predominant value of Āryan society. The Vedic sages want people to escape the pitfalls of premature death and to live to the optimum period of life, set at one hundred years. A vibrant "will to life" is resounded in numerous prayers. Although there is the recognition that men are mortal, there is hope through the "gift to men" of biological immortality—"life succeeding life."[2] A father prays: "May I be immortal through my children."[3] Since Āryan society was patriarchal, it is to be expected that genealogical continuity was sought through the birth of many sons,[4] though it would be incorrect to limit all references to progeny to apply only to sons. "As in the Veda *putra* means "a male child" as well as "a child" (e.g., *putra* for the child in the womb), one has to refer to the context to find out which of the two meanings is intended. (Śayana represents the attitude of later ages in interpreting *putra* in every context as a "male child.")"[5]

This quest for earthly immortality is reflected in positive attitudes toward women, marriage, and parenthood. The poet brings it all together in "The Wedding" hymn:

> *Behold the comely forms of Sūryā!*
> *her border-cloth and her headwear,*
> *and her garment triply parted,*
> *these the priest has sanctified.*

> *I take thy hand for good fortune, that thou*
> *mayst attain old age with me thy husband. Devas—*
> *Bhaga, Aryaman, Savitri, Purandhi—*
> *have given thee to be my house-hold's mistress.*

Pushan, arouse her, the most blissful one;
        through whom a new generation will spring to life.
She, in the ardour of her love, will meet me,
        and I, ardently loving, will meet her.

For thee at first they escorted
        Sūryā with her bridal train;
Give the wife, Agni, to the husband
        and also give her progeny.

Agni has given him the wife
        with long life and brilliance;
long-lived be he who is her husband,
        may he live a hundred autumns.

Soma gave her to the Gandharva,
        the Gandharva gave her to Agni,
And Agni has given her to me
        granting me wealth and sons.[6]

In the Yajurveda the womb is mystically exalted as the place in which *Purusha* (the Supreme Being) takes birth:

He is the Deity who pervades all regions,
        born at first, he is also within the womb.
Verily, he who is born and is to be born,
        meets his offspring facing him on all sides.[7]

The womb is here a metaphor of creation, denoting the manifestation of Deity as a continuous process, repeated from birth to birth, and encompassing the past, present, and the future. The womb is hallowed as the creative center of the universe and as the point of intersection of divine-human activity which unites all creatures with the "Lord of life."[8]

A unique feature of the Vedic hymns is their natural blending of spiritual and moral values with physical well-being—a note that is fully orchestrated in later Āyurveda. Longevity is not simply valued in terms of duration, but by the quality of life. The Vedic code of life does not tolerate distinctions based on spirit and matter, as in later periods, but displays the groundwork of a vision of life in which full biological growth—from womb to tomb—is a spiritual quest. Vigor, virility, valor and virtue are parts of a single mosaic. The ideal of brave warriors living for a hundred years has embryonic beginnings in fine offspring, and it is for such progeny that the seers pray.

Earth, Ether, Sky!
  May we be proud possessors of fine children,
proud possessors of fine heroes,
  and be well nourished by fine food.[9]

The above verse is one of many which illustrates the biological purpose of marriage in which Prajāpati (Lord of Creation) brings forth children through the coupling of husband and wife.[10]

We now move from the three earlier Vedas to the fourth Veda within the orthodox corpus, called the Atharvaveda (Veda of knowledge of magic formulas). It dates from 900 to 600 B.C. and is closely associated with the science of Āyurveda.

A. C. Bose rightly observes that in the address of the bridegroom to the bride—"I am song, thou art verse, I am Heaven, thou art Earth, we two together shall live here becoming parents of children"[11]—is a sacred formula that lifts "the biology of human reproduction to a spiritual plane."[12] Indeed, the formula was continued in later literature.

The Āyurvedic connection is systemically apparent in the Atharvaveda's preoccupation with the preservation and prolongation of human life. The sage sings:

> *For a hundred autumns, may we see,*
> *For a hundred autumns, may we live,*
> *For a hundred autumns, may we know,*
> *For a hundred autumns, may we rise,*
> *For a hundred autumns, may we thrive,*
> *For a hundred autumns, may we be,*
> *For a hundred autumns, may we become,*
> *Aye, and even more than a hundred autumns.*[13]

To preserve and prolong life, the union of body and spirit is the sine qua non of health—"May all my limbs be uninjured and my soul remain unconquered."[14] A healthy couple marries, and the "good fortune" of "ten sons" is sought from "bounteous Indra."[15] "Bearing sons," the wife becomes "queen of the home."[16]

Certain charms prevent miscarriage: that the "embryo be held fast, to produce a child after pregnancy!"[17] Defensive charms are employed against fiends of disease that produce abortions, such as Kanva, "the blood-sucking demon," "the devourer of our offspring."[18] There are charms also for easy parturition: that "the gods who created the embryo" may "open her, that she shall bring forth!"[19]

Given the values of the Atharvaveda, where life is construed as longevity, happiness as health, and boys as bounty, it follows that abortion is to be treated as a heinous crime, bearing the greatest guilt. In two hymns Pushan is invoked to wipe off "the misdeeds upon him that practiseth abortion!"[20] As the commentator explains, in a pyramid of evil, abortion is deemed the basest crime.[21]

Abortion as a crime is repeated in the Brāhmanas (1000–700 B.C.), which constitute the second major body of Vedic literature. The Brāhmanas are mainly ritual texts. The priests show little interest in questions of right and wrong, their imagination having run riot with the theory and practice of ritualism. The allusions to abortion are therefore significant.

In the Śatapatha Brāhmana abortion is used as a criminal yardstick to illustrate the despicable character of ritualistic sins and their punitive consequences. One passage conjures up the fate of an abortionist in order to evoke the hell awaiting a person who has violated the sacred prohibition against eating the flesh of an ox or a cow. "Such a one indeed would be likely to be born (again) as a strange being, (as one of whom there is) evil report, such as 'he has expelled an embryo from a woman,' 'he has committed a sin'; let him therefore not eat (the flesh) of the cow and the ox."[22]

Another passage, aimed at enforcing the carrying of the sacred fire around the neck of the sacrificer during the time of his initiation, warns: "Surely, he who kills a human embryo, is despised, how much more then he who kills him (Agni), for he is a god: 'Let no one become an officiating priest for an (Agni) who has not been carried about for a year,' said Vatsya, 'lest he should be a participator in the killing of this, a god's seed!'"[23]

More important than the textual evidence is the emergence, during the period of the Brāhmanas, of a new set of ethical values which make a permanent contribution to Hinduism's attitude toward the procreation and preservation of progeny. The need arose in Āryan society to strengthen the community and to safeguard its cultural heritage. The response was the introduction of the concept of *obligation* in the doctrine of *rna* (indebtedness). It was held that all Āryans were born with three binding duties: to the gods, to the sages, and to the ancestors. The first duty was discharged by the performance of sacrifices; the second, through the study of the Vedas; and the third, which interests us here, by producing sons, and thus ensuring the survival of the family. In time it was deemed a sin to seek liberation before the fulfillment of these values.

The Upanisads (700–500 B.C.) shed Vedic ceremonialism for the supreme quest of self-realization. *Brahman,* ultimate Reality, objectively perceived, is none other than *Ātman* in the depths of the self. *Tat tvam asi:* "That art thou." Liberation is the discovery of one's identity with the Supreme. To be sure, the Upanisads subscribe to a variety of metaphysical views, but the dominant belief in the unity of life has profound bearing on the status of the unborn and the taking of life. Given the monistic outlook of some Upaniṣads, it is a natural corollary that abortion is regarded as gravely evil.

This attitude is evident in two passages. The Bṛihadāraṇyaka Upaniṣad, describing the soul in the trance state—a state of deep, dreamless sleep—points out that the state is so much out of this world that deepest distinctions are erased, so that "the destroyer of an embryo becomes not the destroyer of an embryo," just as a father is not a father, and a mother is not a mother.[24] In the Kauṣītaki Upaniṣad we learn that the liberated soul, having realized his unity with the Ātman, is freed from his good and evil deeds because these deeds belong to the individual existence, now seen as illusory. In the following passage, Indra, declaring that knowledge of him is the greatest boon to men, says: "So he who understands me—by no deed whatsoever of his is his world injured, not by stealing, not by killing an embryo, not by the murder of his mother, not by the murder of his father; if he has done any evil *(pāpa)*, the dark color departs from his face."[25] In both passages, the Upaniṣads assume that abortion is among the most deplorable evils, subject to consequences that karmically affect both this life and the next, and that only through enlightenment is one delivered from its malevolent force.

The *Smṛti* Literature

We now examine the data from the Sūtra and epic periods found in the *smṛti* literature (that which is remembered), covering the period 500 B.C. to A.D. 300. *Smṛti* incorporates all authoritative texts outside the Vedas. The most important works for our purpose are the Dharma Sūtras, Dharma Śāstras, and the two epics.

The Dharma Sūtras are aphoristic codes *(sūtras,* threads) that impart general principles of moral law *(dharma).* Their sanctions for ethical behavior are religious, not judicial. The treatment of law is not systematic, and their teachings on civil and criminal law are scarce. The most significant of these early lawbooks are the Dharma Sūtras of Gautama, Baudhāyana, Vasiṣṭha, and Āpastamba. They date approximately from the sixth to the second centuries B.C.

The Dharma Śāstras date later than the Dharma Sūtras and are more precise and complete. Like the early lawbooks, the Dharma Śāstras are not as concerned with legal distinctions and technical definitions as with moral duties. The most authoritative text on the subject of *dharma*, professing divine origin, is the Laws of Manu. It is claimed: "What Manu says is medicine." The date of its composition is sometime between the first century B.C. and the second century A.D.

The Mahābhārata and Rāmāyaṇa are the two most cherished works of popular Hinduism. The epics are splendid illustrations of the evolutionary charac-

ter of Hindu thought, having undergone successive accretions and transformations over a period of four to five centuries.

The general picture that emerges from this vast literature is that life begins
at conception, feticide is a major sin, progeny is a great good, women are worthy of respect and care, and pregnant women are especially to be protected and
granted concessions.

Yājñavalkya presents a view of embryology in which the soul takes form at
conception and is progressively invested with all elements for human development.[26]

According to Manu, the process of hominization begins at conception,
whereby, through the act of impregnation, the husband takes birth as the fetus
in the womb of his wife. The wife is therefore called *Jāyā*, "inasmuch as the
husband is again born in her."[27]

The assiduous protection that is enjoined for the wife does not appear to
be so much for the woman's sake as for the purity of progeny, because, as stated
above, it is the man who has impregnated her that is reborn. This seems to
suggest that in the act of conception there is the implantation of the seeds of
personhood.[28] From day one, pregnancy is a particular man in the making.
Gestation is the development of a specific human who enters the womb at
conception.

This view of what takes place in the moment of conception is reflected in
the fixing of the dates for the *saṁskāras* (sacraments) by counting from the
time of conception, and *not from the day of birth*. For instance, Yājñavalkya de-
crees that the Upanayanam ceremony of a Brahmin must be in the eighth year,
calculated from conception.[29]

The belief that fetal existence is elementally human provides the basis for
branding the "killing of an embryo" as mortal sin, to be redressed by severe
penances and punishments. It is classified as one of the five *mahāpātakas* or
atrocious acts. Several authorities aver that the procurer of abortions is a
mahāpātakin. Gautama equates abortion with Brahmanicide, punishable by
the "deprivation of the rights and privileges of a Brahmana, and a degraded
status in the next world."[30] Similarly, Vasistha categorizes the *bhrūnahan* as the
slayer of a learned Brahmin or a destroyer of an embryo.[31] Such a comparison
can only mean the personalization of the embryo. Manu enjoins the same expiatory penance, even when a fetus is *unwillingly* killed, as for the sin of
"Brāhmana-killing."[32] Yājñavalkya places "destruction of the fetus" on par
with a woman's slaying her husband, and therefore subject to identical os-
tracism.[33] The personal factor that makes feticide a *mahāpātaka* similarly accounts for the celebration of progeny as a great good.

A father is expected to give his daughter in marriage upon attainment of pu-
berty in order that she may be fruitful. Should the girl menstruate before she

marries, the father is guilty of the sin of abortion and becomes degraded.[34] Vasiṣṭha endorses this teaching of Vyāsa and adds: "As often as are the menstrual courses of a maiden, who is desirous of, and is solicited in marriage by, a qualified bridegroom of the same caste, so often her father and mother are guilty of [the crime of] killing an embryo: such is the sacred law."[35] Vishṇu goes one step further and permits a maiden who has "passed three monthly courses" to "choose a husband on the expiry of her third menstrual period." Otherwise she lives in disgrace. He also states that a suitor "commits no sin, by carrying her away (from the custody of her guardians)."[36]

Once married, procreation is paramount. "He who does not visit his wife on the day of her menstrual ablution becomes certainly guilty of the dreadful sin of faeticide [sic]."[37]

Given its patriarchal structure, the procreation of sons is especially coveted, partly for economic and social reasons, but mostly for religious reasons. The *śrāddha* ceremony is a religious rite performed for deceased ancestors. It is believed to have the power to avert the sins of omission and commission of the parents which are visited upon their family. The rite also assists the admission of the deceased father into the company of the forefathers. It follows that a father not having a son to effectuate his passage into the assembly of the *pitṛ*, through *śrāddha* offerings, is indeed cursed.

This need for many sons accounts for the old Hindu law's recognition of twelve kinds of sons. Yājñavalkya describes one type of offspring *(kshetraja)* of a wife by a kinsman duly appointed to raise up issue to the husband.[38]

Because of their vital role in bringing sons into the world, pregnant women are accorded care and concessions. Yājñavalkya urges all indulgence: "By not giving what a woman, in pregnancy, wishes for, the embryo meets with some shortcomings, either [in the shape of] disfigurement or death. Therefore what is liked by [a pregnant] woman must be gratified."[39] Likewise Vishṇu exempts pregnant women from having to pay toll;[40] and Manu enjoins that the needs of the pregnant woman in the home must take precedence over those of the *atithis* (chance guests).[41] Again, the reason for Manu's insistence that the wife should be "assiduously protected" is that the husband takes birth within her womb, and "for the purity of his progeny. . . . "[42]

Female protection does not seem to be based on caste. Life is at stake, and hence all women have a right to protection. Yājñavalkya enjoins punishment upon one "who destroys the embryo of a female servant."[43] Killing any woman in her menses or who is pregnant is "equal to that of killing a Brahmana."[44]

From the time of conception, and thereafter as the child develops and grows, certain Vedic rites are called for to purify the individual both in this life and the next. Manu: "By means of the Vedic rites of consecration of the womb, post-natal purification, tonsure, and initiation with the thread, the sin of the

twice-born ones, pertaining to the seed and womb (of their parents) is ab-
solved."[45] Likewise, Yājñavalkya states that with the performance of the prescribed rites "the sin begotten of semen and blood, is dissipated. . . . "[46] This
expiatory function of prenatal rites attributes a personal character to the unborn; otherwise it would make no sense to claim the mystical removal of sin.

The common themes of the legal literature—identifying abortion as a
heinous sin, rejoicing in many sons, deference to pregnant women, and the
practice of *niyoga* (levirate marriage)—are all present in the Mahābhārata and
need not be repeated. They collectively affirm the ancient view that life in the
womb is not tissue of the mother's body, but a separate life bearing the essential marks of humanity from the time of conception.

The value that cradles this view of the unborn is *ahiṃsā* (nonviolence). It is
present in the rules of hospitality, gentleness, care for the young and aged, and
kindness to the land, birds, insects, animals; above all, it is the birthright of
that most vulnerable form of all existence—a child in the womb. And so it is
that Kṛṣṇa informs Arjuna that among the endowments of those who are born
with the divine nature, the first is nonviolence.[47]

The Āyurveda

Āyurveda (the science of life) is a branch of the Vedas. Over the centuries, it
has shaped the ancient ideas along the lines of medical, scientific, and rational
investigation. It treats the person as a psychosomatic unity, with due regard for
constitutional differences among individuals. It is a natural system that promotes a total style of life aimed at happiness and longevity. In the context of
this study, Āyurveda is concerned with the promotion of fertility and the
preservation of progeny. From among the numerous collections, the best-
known texts that have come down to us are those of Caraka, Suśruta, and
Vāgbhata. The first has known the greatest popularity, and has been commented upon by notable scholars.

We now explore the various concepts and theories in the Caraka Saṃhitā to
ascertain its line of thinking on the subject of abortion. The relevant section is
Śarīrasthānam (study of the human body).

We start with the concepts of *person* and *nature*. Both the human individual
and the natural world are seen as manifestations of the eternal Brahman. The
person and nature are constituted of six elements—earth, water, fire, air, ether,
and the spirit or self in the person and Brahman in the universe. Thus "person is
equal to the universe."[48] Man is a microcosmos of the macrocosmos, which
means that spirit and matter are not alien or opposite, but parts of an integral
whole.

In addition to the five *mahābhūtas* (gross elements) and the *ātman* (self), the individual is invested with *buddhi* (intelligence) and *ahankāra* (ego).[49] The ego is separable from the body and is made up of action, the fruit of action, reincarnation, and memory.[50] Conscious perception is brought about in the individual by the agency of the *Puruṣa* (transcendent self) which integrates the *ātman*, mind, senses, and sense objects.[51]

> There cannot be light, darkness, truth, falsehood, scripture, auspicious and in-auspicious actions if there be not the active and intelligent person. There would be no substratum (body), happiness, misery, going and coming, speech, understanding, treatises, life and death, knowledge and emancipation if the person were not there. That is why the person is recognised as the cause by the experts in (theory) of causation. If there be no self, light, etc., would be causeless; they cannot be perceived nor can they serve any purpose.[52]

Thus according to Caraka's theory of causality, the agent behind all happenings, including birth and death, the continuity of life, pleasure and pain, knowledge and ignorance, morality and immorality, is the everlasting, all-pervading, and changeless *Puruṣa*.

Life comes into being by the "conjunction" of body, mind, senses, and the self *(ātman)*. Caraka uses the figure of the "tripod" to illustrate the vital combination of the body, mind, and the self.[53] Life vanishes when any one part is missing.

Turning to the subject of the development of the fetus, Caraka delineates the factors from which the embryo is originated, the definition of the embryo, the factors producing the embryo, and the order of its development.

> Embryo is originated by the aggregate of these entities—mother, father, self, suitability, nutrition and psyche. . . .
>
> The combination of sperm, ovum and life-principle implanted in the womb is known as embryo.
>
> Embryo is the product of *ākāśa*, *vāyu*, *tejas*, *ap* and *pṛthvī* being the seat of consciousness. Thus, embryo is the aggregate of the five mahābhūtas being the seat of the consciousness which is regarded as the sixth constituent of embryo.
>
> Now the order in which the embryo is formed is explained. After the accumulated menstrual blood is discharged and the new one is situated, the woman having cleanly bathed and with undamaged genital passage, ovum and uterus is called as having opportune period. When the man having undamaged sperms cohabits with such a woman, his semen, the essence of all the śarīradhātus, is extracted from the whole body impelled by orgasm. Thus being impelled by the self in the form of orgasm and also seated by him, the semen having potentiality of a seed, is ejaculated from the man's body and through the proper track enters into the uterus and combines with the ovum.[54]

Thus conception occurs when the male semen (sperm cell) and the female ovum (germ cell), having come together in the act of intercourse, are united with the spirit which, in association with the mind, "descends into the zygote situated in the uterus," and "the embryo is formed."[55] "The entire process of receiving the qualities (of mahābhūtas by uniting with them) is completed within a subtle measure of time."[56]

It is important to note that the spirit is an original and necessary constituent of embryonic existence. It abides as the embodied soul, and provides the unborn life with spiritual continuity. The embryo is called "the self" precisely because it is the spirit that has entered the uterus, and having combined with the sperm and ovum, produces itself in the form of the embryo.[57]

Caraka has many interesting observations pertaining to heredity and embryonic growth, but significant for our purpose is the notion that it is the past karma of the individual, carried into the present embodiment, that imparts to the newborn child its special features, in addition to the contributions made by its parents.[58]

By virtue of its karmic inheritance, the unborn is invested with moral qualities, and as such is the object of medical care and protection. Similar care is extended to the mother. "The pregnant woman has to be managed very cautiously like one carrying a vessel full of oil without agitating it."[59]

On the basis of the evidence before us, Caraka Saṃhitā is allied with the earlier tradition found in the Śruti and Smṛti texts in opposing abortion as morally evil. It does so on the assumption that spirit is present in matter from the moment of conception, and is the causal agent in its progressive development. This creative manifestation of the spirit in the microcosmos is similar to the process of creation in the macrocosmos. On the human side, the moral character of the individual is also given in conception. Karma is carried over from one life to the next. Together, the spiritual and moral constituents of the individual make for the production of a person through a continuous process that is developmental but not disjunctive. It is therefore pointless to discriminate between different degrees of human potentiality in terms of "ensoulment," "viability," and "brain waves." The new life is an intimate, inseparable blending of human and physical-biological existence.

The upshot of Caraka's view is that at no time within embryonic development is there a state of pure matter in which the termination of that life is morally justified.

Caraka and the West

We have seen that the current abortion debate in the West is irreconcilably split between two camps: pro-life and pro-choice. One group stands for the inviolable right to life of the fetus as a full human person, and is therefore antiabortion. The other group upholds the woman's right to control her own body and its reproductive processes, and therefore stands for abortion-on-request. The Hindu position, represented by Caraka in particular, assumes a mediating position. It affirms the arguments of each camp while differing from both.

Along with the pro-life people, Hinduism believes in the spiritual creation of nascent life, which invests it with inviolable dignity and sanctity. The womb can be called an "incubator," but it is not for the woman's handiwork but for the Creator's. The embryo or fetus is more than tissue in the mother; it has a separate, individual life of its own. Just as there is no such thing as being "a little pregnant," gestation—from the first mitosis of the fertilized ovum-cell to birth—is one continuous process. To say that termination of the process is morally permissible at one stage but not at another is to truncate the untruncatable. Termination at an early stage may be easier and safer, but it is no less the termination of a person-in-being. The anguish of a pregnant woman may be real, but it is seldom commensurable with the fetus's life that is being taken.

At the same time, Hinduism breaks rank with Roman Catholic and Protestant fundamentalist representatives of the pro-life group on the grounds that the right to life of the fetus ought not to be absolutized. In place of absolute rights, Hinduism advocates addressing competing rights and values. Ethical dilemmas arise in cases of rape and incest and when the mother runs the risk of grave injury or death. Each situation is unique, with its own moral tragedy. The best we can do in such situations is evil, but then it boils down to a question of degree.

In a pregnancy where the mother's life is in a balance, Hindu ethics places greater weight on maternal rights than on fetal rights. The adult human being, having arrived at a karmic state in which there is much more at stake for her spiritual destiny, and in which there are existing obligations to be performed for family and society, is in a position to be favored over an equal human being whose evolution in this life is by comparison rudimentary, and who has not yet established a social network of relationships and responsibilities.

The Suśruta Saṁhitā, which comes to us from the beginning of the Christian era, recommends abortion in difficult cases where the fetus is irreparably damaged or defective and the chances for a normal birth are nil. In such instances the surgeon should not wait for nature to take its course but should intervene by performing craniotomic operations for the surgical removal of the fetus.[60]

The quality that Hinduism calls upon in tragic situations involving the necessary destruction of the fetus is *dayā* or compassion. Legislatively, this was the clear intent of the Medical Termination of Pregnancy Act of 1971 passed by the government of India. The bill states two indications for terminating pregnancy: "(1) The continuance of the pregnancy would involve a risk to the life of the pregnant woman or grave injury to her physical or mental health; or (2) there is substantial risk that, if the child were born, it would suffer from such physical or mental abnormalities as to be seriously handicapped." Two appendices follow:

Explanation 1—"Where any pregnancy is alleged by the pregnant woman to have been caused by rape, the anguish caused by such pregnancy shall be presumed to constitute a grave injury to the mental health of the pregnant woman."

Explanation 2—"Where any pregnancy occurs as a result of failure of any device used by any married woman or her husband for the purpose of limiting the number of children, the anguish caused by such unwanted pregnancy may be presumed to constitute a grave injury to the mental health of the pregnant woman."[61]

The quality of *dayā* lies at the heart of this Pregnancy Bill and is manifest in its humanitarian achievements. The legalization of abortion has removed the practice from unsanitized back rooms and the butchery of unscrupulous opportunists, and has placed it in government hospitals and clinics run by qualified medical personnel.

However, science is only as good as its practitioners, and today we witness the invocation of *dayā* through a convoluted ethic that attempts to hallow professional greed and public prejudice. Indian newspapers carry the familiar advertisement: "Boy or Girl—know the sex of the unborn child." The "boy-girl test" is determined by a scientific procedure known as amniocentesis. The *medical intent* of this test is to detect congenital deformities by sampling amniotic fluid which is withdrawn from the womb by a hypodermic needle during the sixteenth week of pregnancy. The fetus which is enveloped in the fluid casts off cells containing chromosomes which can be tested for birth defects; but the procedure also reveals the sex of the unborn. The test takes three weeks, costs Rs. 3000, and is totally accurate.

A second sex test is ultrasound. A machine takes a sonar picture of the fetus when the mother is sixteen weeks pregnant, and this picture shows what the fetus's sex is. The cost is about Rs. 300, and its accuracy is 90 percent.

Either way, should the test indicate that the fetus is female, the chances are high that the family will request the attending physician to perform an abortion, and this because the prejudice against females is old and deep. This medical practice is now a growth industry. Physicians who profit from this business do so on claims of compassion. The sugar-coated prescription of morality reads like this: "It is better to abort a female fetus than to subject an unwanted child to a life of suffering. People are willing to keep producing children until they get a son. Is it not better to let them have a choice so that they don't have six daughters before they have a son? The test, in fact, is helping the population control program of the government."[62]

If *dayā* is to be regulated by such specious logic, then the doctors should help round up all social outcasts—the poor, the sick, the aged—and mercifully kill them off, rather than allow them to be victimized by a heartless society. The population control program of the government should be helped even more!

Similar ethical reasoning was heard during the debate surrounding the Indian government's move to pass legislation that would ban sex-determination tests. The bill was drafted by the Health Ministry as a new amendment to the Medical Termination of Pregnancy Act of 1971, introduced in the Lok Sabha in December 1990. The bill was crafted to overcome the shortcomings of a similar law passed in Maharashtra in May 1988. Journalist Arvind Kala asks his readers to compare two scenarios: one allowing tests, the other not. Scenario 1: A couple having one female child is now trying for a boy, to complete a family of two children. A problem arises when the next child is also a girl. The wife then has a choice. "She can have an abortion and try for a boy again and again and again, each time terminating her pregnancy until she conceives a son."[63] Scenario 2: With tests banned, the wife delivers her second child, who again happens to be a girl. The cycle may be repeated. "Ultimately, a couple may be saddled with one, two, or three daughters they don't want. Is that fair? At this point the writer interjects the question of ethics. Our law allows abortions. To curb the population, the government encourages them. So can you question the motive—not wanting a girl—which leads to abortions?" Kala concludes: "Once sex-determination tests are banned countrywide, the government's position will be this: couples can decide the number of children they want, not their sex. Won't this affect family planning? Will couples not end up having more children than they want? Is it fair to bring into the world children the parents do not want?"[64] With such moral arguments to satiate families that might have qualms of conscience, the "boy-girl test" goes on, and baby girls die. Between 1978 to 1983, 78,000 female fetuses were aborted.[65]

The situation is clearly barbaric. No civilized society can condone the horrifying practice of female feticide. There is no accommodation here to the principles of Hindu ethics. What is needed is some legislation banning amniocentesis, except to determine genetic deformities. But the law must be enforceable. This means that when the procedure is used to determine the sex of the fetus, with the anticipation of aborting a female fetus, punishment should be meted out to all parties involved—doctors and clients—following the *satī* act model. The law should also shut down clinics in which these techniques are practiced.

The Maharashtra experience demonstrates that reliance should not be placed on law alone. Illegal operations have a way of springing up, which then charge high fees, and only the poor are penalized. In addition to law, social education is needed to end the age-old prejudice against women. Cultural accretions have created attitudes in the Hindu family which make blessings of boys and burdens of girls. The practice of dowry, outlawed in 1961 but still prevalent, is now exacerbated in a developing consumer society where the stakes are raised to include TVs, refrigerators, cars, and houses. These marital economics have ignited the ultimate evil of "bride burning" whereby young wives meet with convenient "accidents" around kerosene kitchen stoves, contrived by greedy husbands and in-laws. At least two women die such fiery deaths each day in the nation's capital. Social education and public awareness are essential parts of a solution. Where standards of literacy are high, dowry deaths do not take place, as in the state of Kerala.

Finally, it all boils down to the role of the physician who performs the "boy-girl test." Clinic advertisements meant to grab people's attention read: "Better to spend Rs. 500 now than Rs. 5000 later." The message is that the small sum spent now on aborting a female fetus will save the parents the huge price of a dowry down the road. This is exploitation at its worst because it elevates materiality above life, and destroys in the guise of good.

Doctors should be made to face these dilemmas at the time of their medical training. At the present time, Indian doctors are schooled in Western science but are ignorant of the medical ethics of their own culture. This may be due partly to the effort to distance themselves from Āyurvedic medicine, in which the ethical codes are found. But values have universal applicability, regardless of the mode of practice, Western or traditional; and the patients are the same people. The Caraka Saṁhitā is a rich repository of ethical codes pertaining to the training, duties, and privileges of the physician. While it regards the desire for success, wealth, and fame on the part of the doctor as proper and normal, it balances ambition with obligations to patients and to society. Caraka states: "When you join the medical profession and wish success in work, earnings of wealth, fame, . . . you should always think of the welfare of all living beings. . . . You should make effort to provide health to the patients by all means."[66] The passage is especially sensitive to the mental, physical, and social position of females. In no way must she be violated. The very thought of a young woman having to endure the pain of abortion with her only solace being the sparing of her unborn daughter the wrath of an angry family, would be utterly and unequivocally abhorrent to the medical codes of ancient India.

Notes

1. Julius Lipner, "The Classical Hindu View on Abortion and the Moral Status of the Unborn," in *Hindu Ethics,* ed. Harold G. Coward, Julius Lipner, and

Katherine K. Young (New York: State University of New York Press, 1989), 42.

2. RV. 4.54.2, in A. C. Bose, *Hymns from the Vedas* (Bombay: Asia Publishing House, 1966), 333.

3. RV. 5.4.10, ibid., 334.

4. RV. 10.85.45, ibid., 139.

5. Ibid., 334.

6. RV. 10.85.35–41, ibid., 135–37.

7. Yajurveda vs. 32.4, ibid., 301.

8. Ibid. vs. 5.

9. YV. vs. 8.53, ibid., 92.

10. RV. 10.85.43, ibid., 137.

11. AV. 14.2.71, ibid., 12.

12. Ibid.

13. Atharvaveda 19.67.1–8, ibid., 97.

14. Atharvaveda 19.60.2, ibid.

15. RV. 10.85.45, ibid., 139.

16. Atharvaveda 2.36.3, ibid., 125.

17. Atharvaveda 6.17.2, in *Sacred Books of the East,* ed. F. Max Muller (New Delhi: Motilal Banarsidass, 1987 reprint), vol. 42, p. 98.

18. Atharvaveda 2.25.3, ibid., 36.

19. Atharvaveda 1.11.2, ibid., 99.

20. Atharvaveda 6.112.3, ibid., 165.

21. 6.112 Commentary, ibid., 521.

22. Śatapatha-Brāhmaṇa 3.1.2,21, ibid., vol. 26, p. 11.

23. Śatapatha-Brāhmaṇa 4.5.1, 62, ibid., vol. 43, p. 272.

24. Bṛihad-Āraṇyaka Upanishad 4.3.19, in *The Thirteen Principal Upanishads,* trans. Robert E. Hume (London: Oxford University Press, 1971), 136.

25. Kaushītaki Upanishad 3.1, ibid., 321.

26. Yājñavalkya Saṁhitā 3.75, in *The Dharam Shastra: Hindu Religious Codes,* ed. M. N. Dutta (New Delhi: Cosmo Publications, 1978), vol. 1, p. 130.

27. Manu Saṁhitā, 9.8, ibid., vol. 5, p. 316.

28. Ibid. vs. 9.

29. Yājñavalkya 1.14, in Dutta, op. cit., vol. 1, p. 4.

30. Gautama Saṁhitā 22, ibid., vol. 3, p. 706.

31. Vaśishtha 20.23, in Muller, op. cit., vol. 14, p. 105.

32. Manu Saṁhitā 11.87, in Dutta, op. cit., vol. 5, p. 397.

33. Yājñavalkya 3.298, ibid., vol. 1, p. 159.

34. Vyāsa Saṁhitā 1.7, ibid., vol. 3, p. 508.

35. Vaśishtha Saṃhitā 15, ibid., 800.

36. Vishṇu Saṃhitā 24.41, ibid., vol. 4, p. 875.

37. Parāśara Saṃhitā 4.14, ibid., vol. 3, p. 555.

38. Yājñavalkya Saṃhitā 1.68–69, ibid., vol. 1, p. 12.

39. Ibid. 3.79.

40. Vishṇu Saṃhitā 4.130, p. 831.

41. Manu Saṃhitā 3.114, ibid., vol. 5, p. 102.

42. Ibid. 9.9, vol. 5, p. 316.

43. Yājñavalkya Saṃhitā 2.237–240, ibid., vol. 1, p. 104.

44. Vishṇu Saṃhitā 36.1, ibid., vol. 4, p. 891.

45. Manu Saṃhitā 2.27, ibid., vol. 5, p. 39.

46. Yājñavalkya Saṃhitā 1.13, ibid., vol. 1, p. 3.

47. The Bhagavadgītā 16.2.

48. Caraka Saṃhitā, Priyavrat Sharma, ed. and trans. (Varanasi: Chaukhamba Orientalia, 1981), Śārīrasthānam 5.4, vol. 1, p. 440.

49. Ibid., Sa. 2.63–64, p. 403.

50. Ibid., Sa. 1.52, p. 401.

51. Ibid., Sa. 1.39–42, p. 400.

52. Ibid.

53. Ibid., Sūtrasthāna 1.46–47, p. 6.

54. Ibid., Sa. 4.4–7., pp. 428–429.

55. Ibid., Sa. 3.3, p. 419.

56. Ibid., Sa. 4.8, p. 429.

57. Ibid., Sa. 3.8, p. 422

58. Ibid., Sa. 11.23–27, p. 415.

59. Ibid., Sa. 8.22, p. 469.

60. Suśruta-Saṃhitā: A Scientific Synopsis, ed. P. Ray, H. Gupta, and M. Roy (New Delhi: Indian National Science Academy, 1980), 22 (Cikitsasthana 15.6–7).

61. O. P. Jaggi, "History of Medical Ethics: India," in Encylopedia of Bioethics, W. T. Reich, gen. ed. (New York: The Free Press, 1978), vol. 3, p. 910.

62. Seema Sirohi, "Indians Embrace the Boy-Girl Test," Honolulu Star-Bulletin, 22 March 1988.

63. Arvind Kala, "Banning Sex Tests: Unfair, Unworkable," Times of India, 25 January 1991.

64. Ibid.

65. Sirohi, op. cit.

66. Caraka Saṃhitā, op. cit., vol. 2, p. 354.

PART THREE

ABORTION AND FAITH

Moral Analysis in Christian Perspective

[30]

Abortion: Its Moral Aspects

Charles E. Curran

A position paper on the morality of abortion from the Roman Catholic perspective must of necessity be somewhat selective. The following pages will center on three specific facets: the correct statement of the official teaching of the hierarchical magisterium, the possibility of dissent, and the present state of debate within Roman Catholicism.

Proper Statement of the Teaching

The most succinct and correct statement of the official teaching of the hierarchical magisterium is: Direct abortion is always wrong. Pope Paul VI's encyclical *Humanae Vitae* condemns "directly willed and procured abortion, even if for therapeutic reasons."[1]

A very accurate summary of the reasoning and statement of the Catholic position was given by Pope Pius XII in a 1951 address to an Italian family group.

> Innocent human life, in whatsoever condition it is found, is withdrawn, from the very first moment of its existence, from any direct deliberate attack. This is a

Source: Originally published in *The Jurist* 33 (1973). Reprinted by permission of the author. The same essay was reprinted in *New Perspectives in Moral Theology* (Notre Dame, Ind.: Fides, 1974).

fundamental right of the human person, which is of general value in the Christian conception of life; hence as valid for the life still hidden within the womb of the mother, as for the life already born and developing outside of her; as much opposed to direct abortion as to the direct killing of the child before, during or after its birth. Whatever foundation there may be for the distinction between these various phases of the development of life that is born or still unborn, in profane and ecclesiastical law, and as regards certain civil and penal consequences, all these cases involve a grave and unlawful attack upon the inviolability of human life.[2]

The ultimate basis of the teaching on abortion comes from the sanctity or dignity of human life. However, the precise teaching on abortion requires two more specific judgments before it can be accurately articulated and formulated. The first judgment concerns the question of when human life begins. The second judgment involves the solution of conflict situations.

On this question of the beginning of human life there has been and still is a difference of opinion among Catholic theologians. Catholic canon law in its history often acknowledged a theory of delayed animation and did not propose the same penalties for abortion before animation and abortion after animation although both abortions were considered wrong. Thomas Aquinas and a majority of medieval theologians held such a view of delayed animation.[3] Even in the twentieth century there were still many Catholic theologians maintaining the theory of delayed animation.[4] Pope Pius XII acknowledges this in a long citation from his address to "The Family Front." Although Catholic teaching allows diversity on the theoretical question of when human life begins, in practice the question was solved by saying that one must act as if life is present from the beginning. If there is doubt whether or not life is present, the benefit of the doubt must be given to the fact that there is human life present.[5]

Such an understanding should guide Catholic statements on abortion, especially when voices become raised and shrill with the attendant problems of oversimplification and sloganeering. Abortion from the viewpoint of Catholic teaching thus should not be called murder or infanticide, because even Church teaching acknowledges that human life might not be present there. One must strive to be as accurate as possible in these matters.

Likewise, one distorts the true Catholic teaching by claiming that Catholic teaching forbids all abortion. In reality Catholic teaching does acknowledge the existence of some conflict situations which are solved by the application of the principle of the double effect. Direct abortion is always wrong, but indirect abortion can be permitted when there is a proportionate reason. The two most famous examples of indirect abortion are the cancerous uterus and the ectopic pregnancy. Pope Pius XII emphasized that he purposely used the term direct abortion, or direct killing, because indirect abortion could be permitted.[6] He defined direct killing as a deliberate disposition concerning innocent human life which aims at its destruction either as an end in itself or as the means of attaining another end that is perhaps in no way illicit in itself.[7]

Unfortunately, statements in the past about the Catholic position have not always been as accurate and precise as they should have been.

Possibility of Dissent

Recently Roman Catholic theology has publicly recognized that a good Roman Catholic can dissent from the authoritative or authentic, noninfallible papal teaching on artificial contraception. The question also arises: Is dissent possible on the question of the condemnation of direct abortion?

The teaching on direct abortion does belong to the category of authentic or authoritative, noninfallible hierarchical teaching. This teaching has been proposed in various responses of different Roman congregations and especially in the encyclical *Casti Connubii* of Pope Pius XI. Pius XII frequently reiterated and explained in his allocutions the condemnation of direct abortion. The Pastoral Constitution on the Church in the Modern World of Vatican Council II spoke of abortion as an infamy and an unspeakable crime but unfortunately did not make explicit the necessary distinction between direct and indirect abortion.[8] However, this question was really not a central consideration in this document. Obviously, the comments made in this document are to be interpreted in light of the general Catholic teaching on the subject. *Humanae Vitae* carefully restated the condemnation of direct abortion even if done for therapeutic reasons.[9]

The historical tradition indicates there was a solid historical basis for the teaching that has been expressed with greater precision from the time of St. Alphonsus as the condemnation of directly willed and procured abortion.[10] Perhaps the greatest deviation in the historical tradition concerns the expulsion of an inanimate fetus to save the life of the mother and even the reputation of the mother. John of Naples, an obscure fourteenth-century theologian whose work is known to us only through citations from others, apparently allows the abortion of an inanimate fetus to save the life of the mother. The animated fetus cannot be aborted.[11] This opinion was also maintained by Antoninus of Florence. However, Antoninus expressly denied the liceity of abortion to save the life of the mother if the fetus is already animated. He also expressly condemned the abortion of an inanimate fetus if the purpose was merely to hide the sin of the mother.[12] Later, Sylvester da Prieras presented his opinion in the same manner.[13] The same opinion was maintained by the influential Martin Azpilcueta, better known as Doctor Navarrus.[14]

A theologian named Torreblanca exerted a great influence on some seventeenth-century theologians. Torreblanca taught that before animation a woman may procure an abortion if because of the birth she is in danger of death or even of losing her reputation. In this case the fetus is not yet animated and her action is not homicide. Torreblanca cites seven authors in favor of his opinion, but he mistakenly cites Antoninus, Sylvester, Navarrus, and Sanchez as favoring his position, which they did not do in the case of abortion to protect the reputation of the woman.[15]

Leo Zambellus, explicitly following Torreblanca, held that if it is licit to procure an abortion before animation to save the life of the mother, it is also licit to save her reputation.[16] John the Baptist de Lezana allowed abortion before animation in the case of a noblewoman or a nun who sinned with a man and feared death or loss of reputation or scandal if her sin were known, but he accepted the expulsion in these cases only if it is the last available means.[17] John Trullenchus cited Torreblanca and Pontius (wrongly in this case) as permitting the abortion of an inanimate fetus as the last remedy in preserving a pregnant girl's life or reputation. Trullenchus himself denied such an opinion, but he admitted that the affirmative opinion is not improbable.[18] Gabriel of St. Vincent also argued against the possibility of abortion of the inanimate fetus, but he did admit some extrinsic probability as did Trullenchus.[19] The majority of theologians did not accept such an opinion.[20] On March 2, 1679, among sixty-five errors condemned by the Holy Office was the following: "It is licit to procure an abortion before the fetus is animated lest the girl be killed or lose her reputation if the pregnancy is detected."[21]

This historical section is included because other writers do not mention Torreblanca and those depending on him. The recognition of this fact indicates that even in the historical development there was some vacillation among Roman Catholic theologians, but the opinion permitting abortion of the inanimate fetus to save the reputation of the mother did not really arise again after the condemnation of 1679. In the question of therapeutic abortion even of an animated fetus to save the life of the mother, John R. Connery claims there was no official condemnation by the Church until the nineteenth century.[22]

In comparing the teaching on abortion with the Church's teaching on contraception it should be noted that John T. Noonan Jr., who has extensively studied the historical tradition on both questions, argues strenuously in favor of the Catholic teaching on abortion, while he disagrees with the traditional condemnation of contraception.[23] There do exist some few vacillations in the historical development, but one could still find there the general basis for the present teaching of the Catholic Church. The crucial problem remains the fact that life itself changes and develops, so that one cannot give absolute value to a tradition which merely repeats the past and does not enter into dialogue with present experience and with the discontinuities which can exist in the present, even though one could also conclude there are no such discontinuities.[24]

Thus from the fact the condemnation of direct abortion belongs to the authoritative and authentic, noninfallible papal teaching, and from the fact there is a long historical tradition that despite some vacillations serves as a basis for such a teaching, one cannot legitimately conclude there cannot be dissent from, or possible change in, the Catholic Church's teaching on direct abortion. In fact, I argue there can be both dissent from and change in the accepted Catholic teaching denying direct abortion.

The possibility of dissent from authoritative, noninfallible Church teaching has been demonstrated on the basis of the Church's own self-understanding of the assent due to such teaching.[25] But it is necessary to understand the theological reason justifying the possibility of such dissent. The possibility of dissent rests on the fact that in specific moral judgments on complex matters one cannot hope to attain a degree of certitude that excludes the possibility of error. In more complex matters one must consider many different facets of the question and circumstances so that one cannot expect to exclude all fear of error.

The present teaching of the Church on abortion depends on two very important judgments: the judgment about when human life begins, and the judgment about the solution of conflict situations involving the fetus and other values, such as the life of the mother. Even our brief historical summary indicates that in the past there has been some dispute on both these issues. The following section will furnish additional proof of the possibility of dissent based on the fact that some Roman Catholic theologians are now dissenting from and disagreeing with the accepted teaching of the Church on the condemnation of direct abortion. One can rightly suppose that the dissent will become even more prevalent in the future. Thus even in the question of the morality of abortion it is impossible to speak about *the* Roman Catholic position as if there cannot exist within Catholicism a dissent from this teaching.

Present State of the Debate

Until a few years ago there was no debate within Catholicism on the question of abortion. Earlier there had been other discussions on the question of craniotomy and the possibility of killing the fetus to save the life of the mother, but there was no dissent from the authoritative teaching proposed in *Casti Connubii*. Today there is an incipient debate within Catholicism that deserves to be brought to public attention and discussed, but there is comparatively much less dissent on abortion than on artificial contraception.

Within the last few years most episcopal conferences have made statements defending the accepted Catholic teaching.[26] In the United States, Germain Grisez has published a detailed study on abortion that, with one small exception (the possibility of killing the fetus to save the mother), defends the traditional opinion. As mentioned, John Noonan and others have also defended the existing teaching. However, there are some theological voices both here and abroad that have begun to disagree with the official teaching.

The remainder of this essay will review the recent discussion within Roman Catholicism. The fact that this discussion is comparatively new in Roman Catholicism can be documented by comparing what is mentioned here with the discussion of Roman Catholic theologians as recorded by Daniel Callahan in his far-reaching study on abortion published in 1970.[27] Our present discussion will neither repeat the work done by others such as Callahan nor will it attempt to be totally exhaustive. Rather representative opinions will be outlined and criticized.

The first crucial question in the moral judgment on abortion concerns the beginning of human life. Here there have been some recent divergences from the Catholic teaching that insisted, at least in practice, on the fact that one had to act as if human life is present from the time of conception. Callahan, in his study, has described three generic theories about the beginning of human life—the genetic, the developmental, and the social consequences approach.[28] In the recent Catholic discussions I see two different approaches proposed. The first approach can be called the individualistic approach, with almost exclusive dependence on biological or physical criteria. The second type can be called a relational approach, which is unwilling to accept just physical criteria and argues for what it would call more personalistic criteria for the beginning of human life.

The first characteristic of the relational school is the unwillingness to accept a determination of when human life begins on the basis of biological criteria alone. The destination of the embryo to become a human being is not something that is inscribed in the flesh alone but depends not only on the finality inscribed in the biological aspects, but even more so on the relation of acceptance and recognition by the parents who engage themselves in the act of procreation. Thus it is fruitless to look for a biological moment in which human life begins even if it would be possible to determine such a moment.[29]

Bernard Quelquejeu likewise denies that fecundation alone marks the beginning of human life, for the fruit of conception becomes human only through a procreative will expressed by the mother, the parents, and in some way by society itself.[30] Jacques-Marie Pohier explicitly mentions the fact that in other societies the decision about accepting one into the life of the tribe or the society was made after birth. Although disagreeing with such an approach, he contends that the motivation behind it was an attempt to show respect for life and the obligation of the society to care for the life that is accepted into it. Such approaches do show the relational aspect of acceptance that is required for truly human life.[31]

If the biological criteria are not sufficient, then one must ask what are the criteria for determining the existence of human life. Based on the notion of procreation as a free act of the parents and on the importance of relationship, these authors indicate the need for an acceptance by the parents and to some extent by society itself. Louis Beirnaert rejects an objectivist view that sees the fruit of conception as a being in itself when contemporary epistemology shows the participation of culture and of a knowing or recognizing element in the very constitution of the object of discourse. A human interrelation implies the recognition of the other as similar—the human face of the other. But this similarity is not present in the fetus or embryo. But even before this face is present, the parents, by their acceptance of the fetus—especially through giving a name—make the fetus a subject who has a place in the world. It is not a child until the decision of the parents anticipates the human form to come and names it as a subject.[32]

One can raise the question about when the relational recognition and acceptance take place. At least in some explanations it appears that this can take place any time before birth. For example, Pohier argues that there are economic, psychological, cultural, and even faith aspects of human life in addition to the biological aspects. What is the human life God wants for a man or woman? In effect, all depends, even from the point of view of God, on the possibility that men and women have to sustain a human life for that which will be born from this embryo.[33] Bruno Ribes asserts that in all the cases in which the relationship between the infant and the parents does not exist now or will not exist at birth, one has the duty to ask about the legitimacy of allowing such a child to be born.[34]

These authors generally take very seriously the fact that many people in our contemporary society obviously do not have difficulty in terminating a pregnancy under certain somewhat broad criteria. Quelquejeu calls for an entirely new theological methodology in light of such experience. One can no longer begin with established moral principles and apply them to these different cases, but rather one must begin with the moral experience as manifested in these different decisions. The experience of women who decide to have an abortion definitely constitutes a true source of moral reflection—a *locus theologicus*.[35]

Although I admit to some uneasiness in making the judgment about the beginning of human life, I cannot accept the relational approach described above. In reality it seems that some of the authors themselves do still hold a biological and individualistic criterion, namely birth. Apparently, none of them is willing to apply the relational criterion once the child is born, but some would be willing to apply it before this time. If one accepts only a relational approach in terms of recognition by parents and somewhat by society itself, there seems to be no reason to draw the line at birth. After birth these relationships could so deteriorate that one could judge there was not enough of a relationship for truly human existence.

Likewise, it is necessary to realize the problems existing on the other end of life; namely, the time of death. All the standards acceptable today for determining death are based on individualistic understanding as determined primarily by physical or biological criteria. Death is understood by some as the breakdown of the three basic human systems of circulation, respiration, and brain function. Some might want to define death only in terms of brain death, but all these understandings of death and tests for the presence of death follow an individualistic model. There would seem to be great problems in allowing a relational criterion that could then claim death has occurred when human relationships are no longer present.

In addition, the relational criterion that is proposed does not itself accept a full mutuality of relationships. One could press on with this criterion to say that truly human relations must be mutual and thus the child needs to acknowledge and recognize the gift of the parents before there is a truly human relationship present.

I do not want to deny the importance of relationality in human life and existence, but at the very beginning of human life or at the end of human life we are obviously not dealing with human life in its fullest actuality. Here we are dealing with the bare minimum that is necessary for individual human existence. People do exist in relationships, but more fundamental and basic is the fact that human beings are individuals called to enter into relationships with others in the growth and development of their own human lives.

Some proponents of this approach are not the only ones who mention the theoretical importance of the fact that many women see no moral problems in their decision to have an abortion. I agree that, on the one hand, the experience of people is an important consideration in moral theology. Catholic moral theology itself must recognize this, for it has accepted a natural law on the basis of which all people can arrive at ethical wisdom and knowledge. Thus one cannot write off the experience of people who are not "good Catholics" or "good Christians." On the other hand, one must also recognize that the experience of people can be wrong. Human limitation and sinfulness affect all our judgments and decisions. In many aspects of life we realize that even conscientious people are not able to agree on what is right or wrong. We know from history that the human race has unfortunately accepted some human behavior, such as slavery and torture, which we are not willing to accept today. Yes, one cannot neglect the experience of people who have made their decision in a particular matter, but such experience must always be subject to critical reflection.

The second generic approach to the question of the beginning of human life sees the basis of human life in terms of the presence of a human individual and usually employs physical or biological criteria to establish this fact. Such an approach, like the previous one, could insist on a developmental or process understanding of the development of human life, but it will still be necessary to draw some lines about when individual human life is present.

One could, from this perspective, adopt the time of birth or even the time of viability. In my judgment, birth and viability tell us where the individual is or can be and not necessarily what the individual is. It is important to acknowledge that at this time, to my knowledge, no Catholic theologians explicitly propose birth as the beginning of human life.

Joseph Donceel has written often on the subject and espouses a theory of delayed animation that, in his judgment, is the teaching Thomas Aquinas proposed, not on the basis of his admittedly inaccurate biological knowledge, but on the basis of his philosophical theory of hylomorphism.[36] According to the Thomistic theory, the soul is the substantial form of the body, but a substantial form can be present only in matter capable of receiving it. Thus the fertilized ovum or early embryo cannot have a human soul. A human being's spiritual faculties have no organs of their own, but the activity of cogitative power presupposes that the brain be fully developed, that the cortex be ready. Donceel admits he is not certain when the human soul is infused into the matter, and he draws what appears to be a somewhat strict criterion in light of his above understanding. The least we may ask before admitting the presence of a human soul is the availability of these organs: the senses, the nervous system, the brain, and especially the cortex. Since these organs are not ready early in pregnancy, he feels certain there is no human person until several weeks have elapsed.[37]

John Dedek, after reviewing some of the theological literature on the question of the beginning of human life, admits there is doubt. He resolves the problem in practice by balancing off the probability of life and the reasons justifying abortion. He allows abortion up to the beginning of the third week for such circumstances as rape or even grave socioeconomic reasons. He even states there is a prudent doubt until the twelfth week and perhaps even until the fetus is technically viable, although he has really given no proof for the latter part of this statement. Only very serious reasons, such as grave danger to the physical or mental health of the mother or some serious physical or mental deformity of the child, could justify an abortion during this time.[38]

Wilfried Ruff has proposed that the individual life begins with the cortical function of the brain. Spiritual animation takes place at this time. Contemporary medicine also tests for death by the irreversible loss of the functioning of the cortex. The same test seems to be logical for the beginning of human life.[39]

In a matter as complex as this I have to admit there is some basis for these proposals, but I cannot accept them. Actual human and personal relations do not really take place until after birth. Truly spiritual activity does not take place until after birth. In my judgment, the basis for these actions is not qualitatively that much more present because there is now a cortex in the brain. A great deal of potentiality and development is still required. I do not see the rudimentary emergence of these organs as a qualitatively different threshold that can determine the difference between human life and no human life.

The argument about the consistency of tests for the beginning of human life and the end of human life does have some attractiveness. Frankly, I see it as a good approach with those who do not believe human life is present until much later. In this whole question of life it is important to respond with some logical consistency to the questions raised about the beginning of human life and about the end of human life, but one must realize what the test is trying to measure. The irreversibility of the coma is the decisive factor in the test for death. The test tries to measure if there is present any immediate potentiality for spontaneous life functioning. At the beginning of life this can already be present before there is measurable electrical brain activity.

My own particular opinion is that human life is not present until individuality is established. In this context we are talking about individual human life, but irreversible and differentiated individuality is not present from the time of fecundation. This single fertilized cell undergoes cell division, but in the process twinning may occur until the fourteenth day. This indicates that individual human life is not definitely established before this time. There is also some evidence for recombination—one human being is formed from the product of more than one fertilization.[40] Thus I would argue that individuated human life is not present before this time. Corroborating evidence is the fact that a great number of fecundated ova are expelled from the uterus before they could ever reach this stage of the fourteenth day.

Notice that my argument is based on the concept of individuality that employs biological data to determine when individuality is present. The appearance of rudimentary organs, in my judgment, does not constitute a qualitative threshold marking the beginning of individual human life, for much development is still necessary. I have purposely refrained from using the term person or personal life, because as argued above, the actual signs of such personal life do not seem to be present until well after birth. Obviously, many Roman Catholic theologians still argue that human life begins or probably begins at conception, and confirm this argument from genetics that reminds us there is present from the very beginning a unique genetic package. However, I do not believe the individuality that is required is yet present.

An important study that needs to be done in this whole area is the question of probabilism and what to do when there is some doubt. My own tendency is to draw the line earlier so as to give the benefit of the doubt to individual existing human life. The older official Catholic teaching, which is still maintained by many Catholics, explicitly employs probabilism in this question. In one way or another this must enter into all the judgments made on this question. It would be an important contribution to indicate how various authors deal with this concept.

The second crucial moral question concerns the solution of conflict situations in which the life of the fetus is in conflict with the life of the mother or with some other value. Catholic theology has traditionally solved such conflict situations in the question of abortion by the concept of direct and indirect abortion. Direct abortion is always wrong, but indirect abortion may be permitted for a sufficient reason. The basis of the distinction between direct and indirect, as noted earlier, is found in the nature and direction of the physical act and its effects.

In the question of abortion according to traditional Roman Catholic teaching, the only possible conflict situation involves two innocent individuals and is solved by the application of the principle of direct and indirect effects. In cases outside the womb, Catholic theology admits the unjust aggressor situation in which the unjust aggressor, even if the aggressor is in no way subjectively guilty for what is being done, can be repulsed by killing if necessary to protect life or other values proportionate to life. Thus anyone familiar with Roman Catholic moral theology recognizes that more possible conflict situations have been admitted for life outside the womb than for life inside the womb.

There is comparatively widespread dissatisfaction among Roman Catholic theologians today about the resolution of conflict situations by the concept of direct and indirect effects. Even some who maintain most of the traditional Catholic teaching admit that in some cases the fetus may be killed to save the life of the mother even though the general and even official interpretation of the older teaching would not allow it.[41] Germain Grisez argues that the principle of double effect in its modern formulation is too restrictive insofar as it demands that even in the order of physical causality the evil aspect of the act not precede the good. Grisez then gives some illustrations in which he would admit abortion to save the life of the mother provided no other act must intervene to accomplish the good effect.[42]

Other Catholic theologians have given even more radical theoretical interpretations to the understanding of the principle of the double effect. Many Catholic theologians today would be willing to accept in principle my earlier stated solution to the problem of conflict situations in abortion.[43] "Conflict situations cannot be solved merely by the physical structure and causality of the act. The human values involved must be carefully considered and weighed. . . . As a Christian any taking of life must be seen as a reluctant necessity. However, in the case of abortion there can arise circumstances in which the abortion is justified for preserving the life of the mother or for some other important value commensurate with life even though the action itself aims at abortion 'as a means to an end.'"[44] Richard McCormick, after studying six different modifications of the concept of the direct effect, also concludes that one cannot decisively decide the morality of the conflict situation on the basis of the physical structure of the act but ultimately on the basis of proportionate reason.[45]

In this light the question arises about what constitutes a proportionate reason. In other conflict situations in the past, especially in the case of unjust aggression, Catholic theology has been willing to equate other values with physical human life itself. Manuals of moral theology justified the killing of an unjust aggressor as a last resort in defense of one's life, bodily integrity, spiritual goods "of greater value than life or integrity," such as the use of reason or conservation of reputation in very important matters, and material goods of great value.[46] In my opinion such a balancing of values could also be present in conflict situations involving abortion. Thus abortion could be justified to save the life of the mother or to avert very grave psychological or physical harm to the mother, with the realization that this must truly be grave harm that will perdure over some time and not just a temporary depression.

From my theological perspective there is also another theoretical justification for abortion in some conflict situations based on a theological notion of compromise. The theory of compromise recognizes the existence of human sinfulness in our world because of which we occasionally might be in a position in which it seems necessary to do certain things that in normal circumstances we would not do. In the case of abortion, for example, the story as reported about women in Bangladesh who were raped and would no longer be accepted in their communities if they bore children out of wedlock illustrates a concrete application of the theory of compromise.

A fair assessment of contemporary Catholic moral theology indicates a growing dissatisfaction with the concept of direct killing, which in the case of abortion would call for a greater number of conflict situations, even though some might disagree with my understanding of proportionate values or with my other justification for abortion on the basis of compromise.

Although some Catholic theologians today are questioning and denying the traditional Catholic teaching in the area of abortion, it is necessary to realize precisely what they are saying. I have not read any Catholic theologian who holds that the fetus is just tissue in the womb of the mother, or that the woman may abort for any reason whatsoever. No Catholic theologian, to my knowledge, accepts abortion of the fetus as just another form of contraception needing no more justification than any other use of contraception. At times I feel that some Catholic theologians are so involved in intramural discussions about abortion they do not emphasize that their opinions also differ quite markedly from many others in our society who seem to see nothing at all wrong with abortion. My own position does differ somewhat from the accepted Catholic position both about the beginning of human life and the solution of conflict situations, but I am adamantly opposed to any position that does not recognize some independent life in the fetus and that justifies abortion as just another form of contraception.

In closing this summary of contemporary Catholic moral theology on the moral aspects of the question of abortion, it is important to recall that this essay has presented just the newer and different opinions that have recently appeared. These positions are not held by the majority of Catholic theologians, but there is sizable and growing number of Catholic theologians who do disagree with some aspects of the officially proposed Catholic teaching that direct abortion from the time of conception is always wrong.

Notes

1. *A.A.S.* LX (1968): 490.

2. *A.A.S.* XIII (1951): 857.

3. John T. Noonan Jr., "Abortion and the Catholic Church: A Summary History," *Natural Law Forum* 12 (1967): 85–131.

4. H. M. Hering, "De tempore animationis foetus humani," *Angelicum* 18 (1951): 19.

5. John Canon McCarthy, Problems in Theology, vol. 1, *The Sacraments* (Westminster, Md.: Newman Press, 1956), 15–21.

6. *A.A.S.* XLIII (1951): 859.

7. Ibid., 838.

8. Richard A. McCormick, "Past Church Teaching on Abortion," *Proceedings of the Catholic Theological Society of America* 23 (1968): 133–37.

9. *A.A.S.* LX (1968): 490.

10. John T. Noonan Jr., "Abortion and the Catholic Church." Note that in my judgment Noonan misinterprets the position of Thomas Sanchez and of Arthur Vermeersch. Germain G. Grisez, in *Abortion: The Myths, the Realities, and the Arguments* (New York: Corpus Books, 1970), 117–84, also misinterprets Sanchez, for he holds like Noonan that Sanchez would allow the abortion of an inanimate fetus to save the life of the mother that might be threat-

ened if it were known she had conceived through sinful intercourse. On p. 168 Grisez maintains about Sanchez that apparently he alone in the Catholic tradition holds such an opinion. Although Sanchez did not hold such an opinion, in the next paragraph in the text I mention some Catholic theologians who did hold such a position.

11. John of Naples is cited by both Antoninus of Florence and Sylvester da Prieras in the places referred to in the next two notes.

12. S. Antoninus, *Summa Theologica* (Verona, 1760), Pars III, Tit. VII, Cap. III.

13. Sylvester da Prieras, *Summa Sylvestrina* (Antwerp, 1569), Medicus, n. 4.

14. Martinus Azpilcueta, *Enchiridion sive Manuale Confessoriorum et Poenitentium* (Venice, 1593), c. XXV, n. 60–64.

15. Franciscus Torreblanca, *Epitome Delectorum sive De Magia* (Lyons, 1678), Lib. II, Cap. XLIII, n. 10.

16. Leo Zambellus, *Reportorium Morale Resolutorium Casum Conscientiae* (Venice, 1640), Medicus, n. 11.

17. Joannes Baptista de Lezana, *Summa Questionum Regularium seu de Casibus Conscientiae* (Venice, 1646), Tom. III, Abortus, n. 5.

18. Joannes Aegidius Trullenchus, *Opus Morale* (Barcelona, 1701), Tom. II, Lib. V, Cap. I, Dub. 4.

19. Gabriellus a S. Vincentio, *De Sacramentis,* Pars IV, De Matrimonio, Disp. VII, Q. V, n. 42.

20. The following theologians cite the opinion proposed by Torreblanca but do not follow it: Zanardus, Amicus, Franciscus Bonae Spei, Azor, Diana, Sporer.

21. *E.S.,* No. 2134.

22. John R. Connery, "Grisez on Abortion," *TS* 31 (1970): 173.

23. John T. Noonan Jr., *Contraception: A History of Its Treatment by the Catholic Theologians and Canonists* (Cambridge: Harvard University Press, 1965).

24. The understanding of the value of the historical tradition as expressed in this sentence is similar to the opinion expressed in a roundtable discussion by René Simon, *Avortement et respect de la vie humaine,* 233.

25. Joseph A. Komonchak, "Ordinary Papal Magisterium and Religious Assent," *Contraception: Authority and Dissent,* ed. Charles E. Curran (New York: Herder & Herder, 1969), 101–26.

26. For a summary of these, see D. Mongillo et al., "L'Aborto," *Rivista de Teologia Morale* 4 (1972): 374–77.

27. Daniel Callahan, *Abortion: Law, Choice, and Morality* (New York: Macmillan, 1970), 409–47.

28. Ibid., 378–401.

29. Bruno Ribes, "Recherche philosophique et théologique," *Avortement et respect de la vie humaine,* 200.

30. Bernard Quelquejeu, "La volonté de procréer," *Lumière et Vie* 21, no. 109 (Août-Octobre, 1972): 67.

31. Jacques-Marie Pohier, "Réflexions théologiques sur la position de l'église Catholique," *Lumière et Vie* 21, no. 109 (Août-Octobre, 1972): 84.

32. Louis Beinart, "L'avortement est-il infanticide?," *Études* 333 (1970): 522.

33. Pohier, *Avortement et respect de la vie humaine*, 179.

34. Ribes, *Avortement et respect de la vie humaine*, 202.

35. Quelquejeu, "La volonté de procréer," 57–62.

36. Joseph F. Donceel, "Abortion: Mediate vs. Immediate Animation," *Continuum* 5 (1967): 167–71. Cf. Donceel, "A Liberal Catholic View," *Abortion in a Changing World*, vol. 1, ed. Robert E. Hall (New York: Columbia University Press, 1970), 39–45; see also Donceel, "Immediate Animation and Delayed Hominization," *TS* 31 (1970): 76–105.

37. Joseph F. Donceel, *TS* 31 (1970): 83, 101.

38. John F. Dedek, *Human Life: Some Moral Issues* (New York: Sheed & Ward, 1972), 88–89.

39. Wilfried Ruff, "Das embryoale Werden des Individuums," *Stimmen der Zeit* 181 (1968): 107–19; Ruff, "Das embryoale Werden des Menschen," *Stimmen der Zeit* 181 (1968): 327–37: Ruff, "Individualität und Personalität in embryoanalen Werden," *Theologie et Philosophie* 45 (1970): 24–59.

40. Andre E. Hellegers,"Fetal Development." *TS* 31 (1970): 4–6.

41. Edouard Pousset, "Etre humain déjà," *Études* 333 (1970): 512–13; Roger Troisfontaines, "Faut-it légaliser l'avortement?" *Nouvelle Revue Théologique* 103 (1971): 491.

42. Grisez, *Abortion*, 333–46.

43. For a perceptive summary of recent debate on this question, see Richard A. McCormick, "Notes on Moral Theology," *TS* 32 (1971): 80–97; Cf. *TS* 33 (1972): 68–86.

44. *A New Look at Christian Morality* (Notre Dame, Ind.: Fides, 1968), 243.

45. Richard A. McCormick, *Ambiguity in Moral Choice* (Milwaukee: Marquette University, 1973).

46. Marcellinus Zalba, *Theologia Moralis Summa* II: *Theologia Moralis Specialis* (Madrid: Biblioteca de Autores Christianos, 1953), 276–77.

[31]

Personhood, Covenant, and Abortion

Marjorie Reiley Maguire

ABORTION CONTINUES TO BE one of the most difficult moral problems of the day for ethicists, particularly Christian ethicists. The moral debate concerns the questions of whether persons have an inviolable right to life which should always be protected by both ethics and law, and whether every act of abortion can be described as the sin of killing and a violation of a person's right to life. Behind the debates on this topic frequently lie contradictory or, more often, unexamined understandings of the meaning of person and when personhood begins.

What I intend to do here is to explore the frequently overlooked questions, "What is a human person?" "When does personhood begin?" and "Who or what is the agent or efficient cause of personhood?" I strongly disagree with Richard McCormick, who says that the word person "only muddies the moral discussion."[1] What muddies the discussion is to avoid the word person. The ontological reality of what is being aborted profoundly affects the moral evaluation of the act of abortion. The only reasons to resist questions about personhood are to avoid subjecting unexamined presuppositions about the nature of fetal life to critical analysis and to avoid threatening a preestablished agenda to either prohibit or allow all abortions.

My primary intention in this presentation is not a matter of ethics *per se*. It is a metaphysical task that might be described as preethical. But from the pro-

SOURCE: Slightly abridged version published in *Annual of the Society of Christian Ethics 1983*. Copyright © 1983 by Georgetown University Press. Reprinted by permission.

posed answers to the metaphysical questions ethical conclusions concerning abortion will follow.

By way of introduction, I begin this paper with the epistemological recognition that both good ethics and objective thought occur not when one lacks any presuppositions or emotions on a subject, since that is humanly impossible, but when one recognizes the assumptions, biases, and feelings that are part of one's life, and considers how they may have influenced one's thought. In an effort to be objective on this important subject, especially since I will attempt to put forth a new understanding of the beginning of personhood that is compatible with a prochoice and a feminist point of view, I wish to share briefly with you five aspects of my individual experience and my beliefs which I acknowledge have influenced my pursuit of the questions here.

First is the experience of having been pregnant, which has served to convince me that it is romantic to speak of a human life in its early stage of development as a person. I realize that the experience of pregnancy is not unique to me, and that other women who have shared this experience may or do not share this conclusion. I hope that the definition of personhood and the description of its beginnings I will give will allow for that difference. The experience of pregnancy has also convinced me, however, that the fetus becomes a person before birth.

Second is the experience of having had a child with a genetic disorder that causes progressive degeneration of the brain and central nervous system and brings about an early death. From this child I learned in an immediate way that personhood and the value it connotes are not simply a function of a capacity for intelligent activity or an ability to perform useful tasks for society.

Third is the experience of having to face the possibility of abortion myself. We learned that our first child had his genetic disorder, and that I am a carrier of it, when I was three months pregnant with our second child. We were fortunate that amniocentesis revealed that our second child is free of this disorder, and that I did not have to have the abortion I was sure I would have had if the diagnosis had been different. However, I then had to ask the question whether it was moral to try to have any other children, if a future pregnancy would carry with it the possibility of abortion, especially since such an abortion would have to be performed relatively late in the pregnancy after amniocentesis. My decision was that it is moral to try to become pregnant under these circumstances. (Mother Nature has kept me from having to face the moral problem beyond this theoretical level.)

My fourth "bias" is a strong identification with feminism that has taken root in me in recent years. Feminism does not mean that one automatically approves of abortion, but it does mean that one looks at the reality of pregnancy from the woman's point of view. As a feminist then, one is forced at least to ask whether the availability of abortion as a legal choice represents a loss of respect for life, or whether it actually represents an increase of respect for the life of the woman, and a conviction that she can be trusted to make a responsible moral choice in an area that so intimately affects her and the life she bears within her. A feminist viewpoint would help one understand the woman who recently said to me, "The antiabortion movement presents itself as only trying to value prenatal life as much as it values my life, but what it says to me is that I am no more valuable than a fertilized egg." I might add that many Jews and blacks have the same problem as this woman when antiabortionists compare abortion to the lives taken in Nazi death camps or degraded by slavery. Finally, feminism makes one realize that any right a woman may have to choose an abortion derives ultimately not from individualistic principles of liberation that simply give persons unlimited rights over their bodies; it derives rather from the realization that self-determination is inextricably linked to embodiment. As Beverly Harrison has written, "In any social relation, body-space must be respected or nothing deeply human or moral can be created."[2]

My fifth and final presupposition, or, more correctly, creedal assumption, is the belief that persons are immortal, and that Christian ethics and any discussion about abortion is meaningless without the conviction that persons transcend death.[3] This conviction does not mean that abortion is an easier thing to justify on the grounds that the fetus, if a person, will be with God anyway. Rather, it means that abortion is harder to justify, if the fetus is a person, because there are eternal repercussions to one's act of abortion. These eternal repercussions do not involve damnation for the woman who has an abortion, but aborted connections with earthly life for the fetus who is aborted. If an afterlife has any connections with life in this world, then the quality of a person's life at the time earthly life is ended affects the quality of life in the next world. This makes voluntary and premature termination of personal life a more serious act than it would be without belief in an afterlife.

These are the elements which have influenced the questions of this paper and which have undoubtedly influenced the conclusions. I trust the conclusions reached are no less objective or true for all of that.

The Legality of Abortion

While this presentation will touch on the moral question surrounding abortion, it will not address the legal question of abortion. As I have argued briefly elsewhere,[4] even if prenatal human life at every stage of its development—from the first moment of fertilization to birth—is considered a person, the life of such a "person" is not entitled to protection from the law until it is viable.

(Viability, of course, is a somewhat fluid category.) In other words, I would have agreed with McCormick if he had said that the word "person" muddies the *legal* discussion rather than the *moral* discussion. The reason I hold this is that previable "persons" are unlike any other persons in our experience, because they alone are absolutely dependent upon the body of another human being for their physical life-support systems. The law would have to violate its obligations to a woman, who is an independent life and a citizen, in order to protect any purported "rights" of nonviable, prenatal life. I believe that no one has a "right" to life, deserving of full protection of the law, when that life is totally dependent on the body of another human being for its life support.[5] Moreover, the legitimate rights of all citizens under the law would be undermined if the law required all persons to give bodily life support to those who needed it in the form of blood transfusions and organ or bone-marrow transplants, and even made it a criminal offense to refuse to give such support,[6] or if the law limited this obligation to only one class of citizens, i.e., pregnant women. A history of the law limiting this obligation to one class of citizens does not give warrant for the law to continue to do this, any more than it would be appropriate for the law to reinstitute slavery just because it was on the books for so many years. Thus, clarifying whether or not the fetus is a person will not solve problems of law. But it can help to solve moral problems, or at least to delineate them.

What Is a Person?

The most influential definition of *person* in Christian theology was the one given by Boethius near the end of the fifth century: "an individual substance of a rational nature." The problem with this definition is that "rational nature" for Boethius included the notion of the presence of a spiritual soul in a being. For him and his followers, like Aquinas, the problem was not so much deciding what constituted a person, since the formal cause of human personhood was considered to be the rational soul; the problem was deciding when the soul, which could only be created by God, was infused into the body. Today we are less inclined to speak in the language of body and soul. It is too heavily tainted with dualism. So we face not only the problem of the beginning of personhood but also a decision about the precise formal element that constitutes personhood.

For the Christian, modern definitions of person are not very helpful. They usually center on the ability of a being to perform self-conscious acts. However, the Christian believes that all persons are of equal worth and equally loved by God even when it is obvious that not all persons possess an equal capacity for self-conscious activity. Infants, brain-damaged persons, and perhaps even some or all fetuses are valued by God in the Christian perspective. Yet they are not capable of the kind of conscious activity that is associated with the notion of "person" in the modern mind.

Perhaps the meaning of personhood can best be approached by examining what can be said of persons in both common parlance and in the Christian tradition. Persons are beings that have embodied existence.[7] What this means is both that persons are determined by their bodies and that they transcend their bodies. In addition to believing that persons can transcend the limitations of their bodies in the ordinary experiences of life in which they are able to think thoughts and/or perform acts which exceed the limitations of their bodies to one time, place, and condition, most Christians also believe that persons transcend the death that strikes down the life of the body. In Christian theology, a person is a being who is so valued and loved by God that God would be willing to die for this being—symbolized by Jesus' death on the Cross. In addition, God loves this being even into eternity. Furthermore, a person is a being who should be loved and valued by all other persons in the same way that God loves and values persons. A person is one who should be treated as sacred by the human community. In fact, without even appealing to Christian belief in God, it can be argued that the foundation of morality is the experience of the sacred value of persons.[8]

The important point in all of this is that for a Christian a person is a being who is called into community with God and with other human persons. So valued and sacred are persons in the Christian tradition that the language of "person" has itself been used in this tradition for the communitarian aspects of God's own existence.

Because the notion of persons' sacredness is so central in Christian theology, it is common to find attempts in philosophical and theological literature to state this insight through different language. The most common language used is the expression "the sanctity of life." Some persons, however, prefer the expression "the right to life," while others use language that implies an exact equivalence between person and human being.

The expression "the sanctity of life" is not only an erroneous expression, since life has not been treated as sacred in Christian theory or practice, but it is also most unhelpful and misleading when used to capture the idea of the sanctity of persons. The first reason it is misleading is scriptural. There is no place in Scripture where it is asserted that life is sacred.[9] Second, life ends. What ends and is conquered by death is threatened in its claim to sacredness and inviolability. In Christian theology, persons do not end. Persons are sacred, life is not. Third, life is a word that is too broad to describe what is sacred, even when the adjective "human" is attached to it. Life is a continuum that has been in existence for billions of years. Not every being on that continuum is considered as sacred as persons by the Christian tradition. Life on this continuum that is in and of a human being is human life, but all separable human life does not constitute an individual person. Human life covers everything from the separate genetic material of sperm and ovum to the developing fetus, the newborn infant, the cells that are presently taken from human beings and grown in laboratories and may even outlive the individuals from whom they were taken. In summary, for much of the Eastern religious tradition and for vegetarian pacifists, the "sanctity of life" is a basic moral principle; for Western religious thought, it is simply not a basic moral principle, no matter how often such a claim is asserted.

Another expression like the "sanctity of life" that I would also characterize as a false truism or an aphoristic fallacy is the expression "right to life." Rights inhere primarily in persons. Rights that inhere in nonpersons never take precedence over rights that inhere in persons. For this reason, it is important to decide whether the fetus is a person to determine just what rights it has. One cannot say that life has a "right" to produce new persons—unless perhaps the species were threatened with extinction on the planet or in the universe. If one really wants to say that life has such a "right" then one might have to outlaw celibacy and any other voluntary activity that limited all potential reproduction.

Others feel that "human being" is an expression that could be considered the equivalent of the word "person." In some contexts it could be equivalent. However, human being could also be considered simply the equivalent of "human life," the only difference being that it is a narrower term than human life and only applies to an individuated human life, including a prenatal individuated human life. Thus, it is not a helpful expression for deciding when personhood begins, that is, for deciding when a human life becomes sacred, valued by God, and an equal part of the human community. Another reason for using the word "person," rather than the expression "human being," is that the word "person" is applied even to God. It therefore better captures the sense of sacredness of persons, whose beginnings we want to chart.

The Individual-Biological Approach to Personhood

Various approaches have been taken to determine criteria for the beginning of personhood, although the expressions "life" or "human life" are often mistakenly used in place of personhood in the discussion of this question, and in fact prejudice the outcome. Charles Curran outlines four of the approaches taken: an individual-biological approach, a relational approach, a multiple approach, and a societal approach.[10] My presentation will adopt a relational approach to discuss the beginning of personhood, but hopefully I will overcome the objection of Curran and others to that approach by allowing some validity to the individual-biological approach to save the relational approach from complete subjectivity. Before presenting my own approach to the beginning of personhood, however, I will consider the shortcomings of the individual-biological approach, both in the arguments of those who appeal solely to biology, as well as in the arguments of those who couple their appeal to biology with an appeal to God.

The appeal to biology[11] that is most basic is to argue that the person begins at the moment of conception, because at this moment a unique genetic code comes into being. Followers of this approach would say that any human termination of a pregnancy after this point—whether by an intrauterine device, drugs, or surgery—involves the killing of a person. Sometimes the fertilized ovum in its early stages of development is called a "potential person" rather than a "person," but there is no comparable modification of the language of killing applied to the termination of this life. If potentiality is the touchstone of sacredness, then adherents of this rigorous view of abortion should logically follow the position of recent Catholic popes who condemn contraception as evil. However, no one, including recent Catholic popes, speaks of contraception as the "killing" of a "potential person." Even farther back in the Catholic tradition, as Susan Nicholson has shown so well,[12] when words such as "homicide," "parricide" and "murder" were used in conjunction with contraception (or homosexuality), the intent was to show the evil of nonprocreative sex, rather than to make a statement that a "person" had been killed.

There are variations on the biological-approach theme among those who would locate the beginning of personhood at a biological moment later than fertilization. Some locate the earliest beginning of personhood at the moment of individuation, since twinning can no longer occur after that. Others will locate it at the first heartbeat. Others, following a more modern criterion for determining significant life, and looking for consistency with criteria for terminating life at the other end of the life spectrum, will locate the beginning of personhood at the first discernible brain wave. Still others will look to a more complex development of the brain. Some of these adherents of a later biological moment signaling the beginning of personhood would allow for some moral freedom in the area of abortion.

The problem with the biological approach, at any point on its spectrum, is that it treats personhood as if it were a purely biological reality. Yet personhood signifies a spiritual, transcendent reality, which is the basis of the sacredness of persons. The appeal to biology, furthermore, makes no real distinction between full personhood and potential personhood. It never clearly shows why the newly conceived or developing prenatal life should be considered the moral and legal peer of a newborn baby rather than ontologically closer to a separate sperm and egg.

Another more "spiritual" way that the individual-biological approach is presented is with an appeal to God as the Creator and Lord of life.[13] In this perspective God creates personhood, or "infuses a soul" into the material reality of the fertilized ovum, either at the first moment of conception or at one of the later moments of biological development. It is the special creation of every person by God that makes persons the "image of God" and makes them sacred. For persons who take this approach, the merest presence of life is the sign that God has "breathed" into the material reality, giving it a spiritual life, just as God did in the Book of Genesis for the creation of Adam and Eve. There is a fivefold problem with this approach.

First, it can appeal only to the confessional believer. Second, it fails to recognize that life is a continuum. God's breath of life touched creation at its beginning, which caused creation to be. Since then creation has continued from this original impetus. New individual lives have appeared from the life that surrounds all of us. Life comes from life, not from nothingness. Thus, the appearance of a fertilized ovum does not signal that God has visited creation with a new breath of life. From the biological point of view it is a continuation of life.

Third, and related to the second objection, is that it is circular reasoning to argue that the fertilized ovum is a person because God is the Creator and Lord of life. We cannot know God except through human reality. Therefore, it is impossible to argue that a new act of God proves that a certain material reality constitutes a new person in our midst. God has never decreed what biological moment of human reality is a new sign of the divine presence.

Fourth, if the presence of a fertilized ovum is the signal that God has created a new person, then God does not consider persons to be sacred, and so we might well ask why we should. If God creates a person every time there is the fertilization of an ovum by a sperm, then persons must be cheap and disposable, since approximately 58 percent of fertilized ova spontaneously abort prior to implantation.[14]

Fifth and finally, the creation of much human life is not very godly. This view would have God approving life begun anew in the ugly acts of rape and incest as much as in the union of two persons who have joined their lives together to become as one flesh. It would have God approving new life begun in the bodies of women who are too frail to sustain even their own life, let alone the life of another person. It would have God creating persons by whimsy, in order to surprise with contraceptive failure women who wanted no children, either because they were unmarried, or because they were at the stage in their life when they were sending the last child of a large family off to college, or because they were just catching their breath after several toddlers a year apart, or because they did not have sufficient material advantages to welcome a new child. We would find it hard to love and admire a human being who played such tricks on other humans. How can we attribute to God such a cruel or arbitrary attitude toward existing persons or new persons?

The lure of the appeal to biology for the beginning of personhood is the apparent objectivity and simplicity of this approach. But persons are not simple objects. This approach is reductionistic. It fails to establish a base for personhood that accounts for the spiritual, transcendent, sacred reality of personhood that is recognized even by those who do not believe in God. The lure of the appeal to God is its apparent spirituality and piety. However, this approach is extrinsicist and tendentially nominalistic. It states that persons are sacred but does not show what personhood is or when personhood begins.

A Relational Approach to the Beginning of Personhood

What is needed is a way of defining the beginning of personhood that takes into account the objective individual aspect of human personhood that the biological approach recognizes, as well as the spiritual, transcendent, and sacred aspect of personhood that the appeal to God attempts to convey. It must bear some relationship to the bodily existence that characterizes human beings, but it has to allow room for personhood to transcend bodily limitations. It has to be an approach aware of the processual nature of personhood, but one that can also describe the formal reality which begins this process. It must be an approach that unites the human and divine moments of a person's creation in a nonartificial or dualistic way, and it must be an approach which frees God from the limitations of biology. I believe such a way can be found in a variation of the relational approach to this question.[15]

In Christian theology it has been common to move from the seen to the unseen, to move from what we know about human beings to predicating statements about God based on the likeness of God to human persons. A movement in the other direction might offer some help in solving the question of when human personhood begins. Christian theology has hypothesized that there are three persons in God and that these persons are constituted by relations within the godhead (*S. T.* I, 29, 4). In the spirit of this theology, it might be suggested that if divine persons are constituted by relations, perhaps human persons are also constituted by relations.

In looking for analogues other than in the godhead for the constitution of personhood through relationship, one might, with admitted literary freedom, look to the covenant symbolism and to the constitution of Israel as a people in the Exodus account. Here we have the beginning of the collective personhood of Israel, or the creation of a new ontological reality, through a willed relation on the part of Yahweh that is characterized as covenant love, or *hesed*. This new identity for the people of Israel calls them into a community of persons, a community which involved their relationship with God and the relationship of each member of the community with each other. This new identity was a completely free and gracious gift on the part of Yahweh, in no way predetermined or forced by the fact that Yahweh had already had a relationship to them as the Creator of their separate existences as individuals, or even that Yahweh had already entered into a voluntary relationship with them through their forefathers, Abraham, Isaac, and Jacob. Israel's creation as the People of God, a spiritual, transcendent, sacred reality beyond the fact of their material existence, can be instructive for our attempt to locate the beginning of human personhood.

From trinitarian theology we can take the insight that persons are constituted by relations. From Exodus peoplehood theology we can take the suggestion that personhood is constituted by a free and gracious act of love that establishes a covenant with the new reality that is being personed, calling that person into community that creates a covenantal relationship with God and all other persons. The problem is to determine the point at which this might be said to occur and signal a new human person in our midst.

What I am looking for is a point on the continuum of sexual union, conception, pregnancy, and birth that could be considered as producing a relationship of covenantal love marking the beginning of personhood. I am not concerned about God's part in this, since I see God as a presence along the whole continuum of life. I am concerned about the human reality that marks God's presence in a special way, a way that can be said to be ontologically new. What I am doing then is looking for the *human* agency that is responsible for the creation of personhood or "soul." We look upon each new human life as a gift of God, and yet we know that it is human agency directly and God only indirectly that is responsible for that life. Thus, I see no reason why we should not look for human agency as the direct cause of the spiritual, transcendent aspect of human life to which God then gives assent. It makes more sense to have God's personing creativity determined by a personal moment of human covenant love than simply by biology, as has often been the view in the past.

In searching for the moment of human "love making" which constitutes personhood and establishes a sacred and spiritual relationship between God and human life, I reject the time of sexual intercourse as this moment. I believe sexual intercourse is misnamed as "love making." Some, but not all sexual intercourse, not even all that between married persons, can be characterized as "making love." This was especially impressed on me once as I watched a television show on incest. I winced each time one of the young women interviewed spoke of the times her father had "made love" to her, occasions that had even included violence and threats of harm if she revealed what had happened. Nor is intercourse that *is* truly "love making" the kind of love which constitutes a person. This love is not directed to the as-yet-unconceived life that may result from the intercourse. It is directed by the spouses toward each other. Finally, there are persons who were not biologically initiated by sexual intercourse, but by artificial insemination, *in vitro* fertilization, insemination in a surrogate mother—or some day, perhaps, by cloning.

I would propose that the only person who can be the initiator of covenant love for prenatal life, bringing that life into the reality of human community and thereby making it a person, is the woman in whose womb the pregnancy exists. The personhood begins when the bearer of life, the mother, makes a covenant of love with the developing life within her to bring it to birth. Obviously the mother shows more love if she is willing to make a covenant with the fetus for more than the minimal demands of birth. However, that minimum is a gift of self which must be characterized as love. It is an act which recognizes the life within her as having a personal relationship to her. And it is an act which makes possible the introduction of the fetus into the relationship of the larger human community. The moment which begins personhood, then, is the moment when the mother accepts the pregnancy.

At the moment when the mother bonds with the fetus, the fetus becomes a Thou to her rather than an It. It is then that its potentiality for relationality and sociality is activated, because it is brought into a personal relationship with a human person, with the only human person who can actuate this potentiality while the fetus is still in the mother's body and in a previable state. The fetus cannot become related to the human social community except through the mediation of the mother. It is the mother who makes the fetus a social being by accepting its relatedness to her. Thus, it is the mother who makes the fetus a person. After that point its life is sacred because it is sacred to her.

What I am saying, in other words, is that the conception of the personhood (or "soul") of each of us was symbolically a virginal conception. Looking again to Scripture we could say that the model for the beginning of the personhood of every human being is found in Luke 1:38. Personhood is the product of the *fiat* ("Let it be done unto me . . . ") of a mother. It is because of that *fiat* that all future possibilities for growth in personhood exist. It is because of that co-creative *fiat* that God can say, "Thou art my child, this day have I begotten thee" (see Psalm 2:7).

I am not proposing that a covenant made by the mother with the fetus constitutes the beginning of personhood only because abortion is now a legal option. I am proposing that it is in the nature of things as established by God that woman creates the "soul" just as much as she nourishes the body of developing human life. I am proposing that if ethics is built upon "natural law," as some ethicists hold, then this "natural law," which links the beginning of personhood to a covenant made by a woman, must affect our ethical evaluation of abortion.

If what I have proposed sounds preposterous, let us look to nature itself, and to aspects of human activity which point to the fact that the mother, the life bearer, does bear a more distinctive relationship to a person than the biological father. Dr. James Diamond, M.D., noted in an article in *Theological Studies* that the free ovum is many times larger than the free sperm, and, if fertilization occurs, the ovum supplies the energy to the nucleus of the fertilized egg. He went on to say,

> the vital activity in these early days is ordered by what is called messenger ribonucleic acid (RNA) from the mother's ovum. The sperm apparently does not enter into the ordering of this activity. The sperm resembles a man who impregnates a woman and then leaves to her all the work of raising the child. When we note of such a shiftless male "Isn't that just like a man," we may also say of the sperm, "Isn't that just like a sperm."[16]

To indulge in a mercantile image, one could say that if the biological father has a fifty-fifty share in the "corporation" that is the developing life at the first moment of conception, he quickly loses his shares, so that by the moment of birth it is difficult to say whether he holds even one share of "stock" in what has been produced and what has gone into the production, strictly from a material point of view. In other words, the relationship of the father to a new human life can simply be that of a biological donor, even if conception has taken place through sexual intercourse. The woman in whose womb the pregnancy exists can never be considered simply a donor, even if she were a surrogate mother who was pregnant as the result of *in vitro* fertilization using another woman's ovum. The continued existence of a conceptus in the womb of a woman depends not merely on biological donation but on consensual and hospitable agreement by the woman, involving a gift of self which constitutes the minimum of a personal relationship.

Further strength could be given to the theory I have proposed by a look at tradition. Quickening has been considered a significant event that signaled animation in major ethical systems through the centuries.[17] Quickening is an event that only the mother experiences. A bit of soft evidence for my theory is found by looking at the search of adoptees for their natural, biological parents. Most often the concern is to find the mother. It is not that there is a lack of interest in the biological father, or simply that he is even harder to find than the mother, but there is in most people a special attachment to the birth mother who nurtured life within her body for nine months and, according to my theory, even created the "soul."

Some may object to using the word "covenant" to describe the relationship between the mother and the intrauterine person. Does not a covenant involve an agreement between two persons? Since this unborn person cannot respond to the mother's act of self-giving love, is it proper to describe their relationship by the name covenant?

Perhaps this objection can best be addressed by looking at the Christian theology of baptism. Many Christian churches practicing infant baptism speak of this sacrament as a covenant, and many even see it as a covenant which constitutes the infant as an ontologically new being, a "new creature." (Moreover, in the Catholic tradition it is Holy *Mother* Church who makes possible this covenant.) Yet an infant can in no way actively respond to the baptismal covenant in a personal way at the moment of baptism. It can simply continue to exist and grow, until its growth in personhood through community enables it to respond.

The expressions "covenant" and "covenant love" in this discussion have the advantage of continuity with the religious tradition. Moreover, they convey the serious obligation that falls upon the mother who creates a person from the life that is growing within her body. Her decision to bring the fetus to birth constitutes it as a person, but her obligations do not end with her decision or with its birth. For her part, her decision to enter into this covenant involves the obligation either to continue her self-giving love to bring the newborn to fuller personhood or else a willingness to give the child up for adoption to someone who can assume the continuing obligations of the personing covenant. In spite of these advantages, however, the expressions "covenant" and "covenant love" could be considered too poetic or too religious to describe the relationship that constitutes human personhood. A more universally acceptable and secular expression might be "consent of the mother." The moment which begins personhood, then, could be described for the rest of the discussion of this paper as the moment when the mother *consents* to the pregnancy.

The Biological or Objective Aspect of Personhood

If the consent of the mother to the pregnancy marks the formal moment when personhood begins, does that mean that personhood is a very fluid concept and that it could even be denied to a newborn infant if the mother had not consented to the pregnancy? Does biological reality count as nothing in the personing of beings with an *embodied* existence? What I have done in placing the beginning of personhood at the moment of maternal consent is to try to pinpoint the formal constitutive element for the beginning of personhood, a moment that could not be captured by television. This might be termed the spiritual side of personhood, or even the subjective side of personhood. However, I would argue that there is, as well, a biological or objective side to personhood for embodied individuals. There is a point in the pregnancy when the biological development of the fetus is such that the consent of the mother to the pregnancy is implicit, and therefore the fetus should be considered a person, even though consent has not consciously and actively been given by the mother. I would still argue that the formal constitutive element of personhood is the mother's consent and not the stage of biological development of the fetus, but sufficient biological development can create a presumption of consent.[18] In other words, if the woman allows a pregnancy to continue long enough she has implicitly consented to the pregnancy even if she has not consciously accepted it. This would also apply to a woman who fell into a coma after a sufficiently advanced stage of pregnancy and was delivered of a baby without her explicit consent. The use of expressions such as "covenant" or "covenant love" to describe presumed consent, is, of course, completely inappropriate and illustrates the need for this legalistic expression.

To the question of what stage of biological development is a reasonable point to mark presumed consent, I believe there is room for disagreement among ethicists and theologians. However, making presumed consent the formal element in constituting personhood does change the terms of the moral debate.

In looking for the *minimum* of biological reality that would have to exist for presumed consent, I would at least have to listen to those who would argue that this minimum exists at the first moment of fertilization. However, I could only *presume* the consent of the mother at this stage *if* she had directly sought and willed the pregnancy. Willingness to engage in sexual intercourse is not sufficient to create a presumption of consent to a pregnancy.

A more reasonable but not completely acceptable biological development for marking presumed consent is the point about two to three weeks after conception when implantation has occurred—and so there is less chance for a miscarriage—when individuation has occurred, and when the mother becomes aware that she might be pregnant. If the mother consents to the pregnancy at that point, I am willing to call the developing embryo a person which is sacred to God, which should be sacred to humanity, and which will share eternal life with all other persons, even if its life should be subsequently terminated by a miscarriage. However, I am not willing to *presume* consent at this early stage of pregnancy. If a woman does not consent to the pregnancy at this time, and aborts the developing life within her, I do not believe she has killed a person who will then point a condemnatory finger at the mother as she enters eternal life. The person-making relationship had not yet occurred. This, of course, means that in one case I find it acceptable to call a three-week-old embryo a person, while in another case I do not find it acceptable. In other words,

I am willing to employ only a relational criterion for determining personhood at this stage of embryonic development.

For my own part I would demand significant development of the brain and central nervous system before I would say that a biological reality existed which presumed consent of the mother to the pregnancy. It is only when the brain and central nervous system are sufficiently developed that the fetus reaches the threshold of viability. And it is only when the fetus is viable that it is no longer dependent on its mother to actuate its potentiality for relatedness and sociality. Only after viability can it be in a personal relationship with members of the human social community other than its mother. Viability, of course, is not marked by a single moment in the pregnancy that turns on like a light. It is a shifting area and, in fact, is not even purely biological but is itself dependent on society's standards as technology allows society to take over biology.

The difficult area for determining presumed consent and for ethical evaluation of abortion is the second trimester of pregnancy, when viability looms on the horizon. This is the difficult area not only for philosophers and theologians, who deal with the issue abstractly, but also for the providers of abortion services,[19] and, most especially, for the woman herself, for whom the methods of abortion at this stage are a difficult experience and, in some cases, even like vaginal or caesarean delivery of a full-term baby. I will return to an ethical consideration of second trimester abortions at the end of this paper.

If I were to end my examination of personhood here my paper would probably be criticized for exhibiting the ultimate in female chauvinism, because of its seeming suggestion that men are only useful for producing sperm in the process that we call person making. If past patriarchal scholarship's favorable treatment of male chauvinists were taken as a model, then, of course, I should expect no criticism for centuries. After all, Augustine got away with teaching that women were only useful for generating and would be no help to man apart from that.[20] And then there was Luther, who taught that the father's semen was the source of the human soul and the mother provided only nourishment for the life.[21] However, having the advantage of better knowledge (and perhaps greater wisdom and insight!) than either Augustine or Luther on this point, I cannot end this paper leaving the impression that I am wallowing in female chauvinism. Men, and particularly the father, do have a part to play in the personing process.

Persons and the Image of God

Personing is not a moment. It is not a once-and-forever event. It is a process. It is a process that is begun in a moment and by a person, and it is that moment and that causality that I have thus far investigated. However, personing can only come to full flower if it continues beyond that moment and if it involves other persons. When we looked to the covenant symbolism of Exodus to locate the kind of action that begins personhood, we saw that covenant love introduced the newly created reality of Israel into community. It created a people. Peoplehood requires community but personhood also requires community. Persons cannot be persons alone. No person is an island. Sociality is the touchstone of personhood. That is why the biological side of personhood is not sufficient of itself to constitute the formal element of the beginning of personhood.

Recourse to another passage of Scripture will help to shed light on the essential link between community and personhood, between individuality and sociality. In Genesis 1:27 we read "In the image of God they were created, male and female God created them." This passage has been wrongly interpreted over the centuries to indicate that each individual in his or her own individuality is the image of God. It has been further distorted to mean that each individual is the image of God only in his or her spiritual faculties, in his or her soul. What I think this passage is really saying, however, is that the image of God is found only in community, and it is only found in community that can accept diversity, especially the most basic diversity of male and female.

A woman is the initial creator of personhood in the view that I have proposed. However, she can create personhood only because she herself is a social being. Further personing involves other persons working with or in place of the mother. Even during the pregnancy this can involve the father, insofar as he takes an interest in the personing process that is occurring, but which he cannot see and which is being mediated to him by the mother. If he has entered into a marriage covenant with the mother, he is more one with her in the personing process she is effecting than if he is not willing to become spiritually one flesh with her. After birth, during what I would call the postnatal pregnancy, an even larger social community than the mother and father is involved in the personing process. The "soul" is conceived during the prenatal pregnancy, but it is formed during the postnatal pregnancy. Thus, while the mother begins the process, the father, if possible, and many others too, are needed to make the child a full human person and the image of God. Furthermore, it is when the father primarily but also the rest of society fail in their obligations of community toward the woman that she most often resorts to abortion, out of an implicit realization that she cannot make a covenant with the fetus.

Finally, if there is a time in the future when a pregnancy can take place completely in an artificial environment, in a "test tube" or artificial womb, then men themselves or society as a whole would have to be considered the initial creators of personhood rather than the mother. While liberating woman from the cares of pregnancy, such technology would actually usurp a spiritual power that is now uniquely hers. While this could represent the ultimate sharing and community between male and female, it could also lead to the final invasion of woman's dignity.[22]

Ethical Conclusions

Briefly and obviously, a number of ethical conclusions could be drawn from the position I have proposed. First, prior to actual or presumed consent to the pregnancy the mother ultimately has the moral right to make the decision to terminate the pregnancy. After consent she should still have the legal right to terminate the pregnancy, but in this view her moral right is limited.

Prior to the beginning of personhood, abortion does not require moral justifications similar to those that would be needed for the killing of persons. This does not mean that abortion needs no moral evaluation or is just another form of contraception. However, any moral evil attached to abortion, prior to the beginning of personhood, would derive from the two facts that abortion is the snuffing out of life and that it requires an invasion of the woman's body. All life should be revered and should not be arbitrarily created and then arbitrarily taken, whether it is the life of a flower, a baby seal, or a human embryo. When life is irresponsibly taken there is moral evil. When medical procedures that invade the human body are made necessary through careless human actions, there is moral evil. Neither of these evils, however, can be called murder.

The difficult area for ethical evaluation of abortion is the second trimester of pregnancy, as viability nears. Perhaps the philosophical and theological problems are solved by the fact that during the second trimester there are usually only four reasons why a woman terminates a pregnancy: to preserve her life, for fetal indications following amniocentesis or disease, when social and economic barriers prevent a woman from completing a pregnancy she wanted and had previously accepted, or finally, because of the woman's prior ignorance of her pregnancy.

There are two ways to handle these problem areas of abortion. One is a legalistic solution that accepts these abortions and justifies them by philosophical considerations revolving around individualistic and contractual interpretations of actual or presumed consent. The other is an activist solution which seeks to eliminate the conditions which create a need for second trimester abortions. Both solutions could appeal to ethicists.

The legalistic solution could accept the notion that it is the consent of the mother that is formally constitutive of personhood, and that sufficient biological development can create a presumption of consent. This solution could then offer the following distinctions: (1) presumed consent would never take away a woman's moral right to abort to save her life; (2) the notion of conditional consent could be employed morally to justify an abortion for fetal indications or for radically changed economic conditions after the stage of biological development signaling presumed consent had been reached; and (3) the notion of consent marred by ignorance could be used to justify a second trimester abortion for a woman who did not know she was pregnant before that. There are, of course, other abstract ethical principles which can be used to justify abortion of a fetus that is considered a person. Susan Nicholson ably and thoroughly presents many of these in her book *Abortion and the Roman Catholic Church*.[23]

What is really needed, however, is a more revolutionary approach to the ethical problem of second trimester abortions. If those persons and churches who are avowedly antiabortion really made an effort, they could eliminate the need for most second trimester abortions except those necessary to save the life of the mother. If society made it a priority and committed sufficient research funds to the effort, the time for fetal diagnosis by amniocentesis or other yet-to-be-discovered methods could be pushed back earlier than the sixteenth week of pregnancy. Then there would be no need to have a late abortion for fetal indications. Similarly, society could set its priorities so that no woman ever had to consider an abortion of a fetus she wanted because she discovered that she could not afford to have a child. Finally, vigorous and aggressive sex education and contraceptive information programs could help to insure that no woman would reach the second trimester of a pregnancy without knowledge of her condition or with the hope that her problem would just go away by itself if she waited that long.

Aside from influencing ethical conclusions concerning first and second trimester abortions, the position on the beginning of personhood that I have proposed also affects the evaluation of such issues as artificial insemination, *in vitro* fertilization, and "surrogate mothers." Since sexual intercourse is not a sacred moment of human community marking the beginning of personhood, conception can take place in an artificial way. Fertilization of ova outside a woman's body, the discarding of some of those fertilized ova, and even experimentation on them are not necessarily immoral if there are no persons floating on petri dishes. Finally, all of these techniques enable sterile women to fulfill a role that, with the limitations of our present technology, is unique to womankind—that is, creating a person, a "soul."

It is the relationship between maternal acceptance of a pregnancy and fetal sacredness that makes understandable the disjunctions in life that Richard McCormick has wrongly called "cultural schizophrenia."[24] Many of the same persons who approve the abortion of an unwanted fetus would advocate laws protecting the life and health of an accepted fetus. Medical personnel who countenance or even perform abortions of unwanted fetuses are some of the same persons who perform fetal surgery to save an accepted fetus or practice *in vitro* fertilization to help a woman become pregnant. A mother who loves, cherishes, and cares for a retarded or handicapped child who is already a member of her family might abort her fetus that is diagnosed as being similarly damaged. A woman who could never give her newborn up for adoption can abort the fetus she bears so intimately within her body.

In the popular children's book *Horton Hears a Who*[25] there is the constant refrain, "A person's a person, no matter how small." This could be the slogan of some ethicists in the abortion debate, who seem to make biological smallness the touchstone of personhood. What I have tried to show in this presentation is that a person's a person when personally related to other persons. (Even Horton's Who was a part of Whoville.) The fetus cannot become related to other persons except through the womb-mother. Once brought into sociality by its mother, the unborn person must be treated as sacred by other persons. No one has a right to violate her decision to bring this intrauterine person to birth. After its birth, when the mother has brought it into the fabric of the larger social whole, its rejection by its mother does not take away its right to life. It then holds it independently, although still in virtue of its reality as a social being.[26]

Early in this presentation I stated that Scripture nowhere asserts that life is sacred. What Scripture does assert, however, is that the People of God are sacred.[27] It is covenant love calling people into community which makes life sacred. In the view I have proposed, God has made woman the human co-creator who has the privilege of bringing new persons into this covenant. This privilege, however, is also a source of responsibility. But that responsibility cannot be defined as simply the obligation to bring to birth every pregnancy that takes root in her body. Rather, it is the obligation to bring to birth only those fetuses for whom she is physically, emotionally, psychologically, and economically prepared either to carry out the demands of covenant after birth, or to give the child to someone who can. She has an obligation not to make a personing covenant with a fetus if the personing covenant will not or cannot be continued with the infant after birth. When the human personing covenant is broken by the mother or by society in the postnatal pregnancy, it can critically harm a person's appreciation of God's creation covenant with humanity, which is the condition of the possibility for all covenants and for the existence of all persons.

Notes

1. Richard A. McCormick, S.J., *How Brave a New World? Dilemmas in Bioethics* (New York: Doubleday, 1981), 194.

2. Beverly Wildung Harrison, "Theology of Pro-Choice: A Feminist Perspective," in *Abortion: The Moral Issues,* ed. Edward Batchelor Jr. (New York: Pilgrim Press, 1982), 222. For one of the most important contributions to the abortion discussion, see Beverly Harrison's *Our Right to Choose: Toward a New Ethic of Abortion* (Boston: Beacon Press, 1983).

3. At the 1978 meeting of the Society of Christian Ethics, I presented a paper arguing that there is an essential link between Christian ethics and belief in immortality. Marjorie Reiley Maguire, "Ethics and Immortality," in *Proceedings of the American Society of Christian Ethics Annual Meeting* (Waterloo, Ont.: Wilfrid Laurier University Press, 1978).

4. Marjorie Reiley Maguire, "Can Technology Solve the Abortion Dilemma," *Christian Century* 93, no. 34 (1976): 918–19.

5. Judith Jarvis Thomson was the first to use the image of pregnancy as a state in which one person is connected to another for life support, although I must mention that I was not aware of Thomson's position when I developed a similar image for the article cited above in the *Christian Century.* See Judith Jarvis Thomson, "A Defense of Abortion," *Philosophy and Public Affairs* 1 (1971): 47–66. The implications of Thomson's position have been systematically examined by Susan Teft Nicholson, *Abortion and the Roman Catholic Church* (Notre Dame, Ind.: University of Notre Dame Press, 1978), 49–62.

6. In August 1978, Judge Flaherty of Pittsburgh ruled that the law could not require David Shimp to donate bone marrow to his dying cousin, Robert McFall, even though Flaherty indicated that he thought Shimp's refusal was morally revolting. It is my opinion that even if some people consider a woman's decision for abortion to be "morally revolting" the law should not give less protection to a pregnant woman than it gave to David Shimp. See Alan Meisel and Loren H. Roth, "Must a Man Be His Cousin's Keeper," in *Hastings Center Report* 8, no. 5 (Oct. 1978): 5–6.

7. For a history and development of the idea of embodiment as well as further bibliography, see Richard N. Zaner, "Embodiment," in *Encyclopedia of Bioethics* I, ed. Warren T. Reich (New York: Free Press, 1978), 361–65.

8. This has been argued by Daniel C. Maguire, *The Moral Choice* (New York: Doubleday, 1978).

9. This is the finding of Richard Lux in an unpublished paper entitled "What Do We Mean When We Say That Life Is Sacred?" which was presented at a dialogue between representatives of the U.S. Catholic Conference and the Synagogue Council of America on Nov. 8–10, 1982.

10. Charles Curran, "Abortion: V: Contemporary Debate in Philosophical and Religious Ethics," in *Encyclopedia of Bioethics* I, 17–26. See also Charles Cur-

ran, "Abortion: Its Moral Aspects," in *Abortion: The Moral Issues,* 115–28. For other divisions and other treatments of the various abortion positions, see Daniel Callahan's classic study, *Abortion: Law, Choice and Morality* (New York: Macmillan, 1970).

11. Some examples of this approach are John T. Noonan Jr., ed., *The Morality of Abortion: Legal and Historical Perspectives* (Cambridge: Harvard University Press, 1970); and Germain G. Grisez, *Abortion: The Myths, the Realities, and the Arguments* (New York: Corpus Books, 1970). Two more liberal examples of the biological approach are Charles Curran and Richard McCormick. See their works cited in these notes. They both see personhood as beginning only after individuation has occurred.

12. Nicholson, *Abortion and the Roman Catholic Church,* 6–7. Beverly Harrison disputes Nicholson's conclusions on this point. She says, "This carefully crafted study assumes that there has been a clear 'anti-killing' ethic separable from any antisexual ethic in Christianity. This is an assumption that my historical research does not sustain." Harrison, "Theology of Pro-Choice: A Feminist Perspective," 240–41, n. 11.

13. Two examples of this approach are Paul Ramsey, "The Morality of Abortion," in *Abortion: The Moral Issues,* 73–91; and Edward Shils, "The Sanctity of Life," in *Life or Death, Ethics and Options,* ed. Daniel H. Labby (Portland, Oreg.: Reed College Press, 1968), 2–39.

14. James J. Diamond, M.D., "Abortion, Animation, Hominization," *Theological Studies* 36, no. 2 (June 1975): 311, n. 12. Another 12 percent of fertilized ova spontaneously abort after implantation so that only about 30 percent survive to birth.

15. The relational approach is found chiefly among some French Catholic moral theologians: Bruno Ribes, Bernard Quelquejeu, Jacques-Marie Pohier, and Louis Beinart. Their positions can be found in *Études* (1970), *Lumière et Vie* (1972), and *Avortement et respect de la vie humaine,* Colloque du Centre catholique des médecins français (commission conjugale), (Paris: Editions du Seuil, 1972). Excellent summaries of the positions of these men can be found in Curran, "Abortion: Its Moral Aspects," 120–22; Curran, "Abortion: V: Contemporary Debate in Philosophical and Religious Ethics," 20; McCormick, *How Brave a New World?,* 141–49. An American, H. Tristram Englehardt Jr., also takes a relational approach to the beginning of personhood. His, like the one I will propose, also emphasizes the mother-child relationship. However, he only sees this relationship as having a personing function after the birth of the child, when he sees their relationship as a social one. He sees the mother-fetus relationship as only biological. Englehardt, "The Ontology of Abortion," *Ethics* 84, no. 3 (April 1974): 217–23.

16. Diamond, "Abortion, Animation, Hominization," 310.

17. See John R. Connery, *Abortion: The Development of the Roman Catholic Perspective* (Chicago: Loyola University Press, 1977). For an excellent examina-

tion of the theory of delayed animation see Joseph T. Donceel, "Abortion: Mediate vs. Immediate Animation," in *Abortion: The Moral Issues,* 110–14.

18. I am indebted to James Bresnahan, S.J., who was the commentator for a slightly abridged version of this paper presented at the 1983 meeting of the Society of Christian Ethics, for pointing out that "presumed consent" is a very legalistic concept and perhaps works against the kind of personalism I am trying to introduce into this debate. The legalistic implications of this will be brought out more clearly later in this paper and, I hope, sufficiently counterbalanced with other considerations.

19. At the Seventh Annual Conference of the National Abortion Federation held Apr. 10–13, 1983, there was a session on personhood. Two of the panelists responding to the keynote speaker were Ruth Hoesen, a nurse at an Atlanta abortion clinic, and Naim Kassar, a physician at a Kansas abortion clinic. Both spoke of the psychological and emotional problems for staff members attendant upon participating in second trimester abortions, especially ones using the technique of D & E (dilation and evacuation). Their remarks were not to deny the need for or legality of second trimester abortions but to face them as a human problem. Audiocassette tapes of the Proceedings of this meeting are available from the American Audio Association, Box 511, Floral Park, N.Y. 11002.

20. Nicholson, *Abortion and the Roman Catholic Church,* 6.

21. James B. Nelson, "Abortion: IV: Protestant Perspectives," in *Encyclopedia of Bioethics* I, 14.

22. For an article presenting "a not-so-far-out fantasy of reproductive tyranny," see Diane Sauter and Steven Feinberg, "Prima Gravids," *Ms* 11, no. 4 (Oct. 1982): 45.

23. Nicholson, *Abortion and the Roman Catholic Church.*

24. McCormick, *How Brave a New World?,* 189.

25. Dr. Seuss, *Horton Hears a Who* (New York: Random House, 1954).

26. This does not mean that extraordinary efforts must be taken to save the life of an infant, or other person, whose ability to further enter into the personing process has been severely physically impaired. Just as the mother cannot initiate the personing process without a biological base, so the personing process cannot continue if the biological base is severely damaged.

27. Lux, "What Do We Mean When We Say That Life Is Sacred?"

[32]

The Consistent Ethic: What Sort of Framework?

Cardinal Joseph Bernardin

I AM DEEPLY GRATEFUL for the invitation to address you on a topic to which I have devoted much time and energy during the past three years: the "consistent ethic of life."

This morning I will (1) give an overview of the concept, (2) explore the movement from moral analysis to public-policy choices, and (3) identify issues needing further development: the implications of the consistent ethic for citizens, office seekers, and officeholders.

The Consistent Ethic: An Overview

The idea of the consistent ethic is both old and new. It is "old" in the sense that its substance has been the basis of many programs for years. For example, when the U.S. bishops inaugurated their Respect Life Program in 1972, they invited the Catholic community to focus on the "sanctity of human life and the many threats to human life in the modern world, including war, violence, hunger and poverty" (National Conference of Catholic Bishops' resolution, April 13, 1972).

SOURCE: From *Consistent Ethic of Life*. Copyright © 1988 by Sheed and Ward. Reprinted by permission.

Fourteen years later, the focus remains the same. As the 1986 Respect Life brochure states, "The pastoral plan is set in the context of a consistent ethic that links concern for the unborn with concern for all human life. The inviolability of innocent human life is a fundamental norm."

Moreover, the bishops' pastoral letter "The Challenge of Peace: God's Promise and Our Response" emphasized the sacredness of human life and the responsibility we have personally and as a society to protect and preserve its sanctity. In paragraph 285, it specifically linked the nuclear question with abortion and other life issues:

> When we accept violence in any form as commonplace, our sensitivities become dulled. When we accept violence, war itself can be taken for granted. Violence has many faces: oppression of the poor, deprivation of basic human rights, economic exploitation, sexual exploitation and pornography, neglect or abuse of the aged and the helpless, and innumerable other acts of inhumanity. Abortion in particular blunts a sense of the sacredness of human life. In a society where the innocent unborn are killed wantonly, how can we expect people to feel righteous revulsion at the act or threat of killing noncombatants in war?

However, the pastoral letter—while giving us a starting point for developing a consistent ethic of life—does not provide a fully articulated framework.

It was precisely to provide a more comprehensive theological and ethical basis for the Respect Life Program and for the linkage of war and abortion as noted by the pastoral letter that I developed the theme of the consistent ethic. Another important circumstance which prompted me to move in this direction was that I had just been asked to serve as chairman of the bishops' Pro-Life Committee. It was October of 1983, and I knew that both abortion and defense-related issues would undoubtedly play an important role in the upcoming presidential campaign.

It was urgent, I felt, that a well-developed theological and ethical framework be provided which would link the various life issues while at the same time pointing out that the issues are not all the same. It was my fear that without such a framework or vision the U.S. bishops would be severely pressured by those who wanted to push a particular issue with little or no concern for the rest. With such a theological basis, we would be able to argue convincingly on behalf of all the issues on which we had taken a position in recent years.

I first presented the theme in a talk at Fordham University in December 1983. At that time I called for a public discussion of the concept both in Catholic circles and the broader community. In all candor I must admit that the public response greatly exceeded my hopes and expectations.

Since that time there has been a lively exchange by both those who agree and disagree with the theme and its implications. By far, the majority of the reactions have been supportive. Nonetheless, it has been used and misused by those who have tried to push their own, narrower agendas. I myself have made further contributions to the discussion through subsequent talks and articles.

The concept itself is a challenging one. It requires us to broaden, substantively and creatively, our ways of thinking, our attitudes, our pastoral response. Many are not accustomed to thinking about all the life-threatening and life-diminishing issues with such consistency. The result is that they remain somewhat selective in their response. Although some of those who oppose the concept seem not to have understood it, I sometimes suspect that many who oppose it recognize its challenge. Quite frankly, I sometimes wonder whether those who embrace it quickly and wholeheartedly truly understand its implicit challenge.

Last November, when the U.S. bishops updated and reaffirmed the Pastoral Plan for Pro-Life Activities, they explicitly adopted the consistent ethic for the first time as the theological context for the plan.

In sum, to the delight of those who agree with its theological reasoning and to the dismay of the small minority who do not, the consistent ethic has entered into our theological vocabulary.

Let me now explain in greater depth the theological basis and strategic value of the consistent ethic. Catholic teaching is based on two truths about the human person: Human life is both sacred and social. Because we esteem human life as sacred, we have a duty to protect and foster it at all stages of development from conception to natural death and in all circumstances. Because we acknowledge that human life is also social, society must protect and foster it.

Precisely because life is sacred, the taking of even one life is a momentous event. Traditional Catholic teaching has allowed the taking of human life in particular situations by way of exception—for example, in self-defense and capital punishment. In recent decades, however, the presumptions against taking human life have been strengthened and the exceptions made ever more restrictive.

Fundamental to these shifts in emphasis is a more acute perception of the many ways in which life is threatened today. Obviously, such questions as war, aggression, and capital punishment are not new; they have been with us for centuries. Life has always been threatened, but today there is a new context that shapes the content of our ethic of life.

The principal factor responsible for this new context is modern technology, which induces a sharper awareness of the fragility of human life. War, for example, has always been a threat to life, but today the threat is qualitatively different because of nuclear and other sophisticated kinds of weapons. The weapons produced by modern technology now threaten life on a scale previously unimaginable. Living as we do, therefore, in an age of extraordinary technological development means we face a qualitatively new range of moral problems.

The essential questions we face are these: In an age when we *can* do almost anything, how do we decide what we *should* do? In a time when we can do anything technologically, how do we decide morally what we should not do?

We face new technological challenges along the whole spectrum of life from conception to natural death. This creates the need for a consistent ethic, for the spectrum cuts across such issues as genetics, abortion, capital punishment, modern warfare, and the care of the terminally ill. Admittedly these are all *distinct* problems, enormously complex, and deserve individual treatment. Each requires its own moral analysis. No single answer or solution applies to all. *But they are linked!*

Given this broad range of challenging issues, we desperately need a societal attitude or climate that will sustain a consistent defense and promotion of life. When human life is considered "cheap" or easily expendable in one area, eventually nothing is held as sacred and all lives are in jeopardy. Ultimately it is society's attitude about life—whether of respect or nonrespect—that determines its policies and practices.

The theological foundation of the consistent ethic, then, is defense of the person. The ethic grows out of the very character of Catholic moral thought. I do not mean to imply, of course, that one has to be a Catholic to affirm the moral content of the consistent ethic. But I do think that this theme highlights both the systematic and analogical character of Catholic moral theology.

The systematic nature of Catholic theology means it is grounded in a set of basic principles and then articulated in a fashion which draws out the meaning of each principle and the relationships among them. Precisely because of its systematic quality, Catholic theology refuses to treat moral issues in an ad hoc fashion. There is a continual process of testing the use of a principle in one case by its use in very different circumstances. The consistent ethic seeks only to illustrate how this testing goes on when dealing with issues involving the taking of life or the enhancement of life through social policy.

The analogical character of Catholic thought offers the potential to address a spectrum of issues which are not identical but have some common characteristics. Analogical reasoning identifies the unifying elements which link two or more issues, while at the same time recognizing why similar issues cannot be reduced to a single problem.

The taking of life presents itself as a moral problem all along the spectrum of life, but there are differences between abortion and war, just as there are elements that radically differentiate war from decisions made about the care of a terminally ill patient. The differences among these cases are universally acknowledged. A consistent ethic seeks to highlight the fact that differences do not destroy the elements of a common moral challenge.

A Catholic ethic which is both systematic in its argument and analogical in its perspective stands behind the proposal that, in the face of the multiple threats to life in our time, spanning every phase of existence, it is necessary to develop a moral vision which can address these several challenges in a coherent and comprehensive fashion.

The theological assertion that the human person is made in the image and likeness of God, the philosophical affirmation of the dignity of the person, and the political principle that society and state exist to serve the person—all these themes stand behind the consistent ethic. They also sustain the positions that the U.S. Catholic bishops have taken on issues as diverse as nuclear policy, social policy, and abortion. These themes provide the basis for the moral perspective of the consistent ethic.

From Moral Analysis to Public Policy

Some commentators on the consistent ethic saw it primarily as a political policy. They missed its primary meaning: It is a moral vision and an ethical argument sustaining the vision. But the moral vision does have political consequences. The consistent ethic is meant to shape the public witness of the Catholic Church in our society.

Before exploring some of the political consequences, I would like to comment briefly on some related issues which provide a broader context for such a discussion. The movement from moral analysis to public-policy choices is a complex process in a pluralistic society like ours.

First, civil discourse in the United States is influenced, widely shaped, by religious pluralism. The condition of pluralism, wrote John Courtney Murray, is the coexistence in one society of groups holding divergent and incompatible views with regard to religious questions. The genius of American pluralism, in his view, was that it provided for the religious freedom of each citizen and every faith. However, it did not purchase tolerance at the price of expelling religious and moral values from the public life of the nation. The goal of the American system is to provide space for religious substance in society, but not a religious state.

Second, there is a legitimate secularity of the political process, just as there is a legitimate role for religious and moral discourse in our nation's life. The dialogue which keeps both alive must be a careful exchange which seeks neither to transform secularity into secularism nor to change the religious role into religiously dominated public discourse.

John Courtney Murray spent a substantial amount of time and effort defending the church's right to speak in the public arena. But he also stressed the limits of the religious role in that arena. Today religious institutions, I believe, must reaffirm their rights and recognize their limits. My intent is not, of course, to produce a passive church or a purely private vision of faith. The limits relate not to whether we enter the public debate but how we advocate a public case. This implies, for example, that religiously rooted positions somehow must be translated into language, arguments, and categories which a religiously pluralistic society can agree on as the moral foundation of key policy positions.

Third, all participants in the public discourse must face the test of complexity. From issues of defense policy through questions of medical ethics to issues of social policy, the moral dimensions of our public life are interwoven with empirical judgments where honest disagreement exists. I do not believe, however, that empirical complexity should silence or paralyze religious or moral analysis and advocacy of issues. But we owe the public a careful accounting of how we have come to our moral conclusions.

Fourth, we must keep in mind the relationship between civil law and morality. Although the premises of civil law are rooted in moral principles, the scope of law is more limited and its purpose is not the moralization of society. Moral principles govern personal and social human conduct and cover as well interior acts and motivation. Civil statutes govern public order; they address primarily external acts and values that are formally social.

Hence it is not the function of civil law to enjoin or prohibit everything that moral principles enjoin or prohibit. History has shown over and over again that people cherish freedom; they can be coerced only minimally. When we pursue a course of legal action, therefore, we must ask whether the requirements of public order are serious enough to take precedence over the claims of freedom.

Fifth, in the objective order of law and public policy, how do we determine which issues are public moral questions and which are best defined as private moral questions?

For Murray, an issue was one of public morality if it affected the public order of society. Public order, in turn, encompassed three goods: public peace, essential protection of human rights, and commonly accepted standards of moral behavior in a community. Whether a given question should be interpreted as one of public morality is not always self-evident. A rationally persuasive case has to be made that an action violates the rights of another or that the consequences of actions on a given issue are so important to society that the authority of the state and the civil law ought to be invoked to govern personal and group behavior.

Obviously, in a religiously pluralistic society, achieving consensus on what constitutes a public moral question is never easy. But we have been able to do it—by a process of debate, decision making, then review of our decisions.

Two cases exemplify how we struggled with public morality in the past. First, Prohibition was an attempt to legislate behavior in an area ultimately decided to be beyond the reach of civil law because it was not sufficiently public in nature to affect the public order. Second, civil rights, particularly in areas of housing, education, employment, voting, and access to public facilities, were determined—after momentous struggles of war, politics, and law—to be so central to public order that the state could not be neutral on the question.

Today we have a public consensus in law and policy which clearly defines civil rights as issues of public morality and the decision to drink alcoholic beverages as clearly one of private morality. But neither decision was reached without struggle. The consensus was not automatic on either question. Philosophers, activists, politicians, preachers, judges, and ordinary citizens had to state a case, shape a consensus, and then find a way to give the consensus public standing in the life of the nation.

The fact that a spontaneous public consensus is lacking at a given moment does not prohibit its being created. When he was told that the law could not legislate morality, Dr. Martin Luther King, Jr., used to say that the law could not make people love their neighbors, but it could stop their lynching them. Law and public policy can also be instruments of shaping a public consensus; they are not simply the product of consensus.

In sum, in charting the movement from moral analysis to public-policy choices, we must take into account the facts that (1) civil discourse in this nation is influenced and shaped by religious pluralism; (2) there is a legitimate secularity of the political process; (3) all participants in it must face the test of complexity; (4) there is a distinction between civil law and morality; and (5) some issues are questions of public morality, others of private morality.

This brings us to the third part of my address.

Implications for Citizens, Office Seekers, and Officeholders

In light of the nearly three-year debate about the consistent ethic, questions have surfaced at the level of theological principle and ethical argument. As noted earlier, I have addressed these as they have arisen. The area that now needs attention is precisely how the framework of the consistent ethic takes shape (a) in the determination of public-policy positions taken by the church and (b) in the decisions that legislators and citizens take in light of the church's positions.

Let me hasten to acknowledge that I do not have all the answers to the next set of questions. At this point in the dialogue I have chosen simply to identify questions which need further reflection and discussion. I also acknowledge that others have raised some of the questions; they are not all mine. Although

I am not prepared to give answers to these questions, I do intend to address them at a later date.

What role does consensus play in the development of public policy and civil law? Earlier I suggested that its role is essential in the long run. But what about the short term? Moreover, what are the appropriate roles of civic and religious leaders in providing moral leadership in the public-policy debate within a pluralistic community? What is the difference between a bishop's role and a politician's in the public debate about moral issues which the consistent ethic embraces? Should a politician wait until a consensus is developed before taking a stand or initiating legislation?

Must a Catholic office seeker or officeholder work for all clearly identified Catholic concerns simultaneously and with the same vigor? Is that possible? If such a person need not work for all these concerns aggressively and at the same time, on what basis does one decide what to concentrate on and what not? Does theology provide the answer, or politics, or both? What guidelines does one use to determine which issues are so central to Catholic belief that they must be pursued legislatively regardless of the practical possibilities of passage? What are the consequences if a Catholic office seeker or officeholder does not follow the church's teaching in the campaign for or exercise of public office?

What is a Catholic officeholder's responsibility, in light of the Second Vatican Council's Declaration on Religious Liberty, to protect the religious beliefs of non-Catholics? What is his or her responsibility under the Constitution? How are these responsibilities related?

How is the distinction between accepting a moral principle and making prudential judgments about applying it in particular circumstances—for example, in regard to specific legislation—worked out in the political order? What is the responsibility of a Catholic officeholder or office seeker when the bishops have made a prudential judgment regarding specific legislation? How are Catholic voters to evaluate a Catholic officeholder or office seeker who accepts a moral principle, and not only disagrees with the bishops regarding specific legislation but supports its defeat?

Until questions like these are explored and ultimately answered, using the consistent ethic of life to test public policy, party platforms and the posture of candidates for office will remain problematic and controversial. I firmly believe, however, that the consistent ethic, when pursued correctly and in depth, can make a genuine contribution. Solid, credible answers to the questions raised above will require an honest exchange of the best there is to offer in theological, political, and social thought.

I assure you that the Catholic bishops will remain in the public debate, and we need help. Public officials will remain in the line of fire, and they need help. Citizens will ultimately make the difference, and they too need help if the dialogue about how we are to respond to the broad range of contemporary issues is to proceed in a constructive fashion.

As the debate proceeds, we have a wonderful opportunity to bring together the best of our religious, political, and social traditions in the service of each other and the wider society to which we are bound in hope and love.

[33]

Abortion and the True Believer

Joseph F. Fletcher

MOST OF US LEARN sooner or later how wise it is not to debate with True Believers. Debate with them ends as an exercise in futility. What follows is therefore not an argument for abortion, either therapeutic or personal; nor is it a retort to the arguments of the antiabortionists. It is simply a comment, as from the sidelines or the balcony, on the debate—which is essentially over the question whether a fetus is a person or not and, consequently, what rights if any ought to be assigned to uterine life.

I

Thoughtful people, not just dull old philosophers, are always bemused when they learn how a medieval notion called substance enters into the abortion debate, lurking behind and beneath the rhetoric of the right-to-life forces.

Spokespersons for the Roman Catholic hierarchy, backed by one Lutheran synod and most Orthodox Jews, say that a fetus is a person and that therefore abortion is murder, the killing of an innocent person. They claim that a human embryo or fetus is a person because it is potentially a person. By this they mean that the substance of a person is already present in a fetus or unformed

SOURCE: Copyright © 1974 by the Christian Century Foundation. Reprinted by permission from the November 27, 1974 issue of *The Christian Century.*

human. How sound or valid is this preformist idea? Well, it is like saying that the house is in the blueprint, the statue is in the marble, the book is in the writer's conception of it, the oak is in the acorn—and by the same token, and *a fortiori,* the person is in the fetus.

The substance doctrine is the one that holds up the sacramental theology of transubstantiation—the belief that even though the wafer in the Mass has the "accidents" of bread (its taste, color, consistency, cereal content), down underneath these accidents lies the real substance, the body of Christ, which cannot be seen or touched or tasted or smelled but is nonetheless *there*—not just prospectively or virtually, but actually.

In the same way, it is contended, the verifiable properties of a fetus are admittedly not personal; it has no cerebration or memory or ability to communicate or self-consciousness. But these things are, after all, only accidents. The person is actually there, unverifiably (mysteriously) yet knowable by faith. It follows, of course, that abortion is killing an innocent person, i.e., that abortion is murder.

The medieval theology of transubstantiation offers a kind of objective argument against abortion, if you can accept its ontology or supernaturalistic theory of material reality. Its basis lies solely in a faith assertion: in an unverifiable *belief* in something we might call a preformed person. However, if you accept the faith assertion of substance (a very big If, to be sure), the deductive argument from it may be said to be a logical one in the syllogistic sense. (All fetuses are persons; this is a fetus; therefore this is a person: everything hangs on the first premise.)

For those who believe in the metaphysics of substance and accidents, who are convinced that the medieval sacramental theology was a true account of real things, it makes sense to refuse to terminate fetal development. But one more assumption is required for the antiabortion argument. Even if you are willing to revive the medieval notion of the homunculus (a minuscule person down *in* the fetus, maybe even in the sperm or ovum), you still have to assume (judge) that life is the highest good (*summum bonum*), thus taking priority over all other values—health, quality of life, resources for well-being, and so on. This is a vitalistic ethics, and it makes human life sacrosanct, taboo, untouchable.

On examination, all of this comes down to two highly challengeable jumps in reasoning. They are known, among those who do not indulge in them, as the error of potentiality (taking what could be as what already is) and the fallacy of the single cause (seeing the constant, ignoring the variable).

Thomas Aquinas rejected this line of argument. He distinguished between life *in potentia* and *in situ* (in being), and held that the difference between potential humanness and actual humanness is an essential difference, not merely a superficial or accidental one. For St. Thomas, what changed the fetus from merely biological life into a person was the infusion of the soul or animation— which he, like Aristotle, thought takes place about the time of quickening. Some Catholics still hold to this opinion, but the Vatican's official teaching has discarded it.

Among antiabortionists there is, it should be noted, an alternative position. A few of them claim to have a revelation of some kind, written either in a book or in their hearts, that God's eternal will has sanctified the fetus. This group does *not* take its stand on the metaphysical ground. It is amusing to observe how Protestants who fiercely reject the substance theory at the altar accept it in the uterus; they repudiate transubstantiation sacramentally but swallow it whole fetally.

These two antiabortion arguments, the one metaphysical and the other revelational, are fused together in the debate, yet in fact they are quite independent of each other. Some nontheists (a few humanists also, as well as Mahayana Buddhists and the like) accept the metaphysical position but not the revelational, while a few theistic debaters (for example, evangelical Protestants, Orthodox Jews, and Jains in India) reverse things, holding to a revelation without recourse to any metaphysics.

II

Leaving metaphysical and supernatural grounds altogether, we find another group who opposes abortion on a different basis: on ethical rather than either metaphysical or revelational premises. They take their stand on what *ought* to be rather than on what is or at least is believed to be. Their starting point is a *value* commitment. Their contention is that because the potential of a fetus is personal value, we ought to preserve the fetus when we can for the sake of what is not yet actual but presumably will come to be.

Once you stake your antiabortion case on values rather than on alleged facts not in evidence, on what ought to be rather than on what is, you are landed in the whole ethical problem of values and preferences and choices, the problem of relative values and of proportionate good. This is a radically different order of argument against abortion.

It is one thing to say, "No matter what else has to be sacrificed (health, happiness, growth, resources), I will not murder a 'substantially' real person"; but it is a quite different thing to say, "No matter what has to be lost in terms of present values, I will not weigh them against the future value of this embryo." The essential feature of this latter argument is not that it rests on moral rather than metaphysical or religious grounds, but that it *always* gives a first-order value to a fetus regardless of the situation or circumstances. When this posture is combined with substance metaphysics, we have a True Believer whose dogmatism rules out any kind of pragmatic or responsible judgment about down-to-earth cases.

The great majority of us—doctors, nurses, patients, people as people—look at the abortion issue in ethical rather than metaphysical or revealed terms. But even if we regard it ethically, we cannot deal with abortion dogmatically or absolutistically or by universalized generalizations. Whether present human values should be traded off for or subordinated to future fetal values would depend on a responsible assessment of proportionate good. Approached in this way, a good case can sometimes be made for abortion, whether it happens to be for medical reasons or personal reasons.

Surely no law should be tolerated that forces the substance theory on those who do not find it reasonable, either in the fetus or in the sacrament. At the political level—at any rate in a democracy—it is obvious that like the substance doctrine, the revealed and vitalist doctrines are very much matters of private opinion.

Opposition to abortion is certainly a part of the freedom of religious belief and practice we want to protect: people should be free to embrace it. But this freedom has to be protected for all, not just for some. It is difficult if not impossible to see how church metaphysics or divine revelations or individual value preferences can be imposed by law on those who do not believe them to be either true or wise.

This is, in a word, the recommendation of wise and thoughtful people on both sides of the opinion line—those who disapprove abortion as well as those who approve it.

[34]

Abortion: Why the Arguments Fail

Stanley Hauerwas

1. Have the Arguments Failed?

Essays on the morality of abortion, whether they be anti or pro, have begun to take on a ritualistic form. Each side knows the arguments and counterarguments well, but they continue to go through the motions. Neither side seems to have much hope of convincing the other, but just as in some rituals we continue to repeat words and actions though we no longer know why, in like manner we continue to repeat arguments about why abortion is right, wrong, or indifferent. It is almost as though we assume that the repetition of the arguments will magically break the moral and political impasse concerning the status of abortion in our society.

The intractability of the debate frustrates us and our frustration gives way to shrillness. Having tried to develop good philosophical, theological, legal, and social arguments we find our opponents still unconvinced. In the heat of political exchange, both sides resort to rhetoric designed to make their opponents appear stupid or immoral. Thus we are besieged by slogans affirm-

SOURCE: Copyright © 1981by University of Notre Dame Press. Reprinted from *A Community of Character: Toward a Constructive Christian Social Ethic* with permission of author and University of Notre Dame Press.

ing the "right to life" or that every woman has the "right over her body"; or it seems we must choose between being "pro-life" or "pro-choice." Some, concluding that there is no hope of conducting the public debate in a manner befitting the moral nuances of the abortion issue, have withdrawn from the field of battle.

Yet before anyone beats too hasty a retreat it is worth considering why the arguments seem to have failed and why we have been left with little alternative to the oversimplifications of the public debate. There may be a moral lesson to be learned from the intractable character of the debate that is as important as the morality of abortion itself. And I suspect it offers a particularly important lesson for Christians. It is my contention that Christian opposition to abortion on demand has failed because, by attempting to meet the moral challenge within the limits of public polity, we have failed to exhibit our deepest convictions that make our rejection of abortion intelligible. We have failed then in our first political task because we accepted uncritically an account of "the moral question of abortion" determined by a politics foreign to the polity appropriate to Christian convictions. We have not understood, as Christians, how easily we have presumed that the presuppositions of our "liberal" cultural ethos are "Christian." As a result, our temptation has been to blame the intractability of the abortion controversy on what appears to us as the moral blindness or immorality of pro-abortionists. We fail to see how much of the problem lies in the way we share with the pro-abortion advocates the moral presumptions of our culture.

As Christians we have assumed that we were morally and politically required to express our opposition to abortion in terms acceptable in a pluralist society. To be sure, we did this with depth of conviction, as we assumed those terms were the ones which should inform our understanding of the moral injustice involved in abortion. Hence we could claim that our opposition to abortion was not based on our special theological convictions, but rather founded on the profoundest presumptions of Western culture. All agree murder is wrong; all agree life is sacred; all agree that each individual deserves the protection of law; such surely are the hallmarks of our civilization.

Yet we discovered that not every one agrees about when human life begins. This, we have supposed, is the point of dispute. And no matter how earnestly we tried to document genetically that human life begins at conception, we found many accepting Justice Blackmun's claim that the unborn are not "persons in the whole sense."[1] Philosophically we are told that our assumption that the fetus has moral status confuses the moral sense of being "human" or a "person" with the genetic,[2] and that we have to understand how the intelligibility of the notion of being a human or of being a person is anchored in our civilization's deepest moral values.[3]

Indeed even as strong an anti-abortion advocate as John Noonan has recently suggested that the issue of when human life begins is part of the public controversy that cannot be settled. "It depends on assumptions and judgments about what human beings are and about what human beings should do for one another. These convictions and conclusions are not easily reached by argument. They rest on particular perspectives that are bound to the whole personality and can shift only with a reorientation of the person."[4] But if that is true, then surely we Christians have already lost the battle by letting the enemy determine the terrain on which the battle must be fought.

If the issue is limited to the determination of when human life begins, we cannot prevail, given the moral presuppositions of our culture. When the debate is so limited, it has already been uncritically shaped by the political considerations of our culture, the "moral" has already been determined by the "political," and the very convictions that make us Christian simply never come up. Indeed we have made a virtue of this, since some allege that appeals to religious convictions invalidate our views for the formulation of public policy.[5] As a result the Christian prohibition of abortion appears as an irrational prejudice of religious people who cannot argue it on a secular, rational basis.

But if Noonan is right that the convictions about human life rest on a perspective that is bound up with the "whole personality," then it seems that we Christians must make clear what we take such a "personality" to involve. For the Christian prohibition of abortion is a correlative to being a particular kind of people with a particular set and configuration of virtues. Yet we have tried to form our moral arguments against abortion within the moral framework of a liberal culture, as though the issue could be abstracted from the kind of people we should be. How the moral description and evaluation of abortion depends on more profound assumptions about the kind of people we ought to be was thus not even recognized by ourselves, much less by those who do not share our convictions. As a result Christian arguments about abortion have failed. They have not merely failed to convince, but have failed to suggest the kind of "reorientation" necessary if we are to be the kind of people and society that make abortion unthinkable.

Of course it may be objected that the arguments have not failed. The fact that not everyone agrees that abortion is immoral and the failure to pass a constitutional amendment are of themselves no indication that the anti-abortion arguments have been invalid. Even at the political level there is still good reason to think that all is not lost, for there are political and legal strategies that are just beginning to have an effect on reversing our society's current abortion stance.[6] Yet even if such strategies succeed, our success may still be a form of failure if we "win" without changing the presuppositions of the debate.

To understand why this is the case it is necessary to look more generally at the obstacle to moral agreement in our society. Only from such a perspective can we appreciate why the Christian stance concerning abortion may be a far more fundamental challenge to our society's moral presuppositions than even the most radical anti-abortionists have considered.

2. Abortion in a Liberal Society

According to Alasdair MacIntyre there is nothing peculiar about the failure of our society to reach a moral consensus concerning the appropriate manner to deal with abortion. Indeed the very character of debate in a liberal, secular, pluralist culture like ours shows that there is no rational method for resolving most significant matters of moral dispute. Any rational method for resolving moral disagreements requires a shared tradition that embodies assumptions about the nature of man and our true end.[7] But it is exactly the presumption of liberalism that a just society can be sustained by freeing the individual from all tradition.[8]

MacIntyre illustrates his argument by calling attention to three different positions concerning abortion:

A: Everybody has certain rights over their own person, including their own body. It follows from the nature of these rights that at the stage when the embryo is essentially part of the mother's body, the mother has a right to make her uncoerced decision on whether she will have an abortion or not. Therefore each pregnant woman ought to decide and ought to be allowed to decide for herself what she will do in the light of her own moral views.

B: I cannot, if I will to be alive, consistently will that my mother should have had an abortion when she was pregnant with me, except if it had been certain that the embryo was dead or gravely damaged. But if I cannot consistently will this in my own case, how can I consistently deny to others the right to life I claim for myself? I would break the so-called Golden Rule unless I denied that a mother has in general a right to abortion. I am not of course thereby committed to the view that abortion ought to be legally prohibited.

C: Murder is wrong, prohibited by natural and divine law. Murder is the taking of innocent life. An embryo is an identifiable individual, differing from a new-born infant only in being at an earlier stage on the long road to adult capacities. If infanticide is murder, as it is, then abortion is murder. So abortion is not only morally wrong, but ought to be legally prohibited.[9]

MacIntyre suggests the interesting thing about these arguments is that each of the protagonists reaches his conclusion by valid forms of inferences, yet there is no agreement about which premises are the right starting points. And in our culture there is no generally agreed upon procedure for weighing the merits of the rival premises. Each of the above positions represents fragments of moral systems that exist in uneasy relation to one another. Thus position A, premised as "an understanding of rights which owes something to Locke and something to Jefferson is counterposed to a universalibility argument whose debt is first to Kant and then to the gospels and both to an appeal to the moral law as conceived by Hooker, More, and Aquinas."[10]

The fact that these are "fragments" of past moral positions is particularly important. For as fragments they have been torn from the social and intellectual contexts in which they gained their original intelligibility and from which they derive such force and validity as they continue to possess. But since they now exist *only* as fragments, we do not know how to weigh one set of premises against another. We do not know what validity to grant to each in isolation from those presuppositions that sustained their original intelligibility.

To understand the roots of our dilemma, MacIntyre argues that we must look to the moral presuppositions on which our society was founded. For in spite of the appeal to self-evident truths about equality and rights to life, liberty, and the pursuit of happiness, there was the attempt to provide some cogent philosophical basis for these "truths." The difficulty, however, begins when appeals such as Jefferson's to Aristotle and Locke fail to acknowledge these to be mutually antagonistic positions. We are thus a society that may be in the unhappy position of being founded upon a moral contradiction.

The contradiction, in its most dramatic form, involves the impossibility of reconciling classical and modern views of man. Thus as MacIntyre points out:

> the central preoccupation of both ancient and medieval communities was characteristically: how may men together realize the true human good? The central preoccupation of modern men is and has been characteristically: how may we prevent men interfering with each other as each of us goes about our own concerns? The classical view begins with the community of the *polis* and with the individual viewed as having no moral identity apart from the communities of kinship and citizenship; the modern view begins with the concept of a collection of individuals and the problem of how out of and by individuals social institutions can be constructed.[11]

The attempt to answer the last question has been the primary preoccupation of social theorists since the seventeenth century, and their answers to it are not always coherent with one another.

In the face of this disagreement the political consensus has been that the most nearly just social arrangement is one which requires no commitment to any good except the protection of each individual to pursue his or her interests fairly. Thus John Rawls describes the way we ought to envisage the terms of an original contract between individuals on which a just society can be founded as one where they "do not share a conception of the good by reference to which the fruition of their powers or even the satisfaction of their desires can be evaluated. They do not have an agreed criterion of perfection that can be used as a principle for choosing between institutions. To acknowledge any such standard would be, in effect, to accept a principle that might lead to a lesser religious or other liberty."[12]

Such a view can no longer provide a place for the classical perspective's insistence on the development of virtuous people. From the classical perspective judgments about virtues and goods are interdependent, since the good is known only by observing how a virtuous man embodies it. But in the absence of any shared conception of the good, judgments about virtues and judgments about goods are logically independent of one another. Thus it becomes a political necessity, anchored in our society's profoundest moral convictions, that an issue such as abortion be considered on grounds independent of the kind of persons we would like to encourage in our society. The morality of the "act" of abortion must be considered separately from the "agent," for to take the character of the agent into account offends the basic moral and political consensus of our society.

We should be hesitant to criticize the moral achievement of political liberalism too quickly. By making the moral purpose of government the securing of the equal right of all individuals to pursue their happiness as they understand it, liberalism was able to secure political peace in a morally pluralistic and fragmentary society. Its deepest advantage is to remove from the political arena all issues that might be too deeply divisive of the citizenry.[13] The ideal of liberalism is thus to make government neutral on the very subjects that matter most to people, precisely *because* they matter most.

Of course our society has never acted with complete consistency on the principle of neutrality. Thus, we ended slavery, and polygamy was outlawed. And, more recently, the modern welfare function of the state appears to require that certain beliefs about what is good for people be the basis of public policy. But it can still be claimed that the state leaves to individuals and groups the power to determine what private vision of happiness to pursue. "Hence governmental programs to assure full employment, to guarantee equal opportunity to enter the professions, to give everyone as much education as he wants, etc., imply no communal understanding of the good which is to be imposed on all. These programs aim only at establishing the conditions that enable everyone to pursue his own good as he understands it."[14]

One of the ironies, however, is that the liberal state so conceived has worked only because its citizens continued to assume that the classical conception still held some validity for the regulation of their lives. Thus even though the virtues could not be encouraged as a "public" matter, they were still thought important as a private concern and of indirect benefit for our public life. Religion and the family institutions appropriate for the training of virtue were encouraged on the assumption they were necessary to sustain a polity based on the overriding status of the individual.

Thus, as Francis Canavan has argued,

> Liberal democracy has worked as well as it has and as long as it has because it has been able to trade on something that it did not create and which it tends on the whole to undermine. That is the moral tradition that prevailed among the greater part of the people. It is not necessary to pretend that most Americans in the past kept the Ten Commandments, certainly not that they kept them all the time. It is enough that by and large Americans agreed that there were Ten Commandments and that in principle they ought to be kept. The pluralist solution of withdrawing certain areas of life from legal control worked precisely because American pluralism was not all that pronounced. In consequence, many important areas of life were not withdrawn from the reach of law and public policy and were governed by a quasi-official public ethos.[15]

But in our day the moral consensus has disintegrated in a number of significant respects: we no longer have agreement on the value of human life, or on such basic social institutions as marriage and the family, or for that matter on the meaning of being human.

> At this point, it is doubtful whether the typical response of the liberal pluralist society is any longer adequate, that is, to take the dangerously controversial matters out of politics and relegate them to the conscience of individuals. For this way of eliminating controversy in fact does much more. Intentionally or not, it contributes to a reshaping of basic social institutions and a revision of the moral beliefs of multitudes of individuals beyond those directly concerned. It turns into a process by which one ethos, with its reflection in law and public policy, is replaced by another. Liberal pluralism then becomes a sort of confidence game in which, in the guise of showing respect for individual rights, we are in reality asked to consent to a new kind of society based on a new set of beliefs and values.[16]

Perhaps this is nowhere better seen than in the phenomenon that Noonan has called the "masks" of liberty. By masks he means the linguistic conventions that are developing to redescribe the object and means of injustice.[17] Language such as child, baby, and killing have to be avoided, for if such language is used it will require a break with the moral culture we assume we wish to preserve.[18] "If all that has happened may fairly be described as 'termination of a pregnancy' with 'fetal wastage' the outcome, abortion may be accepted without break with the larger moral culture. If, however, such a description is a mask, if the life of an unborn child is being taken, it is difficult to reconcile the acceptance of abortion with the overarching prohibition against the taking of life."[19]

Thus we attempt to change our language so our commitment to greater individual liberty concerning abortion will not contradict our traditional views about what kind of people we should be to deserve to be free. The reason that our arguments concerning abortion are bound to fail is that we cannot resolve the morally antithetical traditions that form our society and our Christian ambitions for ourselves. Attempting to resolve the issue as though the act of abortion could be separated from our conviction about character has been a futile attempt to settle a substantive moral issue on "objective" or procedural grounds acceptable to a liberal culture.

Thus Justice Blackmun's opinion, while no doubt out of harmony with the majority of opinion concerning abortion in America, may actually be in accordance with our deepest views if we apply them more consistently. An indication, perhaps, that we are better off as a people if we fail to think and act consistently! For the underlying presupposition of *Roe v. Wade* is consistent liberalism in assuming that the only entity with political standing is the individual. And individuals are understood to consist of characteristics sufficient to make him or her a "person." Of course, as Noonan points out, a liberalism so consistently applied also challenges some of our presumptions about the family,[20] but that may be but another price we have to pay in order to be "free."

Noonan has located the paradox of Justice Blackmun's opinion:

> To invalidate the state abortion statutes it was necessary for him not only to ignore the unborn child but to recognize a liberty anterior to the state in the carrier of the child. The invocation of liberty which was the very heart of his opinion was the invocation of a standard superior to enacted law. His radical use of "higher law" was only disguised by his claim that something in the Constitution supplied the standard by which the state laws on abortion were invalid. The ultimate basis of his decision was nothing in the Constitution but rather his readings of the natural law liberties of an individual.[21]

Blackmun has based his opinion on the most cherished moral presumption of our society: freedom of the individual.[22] Ironically, in the absence of a tradition, the ideal of a society constituted by individuals free of all tradition remains the sole moral basis we have for settling issues of moral significance.

3. Christians and Abortion: The Philosophical Issues

I showed above how in attempting to form their arguments against abortion in a manner that could be translated into public policy, Christians have accepted the moral limits imposed by our liberal heritage. As a result the reasons that Christians qua Christians should oppose abortion have not become a matter of public record. It should be noted that this was not just a strategic policy, but it also witnesses to our standing conviction of a profound commonality between Christianity and liberalism. Christians have assumed that the liberal commitment to the individual carried with it the prohibition of abortion. Yet what they have found is that the "individual" whom liberalism has an interest in protecting does not, either conceptually or normatively (though perhaps legally), necessarily include the fetus.

Such a discovery is shocking in itself; worse, it seems to leave Christians without further appeal. For we must admit that the fact and way abortion became a matter of moral controversy caught us by surprise and unprepared. We were prepared to argue about whether certain kinds of abortion might or might not be legally prohibited or permitted, but that we would be required to argue whether abortion as an institution is moral, amoral, or immoral was simply unthinkable. As Christians we knew generally that we were against abortion, but we were not clear why. We assumed it surely had to do with our prohibition against the taking of life, and we assumed that that was surely all that needed to be said.

There is nothing unusual about the Christian failure to know why abortion is to be prohibited. Most significant moral prohibitions do not need to be constantly justified or rethought. They are simply part and parcel of the way we are. When asked why we do or do not engage in a particular form of activity we often find that it makes perfectly good sense to say "Christians just do or do not do that kind of thing." And we think that we have given a moral reason. But it is moral because it appeals to "what we are," to what kind of people we think we should be; yet liberalism wishes to exclude such contentions from moral consideration in the interest of securing cooperation in a morally pluralistic society. Liberalism seeks a philosophical account of morality that can ground the rightness or wrongness of particular actions or behavior in a "theory" divorced from any substantive commitments about what kind of people we are or should be—except perhaps to the extent that we should be rational or fair.[23] However, as Stuart Hampshire has argued, such theories falsify the way in which moral injunctions function, such as those about life-taking, sexual relations, relations between parents and children, truth-telling. The meaning and unity between such injunctions cannot be easily inferred from the axioms of a theory. Rather,

taken together, a full set of such injunctions, prohibiting types of conduct in types of circumstance, describes in rough and indeterminate outline, an attainable and recognizable way of life, aspired to, respected and admired: or at least the minimum general features of a respectworthy way of life. And a way of life is not identified and characterized by one distinct purpose, such as in the increase of general happiness, or even by a set of such distinct purposes. The connection between the injunctions, the connection upon which a reasonable man reflects, is to be found in the coherence of a single way of life, distinguished by the characteristic virtues and vices recognized within it.[24]

Of course ways of life are complicated matters marked out by many details of style and manner. Moreover the "connectedness" of any set of injunctions often has the character, not of "rational" necessity, but rather of a "reasonableness" that derives from the history of a community's moral experience and wisdom. Such a community may well have prohibitions that have an almost absolute character, such as the Christian prohibition of abortion, but such prohibitions need not be categorical, in the Kantian sense, nor based on principles of rationality. Rather they are judgments of unconditioned necessity,

> in the sense that they imply that what must be done is not necessary because it is a means to some independently valued end, but because the action is a necessary part of a way of life and ideal of conduct. The necessity resides in the nature of the action itself, as specified in the fully explicit moral judgment. The principal and proximate grounds for claiming that the action must, or must not, be performed are to be found in the characterization of the action offered within the prescription; and if the argument is pressed further, first a virtue or vice, and then a whole way of life will have to be described.[25]

But I am suggesting that this is exactly what we as Christians failed to do when it came to explaining why abortion is to be avoided. We failed to show, for ourselves or others, why abortion is an affront to our most basic convictions about what makes life meaningful and worthwhile. We tried to argue in terms of the "facts" or on the basis of "principles" and thus failed to make intelligible why such "facts" or "principles" were relevant in the first place. We have spent our time arguing abstractly about when human life does or does not begin.[26] As a result, we have failed to challenge the basic presuppositions that force the debate to hinge on such abstractions.

Hampshire suggests that the best means to avoid the kind of abstract thinking encouraged by moral theories given birth by liberalism is to tell stories. For

> telling stories, with the facts taken from experience and not filtered and at second hand, imposes some principles of selection. In telling the story one has to select the facts and probabilities which, taken together, constitute the situation confronting the agent. Gradually, and by accumulation of examples, belief that the features of the particular case, indefinite in number, are not easily divided into the morally relevant and morally irrelevant will be underlined by the mere process of story-telling. One cannot establish conclusively by argument in gen-

eral terms the general conclusion that the morally relevant features of situations encountered cannot be circumscribed. One can only appeal to actual examples and call the mind back to personal experience, which will probably include occasions when the particular circumstances of the case modified what would have been the expected and principled decisions, and for reasons which do not themselves enter into any recognized principle.[27]

In a like manner I am suggesting that if Christians are to make their moral and political convictions concerning abortion intelligible we must show how the meaning and prohibition of abortion is correlative to the stories of God and his people that form our basic conviction. We must indicate why it is that the Christian way of life forms people in a manner that makes abortion unthinkable. Ironically it is only when we have done this that we will have the basis for suggesting why the fetus should be regarded as but another of God's children.

For as Roger Wertheimer has shown, arguments concerning the status of the fetus's humanity are not factual arguments at all, but actually moral claims requiring the training of imagination and perception. Wertheimer suggests that the argument over the status of the fetus is a

paradigm of what Wittgenstein had in mind when he spoke of the possibility of two people agreeing on the application of a rule for a long period, and then, suddenly and quite inexplicably, diverging in what they call going on in the same way. This possibility led him to insist that linguistic communication presupposes not only agreement in definitions, but also agreement in judgments, in what he called forms of life—something that seems lacking in the case at hand (i.e., the fetus). Apparently, the conclusion to draw is that it is not true that the fetus is a human being, but it is not false either. Without agreement in judgments, without a common response to the pertinent data, the assertion that the fetus is a human being cannot be assigned a genuine truth value.[28]

Wertheimer suggests that there seems to be no "natural" response, no clear forms of life, which provide the basis for why the fetus should be regarded one way rather than another. Thus failure to respect the fetus is not analogous to failure to respect blacks or Jews, since we share forms of life, common responses, with them that make the denial of their humanity unintelligible. Thus the forms of life that lead some to believe and treat blacks and Jews as less than human can be shown to be perverse by appeal to obvious factual counterclaims based on our common experiences.

Wertheimer may be right that the case for respect for blacks and Jews is more immediately obvious than the case for the fetus, but I hope to show that the Christian form of life provides powerful reasons why the fetus should be regarded with respect and care. Moreover such respect is as profoundly "natural" as our current belief that blacks and Jews have moral status. What we must understand is that all "natural" relations are "historical" insofar as the natural is but what we have come to accept as "second nature."[29] The recognition of blacks and Jews was no less dependent on a history than the recognition of the status of the fetus. Both are the result of the experience of communities which are formed by substantive convictions of the significance of being open to new life. Because such an "openness" has become so "natural," and often so perverted, we have forgotten what profound moral commitments support and are embodied in the simple and everyday desire and expectation of new life that appears among us through and after pregnancy. Such a desire is obviously not peculiar to Christians, but by attending more directly to the Christian form of life I hope to show why and how the Christian desire for children makes it imperative that the fetus be regarded with respect and care.

4. Christians and Abortion: The Narrative Context

If my analysis has been correct we should now have a better hold on why arguments concerning abortion have failed in our society. At one level I have tried to show they must fail given the moral presuppositions and language offered by our liberal ethos. But I have also tried to suggest that failure at this level is but an indication of a deeper failure for Christians. Christians have failed their social order by accepting too easily the terms of argument concerning abortion offered by our society. If we are to serve our society well, and on our own terms, our first task must be to address ourselves by articulating for Christians why abortion can never be regarded as morally indifferent for us. Only by doing this can we witness to our society what kind of people and what kind of society is required if abortion is to be excluded.

Such a suggestion may sound extremely odd, since it seems to ask that we reinvent the wheel. Surely that is not the case, for both anti- and pro-abortion advocates know that, rightly or wrongly, Christians have had their minds made up about abortion from the beginning. It is certainly true that Christians, drawing on their Jewish roots, have condemned abortion from earliest days.[30] Yet this condemnation does not come from nowhere; it is a correlative of a way of life that must be constantly renewed and rethought. The task of each new generation of Christians is to rediscover that way of life and why prohibitions such as that against abortion are critical reminders of what kind of life it is that they are called to lead. The Christian way of life, though often lived simply, is no simple matter but involves a complex set of convictions that are constantly being reinterpreted as our understanding of one aspect of the tradition illuminates another. What we must do is show how this process makes a difference for our understanding of the prohibition of abortion.

It is important, furthermore, to distinguish my argument in this respect from those who make the often unfair criticism that the church must rethink its position on abortion because it allows the taking of life in other contexts. Though I do not wish to deny that Christians have often been inconsistent, especially in practice, about the protection and taking of life, there is nothing conceptually inconsistent about the prohibition of abortion as the unjust taking of life and the permissibility of just war and capital punishment. My call for the church to rethink her understanding of abortion involves the more fundamental concern that the church understand why abortion is incompatible with a community whose constitution is nothing less than the story of God's promise to mankind through the calling of Israel and the life of Jesus.

Such a discussion must be both theological and political. One cannot be separated from the other. Our beliefs about God are political, as they form the kind of community that makes the prohibition of abortion intelligible. But the discussion is also political, as it must be done in such a manner that Christians listen and learn from one another concerning their different understanding of what is at stake in abortion. Only by proceeding in this way can we be a paradigm, and perhaps even a witness, to our society of what a genuine moral discussion might look like.

I do not mean to imply that such discussion has been missing entirely in recent Christian history. Yet I think it is fair to say that we have not paid sufficient attention to how Christians as Christians should think about abortion.[31] Indeed I suspect many are not even sure what a call for this kind of discussion entails. Therefore I will try to suggest the kind of theological concerns that any discussion of abortion by Christians should involve.

To begin with, the first question is not, "Why do Christians think abortion is wrong?" To begin there already presupposes that we know and understand what abortion is. Rather, if we are to understand why Christians assume that by naming abortion they have already said something significant, we have to begin still a step back. We have to ask what it is about the kind of community, and corresponding world, that Christians create that makes them single out abortion in such a way as to exclude it.

For we must remember that "abortion" is not a description of a particular kind of behavior; rather it is a word that teaches us to see a singular kind of behavior from a particular community's moral perspective. The removal of the fetus from the mother's uterus before term can be called an "interruption of pregnancy," the child can be called "fetal matter," and the mother can be called a "patient." But from the Christian perspective, to see the situation in that way changes the self and the community in a decisive way. The Christian insistence on the term "abortion" is a way to remind them that what happens in the removal of the fetus from the mother in order to destroy it strikes at the heart of their community. From this perspective the attempt of Christians to be a community where the term "abortion" remains morally intelligible is a political act.

In this respect the pro-abortionists have always been at a disadvantage.[32] For they have had to carry out the argument in a language created by the moral presuppositions of the Jewish and Christian communities. "Abortion" still carries the connotation that this is not a good thing. Thus to be "pro-abortion" seems to put one in an embarrassing position of recommending a less than good thing. It is not without reason, therefore, that pro-abortion advocates seek to redescribe both the object and act of abortion. We must remind them, however, that by doing so they not only change the description of the act, they also change themselves.

Christians insist on the significance of such a change by refusing to live in a world devoid of abortion as a moral description—a world which admittedly may, as a result, involve deep tragedy. There can be no doubt that the insistence that unjust termination of pregnancy be called "abortion" has to do with our respect for life, but that is surely too simple. Jews and Christians are taught to respect life, not as an end in itself, but as a gift created by God. Thus life is respected because all life serves God in its way. Respect for human life is but a form of our respect for all life.

But note that just as no particular life can claim highest value, except as it exists for the love and service of God, neither can human life be thought to have absolute value. The Christian prohibition against taking life rests not on the assumption that human life has overriding value, but on the conviction that it is not ours to take. The Christian prohibition of abortion derives not from any assumption of the inherent value of life, but rather from the understanding that as God's creatures we have no basis to claim sovereignty over life.

And we cannot forget that this creator is also our redeemer. The life that lies in the womb is also a life that has come under the lordship of Jesus Christ. As Karl Barth has said,

> this child is a man for whose life the Son of God has died, for whose unavoidable part in the guilt of all humanity and future individual guilt He has already paid the price. The true light of the world shines already in the darkness of the mother's womb. And yet they want to kill him deliberately because certain reasons which have nothing to do with the child himself favor the view that he had better not be born! Is there any emergency which can justify this? It must surely be clear to us that until the question is put in all its gravity a serious discussion of the problem cannot even begin, let alone lead to serious results.[33]

The temptation, in this secular age, is to ignore this kind of rhetorical flourish on the assumption that all it really amounts to is that Christians also believe in the value or sacredness of life. But from the perspective of Christian convictions about life as the locus of God's creating and redeeming purpose, claims of life's "value" or "sacredness" are but empty abstractions. The value of life is God's value and our commitment to protect it is a form of our worship of God as a good creator and a trustworthy redeemer. Our question is not "When does life begin?" but "Who is its true sovereign?" The creation and meaningfulness of the term "abortion" gain intelligibility from our conviction that God, not man, is creator and redeemer, and thus, the Lord of life. The Christian respect for life is first of all a statement, not about life, but about God.[34]

Yet the way of life of Christians involves more than the conviction of God's creating and redeeming purposes. We also believe that God has created and called us to be a people whose task it is to manifest and witness to his providential care of our existence. Thus to be a Christian is not just to hold certain beliefs, but it is to be part of a historic community that has the task of maintaining faithful continuity with our forebears. To be a Christian is to be part of a people who live through memory, since we only know how to face and create our future by striving to be as faithful and courageous as our forebears. The necessity of memory for our continued existence is but a form of our worship of our God, who wills to be known through the lives of his followers.

Christians are thus a people who have an immense stake in history. We look neither to escape nor to transcend history. Rather we are determined to live within history, hopefully living faithful to the memory of our founder. There is no conviction, therefore, more significant for Christians than our insistence on having children. For children are our anchors in history, our pledge and witness that the Lord we serve is the Lord, not only of our community, but of all history. The family is, therefore, symbolically central for the meaning of the existence of the Christian people.

From a Christian perspective children represent our continuing commitment to live as a historic people.[35] In the Christian community children are, for those who are called to be married, a duty. For the vocation of marriage in part derives its intelligibility from a couple's willingness to be open to new life. Indeed that is part of the test of the validity of their unity as one worthy to be called "love" in the Christian sense. It must necessarily be open to creation of another.

The Christian community's openness to new life and our conviction of the sovereignty of God over that life are but two sides of the same conviction. Christians believe that we have the time in this existence to care for new life, especially as such life is dependent and vulnerable, because it is not our task to rule this world or to "make our mark on history." We can thus take the time to live in history as God's people who have nothing more important to do than to have and care for children. For it is the Christian claim that knowledge and love of God is fostered by service to the neighbor, especially the most helpless, as in fact that is where we find the kind of Kingdom our God would have us serve.

It is the Christian belief, nurtured by the command of Jesus, that we must learn to love one another, that we become more nearly what we were meant to be through the recognition and love of those we did not "choose" to love. Children, the weak, the ill, the dispossessed provide a particularly intense occasion for such love, as they are beings we cannot control. We must love them for what they are rather than what we want or wish them to be, and as a result we discover that we are capable of love. The existence of such love is not unique or limited to Christians. Indeed that is why we have the confidence that our Christian convictions on these matters might ring true even for those who do not share our convictions. The difference between the Christian and the non-Christian is only that what is a possibility for the non-Christian is a duty for the Christian.

But the Christian duty to welcome new life is a joyful duty, as it derives from our very being as God's people. Moreover correlative to the language of duty is the language of gift. Because children are a duty they can also be regarded as gift, for duty teaches us to accept and welcome a child into the world, not as something that is "ours," but as a gift which comes from another.[36] As a result Christians need not resort to destructive and self-deceiving claims about the qualities they need to have, or the conditions of the world necessary to have children. Perhaps more worrisome than the moral implications of the claim "no unwanted child ought ever to be born," are the ominous assumptions about what is required for one to "want" to have a child.

Christians are thus trained to be the kind of people who are ready to receive and welcome children into the world. For they see children as a sign of the trustworthiness of God's creation and his unwillingness to abandon the world to the powers of darkness. The Christian prohibition of abortion is but the negative side of their positive commitment to welcome new life into their community: life that they know must challenge and perhaps even change their own interpretation of their tradition, but also life without which the tradition has no means to grow.

It is, of course, true that children will often be conceived and born under less than ideal conditions, but the church lives as a community which assumes that we live in an age which is always dangerous. That we live in such a time is all the more reason we must be the kind of community that can receive children into our midst. Just as we need to be virtuous, not because virtue pays but because we cannot afford to be without virtue where it does not pay, so we must learn how to be people open to new life. We can neither protect them from that suffering nor deny them the joy of participating in the adventure of God's Kingdom.

For Christians, therefore, there can be no question of whether the fetus is or is not a "human being." That way of putting the matter is far too abstract and formal. Rather, because of the kind of community we are, we see in the fetus nothing less than God's continuing creation that is destined in hope to be another citizen of his Kingdom. The question of when human life begins is of little interest to such a people, since their hope is that life will and does continue to begin time after time.[37]

This is the form of life that brings significance to our interaction with the fetus. Our history is the basis for our "natural" sympathies, which have been trained to look forward to the joy and challenge of new life. Wertheimer may well be right that there is no corresponding "natural" welcome for life in our society that would make intelligible the recognition of the fetus as having moral status. Yet I suspect that the expectation of parents, and in particular of women, for the birth of their children remains a powerful form of life that continues to exert a force on everyone. Such an "expectation," however, in the absence of more substantive convictions about parenting, too easily becomes a destructive necessity that distorts the experience of being a parent and a child. Particularly repugnant is the assumption that women are thus primarily defined by the role of "mother," for then we forget that the role of being a parent, even for the childless, is a responsibility for everyone in the Christian community.

Nor should it be thought that the Christian commitment to welcome new life into the world stems from a sentimental fondness for babies. Rather, for Christians the having of children is one of their most significant political acts. From the world's perspective the birth of a child represents but another drain on our material and psychological resources. Children, after all, take up much of our energy that could be spent on making the world a better place and our society more just. But from the Christian perspective the birth of a child represents nothing less than our commitment that God will not have this world "bettered" by destroying life. That is why there is no more profound political act for Christians than taking the time for children. It is but an indication that God, not man, rules this existence, and we have been graciously invited to have a part in God's adventure and his Kingdom through the simple action of having children.

5. Christians and Abortion: The Immediate Political Task

To some it may seem that I have argued Christians right out of the current controversy, for my argument has made appeal to religious convictions that are inadmissible in the court of our public ethos. But it has certainly not been my intention to make it implausible for Christians to continue to work in the public arena for the protection of all children; nor do I think that this implication follows from the position I have developed. Of course, Christians should prefer to live in societies that provide protection for children. And Christians should certainly wish to encourage those "natural" sentiments that would provide a basis for having and protecting children.

Moreover Christians must be concerned to develop forms of care and support, the absence of which seem to make abortion such a necessity in our society. In particular Christians should, in their own communities, make clear that the role of parent is one we all share. Thus the woman who is pregnant and carrying the child need not be the one to raise it. We must be a people who stand ready to receive and care for any child, not just as if it were one of ours, but because in fact each is one of ours.

But as Christians we must not confuse our political and moral strategies designed to get the best possible care for children in our society with the substance of our convictions. Nor should we hide the latter in the interest of securing the former. For when that is done we abandon our society to its own limits. And then our arguments fall silent in the most regrettable manner, for we forget that our most fundamental political task is to be and to point to that truth which we believe to be the necessary basis for any life-enhancing and just society.

In particular, I think that we will be wise as Christians to state our opposition to abortion in a manner that makes clear our broader concerns for the kind of people we ought to be to welcome children into the world. Therefore, rather than concentrating our energies on whether the fetus is or is not a "person," we would be better advised by example and then argument to make clear why we should hope it is a child. We must show that such a hope involves more than just the question of the status of the fetus, but indeed is the very reason why being a part of God's creation is such an extraordinary and interesting adventure.

Notes

1. *Roe v. Wade*, 410 U.S. 113.
2. For example see Mary Anne Warren, "On the Moral and Legal Status of Abortion," in *Contemporary Issues in Bioethics*, ed. I. Beauchamp and L. Walters (Encino, Calif.: Dickenson Publishing Co., 1978), 222–25. Warren's argument in this respect is common in current philosophical literature. Perhaps the most celebrated form of it is Michael Tooley's article, "Abortion and Infanticide," in *The Rights and Wrongs of Abortion*, ed. M. Cohen, T. Nagel, and T. Scanlon (Princeton, N.J.: Princeton University Press, 1974), 52–84.
3. Thus Warren argues that "the moral community consists of all and only *people*, rather than all and only human beings," and the characteristics of the former

she takes to be consciousness, reasoning, self-motivated activity, the capacity to communicate whatever the means, and presence of self-concepts, 223–24. For an extremely interesting article dealing with the ambiguity of deciding whether a class of beings are human see Edmund Pincoffs, "Membership Decisions and the Limits of Moral Obligation," in *Abortion: New Directions for Policy Studies*, ed. E. Manier, W. Liu, and D. Solomon (Notre Dame, Ind.: University of Notre Dame Press, 1977), 31–49. I have argued elsewhere against the significance of "person" as a moral ascription, but it is hard to deny its significance in a society such as ours. For the idea of "person" embodies our attempt to recognize that everyone has a moral status prior to any role they might assume. It therefore represents the profound egalitarian commitment of our culture. The difficulty, of course, is that the notion of being a "person" seems to carry with it psychological implications that simply exclude certain beings from being treated with respect. See my *Truthfulness and Tragedy* (Notre Dame, Ind.: University of Notre Dame Press, 1977), 127–32, 157–63.

4. John Noonan, *A Private Choice: Abortion in America in the Seventies* (New York: Free Press, 1979), 2–3. In his earlier essay, "An Almost Absolute Value in History," Noonan had argued that conception is the decisive moment of humanization because "at conception the being receives the genetic code. It is this genetic information which determines his characteristics, which is the biological carrier of the possibility of human wisdom, which makes him a self-evolving being. A being with a human genetic code is man." In John T. Noonan, ed., *The Morality of Abortion* (Cambridge: Harvard University Press, 1970), 1–59. Noonan obviously no longer regards such empirical claims as decisive for establishing the moral status of the fetus, though they may certainly be sufficient for claiming that the fetus is a human being. Underlying the issue of the relation between the moral and descriptive status of the fetus may be the larger assumption that the distinction between facts and values, or better, how values include factual claims, makes sense. Thus the claim that the anti-abortionist is confusing a "moral" claim with a "factual" claim may involve the unwarranted assumption that such "facts" are not moral.

5. Thus Roger Wertheimer suggests that the anti-abortionist "realizes that, unless he uses religious premises, premises inadmissible in the court of common morality, he has no way of categorically condemning the killing of a fetus except by arguing that a fetus is a person." From "Understanding the Abortion Argument," *The Rights and Wrongs of Abortion*, 37. But, as we shall see, the assumption that there is a common morality with an agreed upon content can hardly be accepted in our society. Moreover, I hope to show that theological convictions play quite a different role than Wertheimer and many others seem to assume. For there is no theological means to determine when life begins. Indeed, a Christian understanding of the morality of abortion should make such a question irrelevant.

6. Noonan has made a strong case, for example, for a constitutional amendment that would not prohibit states from protecting unborn life if it is the will of

their legislatures. Such an amendment would at least provide the possibility of a more refined moral debate on this issue in our society. Moreover it might result in laws that do not have the negative effect on other institutions, such as the family, that the current abortion ruling seems to involve. See Noonan, *A Private Choice,* 178–88.

7. Alasdair MacIntyre, "How Virtues Become Vices," in *Evaluation and Explanation in Biomedical Sciences,* ed. Engelhardt and Spicker (Dordrecht: Reidel, 1974), 104.

8. Ironically the anti-traditional stance of liberalism results in self-deception, since liberalism is only intelligible in the light of its history. It is, of course, true that liberalism is an extremely complex phenomenon that is not easily characterized even by the most sophisticated forms of political theory. I associate liberalism, however, with the political philosophy of Rawls and Nozick, the political science of Dahl, and the economics of neo-capitalism. There often appear to be deep disagreements between the advocates of liberalism in America, but such disagreements are finally arguments between brothers.

9. Alasdair MacIntyre, "How to Identify Ethical Principles," *The Belmont Report: Ethical Principles and Guidelines for the Protection of Human Subjects of Research,* I (Washington, D.C.: DHEW Publication No. (OS) 78-0013, 1978), article 10, 9–10. For an extremely able development of this argument, see Philip Devine, *The Ethics of Homicide* (Ithaca, N.Y.: Cornell University Press, 1978). Devine argues "that acts of homicide are prima facie seriously wrong because they are acts of homicide, and not for any supposedly more fundamental reason, such as that they tend to produce disutility or are unjust or unkind, and that this prima facie wrongness cannot be overridden by merely utilitarian considerations," p. 11. He correctly refuses to try to give a further theoretical account for why unjustified homicide is wrong, since such an account necessarily has the effect of qualifying the prohibition.

10. MacIntyre, "How to Identify Ethical Principles," 10. Garry Wills's recent study of Jefferson certainly requires a reconsideration of Jefferson's position vis-à-vis Locke. Wills makes clear that Jefferson's position owes more to the communitarian strains of the Scottish Common Sense philosophers, such as Hutcheson, than had been suspected. An indication of the power of Locke and the general liberal-contractarian tradition in America is that, in spite of what Jefferson's own views might have been, they were simply interpreted through the eyes of Locke. See Garry Wills, *Inventing America: Jefferson's Declaration of Independence* (Garden City, N.Y.: Doubleday, 1978).

11. MacIntyre, "How to Identify Ethical Principles," 22. This change in perspective also makes clear why so many attempt to form all moral arguments in the language of "right." "Rights" become our way to protect ourselves from one another.

12. John Rawls, *A Theory of Justice* (Cambridge: Harvard University Press, 1971), 327. One of the difficulties with Rawls' assumption that the meaning of jus-

tice can be separated from a conception of the good is that he ends up endorsing an understanding of the good to which he would object on other grounds. For, in spite of Rawls' richer view of the relation of individual and community in the last sections of *A Theory of Justice*, methodologically his position does not exclude the economic man enshrined in liberal theory.

13. Francis Canavan, "The Dilemma of Liberal Pluralism," *The Human Life Review* 5/3 (summer 1979): 7. The social and political experience of the American people has often contained more profound moral commitments than our commitment to liberal ideology could express. As a result we have often been unable to give some of our most significant achievements political standing.

14. Ibid., 9.

15. Ibid., 14.

16. Ibid., 15.

17. Noonan, *A Private Choice*, 153–69.

18. It is interesting, however, that women undergoing abortion often continue to describe the fetus as a baby or child. See, for example, Linda Bird Francke, *The Ambivalence of Abortion* (New York: Random House, 1978).

19. Noonan, *A Private Choice*, 175. Warren's attempt to deny that her arguments imply infanticide are interesting in this respect. She says that it would be wrong to kill a newborn infant, "because even if its parents do not want it and would not suffer from its destruction, there are other people who would like to have it, and would in all probability, be deprived of a great deal of pleasure by its destruction. Thus, infanticide is wrong for reasons analogous to those which make it wrong to wantonly destroy natural resources, or great works of art. Secondly, most people, at least in this country, value infants and would much prefer that they be preserved, even if foster parents are not immediately available," 227. Warren seems to feel no difficulty in making the prohibition against infanticide depend on whether someone might want a child. Moreover she is rigorously consistent and clear that if an "unwanted or defective infant is born into a society which cannot afford and/or is not willing to care for it, then its destruction is permissible," 227. It does not seem to occur to her that we ought to be the kind of society, no matter what our material appetites, that is able to receive children, even retarded children, into our midst. Her argument is a clear example, therefore, of the assumption that the rightness or wrongness of acts can be abstracted from the kind of people we ought to be.

20. Noonan, *A Private Choice*, 90–96.

21. Ibid., 17.

22. The abortion decisions of the current Supreme Court can in some ways be interpreted as further extensions of the arguments of the laissez-faire capitalist, only now they are being applied to issues of personal morality. Just as those earlier decisions that enshrined for a time such views as the law of the land regarding the regulation of business distorted the law, so do these recent

decisions. Indeed there has always been an uneasy tension between our legal tradition and the ideology of liberalism. It may well be, however, that as liberalism has become an increasingly self-fulfilling prophecy in so many other aspects of our life, so it will ultimately transform our legal tradition.

23. It is my contention that current ethical theory involves an attempt to write about "morality" in a manner required by a liberal society. The very assumption that "ethics" can be a "discipline" separate from political theory and economics seems to me to be an indication of the power of liberalism over our imagination. Such moral philosophies attempt to provide highly formal accounts of the conditions of moral argument and judgment separate from the beliefs of actual agents. One cannot help but admire their attempt to find a way to make moral argument work between people who share no common values, but they fail to see that such accounts too easily become ideologies for the status quo.

24. Stuart Hampshire, "Morality and Pessimism," in *Public and Private Morality*, ed. Stuart Hampshire (Cambridge: Cambridge University Press, 1978), 11.

25. Ibid., 13.

26. Ironically, Christians have often tried to construct their arguments by using moral theories, especially the more deontological theories, that make rationality the basis for any moral claim. Though these theories often provide powerful accounts for why everyone deserves a minimum of respect, by their very structure they exclude the fetus from their account.

27. Stuart Hampshire, "Public and Private Morality," in *Public and Private Morality*, 38–39.

28. Wertheimer, "Understanding the Abortion Argument," 42. See Wertheimer's fine article, "Philosophy on Humanity," in *Abortion: New Directions for Policy Studies* (Notre Dame, Ind.: University of Notre Dame Press, 1977), 117–36.

29. I suspect that Wertheimer would not deny this point as he is not using "nature" in a theory-laden sense but simply means by it "what is common." Thus whereas we have many everyday experiences with blacks, we do not "bump into" the fetus in the same manner. Yet as I will argue below, there are powerful forms of life which are unintelligible apart from the existence of the fetus.

30. See for example John Connery's excellent history of moral reflection on the subject, *Abortion: The Development of the Roman Catholic Perspective* (Chicago: Loyola University Press, 1977).

31. In a sense, Christian discussion of abortion has been too "ethical" and insufficiently theological. In effect we became the victim of our own highly refined casuistry on the subject and failed to rethink the theological context that made the casuistry intelligible in the first place. Thus consideration of whether certain acts of abortion might be permissible were abstracted from the community's narrative that made the prohibition of abortion intelligible. No community can or should avoid casuistical reflection, but it should always remember that the function of casuistry is to help the community save

its language and judgments from distortion through analogical comparisons. And control of the analogies ultimately depends on paradigms rooted in the community's experience as interpreted through its central narratives.

32. There is a broader issue involved here, which can only be mentioned. For just as liberalism has often "worked" only because it could continue to count on forms of life that it did not support and even worked against, so current ethical theory has often seemed intelligible because it continued to be able to rely on moral language and descriptions for which it can give little basis. Thus contemporary ethical theory tends to concentrate on questions of decision and justification and avoids issues of how we learn to see and describe our experience morally.

33. Karl Barth, *Church Dogmatics,* III/4, trans. MacKay et al. (Edinburgh: T. & T. Clark, 1961), 416.

34. There is nothing about this claim that requires that all abortions are to be prohibited. Indeed, when abortions may be permitted will depend on the experience and discussion of a community formed by the conviction of God's sovereignty over life. The broad theological claims I am developing here cannot determine concrete cases, though they can determine how abortion as a practice can and should be understood and evaluated.

35. In *The Culture of Narcissism* (New York: Norton, 1978), Christopher Lasch suggests that a people's sense of historical time and their attitudes toward children are closely interrelated. Thus "the narcissistic personality reflects among other things a drastic shift in our sense of historical time. Narcissism emerges as the typical form of character structure in a society that has lost interest in the future. Psychiatrists who tell parents not to live through their offspring; married couples who postpone or reject parenthood, often for good practical reasons; social reformers who urge zero population growth, all testify to a pervasive uneasiness about reproduction—to widespread doubts, indeed, about whether our society should reproduce itself at all. Under these conditions, the thought of our eventual suppression and death becomes utterly insupportable and gives rise to attempts to abolish old age and to extend life indefinitely. When men find themselves incapable of taking an interest in earthly life after their own death, they wish for eternal youth; for the same reason they no longer care to reproduce themselves. When the prospect of being superseded becomes intolerable, parenthood itself, which guarantees that it will happen, appears almost as a form of self-destruction," 211.

36. For a fuller presentation of this theme see my *Truthfulness and Tragedy,* 147–56.

37. The issue of when life begins will of course come up in considering hard cases. Connery, for example, provides a good overview of the history of such reflection in his book. Yet just as hard cases make bad law, so hard cases can distort our moral reflection if, in the process of our reflection on them, we forget the more positive commitments that make the casuistry intelligible. It

is noteworthy, however, as Connery makes clear, that the question of when life begins has always been a side issue for Christian casuistry. Rather, the concern has been whether the taking of the life of the fetus under particular circumstances is analogous to other situations where it is unavoidable or permissible that life be taken.

[35]

Theology and Morality of Procreative Choice

Beverly Wildung Harrison with Shirley Cloyes

Much discussion of abortion betrays the heavy hand of misogyny, the hatred of women. We all have a responsibility to recognize this bias—sometimes subtle—when ancient negative attitudes toward women intrude into the abortion debate. It is morally incumbent on us to convert the Christian position to a teaching more respectful of women's concrete history and experience.

My professional peers who are my opponents on this question feel they own the Christian tradition in this matter and recognize no need to rethink their positions in the light of this claim. As a feminist, I cannot sit in silence when women's right to shape the use of our own procreative power is denied. Women's competence as moral decision makers is once again challenged by the state even before the moral basis of women's right to procreative choice has been fully elaborated and recognized. Those who deny women control of procreative power claim that they do so in defense of moral sensibility, in the name of the sanctity of human life. We have a long way to go before the sanctity of human life will include genuine regard and concern for every female already born, and no social policy discussion that obscures this fact deserves to be called moral. We hope the day will come when it will not be called "Christian" either, for the Christian ethos is the generating source of the cur-

SOURCE: From *Making the Connections* by Beverly Harrison and Carol S. Robb. Copyright © 1985 by Beverly Wildung Harrison and Carol S. Robb. Reprinted by permission of Beacon Press.

rent moral crusade to prevent women from gaining control over the most life-shaping power we possess.

Although I am a Protestant, my own "moral theology"[1] has more in common with a Catholic approach than with much neo-orthodox ethics of my own tradition. I want to stress this at the outset because in what follows I am highly critical of the reigning Roman Catholic social teaching on procreation and abortion. I believe that on most other issues of social justice, the Catholic tradition is often more substantive, morally serious, and less imbued with the dominant economic ideology than the brand of Protestant theological ethics that claims biblical warrants for its moral norms. I am no biblicist; I believe that the human wisdom that informs our ethics derives not from using the Bible alone but from reflecting in a manner that earlier Catholic moral theologians referred to as consonant with "natural law."[2] Unfortunately, however, all major strands of natural law reflection have been every bit as awful as Protestant biblicism on any matter involving human sexuality, including discussion of women's nature and women's divine vocation in relation to procreative power. And it is precisely because I recognize Catholic natural law tradition as having produced the most sophisticated type of moral reflection among Christians that I believe it must be challenged where it intersects negatively with women's lives.

Given the depth of my dissatisfaction with Protestant moral tradition, I take no pleasure in singling out Roman Catholic moral theology and the activity of the Catholic hierarchy on the abortion issue. The problem nevertheless remains that there is really only one set of moral claims involved in the Christian antiabortion argument. Protestants who oppose procreative choice[3] either tend to follow official Catholic moral theology on these matters or ground their positions in biblicist anti-intellectualism, claiming that God's "word" requires no justification other than their attestation that divine utterance says what it says. Against such irrationalism, no rational objections have a chance. When, however, Protestant fundamentalists actually specify the reasons why they believe abortion is evil, they invariably revert to traditional natural law assumptions about women, sexuality, and procreation. Hence, direct objection must be registered to the traditional natural law framework if we are serious about transforming Christian moral teaching on abortion.

To do a methodologically adequate analysis of any moral problem in religious social ethics it is necessary to (1) situate the problem in the context of various religious communities' theologies or "generative" stories, (2) do a critical historical review of the problem as it appears in our religious traditions and in the concrete lives of human agents (so that we do not confuse the past and the present), (3) scrutinize the problem from the standpoint of various moral theories, and (4) analyze existing social policy and potential alternatives to determine our "normative moral sense" or best judgment of what ought to be done in contemporary society. Although these methodological basepoints must be addressed in any socioethical analysis, their treatment is crucial when abortion is under discussion because unexamined theological presumptions and misrepresentations of Christian history figure heavily in the current public policy debate. Given the brevity of this essay, I will address the theological, Christian historical, and moral theoretical problematics first and analyze the social policy dimensions of the abortion issue only at the end, even though optimum ethical methodology would reverse this procedure.

Abortion in Theological Context

In the history of Christian theology, a central metaphor for understanding life, including human life, is as a gift of God. Creation itself has been interpreted primarily under this metaphor. It follows that in this creational context procreation itself took on special significance as the central image for the divine blessing of human life. The elevation of procreation as the central symbol of divine benevolence happened over time, however. It did not, for instance, typify the very early, primitive Christian community. The synoptic gospels provide ample evidence that procreation played no such metaphorical role in early Christianity.[4] In later Christian history, an emergent powerful antisexual bias within Christianity made asceticism the primary spiritual ideal, although this ideal usually stood in tension with procreative power as a second sacred expression of divine blessing. But by the time of the Protestant Reformation, there was clear reaffirmation of the early Israelite theme of procreative blessing, and procreation has since become all but synonymous among Christians with the theological theme of creation as divine gift. It is important to observe that Roman Catholic theology actually followed on and adapted to Protestant teaching on this point.[5] Only in the last century, with the recognition of the danger of dramatic population growth in a world of finite resources, has any question been raised about the appropriateness of this unqualified theological sacralization of procreation.

The elevation of procreation as the central image for divine blessing is intimately connected to the rise of patriarchy. In patriarchal societies it is the male's power that is enhanced by the gift of new life. Throughout history, women's power of procreation has stood in definite tension with this male social control. In fact, what we feminists call patriarchy—that is, patterned or institutionalized legitimations of male superiority—derives from the need of men, through male-dominated political institutions such as tribes, states, and religious systems, to control women's power to procreate the species. We must assume, then, that many of these efforts at social control of procreation, including some church teaching on contraception and abortion, were part of this institutional system. The perpetuation of patriarchal control itself depended on wresting the power of procreation from women and shaping women's lives accordingly.

In the past four centuries, the entire Christian story has had to undergo dramatic accommodation to new and emergent world conditions and to the scientific revolution. As the older theological metaphors for creation encountered the rising power of science, a new self-understanding including our human capacity to affect nature had to be incorporated into Christian theology or its central theological story would have become obscurantist. Human agency had to be introjected into a dialectical understanding of creation.

The range of human freedom to shape and enhance creation is now celebrated theologically, but only up to the point of changes in our understanding of what is natural for women. Here a barrier has been drawn that declares No Radical Freedom! The only difference between mainstream Protestant and Roman Catholic theologians on these matters is at the point of contraception, which Protestants more readily accept. However, Protestants like Karl Barth and Helmut Thielicke exhibit a subtle shift of mood when they turn to discussing issues regarding women. They follow the typical Protestant pattern: They have accepted contraception or family planning as part of the new freedom, granted by God, but both draw back from the idea that abortion could be morally acceptable. In *The Ethics of Sex*, Thielicke offers a romantic, ecstatic celebration of family planning on one page and then elaborates a total denunciation of abortion as unthinkable on the next.[6] Most Christian theological opinion draws the line between contraception and abortion, whereas the *official* Catholic teaching still anathematizes contraception.

The problem, then, is that Christian theology celebrates the power of human freedom to shape and determine the quality of human life except when the issue of procreative choice arises. Abortion is anathema, while widespread sterilization abuse goes unnoticed. The power of man to shape creation radically is never rejected. When one stops to consider the awesome power over nature that males take for granted and celebrate, including the power to alter the conditions of human life in myriad ways, the suspicion dawns that the near hysteria that prevails about the immorality of women's right to choose abortion derives its force from the ancient power of misogyny rather than from any passion for the sacredness of human life. An index of the continuing misogyny in Christian tradition is male theologians' refusal to recognize the full range of human power to shape creation in those matters that pertain to women's power to affect the quality of our lives.

In contrast, a feminist theological approach recognizes that nothing is more urgent, in light of the changing circumstances of human beings on planet

Earth, than to recognize that the entire natural-historical context of human procreative power has shifted.[7] We desperately need a desacralization of our biological power to reproduce[8] and at the same time a real concern for human dignity and the social conditions for personhood and the values of human relationship.[9] And note that desacralization does not mean complete devaluation of the worth of procreation. It means we must shift away from the notion that the central metaphors for divine blessing are expressed at the biological level to the recognition that our social relations bear the image of what is most holy. An excellent expression of this point comes from Marie Augusta Neal, a Roman Catholic feminist and a distinguished sociologist of religion:

> As long as the central human need called for was continued motivation to propagate the race, it was essential that religious symbols idealize that process above all others. Given the vicissitudes of life in a hostile environment, women had to be encouraged to bear children and men to support them: childbearing was central to the struggle for existence. Today, however, the size of the base population, together with knowledge already accumulated about artificial insemination, sperm banking, cloning, make more certain a peopled world.
>
> The more serious human problems now are who will live, who will die and who will decide.[10]

A Critical Historical Review of Abortion: An Alternative Perspective

Between persons who oppose all abortions on moral grounds and those who believe abortion is sometimes or frequently morally justifiable, there is no difference of moral principle. Pro-choice advocates and antiabortion advocates share the ethical principle of respect for human life, which is probably why the debate is so acrimonious. I have already indicated that one major source of disagreement is the way in which the theological story is appropriated in relation to the changing circumstances of history. In addition, we should recognize that whenever strong moral disagreement is encountered, we simultaneously confront different readings of the history of a moral issue. The way we interpret the past is already laden with and shaped by our present sense of what the moral problem is.

For example, professional male Christian ethicists tend to assume that Christianity has an unbroken history of "all but absolute" prohibition of abortion and that the history of morality of abortion can best be traced by studying the teaching of the now best-remembered theologians. Looking at the matter this way, one can find numerous proof-texts to show that some of the "church fathers" condemned abortion and equated abortion with either homicide or murder. Whenever a "leading" churchman equated abortion with homicide or murder, he also *and simultaneously* equated *contraception* with homicide or murder. This reflects not only male chauvinist biology but also the then almost phobic antisexual bias of the Christian tradition. Claims that one can separate abortion teaching into an ethic of killing separate from an antisexual and antifemale ethic in the history of Christianity do not withstand critical scrutiny.[11]

The history of Christian natural law ethics is totally conditioned by the equation of any effort to control procreation with homicide. However, this antisexual, antiabortion tradition is not universal, even among theologians and canon lawyers. On the subject of sexuality and its abuse, many well-known theologians had nothing to say; abortion was not even mentioned in most moral theology. An important, untold chapter in Christian history is the great struggle that took place in the medieval period when clerical celibacy came to be imposed and the rules of sexual behavior rigidified.

My thesis is that there is a relative disinterest in the question of abortion overall in Christian history. Occasionally, Christian theologians picked up the issue, especially when these theologians were state-related, that is, were articulating policy not only for the church but for political authority. Demographer Jean Meyer, himself a Catholic, insists that the Christian tradition took over "expansion by population growth" from the Roman Empire.[12] Christians opposed abortion strongly only when Christianity was closely identified with imperial state policy or when theologians were inveighing against women and any sexuality except that expressed in the reluctant service of procreation.

The Holy Crusade quality of present teaching on abortion is quite new in Christianity and is related to cultural shifts that are requiring the Christian tradition to choose sides in the present ideological struggle under pressure to rethink its entire attitude toward women and sexuality. My research has led me to the tentative conclusion that, in Protestant cultures, except where Protestantism is the "established religion," merging church and state, one does not find a strong antiabortion theological-ethical teaching at all. At least in the United States, this is beyond historical debate.[13] No Protestant clergy or theologian gave early support for proposed nineteenth-century laws banning abortion in the United States. It is my impression that Protestant clergy, usually married and often poor, were aware that romanticizing nature's bounty with respect to procreation resulted in a great deal of human suffering. The Protestant clergy who finally did join the antiabortion crusade were racist, classist white clergy, who feared America's strength was being threatened because white, middle-class, respectable women had a lower birth rate than black and ethnic women. Such arguments are still with us.

One other historical point must be stressed. Until the late nineteenth century the natural law tradition, and biblicism following it, tended to define the act of abortion as interruption of pregnancy after ensoulment, which was understood to be the point at which the breath of God entered the fetus. The point at which ensoulment was said to occur varied, but most typically it was marked by quickening, when fetal movement began. Knowledge about embryology was primitive until the past half-century, so this commonsense understanding prevailed. As a result, when abortion was condemned in earlier Christian teaching it was understood to refer to the termination of a pregnancy well into the process of the pregnancy, after ensoulment. Until the late nineteenth century, when Pope Pius IX, intrigued with the new embryonic discoveries, brought the natural law tradition into consonance with "modern science," abortion in ecclesiastical teaching often applied only to termination of prenatal life in more advanced stages of pregnancy.

Another distortion in the male-generated history of this issue derives from failure to note that, until the development of safe, surgical, elective abortion, the act of abortion commonly referred to something done to the woman, with or without her consent (see Exodus 22), either as a wrong done a husband or for the better moral reasons that abortion was an act of violence against both a pregnant woman and fetal life. In recent discussion it is the woman who does the wrongful act. No one would deny that abortion, if it terminates a pregnancy against the woman's wishes, is morally wrong. And until recent decades, abortion endangered the woman's life as much as it did the prenatal life in her womb. Hence, one premodern moral reason for opposing abortion was that it threatened the life and well-being of the mother more than did carrying the pregnancy to term. Today abortion is statistically safer than childbearing. Consequently, no one has a right to discuss the morality of abortion today without recognizing that one of the traditional and appropriate moral reasons for objecting to abortion—concern for women's well-being—now inheres in the pro-choice side of the debate. Antiabortion proponents who accord the fetus full human standing without also assigning positive value to women's lives and well-being are not really pressing the full sense of Christian moral tradition in the abortion debate.

Beyond all this, the deepest moral flaw in the "pro-life" position's historical view is that none of its proponents has attempted to reconstruct the concrete, lived-world context in which the abortion discussion belongs: the all but desperate struggle by sexually active women to gain some proximate control over nature's profligacy in conception. Under the most adverse conditions, women have had to try to control our fertility—everywhere, always. Women's relation to procreation irrevocably marks and shapes our lives. Even those of us who do not have sexual contact with males, because we are celibate or lesbian, have been potential, even probable, victims of male sexual violence or have had to bear heavy social stigma for refusing the centrality of dependence on men and of procreation in our lives. The lives of infertile women, too, are shaped by our failure to meet procreative expectations. Women's lack of social power, in all recorded history, has made this struggle to control procreation a life-bending, often life-destroying one for a large percentage of females.

So most women have had to do whatever we could to prevent too-numerous pregnancies. In societies and cultures, except the most patriarchal, the processes of procreation have been transmitted through women's culture. Birth control techniques have been widely practiced, and some primitive ones have proved effective. Increasingly, anthropologists are gaining hints of how procreative control occurred in some premodern societies. Frequently women have had to choose to risk their lives in order not to have that extra child that would destroy the family's ability to cope or bring about an unmanageable crisis.

We have to concede that modern medicine, for all its misogyny, has replaced some dangerous contraceptive practices still widely used where surgical abortion is unavailable. In light of these gains, more privileged western women must not lose the ability to imagine the real-life pressures that lead women in other cultures to resort to ground-glass douches, reeds inserted in the uterus, and so on, to induce labor. The radical nature of methods women use bespeaks the desperation involved in unwanted pregnancy and reveals the real character of our struggle.

Nor should we suppress the fact that a major means of birth control now is, as it was in earlier times, infanticide. And let no one imagine that women have made decisions to expose or kill newborn infants casually. Women understand what many men cannot seem to grasp—that the birth of a child requires that some person must be prepared to care, without interruption, for this infant, provide material resources and energy-draining amounts of time and attention for it. The human infant is the most needy and dependent of all newborn creatures. It seems to me that men, especially celibate men, romanticize this total and uncompromising dependency of the infant on the already existing human community. Women bear the brunt of this reality and know its full implications. And this dependency is even greater in a fragmented, centralized urban-industrial modern culture than in a rural culture, where another pair of hands often increased an extended family unit's productive power. No historical interpretation of abortion as a moral issue that ignores these matters deserves moral standing in the present debate.

A treatment of any moral problem is inadequate if it fails to analyze the morality of a given act in a way that represents the concrete experience of the agent who faces a decision with respect to that act. Misogyny in Christian discussions of abortion is evidenced clearly in that the abortion decision is never treated in the way it arises as part of the female agent's life process. The decision at issue when the dilemma of choice arises for women is whether or not to be pregnant. In most discussions of the morality of abortion it is treated as an abstract act[14] rather than as a possible way to deal with a pregnancy that frequently is the result of circumstances beyond the woman's control. John Noonan, for instance, evades this fact by referring to the pregnant woman almost exclusively as "the gravida" (a Latin term meaning "pregnant one") or "the carrier" in his *A Private Choice: Abortion in America in the Seventies*.[15] In any pregnancy a woman's life is deeply, irrevocably affected. Those such as Noonan who uphold the unexceptional immorality of abortion are probably wise to obscure the fact that an unwanted pregnancy always involves a life-shaping consequence for a woman, because suppressing the identity of the moral agent and the reality of her dilemma greatly reduces the ability to recognize the moral complexity of abortion. When the question of abortion arises it is usually because a woman finds herself facing an unwanted pregnancy. Consider the actual circumstances that may precipitate this. One is the situation in which a woman did not intend to be sexually active or did not enter into a sexual act voluntarily. Since women are frequently victims of sexual violence, numerous cases of this type arise because of rape, incest, or forced marital coitus. Many morally sensitive opponents of abortion concede that in such cases abortion may be morally justifiable. I insist that in such cases it is a moral good because it is not rational to treat a newly fertilized ovum as though it had the same value as the existent, pregnant female person and because it is morally wrong to make the victim of sexual violence suffer the further agonies of unwanted pregnancy and childbearing against her will. Enforced pregnancy would be viewed as a morally reprehensible violation of bodily integrity if women were recognized as fully human moral agents.

Another more frequent case results when a woman—or usually a young girl—participates in heterosexual activity without clear knowledge of how pregnancy occurs and without intention to conceive a child. A girl who became pregnant in this manner would, by traditional natural law morality, be held in a state of invincible ignorance and therefore not morally culpable. One scholarly Roman Catholic nun I met argued—quite appropriately, I believe—that her church should not consider the abortions of young Catholic girls as morally culpable because the Church overprotected them, which contributed to their lack of understanding of procreation and to their inability to cope with the sexual pressures girls experience in contemporary society. A social policy that pressures the sexually ill-informed child or young woman into unintended or unaware motherhood would be morally dubious indeed.

A related type of pregnancy happens when a woman runs risks by not using contraceptives, perhaps because taking precaution in romantic affairs is not perceived as ladylike or requires her to be too unspontaneous about sex. Our society resents women's sexuality unless it is "innocent" and male-mediated, so many women, lest they be censured as "loose" and "promiscuous," are slow to assume adult responsibility for contraception. However, when pregnancies occur because women are skirting the edges of responsibility and running risks out of immaturity, is enforced motherhood a desirable solution? Such pregnancies could be minimized only by challenging precisely those childish myths of female socialization embedded in natural law teaching about female sexuality.

It is likely that most decisions about abortion arise because mature women who are sexually active with men and who understand the risk of pregnancy nevertheless experience contraceptive failure. Our moral schizophrenia in this matter is exhibited in that many people believe women have more responsibility than men to practice contraception and that family planning is always a moral good, but even so rule out abortion altogether. Such a split consciousness ignores the fact that no inexorable biological line exists between prevention of conception and abortion.[16] More important, such reasoning ignores the genuine risks involved in female contraceptive methods. Some women are at higher risk than others in using the most reliable means of birth control. Furthermore, the reason we do not have more concern for safer contraceptive methods for men and women is that matters relating to women's health and well-being are never urgent in this society. Moreover, many contraceptive failures are due to the irresponsibility of the producers of contraceptives rather than to bad luck.[17] Given these facts, should a woman who actively attempts to avoid pregnancy be punished for contraceptive failure when it occurs?

In concluding this historical section, I must stress that if present efforts to criminalize abortion succeed, we will need a state apparatus of massive proportions to enforce compulsory childbearing. In addition, withdrawal of legal abortion will create one more massively profitable underworld economy in which the Mafia and other sections of quasi-legal capitalism may and will profitably invest. The radical right promises to get the state out of regulation of people's lives, but what they really mean is that they will let economic activity go unrestrained. What their agenda signifies for the personal lives of women is quite another matter.

An adequate historical perspective on abortion recognizes the long struggle women have waged for some degree of control over fertility and their efforts to regain control of procreative power from patriarchal and state-imperial culture and institutions. Such a perspective also takes into account that more nearly adequate contraceptive methods and the existence of safe, surgical, elective abortion represent positive historic steps toward full human freedom and dignity for women. While the same gains in medical knowledge also open the way to new forms of sterilization abuse and to social pressures against some women's use of their power of procreation, I know of no women who would choose to return to a state of lesser knowledge about these matters.

There has been an objective gain in the quality of women's lives for those fortunate enough to have access to procreative choice. That millions upon millions of women as yet do not possess even the rudimentary conditions—moral or physical—for such choice is obvious. Our moral goal should be to struggle against those real barriers—poverty, racism, and antifemale cultural oppression—that prevent authentic choice from being a reality for every woman. In this process we will be able to minimize the need for abortions only insofar as we place the abortion debate in the real lived-world context of women's lives.

Abortion and Moral Theory

The greatest strategic problem of pro-choice advocates is the widespread assumption that pro-lifers have a monopoly on the moral factors that ought to enter into decisions about abortion. *Moral* here is defined as that which makes for the self-respect and well-being of human persons and their environment. Moral legitimacy seems to adhere to their position in part because traditionalists have an array of religiomoral terminology at their command that the sometimes more secular proponents of choice lack. But those who would displace women's power of choice by the power of the state and/or the medical profession do not deserve the aura of moral sanctity. We must do our homework if we are to dispel this myth of moral superiority. A major way in which Christian moral theologians and moral philosophers contribute to this monopoly of moral sanctity is by equating fetal or prenatal life with human personhood in a simplistic way and by failing to acknowledge changes regarding this issue in the history of Christianity.

We need to remember that even in Roman Catholic natural law ethics, the definition of the status of fetal life has shifted over time and in all cases the status of prenatal life involves a moral judgment, not a scientific one. The question is properly posed this way: What status are we morally wise to predicate to prenatal human life, given that the fetus is not yet a fully existent human being? Those constrained under Catholic teaching have been required for the past ninety years to believe a human being exists from conception, when the ovum and sperm merge.[18] This answer from one tradition has had far wider impact on our culture than most people recognize. Other Christians come from traditions that do not offer (and could not offer, given their conception of the structure of the church as moral community) a definitive answer to this question.

Even so, some contemporary Protestant medical ethicists, fascinated by recent genetic discoveries and experiments with deoxyribonucleic acid (DNA), have all but sacralized the moment in which the genetic code is implanted as the moment of humanization, which leaves them close to the traditional Roman Catholic position. Protestant male theologians have long let their enthrallment with science lead to a sacralization of specific scientific discoveries, usually to the detriment of theological and moral clarity. In any case, there are two responses that must be made to the claim that the fetus in early stages of development is a human life or, more dubiously, a human person.

First, the historical struggle for women's personhood is far from won, owing chiefly to the opposition of organized religious groups to full equality for women. Those who proclaim that a zygote at the moment of conception is a person worthy of citizenship continue to deny full social and political rights to women. Whatever one's judgment about the moral status of the fetus, it cannot be argued that that assessment deserves greater moral standing in analysis than does the position of the pregnant woman. This matter of evaluating the meaning of prenatal life is where morally sensitive people's judgments diverge. I cannot believe that any morally sensitive person would fail to value the woman's full, existent life less than they value early fetal life. Most women can become pregnant and carry fetal life to term many, many times in their lifetimes. The distinctly human power is not our biologic capacity to bear children, but our power to actively love, nurture, care for one another, and shape one another's existence in cultural and social interaction.[19] To equate a biologic process with full normative humanity is crass biologic reductionism, and such reductionism is never practiced in religious ethics except where women's lives and well-being are involved.

Second, even though prenatal life, as it moves toward biologic individuation of human form, has value, the equation of abortion with murder is dubious. And the equation of abortion with homicide—the taking of human life—should be carefully weighed. We should also remember that we live in a world where men extend other men wide moral range in relation to justifiable homicide. For example, the just-war tradition has legitimated widespread forms of killing in war, and Christian ethicists have often extended great latitude to rulers and those in power in making choices about killing human beings.[20] Would that such moralists extended equal benefit of a doubt to women facing life-crushing psychological and politicoeconomic pressures in the face of childbearing! Men, daily, make life-determining decisions concerning nuclear power or chemical use in the environment, for example, that affect the well-being of fetuses, and our society expresses no significant opposition, even when such decisions do widespread genetic damage. When we argue for the appropriateness of legal abortion, moral outrage rises.

The so-called pro-life position also gains support by invoking the general principle of respect for human life as foundational to its morality in a way that suggests that the pro-choice advocates are unprincipled. I have already noted that pro-choice advocates have every right to claim the same moral principle, and that this debate, like most debates that are morally acrimonious, is in no

sense about basic moral principles. I do not believe there is any clear-cut conflict of principle in this very deep, very bitter controversy.

It needs to be stressed that we all have an absolute obligation to honor any
moral principle that seems, after rational deliberation, to be sound. This is the
one absolutism appropriate to ethics. There are often several moral principles
relevant to a decision and many ways to relate a given principle to a decisional
context. For most right-to-lifers only one principle has moral standing in this
argument. Admitting only one principle to one's process of moral reasoning
means that a range of other moral values is slighted. Right-to-lifers are also
moral absolutists in the sense that they admit only one possible meaning or application of the principle they invoke. Both these types of absolutism obscure
moral debate and lead to less, not more, rational deliberation. The principle of
respect for human life is one we should all honor, but we must also recognize
that this principle often comes into conflict with other valid moral principles
in the process of making real, lived-world decisions. Understood in an adequate way, this principle can be restated to mean that we should treat what falls
under a reasonable definition of human life as having sanctity or intrinsic
moral value. But even when this is clear, other principles are needed to help us
choose between two intrinsic values, in this case between the prenatal life and
the pregnant woman's life.

Another general moral principle from which we cannot exempt our actions
is the principle of justice, or right relations between persons and between
groups of persons and communities. Another relevant principle is respect for
all that supports human life, namely, the natural environment. As any person
knows who thinks deeply about morality, genuine moral conflicts, as often
as not, are due not to ignoring moral principles but to the fact that different
principles lead to conflicting implications for action or are selectively related
to decisions. For example, we live in a time when the principle of justice
for women, aimed at transforming the social relations that damage women's
lives, is historically urgent. For many of us this principle has greater moral ur-
gency than the extension of the principle of respect for human life to include
early fetal life, even though respect for fetal life is also a positive moral good.
We should resist approaches to ethics that claim that one overriding principle
always deserves to control morality. Clarification of principle, for that matter,
is only a small part of moral reasoning. When we weigh moral principles
and their potential application, we must also consider the implications of
a given act for our present historical context and envision its long-term consequences.

One further proviso on this issue of principles in moral reasoning: There are
several distinct theories among religious ethicists and moral philosophers as to
what the function of principles ought to be. One group believes moral princi-

ples are for the purpose of terminating the process of moral reasoning. Hence, if this sort of moralist tells you always to honor the principle of respect for human life, what he or she means is for you to stop reflection and act in a certain way—in this case to accept one's pregnancy regardless of consequences. Others believe that it is better to refer to principles (broad, generalized moral criteria) than to apply rules (narrower, specific moral prescriptions) because principles function to open up processes of reasoning rather than close them off. The principle of respect for life, on this reading, is not invoked to prescribe action but to help locate and weigh values, to illuminate a range of values that always inhere in significant human decisions. A major difference in the moral debate on abortion, then, is that some believe that to invoke the principle of respect for human life settles the matter, stops debate, and precludes the single, simple act of abortion. By contrast, many of us believe the breadth of the principle opens up to reconsideration the question of what the essential moral quality of human life is all about [while increasing] moral seriousness about choosing whether or when to bear children.

Two other concerns related to our efforts to make a strong moral case for women's right to procreative choice need to be touched on. The first has to do with the problems our Christian tradition creates for any attempt to make clear why women's right to control our bodies is an urgent and substantive moral claim. One of Christianity's greatest weaknesses is its spiritualizing neglect of respect for the physical body and physical well-being. Tragically, women, more than men, are expected in Christian teaching never to honor their own well-being as a moral consideration. I want to stress, then, that we have no moral tradition in Christianity that starts with body-space, or body-right, as a basic condition of moral relations. (Judaism is far better in this regard, for it acknowledges that we all have a moral right to be concerned for our life and our survival.) Hence, many Christian ethicists simply do not get the point when we speak of women's right to bodily integrity. They blithely denounce such reasons as women's disguised self-indulgence or hysterical rhetoric.[21]

We must articulate our view that body-right is a basic moral claim and also remind our hearers that there is no unchallengeable analogy among other human activities to women's procreative power. Pregnancy is a distinctive human experience. In any social relation, body-space must be respected or nothing deeply human or moral can be created. The social institutions most similar to compulsory pregnancy in their moral violations of body-space are chattel slavery and peonage. These institutions distort the moral relations of a community and deform a community over time. (Witness racism in the United States.) Coercion of women, through enforced sterilization or enforced pregnancy, legitimates unjust power in intimate human relationships and cuts to the heart of our capacity for moral social relations. As we should recognize, given our violence-prone society, people learn violence at home and at an early age when women's lives are violated!

Even so, we must be careful, when we make the case for our right to bodily integrity, not to confuse moral rights with mere liberties.[22] To claim that we have a moral right to procreative choice does not mean we believe women can exercise this right free of all moral claims from the community. For example, we need to teach female children that childbearing is not a purely capricious, individualistic matter, and we need to challenge the assumption that a woman who enjoys motherhood should have as many children as she and her mate wish, regardless of its effects on others. Population self-control is a moral issue, although more so in high-consuming, affluent societies like our own than in nations where a modest, simple, and less wasteful lifestyle obtains.

A second point is the need, as we work politically for a pro-choice social policy, to avoid the use of morally objectionable arguments to mobilize support for our side of the issue. One can get a lot of political mileage in U.S. society by using covert racist and classist appeals ("abortion lowers the cost of welfare rolls or reduces illegitimacy" or "paying for abortions saves the taxpayers money in the long run"). Sometimes it is argued that good politics is more important than good morality and that one should use whatever arguments work to gain political support. I do not believe that these crassly utilitarian[23] arguments turn out, in the long run, to be good politics for they are costly to our sense of polis and of community. But even if they were effective in the short run, I am doubly sure that on the issue of the right to choose abortion, good morality doth a good political struggle make. I believe, deeply, that moral right is on the side of the struggle for the freedom and self-respect of women, especially poor and non-white women, and on the side of developing social policy that ensures that every child born can be certain to be a wanted child. Issues of justice are those that deserve the deepest moral caretaking as we develop a political strategy.

Only when people see that they cannot prohibit safe, legal, elective surgical abortion without violating the conditions of well-being for the vast majority of women—especially those most socially vulnerable because of historic patterns of oppression—will the effort to impose a selective, abstract morality of the sanctity of human life on all of us cease. This is a moral battle par excellence, and whenever we forget that we make it harder to reach the group most important to the cause of procreative choice—those women who have never suffered from childbearing pressures, who have not yet put this issue into a larger historical context, and who reverence women's historical commitment to childbearing. We will surely not reach them with pragmatic appeals to the taxpayer's wallet! To be sure, we cannot let such women go unchallenged as they support ruling-class ideology that the state should control procreation. But they will not change their politics until they see that pro-choice is grounded in a deeper, tougher, more caring moral vision than the political option they now endorse.

The Social Policy Dimensions of the Debate

Most people fail to understand that in ethics we need, provisionally, to separate our reflection on the morality of specific acts from questions about how we express our moral values within our social institutions and systems (that is, social policy). When we do this, the morality of abortion appears in a different light. Focusing attention away from the single act of abortion to the larger historical context thrusts into relief what "respect for human life" means in the pro-choice position. It also illuminates the common core of moral concern that unites pro-choice advocates to pro-lifers who have genuine concern for expanding the circle of who really counts as human in this society. Finally, placing abortion in a larger historical context enables proponents of pro-choice to clarify where we most differ from the pro-lifers, that is, in our total skepticism that a state-enforced antiabortion policy could ever have the intended "pro-life" consequences they claim.

We must always insist that the objective social conditions that make women and children already born highly vulnerable can only be worsened by a social policy of compulsory pregnancy. However one judges the moral quality of the individual act of abortion (and here, differences among us do exist that are morally justifiable), it is still necessary to distinguish between how one judges the act of abortion morally and what one believes a societywide policy on abortion should be. We must not let those who have moral scruples against the personal act ignore the fact that a just social policy must also include active concern for enhancement of women's well-being and, for that, policies that would in fact make abortions less necessary. To anathematize abortion when the social and material conditions for control of procreation do not exist is to blame the victim, not to address the deep dilemmas of female existence in this society.

Even so, there is no reason for those of us who celebrate procreative choice as a great moral good to pretend that resort to abortion is ever a desirable means of expressing this choice. I know of no one on the pro-choice side who has confused the desirability of the availability of abortion with the celebration of the act itself. We all have every reason to hope that safer, more reliable means of contraception may be found and that violence against women will be reduced. Furthermore, we should be emphatic that our social policy demands include opposition to sterilization abuse, insistence on higher standards of health care for women and children, better prenatal care, reduction of unnecessary surgery on women's reproductive systems, increased research to improve contraception, and so on. Nor should we draw back from criticizing a health care delivery system that exploits women. An abortion industry thrives on the profitability of abortion, but women are not to blame for this.

A feminist position demands social conditions that support women's full, self-respecting right to procreative choice, including the right not to be sterilized against our wills, the right to choose abortion as a birth control means of last resort, and the right to a prenatal and postnatal health care system that will also reduce the now widespread trauma of having to deliver babies in rigid, impersonal health care settings. Pro-lifers do best politically when we allow them to keep the discussion narrowly focused on the morality of the act of abortion and on the moral value of the fetus. We do best politically when we make the deep connections between the full context of this issue in women's lives, including this society's systemic or patterned injustice toward women.

It is well to remember that it has been traditional Catholic natural law ethics that most clarified and stressed this distinction between the morality of an individual act on the one hand and the policies that produce the optional social morality on the other. The strength of this tradition is probably reflected in the fact that even now most polls show that slightly more Catholics than Protestants believe it unwise for the state to attempt to regulate abortion. In the past, Catholics, more than Protestants, have been wary of using the state as an instrument of moral crusade. Tragically, by taking their present approach to abortion, the Roman Catholic hierarchy may be risking the loss of the deepest wisdom of its own ethical tradition. By failing to acknowledge a distinction between the church's moral teaching on the act of abortion and the question of what is a desirable social policy to minimize abortion, as well as overemphasizing it to the neglect of other social justice concerns, the Roman Catholic church may well be dissipating the best of its moral tradition.[24]

The frenzy of the current pope and many Roman Catholic bishops in the United States on this issue has reached startling proportions. The United States bishops have equated nuclear war and the social practice of abortion as the most heinous social evils of our time.[25] While this appallingly misguided analogy has gained credibility because of the welcome if modest opposition of the bishops to nuclear escalation, I predict that the long-term result will be to further discredit Roman Catholic moral wisdom in the culture.

If we are to be a society genuinely concerned with enhancing women's well-being and minimizing the necessity of abortions, thereby avoiding the danger over time of becoming an abortion culture,[26] what kind of a society must we become? It is here that the moral clarity of the feminist analysis becomes most obvious. How can we reduce the number of abortions due to contraceptive failure? By placing greater emphasis on medical research in this area, by requiring producers of contraceptives to behave more responsibly, and by developing patterns of institutional life that place as much emphasis on male responsibility for procreation and long-term care and nurturance of children as on female responsibility.

How can we reduce the number of abortions due to childish ignorance about sexuality among female children or adult women and our mates? By adopting a widespread program of sex education and by supporting institutional policies that teach male and female children alike that a girl is as capable as a boy of enjoying sex and that both must share moral responsibility for preventing pregnancy except when they have decided, as a deliberative moral act, to have a child.

How would we reduce the necessity of abortion due to sexual violence against women in and out of marriage? By challenging vicious male-generated myths that women exist primarily to meet the sexual needs of men, that women are, by nature, those who are really fulfilled only through our procreative powers. We would teach feminist history as the truthful history of the race, stressing that historic patterns of patriarchy were morally wrong and that a humane or moral society would be a fully nonsexist society.

Technological developments that may reduce the need for abortions are not entirely within our control, but the sociomoral ethos that makes abortion common is within our power to change. And we would begin to create such conditions by adopting a thoroughgoing feminist program for society. Nothing less, I submit, expresses genuine respect for all human life.

Notes

1. I use the traditional Roman Catholic term intentionally because my ethical method has greater affinity with the Roman Catholic model.

2. The Christian natural law tradition developed because many Christians understood that the power of moral reason inhered in human beings qua human beings, not merely in the understanding that comes from being Christian. Those who follow natural law methods address moral issues from the consideration of what options appear rationally compelling, given present reflection rather than from theological claims alone. My own moral theological method is congenial to certain of these natural law assumptions. Roman Catholic natural law teaching, however, has become internally incoherent by its insistence that in some matters of morality the teaching authority of the hierarchy must be taken as the proper definition of what is rational. This replacement of reasoned reflection by ecclesiastical authority seems to me to offend against what we must mean by moral reasoning on best understanding. I would argue that a moral theology cannot forfeit final judgment or even penultimate judgment on moral matters to anything except fully deliberated communal consensus.

On the abortion issue, this of course would mean women would be consulted in a degree that reflects their numbers in the Catholic church. No a priori claims to authoritative moral reason are ever possible, and if those affected are not consulted, the teaching cannot claim rationality.

3. For a critique of these positions, see Paul D. Simmons, "A Theological Response to Fundamentalism on the Abortion Issue," in *Abortion: The Moral Issues,* ed. Edward Batchelor Jr. (New York: Pilgrim Press, 1982), 175–87.

4. Most biblical scholars agree that either the early Christians expected an imminent end to history and therefore had only an "interim ethic," or that Jesus' teaching, in its radical support for "the outcasts" of his society, did not aim to justify existing social institutions. See, for example, Luke 4 and 12; Mark 7, 9, 13, and 14; Matthew 25. See also Elisabeth Schüssler Fiorenza, "You Are Not to Be Called Father," *Cross Currents* (fall 1979): 301–23. See also her *Bread Not Stone: The Challenge of Feminist Biblical Interpretation* (Boston: Beacon Press, 1985).

5. Few Roman Catholic theologians seem to appreciate how much the recent enthusiastic endorsement of traditional family values implicates Catholicism in Protestant Reformational spirituality. Rosemary Ruether is an exception; she has stressed this point in her writings.

6. Helmut Thielicke, *The Ethics of Sex* (New York: Harper and Row, 1964), 199–247. Compare pp. 210 and 226ff. Barth's position on abortion is a bit more complicated than I can elaborate here, which is why one will find him quoted on both sides of the debate. Barth's method allows him to argue that any given radical human act could turn out to be "the will of God" in a given context or setting. We may at any time be given "permission" by God's radical freedom to do what was not before permissible. My point here is that Barth exposits this possible exception in such a traditional prohibitory context that I do not believe it appropriate to cite him on the pro-choice side of the debate. In my opinion, no woman could ever accept the convoluted way in which Barth's biblical exegesis opens the door (a slight crack) to woman's full humanity. His reasoning on these questions simply demonstrates what deep difficulty the Christian tradition's exegetical tradition is in with respect to the full humanity and moral agency of women. See Karl Barth, "The Protection of Life," in *Church Dogmatics,* part 3, vol. 4 (Edinburgh: T. and T. Clark, 1961), 415–22.

7. Compare Beverly Wildung Harrison, "When Fruitfulness and Blessedness Diverge," *Religion and Life* 41, no. 4 (1972): 480–96. My views on the seriousness of misogyny as a historical force have deepened since I wrote this essay.

8. Marie Augusta Neal, "Sociology and Sexuality: A Feminist Perspective," *Christianity and Crisis* 39, no. 8 (14 May 1979): 118–22.

9. For a feminist theology of relationship, see Carter Heyward, *Toward the Redemption of God: A Theology of Mutual Relation* (Washington, D.C.: University Press of America, 1982).

10. Neal, "Sociology and Sexuality." This article is of critical importance in discussions of the theology and morality of abortion.

11. Susan Teft Nicholson, *Abortion and the Roman Catholic Church*, JRE Studies in Religious Ethics II (Knoxville: Religious Ethics Inc., University of Tennessee, 1978). This carefully crafted study assumes that there has been a clear "antikilling" ethic separable from any antisexual ethic in Christian abortion teaching. This is an assumption that my historical research does not sustain.

12. Jean Meyer, "Toward a Non-Malthusian Population Policy," in *The American Population Debate*, ed. Daniel Callahan (Garden City, N.Y.: Doubleday, 1971).

13. See James C. Mohr, *Abortion in America* (New York: Oxford University Press, 1978), and James Nelson, "Abortion: Protestant Perspectives," in *Encyclopedia of Bioethics*, vol. 1, ed. Warren T. Reich (New York: Free Press, 1978), 13–17.

14. H. Richard Niebuhr often warned his theological compatriots about abstracting acts from the life project in which they are embedded, but this warning is much neglected in the writings of Christian moralists. See "The Christian Church in the World Crises," *Christianity and Society* 6 (1941).

15. John T. Noonan Jr., *A Private Choice: Abortion in America in the Seventies* (New York: Free Press, 1979). Noonan denies that the history of abortion is related to the history of male oppression of women.

16. We know now that the birth control pill does not always work by preventing fertilization of the ovum by the sperm. Frequently, the pill causes the wall of the uterus to expel the newly fertilized ovum. From a biological point of view, there is no point in the procreative process that can be taken as a clear dividing line on which to pin neat moral distinctions.

17. The most conspicuous example of corporate involvement in contraceptive failure was the famous Dalkon Shield scandal. Note also that the manufacturer of the Dalkon Shield dumped its dangerous and ineffective product on family planning programs of third world (overexploited) countries.

18. Catholic moral theology opens up several ways for faithful Catholics to challenge the teaching office of the church on moral questions. However, I remain unsatisfied that these qualifications of inerrancy in moral matters stand up in situations of moral controversy. If freedom of conscience does not function *de jure*, should it be claimed as existent in principle?

19. I elaborate this point in greater detail in "The Power of Anger in the Work of Love," in my *Making the Connections: Essays in Feminist Social Ethics*, ed. Carol S. Robb (Boston: Beacon Press, 1985).

20. For example, Paul Ramsey gave unqualified support to U.S. military involvement in Southeast Asia in light of just-war considerations but finds abortion to be an unexceptional moral wrong.

21. See Richard A. McCormick, S.J., "Rules for Abortion Debate" (from Batchelor, *Abortion: The Moral Issue*, 27–37), in this volume.

22. One of the reasons why abortion-on-demand rhetoric—even when it is politically effective in the immediate moment—has had a backlash effect is that it seems to many to imply lack of reciprocity between women's needs and society's needs. While I would not deny, in principle, a possible conflict of interest between women's well-being and the community's needs for reproduction, there is little or no historical evidence that suggests women are less responsible to the well-being of the community than are men. We need not fall into a liberal, individualistic trap in arguing the central importance of procreative choice to issues of women's well-being in society. The right in question is body-right, or freedom from coercion in childbearing. It is careless to say that the right in question is the right to an abortion. Morally, the right is bodily self-determination, a fundamental condition of personhood and a foundational moral right. See Beverly Wildung Harrison, *Our Right to Choose: Toward a New Ethic of Abortion* (Boston: Beacon Press, 1983).

23. A theory is crassly utilitarian only if it fails to grant equal moral worth to all persons in the calculation of social consequences—as, for example, when some people's financial well-being is weighted more than someone else's basic physical existence. I do not mean to criticize any type of utilitarian moral theory that weighs the actual consequences of actions. In fact, I believe no moral theory is adequate if it does not have a strong utilitarian component.

24. For a perceptive discussion of this danger by a distinguished Catholic priest, read George C. Higgins, "The Prolife Movement and the New Right," *America*, 13 Sept. 1980, 107–10.

25. Philip J. Murnion, ed., *Catholics and Nuclear War: A Commentary on the Challenge of the U.S. Bishops' Pastoral Letter on War and Peace* (New York: Crossroads, 1983), 326.

26. I believe the single most valid concern raised by opponents of abortion is that the frequent practice of abortion, over time, may contribute to a cultural ethos of insensitivity to the value of human life, not because fetuses are being "murdered" but because surgical termination of pregnancy may further "technologize" our sensibilities about procreation. I trust that all of the foregoing makes clear my adamant objection to allowing this insight to justify yet more violence against women. However, I do believe we should be very clear that we stand ready to support—emphatically—any social policies that would lessen the need for abortion *without* jeopardizing women's right to control our own procreative power.

[36]

Abortion and the Sexual Agenda:
A Case for Prolife Feminism

Sidney Callahan

THE ABORTION DEBATE CONTINUES. In the latest and perhaps most crucial development, prolife feminists are contesting prochoice feminist claims that abortion rights are prerequisites for women's full development and social equality. The outcome of this debate may be decisive for the culture as a whole. Prolife feminists, like myself, argue on good feminist principles that women can never achieve the fulfillment of feminist goals in a society permissive toward abortion.

These new arguments over abortion take place within liberal political circles. This round of intense intra-feminist conflict has spiraled beyond earlier right-versus-left abortion debates, which focused on "tragic choices," medical judgments, and legal compromises. Feminist theorists of the prochoice position now put forth the demand for unrestricted abortion rights as a *moral imperative* and insist upon women's right to complete reproductive freedom. They morally justify the present situation and current abortion practices. Thus it is all the more important that prolife feminists articulate their different feminist perspective.

These opposing arguments can best be seen when presented in turn. Perhaps the most highly developed feminist arguments for the morality and legality of abortion can be found in Beverly Wildung Harrison's *Our Right to*

Choose (Beacon Press, 1983) and Rosalind Pollack Petchesky's *Abortion and Woman's Choice* (Longman, 1984). Obviously it is difficult to do justice to these complex arguments, which draw on diverse strands of philosophy and social theory and are often interwoven in prochoice feminists' own version of a "seamless garment." Yet the fundamental feminist case for the morality of abortion, encompassing the views of Harrison and Petchesky, can be analyzed in terms of four central moral claims: (1) the moral right to control one's own body; (2) the moral necessity of autonomy and choice in personal responsibility; (3) the moral claim for the contingent value of fetal life; (4) the moral right of women to true social equality.

1. The moral right to control one's own body. Prochoice feminism argues that a woman choosing an abortion is exercising a basic right of bodily integrity granted in our common law tradition. If she does not choose to be physically involved in the demands of a pregnancy and birth, she should not be compelled to be so against her will. Just because it is *her* body which is involved, a woman should have the right to terminate any pregnancy, which at this point in medical history is tantamount to terminating fetal life. No one can be forced to donate an organ or submit to other invasive physical procedures for however good a cause. Thus no woman should be subjected to "compulsory pregnancy." And it should be noted that in pregnancy much more than a passive biological process is at stake.

From one perspective, the fetus is, as Petchesky says, a "biological parasite" taking resources from the woman's body. During pregnancy, a woman's whole life and energies will be actively involved in the nine-month process. Gestation and childbirth involve physical and psychological risks. After childbirth a woman will either be a mother who must undertake a twenty-year responsibility for child rearing, or face giving up her child for adoption or institutionalization. Since hers is the body, hers the risk, hers the burden, it is only just that she alone should be free to decide on pregnancy or abortion.

This moral claim to abortion, according to the prochoice feminists, is especially valid in an individualistic society in which women cannot count on medical care or social support in pregnancy, childbirth, or child rearing. A moral abortion decision is never made in a social vacuum, but in the real life society which exists here and now.

2. The moral necessity of autonomy and choice in personal responsibility. Beyond the claim for individual *bodily* integrity, the prochoice feminists claim that to be a full adult *morally*, a woman must be able to make responsible life commitments. To plan, choose, and exercise personal responsibility, one must have control of reproduction. A woman must be able to make yes-or-no decisions about a specific pregnancy, according to her present situation, resources, prior commitments, and life plan. Only with such reproductive freedom can a woman have the moral autonomy necessary to make mature commitments, in the area of family, work, or education.

Contraception provides a measure of personal control, but contraceptive failure or other chance events can too easily result in involuntary pregnancy. Only free access to abortion can provide the necessary guarantee. The chance biological process of an involuntary pregnancy should not be allowed to override all the other personal commitments and responsibilities a woman has: to others, to family, to work, to education, to her future development, health, or well-being. Without reproductive freedom, women's personal moral agency and human consciousness are subjected to biology and chance.

3. The moral claim for the contingent value of fetal life. Prochoice feminist exponents like Harrison and Petchesky claim that the value of fetal life is contingent upon the woman's free consent and subjective acceptance. The fetus must be invested with maternal valuing in order to become human. This process of "humanization" through personal consciousness and "sociality" can only be bestowed by the woman in whose body and psychosocial system a new life must mature. The meaning and value of fetal life are constructed by the woman; without this personal conferral there only exists a biological, physiological process. Thus fetal interests or fetal rights can never outweigh the woman's prior interest and rights. If a woman does not consent to invest her pregnancy with meaning or value, then the merely biological process can be freely terminated. Prior to her own free choice and conscious investment, a woman cannot be described as a "mother" nor can a "child" be said to exist.

Moreover, in cases of voluntary pregnancy, a woman can withdraw consent if fetal genetic defects or some other problem emerges at any time before birth. Late abortion should thus be granted without legal restrictions. Even the minimal qualifications and limitations on women embedded in *Roe v. Wade* are unacceptable—repressive remnants of patriarchal unwillingness to give power to women.

4. The moral right of women to full social equality. Women have a moral right to full social equality. They should not be restricted or subordinated because of their sex. But this morally required equality cannot be realized without abortion's certain control of reproduction. Female social equality depends upon being able to compete and participate as freely as males can in the structures of educational and economic life. If a woman cannot control when and how she will be pregnant or rear children, she is at a distinct disadvantage, especially in our male-dominated world.

Psychological equality and well-being is also at stake. Women must enjoy the basic right of a person to the free exercise of heterosexual intercourse and full sexual expression, separated from procreation. No less than males, women should be able to be sexually active without the constantly inhibiting fear of pregnancy. Abortion is necessary for women's sexual fulfillment and the growth of uninhibited feminine self-confidence and ownership of their sexual powers.

But true sexual and reproductive freedom means freedom to procreate as well as to inhibit fertility. Prochoice feminists are also worried that women's freedom to reproduce will be curtailed through the abuse of sterilization and needless hysterectomies. Besides the punitive tendencies of a male-dominated health-care system, especially in response to repeated abortions or welfare pregnancies, there are other economic and social pressures inhibiting reproduction. Genuine reproductive freedom implies that day care, medical care, and financial support would be provided mothers, while fathers would take their full share in the burdens and delights of raising children.

Many prochoice feminists identify feminist ideals with communitarian, ecologically sensitive approaches to reshaping society. Following theorists like Sara Ruddick and Carol Gilligan, they link abortion rights with the growth of "maternal thinking" in our heretofore patriarchal society. Maternal thinking is loosely defined as a responsible commitment to the loving nurture of specific human beings as they actually exist in socially embedded interpersonal contexts. It is a moral perspective very different from the abstract, competitive, isolated, and principled rigidity so characteristic of patriarchy.

How does a prolife feminist respond to these arguments? Prolife feminists grant the good intentions of their prochoice counterparts but protest that the prochoice position is flawed, morally inadequate, and inconsistent with feminism's basic demands for justice. Prolife feminists champion a more encompassing moral ideal. They recognize the claims of fetal life and offer a different perspective on what is good for women. The feminist vision is expanded and refocused.

1. From the moral right to control one's own body to a more inclusive ideal of justice. The moral right to control one's own body does apply to cases of organ transplants, mastectomies, contraception, and sterilization; but it is not a conceptualization adequate for abortion. The abortion dilemma is caused by the fact that 266 days following a conception in one body, another body will emerge. One's own body no longer exists as a single unit but is engendering another organism's life. This dynamic passage from conception to birth is genetically ordered and universally found in the human species. Pregnancy is not like the growth of cancer or infestation by a biological parasite; it is the way every human being enters the world. Strained philosophical analogies fail to apply: having a baby is not like rescuing a drowning person, being hooked up to a famous violinist's artificial life-support system, donating organs for transplant—or anything else.

As embryology and fetology advance, it becomes clear that human development is a continuum. Just as astronomers are studying the first three minutes in the genesis of the universe, so the first moments, days, and weeks at the beginning of human life are the subject of increasing scientific attention. While neonatology pushes the definition of viability ever earlier, ultrasound and fetology expand the concept of the patient in utero. Within such a continuous growth process, it is hard to defend logically any demarcation point after conception as the point at which an immature form of human life is so different from the day before or the day after, that it can be morally or legally discounted as a nonperson. Even the moment of birth can hardly differentiate a nine-month fetus from a newborn. It is not surprising that those who countenance late abortions are logically led to endorse selective infanticide.

The same legal tradition which in our society guarantees the right to control one's own body firmly recognizes the wrongfulness of harming other bodies, however immature, dependent, different looking, or powerless. The handicapped, the retarded, and newborns are legally protected from deliberate harm. Prolife feminists reject the suppositions that would except the unborn from this protection.

After all, debates similar to those about the fetus were once conducted about feminine personhood. Just as women, or blacks, were considered too different, too underdeveloped, too "biological," to have souls or to possess legal rights, so the fetus is now seen as "merely" biological life, subsidiary to a person. A woman was once viewed as incorporated into the "one flesh" of her husband's person; she too was a form of bodily property. In all patriarchal unjust systems, lesser orders of human life are granted rights only when wanted, chosen, or invested with value by the powerful.

Fortunately, in the course of civilization there has been a gradual realization that justice demands the powerless and dependent be protected against the uses of power wielded unilaterally. No human can be treated as a means to an end without consent. The fetus is an immature, dependent form of human life which only needs time and protection to develop. Surely, immaturity and dependence are not crimes.

In an effort to think about the essential requirements of a just society, philosophers like John Rawls recommend imagining yourself in an "original position," in which your position in the society to be created is hidden by a "veil of ignorance." You will have to weigh the possibility that any inequalities inherent in that society's practices may rebound upon you in the worst, as well as in the best, conceivable way. This thought experiment helps ensure justice for all.

Beverly Harrison argues that in such an envisioning of society everyone would institute abortion rights in order to guarantee that if one turned out to be a woman one would have reproductive freedom. But surely in the original position and behind the "veil of ignorance," you would have to contemplate the possibility of being the particular fetus to be aborted. Since everyone has passed through the fetal stage of development, it is false to refuse to imagine oneself in this state when thinking about a potential world in which justice would govern. Would it be just that an embryonic life—in half the cases, of course, a female life—be sacrificed to the right of a woman's control over her own body? A woman may be pregnant without consent and experience a great many penalties, but a fetus killed without consent pays the ultimate penalty.

It does not matter (*The Silent Scream* notwithstanding) whether the fetus being killed is fully conscious or feels pain. We do not sanction killing the innocent if it can be done painlessly or without the victim's awareness. Consciousness becomes important to the abortion debate because it is used as a criterion for the "personhood" so often seen as the prerequisite for legal protection. Yet certain philosophers set the standard of personhood so high that half the human race could not meet the criteria during most of their waking hours (let alone their sleeping ones). Sentience, self-consciousness, rational decision-making, social participation? Surely no infant, or child under two, could qualify. Either our idea of person must be expanded or another criterion, such as human life itself, be employed to protect the weak in a just society. Prolife feminists who defend the fetus empathetically identify with an immature state of growth passed through by themselves, their children, and everyone now alive.

It also seems a travesty of just procedures that a pregnant woman now, in effect, acts as sole judge of her own case, under the most stressful conditions. Yes, one can acknowledge that the pregnant woman will be subject to the potential burdens arising from a pregnancy, but it has never been thought right to have an interested party, especially the more powerful party, decide his or her own case when there may be a conflict of interest. If one considers the matter as a case of a powerful versus a powerless, silenced claimant, the prochoice feminist argument can rightly be inverted: since hers is the body, hers the risk, and hers the greater burden, then how in fairness can a woman be the sole judge of the fetal right to life?

Human ambivalence, a bias toward self-interest, and emotional stress have always been recognized as endangering judgment. Freud declared that love and hate are so entwined that if instant thoughts could kill, we would all be dead in the bosom of our families. In the case of a woman's involuntary pregnancy, a complex, long-term solution requiring effort and energy has to compete with the immediate solution offered by a morning's visit to an abortion clinic. On the simple, perceptual plane, with imagination and thinking curtailed, the speed, ease, and privacy of abortion, combined with the small size of the embryo, tend to make early abortions seem less morally serious—even though speed, size, technical ease, and the private nature of an act have no moral standing.

As the most recent immigrants from nonpersonhood, feminists have traditionally fought for justice for themselves and the world. Women rally to feminism as a new and better way to live. Rejecting male aggression and destruction, feminists seek alternative, peaceful, ecologically sensitive means to resolve conflicts while respecting human potentiality. It is a chilling inconsistency to see prochoice feminists demanding continued access to assembly-line, technological methods of fetal killing—the vacuum aspirator, prostaglandins, and dilation and evacuation. It is a betrayal of feminism, which has built the struggle for justice on the bedrock of women's empathy. After all, "maternal thinking" receives its name from a mother's unconditional acceptance and nurture of dependent, immature life. It is difficult to develop concern for women, children, the poor and the dispossessed—and to care about peace—and at the same time ignore fetal life.

2. *From the necessity of autonomy and choice in personal responsibility to an expanded sense of responsibility.* A distorted idea of morality overemphasizes individual autonomy and active choice. Morality has often been viewed too exclusively as a matter of human agency and decisive action. In moral behavior persons must explicitly choose and aggressively exert their wills to intervene in the natural and social environments. The human will dominates the body, overcomes the given, breaks out of the material limits of nature. Thus if one does not choose to be pregnant or cannot rear a child, who must be given up for adoption, then better to abort the pregnancy. Willing, planning, choosing one's moral commitments through the contracting of one's individual resources becomes the premier model of moral responsibility.

But morality also consists of the good and worthy acceptance of the unexpected events that life presents. Responsiveness and response-ability to things unchosen are also instances of the highest human moral capacity. Morality is not confined to contracted agreements of isolated individuals. Yes, one is obligated by explicit contracts freely initiated, but human beings are also obligated by implicit compacts and involuntary relationships in which persons simply find themselves. To be embedded in a family, a neighborhood, a social system, brings moral obligations which were never entered into with informed consent.

Parent-child relationships are one instance of implicit moral obligations arising by virtue of our being part of the interdependent human community. A woman, involuntarily pregnant, has a moral obligation to the now-existing dependent fetus whether she explicitly consented to its existence or not. No prolife feminist would dispute the forceful observations of prochoice feminists about the extreme difficulties that bearing an unwanted child in our society can entail. But the stronger force of the fetal claim presses a woman to accept these burdens; the fetus possesses rights arising from its extreme need and the interdependency and unity of humankind. The woman's moral obligation arises both from her status as a human being embedded in the interdependent human community and her unique lifegiving female reproductive power. To follow the prochoice feminist ideology of insistent individualistic autonomy and control is to betray a fundamental basis of the moral life.

3. *From the moral claim of the contingent value of fetal life to the moral claim for the intrinsic value of human life.* The feminist prochoice position which claims that the value of the fetus is contingent upon the pregnant woman's bestowal—or willed, conscious "construction"—of humanhood is seriously flawed. The inadequacies of this position flow from the erroneous premises (1) that human value and rights can be granted by individual will; (2) that the individual woman's consciousness can exist and operate in an *a priori* isolated fashion; and (3) that "mere" biological, genetic human life has little meaning. Prolife feminism takes a very different stance toward life and nature.

Human life from the beginning to the end of development *has* intrinsic value, which does not depend on meeting the selective criteria or tests set up by powerful others. A fundamental humanist assumption is at stake here. Either we are going to value embodied human life and humanity as a good thing, or take some variant of the nihilist position that assumes human life is just one more random occurrence in the universe such that each instance of human life must explicitly be justified to prove itself worthy to continue. When faced with a new life, or an involuntary pregnancy, there is a world of difference in whether one first asks, "Why continue?" or "Why not?" Where is the burden of proof going to rest? The concept of "compulsory pregnancy" is as distorted as labeling life "compulsory aging."

In a sound moral tradition, human rights arise from human needs, and it is the very nature of a right, or valid claim upon another, that it cannot be denied, conditionally delayed, or rescinded by more powerful others at their behest. It seems fallacious to hold that in the case of the fetus it is the pregnant woman alone who gives or removes its right to life and human status solely through her subjective conscious investment or "humanization." Surely no pregnant woman (or any other individual member of the species) has created her own human nature by an individually willed act of consciousness, nor for that matter been able to guarantee her own human rights. An individual woman and the unique individual embryonic life within her can only exist because of their participation in the genetic inheritance of the human species as a whole. Biological life should never be discounted. Membership in the species, or collective human family, is the basis for human solidarity, equality, and natural human rights.

4. *The moral right of women to full social equality from a prolife feminist perspective.* Prolife feminists and prochoice feminists are totally agreed on the moral right of women to the full social equality so far denied them. The disagreement between them concerns the definition of the desired goal and the best means to get there. Permissive abortion laws do not bring women reproductive freedom, social equality, sexual fulfillment, or full personal development.

Pragmatic failures of a prochoice feminist position combined with a lack of moral vision are, in fact, causing disaffection among young women. Middle-aged prochoice feminists blamed the "big chill" on the general conservative backlash. But they should look rather to their own elitist acceptance of male models of sex and to the sad picture they present of women's lives. Pitting women against their own offspring is not only morally offensive, it is psychologically and politically destructive. Women will never climb to equality and social empowerment over mounds of dead fetuses, numbering now in the millions. As long as most women choose to bear children, they stand to gain from the same constellation of attitudes and institutions that will also protect the fetus in the woman's womb—and they stand to lose from the cultural assumptions that support permissive abortion. Despite temporary conflicts of interest, feminine and fetal liberation are ultimately one and the same cause.

Women's rights and liberation are pragmatically linked to fetal rights because to obtain true equality, women need (1) more social support and changes in the structure of society, and (2) increased self-confidence, self-expectations, and self-esteem. Society in general, and men in particular, have to provide women more support in rearing the next generation, or our devastating feminization of poverty will continue. But if a woman claims the right to decide by herself whether the fetus becomes a child or not, what does this do to paternal and communal responsibility? Why should men share responsibility for child support or child rearing if they cannot share in what is asserted to be the woman's sole decision? Furthermore, if explicit intentions and consciously accepted contracts are necessary for moral obligations, why should men be held responsible for what *they* do not voluntarily choose to happen? By prochoice reasoning, a man who does not want to have a child, or whose contraceptive fails, can be exempted from the responsibilities of fatherhood and child support. Traditionally, many men have been laggards in assuming parental responsibility and support for their children; ironically, ready abortion, often advocated as a response to male dereliction, legitimizes male irresponsibility and paves the way for even more male detachment and lack of commitment.

For that matter, why should the state provide a system of day care or child support, or require workplaces to accommodate women's maternity and the needs of child rearing? Permissive abortion, granted in the name of women's privacy and reproductive freedom, ratifies the view that pregnancies and children are a woman's private individual responsibility. More and more frequently, we hear some version of this old rationalization: if she refuses to get rid of it, it's her problem. A child becomes a product of the individual woman's freely chosen investment, a form of private property resulting from her own cost-benefit calculation. The larger community is relieved of moral responsibility.

With legal abortion freely available, a clear cultural message is given: conception and pregnancy are no longer serious moral matters. With abortion as an acceptable alternative, contraception is not as responsibly used; women take risks, often at the urging of male sexual partners. Repeat abortions increase, with all their psychological and medical repercussions. With more abortion there is more abortion. Behavior shapes thought as well as the other way round. One tends to justify morally what one has done; what becomes commonplace and institutionalized seems harmless. Habituation is a powerful psychological force. Psychologically it is also true that whatever is avoided becomes more threatening; in phobias it is the retreat from anxiety-producing events which reinforces future avoidance. Women begin to see themselves as too weak to cope with involuntary pregnancies. Finally, through the potency of social pressure and the force of inertia, it becomes more and more difficult, in fact almost unthinkable, *not* to use abortion to solve problem pregnancies. Abortion becomes no longer a choice but a "necessity."

But "necessity," beyond the organic failure and death of the body, is a dynamic social construction open to interpretation. The thrust of present feminist prochoice arguments can only increase the justifiable indications for "necessary" abortion; every unwanted fetal handicap becomes more and more unacceptable. Repeatedly assured that in the name of reproductive freedom, women have a right to specify which pregnancies and which children they will accept, women justify sex selection, and abort unwanted females. Female infanticide, after all, is probably as old a custom as the human species possesses. Indeed, all kinds of selection of the fit and the favored for the good of the family and the tribe have always existed. Selective extinction is no new program.

There are far better goals for feminists to pursue. Prolife feminists seek to expand and deepen the more communitarian, maternal elements of feminism—and move society from its male-dominated course. First and foremost, women have to insist upon a different, woman-centered approach to sex and reproduction. While Margaret Mead stressed the "womb envy" of males in other societies, it has been more or less repressed in our own. In our male-dominated world, what men don't do, doesn't count. Pregnancy, childbirth, and nursing have been characterized as passive, debilitating, animallike. The disease model of pregnancy and birth has been entrenched. This female disease or impairment, with its attendant "female troubles," naturally handicaps women in the "real" world of hunting, war, and the corporate fast track. Many prochoice feminists, deliberately childless, adopt the male perspective when they cite the "basic injustice that women have to bear the babies," instead of seeing the injustice in the fact that men cannot. Women's biologically unique capacity and privilege has been denied, despised, and suppressed under male domination; unfortunately, many women have fallen for the phallic fallacy.

Childbirth often appears in prochoice literature as a painful, traumatic, life-threatening experience. Yet giving birth is accurately seen as an arduous but normal exercise of life-giving power, a violent and ecstatic peak experience, which men can never know. Ironically, some prochoice men and women think and talk of pregnancy and childbirth with the same repugnance that ancient ascetics displayed toward orgasms and sexual intercourse. The similarity may not be accidental. The obstetrician Niles Newton, herself a mother, has written of the extended threefold sexuality of women, who can experience orgasm, birth, and nursing as passionate pleasure-giving experiences. All of these are involuntary processes of the female body. Only orgasm, which males share, has been glorified as an involuntary function that is nature's great gift; the involuntary feminine processes of childbirth and nursing have been seen as bondage to biology.

Fully accepting our bodies as ourselves, what should women want? I think women will only flourish when there is a feminization of sexuality, very different from the current cultural trend toward masculinizing female sexuality. Women can never have the self-confidence and self-esteem they need to achieve feminist goals in society until a more holistic, feminine model of sexuality becomes the dominant cultural ethos. To say this affirms the view that men and women differ in the domain of sexual functioning, although they are more alike than different in other personality characteristics and competencies. For those of us committed to achieving sexual equality in the culture, it may be hard to accept the fact that sexual differences make it imperative to talk of distinct male and female models of sexuality. But if one wants to change sexual roles, one has to recognize preexisting conditions. A great deal of evidence is accumulating which points to biological pressures for different male and female sexual functioning.

Males always and everywhere have been more physically aggressive and more likely to fuse sexuality with aggression and dominance. Females may be more variable in their sexuality, but since Masters and Johnson, we know that women have a greater capacity than men for repeated orgasm and a more tenuous path to arousal and orgasmic release. Most obviously, women also have a far greater sociobiological investment in the act of human reproduction. On the whole, women as compared to men possess a sexuality which is more complex, more intense, more extended in time, involving higher investment, risks, and psychosocial involvement.

Considering the differences in sexual functioning, it is not surprising that men and women in the same culture have often constructed different sexual ideals. In Western culture, since the nineteenth century at least, most women have espoused a version of sexual functioning in which sex acts are embedded within deep emotional bonds and secure long-term commitments. Within these committed "pair bonds" males assume parental obligations. In the idealized Victorian version of the Christian sexual ethic, culturally endorsed and maintained by women, the double standard was not countenanced. Men and women did not need to marry to be whole persons, but if they did engage in sexual functioning, they were to be equally chaste, faithful, responsible, loving, and parentally concerned. Many of the most influential women in the nineteenth-century women's movement preached and lived this sexual ethic, often by the side of exemplary feminist men. While the ideal has never been universally obtained, a culturally dominant demand for monogamy, self-control, and emotionally bonded and committed sex works well for women in every stage of their sexual life cycles. When love, chastity, fidelity, and commitment for better or worse are the ascendant cultural prerequisites for sexual functioning, young girls and women expect protection from rape and seduction, adult women justifiably demand male support in child rearing, and older women are more protected from abandonment as their biological attractions wane.

Of course, these feminine sexual ideals always coexisted in competition with another view. A more male-oriented model of erotic or amative sexuality endorses sexual permissiveness without long-term commitment or reproductive focus. Erotic sexuality emphasizes pleasure, play, passion, individual self-expression, and romantic games of courtship and conquest. It is assumed that a variety of partners and sexual experiences are necessary to stimulate romantic passion. This erotic model of the sexual life has often worked satisfactorily for men, both heterosexual and gay, and for certain cultural elites. But for the average woman, it is quite destructive. Women can only play the erotic game successfully when, like the "*Cosmopolitan* woman," they are young, physically attractive, economically powerful, and fulfilled enough in a career to be willing to sacrifice family life. Abortion is also required. As our society increasingly endorses this male-oriented, permissive view of sexuality, it is all too ready to give women abortion on demand. Abortion helps a woman's body be more like a man's. It has been observed that *Roe v. Wade* removed the last defense women possessed against male sexual demands.

Unfortunately, the modern feminist movement made a mistaken move at a critical juncture. Rightly rebelling against patriarchy, unequal education, restricted work opportunities, and women's downtrodden political status, feminists also rejected the nineteenth-century feminine sexual ethic. Amative, erotic, permissive sexuality (along with abortion rights) became symbolically identified with other struggles for social equality in education, work, and politics. This feminist mistake also turned off many potential recruits among women who could not deny the positive dimensions of their own traditional feminine roles, nor their allegiance to the older feminine sexual ethic of love and fidelity.

An ironic situation then arose in which many prochoice feminists preach their own double standard. In the world of work and career, women are urged to grow up, to display mature self-discipline and self-control; they are told to persevere in long-term commitments, to cope with unexpected obstacles by learning to tough out the inevitable sufferings and setbacks entailed in life and work. But this mature ethic of commitment and self-discipline, recommended as the only way to progress in the world of work and personal achievement, is discounted in the domain of sexuality.

In prochoice feminism, a permissive, erotic view of sexuality is assumed to be the only option. Sexual intercourse with a variety of partners is seen as "inevitable" from a young age and as a positive growth experience to be managed by access to contraception and abortion. Unfortunately, the pervasive cultural conviction that adolescents, or their elders, cannot exercise sexual self-control undermines the responsible use of contraception. When a pregnancy occurs, the first abortion is viewed in some prochoice circles as a *rite de passage*. Responsibly choosing an abortion supposedly ensures that a young woman will take charge of her own life, make her own decisions, and carefully practice contraception. But the social dynamics of a permissive, erotic model of sexuality, coupled with permissive laws, work toward repeat abortions. Instead of being empowered by their abortion choices, young women having abortions are confronting the debilitating reality of *not* bringing a baby into the world; *not* being able to count on a committed male partner; *not* accounting oneself strong enough, or the master of enough resources, to avoid killing the fetus. Young women are hardly going to develop the self-esteem, self-discipline, and self-confidence necessary to confront a male-dominated society through abortion.

The male-oriented sexual orientation has been harmful to women and children. It has helped bring us epidemics of venereal disease, infertility, pornography, sexual abuse, adolescent pregnancy, divorce, displaced older women, and abortion. Will these signals of something amiss stimulate prochoice feminists to rethink what kind of sex ideal really serves women's best interests? While the erotic model cannot encompass commitment, the committed model can—happily—encompass and encourage romance, passion, and playfulness. In fact, within the security of long-term commitments, women may be more likely to experience sexual pleasure and fulfillment.

* * *

The prolife feminist position is not a return to the old feminine mystique. That espousal of "the eternal feminine" erred by viewing sexuality as so sacred that it cannot be humanly shaped at all. Woman's *whole* nature was supposed to be opposite to man's, necessitating complementary and radically different social roles. Followed to its logical conclusion, such a view presumes that reproductive and sexual experience is necessary for human fulfillment. But as the early feminists insisted, no woman has to marry or engage in sexual intercourse to be fulfilled, nor does a woman have to give birth and raise children to be complete, nor must she stay home and function as an earth mother. But female sexuality does need to be deeply respected as a unique potential and trust. Since most contraceptives and sterilization procedures really do involve only the woman's body rather than destroying new life, they can be an acceptable and responsible moral option.

With sterilization available to accelerate the inevitable natural ending of fertility and childbearing, a woman confronts only a limited number of years in which she exercises her reproductive trust and may have to respond to an unplanned pregnancy. Responsible use of contraception can lower the probabilities even more. Yet abortion is not decreasing. The reason is the current permissive attitude embodied in the law, not the "hard cases" which constitute 3 percent of today's abortions. Since attitudes, the law, and behavior interact, prolife feminists conclude that unless there is an enforced limitation of abortion, which currently confirms the sexual and social status quo, alternatives will never be developed. For women to get what they need in order to combine childbearing, education, and careers, society has to recognize that female bodies come with wombs. Women and their reproductive power, and the children women have, must be supported in new ways. Another and different round of feminist consciousness raising is needed in which all of women's potential is accorded respect. This time, instead of humbly buying entrée by conforming to male lifestyles, women will demand that society accommodate itself to them.

New feminist efforts to rethink the meaning of sexuality, femininity, and reproduction are all the more vital as new techniques for artificial reproduction, surrogate motherhood, and the like present a whole new set of dilemmas. In the long run, the very long run, the abortion debate may be merely the opening round in a series of far-reaching struggles over the role of human sexuality and the ethics of reproduction. Significant changes in the culture, both positive and negative in outcome, may begin as local storms of controversy. We may be at one of those vaguely realized thresholds when we had best come to full attention. What kind of people are we going to be? Prolife feminists pursue a vision for their sisters, daughters, and granddaughters. Will their great-granddaughters be grateful?

[37]

Feminists for Life of America: Official Statement

What Do Women *Really* Want?

When a man steals to satisfy hunger, we may safely conclude that there is something wrong in society—so when a woman destroys the life of her unborn child, it is evidence that either by education or circumstances she has been greatly wronged.

—Mattie Brinkerhoff, *The Revolution*, 1869

Abortion.
Every woman's right?
A fundamental freedom?
The solution to sexism, discrimination, and poverty?
For some, abortion is accepted without scrutiny as necessary for women's advancement. But a growing number of women are giving abortion a second look—and reconsidering whether it has fulfilled the many promises made to us.

Abortion rights activists promised us a world of equality, reduced poverty. A world where every child would be wanted. Instead, child abuse has escalated, and rather than shared responsibility for children, even more of the burden has shifted to women.

Women have sought real solutions since we entered the workforce. Women want economic empowerment through equal opportunities for pay and position in the workplace. Flex time and job sharing. Comprehensive health care.

SOURCE: Feminists for Life of America, 733 15th St., NW, Suite 1100, Washington, D.C. 20005, 202/737-3352.

Maternity benefits and parental leave. Affordable, quality child care. Shared parental responsibility. Child support.

By promoting abortion instead of working for social changes that would make it possible to combine children and career, abortion advocates have betrayed a majority of wage earning women who *want* to have children.

While members of the 70's women's movement continue to promote abortion, another movement is going forward with *real* solutions. This movement, a renaissance of the original American feminism, is built on a progressive ethic that challenges the status quo.

Pro-life feminists recognize abortion as a symptom of, not a solution to, the continuing struggles we face in the workplace, at home and in society. Like Susan B. Anthony and other early American suffragists, today's pro-life feminists envision a better world, where no woman would feel forced into the personal tragedy of abortion:

A world in which pregnancy and motherhood are accepted and supported.
A structured workplace that supports mothers rather than forcing them to choose between their children and their careers.
A society that supports the role of mothers and values the role of fathers, and helps fathers provide both financial and emotional support for their children.
A culture where "stay-at-home moms" are afforded respect.

Since both sides of the abortion issue agree that no woman wants to have an abortion, it is a cruel hoax to call abortion a woman's "choice." No woman should be forced to choose between relinquishing life and career plans or suffering through a humiliating, invasive procedure and sacrificing her child.

Abortion is a last resort, not a free choice.

Feminists for Life.

Because women don't have to settle for less.

Because there is a better way.

Join us.

PART FOUR

ABORTION AND SOCIETY

Justice, Law, and Public Policy

[38]

Abortion, Autonomy, and Community

Lisa Sowle Cahill

WITHIN THE CIRCLE OF Christian theological ethicists who converse in "the academy," as I do, it is definitely not in vogue to voice opposition to the prochoice position. This position is often believed to be entailed in a serious commitment to sexual autonomy, to feminism, and to enlightened, humanistic causes in general. To some extent, my contribution to this project is a reaction against that assumption.

In formulating my position, and in evaluating the relation of positions on abortion generally to the values affirmed and denied in contemporary North American culture, I have drawn on resources both theological and philosophical. The relevant religious resources are those biblical stories, symbols, and thematic patterns that support a willingness to sacrifice personal interests in order to protect the weakest or the "neighbor" most in need. (The latter category includes both women, who suffer the effects of injustices in the spheres of sexuality, domesticity, and reproduction, and fetuses, as dependent and unable effectively to assert claims.) Also central are the resources of the Roman Catholic tradition in social ethics, which has been considerably more "progressive" than the tradition in personal ethics, medical and sexual.[1] However, I dissent from the proposition that abortion is a narrowly religious issue. Both biblical themes and Catholic natural-law social analysis are presented here in

Source: From Daniel and Sidney Callahan, eds., *Abortion: Understanding Differences* (New York: Plenum Press, 1984). Reprinted by permission of Human Sciences Press, Inc., and the author.

359

terms congruent with many secular or humanistic perspectives on the relations of persons in community (though not all, e.g., utilitarianism). The possibility of assuming in principle an alliance between religious and rational ethics is itself a fruit of the Catholic, Thomistic, natural-law tradition of moral insight.

The principal value at stake in this essay is the existence of the fetus itself, for it must be established *who* are considered members of the "human community" before the moral relationships among these members can be addressed. The question of the status of fetal life in the human community is the most divisive and the least easy to resolve in the entire abortion debate; it is also the most fundamental. Although it is not my purpose here to defend a certain view of the fetus, of its rights, or of the rights of its mother, I have yet to be persuaded that these issues can be avoided successfully. For this reason, I feel a need to briefly indicate my own evaluation of fetal life, fully realizing that any position on the status of the fetus is vulnerable. I then proceed to my major task of broader reflections on abortion and the culture, where assumptions about the fetus also influence social attitudes and policies.

I am convinced that the fetus is from conception a member of the human species (having an identifiably human genotype, and being of human parentage), and, as such, is an entity to which at least some protection is due, even though its status may not at every phase be equivalent to that of postnatal life. (See the following section on "Dualism and Corporeality" for a further discussion of the relation between biological facts and moral value.) Further, I believe that there exists, even in our pluralist culture, a relatively broad consensus that the fetus does have some value and status in the human community, even among those who maintain that "hard choices" about sustaining its life must be left finally to the woman who bears it. My position on fetal status might be characterized as "developmentalist"[2] insofar as I view its value as incremental throughout gestation. The fact that few, if any, give absolutely equal value to the mother and the fetus is attested to by the fact that all are willing to prefer the mother in at least some "life-against-life" cases, and by the fact that virtually no one perceives the abortion of a seven-month-old fetus as the moral equivalent of the use of an abortifacient method of birth control, such as the IUD (even though both may be viewed as wrong). Nonetheless, I see the fetus as having a value at conception that is quite significant and that quickly increases; but it never overrides the right of the mother to preserve her own life. Even relatively early in pregnancy (for example, in the first trimester), I think serious considerations must be present to justify abortion. Threat to life is the classic case, although I would not exclude the possibility that other threats might justify abortion, particularly when the interest that the mother has at stake is equal to or greater than her interest in her life. (To specify such interests and to stipulate circumstances in which they might be threatened remains a perplexing task.) In summary, I endorse a strong bias in favor of the fetus and rest a heavy burden of proof on those who would choose abortion. This endorsement will in obvious ways influence my assessment of the values that form the backdrop for our culture's permissive policies regarding abortion. At the same time, I trust that much of what I have to say about such things as community, corporeality, suffering, physical or mental disabilities, and family will find agreement among many who do not share my evaluation of fetal life or my grounding in Catholic Christianity.

Liberalism and the Common Good

A central focus of my analysis of abortion and the culture is the relations between individuals and the communities in which they associate. Often, these relations are articulated in terms of "rights" and "duties." It has been observed, however, that these terms encourage moral individualism and isolation of the moral agent(s) from the social relationships in which decision making occurs.[3]

I continue to think it legitimate to use "rights" language to discuss abortion, but I want to remove that language from the context of moral and political liberalism. To shift attention away from the rights of the fetus or the woman understood individualistically does not mean that the value and rights of either thereby become irrelevant. It means, rather, that their respective rights must be defined in relation to one another (and, in a less immediate sense, to the rights of others, for example, family members). Where those rights can conflict, neither can be absolute. The rights of both are *limited,* but still significant.

Fundamentally, then, I want to speak of rights in the context of sociality and of community. Of particular relevance to the abortion dilemma is the fact that duties or obligations can bind humans to their fellows in ways to which they have not explicitly consented. Such obligations originate simply in the sorts of reciprocal relatedness that constitute being a human. The mother-fetus relation is characterized by obligations of this sort, as are all parent-child relations.

Abortion represents a conflict between, most directly, the rights of the mother and the rights of the fetus. In contemporary American culture, this conflict is settled in favor of the pregnant woman's right to dispose of the fetus as she deems necessary to protect her own rights or interests. A warrant often adduced in support of such an adjudication of claims is the woman's right to autonomous self-determination, particularly regarding her body and its reproductive capacities. Thus, a restriction of the right to choose abortion is perceived as an infringement of personal liberty in a most intimate and private sphere.

The present dominance of the prochoice position on abortion (that is, every woman has a right to decide for herself, and on the basis of her own religious and moral convictions, whether or not to have an abortion) represents *positively* the view that women must be taken seriously as autonomous moral agents. Societal and legal protection of the freedom to control childbearing, through abortion if necessary, represents a challenge to those dimensions of marriage, family, and employment that continue to oppress and subordinate the female sex. In addition, to leave abortion decisions to the discretion of the agent most directly involved is to acknowledge the individuality that attends every moral decision, especially decisions that are complex, filled with conflict, and even tragic.

However, I believe that our culture's general willingness to grant to women the exclusive power to terminate their pregnancies has other, too frequently unexamined, implications that can be described *negatively.* First, and perhaps most fundamentally, the single-minded affirmation of the rights of the pregnant woman (e.g., her "right to privacy" or "right to reproductive freedom") virtually circumvents the equally important but incorrigibly difficult problem of the status of fetal life. What sort of being is it that threatens the welfare of the pregnant woman? Does it in turn have rights? And if so, how do they weigh in the balance against those of the woman? Furthermore, the subordination in the legal and practical spheres of any right to life of the fetus (at least, if previable) to a whole spectrum of rights, needs, or interests of the mother manifests a widespread and often uncritical cultural acceptance of political and moral liberalism.

By *liberalism,* I mean a family of views concerning the person and the society resembling or rooted in the social contract theories of John Locke, Thomas Hobbes, and Jean Jacques Rousseau, who have influenced, at least indirectly, Western democracy and the American constitutional tradition. In such views, persons are seen essentially as free and autonomous agents who come into society to protect self-interest by a series of mutually advantageous agreements. Society or community is thus secondary to the existence of the individual; persons are not social by nature and have no natural obligations antecedent to their free consent.[4] A woman, for example, has no *prima facie* moral obligation to sustain a pregnancy that she has not undertaken voluntarily; to do so would constitute a supererogatory act (Judith Jarvis Thomson).[5]

Other competing theories—for example, some Marxist and feminist social theories, or the Thomistic notion of the "common good" as reinterpreted by the modern papal social encyclicals—begin from the contrary premise. That is, persons are by definition interrelated in a social whole whose fabric of reciprocal rights and duties constitutes the very condition of their individual and communal fulfillment. The concept of the *common good* envisions society in a way that is neither liberal nor utilitarian. The community is understood as prior to the individual; however, each individual is equally entitled to share in the benefits that inhere in the community. The common good is not identified with the interests of any particular group. Rather, it is a normative standard or ideal by which to criticize and reform any existing social order. Undeniably associated with this notion are some intransigent problems of definition shared with other attempts to elucidate "normative" or "essential" humanity or human community. Still, fidelity to the common good as the primary framework for social analysis guarantees, at least, that *individual* and *community*, as well as *rights* and *duties,* will be taken as a pair of complementary terms. Above all, it suggests that human society is characterized by an intrinsic interdependence or cohesiveness for which paradigms that construe society as voluntary affiliations of individuals whose mutual obligations are purely contractual do not adequately account.[6]

From the viewpoint of the common good, understood in these terms, one indeed has a duty, premised on the mutual interdependence and obligations implied by common humanity, to help another person when to do so involves relatively little self-sacrifice and a proportionate gain for the other. Because gestation is a primordial, prototypical, and physically concrete form of sociality and interdependence, some obligations to the fetus may exist even when they have not been undertaken deliberately. One consequence of the individualistic liberal view of the pregnant woman as moral agent, besides the obvious one of minimizing restraints on her free power of self-determination, is that it reduces the obligations of other individuals or of the community to offer support during and after a burdensome pregnancy. Moral and social dilemmas are regarded as the business and the burden of individuals, to be resolved or borne alone.[7]

Dualism and Corporeality

Twentieth-century philosophy and theology have been accustomed to repudiating the "dualism" of ancient Greece and its remnants in Christianity or its facsimile in René Descartes. In sexual ethics, for example, we resist any attempts to define the body as "bad" and the spirit as resistant to it, and instead, we insist on attention to bodily experience in definitions of moral obligation.[8] The unity of body and spirit in human experience should also be taken into account seriously in discussions of pregnancy. The facts that a fetus is ineluctably dependent for its very existence on the body of another, and that this relation of dependence is not *prima facie* pathological or unjust, but physiologically normal and natural for a human being in its earliest stages of existence, should count as *one* factor in a moral evaluation of pregnancy and abortion. The morality of abortion is not reducible to the issue of "free consent" to pregnancy. This is not to say that abortion can never be justified (given the presence of countervailing factors), but only that we have not grasped the reality of the moral situation when we define freedom only as "freedom over" the body and not also as "freedom in" or "freedom through" the body. The body makes peculiar demands, creates peculiar relationships, and grounds peculiar obligations.

The Catholic moral theologian Louis Janssens has reformulated the notion of a normative human nature in a way that affirms the historicity, equality, sociality, and corporeality of all persons:

> That we are corporeal means in the first place that our body forms a part of the integrated subject that we are; corporeal and spiritual, nonetheless a singular being. What concerns the human body, therefore, also affects the person himself.
>
> That we are a subjectivity, or a conscious interiority, in corporeality . . . is the basis for a number of moral demands.[9]

Conversely, our culture as liberal denies both determinations of "freedom" by our concrete embodied nature and obligation without consent (as a contradiction in terms). The former denial is related to the latter as partial cause. Examples of the tendency to ignore, repress, or negate the demands of corporeality can be seen at many levels: in the rapid increase in medical litigation over the past two decades, which seems to represent the unrealistic demand that the physician free us from the vulnerability of the human body and the fallibility of the medical arts; in the denial in popular mores and in sexual ethics that there is any morally significant connection whatsoever between sex and procreation; and in the recalcitrant refusal of denizens of the developed nations to curtail their supposed right to pursue life, liberty, and happiness at the expense of the material needs of Third World citizens.

At the same time that we avoid the exaltation of autonomy to the detriment of corporeality, it is important to avoid biologism, another form of dualism, in which freedom is completely constrained by physiological functions or conditions. Examples of the latter can be found in traditional Roman Catholic analyses of sexual and medical ethics. Since the negative response of the Holy Office of the Vatican in 1869 to the inquiry whether craniotomy is licit, magisterial teaching regarding abortion has been that a fetus may be sacrificed to preserve its mother's life only when the procedure that destroys it is aimed *physically* at some other objective. Thus, the removal of the cancerous uterus of a pregnant woman would be allowed, insofar as the physically indirect method of killing the fetus (though a surgical procedure related directly to a condition other than pregnancy) "guarantees" that the intention of the agents involved is not primarily to bring about the death of the fetus, but to protect the woman.

By the same token, it would be permissible to remove the entire fallopian tube in a case of ectopic pregnancy; but it would not be permissible to remove the embryo from the tube, leaving intact the tube and the woman's potential to conceive again. Much less would it be justified to remove a potentially viable fetus directly from the womb to curtail the potentially fatal strain of pregnancy on a woman suffering from renal or coronary disease. The crucial question in such dilemmas is whether the moral key ought to be the indirectness of the physical procedure of resolution or the simple fact of two lives in conflict.[10]

Another nexus of dualistic arguments about abortion is the problematic relationship of the biological development of the fetus (for example, its appearance) to its status in the human community. Equally prone to oversimplification are those who claim that a recognizably human genotype or human form is of no relevance at all to the respect accorded some particular being and those who assume that a demonstration of the membership of the fetus in the species *Homo sapiens,* or its resemblance to a baby, settles the issue of full "humanity" or "personhood," and thus of abortion. Few are unfamiliar with the attempts of some prolife advocates to substitute enlarged photographs of aborted fetuses for rational argument. More subtle are the efforts of prochoice proponents to eliminate critical recognition of the matter–spirit link in abortion. Michael Tooley and Laura Purdy asked rhetorically, "If pig fetuses resembled adult humans, would it be seriously wrong to kill pig fetuses?"[11] Dualism is the premise that allows such a question to be posed at all, as it requires us to dissociate from our notion of "humanity" what it means to exist materially and corporeally in a human (or porcine) manner. The reader is induced to answer, "No," and thus to agree with the proabortion argument framing the question, because the hypothetical situation is nonsensical.

A more thoughtful treatment of the problem is presented by Joseph Donceel's revival of the Aristotelian-Thomistic notion of "hylomorphism."[12] Donceel suggested that the material aspect of any being is naturally appropriate to its "form" or spirit. Thus, the increasingly human appearance of human offspring during gestation may be relevant to their developing status within the community of persons. Donceel suggested that the possibility of the "delayed hominization" of the fetus is not inconsistent with the acceptance by some traditional Christian authors (such as Anselm, Aquinas, and Alphonsus Liguori) of the idea that "ensoulment" takes place at some point subsequent to conception, for example, at "quickening." Abortion, although always sinful, becomes the sin of homicide only after that point.

The merit of a position such as Donceel's lies in its recognition that scientific or empirical evidence (e.g., about genotype or appearance) can be relevant to moral decisions, even if it is not in itself decisive. An integral view of the person urges recognition that neither human spirit, freedom, and valuing, on the one hand, nor the material conditions, realizations, and manifestations of same, on the other, ought to be taken alone as definitive of moral obligation. Normative ethics is dependent on the empirical sciences and other "descriptive" (as distinct from "normative") accounts of the human situation for two reasons at least: (1) the ethicist must have a realistic appreciation of the act or the relation that he or she proposes to evaluate; and (2) the fact that an entity or relation is "normal" or "abnormal" in, for example, a sociological, physiological, or psychological sense will count for or against the conclusion that its existence ought or ought not to be chosen or encouraged. (However, to determine the precise weight that empirical or statistical normality or abnormality ought to have in normative ethics is not a simple matter. It joins the ranks of the highly debated questions in ethics.) Donceel's point is not only that the entity to be evaluated, the fetus, has a corporeal dimension, but also that what is known about normal fetal development should be correlated with any normative account of fetal status.

Suffering

The liberal ethos discourages making personal sacrifices and encourages at best a minimal appreciation of the virtue and even the necessity of constructive suffering. Our culture has a low tolerance of the burdens and failures of life and tends to deny that life has value when conducted in irremediably painful conditions. There is an expectation of ready resort to the "technological fix" and an inability to appropriate suffering in meaningful ways.[13] To these sorts of attitudes might be contrasted the Christian ideals of reconciliation or redemption of the conditions of brokenness and evil in which we consistently find ourselves.

The notion of ability and responsibility to constructively redeem tragedy under circumstances of difficulty is not incompatible with the feminist concern that women be regarded as and regard themselves as mature moral agents who do not need protection from and do not avoid the exigencies of adulthood in the human community. I do not recommend masochism, nor the martyrdom of women who sacrifice themselves out of unwillingness or inability to assert their legitimate claims; rather, I recommend a recognition that some human situations have unavoidably tragic elements and that to be human is to bear these burdens. We cannot be freed from all infringements on our self-fulfillment, and to persistently demand that is to avoid moral agency in the complete sense. The decision to continue a pregnancy might be construed as a decision by the stronger to assume burdens that would otherwise fall on the most defenseless. However, "the stronger" includes not only the woman, who is also a victim, but the larger community of which she and the fetus are a part. (This is not to deny that the tragic elements of conflictual pregnancies may justify some decisions to abort.) As a final note, an important element in constructively assimilating suffering, and also in alleviating suffering to the extent possible, is communal support, both of the difficult pregnancy and of the abnormal fetus, child, or adult. In another context, Daniel Callahan (himself a prochoice advocate) has perceptively commented on the kind of community needed to successfully weather moral conflicts for which there appears to be a dearth of satisfactory resolutions:

> Hard times require self-sacrifice and altruism—but there is nothing in an ethic of moral autonomy to sustain or nourish those values. Hard times necessitate a sense of community and the common good—but the putative virtues of autonomy are primarily directed toward the cultivation of independent selfhood. . . . Hard times need a broad sense of duty toward others, especially those out of sight—but an ethic of autonomy stresses responsibility only for one's freely chosen, consenting-adult relationships.
>
> Whether suffering brings out the best or the worst in people is an old question, and the historical evidence is mixed. Yet a people's capacity to endure suffering without turning on each other is closely linked to the way they have envisioned, and earlier embodied, their relationship to each other.[14]

Standards of Human Existence

Our culture tends to estimate the value of human life in direct proportion to its level of physical and intellectual perfection or achievement. This attitude leads to the inability of parents and others to envision creatively or positively the task of raising an abnormal child, and it creates widespread support of abortion for so-called fetal indications. A question that often could be pressed more critically is whether the abortion is intended primarily to serve the interests of the family (in its "freedom") or of the fetus (in a "happy" life), and in either case, what criteria of evaluation are used.[15]

The liberal individualistic theory of moral responsibility comes into play not only in the moral weight usually given to freedom, but also because society often seems to see parents as responsible for avoiding the births of defective (and hence burdensome) children; social willingness to provide structures of assistance for severely handicapped individuals and their families decreases correspondingly.[16]

One Christian ethicist, Stanley Hauerwas, has developed a critique of the further implications of liberalism for the nature of the family.[17] Hauerwas, who is noted for his emphasis on the narrative qualities of religion and theology, on the centrality of character in morality and ethics, and on the importance of community in embodying religious and moral commitment in life and action, observed that the modern nuclear family is perceived as a complex of intimate relationships whose purpose is the personal fulfillment of its members. Such an account of family life has lost both the connection of the "self-sufficient" family with the larger community and its institutions and any resources for understanding the purposes of family life, including having children, beyond the gratification of the couple. Hauerwas proposed that the family ought not to be understood as "a contractual social unit"[18] and that "marriage is not sustained by being a fulfilling experience for all involved, but by embodying moral and social purposes that give it a basis in the wider community."[19]

The language of rights is criticized by Hauerwas because it seems to represent the liberal commitment to the autonomy of the individual and his or her freedom to enter into moral obligations electively via contracts.[20] He also seems to detect a liberal agenda hidden behind attempts to hinge the abortion discussion on whether the fetus has or has not a "right to life." Hauerwas suggested that the precise status of the fetus as a "human being" may not be crucial as long as it is agreed that it is a "child." (These terms are not clarified precisely, but by *human being* I take Hauerwas to mean a member of the human community with full status and by *child* to mean human offspring.)

> Thus the preliminary question must be inverted: "What kind of people should we be to welcome children into the world?" Note that the question is *not* "Is the fetus a human being with a right to life?" but "How should a Christian regard and care for the fetus as a child?"[21]

I concur with Hauerwas that our evaluations of the morality of abortion, and particularly a commitment to its avoidance, cannot be understood apart from communal values and commitments. My discussion, too, concerns essentially the kinds of community (the kinds of values, attitudes, and virtues that community encourages) that will support or not support nascent life in difficult circumstances. However, I am not convinced of the wisdom or even the possibility of setting aside the question of the status of the unborn offspring, because the presupposition that we *should* support it (even as a sign of hope in the future) seems to involve a certain understanding of its value. Our protectiveness and hope do not include in the same way other forms of sentient and nonsentient life. The point is well taken, however, that the virtue of hope embodied in inauspicious situations enables the perception of at least a *prima facie* obligation to sustain fetal life, even if that life is not clearly of equal value to postnatal human life. Indeed, this takes us far from the position that it must be demonstrated beyond a reasonable doubt that the fetus is a "person" in the full sense of the word as a precondition for according it protection. If relatedness to and concern for others and for the sort of community in which we all associate is more important to us than "defending our own territory" (by defining the precise limits of our minimal obligations not to prevent other equal beings from promoting their own self-interested welfare), then it becomes less important to show whether or not the fetus is a human with exactly the same right to consideration as our own. If we are able to foster a sense of duty to others and to our common society, a duty that precedes and grounds our own rights as individuals, then it also becomes possible to envision a moral obligation to support the cohesion in the human community of even its weakest members, those with the least forceful claim to consideration, whether they be the unborn, the sick, the poor, or the socially powerless.[22]

Conclusions

The precise value and rights of human fetal life remain questions awaiting resolution, perhaps indefinitely. However, without at least a provisional answer, the abortion discussion cannot proceed coherently, for the participants will not avoid hidden presuppositions about the consideration due the fetus as such. My own conviction that the fetus deserves considerable respect from conception may not represent a common denominator in the abortion debate. Nevertheless, I believe that there is now more of a consensus in our culture than is usually recognized that a policy on abortion attributing to the fetus no value that can ever outweigh its mother's choice to terminate pregnancy is not consonant with its membership in the human community, disputed though the exact nature of that membership may be. Failing agreement on the precise status of the fetus, we may hope still for concurrence in a generally protective attitude toward the fetus, a bias in its favor, and an expectation that those seeking to kill it will be able to claim reasonably that its continued existence imposes on others unjust and intolerable burdens. For such an attitude to be genuinely life-enhancing, rather than simply restrictive and destructive of the lives of pregnant women and their families, will require a move beyond the liberal ethos. It will require nourishment by a renewed and even redirected sense of community, one in which not only the fetus is protected, but also all who suffer disadvantage at the hands of fellow humans, nature, or chance. "Human 'flourishing'" is a phrase invented by G. E. M. Anscombe to describe what grounds, defines, and constitutes the virtues that human beings ought to cultivate.[23] A community in which the "right to abort" could be overshadowed by rather than entailed in the "duty to encourage human well-being" would be one in which human interdependence in the spheres not only of personal freedoms and civil liberties, but also of physical prosperity and amelioration of suffering, corporal and spiritual, is recognized as the very condition of human flourishing, and so as bounty, not burden.

Notes

1. The twentieth-century popes have taken a persistent and sometimes prophetic interest in redressing imbalances in the social and economic orders, whether precipitated by socialism or by capitalism. Examples are Leo XIII's *Rerum novarum* (1891), Pius XI's *Quadragesimo anno* (1931), John XXIII's *Mater et magistra* (1961) and *Pacem in terris* (1963), Paul VI's *Populorum progressio* (1967) and *Octogesima adveniens* (1971), and John Paul II's *Laborem exercens* (1982).

2. Daniel Callahan, *Abortion: Law, Choice, and Morality* (New York: Macmillan, 1970), 381–90.

3. See, for example, Larry R. Churchill and José Jorge Siman, "Abortion and the Rhetoric of Individual Rights," *Hastings Center Report* 12 (Feb. 1982): 9–12; and Sandra Harding, "Beneath the Surface of the Abortion Dispute," in *Abortion: Understanding Differences,* ed. Sidney and Daniel Callahan (New York: Plenum Press, 1984).

4. See the critiques of liberalism by Sandra G. Harding, "Beneath the Surface of the Abortion Debate," and Jean Bethke Elshtain, "Reflections on Abortion, Values, and the Family," both in *Abortion: Understanding Differences.*

5. Judith Jarvis Thomson, "A Defense of Abortion," *Philosophy and Public Affairs* 1 (fall 1972): 47–66.

6. The papal social encyclicals have been largely *ad hoc* in nature, addressing themselves in the name of the common good to actual abuses and imbalances of rights and duties, rather than attempting to articulate any exhaustive list of rights and duties or to formulate precisely enduring relationships among them. For instance, in *Rerum novarum* Leo XIII addressed, against socialism, the right of the worker to own private property; in *Quadragesimo anno* Pius XI asserted the rights of the worker against capitalistic property owners who neglected duties to others and to the community as a whole. Among the best concise definitions of "common good" in the encyclicals is that offered by John XXIII in *Pacem in terris* (paras. 55–58). I have further developed this analysis of common good, rights, and duties in "Toward a Christian Theory of Human Rights," *Journal of Religious Ethics* 8 (fall 1980): 277–301.

   In a recent essay ("Abortion and the Pursuit of Happiness," *Logos* 3 [1982]: 61–77), Philip Rossi, S.J., similarly asserted the connection between human freedom and interdependence and linked it with Kant's characterization of moral agency in accord with membership in a "kingdom of ends." Rossi argued effectively that "rights in conflict" language is insufficient to handle the morality of abortion in the absence of a unified view of happiness or the human good.

7. In *The Heretical Imperative* (Garden City, N.Y.: Doubleday, 1979), Peter Berger dubbed the "modern consciousness" a phenomenon akin to the liberal ethos. The modern man or woman is under the necessity of making choices rather than of acquiescing to fate. However, he or she also is confronted with a plurality of world views, rather than with a cohesive tradition that shapes social roles and gives them significance. A crisis of belief results because beliefs about reality, including religious and moral beliefs, require social confirmation, and that is widely unavailable in modern society. As a result, morality and religion become subjectivized and contingent on the sheer choice or "preference" of the individual, 1–31).

8. See, for example, James B. Nelson, *Embodiment: An Approach to Sexuality and Christian Theology* (Minneapolis: Augsburg, 1978), and Robert Baker and Frederick Elliston, eds., *Philosophy and Sex* (Buffalo, N.Y.: Prometheus Books, 1975).

9. Louis Janssens, "Artificial Insemination: Ethical Considerations," *Louvain Studies* 8 (spring 1980): 5–6.

10. More complete discussions of the evolution of the Catholic position on abortion are offered in John T. Noonan Jr., "An Almost Absolute Value in History," in *The Morality of Abortion,* ed. John T. Noonan Jr. (Cambridge: Harvard University Press, 1970); and John Connery, S.J., *Abortion: The Development of the Roman Catholic Perspective* (Chicago: Loyola University Press, 1977). Critiques have been developed by Bernard Häring, "A Theological Evaluation"; James M. Gustafson, "A Protestant Ethical Approach"; and Paul Ramsey, "Reference Points in Deciding about Abortion," in *The Morality of Abortion.* Charles Curran examined the problem of "physicalism" in Roman Catholic ethics generally in "Natural Law and Contemporary Moral Theology," *Contemporary Problems in Moral Theology* (Notre Dame, Ind.: Fides, 1970). Several discussions of the "principle of double effect" operative in the Catholic analysis of abortion appear in Charles E. Curran and Richard A. McCormick, S.J., eds., *Readings in Moral Theology No. 1: Moral Norms and Catholic Tradition* (New York: Paulist, 1979). Unfortunately, to cite these resources is only to skim the surface of those available.

11. Michael Tooley and Laura Purdy, "Is Abortion Murder?" in *Abortion: Pro and Con,* ed. Robert Perkins (Cambridge, Mass., 1974), 134.

12. Joseph Donceel, S.J., "Animation and Hominization," *Theological Studies* 31 (Mar. 1970): 76–105.

13. I perceive a concern similar to mine in David Peretz's "The Illusion of 'Rational' Suicide," *Hastings Center Report* 11 (Dec. 1981): 40–42. Peretz sees planned suicide as an attempt to gain control over feelings of pain and helplessness by idealizing the freedom and autonomy of the "self as agent."

14. Daniel Callahan, "Minimalist Ethics," *Hastings Center Report* 11 (Oct.

1981): 19–20. Callahan addressed the question of whether a morality that stresses the autonomy of the individual is a "good-time philosophy," able to sustain a society in times of affluence but not in times of economic and political stress.

15. A provocative example of a criterion of the life worth preserving has been offered by Richard McCormick in a discussion of whether and when to treat infants suffering from serious congenital anomalies. McCormick suggested that physical life can be a worthwhile good for the person living it if it offers at least "relational potential," that is, the capacity to give and receive love, and even if it does not offer "normal" intelligence or physical competence ("To Save or Let Die," *Journal of the American Medical Association* 229 [July 1974]: 172–76).

16. Those who have counseled or interviewed parents of abnormal infants have commented that the availability of amniocentesis and abortion in cases of genetic defect has altered the nature of the parent–child relationship after such a birth occurs. John Fletcher commented, "If an infant is born with a severe genetic defect which might have been diagnosed pre-natally, will it not occur to the physicians and parents, that this infant might have been tested and aborted? Such thoughts will, presumably, intensify the rejection of the infant" ("Moral and Ethical Problems of Pre-Natal Diagnosis," *Clinical Genetics* 9 [October 1975]: 25). See also John Fletcher, "The Brink: The Parent–Child Bond in the Genetic Revolution," *Theological Studies* 33 (Sept. 1972): 457–85; and Raymond S. Duff and A. G. M. Campbell, "Moral and Ethical Dilemmas in the Special-Care Nursery," *New England Journal of Medicine* 289 (Oct. 1973): 890–94.

17. This is accomplished most extensively in Stanley Hauerwas, *A Community of Character* (Notre Dame, Ind.: University of Notre Dame Press, 1981), especially part 3, "The Church and Social Policy: The Family, Sex, and Abortion."

18. Ibid., 171.

19. Ibid., 191.

20. Ibid., 198–99.

21. Ibid., 198.

22. In an essay entitled "The Christian, Society, and the Weak: A Meditation on the Care of the Retarded," in *Vision and Virtue* (Notre Dame, Ind.: Fides, 1974), 187–94, Hauerwas argued that the Christian's task of caring for the weak exemplifies the obligation to live the love revealed in the cross, rather than either to try to eradicate all suffering or to attribute the existence of suffering to God's hidden purposes.

23. G. E. M. Anscombe, "Modern Moral Philosophy," *Philosophy* 33 (Jan. 1958): 18.

[39]

Religious Belief and Public Morality:
A Catholic Governor's Perspective

Mario Cuomo

I WOULD LIKE TO begin by drawing your attention to the title of this lecture: "Religious Belief and Public Morality: A Catholic Governor's Perspective." I was not invited to speak on church and state generally. Certainly not Mondale vs. Reagan. The subject assigned is difficult enough. I will not try to do more than I've been asked.

It's not easy to stay contained. Certainly, although everybody talks about a wall of separation between church and state, I've seen religious leaders scale that wall with all the dexterity of Olympic athletes. In fact, I've seen so many candidates in churches and synagogues that I think we should change election day from Tuesdays to Saturdays and Sundays.

I am honored by this invitation, but the record shows that I am not the first governor of New York to appear at an event involving Notre Dame. One of my great predecessors, Al Smith, went to the Army–Notre Dame football game each time it was played in New York.

His fellow Catholics expected Smith to sit with Notre Dame; protocol required him to sit with Army because it was the home team. Protocol prevailed. But not without Smith noting the dual demands on his affections. "I'll take my seat with Army," he said, "but I commend my soul to Notre Dame!"

SOURCE: From *The Notre Dame Journal of Law, Ethics, and Public Policy* 1, no. 1 (1984). Copyright © 1984 by The Notre Dame Journal of Law, Ethics, and Public Policy. Reprinted by permission.

Today I'm happy to have no such problem: Both my seat and my soul are with Notre Dame. And as long as Father McBrien doesn't invite me back to sit with him at the Notre Dame–St. John's basketball game, I'm confident my loyalties will remain undivided.

In a sense, it's a question of loyalty that Father McBrien has asked me here today to discuss. Specifically, must politics and religion in America divide our loyalties? Does the "separation between church and state" imply separation between religion and politics? Between morality and government? Are these different propositions? Even more specifically, what is the relationship of my Catholicism to my politics? Where does the one end and other begin? Or are the two divided at all? And if they're not, should they be?

Hard questions.

No wonder most of us in public life—at least until recently—preferred to stay away from them, heeding the biblical advice that if "hounded and pursued in one city," we should flee to another.

Now, however, I think that it is too late to flee. The questions are all around us, and answers are coming from every quarter. Some of them have been simplistic, most of them fragmentary and a few, spoken with a purely political intent, demagogic.

There has been confusion and compounding of confusion, a blurring of the issue, entangling it in personalities and election strategies instead of clarifying it for Catholics, as well as others.

Today I would like to try to help correct that.

I can offer you no final truths, complete and unchallengeable. But it's possible this one effort will provoke other efforts—both in support and contradiction of my position—that will help all of us understand our differences and perhaps even discover some basic agreement.

In the end, I'm convinced we will all benefit if suspicion is replaced by discussion, innuendo by dialogue; if the emphasis in our debate turns from a search for talismanic criteria and neat but simplistic answers to an honest—more intelligent—attempt at describing the role religion has in our public affairs and the limits placed on that role.

And if we do it right—if we're not afraid of the truth even when the truth is complex—this debate, by clarification, can bring relief to untold numbers of confused—even anguished—Catholics, as well as to many others who want only to make our already great democracy even stronger than it is.

I believe the recent discussion in my own state has already produced some clearer definition. In early summer an impression was created in some quarters that official church spokespeople would ask Catholics to vote for or against candidates on the basis of their political position on the abortion issue. I was one of those given that impression. Thanks to the dialogue that ensued over the summer—only partially reported by the media—we learned that the impression was not accurate.

Confusion had presented an opportunity for clarification, and we seized it. Now all of us are saying one thing—in chorus—reiterating the statement of the National Conference of Catholic Bishops that they will not "take positions for or against political candidates" and that their stand on specific issues would not be perceived "as an expression of political partisanship."

Of course the bishops will teach—they must—more and more vigorously and more and more extensively. But they have said they will not use the power of their position, and the great respect it receives from all Catholics, to give an imprimatur to individual politicians or parties.

Not that they couldn't if they wished to—some religious leaders do; some are doing it at this very moment.

Not that it would be a sin if they did—God doesn't insist on political neutrality. But because it is the judgment of the bishops, and most of us Catholic lay people, that it is not wise for prelates and politicians to be tied too closely together.

I think that getting this consensus was an extraordinarily useful achievement.

Now, with some trepidation, I take up your gracious invitation to continue the dialogue in the hope that it will lead to still further clarification.

Let me begin this part of the effort by underscoring the obvious. I do not speak as a theologian; I do not have that competence. I do not speak as a philosopher; to suggest that I could would be to set a new record for false pride. I don't presume to speak as a "good" person except in the ontological sense of that word. My principal credential is that I serve in a position that forces me to wrestle with the problems you've come here to study and debate.

I am by training a lawyer and by practice a politician. Both professions make me suspect in many quarters, including among some of my own coreligionists. Maybe there's no better illustration of the public perception of how politicians unite their faith and their profession than the story they tell in New York about "Fishhooks" McCarthy, a famous Democratic leader on the Lower East Side and right-hand man to Al Smith.

"Fishhooks," the story goes, was devout. So devout that every morning on his way to Tammany Hall to do his political work, he stopped into St. James Church on Oliver Street in downtown Manhattan, fell on his knees and whispered the same simple prayer: "Oh, Lord, give me health and strength. We'll steal the rest."

"Fishhooks" notwithstanding, I speak here as a politician. And also as a Catholic, a lay person baptized and raised in the pre–Vatican II church, educated in Catholic schools, attached to the church first by birth, then by choice, now by love. An old-fashioned Catholic who sins, regrets, struggles, worries, gets confused and most of the time feels better after confession.

The Catholic Church is my spiritual home. My heart is there and my hope.

There is, of course, more to being a Catholic than a sense of spiritual and emotional resonance. Catholicism is a religion of the head as well as the heart, and to be a Catholic is to say "I believe" to the essential core of dogmas that distinguishes our faith.

The acceptance of this faith requires a lifelong struggle to understand it more fully and to live it more truly, to translate truth into experience, to practice as well as to believe.

That's not easy: Applying religious belief to everyday life often presents challenges.

It's always been that way. It certainly is today. The America of the late twentieth century is a consumer society, filled with endless distractions, where faith is more often dismissed than challenged, where the ethnic and other loyalties that once fastened us to our religion seem to be weakening.

In addition to all the weaknesses, dilemmas and temptations that impede every pilgrim's progress, the Catholic who holds political office in a pluralistic democracy—who is elected to serve Jews and Moslems, atheists and Protestants, as well as Catholics—bears special responsibility. He or she undertakes to help create conditions under which all can live with a maximum of dignity and with a reasonable degree of freedom; where everyone who chooses may hold beliefs different from specifically Catholic ones—sometimes contradictory to them; where the laws protect people's rights to divorce, to use birth control and even to choose abortion.

In fact, Catholic public officials take an oath to preserve the Constitution that guarantees this freedom. And they do so gladly. Not because they love what others do with their freedom, but because they realize that in guaranteeing freedom for all, they guarantee our right to be Catholics: our right to pray, to use the sacraments, to refuse birth control devices, to reject abortion, not to divorce and remarry if we believe it to be wrong.

The Catholic public official lives the political truth most Catholics through most of American history have accepted and insisted on: the truth that to assure our freedom we must allow others the same freedom, even if occasionally it produces conduct by them which we would hold to be sinful.

I protect my right to be a Catholic by preserving your right to believe as a Jew, a Protestant or nonbeliever, or as anything else you choose.

We know that the price of seeking to force our beliefs on others is that they might some day force theirs on us.

This freedom is the fundamental strength of our unique experiment in government. In the complex interplay of forces and considerations that go into the making of our laws and politics, its preservation must be a pervasive and dominant concern.

But insistence on freedom is easier to accept as a general proposition than in its applications to specific situations. There are other valid general principles firmly embedded in our Constitution which, operating at the same time, create interesting and occasionally troubling problems. Thus the same amendment of the Constitution that forbids the establishment of a state church affirms my legal right to argue that my religious belief would serve well as an article of our universal public morality. I may use the prescribed processes of government—the legislative and executive and judicial processes—to convince my fellow citizens—Jews and Protestants and Buddhists and nonbelievers—that what I propose is as beneficial for them as I believe it is for me; that it is not just parochial or narrowly sectarian but fulfills a human desire for order, peace, justice, kindness, love, any of the values most of us agree are desirable even apart from their specific religious base or context.

I am free to argue for a governmental policy for a nuclear freeze, not just to avoid sin but because I think my democracy should regard it as a desirable goal.

I can, if I wish, argue that the state should not fund the use of contraceptives devices, not because the pope demands it, but because I think that the whole community—for the good of the whole community—should not sever sex from an openness to the creation of life.

And surely I can, if so inclined, demand some kind of law against abortion, not because my bishops say it is wrong, but because I think that the whole community, regardless of its religious beliefs, should agree on the importance of protecting life—including life in the womb, which is at the very least potentially human and should not be extinguished casually.

No law prevents us from advocating any of these things: I am free to do so. So are the bishops. And so is Rev. Falwell.

In fact, the Constitution guarantees my right to try. And theirs. And his.

But should I? Is it helpful? Is it essential to human dignity? Does it promote harmony and understanding? Or does it divide us so fundamentally that it threatens our ability to function as a pluralistic community?

When should I argue to make my religious value your morality? My rule of conduct your limitation?

What are the rules and policies that should influence the exercise of this right to argue and promote?

I believe I have a salvific mission as a Catholic. Does that mean I am in conscience required to do everything I can as governor to translate all my religious values into the laws and regulations of the state of New York or the United States? Or be branded a hypocrite if I don't?

As a Catholic, I respect the teaching authority of the bishops.

But must I agree with everything in the bishops' pastoral letter on peace and fight to include it in party platforms?

And will I have to do the same for the forthcoming pastoral on economics even if I am an unrepentant supply-sider?

Must I, having heard the pope renew the church's ban on birth control devices, veto the funding of contraceptive programs for non-Catholics or dissenting Catholics in my state?

I accept the church's teaching on abortion. Must I insist you do? By law? By denying you Medicaid funding? By a constitutional amendment? If so, which one? Would that be the best way to avoid abortions or to prevent them?

These are only some of the questions for Catholics. People with other religious beliefs face similar problems.

Let me try some answers.

Almost all Americans accept some religious values as a part of our public life. We are a religious people, many of us descended from ancestors who came here expressly to live their religious faith free from coercion or repression. But we are also a people of many religions, with no established church, who hold different beliefs on many matters.

Our public morality, then—moral standards we maintain for everyone, not just the ones we insist on in our private lives—depends on a consensus view of right and wrong. The values derived from religious belief will not—and should not—be accepted as part of the public morality unless they are shared by the pluralistic community at large, by consensus.

That values happen to be religious values does not deny them acceptability as a part of this consensus. But it does not require their acceptability, either.

The agnostics who joined the civil rights struggle were not deterred because that crusade's values had been nurtured and sustained in black Christian churches. Those on the political left are not perturbed today by the religious bias of the clergy and lay people who join them in the protest against the arms race and hunger and exploitation.

The arguments start when religious values are used to support positions which would impose on other people restrictions they find unacceptable. Some people do object to Catholic demands for an end to abortion, seeing it as a violation of the separation of church and state. And some others, while they have no compunction about invoking the authority of the Catholic bishops in regard to birth control and abortion, might reject out of hand their teaching on war and peace and social policy.

Ultimately, therefore, the question whether or not we admit religious values into our public affairs is too broad to yield a single answer. Yes, we create our public morality through consensus, and in this country that consensus reflects to some extent religious values of a great majority of Americans. But no, all religiously based values don't have an *a priori* place in our public morality.

The community must decide if what is being proposed would be better left to private discretion than public policy; whether it restricts freedoms and if so to what end, to whose benefit; whether it will produce a good or bad result; whether overall it will help the community or merely divide it.

The right answers to these questions can be elusive. Some of the wrong answers, on the other hand, are quite clear. For example, there are those who say there is a simple answer to all these questions; they say that by history and practice of our people we were intended to be—and should be—a Christian country in law.

But where would that leave the nonbelievers? And whose Christianity would be law, yours or mine?

This "Christian-nation" argument should concern—even frighten—two groups: non-Christians and thinking Christians.

I believe it does.

I think it's already apparent that a good part of this nation understands—if only instinctively—that anything which seems to suggest that God favors a political party or the establishment of a state church is wrong and dangerous.

Way down deep the American people are afraid of an entangling relationship between formal religions—or whole bodies of religious belief—and government. Apart from constitutional law and religious doctrine, there is a sense that tells us it's wrong to presume to speak for God or to claim God's sanction of our particular legislation and his rejection of all other positions. Most of us are offended when we see religion being trivialized by its appearance in political throwaway pamphlets.

The American people need no course in philosophy or political science or church history to know that God should not be made into a celestial party chairman.

To most of us, the manipulative invoking of religion to advance a politician or a party is frightening and divisive. The American people will tolerate religious leaders taking positions for or against candidates, although I think the Catholic bishops are right in avoiding that position. But the American people are leery about large religious organizations, powerful churches or synagogue groups engaging in such activities—again, not as a matter of law or doctrine, but because our innate wisdom and democratic instinct teach us these things are dangerous.

Today there are a number of issues involving life and death that raise questions of public morality. They are also questions of concern to most religions. Pick up a newspaper and you are almost certain to find a bitter controversy over any one of them: Baby Jane Doe, the right to die, artificial insemination, embryos *in vitro,* abortion, birth control—not to mention nuclear war and the shadow it throws across all existence.

Some of these issues touch the most intimate recesses of our lives, our roles as someone's mother or child or husband; some affect women in a unique way. But they are also public questions, for all of us.

Put aside what God expects—assume if you like there is no God—then the greatest thing still left to us is life. Even a radically secular world must struggle with the questions of when life begins, under what circumstances it can be ended, when it must be protected, by what authority; it too must decide what protection to extend to the helpless and the dying, to the aged and the unborn, to life in all its phases.

As a Catholic I have accepted certain answers as the right ones for myself and my family and because I have, they have influenced me in special ways, as Matilda's husband, as a father of five children, as a son who stood next to his own father's deathbed trying to decide if the tubes and needles no longer served a purpose.

As a governor, however, I am involved in defining policies that determine other people's rights in these same areas of life and death. Abortion is one of these issues, and while it is one issue among many, it is one of the most controversial and affects me in a special way as a Catholic public official.

So let me spend some time considering it.

I should start, I believe, by noting that the Catholic Church's actions with respect to the interplay of religious values and public policy make clear that there is no inflexible moral principle which determines what our political conduct should be. For example, on divorce and birth control, without changing its moral teaching the church abides the civil law as it now stands, thereby accepting—without making much of a point of it—that in our pluralistic society we are not required to insist that all our religious values be the law of the land.

Abortion is treated differently.

Of course there are differences both in degree and quality between abortion and some of the other religious positions the church takes: Abortion is a "matter of life and death," and degree counts. But the differences in approach reveal a truth, I think, that is not well enough perceived by Catholics and therefore still further complicates the process for us. That is, while we always owe our bishops' words respectful attention and careful consideration, the question whether to engage the political system in a struggle to have it adopt certain articles of our belief as part of public morality is not a matter of doctrine: It is a matter of prudential political judgment.

Recently, Michael Novak put it succinctly: "Religious judgment and political judgment are both needed," he wrote. "But they are not identical."

My church and my conscience require me to believe certain things about divorce, birth control and abortion. My church does not order me—under pain of sin or expulsion—to pursue my salvific mission according to a precisely defined political plan.

As a Catholic I accept the church's teaching authority. While in the past some Catholic theologians may appear to have disagreed on the morality of some abortions (it wasn't, I think, until 1869 that excommunication was attached to all abortions without distinction), and while some theologians still do, I accept the bishops' position that abortion is to be avoided.

As Catholics my wife and I were enjoined never to use abortion to destroy the life we created, and we never have. We thought church doctrine was clear on this, and—more than that—both of us felt it in full agreement with what our hearts and our consciences told us. For me, life or fetal life in the womb should be protected, even if five of nine justices of the Supreme Court and my neighbor disagree with me. A fetus is different from an appendix or a set of tonsils. At the very least, even if the argument is made by some scientists or some theologians that in the early stages of fetal development we can't discern human life, the full potential of human life is indisputably there. That—to my less subtle mind—by itself should demand respect, caution, indeed—reverence.

But not everyone in our society agrees with me and Matilda.

And those who don't—those who endorse legalized abortions—aren't a ruthless, callous alliance of anti-Christians determined to overthrow our moral standards. In many cases the proponents of legal abortion are the very people who have worked with Catholics to realize the goals of social justice set out in papal encyclicals: the American Lutheran Church, the Central Conference of American Rabbis, the Presbyterian Church in the United States, B'nai B'rith Women, the Women of the Episcopal Church. These are just a few of the religious organizations that don't share the church's position on abortion.

Certainly we should not be forced to mold Catholic morality to conform to disagreement by non-Catholics however sincere or severe their disagreement. Our bishops should be teachers, not pollsters. They should not change what we Catholics believe in order to ease our consciences or please our friends or protect the church from criticism.

But if the breadth, intensity and sincerity of opposition to church teaching shouldn't be allowed to shape our Catholic morality, it can't help but determine our ability—our realistic, political ability—to translate our Catholic morality into civil law, a law not for the believers who don't need it but for the disbelievers who reject it.

And it is here, in our attempt to find a political answer to abortion—an answer beyond our private observance of Catholic morality—that we encounter controversy within and without the church over how and in what degree to press the case that our morality should be everybody else's, and to what effect.

I repeat, there is no church teaching that mandates the best political course for making our belief everyone's rule, for spreading this part of our Catholicism. There is neither an encyclical nor a catechism that spells out a political strategy for achieving legislative goals.

And so the Catholic trying to make moral and prudent judgments in the political realm must discern which, if any, of the actions one could take would be best.

This latitude of judgment is not something new in the church, not a development that has arisen only with the abortion issue. Take, for example, the question of slavery. It has been argued that the failure to endorse a legal ban on abortions is equivalent to refusing to support the cause of abolition before the Civil War. This analogy has been advanced by the bishops of my own state.

But the truth of the matter is, few if any Catholic bishops spoke for abolition in the years before the Civil War. It wasn't, I believe, that the bishops endorsed the idea of some humans owning and exploiting other humans; Pope Gregory XVI in 1840 had condemned the slave trade. Instead it was a practical political judgment that the bishops made. They weren't hypocrites; they were realists. At the time Catholics were a small minority, mostly immigrants, despised by much of the population, often vilified and the object of sporadic violence. In the face of a public controversy that aroused tremendous passions and threatened to break the country apart, the bishops made a pragmatic decision. They believed their opinion would not change people's minds. Moreover they knew that there were Southern Catholics, even some priests, who owned slaves. They concluded that under the circumstances arguing for a constitutional amendment against slavery would do more harm than good, so they were silent. As they have been generally in recent years on the question of birth control. And as the church has been on even more controversial issues in the past, even ones that dealt with life and death.

What is relevant to this discussion is that the bishops were making judgments about translating Catholic teachings into public policy, not about the moral validity of the teachings. In so doing they grappled with the unique political complexities of their time. The decision they made to remain silent on a constitutional amendment to abolish slavery or on the repeal of the Fugitive Slave Law wasn't a mark of their moral indifference; it was a measured attempt to balance moral truths against political realities. Their decision reflected their sense of complexity, not their diffidence. As history reveals, Lincoln behaved with similar discretion.

The parallel I want to draw here is not between or among what we Catholics believe to be moral wrongs. It is in the Catholic response to those wrongs.

Church teaching on slavery and abortion is clear. But in the application of those teachings—the exact way we translate them into action, the specific laws we propose, the exact legal sanctions we seek—there was and is no one, clear, absolute route that the church says, as a matter of doctrine, we must follow.

The bishops' pastoral letter "The Challenge of Peace" speaks directly to this point. "We recognize," the bishops wrote, "that the church's teaching authority does not carry the same force when it deals with technical solutions involving particular means as it does when it speaks of principles or ends. People may agree in abhorring an injustice, for instance, yet sincerely disagree as to what practical approach will achieve justice. Religious groups are as entitled as others to their opinion in such cases, but they should not claim that their opinions are the only ones that people of good will may hold."

With regard to abortion, the American bishops have had to weigh Catholic moral teaching against the fact of a pluralistic country where our view is in the minority, acknowledging that what is ideally desirable isn't always feasible, that there can be different political approaches to abortion besides unyielding adherence to an absolute prohibition.

This is in the American Catholic tradition of political realism. In supporting or opposing specific legislation the church in this country has never retreated into a moral fundamentalism that will settle for nothing less than total acceptance of its views.

Indeed, the bishops have already confronted the fact that an absolute ban on abortion doesn't have the support necessary to be placed in our Constitution. In 1981 they put aside earlier efforts to describe a law they could accept and get passed, and supported the Hatch Amendment instead.

Some Catholics felt the bishops had gone too far with that action, some not far enough. Such judgments were not a rejection of the bishops' teaching authority: The bishops even disagreed among themselves. Catholics are allowed to disagree on these technical political questions without having to confess.

Respectfully and after careful consideration of the position and arguments of the bishops, I have concluded that the approach of a constitutional amendment is not the best way for us to seek to deal with abortion.

I believe that legal interdicting of abortion by either the federal government or the individual states is not a plausible possibility and even if it could be obtained, it wouldn't work. Given present attitudes, it would be Prohibition revisited, legislating what couldn't be enforced and in the process creating a disrespect for law in general. And as much as I admire the bishops' hope that a constitutional amendment against abortion would be the basis for a full, new bill of rights for mothers and children, I disagree that this would be the result.

I believe that, more likely, a constitutional prohibition would allow people to ignore the causes of many abortions instead of addressing them, much the way the death penalty is used to escape dealing more fundamentally and more rationally with the problem of violent crime.

Other legal options that have been proposed are, in my view, equally ineffective. The Hatch Amendment, by returning the question of abortion to the states, would have given us a checkerboard of permissive and restrictive jurisdictions. In some cases people might have been forced to go elsewhere to have abortions, and that might have eased a few consciences, but it wouldn't have done what the church wants to do—it wouldn't have created a deep-seated respect for life. Abortions would have gone on, millions of them.

Nor would a denial of Medicaid funding for abortion achieve our objectives. Given *Roe v. Wade,* it would be nothing more than an attempt to do indirectly what the law says cannot be done directly; worse, it would do it in a way that would burden only the already disadvantaged. Removing funding from the Medicaid program would not prevent the rich and middle classes from having abortions. It would not even assure that the disadvantaged wouldn't have them; it would only impose financial burdens on poor women who want abortions.

Apart from that unevenness, there is a more basic question. Medicaid is designed to deal with health and medical needs. But the arguments for the cutoff of Medicaid abortion funds are not related to those needs. They are moral arguments. If we assume health and medical needs exist, our personal view of morality ought not to be considered a relevant basis for discrimination.

We must keep in mind always that we are a nation of laws—when we like those laws and when we don't.

The Supreme Court has established a woman's constitutional right to abortion. The Congress has decided the federal government should not provide federal funding in the Medicaid program for abortion. That, of course, does not bind states in the allocation of their own state funds. Under the law, the individual states need not follow the federal lead, and in New York I believe we cannot follow that lead. The equal protection clause in New York's Constitution has been interpreted by the courts as a standard of fairness that would preclude us from denying only the poor—indirectly, by a cutoff of funds—the practical use of the constitutional right given by *Roe v. Wade.*

In the end, even if after a long and divisive struggle we were able to remove all Medicaid funding for abortion and restore the law to what it was—if we could put most abortions out of our sight, return them to the backrooms where they were performed for so long—I don't believe our responsibility as Catholics would be any closer to being fulfilled than it is now, with abortion guaranteed by law as a woman's right.

The hard truth is that abortion isn't a failure of government. No agency or department of government forces women to have abortions, but abortion goes on. Catholics, the statistics show, support the right to abortion in equal proportion to the rest of the population. Despite the teaching in our homes and schools and pulpits, despite the sermons and pleadings of parents and priests and prelates, despite all the effort at defining our opposition to the sin of abortion, collectively we Catholics apparently believe—and perhaps act—little differently from those who don't share our commitment.

Are we asking government to make criminal what we believe to be sinful because we ourselves can't stop committing the sin?

The failure here is not Caesar's. This failure is our failure, the failure of the entire people of God.

Nobody has expressed this better than a bishop in my own state, Joseph Sullivan, a man who works with the poor in New York City, is resolutely opposed to abortion and argues, with his fellow bishops, for a change of law. "The major problem the church has is internal," the bishop said last month in reference to abortion. "How do we teach? As much as I think we're responsible for advocating public-policy issues, our primary responsibility is to teach our own people. We haven't done that. We're asking politicians to do what we haven't done effectively ourselves."

I agree with the bishop. I think our moral and social mission as Catholics must begin with the wisdom contained in the words "Physician, heal thyself." Unless we Catholics educate ourselves better to the values that define—and can ennoble—our lives, following those teachings better than we do now, unless we set an example that is clear and compelling, then we will never convince this society to change the civil laws to protect what we preach is precious human life.

Better than any law or rule or threat of punishment would be the moving strength of our own good example, demonstrating our lack of hypocrisy, proving the beauty and worth of our instruction.

We must work to find ways to avoid abortions without otherwise violating our faith. We should provide funds and opportunity for young women to bring their child to term, knowing both of them will be taken care of if that is necessary; we should teach our young men better than we do now their responsibilities in creating and caring for human life.

It is this duty of the church to teach through its practice of love that Pope John Paul II has proclaimed so magnificently to all peoples. "The church," he wrote in *Redemptor hominis* (1979), "which has no weapons at her disposal apart from those of the Spirit, of the word and of love, cannot renounce her proclamation of 'the word . . . in season and out of season.' For this reason she does not cease to implore . . . everybody in the name of God and in the name of man: Do not kill! Do not prepare destruction and extermination for each other! Think of your brothers and sisters who are suffering hunger and misery! Respect each one's dignity and freedom!"

The weapons of the word and of love are already available to us: We need no statute to provide them.

I am not implying that we should stand by and pretend indifference to whether a woman takes a pregnancy to its conclusion or aborts it. I believe we should in all cases try to teach a respect for life. And I believe with regard to abortion that, despite *Roe v. Wade,* we can, in practical ways. Here, in fact, it seems to me that all of us can agree.

Without lessening their insistence on a woman's right to an abortion, the people who call themselves "prochoice" can support the development of government programs that present an impoverished mother with the full range of support she needs to bear and raise her children, to have a real choice. Without dropping their campaign to ban abortion, those who gather under the banner of "prolife" can join in developing and enacting a legislative bill of rights for mothers and children, as the bishops have already proposed.

While we argue over abortion, the U.S. infant-mortality rate places us sixteenth among the nations of the world. Thousands of infants die each year because of inadequate medical care. Some are born with birth defects that, with proper treatment, could be prevented. Some are stunted in their physical and mental growth because of improper nutrition.

If we want to prove our regard for life in the womb, for the helpless infant—if we care about women having real choices in their lives and not being driven to abortions by a sense of helplessness and despair about the future of their child—then there is work enough for all of us. Lifetimes of it.

In New York, we have put in place a number of programs to begin this work, assisting women in giving birth to healthy babies. This year we doubled Medicaid funding to private-care physicians for prenatal and delivery services.

The state already spends $20 million a year for prenatal care in outpatient clinics and for inpatient hospital care.

One program in particular we believe holds a great deal of promise. It's called "New Avenues to Dignity," and it seeks to provide a teen-age mother with the special service she needs to continue with her education, to train for a job, to become capable of standing on her own, to provide for herself and the child she is bringing into the world.

My dissent, then, from the contention that we can have effective and enforceable legal prohibitions on abortion is by no means an argument for religious quietism, for accepting the world's wrongs because that is our fate as "the poor banished children of Eve."

Let me make another point.

Abortion has a unique significance but not a preemptive significance.

Apart from the question of the efficacy of using legal weapons to make people stop having abortions, we know our Christian responsibility doesn't end with any one law or amendment. That it doesn't end with abortion. Because it involves life and death, abortion will always be a central concern of Catholics. But so will nuclear weapons. And hunger and homelessness and joblessness, all the forces diminishing human life and threatening to destroy it. The "seamless garment" that Cardinal Bernardin has spoken of is a challenge to all Catholics in public office, conservatives as well as liberals.

We cannot justify our aspiration to goodness simply on the basis of the vigor of our demand for an elusive and questionable civil law declaring what we already know, that abortion is wrong.

Approval or rejection of legal restrictions on abortion should not be the exclusive litmus test of Catholic loyalty. We should understand that whether abortion is outlawed or not, our work has barely begun: the work of creating a society where the right to life doesn't end at the moment of birth; where an infant isn't helped into a world that doesn't care if it's fed properly, housed decently, educated adequately; where the blind or retarded child isn't condemned to exist rather than empowered to live.

The bishops stated this duty clearly in 1974 in their statement to the Senate subcommittee considering a proposed amendment to restrict abortions. They maintained such an amendment could not be seen as an end in itself. "We do not see a constitutional amendment as the final product of our commitment or of our legislative activity," they said. "It is instead the constitutional base on which to provide support and assistance to pregnant women and their unborn children. This would include nutritional, prenatal, childbirth and postnatal care for the mother, and also nutritional and pediatric care for the child through the first year of life. . . . We believe that all of these should be available as a matter of right to all pregnant women and their children."

The bishops reaffirmed that view in 1976, in 1980 and again this year when the U.S. Catholic Conference asked Catholics to judge candidates on a wide range of issues—on abortion, yes; but also on food policy, the arms race, human rights, education, social justice and military expenditures.

The bishops have been consistently "prolife" in the full meaning of that term, and I respect them for that.

The problems created by the matter of abortion are complex and confounding. Nothing is clearer to me than my inadequacy to find compelling solutions to all of their moral, legal and social implications. I—and many others like me—are eager for enlightenment, eager to learn new and better ways to manifest respect for the deep reverence for life that is our religion and our instinct. I hope that this public attempt to describe the problems as I understand them will give impetus to the dialogue in the Catholic community and beyond, a dialogue which could show me a better wisdom than I've been able to find so far.

It would be tragic if we let that dialogue become a prolonged, divisive argument that destroys or impairs our ability to practice any part of the morality given us in the Sermon on the Mount, to touch, heal and affirm the human life that surrounds us.

We Catholic citizens of the richest, most powerful nation that has ever existed are like the stewards made responsible over a great household: From those to whom so much has been given, much shall be required. It is worth repeating that ours is not a faith that encourages its believers to stand apart from the world, seeking their salvation alone, separate from the salvation of those around them.

We speak of ourselves as a body. We come together in worship as companions, in the ancient sense of that word, those who break bread together and who are obliged by the commitment we share to help one another, everywhere, in all we do and in the process to help the whole human family. We see our mission to be "the completion of the work of creation."

This is difficult work today. It presents us with many hard choices.

The Catholic Church has come of age in America. The ghetto walls are gone, our religion no longer a badge of irredeemable foreignness. This new-found status is both an opportunity and a temptation. If we choose, we can give in to the temptation to become more and more assimilated into a larger, blander culture, abandoning the practice of the specific values that made us different, worshiping whatever gods the marketplace has to sell while we seek to rationalize our own laxity by urging the political system to legislate on others a morality we no longer practice ourselves.

Or we can remember where we come from, the journey of two millennia, clinging to our personal faith, to its insistence on constancy and service and on hope. We can live and practice the morality Christ gave us, maintaining his truth in this world, struggling to embody his love, practicing it especially where that love is most needed, among the poor and the weak and the dispossessed. Not just by trying to make laws for others to live by, but by living the laws already written for us by God, in our hearts and our minds.

We can be fully Catholic: proudly, totally at ease with ourselves, a people in the world, transforming it, a light to this nation. Appealing to the best in our people, not the worst. Persuading not coercing. Leading people to truth by love. And still, all the while, respecting and enjoying our unique pluralistic democracy. And we can do it even as politicians.

[40]

Just Cause for Abortion

Lloyd Steffen

IN ORDER FOR AN abortion to be deemed just, the cause for the abortion must be morally compelling. What this means in a formal sense is that the reasons for seeking the abortion must be such that they justify lifting the moral presumption against abortion. Just abortion will be grounded in the fact that the pregnancy has generated a conflict between the good of life, which the pregnancy is promoting, and other desired goods, which the pregnancy, because of circumstance, is discouraging or preventing from being satisfied. For the pregnant woman who experiences this conflict, those other goods that are in conflict with the good of pregnancy may include such things as the woman's life; her personal and moral integrity; her health and sense of well-being; her ability to function ably as a responsible provider and nurturer; and her capacity to envision a meaningful life and future where she will be able to experience pleasure and enjoyment in work, play, and in her social and familial relationships. In order to consider the abortion option, it must be determined that morally serious reasons related to these other goods of life are forcing a value conflict with the good of life ingredient in the pregnancy. Moreover, those reasons must be so formulated that in a particular circumstance they provide just cause for lifting or overriding the moral presumption against abortion.

SOURCE: From *Life/Choice: The Theory of Just Abortion* by Lloyd Steffen. Copyright © 1994 by The Pilgrim Press. Reprinted by permission.

Establishing morally serious reasons for justifying abortion does not depend upon identifying some singular reason that by definition will always and universally lead a woman to consider abortion. Morally serious reasons for considering abortion must arise from a consideration of the particularities of a pregnant woman's situation. In just abortion, the pregnancy always provokes a conflict between goods of life. That conflict provides the occasion necessary for articulating a reasoned moral appeal to the possibility of abortion.

There are reasons for desiring an abortion that are insufficient to justify making such a reasoned moral appeal. In her well-known article "A Defense of Abortion," philosopher Judith Jarvis Thomson, who defended a woman's right to decide what she will do with her body, mentions such a case—the woman who is in her seventh month of pregnancy and wants an abortion "just to avoid the nuisance of postponing a trip abroad."[1] Desiring an abortion because of the restrictions pregnancy inevitably places on normal physical activity, or because of simple inconvenience having to do with cosmetic self-image or the altering of lifestyle preferences, would, all things being equal, be insufficient to establish just cause for abortion. Again, just cause emerges from a conflict involving various goods of life, and to establish successfully a just cause for abortion will require one to show that the good of life ingredient in pregnancy is involved in such serious conflict with other goods of life that killing a developing form of human life becomes a reasonable and morally justifiable option.

It is certainly possible that a pregnancy could interfere with a woman's travel plans, or with a desired cosmetic appearance, or with the fit of her clothes, or even with her desire to continue a habit that she should alter for pregnancy (smoking, drinking alcohol, etc.). But these reasons are not sufficiently strong to justify killing a developing form of human life. They are not grounded in a serious value conflict. They present no challenge to the good of life that the good of life—and the moral presumption against abortion—could not reasonably withstand.

The criticism could be made that the examples just noted, while certainly functional for showing what would constitute a trivial and inadequate cause for abortion, are also unrealistic. The argument could be advanced that since an abortion is not trivial either as a topic for moral reflection or as a medical procedure, it would be hard to imagine a woman deciding for an abortion on, say, cosmetic inconvenience grounds alone.

But other, more realistic examples of insufficiently justified abortion are available. One such example would be that of trying to justify an abortion for reasons of gender preference. Abortions are sometimes performed for the sole reason that the fetus is determined to be of a gender that is not valued by a culture or by a couple in a particular situation. Again, depriving a human fetus of life for this reason seems to devalue the good of life and to honor a morally offensive, sexist attitude that is grounded in cultural bias and inadequately developed value commitments. Gender preference is not a candidate for just cause. It does not generate a value conflict that practical reason recognizes as so grave that abortion presents itself as a rational and morally justifiable response to that conflict. Gender preference as a reason for desiring abortion fails to establish a serious moral appeal to the abortion option. It is, in itself, a highly suspect motive, morally speaking, because of the sexist, exploitative, and unjust attitudes toward gender that it entails, for there are no rational grounds for devaluing persons or even potential persons because of gender. Gender preference would not satisfy the test of just cause, and an abortion performed for this reason would be morally impermissible.

It is also worth commenting on physical or genetic defects as possible candidates for establishing just cause. Medical technology has made it possible to detect physical and genetic anomalies in the developing fetus, which then provokes questions about whether a known defective fetus should be aborted. In general, acquiring information that a developing fetus will be in some way biologically defective is itself insufficient to create a morally compelling conflict of values, although there certainly are some fetal defects so grave that a fully engaged moral consideration of the child's best interests will inevitably raise the abortion option. A diagnosis of anencephaly . . . would certainly present such a case. A fetus known to be afflicted with Down's syndrome, however, is more problematic, and the particulars of the situation again must be considered. Down's syndrome does not necessarily deprive the child afflicted with it of meaningful relational possibilities and the prospect of a meaningful life, so that the defect itself is not sufficient grounds for killing the fetus. But that point must then be weighed against the complication that one defect is usually accompanied by others, which should be taken into consideration when making a reasoned moral appeal to the abortion option and in establishing just cause.

While there are reasons that we must say are insufficient to determine a morally compelling cause for abortion, there also are reasons that do meet this test. A pregnancy that presents serious medical complications that endanger the mother's life and well-being is such a reason. Duty does not require that a mother endanger her own life or well-being to promote the good of life involved in a pregnancy. As a moral agent, a pregnant woman is still required to protect herself from harm and danger and to do so in accordance with the canons of prudential reason and the imperative to treat persons, including oneself, with respect. A fetus need not be considered an "aggressor"—or even "innocent," for that matter—in order for a woman to seek an abortion if her life, health, or well-being are in danger because of a pregnancy.

That a mother has a natural moral right to protect herself if her life is endangered by a pregnancy conforms to moral intuitions and explicitly stated moral justifications shared widely in the moral community. Even many persons who consider themselves pro-life find this a situation where an abortion is morally justifiable, with only moral absolutists holding to the position that the mother has no such right because the fetus is itself the moral equivalent of the pregnant woman so that her life cannot be considered in any way more valuable than that of the fetus. People who hold such an extreme moral view usually do so on religious grounds; that is, their faith commits them to a metaphysics of fetal humanity itself grounded in religious belief.

It is interesting to note, and I offer this as an aside, that those who hold the fetus to be the moral equivalent of the pregnant woman, and who thereby deny her the option of abortion on moral grounds even in the case where her life is in danger, are not actually holding the fetus to be the moral equivalent of the woman. The fetus, rather, is being treated as if it were the mother's moral superior, for the good of fetal life is so construed that its value is thought to be sufficient to deny the mother her basic natural right to self-defense.

Theologies and metaphysical theories that hold to a view that fetal life is innocent, and therefore inviolable, endorse a metaphysical-theological belief that innocence renders the life of the fetus more valuable than that of the pregnant woman, for any endangerment the fetus might present the mother is deemed insufficient to justify the mother's acting in self-defense to preserve her own life by killing the fetus. To hold that a pregnant woman does not have a right to protect herself from a fetus involved in medical complications that may kill her is to invest the fetus with moral standing superior to that of the pregnant woman, which thus renders her a fetus' moral inferior. Although there are no secular grounds for holding such a view, some religious persons and communities endorse this position, in a practical if not theoretical sense. This view, which is also offensive to many religious people and faith communities, is based on a religiously grounded metaphysics of moral personhood. Judged by secular standards and even faith standards in some religious traditions, such a view is based on a dubious metaphysics of moral personhood, so much so that the confused and irrational idea of subordinating the woman to the fetus on the issue of fundamental humanity could reasonably be characterized as fanatical.[2]

A medically complicated pregnancy in which a fetus is threatening the mother's life provides the clearest and most widely accepted example of a just cause for lifting the moral presumption against abortion. Abortions performed for this reason are rare, however; but it is also the case that most women who receive abortions justify them morally on the grounds that the pregnancy is threatening, if not to the pregnant woman's health, then to her well-being. It is on the fuzzy issue of well-being that just cause becomes a complicated issue.

What constitutes well-being is not clear and precisely definable. Content can be given to this concern for the pregnant woman's well-being, however, and we can see how concern for well-being is accommodated even by many persons who consider themselves pro-life. Many people in the moral community who identify themselves as pro-life and anti-abortion would think it reasonable to consider abortion in the case of incest or rape. The reason such a justification is so widely accepted, even among persons on the pro-life side of the issue, is not because the fetus is presenting any necessary threat to the mother's physical health or that the fetus has assumed the status of an attacking aggressor and has thereby lost its status as an innocent. The reason to consider abortion in these cases is because the pregnancy is enmeshed in relational entanglements that are deleterious to the mother's well-being. Even many of those who are opposed to abortion acknowledge that there are "mother's well-being" reasons that should be considered, and that these exceptions are sufficiently weighty to actually establish a just cause.[3]

While rape, incest, and the threat to a mother's life are widely regarded by non-absolutists throughout the moral community as legitimate and morally compelling reasons for considering abortion, it is not often made clear why these causes—and for many, no other causes—are so morally compelling. In the case of pregnancy by means of rape and incest, it is clearly the mother's psychological and relational well-being that determines the compelling moral reason sufficient to lift the moral presumption against abortion.[4]

In arguing for just abortion, the well-being criterion ought not to be associated with particular circumstances, such as rape and incest, if pains are not taken to justify why those circumstances provide serious and compelling moral reasons for overruling the presumption against abortion. This is slippery ground. If the reasons related to mother's well-being hold in these cases and establish just cause for abortion, could not other well-being–related reasons also have weight in other kinds of situations? Once that broader case is made, the possibility presents itself that other specific causes of a morally compelling nature can also be appealed to as just causes for abortion.

I hold that pregnancy in the case of rape or incest does involve considerations that are relevant to establishing just cause for abortion in other, seemingly less grave situations. We can get at these broader considerations by asking, What is the moral issue raised in a pregnancy caused by rape and incest?

Such pregnancies—that they are relatively rare is irrelevant at this point—result from the harming of a woman by violence and coercion and relational impropriety. Persons who commit rape or incest act in such a way that they violate their victim's sense of security and well-being, and, beyond that, violate the person's relational integrity. This violation occurs in the case of rape and incest whether or not a woman becomes pregnant. If pregnancy results, however, this violation of relational integrity is so threatening to the woman's continued well-being that considering abortion is justified as a way of continuing to honor the woman as an autonomous moral person, a member of the moral community who ought to be free of coercion and who should not be forced by the moral community into committing herself to a pregnancy when she became pregnant against her will, without her consent, and in a manner that was disrespectful of her personhood, exploitative, physically endangering, and psychologically harmful.

Rape and incest are extreme but common instances of relational violation, but they are not the only kinds of relational violations that might be appealed to when trying to establish just cause for abortion. Consider, for instance, the woman whose dignity and relational integrity have been assaulted by poverty. The presence of poverty in any society indicates that the social system unjustly restricts access to the opportunities that members of the society desire and require if they are to flourish as persons able to exercise their various capabilities—for work, for experiencing pleasure, for making creative contributions to the common good, for living full lives in which as autonomous persons they are able to make choices about how they shall acquire and promote the various goods of life. Poverty prevents people from exercising these capabilities. Poverty turns people from seeking ways to flourish and forces them to concentrate on survival and acquiring necessities. It reduces the number of opportunities and choices that are practically available, and thus demoralizes and even degrades those caught in its grip.

There are poor women who, because of their economic circumstances, may desire to avoid pregnancy. Yet poverty can so affect a woman that she is prevented from taking sufficient control of her life to avoid unwanted pregnancies, which points to a societal failure to work actively so that all persons can make informed choices about pregnancy and contraception.

Many people view unwanted pregnancies among the community of the poor as the sole responsibility of individual women, a self-deceptive ploy that allows them to shirk corporate responsibility and social accountability. But poverty is a societal creation, and society bears responsibility for creating economic circumstances that restrict choice among the poor and disenfranchise them from participating in the society's decision-making processes. Societies that fail to assume responsibility for providing affordable contraception and opportunities for reproductive education, on the basis of which responsible decisions about sexuality and birth control can be made, contribute to the increase in the numbers of unwanted pregnancies and to the probability that abortion rather than contraception will be seen as the way to deal with unwanted pregnancy. Those who hold poor women responsible for their unwanted pregnancies without taking into account all that societies contribute to creating the conditions where unwanted pregnancies arise miss the forest for the trees—and do so in bad faith. Societies create the conditions that increase the likelihood that those unable to afford contraception will face the practical choice of either abortion or bringing to term an unwanted pregnancy. (Refusing societal aid to fund abortions for these unwanted pregnancies continues the assault on women's dignity, and separates poor women even further from the world where women able to justify abortion can then proceed to get one.) A woman is not being treated as an autonomous moral agent if her economic situation precludes her from receiving a safe and justifiable medical abortion in response to her desire to end an unwanted pregnancy. Forcing a poor woman who can justify an abortion to settle for an unsafe medical procedure or to bear unwanted children, sometimes being induced to do so for baby markets, undermines her moral status as a person and unjustly deprives her of reproductive choices available to more affluent women. The society that restricts a poor woman's ability to make choices to avoid unwanted pregnancies contributes to her ability to establish just cause for abortion; such a woman can claim, as an affluent woman may not be able to, that she did not intend to become pregnant and was prevented from exercising contraception options by economic realities. These facts are relevant to determining just cause, for the woman is positioned to argue that society itself, by its social policy commitments and priorities, has placed her in a position where she is coerced into risking unwanted pregnancy, and that such coercion is an assault on her dignity. Her argument for just cause would then proceed in a formal way much like an argument for justifying abortion in the case of rape or incest—at issue is the violation of relational integrity.

A pregnant woman's relational integrity is rendered vulnerable to violation in an impoverished economic and social experience. A just cause for abortion must never look at a woman's circumstances in isolation from the society of which she is a part, for in the presence of poverty and all that poverty does to limit people's choices and violate their integrity, society, representing the moral community at large, must assume responsibility for helping to create conditions where unwanted pregnancies are not adequately avoided and abortion becomes a means of post-conception birth control.

In establishing just cause for abortion, we must take into consideration the woman's situation and circumstances as well as her desire to terminate her pregnancy because doing so will preserve her well-being and relational integrity. Women who do not want to get pregnant have a responsibility to act so that they avoid pregnancy, and establishing that a woman did not consent to becoming pregnant is certainly relevant to establishing just cause. A failed contraceptive device, for instance, would establish just cause, for the argument could be advanced that by using a device to prevent pregnancy, the woman had acted responsibly with respect to the intention to avoid an unwanted pregnancy. Seeking abortion in this situation would be a way of preventing the woman from being coerced into establishing a moral relation with an unwelcome, intrusive, and unintended relational partner (the fetus). Continuing an unwanted pregnancy in this situation could be said to violate the woman's relational integrity and moral autonomy, and this would also be the case in rape or incest or situations like that of forced marriage.

We cannot focus exclusively on the individual woman's action in relation to her intention to avoid unwanted pregnancy. We must also attend to societal complicity in creating the conditions where abortion becomes an option when those who want to avoid unwanted pregnancies find themselves unable to act consistently with their desires and intentions because of social situation and economic circumstance. In a social situation where society fails to empower women to act so that they might avoid unwanted pregnancies, that failure of social responsibility becomes a critical factor in determining what it means to talk about an assault on a woman's well-being and a violation of her relational integrity; and this social factor then must be allowed to play a role in determining just cause. In the light of the high teenage pregnancy rate, it could also be said that young women who would certainly not want to get pregnant but who do, having failed to receive an education in sexuality and reproduction, and whose ignorance has not been corrected by a society determined to help empower even teenaged women to know what they are doing when they fail to act to prevent unwanted pregnancy, are positioned to launch a similar claim for just cause if the society fails to assist and empower them to make responsible choices.

The woman who would, in my interpretation, have the most difficulty establishing just cause for abortion would be a woman of relative affluence who, with her sexual partner, is able to acquire contraception without undo economic hardship; who has available educational resources so that it can be said with some assurance that she understands what is involved in human sexuality and reproduction and family responsibilities; who consented to the sexual act that led to conception; who chose with her partner not to use a contraceptive device, when doing so would have imposed no hardship; and whose capacities for making decisions about contraception were not impaired. If these conditions are met, just cause would be difficult to establish without some other factor coming into play. The couple has acted in such a way that it seems reasonable to say that they did, in fact, intend a pregnancy, and the moral rationale for aborting the fetus involved in this situation would have to come from other factors, such as a medical complication.

Just cause will concern itself with such traditional matters as whether individuals seeking to avoid a pregnancy act consistently with that intention. Should that be demonstrated, it would be coercive to force a woman or couple who acted to prevent a pregnancy from proceeding with it, for doing so violates the relational integrity of persons. Just cause will attend to medical condition and to the best interests of the prospective child—there are some biological anomalies so severe that aborting the fetus would serve the best interests not only of the mother (and father) and even society, but the prospective newborn itself. This kind of child-centered focus, as reflected in the just non-treatment of severely handicapped newborns, . . . is certainly relevant to our consideration of just cause for abortion. And just cause will attend to the well-being of the mother, not just individually in a physical and psychological sense, but in a corporate dimension, too. For a woman caught in the grip of an unwanted pregnancy cannot be held accountable for that pregnancy as if the society of which she is a part is not in some way contributing to the situation that prevents women like her, who want to avoid pregnancy, from actually doing so. By failing to provide such things as sex education and affordable and available contraception, societal priorities, as manifested in the channeling of economic and educational resources, can be such that they reveal a society not committed to helping persons act consistently with their desire to avoid unwanted pregnancy. Society itself becomes a responsible agent that must be held accountable for creating conditions that can be appealed to as just cause for abortion. Societies make decisions and expend resources that contribute to the increase in the number of unwanted abortions; for society then to coerce women into bringing to term their unwanted pregnancies would constitute action that would violate the relational integrity of human persons. It would do harm to the well-being of women, demean them, and deprive them of their status of autonomous moral persons. Making the abortion option available and allowing women to exercise that option would prevent such gross moral impropriety from occurring. And even though the abortion option will involve the killing of a developing form of human life, that killing, as we see most clearly when a pregnancy is threatening to a woman's life or has come about through rape or incest, is not so grave as the moral offense that would occur were an unwanted pregnancy to continue under coercion and by means that violate women's relational integrity. That would visit harm on the pregnant woman and possibly even the future neonate, with whom the mother would establish moral relationship. Determining just cause for abortion will require that this kind of analysis be presented so that the moral presumption against abortion can be justifiably overruled in a particular instance of unwanted pregnancy.

Notes

1. Judith Jarvis Thomson, "A Defense of Abortion," reprinted in *The Problem of Abortion*, 2d ed., ed. Joel Feinberg (Belmont, Calif.: Wadsworth Publishing, 1984), 187.

2. I say "fanatical" because fanatics are persons who hold to positions with such inflexibility that they would allow themselves to be harmed and destroyed by so doing. A fanatical person would be willing to say, "I accept that a fetus is my moral superior. If my life were threatened by that fetus in some way, I would willingly allow the fetus to come to term and live even if I had to sacrifice my own life to do so." Holding to such a position, which is usually done in the third person (i.e., "She ought to accept that her fetus is her moral superior") rather than the first person, enunciates a position that does not observe prudential reason or even allow the biblical injunction to love the neighbor as oneself. To allow oneself to be sacrificed to a moral superior, represented by the fetus, is to love the fetus more than oneself and oneself-as-neighbor. So much does this offend against prudential and practical reason, and fundamental commitments to self-regard that are the hallmarks of reasonable and faithful people, that one who held to such an absolutist perspective would be termed not only a moral absolutist but a fanatic as well.

3. It is worth noting that pro-life persons who are willing to make the exceptions we have discussed so far—abortion to save a mother's life, incest and rape—are actually advocating a restrictive form of pro-choice by these exceptions because they are not holding the fetus to be the mother's moral superior to which she must sacrifice her life if that life is required to save the fetus, and because they are not demanding that a woman pregnant by rape or incest get an abortion or not get an abortion—but that she decide what she wants to do. In a definite anti-abortion posture, they are holding open the door to choice—that the pregnant woman choose either to abort or not to abort—and if she does abort, the fact that she became pregnant through rape or incest is sufficient to establish just cause.

4. The ongoing civil war in Bosnia-Herzegovina has shown us how rape can be used as an instrument of political-military terrorism. The European Community Commission charged with investigating the allegations of atrocities estimated that 20,000 Muslim women had been raped by Serbs as part of the Serbian expansion policy. Rape was used as a deliberate policy instrument, imposing on Muslim women a lasting wound and religious violation that was designed to force the Moslem women to internalize the degradation and assault of the war itself. Although many women made pregnant through this policy of terrorism have sought abortions, a controversy arose in February 1993 when Pope John Paul II spoke out opposing abortion for victims of rape in Bosnia-Herzegovina while also deploring the violence of rape. The Vatican also denied that it had permitted nuns working in danger zones where the threat of assault and rape was high to take birth control pills. The official Roman Catholic teaching on abortion and birth control was thus reiterated during the civil war in Bosnia-Herzegovina, but it provoked outrage in some quarters. The Roman Catholic teaching on abortion would not ascribe to the life created through rape any evil or taint despite the means by which the pregnancy began. Just abortion would not object to that particular

point. It would, however, hold that this view as a moral perspective on abortion expresses a moral absolutism that fails to appreciate the full dimension of the moral violation experienced by the rape victim. While just abortion would certainly not force a woman who had been raped to abort that fetus, it would object to attempts to restrict access to safe abortion for women who experienced such violation.

[41]

The Law and Fetal Personhood: Religious and Secular Determinations

Peter S. Wenz

Belief in the Personhood of Young Fetuses

Similarly religious is the belief that fetuses younger than twenty-one weeks old are human persons with a right to life. (For reasons of brevity I refer to this as "belief in the personhood of young fetuses" or "belief in the right to life of young fetuses.") As with belief in the existence of God, there are reasonable considerations that can be offered for and against this belief, and the two sides do not differ about any significant matters of fact. But the facts and considerations are inherently incapable of resolving the dispute. Yet the difference is often perceived by the two sides as being in some sense *factual,* not merely attitudinal. The present section illustrates the structural identity between disputes about the existence of God and disputes about the personhood (and right to life) of young fetuses. It shows that when they are viewed as matters of fact, both sorts of disputed beliefs are epistemologically religious and therefore religious for First Amendment purposes.

I begin with reasons for believing in the personhood of young fetuses. Dr. E. Blechschmidt argues:

SOURCE: From *Abortion Rights as Religious Freedom* by Peter Wenz. Copyright © 1984 by Temple University Press. Reprinted by permission.

A human being does not *become* a human being but rather *is* such from the instant of the fertilization. During the entire ontogenesis, no single break can be demonstrated, either in the sense of a leap from the lifeless to the live, or of a transition from the vegetative to the instinctive or to characteristically human behavior. It may be considered today a fundamental law of human ontogenesis . . . that only the appearance of the individual being changes in the course of its ontogenesis.[1]

These are the considerations [connected] with Justice White's dissent in *Thornburgh v. American College of Obstetricians and Gynecologists* (1986).[2] . . . Such considerations are inconclusive. Conceptual, practical, and legal difficulties attend the attribution, which Blechschmidt advocates, of full personhood to newly fertilized ova. Also, the view is defended by a fallacious form of reasoning. It is argued that the zygote is a person because the newborn is a person, and the newborn develops from the zygote by a continuous process. This argument is fallacious because, according to our secular forms of reasoning, continuous processes of change can alter fundamentally what is undergoing change, so that what exists at the end is not the same sort of being as existed at the beginning. Acorns develop through a continuous process into oak trees, but we do not conclude that "acorn" and "oak tree" are different words for the same thing. The possibility of fundamental change cannot be ruled out in the case of the transition from fertilized ovum to newborn child.

The opposite possibility cannot be ruled out either. Defenders of the personhood of young fetuses can point out that gradual change does not always produce a change in essence. Furthermore, there is reason to think that no change in essence takes place in human gestation. Consider the following question: "Why a human ovum always results in a human being, while any other ovum always results in another organism. For instance, no human being originates from a duck's egg. The answer is because in each ovum the essence has already been fixed; only the appearance changes in development. It is characteristic for every ontogenesis that only that develops which is essentially already there."[3]

This consideration is far from conclusive, however. What is present from the beginning in the fertilized ovum's genetic code may be the *potentiality for the development* of a person, not the essence of personhood. Those who agree completely on the scientific details of ontogenesis may thus disagree about the essence of the newly fertilized egg. This is characteristic of disagreements about matters of fact in areas of religious belief. All relevant secular facts of science and common sense can be held in common by people whose attitudes differ and who justify their different attitudes by appeal to "facts" of some other kind. One "sees" the essence of personhood in the fertilized ovum, while the other "sees" merely the potential for personhood.

Reasons against identifying personhood with the presence of a human genetic code are drawn from medicine and science fiction. Consider, first, what I call the common sense of science fiction. Beings who lack a human genetic code are presented in science fiction as persons. They include at the moment Mr. Spock, E.T., and Alf. Common sense accepts these characters as persons, suggesting that, according to our normal concept, the essence of personhood rests on what persons can do, not on what they are biochemically composed of. More specifically, the public acceptance of these characters as persons suggests that a human genetic code is *not necessary* for personhood.

But this does not settle the issue of greatest importance for the classification of the fetus. The fetus has a human genetic code, and the issue is whether the presence of that code is *sufficient,* not whether it is necessary, to make the fetus a person. This is where people in a persistent vegetative state come in. They have a functioning spinal cord and brain stem, but not a functioning cortex. Apart from fictional examples, cortical activity is (believed) necessary for all the distinctively human abilities of thought, imagination, and will. So people in a persistent vegetative state, though they are alive and have a human genetic code, lack all distinctively human abilities. If, as the science fiction cases show, such abilities are sufficient for personhood, perhaps they are necessary as well. The necessity of such abilities for personhood is implied in the treatment of those in a persistent vegetative state. Life-threatening infections and coronary problems that it would be literally criminal to leave untreated in patients with normally functioning brains are often left untreated in persistently vegetative individuals. Life-threatening conditions are left untreated precisely so that the patients can be allowed to die. Such patients are not, then, accorded the right to life that normally accompanies personhood. Few people are troubled by this. Since young fetuses are similarly incapable of the activities that distinguish persons from others, they should be classified with those in a persistent vegetative state. Despite their human genetic code, they should be denied the status of personhood and the accompanying right to life.

Defenders of the young fetus's right to life have two cogent replies to this reasoning. First, nothing is proven by the fact that few people are troubled by common medical practices that violate the right to life of permanently vegetative individuals. Defenders of the fetus can condemn indifference toward the lives of those in a persistent vegetative state just as they condemn indifference toward fetal life. In neither case is common acceptance a proof of moral acceptability. If it were, the treatment of Native Americans during our country's westward expansion, of slaves before the Civil War, and of Jews in Nazi Germany would have been morally acceptable, because they also enjoyed widespread acceptance.

Second, even if indifference were acceptable in the case of persistently vegetative individuals, the same would not follow for the fetus. Characteristically, the fetus is temporarily, not permanently, incapable of engaging in distinctively human activities. Allow it to develop and its activities will be distinctively human. Thus a fetus is more like a person who is temporarily unconscious than one who is persistently vegetative. Just as we do not deny personhood and the right to life to the temporarily unconscious, we should not deny personhood and the right to life to the temporarily immature.

Critics of fetal personhood object to the analogy between young fetuses and normal, but unconscious, children and adults. The latter have already engaged in characteristically human activities and are able, typically, to resume such activities on a moment's notice. They are in what Aristotle calls the state of second potentiality. They have already developed and displayed their abilities, but happen not to be displaying them at the moment. They are like car mechanics who are not currently fixing cars. We call them car mechanics in honor of the abilities that they have developed and displayed, ignoring the fact that they are temporarily asleep or on lunch break.

The young fetus, in contrast, has never yet developed or displayed the abilities distinctive of human beings. The young fetus is in a state of first potentiality, as it has to develop further before it can ever act like a person. Normally, beings in first potentiality are denied the rights associated with the state of being for which they are in a state of first potentiality. For example, those who are not already trained to be doctors may not act as doctors, even those who, because they could acquire such training, are in a state of first potentiality for a medical degree. Similarly, the young fetus is reasonably denied a person's right to life because it is in merely first potentiality for personhood, unlike most unconscious people, who are in a state of second potentiality.

Defenders of the young fetus point out, however, that the fetal potential for personhood is very different from a young person's potential for a medical degree. The young person does not have to become a physician to live. She could follow a different career path. The young fetus has no alternative but death to the development of distinctively human traits and activities. Also, the young person becomes a physician only through conscious choices about the expenditure of time and energy. The young fetus develops personhood automatically, without any choice at all. So its potentiality is based on, and flows naturally from, its actuality. Thus "the potential of a human conceptus to think and talk is an actuality."[4]

The same author points out in this context that "every potential is itself an actuality. . . . A woman's potential to give birth to a baby is an actuality that a man does not have."[5] This example shows, however, apparently contrary to its author's intention, that potentiality and actuality (in the meanings that are important for his argument) are *not* the same thing. A woman's uterus is part of her actuality that underlies her potential for giving birth. Even if a uterus were necessary and sufficient for giving birth, however, a uterus and a birth are different. More generally, an actuality that *underlies* a potentiality (as the uterus is an actuality that underlies the potential for giving birth) is different from the actuality that *fulfills* the potentiality (in this case, giving birth). Analogously, the genetic code is an actuality that underlies the young fetus's potential for personhood, but for that very reason it is not the fulfillment of that potentiality. By secular standards, the young fetus is not yet a person. Furthermore, it is logically impossible for the same thing to be at the same time and in the same respect both potential and actual.[6] So if the young fetus is a potential person, it cannot be at the same time and in the same respect an actual person.

Defenders of the young fetus reply that it is an actual, not a potential, person. But how can it be an actual person when it lacks the current ability to engage in distinctively human pursuits? Advocates for the young fetus point out that newborns are no more able than are young fetuses to engage in distinctively human pursuits. Typically, people "can understand things and reason about them, make plans, and act; they can . . . argue, negotiate, express themselves, make agreements, honor commitments, and stand in relationships of mutual trust."[7] Newborns cannot engage in these activities much better than young fetuses can. So if young fetuses are not actually persons with a right to life, newborns are not either, and infanticide would be morally acceptable. Since infanticide is not morally (or legally) acceptable, newborns must be considered actual persons with a right to life. Young fetuses must for the same reasons be included among persons with a right to life.

The reply is that newborns are significantly closer than are young fetuses to being able to engage in distinctively human pursuits. Unlike young fetuses, typical newborns have already developed all the physiological specializations necessary for human life. They have a heart, liver, kidneys, and lungs that can actually function. Depending on its age, a young fetus may have some of these, but it does not have all of them, since the lungs do not become functional until after twenty weeks, and young fetuses are here defined as those twenty weeks or younger. Also, distinctively human pursuits are directed by the neocortical functions of the brain, and it is only at twenty-two to twenty-four weeks of gestation that neocortical brain functions appear.[8] So it is reasonable to maintain that newborns and fetuses somewhat older than twenty weeks are persons with a right to life, but young fetuses are not.

Defenders of young fetuses point out, however, that the significance of these particular physiological developments is in the eye of the beholder. Someone who finds the heartbeat to be the most significant development could, with equal logic, locate the onset of personhood at five weeks of gestation. Others, more impressed with the similarity of fetal to infant facial features, could justify a few different cutoffs before twenty weeks, depending on how much similarity is believed necessary for the similarity to be significant. Still others, who consider learning to be the most fundamental human trait, could locate personhood at six weeks, when the first reflex occurs, eight weeks, when the head turns toward a source of stimulation, twelve weeks, when swallowing accompanies the "turning toward" reflex, and so forth.[9]

Much more can be, and has been, said on both sides of the debate about the personhood of young fetuses. I think the forgoing sufficient, however, to illustrate my point. The debate is structurally and epistemologically identical to debates about the existence of God. Relevant, secular facts can be used in respectable arguments to address the issue. But the arguments are inconclusive because every argument on one side can be countered with an effective argument on the other. This is inherent in the subject matter, as we have no method of resolving the dispute even in principle. So the issue is not one of ordinary secular fact. Yet it is believed by both sides to be more than an issue of attitude. It seems to be about some "trans-sensual, trans-scientific and metaphysical fact." Thus, like belief in the existence of God, belief in the personhood of young fetuses is, on the epistemological standard, a religious belief.

Since the epistemological standard of religious belief is fundamental to the Court's understanding of "religion" in the First Amendment, the personhood of young fetuses is, for First Amendment purposes, a religious matter. Any state endorsement of a view on this matter and any state law predicated on such a view are unconstitutional establishments of religion.

Distinguishing Religious from Secular Determinations of Fetal Personhood

The present section and the two that follow state and then reply to objections to the position I have taken. The present section is inspired by Justice White's disagreement with Justice Stevens in *Thornburgh v. American College of Obstetricians and Gynecologists*. Stevens maintained what I have just argued, namely, that attributing personhood "during the entire period from the moment of conception until the moment of birth" rests on "a . . . theological argument." It is essentially religious. Stevens added, "I believe our jurisdiction is limited to the evaluation of secular state interests."[10] So enactments that reflect any such theological position would unconstitutionally establish religion.

White replied that attributing personhood from conception onward "is no more a 'theological' position than is the Court's own judgment that viability is the point at which the state interest becomes compelling. (Interestingly, Justice Stevens omits any real effort to defend this judgment.)"[11] White suggests here that if one position on the beginning of personhood is religious, all such positions are equally religious. If this were the case, the religious freedom argument that I have employed would be embarrassed by an unwelcome consequence—abortions could never be restricted in the interests of the unborn, even on the eve of birth. If attributing personhood to a fetus, regardless of its stage of development, is a religious judgment, this would apply to a fetus on the eve of birth. Restricting abortions to save the life of that fetus would be no more constitutional than denying first-trimester abortions because all restrictions aimed at protecting a fetus would unconstitutionally establish a religious belief. This is an embarrassing result because most people believe that the older fetus is a person with a right to life and that restrictions on late abortions are justified by this fact.

This section justifies the distinction that Stevens makes between younger and older fetuses. I argue that while the personhood of young fetuses is inherently a matter of religious belief, the personhood of older fetuses is a secular matter.

I do not base my argument on considerations of secular fact. As shown in the preceding section, when personhood is viewed as a matter of fact, considerations of secular fact and of secular methodologies employed in the determination of secular facts are insufficient. Such considerations cannot establish that a fetus (at any stage of development) *or even a newborn* is a person. In order to address White's concern, then, I treat the issue as a question of value, not a question of fact. Viewed as an issue of fact, the question is posed: "Is, in fact, a fetus (or a newborn) a person?" Viewed as an issue of value, however, the question becomes: "Should we apply the concept of personhood to a fetus (or a newborn)?" Here we are concerned with a matter of choice. We must choose an application of the concept of personhood. Since choice is involved, it is appropriate to consult our values. Since we are concerned with legislation and constitutional interpretation, the values must be secular.

Basing my argument on secular values, I do not maintain in this section that the acquisition of personhood should be placed at a particular week in the gestational process. Instead, I argue that personhood becomes a secular matter, and so a fit subject for legislation, sometime between twenty and twenty-eight weeks. This allows the Court to avoid the embarrassing result, suggested by White's dissent, that the Establishment Clause prohibits legislation designed to save the lives of fetuses on the eve of birth. Because the personhood of such fetuses is a secular matter, the Establishment Clause is no bar to legislation designed to save their lives.

The preceding section showed that arguments can be given for and against the personhood not only of the fetus (at any stage of gestation) but even of the newborn. If the abilities to reason, argue, make compromises, and keep agreements are essential characteristics of persons, then newborns are not, as a matter of fact, persons. Some philosophers have adopted this position and concluded that newborns do not have a right to life.[12] These same philosophers are quick to add, however, that there remain secular reasons to protect newborns *as if* they had a right to life. The details of their reasoning need not detain us. The point is that in our society the protection of newborns, either *because* they have a right to life or *as if* they have a right to life, is *an accepted secular value*. Indeed, few values that legislation embodies or fosters are as central to commonly accepted way of life as the value of protecting (healthy) newborns. That value is woven into the fabric of our society as surely and securely as, for example, the values of general literacy, public health, and national defense.

In none of these cases do I attempt to explain *why* our society adheres to the secular value in question. That kind of sociological inquiry is beyond the scope of the present work. I take secular values as I find them and begin reasoning from that point. I recognize that a different society would likely differ somewhat in the secular values to which it is committed and that our society's value commitments vary over time. Nevertheless, it can be safely maintained that one of our society's secular values at this time is the protection of newborns as (or as if they were) persons.

[It was noted earlier] that we do not believe our right to life to vary with our physical location. One's right to life is the same, according to our values, at home, while out shopping, and during a visit to a foreign country. Also, we do not believe that temporary dependency on external life-support systems affects one's right to life. For example, other things being equal, people in temporary need of a respirator have the same right to life as other people. Finally . . . our secular concepts make size and strength irrelevant to attributions of a right to life. Other things being equal, we do not attribute a right to life more readily to the strong than to the weak, or to the big than to the small.

These secular beliefs can be combined with the secular view that newborns are persons with a right to life to yield the view that fetuses late in the gestational process are persons with a right to life. Fetuses late in the gestational process, eight-month fetuses, for example, differ from newborns primarily in their location, size, strength, and temporary need for support external to themselves. (From the perspective of the fetus, maternal support is external.) Since these features are generally irrelevant to attributions of personhood and a right to life, eight-month fetuses have the same personhood and right to life as newborns. Because all the values employed in this reasoning are secular, this judgment about eight-month fetuses is secular, not religious. The Establishment Clause notwithstanding, states may constitutionally pass laws designed to protect the lives and health of eight-month fetuses. Generally speaking, states may constitutionally forbid late abortions (except to save the life of the mother) where such abortions jeopardize the life or health of the fetus-would-be-newborn. This allows states to rule out most late, elective abortions. Even when steps are taken to preserve the life and health of the fetus-would-be-newborn, premature delivery (which is what such abortions amount to) jeopardizes the life and health of the prematurely delivered infant.

To what part of the gestational process does this reasoning apply? The reasoning turns on the secular value of respecting newborns as (or as if they were) persons. So the reasoning applies to all those fetuses who differ from newborns primarily in location, size, strength, and temporary dependency (on their mothers). By week twenty-eight, a normal fetus has already developed all the basic physiological systems that characterize newborns and other people. Such fetuses are much smaller and weaker than healthy newborns, so they require special care if they are delivered at this time, and their life prospects on delivery are much worse than normal. Nevertheless, they have already developed all the basic physiological systems needed to sustain human life. They differ from newborns only in location, size, strength, and temporary dependency (on their mothers). But these factors are not usually regarded in our secular culture as relevant to the attribution of a right to life. So the twenty-eight-week fetus can, on purely secular grounds, be treated by the state as a person with a right to life.

The twenty-week fetus cannot. The twenty-week fetus has not yet developed all the physiological systems that are necessary to sustain human life. It differs significantly, therefore, from the twenty-eight-week fetus. It is not yet just like a newborn except in location, temporary dependency, size, and strength. It lacks one or more basic systems that newborns have and use.

Since the personhood and right to life of the (healthy) newborn is what anchors abortion legislation in secular concepts (and secures their constitutionality), the absence in twenty-week fetuses of what newborns have and use makes their personhood problematic. Secular concepts regarding the irrelevance of location, temporary dependency, size and strength no longer suffice to justify protecting twenty-week fetuses, as such fetuses differ from newborns in other ways as well. As we saw in the previous section, the significance of these other differences cannot be decided by reference to secular concepts. Where secular concepts leave off, religious ideas take over. But legislation must not be predicated on religious ideas, so abortion legislation designed to protect the lives of fetuses twenty weeks or younger are unconstitutional establishments of religion.

I have argued so far in the present section that considerations of secular value require extension of the concept of personhood to older, but not to younger, fetuses. Combined with the argument of the preceding section, this is sufficient for First Amendment purposes. Lacking secular justification as a matter of fact (preceding section) or value (present section), the attribution of personhood to young fetuses is left, by default, in the realm of religion. I now go further, however. Not only are secular values insufficient to justify attributing personhood to young fetuses, such values argue powerfully against attributing personhood to the youngest among the unborn: newly fertilized ova. Attributing personhood to newly fertilized ova (which are medically termed "zygotes") runs counter to, and so would require significant modifications of, our secular values. The attribution is, from the perspective of secular values, a radical proposal. Several considerations supporting this contention were [previously] explained. . . . I briefly review a few of those considerations.

Since nearly one-half of fertilized ova die early as a result of failure to implant on the uterine wall, failure of implantation would be the gravest medical problem facing humanity if the concept of personhood or humanity were extended to include zygotes. Unprecedented expenditures of resources on medical research would be justified, even if the most favorable result, saving the lives of these "people," increased by 800 percent or more the number of infants born with severe genetic defects. Our society's practices do not reflect, and most people's values do not require, any such commitment to the personhood of zygotes.

Other consequences of attributing personhood to fertilized ova are equally at odds with social practices and secular values. Deliberate abortion at any stage of pregnancy would be murder and would have to be treated as severely as any other deliberate homicide. If the criminal law may be used as evidence of secular values, such treatment of abortion conflicts sharply with secular values. Abortion has never in our legal tradition been equated with murder or with homicide of any sort. So the decision to extend the concept of personhood to zygotes entails practices and values that conflict with those of our society.

The conflict is greatest when the deliberate termination of pregnancy occurs shortly after fertilization, as is the case, for example, with the IUD and the morning-after pill. The use of such contraceptives would be murder if a fertilized ovum were thereby destroyed. Otherwise, the crime would be reckless endangerment. These conclusions, too, conflict with our criminal laws and secular values. But the matter gets worse. Since the crimes of murder and reckless endangerment differ significantly in their seriousness and in the severity of associated punishments, probable cause to believe that someone had used an IUD or morning-after pill would justify the examination of the woman's next menstrual flow to check for the presence of a fertilized ovum. Again, the conflict with our laws, practices, and values is manifest. Thus, the extension of the concept of personhood to include zygotes conflicts sharply with our secular values and with social practices expressive of those values.

More important for purposes of the present work, we saw earlier in this section that secular values fail to justify the choice of attributing personhood to fetuses twenty weeks or younger. We saw in the preceding section that no such attribution can be justified as a matter of secular fact. Having eliminated the bases of both secular fact and secular values, the only grounds for attributing personhood to fetuses twenty weeks or younger are religious. Such grounds may not form the basis for legislation.

But Justice White need not be concerned that if any view about the onset of personhood is deemed religious, all such views must be deemed religious. After twenty-eight weeks, as we have seen, there are grounds in secular values for attributing personhood to the fetus, so laws protecting the fetus at this point do not run afoul of the Establishment Clause.

I cannot say exactly where between twenty and twenty-eight weeks the matter of fetal personhood becomes secular. Those more expert than I must determine when the fetus differs from the newborn in no more than location, temporary dependency, size and strength. Even experts may not be able to agree on a particular week when the fetus differs from healthy newborns in no more than these four ways. Expert opinions may range from twenty to twenty-six weeks.

It is important to avoid confusing this issue with one about viability, which turns on the technological ability to foster the development of a fetus outside its mother. Even if, for example, a form of artificial oxygenation enables us to bring twenty-week fetuses to term outside their mothers, such fetuses still differ from newborns in ways whose significance is a religious matter. Even if such fetuses become viable, then, they are not considered persons on purely secular grounds.

Religious versus Secular Uncertainty

The objection considered in this section is expressed in the following reasoning: Fetuses twenty weeks and younger can be classified as persons only on religious, not on secular, grounds because secular concepts do not suffice to decide the matter one way or the other. On the epistemological standard, undecidability makes a matter religious. But if we cannot decide on secular grounds how to classify young fetuses, the objector continues, we should exercise caution. Feelings of uncertainty about whether abortions early in pregnancy kill a person (the fetus) should lead us to refrain from such abortions, just as uncertainty about whether a movement in the bushes is caused by a person or a deer should lead a hunter to refrain from shooting.

The objector notes also that the government often protects people where uncertainty leads to grave dangers. The government regulates the airline and nuclear power industries, for example, to protect people from such dangers. But there are few, if any, losses more tragic than the premature death of a healthy young person. Given uncertainties about the personhood of young fetuses, the objector concludes, the government has a responsibility to protect such fetuses. It can do this best by outlawing abortions.

Finally, the objector maintains, since all the steps in this reasoning are based on secular premises regarding prudence in the face of uncertainty, the antiabortion legislation promoted here does not establish a religious belief. Such legislation is constitutional and is required if the government is to fulfill its responsibility in situations of uncertainty to protect people against serious harm.

So much for the objection. Now the reply. The flaw in the objector's argument can be seen by first comparing the danger of killing a young fetus who may be a person with the danger of killing a fellow hunter who may be behind a bush. The existence of the danger in the second case does not rely in any way on religious beliefs, whereas in the first case the danger exists only because of uncertainty about the truth of a religious claim. The young fetus is a person according to a certain religious belief. To say that the young fetus may be a person is to say that this religious belief may be true. The objector maintains, then, that dangers implied by the possible truth of religious beliefs may for legal purposes be considered secular dangers. Since they are secular dangers, legislation addressing these dangers does not contravene the Establishment Clause.

The objector fails to appreciate that religious freedom could be suppressed entirely if legislation could be justified by dangers whose existence depends on uncertainty about the truth of religious claims. Consider baptism, for example. Many people believe it necessary for individuals to avoid eternal damnation and suffering when they die. The reduction of suffering is a secular value. We have laws to reduce the suffering even of animals. So, the argument goes, if baptism is necessary for the reduction of suffering, it should be required by law, or at least be promoted and paid for by the government. Of course, the belief that baptism is necessary for the reduction of suffering is a religious belief. From the government's point of view, therefore, its truth is uncertain. But the possibility of its truth, according to this line of reasoning, makes it dangerous for the government to ignore baptism. In sum, if a religiously claimed danger of secular harm (suffering in this case, killing a person in the case of abortion) constitutes a secular danger, then the danger of suffering due to lack of baptism is a secular danger. Like the danger of murder associated with abortion, the danger of suffering associated with failure to baptize would have to be considered a matter that legislation can legitimately address.

This result is clearly unacceptable. Legislation requiring, promoting, or granting public payment for baptism would obviously be an unconstitutional establishment of religion. Any line of reasoning that suggests such legislation would be constitutional is certainly flawed.

The flaw is apparent also from numerous other unacceptable results of this line of reasoning. These results follow from the fact that myriad secular dangers can be associated with religious beliefs. Some concern the welfare in this life of society in general. For example, according to the Old Testament, the world was inundated, two cities were later destroyed, and Egypt was visited with successive plagues, all because people failed to observe God's laws. The Old Testament is often interpreted to indicate continuing dangers from disobedience to God's laws. Chapter 28 of Deuteronomy, for example, is devoted to explaining the earthly rewards of obedience (1–14) and the earthly ruin that attends disobedience to the word of God (15–60). For disobedience: "The Lord shall make the pestilence cleave unto thee. . . . The Lord shall smite thee with a consumption, and with a fever." In addition, the rain will cease, the ground grow hard, and the harvest diminish. National enemies will prevail and enslave the people. In short, the problems associated with disobedience to God's will include secular matters of the utmost importance. Many people in our society hold this sort of belief, for example, those who view the AIDS epidemic as punishment from God for human transgression.

Consider someone who believes that God's law prohibits equality for women, use of contraceptives, or instruction in the theory of evolution. Biblical passages are often cited to justify these, and many similar, beliefs. Combine such beliefs with the view that secular ruin follows disobedience to God's will, and an argument is made for the legal subjugation of women, the prohibition of contraceptives, the suppression of the theory of evolution, and as many other legal restrictions and requirements as someone's religious convictions can justify. According to the type of argument being discussed in this section, uncertainty about the truth of the underlying religious premises means merely that the government's failure to act *risks* (rather than causes) social ruin. Surely the government should act, the argument continues, to reduce or eliminate these grave risks, just as it acts to combat the risks of cancer associated with certain chemicals and the risks of deforestation associated with acid rain. Thus, any number of legal prohibitions can be justified in this way.

But the resulting prohibitions clearly violate the Establishment Clause. The risks that the prohibitions are aimed at reducing or eliminating are risks of secular harm. The existence of these risks, however, is predicated on a religious belief, for example, belief that God requires the subordination of women or forbids the use of contraceptives. This is the crux of the problem. Because religious beliefs are so varied and numerous, any number of legal requirements, restrictions, and prohibitions could be justified if the government were permitted to respond to risks predicated on religious beliefs. The Establishment Clause protects us from this intolerable situation. Accordingly, the Establishment Clause rules out antiabortion statutes aimed at reducing or eliminating the risk of murder associated with aborting young fetuses, as the risk of murder is predicated in this case entirely on a religious belief about young fetuses.

Notes

1. E. Blechschmidt, "Human from the First," in *New Perspectives on Human Abortion,* ed. Hilgers, Horan, and Mall (Frederick, Md.: University Publishers of America, 1981), 7–8.

2. *Thornburgh v. American College of Obstetricians and Gynecologists,* 476 U.S. 747, 792 (1986).

3. Blechschmidt, "Human from the First," 12–13.

4. Robert E. Joyce, "When Does a Person Begin?" in *New Perspectives,* ed. Hilgers et al., 348.

5. Ibid., 348.

6. A sleeping individual can be, at the same time, both a potential and an actual physician only because potentiality is taken in two different senses, first and second potentiality. A trained physician is actually a physician (relative to first potentiality) even when she is asleep. However, because she is asleep, she is a potential physician (relative to second potentiality).

7. Joel Feinberg, "Abortion," in *Matters of Life and Death,* 2d ed., ed. Tom Regan (New York: Random House, 1986), 261–62.

8. Gary B. Gertler, "Brain Birth: A Proposal for Defining When a Fetus Is Entitled to Human Life Status," 59 *Southern California L. Rev.* 1061, 1066 (1986).

9. Wanda Franz, "Fetal Development: A Novel Application of Piaget's Theory of Cognitive Development," in *New Perspectives,* ed. Hilgers et al., 42.

10. Thornburgh, at 778 (1986) (Stevens concurring).

11. Thornburgh, at 795 (White dissenting).

12. See Feinberg, "Abortion," 270–71; Mary Anne Warren, "The Moral and Legal Status of Abortion," *The Monist* 57 (1973); Stanley I. Benn, "Abortion, Infanticide, and Respect for Persons," in *The Problem of Abortion,* ed. J. Feinberg (Belmont, Calif.: Wadsworth, 1973).

[42]

Political Discourse and Public Policy on Funding Abortion: An Analysis

Mary C. Segers

Arguments For and Against Public Funding of Abortions

Those who oppose public funding of abortion have secured passage of the Hyde Amendment to protect fetal life, a legislative purpose they see as perfectly legitimate. While many abortion opponents believe the fetus to be a human being from the moment of conception, this assumption is not necessary to their argument. If Congress can legislate to protect the snail darter, Congress can enact legislation to protect fetal life. In *Roe v. Wade,* Justice Blackmun, writing for the Court, acknowledged the legitimacy of the state's interest in protecting prenatal life and stated:

> Logically, of course, a legitimate state interest in this area need not stand or fall on acceptance of the belief that life begins at conception or at some other point prior to live birth. In assessing the state's interest, recognition may be given to the less rigid claim that as long as at least *potential* life is involved, the state may assert interests beyond the protection of the pregnant woman alone.[1]

Of course, opponents of abortion who do believe in the humanity of the fetus think they are duty-bound to restrict abortion in any way possible and

SOURCE: From James Tunstead Burtchaell, C.S.C., ed., *Abortion Parley.* Copyright © 1980 by James Tunstead Burtchaell, C.S.C. Reprinted by permission.

view funding cutbacks as saving the lives of unborn children rather than as depriving women of constitutional rights. What prochoice advocates view as wrong prolife activists think right. Thus, even in the matter of funding one very quickly comes up against the abortion question itself.

Those who oppose abortion as a grave moral wrong do not think they should be required to subsidize abortion through taxation. They echo here a familiar argument of the 1960s. During the Vietnam War, many in the peace movement argued that they were morally obliged to withhold taxes in protest against an immoral war. This argument holds whether opponents of funding for abortion-on-demand are a minority or a majority. According to recent polls, a majority of Americans do not think government money should be spent for elective abortions.[2] However, even if a minority of Americans held this view, the person morally opposed to abortion might still believe himself or herself bound in conscience to withhold tax monies or to vote against state funding of abortions. Such an individual would be acting according to a libertarian tradition as old as the American nation.

Prolife opponents of funding also question why the public must pay for abortions when the public is so deeply divided on this issue. They argue that if an abortion decision is a private matter, then perhaps private, nongovernmental organizations should engage in fund raising to pay for the abortions of the indigent. Why, they ask, cannot Planned Parenthood, NARAL, various churches, and voluntary associations privately fund this private right to choose to terminate pregnancy? In contemporary American politics, this view accords nicely with conservative trends symbolized by tax revolts and the Proposition 13 movement; in logical terms, however, abortion opponents are simply asking prochoice advocates to adhere consistently to the same individualistic ethic which sustains the right to abortion on privacy grounds.

In response to these arguments against Medicaid funding of abortions, prochoice activists appeal to principles of liberty, equality, utility, and tolerance which have long occupied a prominent place in the tradition of modern Western political thought. The concern with liberty—freedom from dependence upon nature, including one's own biology or human nature—is a powerful impulse in Western thought and a premise of liberalism and Marxism as well as a working assumption of modern science and modern medicine. In this view privacy is a condition of reproductive freedom, and serves to erect a buffer against governmental and societal interference with individual choice. Prochoice advocates also stress equal liberty and the equal worth of liberty. One might be opposed to abortion as morally wrong and socially destructive; however, the fact that abortion has been declared a legal right and is easily available to the middle and upper classes seems to support the idea that, in an ostensibly egalitarian society, it also should be available to the poor. Since equal rights are illusory if one lacks the financial means to exercise such rights, a society committed to liberal principles of equal opportunity and constitutional principles of equal protection must, in fairness, publicly assist the poor in exercising the right to choose whether or not to terminate pregnancy.

Those who favor Medicaid abortions also stress the utility of abortion for the poor. It is said to be less costly than childbirth expenses and welfare payments for child-rearing (an argument which should appeal to fiscal conservatives); in the first trimester, at least, abortion also carries less risk of damage to the woman's health.[3] On practical grounds, prochoice advocates point out that federal funding cutbacks resulting from the Hyde Amendment have the effect of encouraging late abortions, which pose greater risks to maternal health. This is because indigent women in non-Medicaid states are having abortions an average of two weeks later than other women with access to public funding. It is due also to the very nature of the Hyde Amendment, which funds abortions only in life-endangering pregnancies or in pregnancies which threaten "severe and longlasting physical health damage" if carried to term. According to plaintiffs in *McRae:*

> The primary direct causes of maternal mortality are hemorrhage, infection and the hypertensive states of pregnancy—preeclampsia, eclampsia and toxemia. All of these are conditions which occur and cause maternal death late in pregnancy.[4]

By the time such a life-endangering situation had developed late in pregnancy, the risks to maternal health of the abortion then permissible would be much greater than if the abortion had been performed in the first trimester. From a practical standpoint, then, the Hyde Amendment works to encourage high-risk abortions. Since it also encourages more costly reproductive behaviors, it does not, from the standpoint of utility and efficiency, appear to be sound public policy.

Finally, . . . an important prochoice argument against the Hyde Amendment emphasizes the importance of tolerance in a pluralistic society. Those who oppose public funding of abortions are said to be imposing their own religious beliefs upon others who do not subscribe to such views. The enacting of the Hyde Amendment therefore violates the separation of church and state required by the First Amendment. Speaking of the Hyde Amendment, ACLU lawyers state:

> The statute has no secular purpose or effect. The only purpose . . . is to eliminate abortions for poor women and therefore aid those religious groups that consider abortions wrong and sinful because of their theological position that human personhood begins at the moment of conception. At the trial of the *McRae* case, the evidence proved that the primary opposition to abortion is by

religious not secular groups. It was also argued that the question of when life begins has not been, and may never be, scientifically determined. The question truly rests on religious dogma. Religions are clearly divided on this issue.

Catholics and Orthodox Jewish groups support an anti-abortion position while many Protestant and the majority of Jewish groups advocate the religious necessity of choice over the abortion question. Plaintiffs, who include the Women's Division of the Methodist Church, asked the Court to find that the government can have no role in enacting into law an abortion statute which clearly elevates one religious belief over another and aids those religions which forbid abortion while inhibiting those persons who hold opposite religious beliefs or no religious beliefs at all. The state must remain neutral on the abortion issue.[5]

The perception of abortion as an issue involving liberty, privacy, equality, and tolerance helps to explain how the issue is defined by proabortionists as well as what political strategy is adopted. Abortion is conceived to be a civil liberties issue involving a constitutionally protected right to limit childbearing; the political strategy adopted is essentially a legal one since, in the American political system, at least since the 1930s, it is the judiciary which has been most active in protecting individual civil liberties. In the continuing struggle between constitutionalism and democracy in American politics, the prochoice forces come down heavily on the side of constitutionalism, seeking vindication in the courts and distrusting democratic majorities in state and federal legislatures.[6]

Prochoice activists are fond of citing *Brown v. Board of Education of Topeka* as precedent and model for this legal strategy. Fearing majoritarian tyranny, they have chosen the courts as the more congenial arena for their political struggle. This reliance upon the courts to make public policy on abortion, together with the positivism evident in prochoice arguments about compliance with the Court's ruling in *Wade,* poses a dilemma for proabortionists when court rulings on Medicaid funding go against them. Nevertheless, the inability of proabortion arguments to command legislative majorities in Congress and in most state legislatures dictates continuation of their legal strategy. It is no accident that the response of Planned Parenthood and the American Civil Liberties Union to *Maher v. Roe* and *Beal v. Doe* was to continue the legal challenge in *Harris v. McRae.*

Proabortion Arguments for Medicaid Funding: An Evaluation

Let us now analyze and evaluate these prochoice arguments for Medicaid funding in terms of philosophical and political cogency. How persuasive are proabortion arguments for public funding of a woman's exercise of her "right of personal privacy" (to cite the characterization of abortion in *Roe v. Wade*)? How compelling is the conception of individual freedom underlying the proabortion case? How politically effective are the utilitarian cost-benefit and health-risk analyses offered by proabortionists? How plausible is the argument for tolerance of competing views in a pluralistic society, the argument which underlies plaintiffs' First Amendment challenge in *McRae*? Finally, how compelling is the appeal to egalitarian principles which underlies arguments for Medicaid funding?

Answering these questions involves analyzing the values implicit in the prochoice position, a task which is properly and preeminently the work of the political theorist. It should be understood that whenever Supreme Court decisions are cited here to illustrate prochoice arguments, my approach is that of the political theorist seeking to elucidate values underlying political discourse and public policy. The perspective adopted here is not that of the constitutional lawyer interested in the role of the Court, the use of precedent, or the internal consistency of judicial doctrine over time.

The Supreme Court's 1973 abortion rulings were based on a constitutional right of privacy held implicit in the concept of personal liberty protected by the due process clause of the Fourteenth Amendment.[7] While admitting that the Constitution does not explicitly mention the right of privacy, the Court cited a series of past cases to indicate its growing recognition of such a fundamental right.[8] The Court then concluded that the right of privacy "is broad enough to encompass a woman's decision whether or not to terminate her pregnancy."[9]

Many who might applaud the outcome of the Court's ruling in *Wade* find rather odd the Court's appeal to personal privacy rights to justify the legalization of abortion. They echo Justice Rehnquist's dissent:

> I have difficulty in concluding, as the Court does, that the right of "privacy" is involved in this case. Texas by the statute here challenged bars the performance of a medical abortion by a licensed physician on a plaintiff such as Roe. A transaction resulting in an operation such as this is not "private" in the ordinary usage of that word. Nor is the "privacy" which the Court finds here even a distant relative of the freedom from searches and seizures protected by the Fourth Amendment to the Constitution which the Court has referred to as embodying a right to privacy.[10]

Although a majority of the justices also recognized the difficulty of applying privacy notions to abortion,[11] the Court seemed to think that its gradualist, three-stage approach to abortion was a satisfactory response to those who doubted the applicability of privacy. And of course the Court rejected the notion that the fundamental right of privacy is absolute and unlimited.[12]

In any case, on the question of Medicaid funding of abortions, which is of direct concern here, the notion of privacy does not seem to serve women well. In her analysis of *Maher v. Roe,* Sidney Callahan observed:

> Privacy is a double-edged sword with its negative as well as positive dimensions. As this last Court decision seems to indicate: to be private is also to be deprived of support. If an abortion decision is a private matter and the developing fetus nothing more than an appendage of a woman's body, then there is logic in leaving a woman to solve the problem herself, no matter how poor she may be. In private enterprise, power and privilege always operate, and unequal outcomes are the norm.[13]

As a justification for abortion, privacy is very closely related to liberty; this is apparent both in the legal reasoning of *Wade*[14] and in moral philosophizing about reproductive freedom. Here privacy and liberty mean independence of and freedom from the control of others—government and society—who might impose restrictive abortion laws; to use the categorization of liberty made famous by Isaiah Berlin, the conception of freedom here involved is negative.[15] Prochoice advocates stress freedom from biological control as well as freedom from social control. They emphasize autonomy and self-determination in sex- and pregnancy-related medical care.

Again, however, an examination of the values underlying this liberal commitment to reproductive freedom reveals some deficiencies in the conception. The laudable ideal of individual or personal autonomy may be unrealizable so long as society is conceived of as an aggregate of isolated, separate, independent individuals—each having a Lockean natural right to property based on proprietorship of his or her own person. The admittedly extreme proabortion argument that a woman's body is her own to do with as she pleases[16] is reminiscent of Locke's conception of human beings in a state of nature. For Locke, the individual in the state of nature is "free, . . . absolute lord of his own person and possessions, equal to the greatest and subject to nobody."[17] As Macpherson has stated, "The core of Locke's individualism is the assertion that every man is naturally the sole proprietor of his own person and capacities— the absolute proprietor in that he owes nothing to society for them—and especially the absolute proprietor of his capacity to labor."[18] To the extent that prochoice advocates argue that a woman's body (including fetal tissue) is her own private property for which she is not, in the final analysis, accountable to others—and individualist arguments such as these are implicit in both the case for abortion-on-demand and the case for not requiring spousal consent to abortion made in *Planned Parenthood v. Danforth* (1976)—to that extent prochoice activists are making what might be called Lockean liberal arguments for legalized abortion.

The only difficulty with such arguments is that they do very little to advance one's cause when the issue is public funding of abortions for those who are poor, dependent, powerless, and vulnerable. The intensely individualistic perspective of prochoice advocates seems to offer little in the way of social solidarity and support; moreover, such a perspective runs counter to feminist arguments for public assistance to women in their childbearing and child-rearing activities—whether they need public funding of abortions (should they choose to terminate pregnancy) or publicly funded child-care centers (should they choose to bear and rear the children they have conceived). As Sidney Callahan has observed:

> An individualistic ethic which rests the right to an abortion on privacy grounds does not serve women well, and it is unfortunate that most feminists have not addressed the problem. Pregnancy disability payments, family allowances, and public daycare have all been attacked because they are said to infringe on the privacy of the family. Public protection of the fetus and public support for and protection of women's rights are related in principle.[19]

With respect to the values of privacy and liberty, then, I am suggesting that prochoice arguments for the legality of abortion are inconsistent with their arguments for Medicaid funding of abortions. Further, I suggest that this weakness or inconsistency reflects a more general tension between nineteenth-century, individualistic, laissez-faire liberalism and twentieth-century, post–New Deal, welfare-state liberalism.[20] The former conceives society as an aggregate of isolated individuals who seek freedom from the intervention and intrusion of others, while the latter envisions society as an organic community of interdependent, interrelated persons whose freedom is made possible through mutual assistance and cooperation.

In their arguments for Medicaid funding of abortions, prochoice advocates rightly appeal to the egalitarian principles implicit in welfare-state liberalism. Liberalism in contemporary America has stressed the necessity of equality of opportunity if the promise of liberty for all is to be fulfilled.[21] If reproductive freedom includes a right to safe, legal abortions, then equal opportunity to exercise that right and equal access to the abortion option seems appropriate. And equal opportunity in this context requires public funding of abortions for the poor—or so the argument runs. I believe proabortionists are persuasive here when they emphasize the injustice of unequal access to abortions. In fact, appeals to principles of equality and distributive justice were strong planks in the pre-*Wade* movement to legalize abortion as well as in the post-*Wade* movement to subsidize abortion. One of the most effective arguments for legalizing abortion concerned the problem of discriminatory enforcement of antiabortion laws. Mohr has stated this argument forcefully. Noting that in the twentieth century a substantial number of American women continued to seek and to have abortions despite nineteenth-century statutes designed to make them unavailable, he wrote:

> By itself, of course, the violation of a law is not an especially persuasive argument for its repeal; few people would advocate the legalization of homicide, for example, simply because a certain number of Americans continue to kill one another each year in spite of the criminal sanctions against doing so. But the evidence about the continued practice of abortion in the United States throughout the twentieth century raised some rather more difficult problems. Wealthy women, it was alleged, could arrange for safe and "legal" abortions by persuading their physicians to interpret the therapeutic clauses of various antiabortion laws very loosely, while poor women could not. Wealthy women could afford to travel to those jurisdictions where the antiabortion laws were not rigidly enforced; poor women could not. The nation's antiabortion laws were thus perceived as discriminating against poor, frequently non-white women in an era of heightened sensitivity to egalitarianism. It was also the poor who were more likely to die at the hands of the gross incompetents who preyed upon the desperation of those without sufficient funds either to terminate their pregnancy safely and discreetly or to make socially acceptable arrangements both for the period of confinement and for the subsequent care and upbringing of the child, through adoption or other means. Unenforceability, in other words, might be one thing, but discriminatory enforcement was quite another.[22]

Prochoice advocates argue that the same inequality is occurring with respect to post-1973 restrictive legislation in general and the Hyde Amendment in particular. To restrict public funding of poor women's abortions merely perpetuates the selective, discriminatory pattern of earlier days.

Of course, prolife advocates have seized upon the well-known deficiencies of the liberal doctrine of equality of opportunity in arguing against the prochoice side.[23] Chief among such deficiencies is the largely formal character of the doctrine. The equal opportunity principle does not specify the nature or value of the opportunities one is to have. In the case of equal access to abortion, it is precisely the value of abortion which is questioned. Thus, from a socialist perspective, even this crucial and otherwise strong egalitarian argument of proabortionists for Medicaid funding seems tinged with the deficiencies of liberalism.

In addition to the values of privacy, liberty, and equality which underlie proabortion arguments, prochoice advocates often appeal to the liberal virtue of tolerance to support the case for public funding of abortions. The most recent example of this, of course, was the First Amendment brief in *McRae*. There plaintiffs argue that the Hyde Amendment violates the constitutional separation of church and state because it enacts into civil law a religious view of abortion—the view that the fetus is a human being from the moment of conception. Abortion is held to be a religious issue, best left to the private conscience rather than to public legislation. In its public policy, the state must remain neutral on the abortion issue and not intrude upon the domains of individual liberty and conscience. Government neutrality is best achieved through the removal of restrictive abortion laws from the books (as in *Wade*). Finally, repeal of antiabortion statutes is said to pass no judgment on the substantive ethical issues, but merely to allow individuals to make up their own minds.

There are several objections to this train of argument. First, it is hard to know what is meant by the statement that abortion is a religious issue. If it means that for some churches and some religious believers their positions are the direct result of religious teachings, this hardly entails the conclusion that the issue is thus intrinsically religious. One might as well say that racial equality is a religious issue and not subject to legislation, because there are some churches which declare racism immoral on religious grounds. That religious groups take religious positions on many issues (e.g., war, racial equality, poverty, capital punishment, and ecology) does not exempt those problems from public legislation nor turn them into theology.[24]

Abortion seems to be a philosophical and ethical issue, not a religious question. This does not mean the issue is therefore best left to the domain of private conscience. Every serious social issue is philosophical. Questions about the meaning of justice, liberty, or equality arise all the time, and such questions are philosophical and legal in nature. The answers to them shape public policy in a decisive fashion. As one philosopher has remarked:

> It is inconsistent to argue that the right of the fetus is exclusively a philosophical problem, to be left to individual conscience, while the right of women is a matter to be protected or implemented legislatively. If it is legitimate to legislate on the latter (which it is), then it should be equally legitimate to legislate on the former.[25]

One would have to conclude that protection of fetal life, which is the object of the Hyde Amendment, is a legitimate, valid, secular legislative purpose.

Still another objection to arguments for tolerance of abortion in a pluralistic society questions whether it is possible for government to remain neutral on the abortion issue. A governmental decision to remove restrictive antiabortion laws from the books and to leave the question up to individuals hardly seems neutral. Such a policy begs the question of the status of the fetus, or, at the least, assumes that there are no normative standards whatever for determining the rights of fetuses, except the standard that individuals are free to use or to create any standard they see fit. This libertarian policy is not only not neutral; it exhibits a major flaw in liberal political thought—namely, the inability of contemporary liberalism to offer a rationally persuasive conception of universal norms.

The view that it is possible for government to remain neutral on the abortion issue also betrays a certain naïveté about the role of law in society. The Greeks recognized the educative role of the laws[26] and were aware that changes in the law not only often reflect significant shifts in public moral attitudes but also affect individual moral judgments. Mohr has shown the impact in the United States of the nineteenth-century antiabortion statutes upon public attitudes regarding abortion: whereas the great majority of Americans in 1850 did not regard abortion as morally wrong, public opinion in 1950 was invariably opposed to abortion.[27] In the face of such evidence concerning the role of law as a socializing agent—at least with respect to attitudes—it seems naive and disingenuous to pretend that government, law, and public policy are or can be neutral on the question of abortion.

Rather, arguments that America is a pluralistic society in which government must tolerate competing views about the morality or immorality of abortion should be changed to read: America is a liberal, secular society which accords highest importance to individual choice and to worldly values, which cannot achieve public consensus on the abortion question, and which, as a result, must reluctantly leave resolution of the matter to private individual judgment. This clarification of the prochoice argument does not exalt abortion as a civil right grounded in fundamental constitutional privacy rights, but recognizes that abortion is a desperate option, a last resort reluctantly undertaken "in necessity and in sorrow." This may be the best that we can arrive at on the controversial issue; but the point is that such a view offers little justification for coercing others through taxation to fund what they regard as seriously immoral.

Concluding Reflections

In this chapter, I have attempted to discern value-positions beneath the level of common discourse in public debate about funding abortions. Prochoice arguments have been analyzed; the analysis of the prolife case must await another occasion. My analysis has shown that the prochoice case for Medicaid funding is weak primarily because the individualistic ethic used to justify abortion as a legal right is inconsistent with the cooperative, communitarian ethic presupposed by public funding of the abortions of poor women. I believe this inconsistency reflects a larger tension or conflict between two types of liberalism in America. Nineteenth-century laissez-faire liberalism (1) conceives the individual to be the primary unit of sociological analysis; (2) conceives society to be an aggregate of isolated, independent, private individuals who occasionally interact; and (3) conceives liberty to be freedom from interference and intrusion by society and government. Laissez-faire liberalism is, of course, compatible with a free-market system of private enterprise which mostly resists governmental interference and regulation. Twentieth-century welfare-state liberalism also subscribes to an irreducible individualism, but, in contrast to laissez-faire liberalism, it conceives society to be a community of organically related individuals who are interdependent; and it defines liberty as freedom from necessity in order to be available for moral action. Welfare-state liberalism is, of course, compatible with positive governmental action to "hinder the hindrances to freedom" by providing assistance (such as Medicaid payments) to those who are needy.

The prochoice case for Medicaid funding is weak because the appeal to privacy to justify abortion, which has strong affinities with a laissez-faire liberal perspective, seems inconsistent with the arguments for public support, arguments which are distinctly welfare-state liberal in tone. To the political observer, this may seem obvious. What is not always clear is how the original prochoice conception of abortion as a private, self-regarding action involving a pregnant woman's conduct with respect to her own body undermines any plea she might make for public assistance. The original definition of abortion as a private action is, of course, the sticking point. As long as one adheres to that definition, it is difficult to expect others, who in principle oppose not only the action but also the definition of the action, to help one carry it out. Abortion, opponents would say, interrupts the process of development in one person's body of another human being—and this does not strike them as a private matter.

How might the argument of proabortionists be improved? I believe prochoice advocates should define abortion as an ethical dilemma rather than as a civil liberties issue; or at least they should recognize that appeals to privacy, liberty, and tolerance are legal arguments tailored to constitutional analysis and designed primarily to win victory in courts of law. Such appeals are not persuasive on the moral issue of reproductive freedom and the public assistance necessary to make such freedom genuine for all parts of the population. And it is the moral, not the legal, issue which seems more salient on the question of Medicaid funding, subject as it is to the votes of state and federal legislators who react to public opinion. According to a Yankelovich survey, public opinion is much more closely divided on the morality of abortion as compared with public opinion on the legality of abortion.[28] I believe then that the proabortion case for public funding might be more persuasive if abortion were seen as an ethical dilemma and a moral decision reluctantly made rather than as a civil right defiantly asserted.[29]

I would be remiss were I not to mention the strong points in the arguments made by prochoice advocates. Briefly, these are the following. First, the appeal to utility, couched in terms of the health risks and financial costs of late, as opposed to early, abortions—which the Hyde Amendment encourages—seems to be a strong argument against the Hyde Amendment. Unfortunately, a utilitarian approach may not work well for prochoice activists for the simple reason that the opposite side's stress on the value of each human (including fetal) life seems to be part of a larger trend in contemporary political philosophy (argued in John Rawls's *A Theory of Justice*) against utilitarianism and against utilitarian cost-benefit calculations with respect to human life.

Second, the prochoice appeal to egalitarian principles of equal opportunity and equal protection is a very strong argument for Medicaid funding—especially in view of the fact that other medically necessary expenses of poor women, including childbirth costs, are funded. Even here, however, prochoice advocates must be prepared to answer the objection that the equal opportunity principle is formal and begs questions about the "opportunity" to which everyone is to have equal access. Inevitably, the appeal to the equal opportunity doctrine directs the argument about Medicaid funding back to the original issue of the morality and legality of abortion—and I have suggested why that direction would not be a wise route for prochoice advocates to take. Also, any liberal appeal to the principle of equality of opportunity must be prepared to ground that principle in some more fundamental, basic conception of human equality. And here prolife forces may be on a stronger ground. As Daniel Callahan has observed:

> The great strength of the movement against abortion is that it seeks to protect one defenseless category of human or potentially human life; furthermore, it strives to resist the introduction into society of forms of value judgments that would discriminate among the worth of individual lives. In almost any other civil rights context, the cogency of this line of reasoning would be quickly respected. Indeed, it has been at the heart of efforts to correct racial injustices, to improve health care, to eradicate poverty, and to provide better care for the aged. The history of mankind has shown too many instances of systematic efforts to exclude certain races or classes of persons from the human community to allow us to view with equanimity the declaration that fetuses are "not human." Historically, the proposition that all human beings are equal, however "inchoate" they may be, is not conservative but radical. It is constantly threatened in theory and subverted in practice.[30]

Perhaps the strongest planks in the prochoice platform have relatively little to do with systems of logic and a great deal to do with "real life" existential situations. An essential element in all discussions of abortion is the need for a feminist perspective, by which I mean continued emphasis on what motherhood and pregnancy mean for women who hold themselves as persons with life plans to realize. The demands on time and energy, and the frustrations—as well as the satisfactions—of maternity (and also paternity) in contemporary society must always be acknowledged. It is sad and unfortunate that a prominent, well-intentioned prolife spokesman such as John T. Noonan almost entirely ignores this aspect of the abortion issue, referring to the pregnant woman as "the carrier of the child" and as "the gravida." No amount of medical terminology should be permitted to desensitize us to the difficult, sometimes agonizing plight of the poor woman faced with an unwanted pregnancy.

From a feminist perspective, it seems unfortunate that the most effective method of restricting abortion to date has been the Hyde Amendment. It is precisely because indigent women are in poverty and thus dependent upon public assistance that the Hyde Amendment is so effective. Because they are poor and dependent upon public funding, their behavior can be controlled in ways that the behavior of upper- and middle-class women cannot be controlled. The poor and only the poor bear the burden of antiabortion legislation.

A feminist perspective on the practical problem of the involuntarily pregnant woman—rich or poor—will construe her immediate situation as an ethical dilemma, a situation of forced choice. She has certain options, she is under great duress, time is of the essence, and she must decide quickly among her options. Conceiving abortion as an ethical dilemma rather than as an individual civil liberty should focus attention on concrete ways to help women avoid such harrowing dilemmas. It should also provide better arguments and a more favorable atmosphere for public assistance to and support of all women in their professional, vocational, and social roles.

Notes

1. 410 U.S. 113, 150 (1973). Of course, the Court ruled that states may assert this interest only at and subsequent to the point of fetal viability. Also, even during the third trimester, when this state interest in protecting fetal life may be asserted, it must not, according to the Court's ruling in *Wade,* outweigh "the preservation of the life or health of the mother" (id. at 165).

2. Note the responses to a question included in the 1975 Gallup Survey: "Are you in favor of a law which permits a woman to have an abortion even if it has to be at government expense?" 57 percent of respondents answered negatively in 1975 and 35 percent positively, with virtually no variation by age or sex. This is reported in Judith Blake, "The Supreme Court's Abortion Decisions and Public Opinion in the United States," *Population and Development Review* 3, nos. 1–2 (March and June 1977): 45–62. Blake comments as follows: "American women were somewhat less negative than in 1970, when 66 percent opposed government subsidy, but the five-year period clearly did not greatly change Americans' views. It is possible that a share of negative responses to the question relates to hostility toward government expense generally; however, the political implications are the same. Apparently, publicly financed abortion is, like food stamps, an unpopular

government expense." *Commonweal* reports the findings of a poll of 9,000 voters leaving voting places in November 1978. Only 44 percent of Democrats and 37 percent of Republicans favored government funding for abortion; see *Commonweal* 106 (2 February 1979): 36. Finally, according to a public opinion poll conducted by Yankelovich, Skelly, and White and commissioned by *Time,* 58 percent of those polled believe that government funds should not be used to finance elective abortions for the poor. This was so despite the finding that 64 percent believe that, regardless of morality, a woman should be legally free to have an abortion if she wants one (*Time,* 21 November 1977, 115).

3. *Roe v . Wade,* 410 U.S. 113, 163 (1973); "Constitutional Aspects of the Right to Limit Childbearing," A Report of the United States Commission on Civil Rights, April 1975, Appendix I, paragraph 8, p. 103; see also "The Impact of the Hyde Amendment on Medically Necessary Abortions," a report of the American Civil Liberties Union, October 1978, 25–30.

4. ACLU, "The Impact of the Hyde Amendment," 9–10.

5. Janet Benshoof and Judith Levin, "Current Legal Issues in Abortion Litigation," paper prepared for discussion at the Biennial Conference of the American Civil Liberties Union, Mount Vernon College, Washington, D.C., June 16–19, 1979, p. 14.

6. Note that prochoice forces use the constitutionalist doctrines of separation of powers and of checks and balances to their advantage with respect to the branches of the national government; they favor dispersal rather than concentration of power. The opposite is true, however, with respect to federalism and separation of powers between the national government and the states. Here prochoice advocates prefer centralization to decentralization and favor imposition, through Supreme Court decisions, of a national abortion policy upon the states—despite rights left to the states, in *Roe v. Wade,* to regulate abortion in the second and third trimesters. This pattern is especially evident in *Planned Parenthood v. Danforth* (1976) and in *Colautti v. Franklin* (1979). See also the comments by John T. Noonan in *A Private Choice: Abortion in America in the Seventies* (New York: Free Press, 1979), 2–3.

7. The Court summarized the proabortion case as follows: "The principal thrust of appellant's attack on the Texas statutes is that they improperly invade a right, said to be possessed by the pregnant woman, to choose to terminate her pregnancy. Appellant would discover this right in the concept of personal 'liberty' embodied in the Fourteenth Amendment's Due Process Clause; or in personal, marital, familial, and sexual privacy said to be protected by the Bill of Rights or its penumbras . . . ; or among those rights reserved to the people by the Ninth Amendment" (410 U.S. 113, 129 [1973]).

8. Id. at 152–56.

9. "If the right of privacy means anything, it is the right of the individual, married or single, to be free from unwarranted governmental intrusion into mat-

ters so fundamentally affecting a person as the decision whether to bear or beget a child" (*Eisenstadt v. Baird*, 405 U.S. 453 [1972]); the quote from *Wade* is from 410 U.S. 113, 153 (1973).

10. J. Rehnquist, dissenting, 410 U.S. 113, 172 (1973).

11. The Court states: "The pregnant woman cannot be isolated in her privacy. She carries an embryo and, later, a fetus, if one accepts the medical definitions of the developing young in the human uterus. . . . The situation therefore is inherently different from marital intimacy, or bedroom possession of obscene material, or marriage, or procreation, or education, with which *Eisenstadt, Griswold, Stanley, Loving, Skinner, Pierce,* and *Meyer* were respectively concerned. As we have intimated above, it is reasonable and appropriate for a State to decide that at some point in time another interest, that of health of the mother or that of potential human life, becomes significantly involved. The woman's privacy is no longer sole and any right of privacy she possesses must be measured accordingly" (id. at 159).

12. Id. at 154. I have suggested elsewhere that, although the extension of privacy rights to the abortion issue seems strained, there are at least two definitions or denotations of privacy which are at least partly related to decisions regarding abortion: (1) zonal privacy demarcating a public and private sphere; and (2) informational privacy, which concerns the kinds of information (e.g., details of one's personal life) made public in the course of prosecuting in court a certain action (e.g., abortion) regarded as criminal or illegal. See "Some Legal Aspects of Abortion in the United States," paper prepared for a National Endowment for the Humanities Seminar on Constitutionalism, Princeton University, April 1979, 12–15.

13. Sidney Callahan, "The Court and a Conflict of Principles," *The Hastings Center Report* 7 (August 1977): 7.

14. See section 8 of the Court's opinion in *Roe v. Wade.*

15. Isaiah Berlin, "Two Concepts of Liberty," *Four Essays on Liberty* (New York: Oxford University Press, 1969).

16. The Court rejected this argument in *Wade:* "Appellant and some *amici* argue that the woman's right is absolute and that she is entitled to terminate her pregnancy at whatever time, in whatever way, and for whatever reason she alone chooses. With this we do not agree. . . . The Court's decisions recognizing a right of privacy . . . acknowledge that some state regulation in areas protected by that right is appropriate. As noted above, a State may properly assert important interests in safeguarding health, in maintaining medical standards, and in protecting potential life. At some point in pregnancy, these respective interests become sufficiently compelling to sustain regulation of the factors that govern the abortion decision. The privacy right involved, therefore, cannot be said to be absolute. In fact, it is not clear to us that the claim asserted by some *amici* that one has an unlimited right to do with one's body as one pleases bears a close relationship to the right of privacy previ-

ously articulated in the Court's decisions. The Court has refused to recognize an unlimited right of this kind in the past" (410 U.S. 113, 153–54 [1973]).

17. John Locke, *Second Treatise,* chapt. 9, section 123.

18. C. B. Macpherson, *The Theory of Possessive Individualism* (New York: Oxford University Press, 1962), 260.

19. Sidney Callahan, "Conflict of Principles," 7.

20. The former might be associated with Herbert Spencer, to some extent with Locke and J. S. Mill, and in this country with the late nineteenth-century ideology of Social Darwinism, while spokesmen for the latter would be T. H. Green and L. T. Hobhouse. For a general discussion of these two strands in liberal political thought in America, see Dorothy James, *Outside, Looking In: A Critique of American Policies and Institutions, Left and Right* (New York: Harper and Row, 1972), 1–14.

21. For a general review of liberal doctrines of equality, see Mary C. Segers, "Equality in Contemporary Political Thought: An Examination and an Assessment," *Administration and Society* 10 (February 1979): 409–36.

22. James C. Mohr, *Abortion in America* (New York: Oxford University Press, 1978), 255.

23. For a general critique of the principle of equality of opportunity, see John Schaar, "Equality of Opportunity, and Beyond," in *Nomos IX: Equality,* ed. J. R. Pennock and J . W. Chapman (New York: Atherton, 1967), 228–49. See also Jean Bethke Elshtain, "The Feminist Movement and the Question of Equality," *Polity* 7 (summer 1975): 452–77, for a discussion of the deficiencies of this principle as it relates to the women's movement.

24. For a more detailed explication of these points, see the contributions of Mary C. Segers and Robert G. Hoyt to the Symposium "Does the First Amendment Bar the Hyde Amendment?" *Christianity and Crisis* 39 (5 March 1979): 34–43.

25. Daniel Callahan, "Abortion: Some Ethical Issues," in *Abortion, Society, and the Law,* ed. David F. Walbert and J. Douglas Butler (Cleveland: Case Western Reserve University Press, 1973), 92.

26. Recall, for example, Socrates' argument concerning the laws in *The Crito* (Plato, *The Last Days of Socrates,* trans. Hugh Tredennick [Penguin Classics, 1969]), 28–39.

27. Mohr, *Abortion in America,* 262–63.

28. When asked whether it was morally wrong to have an abortion, 48 percent of those who responded to the Yankelovich survey said it was not morally wrong, while 44 percent said it was; on moral grounds women still oppose abortion, 47 percent to 44 percent. By contrast, a far larger majority of those polled (64 percent, including 58 percent of all Catholics) believed that, regardless of morality, a woman should be legally free to have an abortion if she wants one. Results of a Daniel Yankelovich survey as reported in *Time,* 21 November 1977, 115.

29. Daniel Callahan has expressed this well: "Although the contending sides in the abortion debate commonly ignore, or systematically deride, the essentially positive impulses lying behind their opponents' positions, the conflict is nonetheless best seen as the pitting of essentially valuable impulses against one another. The possibility of a society which did allow women the right and the freedom to control their own lives is a lofty goal. No less lofty is that of a society which, with no exceptions, treated all forms of human life as equally valuable. In the best of all possible worlds, it might be possible to reconcile these goals. In the real world, however, the first goal requires the right of abortion, and the second goal excludes that right. This, I believe, is a genuine and deep dilemma. That so few are willing to recognize the dilemma, or even to admit that any choice must be less than perfect, is the most disturbing element in the whole debate" ("Abortion: Some Ethical Issues," 101).

30. Ibid., 100–101.

[43]

Saving America's Souls: Operation Rescue's Crusade against Abortion

Faye Ginsburg

AT SIX O'CLOCK IN the morning on 28 November 1987, Randall Terry, a lanky, twenty-seven-year-old born-again Christian from upstate New York, led his first official "rescue," a blockade of an abortion clinic in Cherry Hill, New Jersey. Three hundred rescuers sealed off access to the building. As Terry describes it, "We sang, prayed, read psalms," and conducted a parachurch service "on the doorstep of hell for nearly eleven hours! No babies died. It was glorious, peaceful, and prayerful."[1] By the end of the day, 211 "mothers, fathers, grandmothers, grandfathers, and singles"[2] had been arrested, charged with trespassing, and released.

The event served as the trial demonstration of a militant anti-abortion organization, Operation Rescue, composed of fundamentalist and evangelical Christians. The group was formally established in the spring of 1988 by Randall Terry and quickly escalated its activities. By 1989, Operation Rescue had gained a prominent, if notorious, reputation, even among fellow travelers in the pro-life movement. By 1990, according to the group's figures, there had been over thirty-five thousand arrests, while sixteen thousand individuals had risked arrest in what they call "rescues."[3] Unlike those allied with other anti-

SOURCE: From Martin E. Marty and R. Scott Appleby, eds., *Fundamentalisms and the State: Remaking Polities, Economies, and Militance.* Copyright © 1993 by The University of Chicago Press. Reprinted by permission of The University of Chicago Press, Faye Ginsburg, Martin E. Marty, and R. Scott Appleby.

abortion groups, which hold regular meetings, call upon political representatives, and in other ways operate as ongoing arenas of action, Operation Rescue relies on the existing infrastructure of independent fundamentalist churches and conservative Roman Catholic congregations and organizations as its base. For most members beyond the leadership, sporadic participation in "rescue" demonstrations constitutes the central activity. Focusing organizational energy into "rescues" takes maximum advantage of the publicity generated by dramatic confrontation.

The blockades carried out by Operation Rescue have been described variously as acts of "biblical obedience," civil disobedience, harassment, and terrorism, and even as a form of racketeering and antitrust action. The distinct positions represented by these terms suggest the complex and often ironic impact of this group.

Whatever the judgment of a particular observer, however, Operation Rescue's political tactics and philosophy distinguish it in two ways. First, it is the most confrontational and right-wing of the contemporary anti-abortion groups. Contrary to stereotypes that portray right-to-life activists as homogeneous and puritanical, a remnant of Victorian mores and family forms, the pro-life cause has generally tolerated a spectrum of practice, belief, and lifestyle through an overall commitment to moderation and single-issue politics. However, Operation Rescue's scorn for civil political process, its uncompromising interventionist tactics, and its absolutist Christian ideology have strained the alliances in the movement. For a decade after the 1973 *Roe v. Wade* decision legalizing abortion, right-to-life activism tended to take a civil approach, attempting to influence political action by working within the legislative and electoral systems. Since 1983, radical elements in the pro-life movement— from the Pro-Life Action League of ex-Benedictine monk Joseph Scheidler (whose work influenced Randall Terry) to individuals responsible for incidents of bombing and arson at abortion clinics—have become increasingly active and more visible than the moderate mainstream represented by the National Right to Life Committee. By the end of the 1980s, Operation Rescue had become the umbrella sheltering the more extreme activists.

As a second distinction, Operation Rescue is the first pro-life group not only to draw large numbers of conservative Protestants into ongoing, organized anti-abortion activity, but also to join them in action with conservative Roman Catholics. Terry himself has been heavily influenced by the teachings of the late evangelical Protestant author Francis Schaeffer, who viewed legal abortion as the epitome of twentieth-century decadence.[4] In his book, *A Christian Manifesto,* published in 1981, Schaeffer recommended civil disobedience in opposition to abortion as a way for evangelicals to "challenge the entire legitimacy of the secular modern state, withholding allegiance until the nation returns to its religious roots in matters like public prayer and religious education."[5] It is not surprising, then, that Terry judged an event like Cherry Hill as a turning point not only because of its impact on abortion politics but also because of the response it generated in the Christian community.[6] In this view, opposition to abortion is not the end so much as the means to a larger goal of returning America to "traditional Christian values." Terry has made this point with a combination of pastoral, industrial, religious, and military metaphors. "God is using us to separate sheep from goats . . . the wheat from the chaff," he writes. "There are a lot of people who believe this is going to be the seedbed of revival in the church, the locomotive to bring reformation in our culture. When the Lord put the vision in my heart, it was not just to rescue babies and mothers but to rescue the country. This is the first domino to fall."[7]

Operation Rescue has catalyzed fundamentalist and evangelical participation in political action that began in America in the mid-1970s, bringing thousands of conservative Christians into the anti-abortion movement and transforming them in the process. In addition to expanding the revival of fundamentalist and evangelical social action, Operation Rescue has had a number of ironic consequences. For example, it has unintentionally served as one stimulus for reinvigorating the organization and focus of the pro-choice movement. It has also introduced a new element of dissension within the right-to-life movement, pushing activism in a more confrontational and militant direction. Like an impatient and unruly youngster (only "born" in 1988), Operation Rescue has disturbed the more settled, mature, and moderate anti-abortion veterans who have been organizing for twenty years.

The Impact of Operation Rescue

The Wichita siege has given Operation Rescue a new sense of power. Although the group did not succeed in closing down any of the clinics it attacked, Operation Rescue's harassment of administrators, doctors, patients, and local peacekeeping forces has been such that the *idea* of an Operation Rescue blockade coming to a clinic in a small city now has the capacity to cause considerable panic. Clearly, Wichita put Operation Rescue back in the public eye, although there is no clear evidence that public opinion turned in its direction. . . . Certainly the position of the administration is contested by many federal judges, not only because of Operation Rescue's flagrant disregard of the law but also because of the tactics it uses, such as flooding the judge's chambers and prosecutor's office with protest calls.

Perhaps the most important effect of the 1991 blockades (now called the "Summer of Mercy" by Operation Rescue) has been financial. (Many fines incurred during the arrests in Wichita were dropped. Final legal resolution awaits the rulings of the Supreme Court for 1991–92.) According to those who have been closely monitoring the group, checks totaling approximately $150,000 with a memo line for Operation Rescue were deposited every day of the three-week siege in the bank accounts of other pro-life groups, thus circumventing the fines on Operation Rescue's accounts. As of fall 1991, it appears that the money is being translated into support for more demonstrations. In a letter to supporters dated 6 September 1991, the agenda for the coming year included: National Days of Rescue IV, scheduled for the week of 17 November and meant to encompass fifty to sixty cities; the Capitol Rescue, to be held 20–22 January 1992 in Washington, D.C.; and rescue events to coincide with the Democratic National Convention in New York City (13–16 July) and the Republican National Convention in Houston (17–20 August). The letter ends with a plea for "as large a gift as you possibly can [make] to help in the upcoming events."[8] Increased money collected in ways that circumvent fines could take on greater significance should *Roe v. Wade* be overturned by the now exceedingly conservative Supreme Court. In that case, the battle for abortion rights could be turned back to individual states and support for state-by-state lobbying could be crucial.

It is hard to judge whether the events in Wichita have actually mobilized new recruits sufficiently to turn around the decline in support that had occurred by 1990. In a letter to supporters written in the spring of 1990, Terry acknowledged the movement's decline. "We are in a lull. The number of rescues and the number of rescuers has decreased. Why? Rescuers are tired and battle-weary. The cost in many areas has gone up."[9]

Not every activist has the general personal commitment of a zealot like Randall Terry or his team members. Grass-roots participants appeared to be disillusioned on the basis of their own experiences. Orin Cooper, president of the Chicago chapter of Operation Rescue, commented, "People found out that when you start going back to court and losing work, it is quite heavy on the budget."[10] It appears that injunctions have hampered demonstrations, and holding people personally liable has tested even the most dedicated. As an indication of the decline in support, an effort for a 1990 Mother's Day rally in Chicago drew one hundred people and resulted in twenty-six arrests; in 1989 there were fifteen hundred people and two hundred arrests.[11] According to Operation Rescue's figures, there was an average of eighty participants in ten rescues reported for spring and summer of 1991.[12]

In a September 1991 letter to supporters, Reverend Keith Tucci seemed to be declaring a reversal of this decline. "There is no doubt that the Summer of Mercy has sparked new and fresh passion and commitment into the pro-life movement. . . . The rescue movement is stronger than ever, and we cannot be stopped by the best efforts of Planned Parenthood, the N.O.W., the A.C.L.U., and various and sundry tyrannical judges."[13] Terry claims that Operation Rescue has had a much greater impact than the moderate groups. (Terry seems somewhat preoccupied with his place in history.)[14] "The pro-life movement has failed to learn the lessons of history, which show how the labor movement, the civil rights movement, Vietnam protest, and gay liberation all occurred because a group of people created social tension," he has argued.[15]

Terry is correct in his assessment that his movement brought the right-to-life cause renewed public attention. However, unlike the social movements he claims as models, Operation Rescue's actions often decrease public support for the pro-life cause. One unintended result of Operation Rescue's prominence has been the mobilization of a long quiescent opposition to the anti-abortion movement. But it is not only pro-choice activists who disagree with Operation Rescue. A second unintended consequence was the divisions that the direct action movements introduced into the ranks of Christians concerned about abortion's legality. Christians from various quarters expressed ambivalence about the group's ongoing active engagement with secular political processes and especially their intentional breaking of the law. While Jerry Falwell, Pat Robertson, and Charles Colson argued that Operation Rescue's tactics are permissible, other prominent Christian leaders, both liberal and conservative, argued that rescuers take too lightly the scriptural mandate to obey civil authorities (Romans 13:10–5, 1 Peter 2:13–15).[16] Terry retorted in true fundamentalist fashion by invoking Proverbs 24:11, which he has taken as his literal mission: "Rescue those who are unjustly sentenced to death; don't stand back and let them die." Some liberal theologians disagree, saying that such writings are not meant to be commands, "but inductive generalizations about wisdom in this life."[17] Taking a conservative position, former president of the Southern Baptist Convention Charles Stanley attempted to distance himself and the Southern Baptists he represented from Terry's biblical readings. While he agreed that abortion is an "abomination before God," Stanley contended that Operation Rescue's approach does not meet the biblical criteria for civil disobedience. In a treatise issued in response to Terry's request for an endorsement during the "siege of Atlanta," Stanley wrote that such actions are justified only when the state "requires an act which is contrary to God's Word" or "prohibits an act which is consistent with God's Word." Stanley also describes women as "free moral agents responsible before Almighty God for their actions, including the exercise [sic] of the rights of their innocent, unborn child."[18] Terry responded:

> In order to obey many of these scriptures, we will have to leave the comfort and safety of our church pews. We are going to have to get our hands dirty and be *active* in society. . . . If Christians stay cloistered in their little groups, it's easy to

keep unstained by the world. But when we go to the trenches of this life, when we reach out to help the unlovely, we run the risk of being defiled. Involving yourself in society rather than abandoning it, presents a far greater challenge to stay pure.[19]

It may seem paradoxical that right-to-life militants, who hope to repeal the "legislated social change" of the 1960s, consider the civil rights movement as a model for their activism. "In many, many ways, the rescue really is like the civil rights movement," Terry has said. "This is a civil rights movement, seeking to restore the civil rights of children, the right to life."[20] Indeed, Operation Rescue mirrors a certain consistency in the style of American social movements, regardless of their position on the ideological spectrum. Commenting on the conditions under which extremism has emerged in American social life, historian Thomas Rose has observed that "violence is a political resource when the bargaining process provides no other alternatives, or at least when some groups perceive no other alternatives. Political violence is an intelligible pattern of interaction that exists in America, but we refuse to understand and confront it as integral to our life."[21] Operation Rescue's resort to militant action may indeed be understood as a strategy to galvanize the larger anti-abortion movement stymied on the mainstream political level by the mid-1980s.

Yet it is this question of violence in Operation Rescue's tactics and strategies that has created the greatest dissension among right-to-life activists. Operation Rescue is not philosophically opposed to the use of violence, as many other pro-life groups, including many direct actionists are.[22] The influential NRLC has maintained its policy of silence on Operation Rescue's activities, but makes clear its differences with the group by underscoring the motives for its own commitment to legal and nonviolent action. "We will want people to obey the new abortion law we are working for, so it is important we let the nation know we are responsible people ourselves," Willke has said. "We will not win with violence. That is the tactic of the abortionist."[23] Indeed, the moderate center of the pro-life movement has tended in public pronouncements to deny the legitimacy of violence. Yet the moderate center has also used, and benefited from, the "antics" of the direct actionists; invariably, the moderates' public exposure, credibility, and relative level of public approval have grown with the rise of Operation Rescue. According to this interpretation, just as the bombings and arsons of even more militant groups made Operation Rescue appear less radical than it otherwise might have appeared, so Operation Rescue's advocacy of radical and sometimes violent behavior lends legitimacy to the moderate right-to-life movement. By contrast, the moderates appear civil, flexible, and representative.[24]

However, many right-to-life activists are skeptical that outsiders can make such fine distinctions, especially given the way right-to-lifers are represented by the secular media. Television and the press in general give disproportionate attention to dramatic political confrontation with little concern for distinctions between groups. News stories tend to conflate those who carry out controversial activities with the movement as a whole; and moderate activists are reluctant to discuss their differences for fear that divisions in the movement will work to the advantage of their opponents. It is not only that violence makes a good story and sells newspapers. Dave Andrusko, editor of the NRLC's newsletter, in an essay entitled "Zealots, Zanies, and Assorted Kooks: How the Major Media Interprets the Pro-Life Movement," writes that for the "media elite" "pro-lifers (and even more so pro-family people) are synonymous with repression, political and sexual. The buzz words practically leap off their typewriters: punitive, prudish, Victorian, rigid, repressed, hysterical, etc."[25] Andrusko is correct insofar as the profession of journalism is dominated by liberals who favor a pro-choice position.[26] Not surprisingly, the more extreme and reprehensible pro-life activities which paint the movement in the worst light, from their perspective, receive the most coverage. Taking advantage of the situation, Operation Rescue has managed to magnify the impact of their minority position in the right to life movement through dramatic, media oriented demonstrations.

Part of Terry's importance thus has to do with his savvy management of image and performance, and his relatively sophisticated understanding of the means by which he can manipulate the media to do his work: "If we can get the press there, we don't need to send out a press release."[27] While the media attention has made people aware of Operation Rescue and catalyzed previously quiescent pro-life sympathizers to action, it is unlikely that the publicity has altered anyone's opinion on abortion, given the immobility of public opinion on this issue.[28] In fact former NRLC president Willke argued that Operation Rescue's publicity has had a negative impact because it is equated with the whole pro-life movement. He is concerned with what ethicists call the logic of "moral calculus": which strategy will save more lives? He draws a different conclusion regarding publicity than does Terry. "In the sixties, the media were behind the civil rights movement. They are not behind the pro-life movement. They portray those demonstrators as a bunch of kooks, religious fanatics." The sit-ins may stop a few abortions, "but if it postpones the reversal of *Roe v. Wade* for just one day by turning people off to the cause, that's 4,000 babies."[29]

In the view of most pro-life moderates, Operation Rescue has undercut one of the larger objectives of the right-to-life movement: to gain credibility for the pro-life position with the American people in order to gain support for a constitutional amendment banning abortion. And as long as public opinion is understood to be shaped by and reflected in the print and electronic media, pro-life activists of all stripes believe that they should pitch their efforts toward gaining favorable coverage. The jury is still out regarding public opinion outside the movement, but evidence suggests that Operation Rescue mobilized its opposition and generated hostility from those uninvolved in the issue. In a recent poll by Terry's hometown newspaper, 70 percent of county residents said they disapproved of Operation Rescue's demonstrating near abortion clinics, and 90 percent disapproved of the organization's blocking or entering the clinics illegally. Sixty-three percent of those polled had a positive impression of the pro-choice movement, while only 37 percent were favorably impressed with the pro-life movement. However, while the Southern Tier clinic of Binghamton is still in business after enduring multiple rescues, local doctors no longer provide abortions in the counties' two clinics. Some doctors, on rare occasion or in cases of therapeutic diagnosis, will do abortions in local hospitals.[30]

In the pro-choice camp, there has been in the last three years a resurgence in organizing formerly complacent activists. The most direct impact has been the multiple lawsuits . . . , the product of sophisticated and strategic organizing on the part of feminist and pro-choice leaders against Operation Rescue. At the grassroots level, it is difficult to determine exactly what role Operation Rescue has played in that revitalization, since its period of greatest visibility has coincided with new conservative U.S. Supreme Court appointments. These developments, and especially the *Webster* decision, have also helped rouse a slumbering pro-choice movement, as was clear in the 1989 March for Women's Lives in Washington, D.C. One recently mobilized activist in her twenties explained that the *Webster* decision inspired her commitment. "I always figured someone else would fight the battle. But the *Webster* decision was such an affront. Before, I didn't pay much attention to Randy Terry. He was just some jerk chaining himself to things."[31] Of course, politically it is advantageous to paint the opposition in the darkest possible colors. As a strategist recently pointed out in a discussion of post-*Webster* pro-choice organizing, "From a tactical standpoint, the movement's most extreme opponents, like Operation Rescue, are its strongest allies."[32]

From a purely financial point of view, this seems to be the case. In the first three months of 1989, the National Abortion Rights Action League (NARAL) raised $300,000, ending the quarter with $347,000 in the bank; during that same three months, the NRLC raised $7,000, ending the quarter with $51,000 in the bank.[33] The ranks and annual budget of the National Organization for Women, which brought several of the legal suits against Operation Rescue, nearly doubled from 1988 to 1989.[34]

While the impact of Operation Rescue on the pro-choice and pro-life movements is important, to analyze the group only within the framework of the abortion debate is to misunderstand its significance. It is intent on mobilizing people not just to stop abortion but to impose on American society at large a conservative Christian culture. Until 1988, most direct action militants were Catholic. Terry has succeeded in catalyzing the direct participation of thousands of evangelicals and fundamentalists in anti-abortion politics who had never before been involved in political action. In his recruiting pitch, Terry addresses this "late arrival" of evangelicals to right-to-life activity with the quip, "There are no heroes in this movement; we are all fifteen years too late."[35] Charging Christians with apathy and their need to repent for the neglect of the abortion issue, he compares them to Christians who did not resist the Nazis in Germany during the Holocaust. He has managed to mobilize evangelical Christians through direct appeal, the mass media, and churches.[36] Some estimate that the pro-life movement is now anywhere from one-third to two-thirds evangelical-fundamentalist. Willke (a Catholic) described it as "an awakening from its slumber of literally millions of deeply committed Protestant folk. . . . This is no longer a Catholic movement. This is very much ecumenical [almost] to the point of being a Protestant Christian Movement."[37] Terry did not create the fundamentalist interest so much as "he caught the wave of evangelical involvement just as it began to crest."[38]

Garry Wills, in a provocative essay on Operation Rescue, suggests that these newly mobilized Christians represent a distinct group on America's religious and political landscape. They are not interested in the eschatological disputes that dominated fundamentalism in a prior generation but in issues that seem to shape their immediate world. All the key leaders and many of the rescuers are, like Terry, in their thirties, with a particular outlook that marks them as a distinct generation in the emergent world of conservative Christian activism in America. Many came of age during the mobilization of the Christian Right in the 1970s and accept that movement as a model of political action. As Wills notes:

> While paying their respect to elders who helped evangelicals get engaged in politics—to Jerry Falwell or Pat Robertson—the Operation Rescue leaders are also gently dismissive of them as armchair warriors, people resting on their laurels and not taking the heat of today's battle. . . . Terry's people talk of the televangelists as tied down to their assets, like bishops in their dioceses. They see themselves as roving carriers of a burning message . . . and the ties they form with other opponents of abortion speed the process, already noticed by sociologists, whereby evangelism has been losing its hostility to Jews, Catholics, blacks and Hispanics.[39]

Others have explored the generational location of Operation Rescue from the perspective of gender and class. Noting that 56 percent of arrested activists are men and half of Operation Rescue's active participants are in their twenties and thirties, author Susan Faludi sketches a profile of these fundamentalist men of the "late baby-boom generation" as sociological mirrors of Randall Terry, with an economic grudge against "careerist" women. They "not only missed the political engagement of the sixties but were cheated out of that era's affluent bounty," she observes. "They are downwardly mobile sons, condemned by the eighties economy to earning less than their fathers, unable to buy homes or support families. . . . These are men who are losing ground and at the same time see women gaining it."[40]

Terry has transformed this marginality into a virtue; his "rescuers" are the righteous remnant, opposed not only to unbelievers but also to many pastors he describes as "pillars of Jell-O." They "seek to upset no one, to step on no toes. . . . With an eye for the offering plate or having the biggest church in town, many seek to protect their own welfare and glory, rather than the welfare and glory of God's Kingdom."[41] Acting against what they see as the tepid Christianity of the mainstream, rescuers hope to "defeat the abortion holocaust, restore religious and civil liberties to individuals, bring justice to our judicial system, see common decency return, and the godless, hedonistic, sexually perverted mindset of today pushed back into the closet—and hopefully back to hell where it came from."[42]

Recriminalizing abortion is only the first domino to fall in the campaign to reverse the effects of the liberal hegemony of the 1960s and 1970s.

> The future of America . . . will depend . . . in part upon the rescue movement. If we do not bring this nation through rescues, through upheavals, through repentance, then America is not going to make it. We are launching a whole political wing. We have thousands of people who have risked their freedom, had their arms broken. For them to work a precinct to get a pro-life official elected is a piece of cake. We have an *army* of people. . . . Child killing will fall, child pornography and pornography will follow, euthanasia, infanticide—we'll totally reform the public education system . . . we'll take back the culture.[43]

Dramatic demonstrations bring these issues to the public by gaining media attention, but perhaps they are most significant for the participants themselves. Political performances reinforce for activists the righteousness of their own cause. Carrying a picket or blockading a doorway is a radicalizing event for the thousands of conservative Christians who follow Terry's lead. "Being dragged by the neck to a paddy wagon is an epiphany."[44]

Operation Rescue and Contemporary Fundamentalism

Whatever face Operation Rescue presents to the outside, it is clear from the writings and speeches of its founder and leader, Randall Terry, that he and those inspired by him see it as a vehicle for Christian social action. Terry puts no exclusive labels on Operation Rescue. His home church is an independent ministry; his training was nondenominational; he seems uninterested in discussing his theological position on the millennium. These characteristics, coupled with his embrace of Catholics and even a few non-Christians in the movement, and his emphasis on political involvement (including law breaking) are a break with the long-standing emphasis on separatism that has characterized American fundamentalism for nearly half a century.

However, if one looks at Operation Rescue historically, one sees parallels to the situation of seventy years ago when fundamentalism first emerged as a powerful presence on the American landscape.[45] Contemporary struggles over abortion, school prayer, and pornography draw fundamentalists (and others) into political battles in much the same way that opposition to the teaching of evolution in the schools mobilized fundamentalist reformers in the early part of the century. The militantly antimodernist fundamentalists of the 1920s had multiple cultural, theological, and organizational roots, but they shared a developing premillennial theology that recommended separation from the world.[46] Nonetheless, fundamentalists formed an active social movement opposed to both the increasing secularization of American life and the liberalizing trends in most Christian denominations. When the activists of the 1920s failed to halt the "modernizing" of American Protestantism and when the press and public reaction following the Scopes trial in 1925 made clear that fundamentalists were increasingly marginal to American culture, the fundamentalists retreated from active engagement in both secular arenas and mainline religion in order to develop their own networks of exclusive institutions.[47] Although there were some calls to activism in the 1940s and 1950s from both the right and the left, the central activity and strategy of fundamentalism for five decades was personal witnessing.[48]

By the 1970s, the expanding organizational structures and the increasing numbers of mainstream middle-class Americans attracted to evangelical Christianity had given fundamentalist activists the infrastructure, intellectual framework, social base, and membership to carry out successful political action. For some, crossing the boundary into the corrupt world undermined the legitimacy of people like Falwell and his organization, the Moral Majority.[49] Operation Rescue has gone much farther than Falwell in breaking the boundary of separation between Christian activists and the world. Fundamentalists who are strict about separatism in particular take Terry to task for making alliances and contact with those outside the group—including Catholics and Jews. Terry justifies this action in biblical terms: "We must serve fellow Christians in whatever way their need requires. But our duty does not stop there. The Lord commands His disciple to serve those *outside* the faith; those who might not value or appreciate our help—or those who might even despise it."[50]

Clearly, it is a mistake to think this movement is simply about abortion. Fundamentalist militance in America has never confined itself to a single issue, and Operation Rescue is the latest incarnation of the fundamentalist impulse to impose its religious culture on others. For "rescuers," fighting abortion is simply a first step in reversing America's "moral decline," much as opposition to the teaching of evolution was considered a way to fight secularization in the 1920s. For these new Christian soldiers, the boundaries of separation that restrained fundamentalist activism for half a century are virtually gone.

In fact, despite Terry's frequent references to the Bible and the ideological and theological basis of the movement in the writings of Francis Schaeffer, there has been a conscious attempt to avoid sectarianism within this activist sect. Operation Rescue has formed an identity rooted in a shared "orthopraxis" more than a shared "orthodoxy."[51] The fact that Roman Catholics and even Jews have joined with conservative Protestant participants—an alliance enabled by the low level of structural organization of the movement itself—has been crucial to the success of the rescues. As a result there is greater emphasis on ritual action than on dogmatic interpretation of the action; the rescues themselves are highly organized and ritualistic, although the ideology and the organizational structure are not. Participants share a sense of moral outrage at abortion, coupled with the conviction that they are together opposing the most brutal results of modern American secularization. There is no evidence to date that Operation Rescue is, as fundamentalist protest movements have been elsewhere in the world, a vehicle for conversion to a specific denominational or sectarian orientation. The point is not to render members more Christian but to render society more fundamentalist, in the larger Judeo-Christian sense. This activist, open fundamentalist movement is indeed a new hybrid on the religious horizon.

For this coalition of fundamentalist and conservative Christians and Catholics, taking action in the "real world" has had real world consequences. In the pluralist setting of America, displaying contempt for the rights of others and the legal system—even in the name of God—carries stiff penalties. However, for a movement that took a martyred and militant Christ, suffering at the hands of the Romans, as a primary image, the punitive actions of the state have been only confirmation of its righteousness.

Whether Operation Rescue manages to surmount the legal obstacles imposed on it and continue its blockades or whether it transforms itself into Terry's Christian Defense Council (with an agenda that, ironically, resembles that of the lobbyists and letter writers he disdains), there is no question that the movement has had a discernible impact. Through an organization committed to direct action, Randall Terry has revived long-term right-to-life loyalists who had become discouraged at the minimal gains of fifteen years of legislative efforts. While he has strengthened the pro-life cause by delivering thousands of new activists, he has also divided the movement because of his law-breaking tactics and the controversial media coverage he has attracted, which has seriously altered the public image of right-to-lifers in the late 1980s and early 1990s. Perhaps of greatest significance, he has offered a new generation of the ever-increasing number of young evangelical Christians in America an incontrovertible experience of militant fundamentalist social action. What the consequences of this transformation will be are difficult to predict. What *is* clear is that the future envisioned by these warriors, now rearming themselves with secular political knowledge, is nothing short of the "rescue" of a nation on fundamentalist Christian terms.

Notes

1. Randall A. Terry, *Operation Rescue* (Springdale, Pa.: Whitaker House, 1988), 24.

2. Ibid. Interestingly, over 25 percent of those arrested were single and in their thirties. Ann Baker, personal communication.

3. Randy Frame, "Rescue Theology," *Christianity Today,* 17 November 1989, 46–48. Many activists have been arrested multiple times, so arrest numbers are larger than the number of protesters.

4. In an interview with Garry Wills ("Evangels of Abortion," *New York Review of Books,* 15 June 1989, 15–21) Randall Terry told Wills, "You have to read Schaeffer's *Christian Manifesto* if you want to understand Operation Rescue," 15, and that he considers Schaeffer "the greatest modern Christian philosopher," 18.

   According to Wills, in his studies at Elim Bible Institute, a homiletics teacher assigned three of Schaeffer's books and screened the film "What Ever Happened to the Human Race?" made in 1979 by Schaeffer with evangelical doctor C. Everett Koop, who later served the Reagan administration as surgeon general. The film, which analyzes abortion as a symptom of the decline of Western civilization, "had a big impact on Terry," 18.

5. Wills, "Evangels of Abortion," 15.

6. Terry, *Operation Rescue,* 25.

7. This quote is from Julie Gustafson's videotaped interview with Randall Terry in Operation Rescue's Binghamton offices, 27 October 1988.

8. Keith Tucci, letter to supporters from Operation Rescue, 6 September 1991, Somerville, S.C.

9. Quoted in Tamara Lewin, "With Thin Staff and Thick Debt, Anti-Abortion Group Faces Struggle," *New York Times,* 11 June 1990.

10. Barbara Brotman, "Abortion Opponents Regroup," *Chicago Tribune,* 20 May 1990, 9.

11. *Rescue Report,* June 1990, Operation Rescue.

12. "National Rescue Recap," *Operation Rescue National Rescuer,* August–September 1991, 5.

13. Tucci letter.

14. When the writer, Francis Wilkinson, in his 1989 interview, "The Gospel according to Randall Terry," published in *Rolling Stone* (October 5), queried Terry about the comparisons made between him and Martin Luther King, Terry replied that he discourages it. "Moments later, however, Terry has the temerity to explain that his proper place will be a matter determined by history. 'The applause or contempt of contemporaries means very little,' he adds with a flourish" (p. 92).

15. Quoted in Lyn Cryderman, "A Movement Divided," *Christianity Today,* 12 August 1988, 48.

16. Such activities were also denounced by right-wing Christian reconstructionists because they are in violation of civil law, and because they "violate the Christian presupposition that change comes only through God's power" [Nancy Ammerman, *Bible Believers: Fundamentalists in the Modern World* (New Brunswick, N.J.: Rutgers University Press, 1987), 80]. See also Randy Frame, "Atlanta Gets Tough," *Christianity Today,* 4 November 1988, 35.

17. David Coffin, director of the Berea Study Center, quoted in interview with Randy Frame, "Rescue Theology," *Christianity Today,* 17 November 1989, 48.

18. These quotes are from a two-page statement released by the staff of Stanley's church, the First Baptist Church, the largest congregation in Atlanta after Terry sought Stanley's endorsement during Operation Rescue demonstrations in Atlanta. The treatise is entitled "A Biblical Perspective on Civil Disobedience." See Randy Frame, "Atlanta Gets Tough," 35.

19. "By misinterpreting 2 Corinthians 6:17 ['Therefore come out from their . . . midst and be separate'] many have neglected their God-given commands to influence society and serve their fellow man. . . . When salt [the Christian influence] stops preserving a nation, that society is going to deteriorate. There's no way around it." Terry, *Operation Rescue,* 51.

20. Quote from videotaped interview with Julie Gustafson in the Operation Rescue offices, Binghamton, N.Y., 27 October 1988.

21. Thomas Rose, "How Violence Occurs: A Theory and Review of the Literature," in *Violence in America,* ed. Thomas Rose (New York: Vintage Books, 1969), 30.

22. For an interesting discussion of right-to-life positions on this issue, see Randy Frame, "Rescue Theology."

23. NRLC president Jack Willke, quoted in Lyn Cryderman, "A Movement Divided," *Christianity Today,* 12 August 1988, 49.

24. These points are raised by Dallas A. Blanchard and Terry J. Prewitt regarding abortion bombers in *Religious Violence and Abortion: The Gideon Project* (Gainesville: University Press of Florida, 1993), 266 and 394.

25. Dave Andrusko, "Zealots, Zanies, and Assorted Kooks: How the Main Media Interprets the Pro-Life Movement," in *The Pro-Life Movement: A Handbook for the 1980s,* ed. Dave Andrusko (Harrison, N.Y.: Life Cycle Press).

26. See Robert S. Lichter and Stanley Rothman, "The Media Elite," *Public Opinion* 96 (1981): 117–25.

27. Terry, from taped interview with Julie Gustafson.

28. On the bases of analyses by the National Opinion Research Center and Gallup Polls between 1973 and 1985, it appears that the level of approval for legalized abortion has remained stable since 1973. Approximately 23 percent believe that abortion should be legal in all cases, while 19 to 22 percent believe it should be illegal. The remainder believe it should be legal in some cases, such as rape, incest, or endangerment to a woman's life. For further analyses of these data, see Daniel Granberg, "The Abortion Issue in the 1984 Elections," *Family Planning Perspectives* 19, no. 2: 59–62.

29. Willke, quoted in Lyn Cryderman, "A Movement Divided."

30. Susan Church, "Poll Shows Terry's Tactics Disliked," *Binghamton Press & Sun Bulletin,* 20 November 1989, 1.

31. Ibid.

32. Ibid.

33. "Anti-Abortion Group Lacks in Raising Funds," *New York Times,* 30 April 1990.

34. Jane Gross, "At NOW Convention, Goal Is Putting More Women in Office," *New York Times,* 1 July 1989, A12.

35. Quoted in Garry Wills, "Save the Babies," *Time,* 1 May 1989, 28.

36. One observer noted that a single speaking engagement before an evangelical congregation, with the endorsement of the pastor, can reap a busload of volunteers. Wilkinson, "The Gospel according to Randall Terry," 86.

37. Kim Lawton, "Can the Prolife Movement Succeed?" *Christianity Today,* 15 January 1988, 36.

38. Wills, "Evangels of Abortion," 21.

39. Ibid.

40. Susan Faludi, "Where Did Randy Go Wrong?" *Mother Jones,* November 1989, 25.

41. Terry, *Operation Rescue,* 172.

42. Ibid., 175.

43. Wilkinson, "The Gospel according to Randall Terry," 92.

44. Ibid.

45. Many scholars use broad understandings of fundamentalism as opposed to narrower ones that are based on definitive characteristics such as separatism and the theology of dispensational premillennialism. Among those who use the broader reading are Ammerman, *Bible Believers*; Steve Bruce, *The Rise and Fall of the New Christian Right* (New York: Oxford University Press, 1988); Susan Harding, "Casting Out the Fundamentalist Other: The Scopes Trial and the Modern Apotheosis," talk delivered at the Society for Cultural Anthropology annual meetings, May 1990; George M. Marsden, *Fundamentalism and American Culture* (New York: Oxford University Press, 1980); Martin Marty, "Fundamentalism as A-Social Phenomenon," *Bulletin of the American Academy of Arts and Sciences* 42, no. 2 (November 1988): 15–29. Ernest Sandeen, in his book *The Roots of Fundamentalism* (Chicago: University of Chicago Press, 1970), espouses the more specific definition of fundamentalism based on doctrinal differences.

46. Marsden, *Fundamentalism and American Culture*, 5.

47. Ibid., 186; Nancy Ammerman, "North American Protestant Fundamentalism," in *Fundamentalisms Observed* (Chicago: University of Chicago Press, 1991), 1–65.

48. According to Ammerman in her essay "North American Protestant Fundamentalism," by the 1950s the "choice facing the movement was between cultural relevance and cultural separation." In 1948, the evangelical leader Carl Henry argued in his influential book *Remaking the Modern Mind* that Christians should be socially and politically active in an effort to reestablish claims in a civilization dominated by secular humanism, while the quintessential separatist was the anticommunist right-wing crusader Carl McIntire (p. 58). Ammerman notes: "A few fundamentalists had joined the anticommunist crusades of the fifties, but most had remained relatively inactive in politics, preferring instead to put energy into the churches and institutions that made their view of the world possible. Evangelism and missions far outweighed social reform on their agendas" (p. 61).

49. Ibid.

50. Terry, *Operation Rescue*, 48.

51. I am indebted to Scott Appleby for this phrasing.

[44]

Text of Anonymous Letter Claiming Responsibility for Pensacola Clinic Bombings

Dear Editor:

So you want to know who bombed the 3 abortion clinics, huh?
I did.

Let me tell you why.

When I was stationed here in the waves, before I got married, I got pregnant. Everyone had told me that a fetus was just a little shapeless blob anyway, so I got an abortion. I was almost 6 months pregnant by then.

Later, after it was too late, a friend gave me some literature one day showing how the baby developed at different stages. I never realized that at that stage, a fetus is so much a baby that some of them have been born at that point and LIVED!

Well, you cannot imagine what that did to me, knowing that I had not just "had an unwanted intra-uterine growth "removed," [sic] but had KILLED MY BABY! It just about ruined my life. Even today, several years later, I lay awake at nights sometimes crying about it.

So maybe you can understand my reason for doing what I did.

It was not because of religious fanaticism . . . I don't even go to church.

It was because I have seen for myself what the psychological effects of an abortion can do to a woman, and I didn't want what happened to me to happen to anyone else.

I did not act alone. And if these clinics reopen, we will see that they are closed again.

Source: From the *Pensacola Journal,* 28 December 1984, and the *Pensacola News,* "Writer Makes Claim," 27 December 1984. Reprinted by permission.

Some will say that it is wrong to use violent means to put an end to the killing. Well, we used a lot of violence in World War II to stop the killing of the Jews.

It is a well-established principal [sic] of justice that force, even deadly force, is justified in order to save innocent lives if necessary. So, I do not feel that I have done anything wrong.

We will stop the slaughter of the innocents. We WILL put an end to the murder of babies. And we WILL prevent any more lives from being ruined.

Signed,
A Woman Who Knew What She Was Doing

[45]

Violence at Abortion Clinics: Clergy Response

[*Editor's note:* Concerned about intimidation from protestors at the Women's Center in Allentown, Pennsylvania—and fearful of violence—directors of that center contacted local clergy leaders to inquire whether there was help that could come from the religious community. In response to that request, the Rev. Timothy Downs of St. John's United Church of Christ, Allentown, called together a group to consider how the Christian community might respond to incidents of intimidation and the threat of violence. Rev. Downs and the editor of this volume drafted the following statement, then sought support from the judicatory heads of various Christian denominations. This statement was released at a press conference in November 1993 at Packer Memorial Church on the campus of Lehigh University in Bethlehem, Pennsylvania.]

Pastoral Letter Regarding Violence around the Issue of Abortion

In this season of growing violence around the issue of abortion, we wish to address this pastoral letter to all citizens of good will. We who are Christian affirm that there is no one view which represents the entire faith community on the issue of abortion. Instead, there is a diversity of convictions even among well-meaning and sincere people on these deeply felt issues.

This letter, however, is neither about abortion nor the debate which surrounds it. It is instead about the issue of how reasonable and faithful people join discussions and debates about their convictions. We respect people of conscience who resort to civil disobedience as an expression of their conscience so long as such disobedience is non-violent. At the same time we believe as Christians that it is wrong to resort to violence or acts which threaten the lives, personal safety, or dignity of others.

It is not our wish to still the debate concerning abortion. Our wish, rather, is to find nonviolent ways for Christians and other people of conscience to engage in civil conversation, debate, and discourse as they seek to persuade one another of the truth of their convictions. In a democratic and pluralistic society, we believe that persuasion rather than coercion, and witness rather than threatening others, are the appropriate and faithful recourse where there are differences of opinion.

We earnestly hope that this letter is not the end of a conversation but the beginning of a dialogue between good people of faith willing—candidly and openly—to share their convictions. By signing this letter we affirm the contents and ideals expressed herein and continue our support of the ideal of nonviolence.

Signators:

The Most Rev. Mark Dyer, Bishop, Diocese of Bethlehem, Episcopal Church

The Rev. Albert L. Kaiser, Presiding Elder, Philadelphia District, African Methodist Episcopal Zion Church

The Rev. Dr. Donald Overlock, Conference Minister, Penn Northeast Conference, United Church of Christ

The Rev. Harold Weiss, Bishop, Northeastern PA Synod, Evangelical Lutheran Church of America

The Rev. Harvey Johnson, Executive, Lehigh Presbytery, Presbyterian Church (USA)

The Rev. Susan Morrison, Bishop, Philadelphia District, United Methodist Church

The Rev. Richard Rusbuldt, Executive Minister (Pennsylvania & Delaware), American Baptist Church

Bibliography

Alton, Bruce, ed. *The Abortion Question.* Toronto: Anglican Book Centre, 1983.

Anderson, Susan Leigh. "Criticism of Liberal Feminist Views on Abortion." *Public Affairs Quarterly* 1 (April 1987).

Andrusko, Dave. "Echoes of Nuremberg." *Fundamentalist Journal* 8 (April 1989): 30–33.

Baertschi, Bernard. "Qu'est-ce qu'une personne humaine? Reflexions sur les fondements philosophiques de la bioethique." *Revue de Théologie et de Philosophie* 121 (1989): 173–93.

Barry, O. "Personhood: The Conditions of Identification and Description." *Linacre Quarterly* 45 (1978): 64–81.

Barry, Robert. *Medical Ethics: Essays on Abortion and Euthanasia.* New York: Lang, 1989.

Barth, Karl. *Church Dogmatics.* Pt. III/4. Edinburgh: T. & T. Clark, 1961.

Batchelor, Edward, ed. *Abortion: The Moral Issues.* New York: The Pilgrim Press, 1984.

Baum, Gregory. "Abortion: An Ecumenical Dilemma." *Commonweal* 99, no. 9 (30 November 30): 231–35.

Becker, Lawrence C. "Human Being: Boundaries of the Concept." *Philosophy and Public Affairs* 4 (1975): 334–59.

Benjamin, Martin. *Splitting the Differences: Compromise and Integrity in Ethics and Politics.* Lawrence: University Press of Kansas, 1990.

Bernardin, Cardinal Joseph. "The Consistent Ethic: What Sort of Framework?" *Origins* 16 (30 October 1986): 347–50.

———. "The Consistent Ethic after *Webster*: Opportunities and Dangers." *Commonweal* 127 (20 April 1990): 242–48.

Biale, Rachel. "Abortion in Jewish Law." *Tikkun* 4 (July–August 1989): 26–28.

Bigelow, John, and Robert Pargetter. "Morality, Potential Persons, and Abortion." *American Philosophical Quarterly* 25 (April 1988): 173–81.

Bleich, David. "Abortion in Halakhic Literature." *Tradition* 10 (1968): 70–120.

Bok, Sissela. "Ethical Problems of Abortion." *Hastings Center Studies* 2 (1974): 33–52.

Bole, Thomas, III. "Metaphysical Accounts of the Zygote as a Person and the Veto Power of Facts." *Journal of Medicine and Philosophy* 14 (December 1989): 647–53.

Bonhoeffer, Dietrich. *Ethics.* Translated by Neville Horton Smith. Edited by Eberhard Bethge. London: S.C.M. Press, 1955.

Borchert, Donald, and Phillip Jones. "Abortion: Morally Right or Wrong?" *Listening* 22 (winter 1985): 22–35.

Brandt, Richard B. "The Morality of Abortion." *The Monist* 36 (1972).

———. "Hare on Abortion." *Social Theory and Practice* 15 (spring 1989): 15–24.

Brody, Baruch A. "Abortion and the Law." *Journal of Philosophy* 68 (1971).

———. "Abortion and the Sanctity of Human Life." *American Philosophical Quarterly* 10 (April 1973): 133–40.

———. *Abortion and the Sanctity of Human Life: A Philosophical View.* Cambridge, Mass.: M.I.T. Press, 1975.

———. "Religious, Moral, and Sociological Issues: Some Basic Distinctions." *Hastings Center Report* 8 (August 1978): 13.

Burtchaell, James. "Continuing the Discussion: How to Argue about Abortion: II." *Christianity and Crisis* 37 (26 December 1977): 313–16.

———. *The Giving and Taking of Life: Essays Ethical.* Notre Dame, Ind.: University of Notre Dame Press, 1989.

———, ed. *Abortion Parley.* Kansas City: Andrews and McMeel, 1980.

Byrne, Harry. "Thou Shalt Not Speak." *America* 155 (6 December 1986): 356–59.

Cahill, Lisa Sowle. "Abortion, Autonomy, and Community." In *Abortion: Understanding Differences,* edited by Daniel and Sidney Callahan. New York: Plenum Press, 1984.

Callahan, Daniel. *Abortion: Law, Choice, and Morality.* London: Collier-Macmillan, Ltd., 1970; New York: Macmillan, 1977.

———. "Abortion: Thinking and Experiencing," *Christianity and Crisis* 32 (8 January 1973): 295–98.

———. "Rights of Fetus Uncertain," *National Catholic Reporter* 13, no. 32 (18 February 1977).

Callahan, Daniel, and Sidney Callahan. *Abortion: Understanding Differences.* New York: Plenum Press, 1984.

Callahan, Joan. "The Fetus and Fundamental Rights." *Commonweal* 123 (11 April 1986): 203–9.

———. "The Silent Scream: A New Conclusive Argument against Abortion?" *Philosophy Research Archives* 11 (1986): 181–95.

Callahan, Sidney. "Abortion and the Sexual Agenda: A Case for Pro-Life Feminism." *Commonweal* 123 (25 April 1986): 232–38.

Canadian Conference of Catholic Bishops. *Contraception, Divorce, Abortion.* Ottawa: CCCB, 1968.

Carrick, Paul. *Medical Ethics in Antiquity: Philosophical Perspectives on Abortion and Euthanasia.* Dordrecht, Neth.: Reidel, 1985.

Carter, Stephen L. *The Culture of Disbelief: How American Law and Politics Trivialize Religious Devotion.* New York: Basic Books, 1993.

"Case Study: The Unwanted Child: Caring for a Fetus Born Alive after an Abortion." *Hastings Center Report* 6 (October 1976): 10–14.

"Case Study: When a Mentally Ill Woman Refuses Abortion." Commentaries by Mary Mahowald and Virginia Abernathy. *Hastings Center Report* 15 (April 1985): 22–23.

Chervenak, Frank A., et al. "When Is Termination of Pregnancy During the Third Trimester of Pregnancy Justifiable?" *New England Journal of Medicine* 310 (23 February 1984): 501–4.

Chopko, Mark, Phillip Harris, and Helen Alvare. "The Price of Abortion Sixteen Years Later." *National Forum* 69 (fall 1989): 18, 20, 22.

Churchill, Larry R., and Jose Jorge Siman. "Abortion and the Rhetoric of Individual Rights." *Hastings Center Report* 12 (February 1982): 9–12.

Church of England, Board of Social Responsibility. *Abortion: An Ethical Discussion.* London: Church Information Office, 1965.

Cohen, Marshall, Thomas Nagel, and Thomas Scanlon, eds. *Rights and Wrongs of Abortion.* Princeton, N.J.: Princeton University Press, 1974.

Colker, Ruth. *Abortion and Dialogue: Pro-Choice, Pro-Life, and American Law.* Bloomington: Indiana University Press, 1992.

Collins, Barbara G. "Transforming Abortion Discourse." *Affilia* 2 (spring 1987): 6–17.

Condit, Celeste. *Decoding Abortion Rhetoric: Communicating Social Change.* Champaign: University of Illinois Press, 1990.

Congdon, Robert. "Exodus 21:22–25 and the Abortion Debate." *Biblioteca Sacra* 146 (April–June 1989): 132–147.

Connery, John. *Abortion: The Development of the Roman Catholic Perspective.* Chicago: Loyola University Press, 1977.

———. "A Seamless Garment in a Sinful World." *America* 153 (14 July 1984): 5–8.

Coughlin, Ellen K. "Research on Emotional Consequences of Abortion Fails to Bolster Cause of Procedure's Opponents [Surgeon General Koop calls evidence inconclusive]." *Chronicle of Higher Education* 35 (1 March 1989): 4–6.

Creighton, Phyllis, ed. *Abortion: An Issue for Conscience.* Toronto: The Anglican Church of Canada, 1974.

Cudd, Ann. "Sensationalized Philosophy: A Reply to Maquis's 'Abortion Is Immoral.'" *Journal of Philosophy* 87 (May 1990): 262–64.

Culliton, Joseph. "Rahner on the Origin of the Soul: Some Implications Regarding Abortion." *Thought* 53 (1978): 203–14.

Cuomo, Mario. "Religious Belief and Public Policy: A Catholic Governor's Perspective." *Notre Dame Journal of Law, Ethics, and Public Policy* 1, no. 1 (1984): 13–31.

Curran, Charles. "Abortion: Ethical Aspects." *Encyclopedia of Bioethics,* vol. 1. Edited by Warren T. Reich. New York: Free Press, 1978.

———. "Abortion, Law, and Morality in Contemporary Catholic Theology." *The Jurist* 33 (1973): 162–82.

———. "Civil Law and Christian Morality." *Clergy Review* 62, no. 6 (June 1977): 227–42.

———. *Contemporary Problems in Moral Theology.* Notre Dame, Ind.: Fides, 1970.

———. "In Vitro Fertilization and Embryo Transter." No. 4 in *Appendix: HEW Support of Research Involving Human In Vitro Fertilization and Embryo Transfer.* Washington, D.C.: U.S. Government Printing Office, 1979.

———. *Issues in Sexual and Medical Ethics.* Notre Dame, Ind.: University of Notre Dame Press, 1978.

———. *New Perspectives in Moral Theology.* Notre Dame, Ind.: Fides, 1974.

———. "Public Dissent in the Church." Origins 16 (31 July 1986): 178–84.

———. *Transition and Tradition in Moral Theology.* Notre Dame, Ind.: University of Notre Dame Press, 1979.

Daum, Annette. "Assault on the Bill of Rights: The Jewish Stake." New York: Union of American Hebrew Congregations, 1982.

———. "The Jewish Stake in Abortion Rights." *Lilith* 8 (1982).

Davis, Nancy. "Abortion and Self-Defence." *Philosophy and Public Affairs* 13 (summer 1984): 175–207.

Dedek, John. "Abortion: A Theological Judgement." *Chicago Studies* 101 (fall 1971): 313–33.

———. *Some Moral Issues.* New York: Sheed & Ward, 1972.

Degnan, Daniel. "Laws, Morals, and Abortion." *Commonweal* 100, no. 13 (31 May 1974): 305–8.

———. "Prudence, Politics, and the Abortion Issue." *America* 155 (6 December 1986): 121–24.

Devine, Philip E. *The Ethics of Homicide.* Ithaca and London: Cornell University Press, 1978.

———. "Relativism, Abortion, and Tolerance." *Philosophy and Phenomenological Research* 48 (summer 1987): 131–38.

Diamond, J. "Abortion, Animation, and Biological Hominization." *Theological Studies* 36 (1975): 305–24.

Di Ianni, Albert. "Is the Fetus a Person?" *American Ecclesiastical Review* 168 (1974): 323–24.

Dobson, Edward G., ed. "Abortion." *Fundamentalist Journal* 7 (January 1988): 26–61.

Dombrowski, Daniel A. "St Augustine, Abortion and libido crudelis." *Journal of Historical Ideas* 49 (January–March 1988): 151–56.

Donceel, Joseph F., S.J. "Abortion: Mediate vs. Immediate Animation." *Continuum* 5, no. 1 (spring 1967): 167–71.

———. "Immediate Animation and Delayed Hominization." *Theological Studies* 31, no. 1 (March 1970): 76–105.

———. "Why Is Abortion Wrong?" *America* 133, no. 4 (16 August 1975): 65–67.

Drinan, Robert F., S.J. "Abortions on Medicaid." *Commonweal* 97, no. 19 (16 February 1973): 438–40.

———. "Catholic Moral Teaching and Abortion Laws in America." *Catholic Theological Society of America Proceedings* 23 (1968): 118–30.

———. "Contemporary Protestant Thinking." *America* 117, no. 24 (9 December 1967): 713.

———. "Jurisprudential Options." *Theological Studies* 31, no. 1 (March 1970): 149–69.

———. "The Right of the Fetus to Be Born." *Dublin Review*, no. 514 (winter 1967–68): 365–81.

Dupre, Louis K. "New Approach to Abortion Question." *Theological Studies* 38 (September 1973): 481–88.

Dworkin, Ronald. *Life's Dominion: An Argument about Abortion, Euthanasia, and Individual Freedom.* New York: Random House, 1993.

Engelhardt, H. Tristram, Jr. "Bioethics and the Process of Embodiment." *Perspectives in Biology and Medicine* 18 (1975): 486–500.

———. "Foundations: Why They Provide So Little." *Journal for the British Society for Phenomenology* 20 (May 1989): 170–72.

———. "The Ontology of Abortion." *Ethics* 8 (1974): 217–34.

Engelhardt, H. Tristram, and Robert Cefalo. "The Use of Fetal and Anencephalic Tissue for Transplantation." *Journal of Medicine and Philosophy* 14 (February 1989): 25–43.

English, Jane. "Abortion and the Concept of a Person." *Canadian Journal of Philosophy* 5, no. 2 (October 1975): 233–43.

Erde, Edmunde L. "Studies in the Exploration of Issues in Biomedical Ethics: The Example of Abortion." *Journal of Medicine and Philosophy* 13 (November 1988): 329–47.

———. "Understanding Abortion via Different Scholarly Methodologies." *Journal of Medical Humanities and Bioethics* 7 (fall–winter 1986): 139–47.

———. "Understanding Abortion via Different Scholarly Methodologies, Part II." *Journal of Medical Humanities and Bioethics* 8 (spring–summer 1987): 56–66.

Evans, Ruth, ed. *Abortion: A Study.* Toronto: United Church of Canada, 1971.

Fortin, Renee. "A Comparison of Church Statements on Abortion, Pt 2: A Working Tool." *Ecumenism* 84 (December 1986): 23–36.

Feinberg, Joel. "Abortion." In *Matters of Life and Death,* edited by Tom Regan. New York: Random House, 1978.

Feldman, David M. *Birth Control and Jewish Law.* New York: New York University Press, 1968.

———. *Marital Relations, Birth Control, and Abortion in Jewish Law.* New York: Schocken, 1975.

Finnis, John, "The Rights and Wrongs of Abortion: A Reply to Judith Thomson." *Philosophy & Public Affairs* 2 (1973): 117–45.

Fleming, Lorette. "The Moral Status of the Fetus: A Reappraisal." *Bioethics* 1 (January 1987): 15–34.

Fletcher, Joseph F. "Abortion and the True Believer." *Christian Century* 91, no. 41 (27 November 1974): 1126–27.

———. *Humanhood: Essays in Biomedical Ethics.* Buffalo: Prometheus Books, 1979.

———. *Situation Ethics.* Philadelphia: Westminster Press, 1966.

Foot, Phillippa. "The Problem of Abortion and the Doctrine of Double Effect." *The Oxford Review* 5 (1967): 5–15.

Frame, Randall L. "Abortion Takes Center Stage for Presbyterians" [1988 General Assembly, St. Louis]. *Christianity Today* 32 (12 August 1988): 64–65.

———. "Rescue Theology." *Christianity Today* 33 (17 November 1989): 46–48.

Galvin, Richard Francis. "Noonan's Argument against Abortion: Probability, Possibility, and Potentiality." *Journal of Social Philosophy* 19 (summer 1988): 80–89.

Garfield, Jay L., and Patricia Hennessey. *Abortion: Moral and Legal Perspectives.* Amherst: University of Massachusetts Press, 1984.

Gilligan, Carol. *In a Different Voice: Psychological Theory and Women's Development.* Cambridge: Harvard University Press, 1982.

Glaeser, Linda L., et al. "What Had I Done?" *Fundamentalist Journal* 8 (January 1989): 16–20, 22–24.

Glover, Jonathan. *Causing Death and Saving Lives.* Hammondsworth, Middlesex, U.K.: Penguin Books, 1977.

Goodman, Michael, ed. *What Is a Person?* Clifton, N.J.: Humana Press, 1988.

Gorman, Michael J. *Abortion and the Early Church: Christian, Jewish, and Pagan Attitudes in the Greco-Roman World.* New York: Paulist Press, 1982.

Gorovitz, Samuel, "Moral Conflict in Public Policy." *National Forum* 69 (fall 1989): 31–32.

Granfield, David. *The Abortion Decision.* Garden City, N.Y.: Doubleday Image Books, 1971.

Green, Ronald, "Conferred Rights and the Fetus." *Journal of Religious Ethics* 2 (spring 1974): 55–73.

Greenburg, Blu. "Abortion: A Challenge to Halakhah." *Judaism* 25, no. 2 (spring 1976): 436–40.

Grisez, Germain C. *Abortion: The Myth, the Realities, and the Arguments.* Washington, D.C.: Corpus Books, 1969; New York: Corpus Books, 1970.

Grossman, Richard. "Preventing Pregnancy: A Neglected Option." [Response to "When a Mentally Ill Woman Refuses Abortion," *Hastings Center Report* 15 (April 1985): 22–23] *Hastings Center Report* 16 (April 1986): 214–15.

Gudorf, Christine. "To Make a Seamless Garment, Use a Single Piece of Cloth." *Cross Currents* 34 (winter 1984): 473–91.

Gustafson, James M. "A Christian Approach to the Ethics of Abortion." *Dublin Review,* no. 514 (winter 1967–68): 346–64.

———. "A Protestant Ethical Approach." In *The Morality of Abortion,* edited by John T. Noonan Jr. Cambridge: Harvard University Press, 1970.

Hall, Robert E., ed. *Abortion in a Changing World.* 2 vols. New York and London: Columbia University Press, 1970.

Hare, Richard M. "Abortion and the Golden Rule." *Philosophy & Public Affairs* 4 (1975): 201–22.

———. "Abortion: Reply to Brandt." *Social Theory and Practice* 15 (spring 1989): 25–32.

Häring, Bernard. *Faithful and Free in Christ.* Vol. 1. New York: Seabury Press, 1978.

———. *Faithful and Free in Christ.* Vol. 11. New York: Seabuty Press, 1979.

———. *Medical Ethics.* Edited by Gabrielle L. Jean. Notre Dame, Ind.: Fides, 1973.

———. "New Dimensions of Responsible Parenthood." *Theological Studies* 37, no. 1 (March 1976): 120–32.

———. "A Theological Evaluation." In *The Morality of Abortion,* edited by John T. Noonan Jr. Cambridge: Harvard University Press, 1970.

Harris, Michael P. "Second Thoughts about Abortion: Many Protestant Groups Are Edging to the Right." *Time* 132 (4 July 1988): 44.

Harrison, Beverly Wildung. *Our Right to Choose: Toward a New Ethic of Abortion.* Boston: Beacon Press, 1983.

———. "Theology of Pro-Choice: A Feminist Perspective." *The Witness* 64, nos. 7 and 8 (July and September 1981).

Hartshorne, Charles. "Concerning Abortion: An Attempt at a Rational View." *Christian Century* 98 (21 January 1981): 42–45.

Hauerwas, Stanley. "Abortion and Normative Ethics." *Cross Currents* 21, no. 4 (fall 1971): 399–414.

———. "Abortion: The Agent's Perspective." *American Ecclesiastical Review* 167, no. 2 (February 1973): 102–20.

———. *A Community of Character: Toward a Constructive Christian Social Ethic.* Notre Dame, Ind.: University of Notre Dame Press, 1981.

———. *Vision and Virtue.* Notre Dame, Ind.: University of Notre Dame Press, 1981.

Heim, David. "American Baptists Maximize the Middle" [Abortion and the National Council of Churches]. *Christian Century* 105 (20–27 July 1988): 660–62.

Hellegers, A. "Fetal Development." *Theological Studies* 31 (1970): 39.

Herbenick, Raymond M. "Remarks on Abortion, Abandonment, and Adoption Opportunities." *Philosophy and Public Affairs* 5 (1975): 89–104.

Higgins, George C. "The Pro-Life and the New Right." *America* 143 (13 September 1980): 107–10.

Hilgers, Thomas, and Dennis Dennis, eds. *New Perspectives on Human Abortion.* Frederick, Md.: University Press of America, 1981.

Jaffe, Frederick. "Enacting Religious Beliefs in a Pluralistic Society." *Hastings Center Report* 8 (August 1978): 14–16.

Jakobowitz, Isaac. *Jewish Medical Ethics.* 2d ed. New York: Block Publishing Company, 1975.

John, Helen. "Reflections on Autonomy and Abortion." *Journal of Social Philosophy* 17 (winter 1986): 3–10.

Jung, Patricia Beattie. "Abortion and Organ Donation: Christian Reflections on Bodily Life Support." *Journal of Religious Ethics* 16 (fall 1988): 273–305.

Jung, Patricia Beattie, and Thomas Shannon. *Abortion and Catholicism: The American Debate.* New York: Crossroad, 1988.

Kelly, James. "Ecumenism and Abortion: A Case Study of Pluralism, Privatization, and the Public Conscience." *Review of Religious Research* 30 (March 1989): 225–35.

Klein, Isaac. "Abortion: A Jewish View." *Dublin Review,* no. 514 (winter 1967–68): 382–90.

Kluge, Eike-Henner W. *The Practice of Death.* New Haven and London: Yale University Press, 1975.

Kohl, Marvin. *The Morality of Killing.* Atlantic Highlands, N.J.: Humanities Press, 1974.

Kolbenschlag, Madonna. "Abortion and Moral Consensus: Beyond Solomon's Choice." *Christian Century* 102 (20 February 1985): 179–83.

Kraus, James E. "Is Abortion Absolutely Prohibited?" *Continuum* 6, no. 3 (fall 1968): 436–40.

Kremar, Elmar. "On Killing the Immature." In *Philosophy and Culture,* vol. 3, edited by Vincent Cauchy. Montreal: Editions Montmorency, 1988.

Lader, Lawrence. *Abortion.* Indianapolis: Bobbs-Merrill, 1966.

Lake, Randall A. "The Metaethical Framework of Anti-Abortion Rhetoric." *Signs: Journal of Women, Culture and Society* 11 (spring 1986): 478–99.

Lamb, David. *Down the Slippery Slope: Arguing in Applied Ethics.* London: Croon Helm, 1988.

Lancaster, Kathy, ed. "National Dialogue on Abortion Perspectives." *Church and Society* 80 (January–February 1990): 1–124.

Langerak, Edward. "Abortion: Listening to the Middle." *Hastings Center Report* 9 (October 1979): 24–29.

Lecso, Phillip A. "A Buddhist View of Abortion." *Journal of Religion and Health* 26 (fall 1987): 214–18.

Leddy, Mary Jo, and James H. Olthuis. "Thoughtful Perspective on Abortion." *Catalyst* 6 (November 1983): 4–5.

Letich, Larry. "Bad Choices" [abortion]. *Tikkun* 4 (July–August 1989): 22–26.

Lombardi, Louis. "The Legal versus the Moral on Abortion." *Journal of Social Philosophy* 17 (winter 1986): 23–29.

Lycan, William. "Abortion and the Civil Rights of Machines." In *Morality and Universality: Essays on Ethical Universalizability,* edited by Nelson T. Potter. Dordrecht, Neth.: Kluwer, 1985.

Macklin, Ruth. "Ethics and Human Reproduction: International Perspectives." *Social Problems* 37 (February 1990): 38–50.

Maguire, Marjorie Reiley. "Personhood, Covenant, and Abortion." *Annual of the Society of Christian Ethics* (1983); and *American Journal of Theology and Philosophy* 6 (1985): 28–46.

Maier, Kelly L. "Pregnant Women: Fetal Containers or People with Rights?" *Affilia* 4 (summer 1989): 8–20.

Maloney, Susan. "Religious Orders and Sisters in Dissent" [1984 statement on abortion]. *Christian Century* 105 (9 March 1988): 238–40.

Markowitz, Sally. "Abortion and Feminism." *Social Theory and Practice* 16 (spring 1990): 1–17.

Marquis, Don. "Why Abortion Is Immoral." *Journal of Philosophy* 86 (April 1989): 183–202.

Mason, J. K. Human Life and Medical Pracnce. Edinburgh: Edinburgh University Press, 1988.

Mavrodes, George I. "Abortion and Imagination: Reflections on Mollenkott's 'Reproductive Choice.'" *Christian Scholar's Review* 17 (1988): 286–93; 18 (1988): 168–70; rejoinder, 171–72.

McConnell, Terrance. "Permissive Abortion Laws, Religion, and Moral Compromise." *Public Affairs Quarterly* 1 (January 1987): 95–109.

McCormick, Richard A. "Aspects of the Moral Question." *America* 117, no. 24 (9 December 1967): 716–19.

———. "A Changing Morality and Policy." *Hospital Progress* 60 (February 1979): 36–44.

———. *How Brave a New World?* Garden City, N.Y.: Doubleday, 1981.

———."Notes on Moral Theology: The Abortion Dossier." *Theological Studies* 35 (June 1974): 312–59.

———."Past Church Teaching on Abortion." *Catholic Theological Society of America Proceedings* 23 (1968): 131–51.

———. "Rules for Debate." *America* 139, no. 2 (15–22 July 1978): 26–30.

McDonagh, Edna. "Ethical Problems of Abortion." *Irish Theological Quarterly* 35 (July 1968): 268–97.

McInerney, Peter. "Does a Fetus Already Have a Future-Like-Ours?" *Journal of Philosophy* 87 (May 1990): 264–68.

Mead, Margaret. "Rights to Life." *Christianity and Crisis* 32 (8 January 1973): 288–92.

Meeks, Thomas. "The Economics Efficiency and Equity of Abortion." *Economics and Philosophy* 6 (April 1990): 95–138.

Mehta, Ajit C. "Ethical Issues in Abortion, Amniocentesis, and Sterilization." *Journal of Family Welfare* 34 (spring 1987): 49–53.

Mensch, Elizabeth, and Alan Freeman. *The Politics of Virtue: Is Abortion Debatable?* Durham, N.C.: Duke University Press, 1993.

Milhaven, John G. "The Abortion Debate: An Epistemological Interpretation." *Theological Studies* 31, no. 1 (March 1970): 106–24.

———. *Towards a New Catholic Morality.* Garden City, N.Y.: Doubleday, 1970.

Mollenkott, Virginia Ramey. "Reproductive Choice: Basic to Justice for Women." *Christian Scholar's Review* 17 (1988): 286–93.

Mollenkott, Virginia, and Frances Beckwith. "Abortion and Public Policy: A Response to Some Arguments." *Journal of the Evangelical Theological Society* 32 (December 1989): 503–18.

Muldoon, Maureen. *The Abortion Debate in the United States and Canada: A Source Book.* New York: Garland Publishing, 1991.

Murphy, Julien S. "Abortion Rights and Fetal Termination." *Journal of Social Philosophy* 17 (winter 1986): 11–16.

National Council of Churches in the U.S.A., Faith and Order Commission. *Guidelines for Ecumenical Debate on Homosexuality and Abortion.* New York: National Council of Churches, 1979.

Nelson, J. Robert. "What Does Theology Say about Abortion?" *Christian Century* 90 (31 January 1973): 124–28.

Nelson, James. "Abortion: Protestant Perspectives." *Encyclopedia of Bioethics,* vol. 1, edited by Warren T. Reich. New York: Free Press, 1978.

———. *Between Two Gardens: Reflections on Sexuality and Religious Experience.* New York: The Pilgrim Press, 1983.

Neuhaus, Richard J. "The Dangerous Assumption." *Commonweal* 86, no. 15 (30 June 1967): 408–13.

Newton, Lisa. "The Irrelevance of Religion in the Abortion Debate." *Hastings Center Report* 8 (August 1978): 16–17.

Nicholson, Susan T. *Abortion and the Roman Catholic Church.* Knoxville, Tenn.: Religious, Inc., 1978.

Noonan, John T., Jr. *Abortion.* Cambridge: Harvard University Press, 1968.

———. "Abortion and the Catholic Church: A Summary History." *Natural Law Forum* 12 (1967): 85–131.

———. "An Almost Absolute Value in History." In *The Morality of Abortion,* edited by John T. Noonan Jr. Cambridge: Harvard University Press, 1970.

———. *A Private Choice: Abortion in America in the Seventies.* New York: Free Press, 1979.

———, ed. *The Morality of Abortion: Legal and Historical Perspectives.* Cambridge: Harvard University Press, 1970.

Norcross, Alastair. "Killing, Abortion, and Contraception: A Reply to Marquis." *Journal of Philosophy* 87 (May 1990): 268–77.

O'Connor, June. "The Debate Continues: Recent Works on Abortion." *Religious Studies Review* 11 (1985): 105–14.

Overall, Christine. "Ethics: Feminist and Non-Feminist Approaches." *Canadian Journal of Women and the Law* 1 (1986): 271–78.

———. *Ethics and Human Reproduction: A Feminist Analysis.* Boston: Allen and Unwin, 1987.

———. "Selective Termination of Pregnancy and Women's Reproductive Autonomy." *Hastings Center Report* 20 (May–June 1990): 6–11.

Pahel, Kenneth. "Michael Tooley on Abortion and Potentiality." *Southern Journal of Philosophy* 25 (spring 1982): 89–107.

Pastrana, G. "Personhood at the Beginning of Human Life." *Thomist* 41 (1977): 247–94.

Perkins, Robert L., ed. *Abortion Pro and Con.* Cambridge: Schenkman Publishing Co., 1974.

Perry, Clifton. "Methods of Aborting." *Reason Papers* 11 (spring 1986): 63–67.

Petchesky, Rosalind Pollack. "Antiabortion, Antifeminism, and the Rise of the New Right." *Feminist Studies* 7 (summer 1981): 206–46.

———. "Reproductive Freedom: Beyond a Woman's Right to Choose." *Signs: Journal of Women, Culture, and Society* 5 (summer 1980): 661–85.

Rahman, Fazlur. "Contraception and Abortion." *Health and Medicine in the Islamic Tradition.* New York: Crossroads, 1984.

Railsbach, Celeste Condit. "Pro-Life, Pro-Choice: Different Conceptions of Value." *Women's Studies in Communication* 5 (spring 1982): 16–28.

Ramsey, Paul. "Abortion: A Review Article." *Thomist* 37, no. 1 (January 1973): 174–226.

———. *The Ethics of Fetal Research.* New Haven: Yale University Press, 1975.

———. "Feticide/Infanticide upon Request." *Religion in Life* 39 (summer 1970): 170–86.

———. "The Morality of Abortion." In *Life or Death: Ethics and Options,* edited by Daniel H. Labby. Seattle: University of Washington Press, 1968.

———. "The Morality of Abortion." In *Moral Problems: A Collection of Philosophical Essays,* edited by James Rachels. New York: Harper & Row, 1971.

———. "Protecting the Unborn." *Commonweal* 100, no. 13 (31 May 1974): 308–14.

———. "Reference Points in Deciding about Abortion." In *The Morality of Abortion,* edited by John T. Noonan Jr. Cambridge: Harvard University Press, 1970.

———. "The Sanctity of Life." *Dublin Review* 241 (spring 1967): 3–23.

Ranck, Lee, ed. A special issue on abortion. *Christian Social Action* 3 (April 1990): 1–16, 25–40.

Rankin, John C. "The Corporeal Reality of Nepes and the Status of the Unborn." *Journal of the Evangelical Theological Society* 31 (June 1988): 153–60.

Ratzinger, Cardinal Joseph. "Bishops, Theologians, and Morality." *Origins* 13 (15 March 1984): 665–66.

Roach, Archbishop John R., and Cardinal Terence Cooke. "Testimony in Support of the Hatch Amendment." *Origins* 11 (19 November 1981): 357–72.

Robertson, John A. "Extracorporeal Embryos and the Abortion Debate." *Journal of Contemporary Health Law and Policy* 2 (spring 1986): 53–70.

———. "Subsidized Abortion: Moral Rights and Moral Compromise." *Philosophy and Public Affairs* 10 (1981): 361–72.

———. "Symbolism, and Public Policy in Fetal Tissue Transplants." *Hastings Center Report* 18 (December 1988): 5–12.

Rodgers, Sandra. "Fetal Rights and Maternal Rights: Is There a Conflict?" *Canadian Journal of Women and the Law* 1 (1986): 456–69.

Rosen, Ruth. "Historically Compromised: The Abortion Struggle; summer 1989." *Tikkun* 4 (July–August 1989): 20–21.

Rossi, Philip. "Abortion and the Pursuit of Happiness." *Logos* 3 (1982): 61–77.

Ruether, Rosemary Radford. "Catholics and Abortion: Authority vs. Dissent." *Christian Century* 102 (2 October 1985): 859–62.

Ryan, Thomas, ed. "The Churches on Abortion." *Ecumenism* 83 (1986): 1–285.

Sacred Congregation for the Doctrine of the Faith. "Declaration on Procured Abortion." *Linacre Quarterly* 2 (1975): 132–47.

———. "Declaration on Abortion." Washington, D.C.: U.S. Catholic Conference, 1975.

Schartz, Stephen, and Tacelli, R. K. "Abortion and Some Philosophers." *Public Affairs Quarterly* 3 (April 1989): 81–98.

Schedler, George. "Will Preserving American Women's Procreative Freedom Conflict with Achieving Equality between the Sexes?" *Reason Papers* 14 (spring 1989): 45–58.

Schwartz, Lewis M. *Arguing about Abortion.* Belmont, Calif.: Wadsworth, 1993.

Shannon, Thomas. "Abortion: A Challenge for Ethics and Public Policy." *Annual of the Society of Christian Ethics* (1982).

———. "Abortion: Ethical Review of Ethical Aspects of Public Policy." *The Annual Selected Papers* (Society of Christian Ethics, 1983).

Shaw, Margery, and A. Edward Doudera, eds. *Defining Life: Medical, Legal, and Ethical Implications.* Ann Arbor, Mich.: AUPHA Press, 1983.

Sher, George, "Hare, Abortion, and the Golden Rule." *Philosophy & Public Affairs* 6 (1977): 185–90.

———. "Subsidized Abortion: Moral Rights and Moral Compromise." *Philosophy & Public Affairs* 10 (1981).

Shinn, Roger L. "Personal Decisions and Social Policies." *Perkins Journal* 27, no. 1 (fall 1973): 58–63.

Sider, Ronald J. *Completely Pro-Life: Building a Consistent Stance.* Westmont, Ill.: Inter-Varsity Press, 1987.

Silverstein, Harry S. "On a Woman's Responsibility for the Fetus." *Social Thought and Practice* (spring 1987): 103–19.

Simmons, Paul D. "A Theological Response to Fundamentalism on the Abortion Issue." *Church and Society* 71, no. 4 (March–April 1981): 22–35.

———. "Dogma and Discord: Religious Liberty and the Abortion Debate." *Church and State* 43 (January 1990): 17–21.

Sinclair-Faulkner, Tom. "Canadian Catholics: At Odds on Abortion." *Christian Century* 107 (9 September 1981): 870–71.

Singer, Peter. *Practical Ethics.* Cambridge and New York: Cambridge University Press, 1975.

Smith, D. T., ed. *Abortion and the Law.* Cleveland: Case Western Reserve University Press, 1967.

Soley, Genny Earnest. "To Preserve and Protect Life: A Christian Feminist Perspective on Abortion." *Sojourners* 15 (October 1986): 34–37.

Steffen, Lloyd. "Abortion and the Conflict of Moral Presumption." *Papers of the Craigville Theological Colloquy VI: Human Beginnings: Deciding about Life in the Presence of God.* Craigville, Mass.: Craigville Conference Center, 1989.

———. *Life/Choice: The Theory of Just Abortion.* Cleveland: The Pilgrim Press, 1994.

Steinfels, Margaret O'Brien. "Consider the Seamless Garrnent." *Christianity and Crisis* 43 (14 May 1984): 172–74.

Stone, Jim. "Why Potentiality Matters." *Canadian Journal of Philosophy* 17 (December 1987): 815–29.

Strasser, Mark. "Noonan on Contraception and Abortion: Comments on Noonan's *The Morality of Abortion: Legal and Historical Perspectives.*" *Bioethics* 1 (April 1987): 199–205.

Suhor, Mary Lou, ed. "Procreative Freedom." *Witness* 72 (June 1989): 5–23.

Sumner, L. W. "Abortion." In *Health Care Ethics,* edited by Donald Van De Veer. Philadelphia: Temple Press, 1982.

———. *Abortion and Moral Theory.* Princeton, N.J.: Princeton University Press, 1981.

Synder, Graydon F. "Covenant Theology and Medical Decision Making." *Brethren Life and Thought* 33 (winter 1988): 27–35.

"Taking the Middle Road" [News: American Baptist Churches abortion position). *Christian Century* 105 (16 March 1988): 273.

Tauer, Carol A. "The Tradition of Probabilism and the Moral Stance of the Early Embryo." *Theological Studies* 45 (March 1984): 3–33.

Thielicke, Helmut. *The Ethics of Sex.* Translated by John W. Doberstein. New York: Harper & Row, 1964.

Thomson, Judith Jarvis. "A Defense of Abortion." *Philosophy & Public Affairs* 1 (fall 1971): 47–66.

———. "Rights and Deaths." *Philosophy & Public Affairs* 2 (1972).

Tickle, Phyllis, ed. *Confessing Conscience: Churched Women on Abortion.* Nashville: Abingdon, 1990.

Tilley, Terrence W. "The Principle of Innocents' Immunity." *Horizons* 15 (spring 1988): 43–63.

Tooley, Michael. *Abortion and Infanticide.* Oxford: Clarendon Press, 1983.

————. "Response to Mary Anne Warren's 'Reconsidering the Ethics of Infanticide.'" *Philosophical Books* 26 (January 1985): 9–14.

Tooley, Michael, and Laura Purdy. "Is Abortion Murder?" In *Abortion Pro and Con,* edited by Robert L. Perkins. Cambridge: Schenkman, 1974.

Wall, James, ed. "Abortion: Is There a Middle Ground?" *Christian Century* 107 (21 February 1990): 180–86.

Warren, Mary Anne. "The Abortion Issue." In *Health Care Ethics,* edited by Donald Van De Veer. Philadelphia: Temple Press, 1982.

————. "The Abortion Struggle in America." *Bioethics* 9 (October 1989): 320–32.

————. "The Moral Significance of Birth." *Hypatia* 4 (1989): 46–65.

————. "Reconsidering the Ethics of Infanticide." *Philosophical Books* 26 (January 1985): 1–9.

Wassner, Thomas. "Contemporary Attitudes of the Roman Catholic Church Toward Abortion." *Journal of Religion and Health* 7, no. 4 (October 1968): 311–23.

Waters, Kristen. "Abortion, Technology, and Responsibility." *Journal of Social Philosophy* 17 (winter 1986): 17–22.

Watt, Helen. "Singer on Abortion: A Utilitarian Critique." *Australasian Journal of Philosophy* 67 (June 1989): 227–29.

Weakland, Archbishop Rembert. "Abortion Issue Far from Black-and-White." *National Catholic Reporter* 26 (1 June 1990): 24.

Weddington, Sarah Ragle. "The Woman's Right of Privacy." *Perkins Journal* 27, no. 1 (fall 1973): 35–41.

Weil, William, and Martin Benjamin, eds. *Ethical Issues at the Outset of Life.* Boston: Blackwell Science, 1987.

Wennberg, Robert N. *Life in the Balance: Exploring the Abortion Controversy.* Grand Rapids, Mich.: Eerdmans, 1985.

Wenz, Peter S. *Abortion Rights as Religious Freedom.* Philadelphia: Temple University Press, 1992.

Wertheimer, Roger. "Understanding the Abortion Argument." *Philosophy and Public Affairs* 1 (1971): 67–95.

Weston, Anthony. "Drawing Lines: The Abortion Perplexity and the Presuppositions of Applied Ethics." *Monist* 67 (October 1984): 589–604.

Wilcox, John. "Nature as Demonic in Thomson's Defense of Abortion." *New Scholasticism* 63 (autumn 1989): 463–84.

Williams, George H. "Religious Residues and Presuppositions in the American Debate on Abortion." *Theological Studies* 31, no. 1 (March 1970): 10–75.

————. "The Sacred Condominium." In *The Morality of Abortion,* edited by John T. Noonan Jr. Cambridge: Harvard University Press, 1970.

Wilson, Bryan. "On a Kantian Argument against Abortion." *Philosophical Studies* 53 (January 1988): 119–30.

Wind, James, ed. "Abortion: A Middle Ground." *Second Opinion* 10 (1989): 38–79.

Zaitchik, Alan. "Viability and the Morality of Abortion." *Philosophy & Public Affairs* 10 (winter 1981): 18–26.